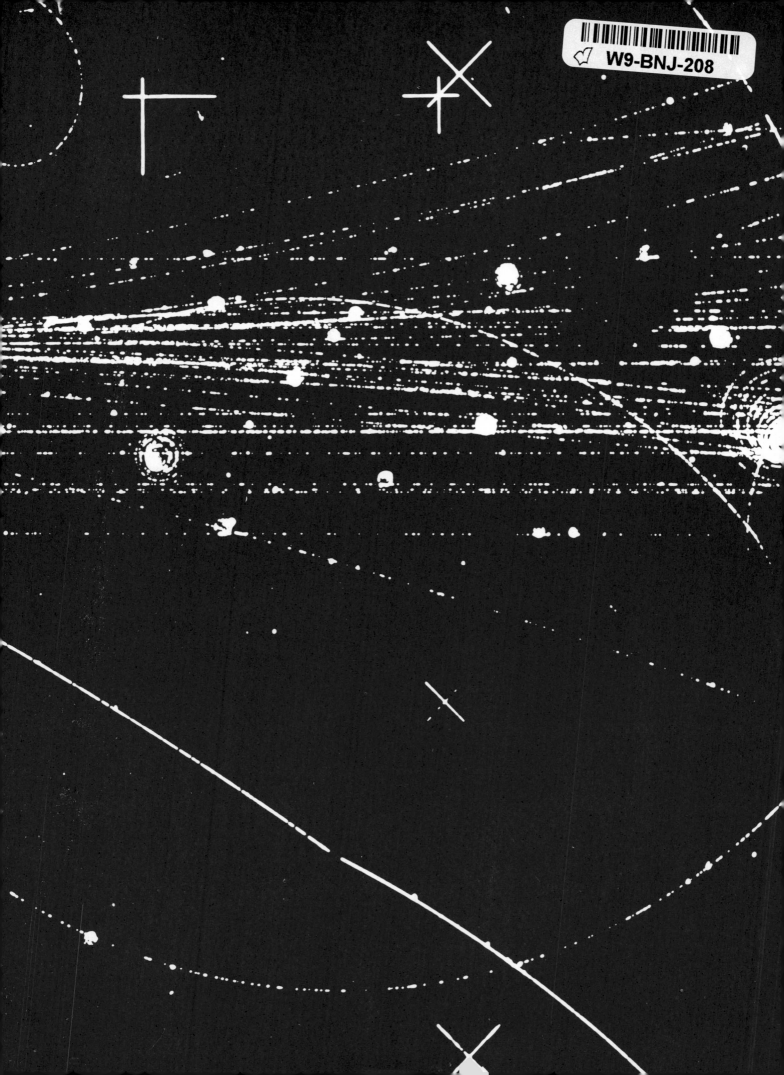

THE
GAIA
PEACE
ATLAS

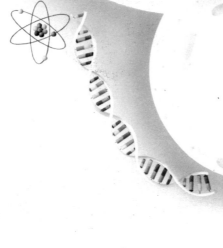

"Peace and security cannot be won
at the barrel of a gun."
Archbishop Desmond Tutu

THE GAIA PEACE ATLAS

Dr. Frank Barnaby, General Editor
Foreword by Javier Pérez de Cuéllar

DOUBLEDAY
New York London Toronto Sydney Auckland

A GAIA ORIGINAL

Conceived by Joss Pearson

Written by Frank Barnaby and Joss Pearson
with Erik Ness, Joanna Godfrey Wood,
Ann Kramer, Anna Kruger, Michele Staple

Direction
Patrick Nugent
Joss Pearson

Project editor
Jonathan Hilton

Art editor
Lucy Oliver

Editorial and research
Joanna Godfrey Wood
Ann Kramer
Anna Kruger
Susan McKeever
Erik Ness
Michele Staple

Design
Annette Peppis
Kate Poole
Marnie Searchwell

Picture research
Shana Magraw

Production
Susan Walby
assisted by Helen Banbury

Copy preparation
Lesley Gilbert

Photomontages for chapter openers
Peter Kennard

Contributors and consultants

General editor Frank Barnaby
International consultant on military technology, former Guest Professor of Peace Research at the Free University in Amsterdam, former Director of the Stockholm International Peace Research Institute (SIPRI), author and editor of several books on military affairs.

Foreword
Javier Pérez de Cuéllar, Secretary-General to the United Nations

Principal reader
Norman Myers

The Peace Atlas Think Tank
The following advised especially on Part 3 of the Atlas, attending a multi-disciplinary Think Tank convened by *Gaia* in 1987 to debate future peace strategies:
Paul Ekins
Former Director of The Other Economic Summit
now at the School of Peace Studies, Bradford University
Neil Finer
European Nuclear Disarmament (END)
Andrew Graham-Yooll
Editor, *South* magazine
John Groom
International Relations, University of Kent
David Hicks PhD
Director of the Centre of Peace Studies, Lancaster
John May
Greenpeace Publications
Norman Myers PhD
Editor, *The Gaia Atlas of Planet Management*, consultant in environment and development
Sheena Phillips
Information Officer, Campaign for Nuclear Disarmament (CND)
Pat Saunders
Development Education Officer, Quaker Peace and Service
Abdul Salim Williams
Labour Research Officer, Sierra Leone

Voices
Statements for peace were contributed by the following:
Rudy Bahro co-founder of Die Grünen
Willy Brandt President of the West German Social Democratic Party
John Eton Archbishop of York
Nichidatsu Fujii Founder, Nipponzan Myohoji Buddhist order
Edward Goldsmith Founder, *The Ecologist*
Mikhail Gorbachev USSR General Secretary
James Grant Director of UNICEF
Immanuel Jacobovitz Chief Rabbi, UK
Bruce Kent Campaign for Nuclear Disarmament
John Marshall Lee Vice Admiral, US Navy (Ret.)
Pope John Paul II
Ronald Reagan, US President
Diana Schumacher Ecologist
Rusty Schweickart Apollo 9 astronaut
Inga Thorsson, Ministry of Foreign Affairs, Sweden
Jack Westoby Economist, statistician and former Director, United Nations Forestry Division.

Chapter introductions

Kenneth E. Boulding Distinguished Professor of Economics, Emeritus, and Project Director of the Institute for Behavioral Sciences at the University of Colorado.

Gro Harlem Brundtland Prime Minister of Norway and Chairman of the World Commission on Environment and Development.

Johan Galtung Professor of Peace Studies, University of Hawaii, and founder of the International Peace Research Institute in Oslo.

Petra Karin Kelly Member of the Bundestag (National Parliament) of West Germany, and co-founder of Die Grünen, the German Green Party.

Mwalimu Julius K. Nyerere Former President of the United Republic of Tanzania, and Chairman of CCM National Party.

Maurice F. Strong Formerly Executive Co-ordinator of the UN Office for Emergency Operations in Africa.

Inga Thorsson Ministry of Foreign Affairs, Sweden, organizer of The Great Peace Journey campaign.

Archbishop Desmond Tutu Secretary of the South African Council of Churches, winner of the Nobel Peace Prize in 1984.

Sir Brian Urquhart Scholar in Residence at the Ford Foundation, and former Assistant Secretary-General to the United Nations.

Research and advice

Material was drawn up with the assistance of the following individuals and organizations: Amnesty International; Anti-Apartheid Movement; Phil Asquith, Sheffield City Council, UK; Australian High Commission, London; Books for a Change; British Council; British Medical Association; British Petroleum; CAAT; Care France; Center for Social Analysis, New York; CITES office, Lausanne; Paul Clark; CND; Committee for Human Rights in Argentina; Commonwealth Secretariat; Andy Crump; Deeper Dimension; Earthscan; Embassy of the Federal Republic of Germany, London; END; Environmental Data Services, London; EPIC; European Proliferation Information Centre; FAO; FREEZE; Friends of the Earth; Jonathan Fryer; Great Peace Journey, Sweden; Green Party UK; Greenpeace; Mark Halle, World Conservation Centre, Geneva; Home Office, UK; Eirwen Harbottle, Centre for International Peacebuilding; IFDA; IGRAT; IIASA; IIED; IISS; Intermediate Technology Development Group; ILO, Geneva; Interpol; IPPF; IUCN; Lawyers for Nuclear Disarmament; John Leggett, Nuclear Materials Working Group, Imperial College London; Tony Long, World Wildlife Fund; Michael Lyons, British Friends of Neve Shalom; Abdul Minti, World Campaign against Military and Nuclear Collaboration with South Africa; National Peace Council, UK; National Remote Sensing Centre, UK Space Department; National Resources Defense Council, US; New Zealand High Commission, London; OXFAM; PANOS; Peace Pledge Union; John-Francis Phipps; Quaker Peace and Service; David Satterthwaite; Southern Africa, the Imprisoned Society (SATIS); TOES; Professor Tom Stonier, Postgraduate School of Studies in Science and Society, University of Bradford; Transnationals Information Centre, London; Survival International; Swedish Embassy, London; UNEP; UNICEF; United Nations Information Centre, London; United States Embassy, London; United World College of the Atlantic, Wales; Universidad Para La Paz, Costa Rica; Warren Spring Laboratory, UK; Melvin Westlake, *South* magazine; WHO; Roy Willis, Department of Social Anthropology, University of Edinburgh; World Federalists; Yugoslav Embassy, London.

About this book

This Atlas maps and analyses the roots of peace and war. It confronts the human, nuclear and environmental crises threatening our species and our planet, and it offers constructive proposals not only for our immediate survival but for long-term sustainable peace.

The Gaia Peace Atlas is divided into three parts. Part 1 examines the lessons we have learned from 5000 years of civilization. Part 2 outlines the major current global dilemmas. Part 3 explores our choices for the future, suggesting short- and long-term solutions for creating a peaceful world.

The message of this Atlas is that the arms race, far from providing security, is ultimately life-threatening. Our survival depends on putting into practice new and viable proposals for peace and security. The presence of social justice, human opportunity, and a harmonious relationship with Gaia, our living planet, will lead us safely into the third millennium.

CONTENTS

FOREWORD
By Javier Pérez de Cuéllar

A reliable system of international security, progressive disarmament and sustainable economic growth are the acknowledged goals of all the peoples of the world. Although there are differences on how to achieve these ends, a consensus has emerged during the past forty years that they are profoundly interrelated and interdependent. This critical interrelationship was recognized by the framers of the Charter of the United Nations more than four decades ago. Specifically, Article 26 of the Charter speaks about the establishment and maintenance of international peace and security "with the least diversion for armaments of the world's human and economic resources". Article 55 envisages "the creation of conditions of stability and well-being which are necessary for peaceful and friendly relations among nations".

At present, almost a thousand billion dollars are expended each year on arms and armed forces, making substantial resources unavailable for sustainable economic and social development. The arms race inhibits confidence-building among States. Instead of providing security, it promotes fear and mistrust. Instead of creating an atmosphere of openness and co-operation, it promotes secrecy and confrontation. And instead of assuring stability, it establishes a precarious balance which is upset by every development in military technology.

The wanton extravagance entailed by the arms race is apparent from the fact that its expense exceeds the total income of the poorer half of humanity and the combined gross national products of large countries in Asia and Africa. The cost is not financial alone. Half a million scientists are employed on weapons research and military projects, when their knowledge and talent could be enlisted to far better effect in the pursuit of life-related goals.

Nor is it just the industrialized countries that indulge in such massive waste. Over the past two decades developing countries have spent more than $200 billion on weaponry, and in some of those countries, military outlays exceed public expenditures on education and health combined. Over and above the direct crippling financial burden, weapons purchases add to the external debt of these countries and create a secondary demand for imports that in turn aggravates their dependence.

The damage to the natural environment as a result of the arms race is also serious and, at times, irreparable. How utterly senseless it is that precious non-renewable resources should be used to build weapons that may destroy more of those resources if they are ever used.

As dangerous as the arms race itself, however, is the feeling that its persistence is humanity's ineluctable fate. Fortunately, this sense of inevitability has been somewhat overcome, and the hope for a radical reversal of course encouraged, by the conclusion of the Intermediate-Range Nuclear Force Treaty. This was the first agreement ever reached to actually reduce the awesome stocks of nuclear weapons in the world. There is reason to hope that it will mark a constructive beginning toward a significant reduction of strategic nuclear weapons with a view to their eventual elimination.

The historic development that has taken place is, of course, a triumph of reason and statesmanship but it also shows that what might be regarded as a visionary and unattainable objective at one stage of international relations can be perceived as quite attainable at another. The important thing is for the world community to maintain focus on ultimate goals and not to allow them to be eclipsed in power politics.

Ultimately, it is the peoples of the world who must save themselves. To do so, they and their governments must have objective data at their disposal and they must also be receptive to fresh ideas. It is my hope that this fine volume will make a significant contribution to knowledge on the interrelated goals of international security, disarmament and sustainable economic growth. It should encourage those in responsible positions to realize that these goals are both urgent and achievable.

"The world now stands on the brink of the final abyss. Let us all resolve to take all possible steps to ensure that we do not, through our own folly, go over the edge."

Earl Mountbatten 1979

Introduction: Peace or a new dark age

Peace is a word of great beauty and power. It has rung down the long ages – but never with such force as now. Because we find ourselves running out of time.

We are children of time, born of the dust of the universe, formed and reformed until life itself began to shape and create this planet of which we are part. We have behind us three and a half billion years of evolution, hundreds of thousands of years of social and co-operative living. We breathe to the pulse of this web of life that sustains and cares for us.

Human time has seen a great accelerating rise of our numbers, our skills our communicating power. A new human child is born every half a second. Each one a child of this Earth, with an inheritance of the past and hope for the future. We are reaching across the globe and to the depths of space with our science, and into the heart of the atom, and of life itself.

Our adventuring has taken us outside the world where we began, to look down on it from space – and see life, the life of Gaia, the living planet. And to see, as if in a mirror, ourselves: our wars and our pollution; our injustice and alienation from each other and from the self-sustaining natural world which shapes us.

This generation has begun to understand, dimly, the great experiment of co-operative living – by perhaps 10 million different species, in uncounted births and lives and deaths, in an endless cycling of materials, energy and creative interdependence – of which we are part. We have begun to understand that peace is indivisible from this living interdependence. We speak of "structural" peace – a positive presence of human well-being, justice, freedom and harmony with the life of Gaia. We speak of "sustainable peace" – of systems of living together that will both serve present generations and cause no theft of future lives.

But the future is stealing away from us like sands through an hour glass. We have been growing too fast and too carelessly. Our timescale is too rapid for the systems of nature, however forgiving, to accommodate the havoc we leave in our wake. And we have acquired the means of self-destruction and with it the taste for power and fear to drive this destruction on.

We are within reach of understanding the true power of peace. But unless we convert this understanding to new directions, our present course will lead straight to an end of human time. We have perhaps 15 years left. Fifteen springtimes. Five thousand days and nights. Five thousand sunrises and glimmering dusks, five thousand wakings in the heart of Gaia. Unless we can change our minds and hearts and actions in time.

The people of Gaia

We live on a small planet circling a minor star at the edge of an unremarkable galaxy. Life here is sustained by energy from the sun, but is otherwise a "closed" system – materials are cycled and recycled through earth, air and water by uncounted lives, from microbes to mammals, nothing lost, nothing new. Though individuals die, the life community continues, almost immortal, experimenting, accumulating experience, increasingly diverse and interdependent. Our own species is young, and very much an experiment. Such innovations in evolution always cause changes around them, until a new equilibrium is reached. But the impact of our species is extraordinary. In the last 80 years alone, our numbers have tripled, our consumption risen 20-fold. Pressed for space and resources, we are becoming violent. And still the expansion continues. We have even reached out into space. This adventure has shown that our planet may even, itself, be alive, a self-sustaining entity, Gaia. Human impact now threatens to outweigh the stabilizing capacity of Gaia. We may render ourselves extinct, if we do not blast ourselves to oblivion first. In either case, Gaia is unlikely to repeat her experiment.

The meaning of Gaia

Life defies definition, yet we distinguish its presence at once. When space travel showed us the world from outside, we saw in the dark of space the colour, beauty and movement of a living thing. This instinct was borne out when the scientist James Lovelock, believing that life on other planets could be detected by its impact on atmospheric chemistry, turned his attention to Earth – and found its atmosphere so "improbable" in geochemical terms that only some regulatory process could explain it. The "regulator" he proposed was life, planetary life as a whole self-regulating organism. He named this entity Gaia, after the ancient Greek goddess of the Earth. The science of Gaia is new, exploring the planet-wide homeostatic processes in which we share. But the concept is old, a rediscovery of what all earlier peoples have known. We are, in Lovelock's words "part and partners in a very democratic entity". Formed of the fabric of Gaia, living amid the web of interdependent species and the traces of past lives, we cannot conquer nature without defeating ourselves. Recognition of this truth is fundamental to peace.

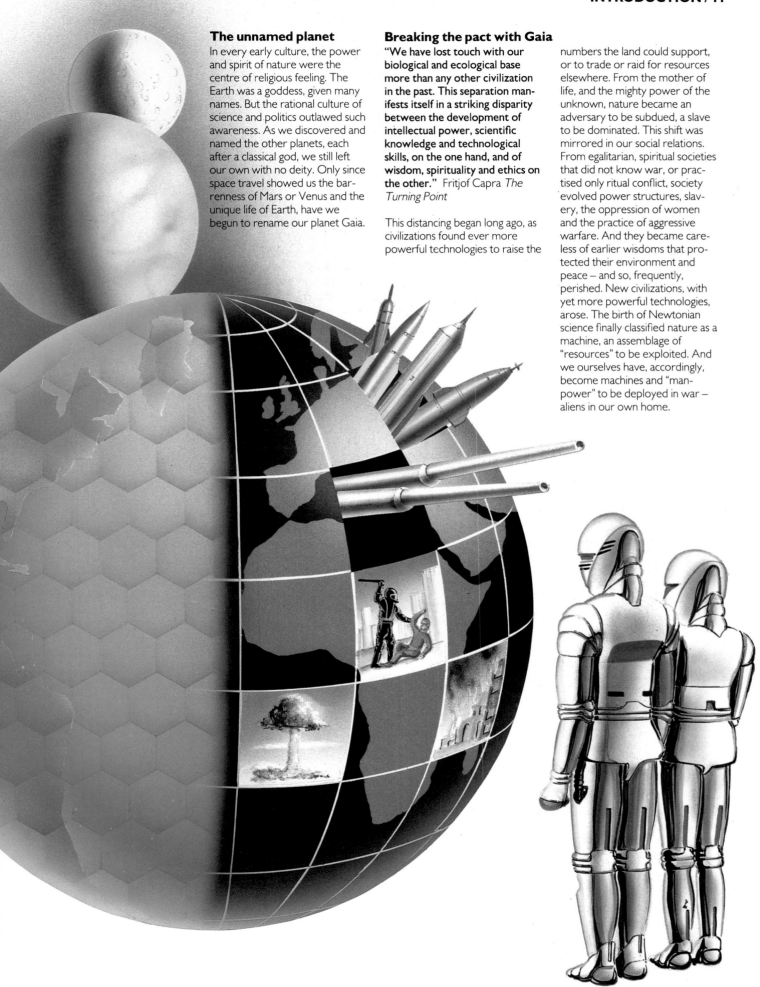

The unnamed planet

In every early culture, the power and spirit of nature were the centre of religious feeling. The Earth was a goddess, given many names. But the rational culture of science and politics outlawed such awareness. As we discovered and named the other planets, each after a classical god, we still left our own with no deity. Only since space travel showed us the barrenness of Mars or Venus and the unique life of Earth, have we begun to rename our planet Gaia.

Breaking the pact with Gaia

"We have lost touch with our biological and ecological base more than any other civilization in the past. This separation manifests itself in a striking disparity between the development of intellectual power, scientific knowledge and technological skills, on the one hand, and of wisdom, spirituality and ethics on the other." Fritjof Capra *The Turning Point*

This distancing began long ago, as civilizations found ever more powerful technologies to raise the numbers the land could support, or to trade or raid for resources elsewhere. From the mother of life, and the mighty power of the unknown, nature became an adversary to be subdued, a slave to be dominated. This shift was mirrored in our social relations. From egalitarian, spiritual societies that did not know war, or practised only ritual conflict, society evolved power structures, slavery, the oppression of women and the practice of aggressive warfare. And they became careless of earlier wisdoms that protected their environment and peace – and so, frequently, perished. New civilizations, with yet more powerful technologies, arose. The birth of Newtonian science finally classified nature as a machine, an assemblage of "resources" to be exploited. And we ourselves have, accordingly, become machines and "manpower" to be deployed in war – aliens in our own home.

Technology and civilization

Homo sapiens has been around for at least a quarter of a million years. Yet war and military might have been known only in the last five thousand – two per cent at most of our history. War is neither a part of human nature nor, necessarily, of civilized urban life. The Anatolian city of Catal Huyuk, for instance, has been excavated back to the seventh millennium BC. In the 800 years of its existence so far examined, there is no evidence of any sack or massacre, nor a single skeleton showing signs of a violent death.

Archaeology throws light on our social evolution. When did patriarchal values of dominance originate? Stone-age symbols are of fertility and earth goddesses. Catal Huyuk had a female priestess class; in Sumerian religion, in Minoan art, goddesses predominate. Early societies laid more emphasis than ours on spiritual life, the cycles of nature and co-operative, sharing values. Power of rule, and the values and militarism to back it, seem both to have begun around 3000 BC.

History is a canvas on which each generation writes its own view of the past. The commonest modern view has been that history represents progress – a long upward struggle of humanity to "master" nature and achieve well-being. This belief has rested, for several hundred years, on our faith in human reason, and in science and technology. Two world wars shook our faith in reason. And the last few decades, of nuclear fear and environmental decline, have challenged the belief in science. Technology has certainly bettered the human lot. But it seems also to carry the seeds of destruction.

Two other views of history are offered by older cultures. The first, the Garden of Eden view of the Bible or the "Golden Age" of the Greeks, sees it as a *regression*, a long decline from some earlier, harmonious state, a long exile. There is no doubt that humans have increasingly lost contact with nature, destroyed their environment and engaged in ever greater savagery in war. Many civilizations have left treeless or desert lands, where once forests flourished, and failed through this destruction – a risk now global in scale.

The second older view sees "nothing new under the sun". History is a cycle of the rise and fall of civilizations; a see-saw of stability and change, of egalitarian societies and hierarchies, democracy and autocracy, socialism and capitalism, patriarchy and feminine values, spiritual and material, peace and war.

This view mirrors Eastern philosophies, which see life as an eternal flux of opposites, and these have influenced the new approaches of systems theory and holistic, organic, ecology. All agree that only by finding a balance do societies achieve stability.

Progression, regression or cycles of imbalance? There is truth in each. And each affects how we see the future. The progress camp expects technology and reason once more to rescue us; the regression camp awaits armageddon. The ecologist looks for a new balance, a turnabout in perception and the use of heart and spirit, as well as reason, to control our technology to serve human and Gaia's well-being.

Historical paradox

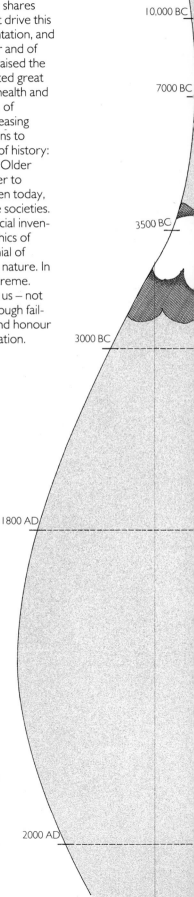

200,000 BC

10,000 BC

7000 BC

3500 BC

3000 BC

1800 AD

2000 AD

Innovation in technology is conventionally used to mark the progress of civilization – the Stone Age, the Bronze Age, the Iron Age, the Industrial Age, and so on. Humanity shares with life itself the characteristics that drive this process – inventiveness, experimentation, and the search for higher levels of order and of interdependence. Technology has raised the "carrying capacity" of the land, created great cities, beauty, wealth, and brought health and ease to many. But it casts a shadow, of environmental destruction and increasing savagery in war, which now threatens to overwhelm us. This is the paradox of history: is "progress" a career into oblivion? Older cultures, few in numbers, lived closer to nature and did not practise war. Even today, there are peaceable and sustainable societies. War, and malign technology, are social inventions – born of arrogance, of the ethics of dominance and competition, of denial of gentler values, and separation from nature. In the Nuclear Age, this sickness is extreme. Technology rules, and may destroy us – not through historical necessity, but through failure to control it, to make it serve and honour the "ecological imperative" of civilization.

The ecological imperative

The time scale of human cultures given here is not absolute – civilizations tend to evolve in similar technological stages, but at widely different times and with different results. Moreover, the oldest styles of human culture are still with us. Hunter-gatherer, nomadic pastoralist and peasant farmer persist alongside the megacities of "modern" life. Though great civilizations have repeatedly failed, these simpler technologies survive. "Advanced" societies have much to learn from such traditional peoples, whose understanding of natural and human systems is of a different order – and whose technology has, over long periods, become closely integrated with those systems. By contrast, technological advance, while it seeks to improve well-being, often brings an illusory sense of power and separation from nature, and erodes the cultural beliefs that encoded sustainable practice. Equally, military technology seduces us with its power, separates us from the act of violence, and erodes our moral norms. Only when war, famine and environmental collapse strike, do we understand, too late, our dependence on nature and on peace – the ecological imperative.

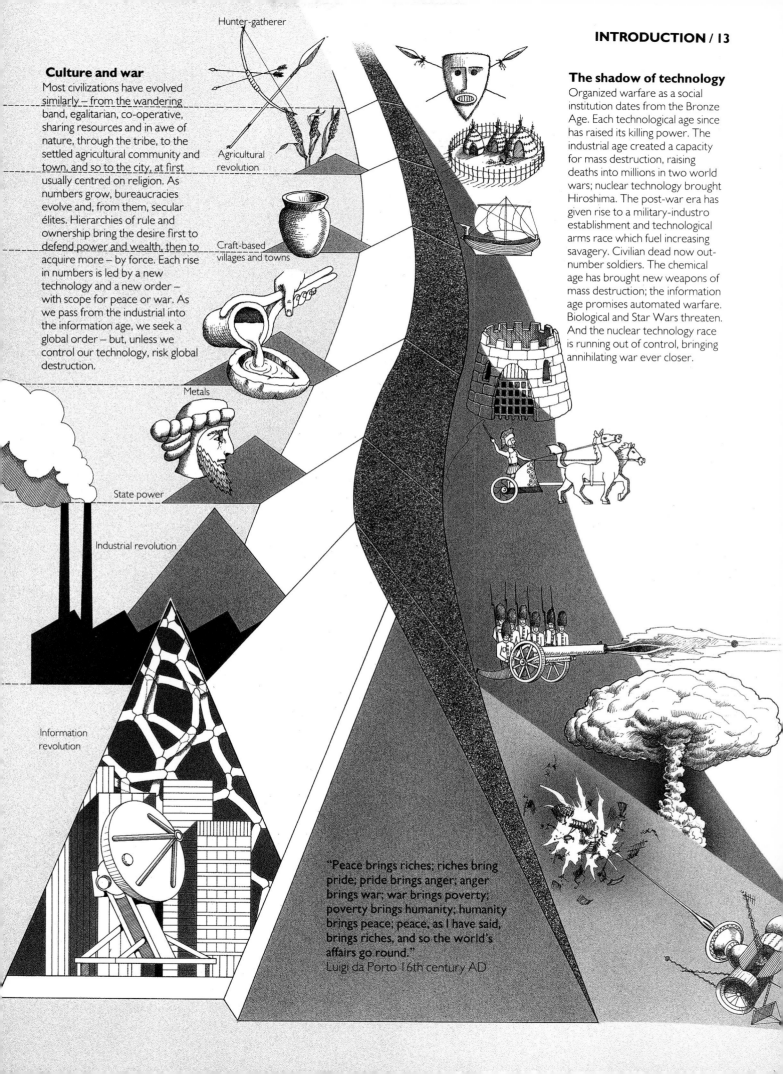

Culture and war

Most civilizations have evolved similarly – from the wandering band, egalitarian, co-operative, sharing resources and in awe of nature, through the tribe, to the settled agricultural community and town, and so to the city, at first usually centred on religion. As numbers grow, bureaucracies evolve and, from them, secular élites. Hierarchies of rule and ownership bring the desire first to defend power and wealth, then to acquire more – by force. Each rise in numbers is led by a new technology and a new order – with scope for peace or war. As we pass from the industrial into the information age, we seek a global order – but, unless we control our technology, risk global destruction.

Hunter-gatherer

Agricultural revolution

Craft-based villages and towns

Metals

State power

Industrial revolution

Information revolution

The shadow of technology

Organized warfare as a social institution dates from the Bronze Age. Each technological age since has raised its killing power. The industrial age created a capacity for mass destruction, raising deaths into millions in two world wars; nuclear technology brought Hiroshima. The post-war era has given rise to a military-industro establishment and technological arms race which fuel increasing savagery. Civilian dead now out-number soldiers. The chemical age has brought new weapons of mass destruction; the information age promises automated warfare. Biological and Star Wars threaten. And the nuclear technology race is running out of control, bringing annihilating war ever closer.

"Peace brings riches; riches bring pride; pride brings anger; anger brings war; war brings poverty; poverty brings humanity; humanity brings peace; peace, as I have said, brings riches, and so the world's affairs go round."
Luigi da Porto 16th century AD

The pursuit of security

In the past 25 years the world has spent, in 1984 prices, 16 trillion dollars on the global arms race. The annual cost has multiplied 2.5 times in 25 years, rising far faster than global income.

What has the expenditure of such great amounts of military money bought us? The ostensible purpose has been to provide "security". But instead, we have become increasingly less secure. Such is the absurdity of today's world: the more we pursue security the less secure we become. It is like some Alice in Wonderland auction, where every bidder pays up, and the higher the bidding goes, the smaller the goods become. We are spending huge sums to buy insecurity.

Ideological rivalry and intransigence drive us on. The plain folly of this was long ago ridiculed by Jonathan Swift in *Gulliver's Travels* – at a time when war could still make us laugh. The minuscule citizens of Lilliput had "been engaged in a most obstinate war for six and thirty moons past" with a neighbouring empire over a religious schism – a disagreement as to whether eggs should be broken at the big or the little end. There is no doubt that the language of our two "empires" today often has a Lilliputian ring.

We are driven on, too, by fear: fear of the evil forces in society, fear of "enemies". We fail to recognize that the enemy is fear itself – fear and alienation and belief in power and force where only co-operation and social skills will serve.

Nuclear warheads are not the only weapons of mass destruction we are stockpiling. Chemical weapons also qualify for this distinction. Chemical arsenals too are huge and growing: the US reportedly has enough to kill the world population 300 times over; the Soviets much the same. About 13 developing countries have them. They are known as the "poor man's atomic bombs". Advances in technology occur at a bewildering rate, increasing the lethality of all weapons. So much so that today's distinction between conventional and non-conventional wars may become obscured.

So the weapons accumulate. A war of empires now would not make us laugh – or weep – but exterminate us. In the nuclear age, any war may escalate to global nuclear war. Insecurity for one is insecurity for all.

"Competitive arms races breed insecurity among nations through spirals of reciprocal fears. Nations need to muster resources to combat environmental degradation and poverty. By misdirecting scarce resources, arms races contribute further to insecurity." So says *Our Common Future*, the report of the recent World Commission on Environment and Development.

While we spend huge sums on irrational fears, our real security is more gravely threatened every hour. Human survival is grim necessity for one billion people who already know their own armageddon – poverty. And planetary life-support systems show signs of strain. The world community must address these crises. All our resources are needed. We cannot afford militarism; we cannot risk militarism. It is obsolete.

The idol of security

"In the face of explosive social needs, the race for security through arms has an alarming air of unreality. How much more difficult it will be for historians of the future to find reality in this militarized world . . . How will their best computers deal with the balance of terror, the specialized language of the weaponeers, the gaming of megadeaths, the military grotesqueries of today? Of course, the historians will conclude, it was not the real world; it was pure theater . . . a diversion no doubt from intractable social problems."
Ruth Sivard

But it is all too real. The latter half of this century has seen a new phenomenon in human society, a relentless rise in militarization, an escalating imperative of fear. In our crowded world of separate, competing nation states, the search for "security" against each other is a madness. What sane society would stockpile enough nuclear and chemical weapons to end human life, and celebrate a Year of Peace by adding to this deadly arsenal? Even as the superpowers seek to reduce nuclear warheads to a number that will kill us all only 6 times over, NATO is worrying about reduced "security" and seeking to introduce new warheads. The arms trade perpetuates wars of mounting savagery; new weaponry makes terrorism and insurgence more deadly; the nuclear state fuels secrecy and abuse of power. Our search for "security" threatens the very freedoms we prize.

Security has become a god, and a cruel and demanding one. Our tribute to fear now runs at around $1 trillion a year. But the real cost is the diversion of resources needed elsewhere. And our insecurity increases. We live under the shadow of nuclear war, of famine, violence, and human and environmental tragedy.

The price of insecurity

Each year, the world spends more on military "security" than the poorer half of humanity earns. The true cost is the loss to all other sectors of human need, a loss compounded over years of neglect. One billion people in developing countries, one in five of world population, live in absolute poverty. Another billion are also inadequately housed and 100 million have no shelter at all. Three out of five governments spend more on military "defence" than on defence against all the enemies of good health. Meantime, 20% of infants born in developing countries fail to live to their fifth birthday. Unnecessary deaths of infants total nearly 15 million a year – 40,000 every day. Four million die from 6 cheaply immunizable diseases, five million from diarrhoea preventable by oral rehydration salts costing virtually nothing. Government inaction and unrelieved poverty drive on environmental destruction. Failure to take preventative measures in Africa allowed a famine that put 35 million people at risk in the mid-1980s. Each year, 6 million hectares of productive dryland turn to desert; each year, 11 million hectares of forest are destroyed. We know solutions to all these problems. But without funding and the attention of world governments and scientists, they remain unsolved.

A new Dark Age?

Some of the team that worked on the preparation of this Peace Atlas also worked five years ago on the creation of the *Gaia Atlas of Planet Management*. At that time, they felt the sense of a crisis coming; on this, they sensed the crisis around us. There is a change of mood, too: a certain hardening of the heart in political circles; a sense of growing helplessness elsewhere; a reckless wealth-gathering in the money markets. We have already begun to live as if there were no tomorrow.

Civilization has known Dark Ages before. Sometime in the 13th century BC, for instance, the Mediterranean world collapsed in war and chaos. For five hundred years life returned to basics. So complete was the fall that not until modern times were the civilizations of the Hittites, Minoans and Mycenae rediscovered. Again, with the fall of Rome, Europe was plunged into a half-millennium of collapse; again, all memory of what had gone before was lost to the survivors.

But what we face now could put these Dark Ages to shame. We live under an ever-growing threat of nuclear holocaust. Unless the nuclear arms race is soon brought under control, it is hard to see how a nuclear world war can be avoided. The explosive power of the nuclear arsenals is equivalent to well over a million Hiroshimas. If these weapons are ever used in war, civilization would be pushed back to the Stone Age in a flash. Nuclear winter, followed by famine, radiation and disease would decimate the survivors.

This nuclear-created Dark Age would not last long – for us. It is more than likely that humankind would be pushed beyond the point of no return, and eventually become extinct. Many species would go with us, leaving the evolutionary energy of Gaia to build a world we shall not be there to see.

There is, however, an alternative Dark Age looming, caused, like those before, by the kick-back of human mismanagement of ourselves and the resources on which civilization is based. But this time, global in scale.

The temperature controls of Gaia are increasingly disturbed by our outpourings of "greenhouse" gases, and by deforestation. In the past 125 years, human activity has raised carbon dioxide levels in the atmosphere by nearly a third. The planet is getting warmer. Climate change is the number one danger concerning future planners today.

Famine, drought, flood, chemical poisoning and the death of once fertile lands are all rapidly rising. Victims of human-induced floods and droughts doubled in the decade of the 1970s. As with our own numbers, it looks as though we may be seeing that familiar, deadly exponential curve – doubling, then doubling again.

And wars are growing ever more frequent: a familiar sign of the instability of a civilization approaching collapse. In the words of Ruth Sivard: "Every hamlet has been brought within the orbit of conflict, every inhabitant made a potential victim of random annihilation. Militarization presumably designed to insulate the nation state has in fact united the world's population in a precarious mutual vulnerability."

On the brink of armageddon

"Most of today's decision-makers will be dead before the planet feels the heavier effects of acid precipitation, global warming, ozone depletion, or widespread desertification and species loss. Most of the young voters of today will still be alive . . . and were the harshest critics of the planet's present management." Our Common Future

Humanity is at the brink of an abyss. If we go over the edge, civilization will plunge back to the dark ages. If our anger and fear unleash nuclear war, our species may become extinct. If our industry and agriculture provoke global climate change, catastrophe may be as complete and almost as swift. If we avoid both, mounting poverty and conflict in a ruined environment may be harder to endure. Images of armageddon have haunted the human mind for centuries. It is tempting to dismiss them. But rising numbers, unsustainable practice and uncontrolled technology all interact to malign effect. Under such pressure, fear, greed and hostility drive us to violence. And our governments fail us.

Nuclear holocaust

Competition in nuclear technology is out of control, driving a race for "fight capability" and "strategic superiority", which one side may win within 15 years. Our peril will then be immensely greater. Even a limited nuclear exchange would wipe out civilization in the northern hemisphere. The nuclear winter, famines and disease that followed would affect all higher life forms on earth, probably exterminating the human species.

Ecocatastrophe

The tragedy of man-made "natural" disasters is accelerating. In the 1960s, drought struck 18.5 million people each year; flooding 5.2 million. In the 1970s, the victims rose to 24.4 million and 15.4 million – doubling in a decade. The 1980s have so far seen 35 million afflicted by drought in Africa alone, while deforestation has produced devastating floods below the Andes and Himalayas. And fuel-burning is producing a global warming that threatens climatic disruption on a massive scale. We are risking catastrophic failure of vital Gaian life-support systems.

Violence and chaos

Human numbers have risen four-fold since the 18th century; war deaths 22 times. There have been 120 wars since World War II – more, and more savage than those before it. In this century, 99 million people have died in war. The arms trade, injustice, oppression, and rising resource crises in a crowded world are spreading war, terrorism, and state violence against citizens worldwide, leaving no person on the planet untouched.

Poverty and famine

From 1975 to 1986 developing world debts increased fourfold; by 1988 they totalled $1 trillion. Debt also burdens developed nations. It is the poor who pay. Even richer states have a growing underclass, and one in five people on Earth live in dire poverty. As numbers increase, their plight deepens. In the drought and flood-ridden tropics, immediate need drives people to further land pressure. Though food surpluses embarrass some nations, famine is striking with increasing severity those who cannot buy across a wide hunger belt around the globe.

"And I saw, and behold a white horse: and he that sat on him . . . went forth conquering . . . And there went out another horse that was red: and power was given to him that sat thereon to take peace from the earth; and that they should kill one another . . . and I beheld, and lo a black horse, and he that sat on him had a pair of balances in his hand . . . And I looked, and behold a pale horse, and his name that sat on him was Death . . . And power was given to them over the fourth part of the earth, to kill with sword, and with hunger, and with death . . ." The Revelation of St John the Divine

Bridges to the future

"If we limit ourselves to the old-paradigm concept of averting war, we are trying to overpower darkness rather than switching on the light. If we reframe the problem – if we think of fostering community, health, innovation, self-discovery, purpose – we are already engaged in waging peace." Marilyn Ferguson

Crisis brings out the human spirit and instinct for survival. The rise of understanding and pressure for change is accelerating, pushing forward a huge creative effort of practicable alternatives. Old leadership is intransigent. But the world is reaching the turning point. The battle of the old and the new is joined.

Ecological wisdom lies in the understanding that just because a thing is good, more of it is not necessarily better. Balance and homeostasis are truer measures of success. Technology is often good for us; but too much of it is definitely not. Our aggressive and competitive side may help us survive, but too much emphasis on it can destroy us. Ecology also teaches us that large problems often need small solutions – in many millions of individual and community efforts – a paradox that governments are poor at grasping.

Faced with complex crises and many apparent options of economic policies, technologies and management styles, we find it difficult to calculate consequences very far ahead. By default, and for political survival, government decisions are short-term and short-sighted. But if we recognize the primacy of the criteria of peace and sustainable living within Gaia, the choice is clear and aimed to the future.

Peace is inseparable from sustainable living – we cannot have one without the other. Yet we have to get there first. We have to build bridges to the future.
● We must break the link between security and military force, and redefine security. Real security is human and planetary security, common security with all nations.
● We must learn non-violence and conflict resolution.
● We must apply Gaian constraints to decisions.
● We must disarm, halt the arms race and divert our military resources to pressing global problems.
● We must place moral controls on technology, especially military technology, and predict with caution any new technology's consequences: if in doubt, don't!
● We need new attitudes. Tomorrow's citizens must accept that survival depends on commitment to moderated national sovereignty and global loyalties.
● We will have to frame new systems of governance that limit the abuse of power and encourage new leadership.
● We must spread the spiritual revolution that is coming: of concern for nature, justice and peace.
● And we must abolish war. We need no longer enquire why or how. We simply have to stop.

Many of these "bridges" demand very difficult decisions for politicians. This will take huge public pressure. Each of us has a choice. Either we give priority to peace and sustainable living, or we will not survive long into the 21st century.

Seize the time

"This chasm between the old and the new is a treacherous historical interval."
Richard Falk

"During the disintegration of a civilization, two separate plays with different plots are being performed simultaneously side by side."
Arnold Toynbee

The future looks black for humankind. Already, famine, poverty, and war are beginning to multiply out of control. Our institutions of governance seem bankrupt of ideas. Locked in rivalry for dominance through technology, wealth and military might, they are leading us into a new Dark Age. From below is rising a tide of approaches based on ecological wisdom and human justice. Whether one sees it as Alvin Toffler's "Third Wave" of civilization, or as Fritjof Capra's "Turning Point", a global constituency is being born – of ordinary people, campaigning organizations and local communities demanding peace. In Falk's imagery, we *can* cross the chasm of the present – if we are able to perceive the future, and build bridges towards it. But the interval is turbulent. Today, the two superpowers are being forced, largely by economic pressures, to consider disarmament and compromise. We must seize the time.

The path to disaster

The approaches of the old wave, founded in the mechanistic and materialist industrial age, and in patriarchal images of dominance, central control, and militarism, still permeate all governments. As Capra says: "overemphasis on the scientific method and on rational, analytical thinking has led to attitudes that are profoundly anti-ecological." These fuel mounting global crises and colour all "solutions". Thus Star Wars proposes to establish peace by force and over-mastering technology; there are even plans for "space colonies" where the élite can escape from a plundered and ruined planet – while the rest, presumably, starve.

The path to the future

We have to live here, on this Earth and with this Earth. And we need a revolution in understanding to achieve it. Peace and security cannot be achieved by nations in competition against each other, but only by all peoples, together. The approaches of the new wave rising to meet this challenge are diverse. There is pressure for democratization of power, a broadened United Nations and new internationalism, and a resurgence of local communities. There are peace movements, green movements, appropriate technology, and hopes of a global citizenry born of the information revolution. All share an ecological, holistic and co-operative ethic – and the vision of one Earth, the living planet, and one humanity, free of war.

The threats to security and survival are grave. We join with others in calling on our institutions of governance to take thought for tomorrow, heed the warnings of our advisory commissions and NGOs and listen to the voice of the people. We challenge the United Nations General Assembly, the Security Council, their member states and all regional organizations to address the issues of real security, and in particular to:

- Cease from the arms race and from the manufacture, deployment and sale of perilous and wasteful weaponry, and deploy resources instead to:

- Eradicate poverty, the scourge of peoples and the engine of environmental destruction

- Reduce economic injustice and usury

- Prevent further acts that threaten the atmosphere

- Introduce policies of sustainable development and guardianship of nature without delay.

"We want a world in which we can declare our identity as 'world citizens', but no such world exists, as yet. For now, we can proclaim ourselves as *citizen pilgrims*, committed to a journey through time to a future as yet uncreated"
Richard Falk, Committee for a Just World Peace

PART ONE: PAST

"Peace is a state of mind, not a state of the nation."
Marilyn Ferguson

This opening section of the *Gaia Peace Atlas* is descriptive, considering the roots of peace, war and peace-keeping and the lessons we have learned from many thousands of years of social history. The first chapter explores the foundations of peace within the co-operative and creative drives of humanity, our social institutions and our relationship with nature. The second chapter examines the political and ecological roots of war and the origins of violence in today's world. The third chapter analyses the means that societies have devised to resolve conflicts peaceably, and our attempts, so far largely unsuccessful, to apply these lessons at the level of international peace-keeping and conflict resolution and the rule of law.

Life is creative, and seeks higher order and new levels of connection. The Darwinian view of natural selection may have taught us to see "nature red in tooth and claw"; Descartian science may have convinced us of nature as a machine. But ecology and Gaian science are now showing us that evolution is as much co-operative as competitive, that species and their environment evolve together in mutual interdependence. And nature is no machine to be understood by its parts, but a living system we can perceive best in its whole behaviour.

How has our species come to threaten damage to this system, and so its own survival and that of many other species besides? Homo sapiens is basically a social animal. We need to live in groups for survival – for food and childcare or for defence against predators. We share with most of animal life both co-operative and aggressive drives. Aggression, however, is not a licence for violence, but a biological tool to create social order. Like all animal societies, we use our aggression to back up rules – of territory, of social precedence, of sexual choices and of social behaviour generally. Aggression is, in fact, a prelude to increased co-operation.

For most of our history we have lived as small bands of perhaps 10 to 30 sharing individuals, hunting and gathering, with leaders chosen on occasion for their strength, knowledge or sheer "charisma". And for most of our history, we have not known or practised warfare – organized killing by order of a leader. As larger tribal groups arose, and more groups occupied neighbouring areas, the need for territorial boundaries led to ritual conflicts. Death was extremely rare – as it still is in many similar groups today.

Laurens van der Post, describing the Bushmen, the "first peoples" of Africa says: "I asked them if they had ever known war, and they said, oh yes, they had fought and were known as very great fighters. But except when they fought against the Black and the White people, they had only one war among themselves. I asked, 'Was it an awful war?' And they said, 'It was a terrible war.' I asked, 'Were many people killed?' And they said, 'One man was killed.' That was enough. One man."

Indeed the archaeological record shows no solid evidence of group murder until after the last Ice Age – by which time Stone Age peoples had evolved fine cave art, mythologies and nature or ancestor worship, crafts, and the beginnings of agriculture. The value systems of early peoples were certainly very different from our own. We know such societies today. In awe of nature, they see living spirituality in every leaf and creature, every aspect of their lives. Dependent on each other for survival, they use codes of sharing, of gift exchange, to bind the group together. While it is risky to extrapolate backwards in history, the cave art, burials and female figurines found from early peoples do suggest similar beliefs.

Change, experiment and growth are also driving forces of nature which we share, alongside the search for order and co-operation, for social codes, and stability. All these drives, coupled with our technical skills, and our simple need to survive, provide the impetus for civilization. But settlement also creates accumulation of wealth, and larger groups need more complex forms of governance. Gradually, perceptions of nature and religious beliefs shift in

THE LESSONS OF EXPERIENCE

favour of secular management – and the hierarchical social structures with which we have struggled ever since.

The earliest settled communities appear to have operated by council and debate, the roots of present day democratic systems. Early full civilizations in urban centres, too, had councils of citizens in many cases. The trend towards power and autocracy emerges with warfare and military might. They go hand in hand. As technology raises our numbers, and capacity to live in larger groups, so it raises the scale and impact of armed might, and intractable power interests. History is written in the struggle of societies to find control of power, checks and balances, while preserving order.

Once war is known as a tool of power, technology and the prestige of warriors powerfully reinforce it. So too does its success: there is no doubt that war has on some occasions brought much gain to those who won. War as a political tool would not otherwise have persisted so long, to our peril. Since the industrial revolution, technology has made war hugely destructive. And in this century, technology and power have both run wild. The global rise of military power, the iniquitous arms trade for profit, the manipulation of whole peoples into ideological hatred, the destruction of civilians and unthinkable acts of savagery; all are driven on by the ethics of dominance, of materialism and of unstoppable technological innovation.

Modern society is very complex. Conflict and disagreement are endemic. All through the evolution of societies, we have sought ways to prevent conflict and disorder, to live under codes of behaviour, moral and spiritual and social; to live peaceably together by consensus. The law and the customary beliefs of humanity have grown and been refined steadily via many cultures. Older ways of settling disputes, seen in hindsight as barbarous, have given way to less violent ones: duels, trial by ordeal, dismemberment, burning, have all been abandoned. If we can "disinvent" them, we can surely do the same for war, militarism, nuclear weaponry and a world of private armies scrapping like medieval warlords.

We are seeking a global order and conflict resolution and control. But the task is difficult. The impetus of the times has brought a new form of government system – a world of equal-in-rights nation states, all pursuing sovereign power. A nation state is a "world actor" in which people of mainly common descent, culture and language occupy a territory with defined borders under one government and set of rules. But in their creation, modern states have often seen one dominant nation subjugate or displace other groups. These "stateless" nations or so-called "minorities" have had their right to self-determination effectively removed. Nearly 200 sovereign states and many disenfranchized minorities are recipe enough for conflict. But our times have also seen the rise of nuclear superpowers battling for influence, and more may soon join the arena of power. The United Nations is paralyzed by all these conflicting interests. It is a hard world indeed to govern.

People have always wanted peace – particularly after experiencing the waste and horror of war first hand. But do we know what peace is? Our concept of peace has grown and evolved. We are beginning to see that peace has two faces: the *absence* of war, violence, injustice and oppression – public, or private in domestic life – and of hostility and damage to nature. And the *presence* of belief in non-violence, in spiritual values, in justice and morality and of a sense of partnership and harmony with nature. Sustainable peace requires a society that can honour these values and control technology and the abuse of power.

1 The roots of peace

Introduced by Johan Galtung

Peace has roots. We do not claim to know them fully; all we know is that they are deep. We also know that there are many kinds of roots. Violence in general and war in particular come in many varieties. To ask "What is the cause of war?" is like asking "What is the cause of illness?". In medical studies, the twin ideas of types of illnesses and careful diagnosis on the basis of symptoms have served us well. The same should apply to peace studies.

But then there is preventive, not only curative, medicine; prophylaxis, not only therapy. And here we are greatly helped by the notion that there may be a certain unity to health, and probably also a certain unity to peace. In other words, building peace may actually be simpler than trying to remedy a situation that has gone wrong. But how?

Maybe Gaia shows the way. There is something ecological to peace. Nature's balance is rooted in diversity (of biota and abiota) and symbiosis between the components of an ecosystem. I would say that peace is also rooted in diversity and symbiosis, meaning the functional interdependence, not only of diverse "actors", like countries, but also of municipalities, international organizations, transnational corporations and so on, not to mention non-human life and non-living resources. However, there is a limit to the organic analogy. Nature is also a brutal place where the strong often devour the weak. So, as well as diversity and symbiosis, let me add to this short list of the roots of peace one more item: equity. As a minimum, this means to maintain the other party. More often it means to promote the other party, also because that is in our own interest. In other words, the symbiosis should not be parasitic. Democracy is based on the assumption that we become strong together precisely when we are diverse (often called "pluralistic" in this context). But we have to use that diversity to co-operate symbiotically, respecting the rights of others. In my opinion, true love is based on exactly the same three principles.

Let me be more specific, and also more political. The parties to a peace structure should be diverse, entering the symbiotic relation with different things to offer. I could go one step further and say: there should be more than two parties (being two so easily leads to bipolar confrontation). Then I could do the same for symbiosis and say: there should be more than just one item on the co-operation agenda. If one, say the economy, fails, there should also be political or cultural co-operation. If relations go sour with one actor, there is the second or the third. Build peace like nature builds a mature ecosystem. Be generous, base it on redundance, always have something extra to fall back on.

Moreover, combine diversity and symbiosis. Spin ties of equitable interdependence between all possible types and subtypes in all parties. Peace is not built by having a summit meeting between two superpowers, but by spinning ties of equitable co-operation at all levels, including cross-levels. This means having ordinary Soviet citizens interact with the US president and ordinary US citizens with the Soviet General Secretary (the latter does happen, the former very rarely). Finally, let new actors emerge. More particularly, actors who transcend the existing actors and provide a setting within which they can practise diversity and symbiosis.

Johan Galtung

"Peace is more than an absence of war. It is a positive quality, with three essential components: relations of harmony and mutual respect among peoples in a society; human co-operation for the common good; and justice based on the concept of equality for all. Indeed, I would argue that the larger meaning of peace is justice and equality. For without justice, peace is impossible."
Mwalimu Julius K. Nyerere 1987

Throughout history most people have lived their lives without experiencing the direct violence of war. Until this century it was unusual for civilians to be targeted in war. Yet millions have died prematurely from a lack of the basic human needs – adequate nutrition, safe water, sanitation and basic health care. Such *structural* violence persists even though humanity is an essentially co-operative and gregarious species. People have always wanted peace – and sought it by consensus, by management of resources, shared wealth and power, and law.

The foundations of civilization

It was the instinct to co-operate, to share the burdens and the fruits of existence, which originally brought people together in large social groups. The individual then has greater liberty and a wider range of choices – about type of work, partner, social standing and cultural activities. There is a sense of control over destiny. In smaller communities with little individual specialization, daily life tends to revolve around survival. When a civilization is booming, human creativity flourishes, spirituality grows into organized religion, art and crafts are in demand, and there is opportunity for individual development. This is the impetus for civilization.

A society that is concerned with social justice will minimize structural violence and protect human rights. When these conditions are satisfied, and basic needs are met sustainably, there is genuine, positive peace.

This desire to co-operate with others is more than just an instinct; it is also a higher value, something most people strive toward. And it is closely linked to morality and spirituality. Within social groups, these three drives interact to produce religious and legal codes, a specific social identity and many cultural expressions. These, in turn, become a system of governance.

It is only because societies are made up of groups of basically co-operative, like-minded individuals that it is possible for us to live together in communities of several million people, as we do today. Without an overall consensus, all social systems would fall apart.

With the rapid increase in global population over the last 200 years, all human societies are coming under immense pressure. Growing economic interdependence, and now the combined threats of nuclear holocaust and global ecological catastrophe, mean that social groups can no longer guarantee their continued existence in isolation. We have to co-operate, now, at a planetary level.

If we are to believe the view of humanity presented in the media, the obstacles to achieving a peaceful

Co-operation and consensus

Co-operation, morality and spirituality are the foundations of civilization. Without the desire to co-operate, human beings would not congregate in large social groups. Without a shared morality, we would not be able to exist peacefully with one another. And without spirituality to provide a sense of common purpose, societies disintegrate in secular conflict. Society can be regarded as the outward expression of these innate human drives. By developing systems of management, belief and responsibility that have a general consensus in the society, we have learned to live relatively peaceably in ever-larger social groups, often containing great internal diversity. The larger the group, the greater the sense of common responsibility for the peacefulness of the society has to be. The ability of a social group to achieve this consensus effectively limits its size.

The fact that we have learned to co-operate in societies with many conflicting interests is a reflection of just how strong these drives are. At a global level, though, there are tremendous difficulties in bringing together diverse cultural groups with systems of belief that are, in some cases, opposed to each other. Now, however, we no longer have the luxury of being able to wait for the mechanisms of co-operation and consensus to evolve. Humanity is presently faced with a question: can we achieve the consensus necessary to co-operate as a single global community of more than 6 billion people by the year 2000?

The evolution of co-operation

The earliest unit of human social organization – the band – was prevalent until at least 10,000BC. Bands consisted of about 30 or 40 individuals at most, comprising related family units. By 7000BC, the farming village of Jericho had a population of approximately 2000 people. The largest Greek city states had populations of around 10,000. In Mexico in the 3rd century AD, the Teotihuacan civilization encompassed a quarter of a million people, 100,000 of whom lived in its capital city. Rome was the only metropolis of over 1 million from 400AD to 1800AD. Today, China is the largest single, cohesive co-operative group in the world. Its population of 1 billion is greater than that of the entire world of only 150 years ago.

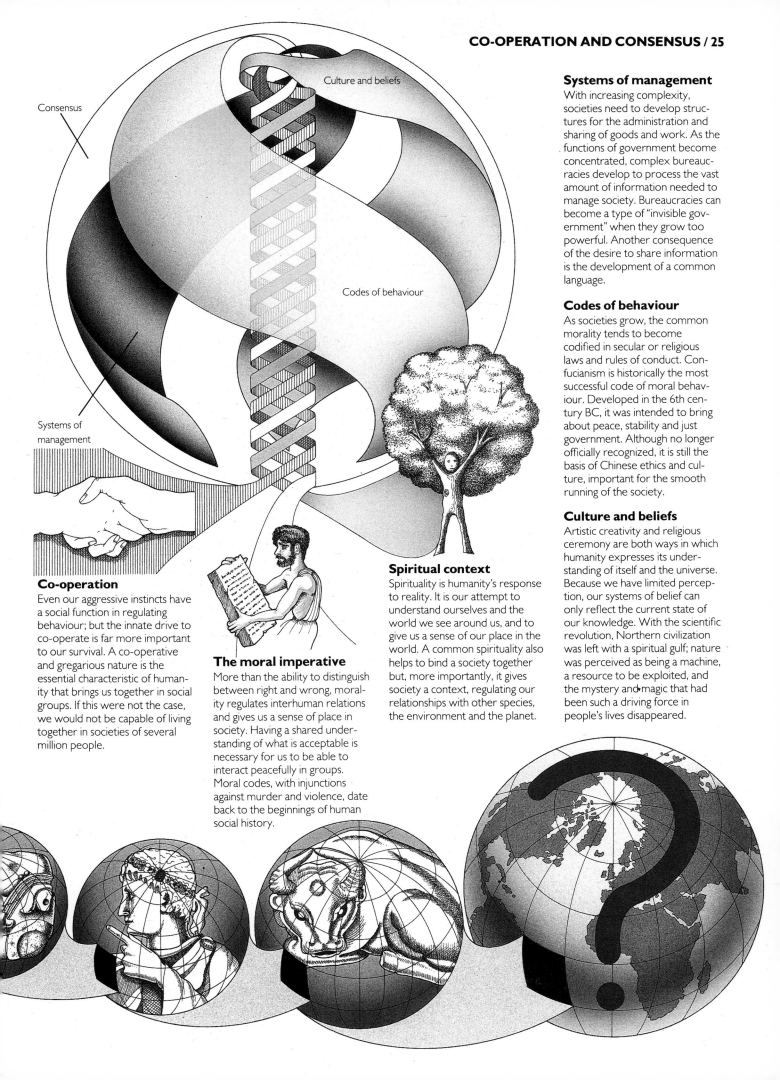

Consensus

Culture and beliefs

Codes of behaviour

Systems of management

Systems of management

With increasing complexity, societies need to develop structures for the administration and sharing of goods and work. As the functions of government become concentrated, complex bureaucracies develop to process the vast amount of information needed to manage society. Bureaucracies can become a type of "invisible government" when they grow too powerful. Another consequence of the desire to share information is the development of a common language.

Codes of behaviour

As societies grow, the common morality tends to become codified in secular or religious laws and rules of conduct. Confucianism is historically the most successful code of moral behaviour. Developed in the 6th century BC, it was intended to bring about peace, stability and just government. Although no longer officially recognized, it is still the basis of Chinese ethics and culture, important for the smooth running of the society.

Culture and beliefs

Artistic creativity and religious ceremony are both ways in which humanity expresses its understanding of itself and the universe. Because we have limited perception, our systems of belief can only reflect the current state of our knowledge. With the scientific revolution, Northern civilization was left with a spiritual gulf; nature was perceived as being a machine, a resource to be exploited, and the mystery and magic that had been such a driving force in people's lives disappeared.

Co-operation

Even our aggressive instincts have a social function in regulating behaviour; but the innate drive to co-operate is far more important to our survival. A co-operative and gregarious nature is the essential characteristic of humanity that brings us together in social groups. If this were not the case, we would not be capable of living together in societies of several million people.

The moral imperative

More than the ability to distinguish between right and wrong, morality regulates interhuman relations and gives us a sense of place in society. Having a shared understanding of what is acceptable is necessary for us to be able to interact peacefully in groups. Moral codes, with injunctions against murder and violence, date back to the beginnings of human social history.

Spiritual context

Spirituality is humanity's response to reality. It is our attempt to understand ourselves and the world we see around us, and to give us a sense of our place in the world. A common spirituality also helps to bind a society together but, more importantly, it gives society a context, regulating our relationships with other species, the environment and the planet.

global community seem insurmountable. But it *is* possible. China, for example, with a population in excess of one billion, has achieved a remarkable degree of consensus. Most of the mechanisms for global communication and conflict resolution already exist.

Conflict and the desire for change are dynamic forces that lead to growth. They do not have to lead to group violence. Warfare is not a product of the human biology of aggression; it is a product of human culture.

Achieving and maintaining positive peace is a dynamic process – society constantly seeks new ways of reducing both direct and structural violence. Today, we must find new methods of resolving conflicts; war is now something nobody can win. We must reduce structural violence by improving social justice – by, for example, achieving a fairer distribution of wealth. And we must ensure that our peaceful society can be sustainable, by having a healthy relationship with our resource base.

The relationship with resources

Human behaviour is intimately related to the availability of basic resources. When a shortage of resources threatens life styles or life itself, rivalry for resources leads to aggression, the development of power élites and, ultimately, to war.

Societies living close to the land, such as the Australian Aborigines and North American Indians before European invasion, have mythologies that protect resources – air, trees, water and land are sacred. Dawning civilizations have religious codes. But cities and secular societies soon lose their communion with nature; the relationship with their resource base consequently deteriorates.

History records the rise and fall of one civilization after another. Civilizations survive only as long as they continue to guard the land and evolve and adjust to changing conditions. When civilizations neglect their base, or stagnate, they collapse. Our own civilization is threatened with collapse unless we can achieve a sustainable relationship with planetary resources.

In today's world, the main threat to the resource base is mismanagement in the face of growing population. Deforestation, desertification, pollution of the land and oceans, and species extinctions are caused by current production and consumption patterns.

Predictions of the Earth's maximum carrying capacity vary. Theoretically, it would be possible to increase global food yields to support a maximum world population of about 11 billion people, close to the UN's median projection for the level at which population will stabilize. But this would involve stretching farmland, rangeland and marine resources to the absolute limit, as well as fundamental changes in eating habits.

Technology can increase the carrying capacity of an area of land in a sustainable way. But raising food yields to two-and-a-half times present rates – which is what would be required if we were to have any hope of supporting 11 billion people – would involve massive use of ecologically damaging fertilizers, pesticides and

A sustainable base

A sustainable ecological base has always been essential for the long-term survival of humanity. Hunter/gatherers and simple agricultural societies have belief systems that sanction ecologically sustainable behaviour. Most major civilizations, too, have initially sought a stable base, relying on a seasonal agricultural "income". But there has been an increasing trend for people to use up capital resources, the planet's wealth – including forests, groundwater, soil and, now, fossil fuels – without perceiving the consequences over a long period of time.

All organisms manipulate the environment, but human beings are altering it at an unparalleled rate. In order to support a highly urbanized society, modern agriculture is far outstripping the ability of the land to regenerate. Increasingly divorced from nature, we are mortgaging the future for short-term ends.

Decline of civilization
The group of related Mesoamerican civilizations flourished from 1000BC until the Spanish conquest in the 16th century AD led to the collapse of the whole society. But it is unusual for an entire civilization to fall from such an event. More often it is the result of a complex interaction of both internal decay and external pressures, one of which is the society's relationship with its environment. Like Egypt, the Mesopotamian civilization of Sumer was originally based on riverine flooding. The introduction of large-scale irrigation allowed the development of a populous urban culture, but the cost was a gradual salinization of the land. Upland deforestation added flooding and siltation to the problem, and the agricultural system collapsed. This weakened the urbanized society and allowed invasion by peoples from the north. The Roman empire, too, was weakened – by over-expansion, internal unrest, epidemic disease and poverty – when it succumbed to waves of Barbarian invaders. Our civilization today is at risk from just such complex factors.

Mesopotamia · Egypt · Indus · China · Mediterranean · Central America

3500BC · 3000BC · 2500BC · 2000BC · 1500BC

Hunters and gatherers

This is the oldest form of relationship between organized societies and the planetary resource base, one which has persisted, in isolated areas, up to the present day. Hunter/gatherers are small, mobile groups with ecologically sustainable lifestyles that respect all living systems. If the population outstrips food supply, the group tends to disperse, restoring a balance with nature.

Early agriculture

From following the seasonal migrations of animals, pastoralists eventually learned to manage them. With a fairly reliable food source, larger groups could be sustained, provided social codes existed to limit slaughter and over-grazing. Simple "slash-and-burn" agricultural techniques allowed communities to settle for a few years, after which time they moved on and the land regenerated. This later evolved into crop rotation and fallow farming. Such early forms of society were all sustainable for relatively small groups of people.

Irrigation and agriculture

The first major civilizations, in Egypt and Sumer, arose in river valleys where flooding brought an annual renewal of soil fertility. Attempts to increase the carrying capacity of the land led to the development of irrigation, and unsustainable land exploitation contributed to the eventual collapse of Sumerian civilization. But in Egypt, strong religious codes ensured that the Nile valley and its headwaters were better protected from over-exploitation. Although Egyptian civilization eventually declined, its system of riverine agriculture continued relatively unchanged until the 20th century. The Aswan dam, however, may have finally destroyed the annual cycle and created a dependence on artificial fertilizers. The paddy irrigation system has also proved sustainable, adding stability to the 5000-year-old Chinese civilization.

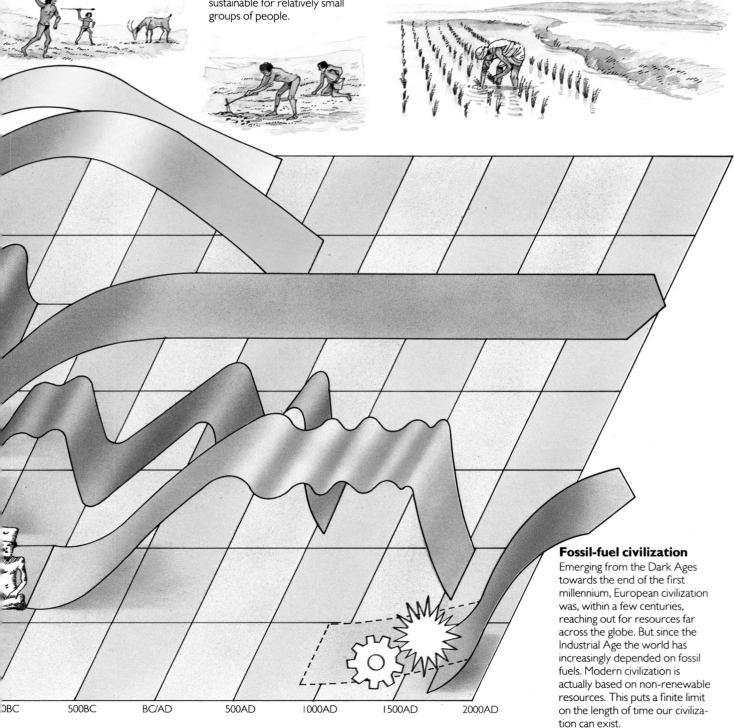

Fossil-fuel civilization

Emerging from the Dark Ages towards the end of the first millennium, European civilization was, within a few centuries, reaching out for resources far across the globe. But since the Industrial Age the world has increasingly depended on fossil fuels. Modern civilization is actually based on non-renewable resources. This puts a finite limit on the length of time our civilization can exist.

0BC   500BC   BC/AD   500AD   1000AD   1500AD   2000AD

other intensive methods, unsustainable in practice.

Theoretically it is also possible to support the existing global population without raising food production at all. Yet 750 million people are undernourished, not obtaining sufficient calories to do a day's work.

The burgeoning world population is a problem. But global inequities in the distribution of wealth, overconsumption in some areas and the South's debt burden – which shifts production from food for local consumption to cash products – are even bigger difficulties.

All carrying capacity estimates assume that we live in a just world. This is not the case. Of those who suffer starvation and malnutrition, 20 per cent do so not because there is a local shortage of food, but because they do not possess the income to command a share.

The world population is now over 5 billion. In the next 35 years, another 3 billion will be added, 90 per cent of them in the South. We cannot raise the Earth's sustainable carrying capacity indefinitely. If population growth continues unabated, their inability to obtain food will cause many to die prematurely, or suffer stunted lives. If we are to limit structural violence in tomorrow's world, we have to tackle the global inequities in wealth, protect resources, and bring average birth rates down to the replacement level of two children per couple. These are our most urgent tasks.

Wealth and social values

Great wealth brings great power. Wealth also brings independence. Those who have no, or little, wealth are totally dependent on an employer, the state or their children for their livelihood. Dependence on children for income, particularly in old age, is a powerful motivation for having large families and, hence, a major contributor to large populations. The link between children and security is now ingrained in many cultures. If we are to achieve replacement fertility, redistribution of wealth for human security is a precondition.

Socialist and communist ideologies usually demand that the means of producing wealth, including land, are publicly owned. Then, the theory goes, the people, represented by the state, have the power and are no longer exploited by an élite. Capitalist theory holds that the ambition to accumulate wealth – and, therefore, power – is a spur to entrepreneurship, which increases the total wealth of the society; the more wealth a society has, the more will "trickle down" to poorer sections. But at either extreme, policy makers are restricted by their ideology. Mixed economies, in which the most important means of production and services are owned by the state but much of industry is in private hands, have had the greatest success with minimizing structural violence.

Early societies did not have the concept of ownership, so individuals did not acquire wealth. Historically, the accumulation of wealth is linked to the development of hierarchical societies. Powerful élites emerged whose main aim was to accumulate more wealth and power.

Wealthy and powerful people will do all that they can

The distribution of wealth

In simple societies goods are shared and land ownership is unknown. But once societies become hierarchical, both income and material wealth tend to flow "upwards" and accumulate in the upper echelons. *Laissez-faire* economics leads to economic and political tensions, to some measure of oppression and, ultimately, to instability. For an equitable, peaceful and sustainable society, money and wealth must be redistributed. Today, there are two ideologically distinct systems for achieving this.

The East-West ideological split has dominated international politics for the last 40 years. But the differences between mixed and centrally planned economies are, for political purposes, exaggerated on both sides. The first step towards a more equitable system is to satisfy the most basic needs of all sectors of society. Both systems have had only limited success with this, but the vast majority of people in the North have an acceptable standard of living.

The differences between East and West pale in comparison with the North-South economic divide. The global economic system is becoming increasingly top-heavy, an issue that is evolving into the greatest source of international tension.

Basic needs: US and USSR compared

Both the US and USSR have social security programmes providing an income for the old, disabled and unwaged; but in neither country is coverage universal. In the USSR, medical care is provided free to everybody, but it can be of a poor standard for lack of medicines and equipment. Americans, once they get to a doctor (there are twice as many patients per physician as in the USSR), can expect far better health care – if they can afford it or do not fall through the "welfare net".

In both societies there is a shortage of low-cost housing, resulting in severe overcrowding in the USSR and estimates of up to 3 million homeless in the USA.

Average per capita calorie supply in both countries is a third over requirements; but the *quality* of nutrition in the USSR is generally quite poor, while 20 million Americans are without adequate nutrition on a regular basis.

Both countries have a state education system, a 99% literacy rate and similar teacher/ pupil ratios.

Officially there is no unemployment in the USSR, although there is an indeterminate number of people "between jobs". The unemployment rate in the US is 7%.

Overall, the Soviet welfare system has greater coverage, but a less adequate service.

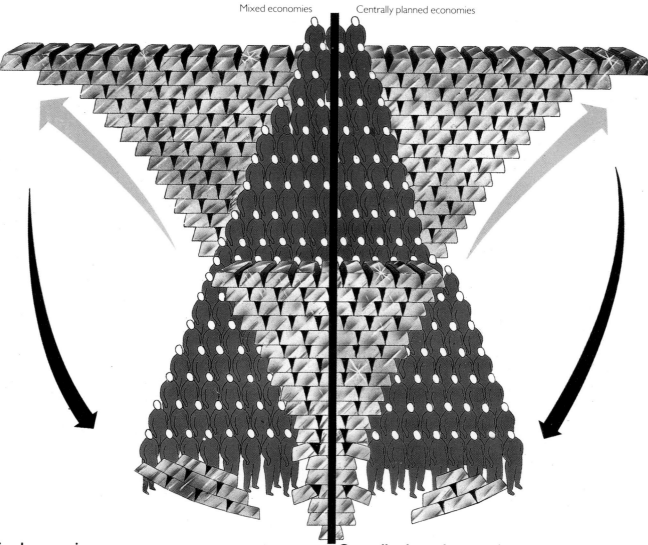

Mixed economies   Centrally planned economies

Mixed economies

All social democracies in the North have mixed economies. So, although the supply of goods and services is determined primarily by private enterprise, the redistribution of wealth is achieved through taxation, bargaining by the labour force and state control of key industries. Part of government revenue is used to fund welfare programmes with varying eligibility criteria.

Centrally planned economies

Communist and socialist economies are characterized by state ownership of all resources, and bureaucratic control of the means of production and distribution of goods. The state determines wage rates and since it controls all public utilities, it should be able to provide welfare services to all and to ensure equitable wealth distribution if the bureaucratic mechanisms work.

The economics of a divided world

In Europe, GNP per capita in the NATO countries is about $7600, compared with $6300 in the Warsaw Pact. The Iron Curtain has always been more of an ideological divide than an economic one. All modern industrial economies are extensively planned, not just the socialist ones.

The real difference in economic organization is between the rich and the poor countries. Their primary concern is with food, shelter and clothing. Most people work in agriculture and those working in industry do not have any real power. Firms are mostly small and, since there are so many of them, they are more subject to impersonal market forces. Government services play a much smaller part in living standards.

This divide creates tremendous economic tension. Wealth and profit flow upwards from the poor South to the rich North, just as they do within hierarchical societies. As the planetary resource base becomes eroded, political tension grows and with it the risk of military conflagration. GNP per capita in the developed world is $9420 compared with $740 in the developing world, where three-quarters of the world population lives, 1 billion of them in absolute poverty. This inequality cannot be maintained indefinitely.

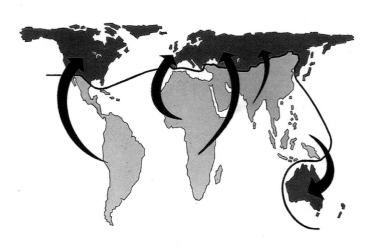

to maintain their position. Powerful capitalists in many Western countries foster and maintain images of "communist enemies" – such sentiments are related more to the élite's fear that it will lose its wealth and power than to any wider threat to security.

Unless the income from wealth is continually returned to a society's capital resource base, this base will become eroded, and the system unsustainable. The real wealth, or capital, of a society – farmland, natural resources, the means of producing goods and food, the skills and knowledge of the population – has to be used productively if it is to survive. Unproductive, or "static wealth" – such as money deposited in foreign bank accounts or circulating in the international financial and currency markets, or providing luxuries for minorities – hampers sustainable development.

Income is derived from real capital, with energy for production. But when capital and income are measured in national accounts today, depletion of natural resources and damage to ecosystems are usually ignored. The use of non-renewable resources, the extinction of species, and environmental pollution all decrease real wealth. A new system of economic accounting is needed.

All economic systems have some moral and ideological basis. If we are to have sustainable growth and positive peace, future economics must be based on the belief that extreme wealth and poverty, usury, unfair trading, and erosion of the resource base are immoral and unacceptable behaviour for human societies.

The power of law

Without a system of social rules there would be anarchy. Laws are just one element of society's total system of social controls, increasingly important as the society becomes more complex. Law provides an interface between the different individuals and groups in society and acceptable sanctions when the social norms are not obeyed. Without a definition of each person's rights and obligations, no large, civilized society could exist. And increasingly today, law guards the fundamental codes and freedoms of a society against the abuse of power.

In a modern state, criminal law is generally administered by courts and enforced by the police and the authority of the state. But civil law is mainly enforced by consensus – law-abiding citizens respect and voluntarily obey established social codes in their dealings with each other. If a civil dispute comes to court and one party is found liable, for example, to pay money, this will normally be done voluntarily.

Consensus is, in fact, essential for all law. Only when most people obey the law and agree that the sanctions are reasonable is a legal system workable.

The earliest rules of society were established by custom and handed down by word of mouth, generation to generation. A number of legal systems, particularly in Africa, still incorporate elements of customary law. Such systems do not, by and large, clearly distinguish between moral and religious principles. In Western

Rule of law

Law is fundamental to peace. Early civilizations flourished with unwritten codes of behaviour, drawn either from customary practice or religious belief. But with the birth of the secular state, written codes of law sanctioned by state authority came into being. Four thousand years ago, the best-known of these was King Hammurabi's code. Roman law

North America and Oceania
Colonized by England, the national legal systems of both regions are based on common law. Louisiana and Quebec, however, colonized by France, adopted French civil law.

6 countries

Latin America
Civil law – Spanish, French or Portuguese – is the basis of all legal systems in Latin America. Many Caribbean countries apply English common law.

26 countries

Europe and Soviet Asia
Civil law is the foundation in Scotland and all countries of the Continent, except the Soviet Union, where the civil codes have been considerably modified.

30 countries

North Africa and Middle East
Apart from Israel, the Koran is the basis of law in this region. Most countries also have a civil or common law system to deal with less serious matters and commerce.

20 countries

Sub-Sahara Africa
The present systems are a mixture of colonial law (derived from one of the European civil codes or English common law) and traditional customs and practices.

41 countries

Asia and Far East
In most countries, civil law has combined with ideas of local origin to produce new types of codes. Many incorporate elements of English common law.

20 countries

Many countries have an amalgam of several legal systems. The Sri Lankan system, for example, incorporates elements of English common law, Roman-Dutch civil law, Muslim law and local custom. The chart summarizes the elements that provide the basis of the law in each region, while an individual country may reflect only one particular influence.

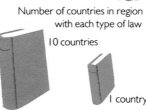

Number of countries in region with each type of law

10 countries

1 country

Note: number of countries that have systems of law that do not fit into these categories are shown next to the regional map.

provides us with a tradition of civil or "statute"-based practices; common law, which derived from precedent, gives the judiciary great independence.

There are often strong regional similarities between legal systems but, taking the world as a whole, our laws are derived from very different, seemingly incompatible, ideologies. The difficulties in achieving a universally acceptable system of international law are immense.

Justice or law?
Justice is defined by the commonly accepted standards of right and wrong in society. We are dependent on the law to try and administer justice. An independent judiciary can be of great importance in championing justice if state government tries to bring in oppressive laws. But generally, the law merely reflects the strengths or weaknesses within society – it cannot create justice.

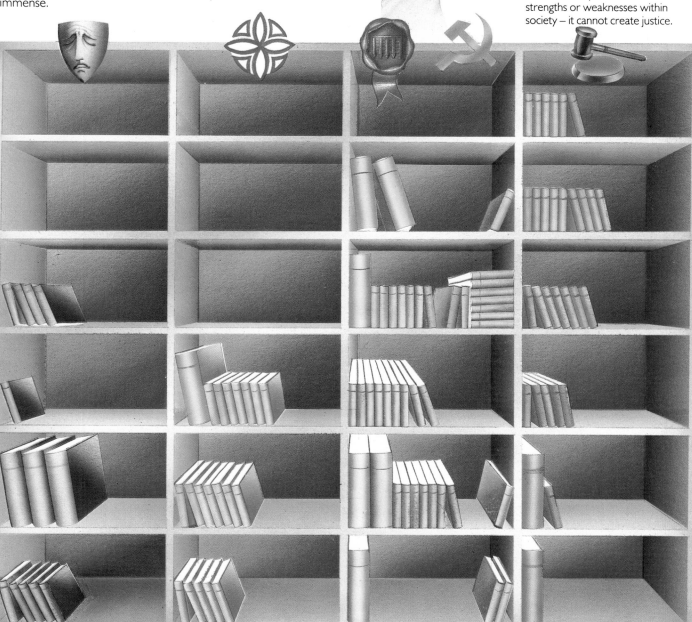

Customary law
Most legal systems are imposed from above. Customary law, on the other hand, arises from customs and behaviour within society, which are then legitimized. Typically unwritten, it is a "living law" expressing a tribal moral code and responding quickly to change. It attaches great importance to both negotiation and arbitration.

Religious law
In these systems, the final arbiter on law is a religious code, such as the Koran for Muslims, with, in some cases, extra statutes derived from the religious authorities. There is thus no distinction between religious and legal authority and the judiciary tends to be independent of the state.

Civil law
Based on statutes (legislative acts), and usually assembled into a code, most civil systems trace their origins to the *Corpus Juris Civilis* (Body of Civil Law) of Roman Emperor Justinian. The statutes are the final arbiter, and they can be extremely difficult to change. When civil law is modified by Communist legal theory, the state is the final arbiter.

Common law
Applied in England and its colonies, the basic feature of the English legal system is the power of judges to make laws. Over time, their judgments build up a body of precedent on which future cases are decided. The judges are the final arbiters. This feature has been retained despite the increasingly important law-making role of the legislature.

systems, law has been largely separated from its religious origins; in Eastern societies the link between religion and law has generally been maintained.

In nearly all countries in Europe and the Americas, the law is derived either from Roman jurisprudence or from the English system of common law. Under both systems, a legislative body can make laws that are then interpreted by the courts. The difference between them is that civil (Roman) law is based on a statute whereas common law is based on precedents established by previous court judgments.

Law often provides social cohesion rather than justice. Justice is very difficult to achieve in large, complex societies; often, the law merely provides the best compromise between competing needs.

Most legal systems have, however, had success with curtailing the use of force in the settlement of disputes. They have also managed to limit the worst cases of oppression within countries. But we have yet to learn how to protect human rights under international law and how to curtail the use of force between countries.

Emerging governance

Governance is all about maintaining social stability. Smaller communities can govern themselves. Decisions can be taken by consensus after negotiation and arbitration. But as societies become larger and more complex, they also become increasingly hierarchical: roles become specialized with greater social value attached to some responsibilities than to others; religious and military leaders emerge; land ownership aggravates the lop-sided accumulation of wealth; bureaucracies form to distribute goods and services.

Once these groups are established, they can determine the way in which governance evolves. The power and influence of the individual citizen declines. This is the historical pattern followed by all the world's major civilizations. Governance eventually fell into the hands of a single leader or small group, maintained by the powerful vested interests in society.

People have struggled throughout history to resolve this dilemma – to achieve a cohesive, stable society and yet prevent the abuse of power. The cyclical swing between citizen council and autocracy, between the divine right of rule and the search for democratic freedoms, has led us to try many systems of government. Civilizations with many small states have tended to many wars; large empires to stagnation or repression. The modern world has elements of all these problems. We are still searching.

Decision makers in a modern state have to take into account the expectations of numerous groups (both at home and abroad), many vested interests, and a rapid rate of social and technological change. But in modern party systems, leaders change too often to be able to apply anything other than short-term solutions to problems. Yet the need for sustainable peace, for just and far-sighted governance at the global level, has never been greater. And with growing awareness of our interconnectedness, it has never been more possible.

Governance

The dynamic tension between the co-operative aspects of human nature and the inherent inclination of more complex societies towards hierarchy is the stuff of history. Evolving civilizations tend to oscillate between extremes of citizen power and autocracy – first, a governing élite is ousted and a more democratic regime established; this then decays and succumbs to a strong individual personality and a "dictatorial" backlash. In older societies, these swings may well become more moderate. But violent see-sawing is currently the pattern in many states that are relatively new to self-determination.

A society is "structurally" peaceful and stable when it is ecologically sustainable, economically equitable and when the government has the general support of the population. The function of governance is to encourage the development of society according to these criteria, and to regulate social affairs through a system of just and enforceable laws. A government can achieve this only by providing a merging of the interests of the individual and those of the state, and by protecting society from both internal and external threat. If the system of governance fails to incorporate these elements it will ultimately collapse.

Public consensus

Sustainable ecology

Co-operatives and power sharing

Human beings are naturally co-operative and gregarious. Co-operativeness, and a common belief in morality and justice, produce a tendency towards power sharing and egalitarianism in society, which act as a counter to the hierarchical inclination. Mechanisms for controlling the power of élites include the establishment of consultative citizens councils, systems of democratic voting and, in extreme circumstances, popular revolution.

Hierarchies and élites

A small community can govern itself successfully. But with increasing size and specialization, it becomes easier to relinquish the decision-making process to a leader or to an élite – often, at first, combining religious and tribal authority (as in many early civilizations from Sumer and Egypt to Mexico). The rise of bureaucracies, needed in order to process the high level of information required by a centralized state machine, is, however, one of the costs of hierarchical structures of government.

Governance

As societies grow larger, one of the most important functions of governance is to maintain a just balance between the different elements at work in society. Individuals need to recognize that they have obligations to the wider community and to the state that will curtail their own freedoms; the state has to recognize that the individual has certain fundamental "human rights" that are its responsibility to protect. When this difficult balance is achieved, the society is "structurally" peaceful.

Security

Paradoxically, one of the most potentially dangerous aspects of governance entrusted to the ruling body is the responsibility for maintaining the security of the state. This implies protecting the way of life of the population in general against internal threats as well as providing a defence against external attack. Having at its disposal a police force and military organization gives the ruling élite immense power – power that can be abused.

Distribution of wealth

Just and enforceable law

Government by an élite: Singapore

Although Singapore is officially a multiparty democracy, the ruling People's Action Party holds all the parliamentary seats, and hence there is no effective opposition. There have been allegations of severe government repression and the state controls many facets of life. Prime Minister Lee Kuan Yew has presided over what is effectively an autocracy for 30 years, yet he has done this with the overwhelming support of the majority of the population. He came to power in 1959 with a programme of social reform and economic development that has succeeded in improving the conditions of the majority of the people. Towards the end of the 1960s, Lee turned his attention to the local ecology and launched a series of programmes for improving the environment with the slogan "Keep Singapore clean and green". Whatever criticisms can be levelled against the rule of "Lee's law", it is clear that he still has popular support, and that his success as a leader has been based on his ability to satisfy all four fundamental criteria for a peaceful society (see below). As long as the political opposition does not reflect a strong measure of dissatisfaction in the society as a whole, it will fail to bring about any significant change in the system. The power imbalances in even the most authoritarian, hierarchical societies cannot be sustained indefinitely without a consensus.

Government by the people: Sweden

Since the liberalization of its government in the 19th century, Sweden has become one of the most prosperous and progressive nations in the world. It has a 349-seat, single-chamber parliament and, arguably, the fairest system of proportional representation in operation. The electorate is assured of representation by a system of voting that gives even small parties a seat in the *Riksdag*. Sweden is striving towards reliance on renewable energy sources, including a phasing out of nuclear power, a reduction in the use of oil and greater dependence on hydroelectricity. It is in the forefront of the campaign against acidification, and in the control of industrial and automobile emissions. Sweden also has the highest life expectancy and one of the highest living standards in the world. It has an extensive social welfare system with the highest per capita public expenditures on health and education in the world. Sweden aims to ensure its security by following a unique route: it takes part in no military alliances, has not fought in a war since 1809, and it refuses to compromise its neutrality by joining either NATO or the Common Market. Sweden is an excellent example of an egalitarian society that has pursued a system of governance based on all the essential criteria for a sustainable and peaceful existence.

Seeking a global community

Visions of global civilization are not new. Babylon, Greece, Rome and all the empires since, each sought to unite the world by conquest, and impose a superior culture. But in the nuclear age, we do not have the option of conquest. Humanity faces the challenge of creating a world order, not by force, but by agreement.

Peace cannot be imposed from above. From Alexander to the Caesars, such efforts have sooner or later failed. Yet for all its brave vision, the United Nations itself began with the old idea of an order imposed by strength: the five victorious powers of World War II would unite to enforce and guard the peace. That they soon became disunited is a sad lesson of history. That we still today, in an increasingly pluralist world, find the potential of the global community blocked by superpower dominance shows we have far to go.

Yet language, culture and trade links have continued to spread and forge a common understanding. Peace grows from within – through the co-operative and creative energies of human beings. If we are to achieve positive peace we must free these energies to build, at a global level, the conditions for it we have begun to learn at a national one – consensus; a fairer wealth distribution; human rights and social justice; far-sighted governance; and a sustainable base, in planetary terms.

Before all, we need to accept the rule of law; only then will war cease. International law began long ago – Rameses II of Egypt, in the 14th century BC, followed an already old tradition in his treaty with the King of Cheta. But in the past 100 years it has multiplied hugely – via multilateral treaties and conventions on trade, or the use of oceans, air space, and radio waves, on border disputes or methods of warfare – into a whole web of agreements regulating the world's activities.

Whereas national laws are enforced and law-breakers fined or imprisoned, international law, however, has few powers. The International Court of Justice cannot compel states to answer charges or obey judgments, nor allow suit by individuals or non-governmental organizations. International law is fundamental to world peace. But it has to be enforceable, recognized and respected, and, ultimately, represent a consensus.

Under such law we could negotiate codes to protect the environment, establish sustainable development, guard human rights, evolve a common security, and diminish social injustice. Then we could begin to seek a sustainable civilization, in harmony with Gaia.

We are still at an early stage. What we have now resembles a medieval state, where wealthy barons exert great influence, private armies multiply, and rivalries are a major source of conflict. Yet we have at least recognized the importance of each actor in the international political arena, in principle – at, for example, the United Nations – even if decisions are *de facto* made by the dominant powers. And, as events in Vietnam and Afghanistan show, even the most powerful states now recognize the limits of their military power and the need to satisfy international opinion. Therein lies hope for the future.

From national to international

As nations grow increasingly interdependent, a system of governance is required to regulate ever more complex international affairs. Such a system must incorporate the same fundamental elements as national governance: unless it is based on a general consensus, and is ecologically and economically sound, the system will ultimately collapse. Without an acceptable and enforceable system of law, collective security cannot be maintained. But international governance is relatively new. Law and security are still jealously guarded aspects of sovereignty, making international agreement difficult. Governments are reluctant to yield power, and slow in gaining a global perspective on ecological issues. The problems demand international governance, even if only out of national self-interest.

The darkest shadow

On a planetary scale, we are destroying our lungs by chopping down the forests, acidifying the water and poisoning our food and water with industrial pollutants, and tampering with the delicate mechanism of atmospheric temperature control. No effective international forum exists specifically for the purpose of discussing the global ecology.

We are no better at looking after members of our own species than we are at protecting our planetary home. There are great internal inequalities in all societies, but even these fade into insignificance when compared with the planetary divide: 25% of the world's population base their wealth on the systematic oppression and continued suffering of the rest of humanity. The average Northerner has a personal wealth 40 times greater, and an income 13 times greater, than the average person in the South. This quarter of humanity also has 94% of world health expenditure, 70% of the world's food grains, 92% of world industry and 89% of world education spending.

All attempts at redressing this imbalance have failed. The inequalities are so fundamental that the token "Aid Budget" determined by the United Nations (0.7% of each country's GNP) is a mere drop in an ocean of suffering.

Consensus

Just as governments cannot long exist without public support, a consensus of opinion is needed for effective international agreements. Even in the UN, though, only national groupings (the "landholders") are given the vote – NGOs, minority groups and ordinary members of the global community are disenfranchized.

Planetary ecology

From the rain forests of the Amazon to the irradiated reindeer in Lapland, and from the hole in the ozone to the encroaching deserts of Africa, the signs of humanity's abuse of the biosphere are legion. The sustainability of society is not even a criterion in a system of global economics that makes no allowance for the costs to the wider environment.

"Wealth"

There has been a complete failure of global social welfare and development economics. People in the South are poor not because they lack potentially valuable resources ("wealth"), but primarily because the global economic system deprives them of the income from that wealth, and because of the inadequacies in their national systems of distribution.

International law

International law has achieved some success in certain uncontroversial areas – agreements on telecommunications, mail, health, weather forecasting, and air and sea transport, for example – that service the global community and do not impinge on national sovereignty. Noticeable failures include all the higher moral conventions, particularly Human Rights legislation such as the Geneva Conventions, the World Court and the laws of peace. This type of "legislation" is difficult to apply because it incorporates a notion of universal justice, a set of overriding human values that outweigh all others.

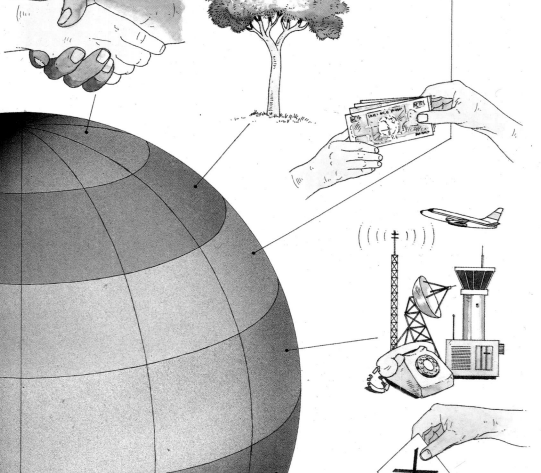

Governance

At the international level, the function of a system of governance is to provide connections between countries, the wider interests of humanity and, ultimately, the planet. The United Nations, Non-aligned Movement and regional alliances such as the EEC, ASEAN, DAU and CARICOM are all attempts at providing a forum for balancing the competing interests of several nation-states and promoting mutual cooperation. Such international forums tend to have a less hierarchical structure than national institutions, although powerful vested interests mean they are still far from being egalitarian.

Security

One of the functions of governance is to ensure the security of society. Despite its inadequacies, the United Nations is our best attempt yet at achieving real international security. By contrast, regional alliances focusing on military security, such as NATO and the Warsaw Pact, are actually threatening the survival of humanity.

2 The roots of conflict

Introduced by Petra Karin Kelly

Enough nuclear and other mass destructive weapons are scattered all over the globe to kill everyone on Earth at least 12 times. These weapons hold all humanity as hostages. The Third World War has already begun – because daily militarization of our skies, our earth, our oceans causes more and more world poverty and debt. As Ruth Sivard has stated, the 20th century has been marked by a rising level of violence. With 11 years still to go before the end of the century, the 20th century already records 237 wars.

In the words of the women's Pentagon protest in 1980-1: "We are in the hands of men whose wealth and power have separated them from the reality of daily life. We are right to be afraid . . . We want to know what anger in these men, what fear, which can only be satisfied by destruction, what coldness of heart and ambition drives their days. We want to know, because we do not want their dominance, which is exploitative and murderous . . . we do not want that sickness, transferred by the violent society to the fathers, to the sons . . ."

Now the *last frontier* is about to be militarized – the outer space, the Strategic Defense Initiative gives rise to a whole new galaxy of weapons. One of the men supporting this proposal stated: "Our Star Wars shield would be analogous to a flotilla of orbiting nuclear plants that must cooperate with the precision of a symphony orchestra" (Kurt Gottfried, 1986).

This is a science, without humanity, without responsibility. I recall the wise words of Bertrand Russell – words that have yet to find their way into military and nuclear research centres, into the meeting rooms of the two major military alliances, into the hearts and minds of military officers and soldiers:

"We have to learn to think in a new way. Remember your humanity and forget the rest. If you can do so, the way lies open to a new paradise; if you cannot, there lies before you the risk of universal death."

As Soviet and Western scholars recently concluded in a joint study, *Breakthrough – Emerging New Thinking*: "Compelled by the threat of a nuclear Armageddon, humans must now raise themselves to a new dimension – a new level of *consciousness beyond war*." Resisting war and militarism is not possible without resisting structures of dominance elsewhere in society. We must resist just as effectively racism, sexism, imperialism and violence in our daily lives. I believe there is a profound relationship, for example, between the fact that individual women and children are commonly attacked, beaten up and raped, and that nuclear or chemical/biological war is threatening our planet, which has no emergency exit! The daily violence we encounter in our lives has its counterpart in the increasing internationalization of violence in the Third World.

When we attempt to get rid of such things as racism or sexism or poverty, we must also look at their structural underpinning – a system of deeply rooted patriarchy which is prevalent in all countries, whether capitalist or state socialist societies. Patriarchy is a hierarchical system of domination, suppressive to women and restrictive to men. Patriarchy, centralism, hierarchy and deterrent thinking shows themselves in all areas of our lives, our daily work, in our political, economic and social structures.

I believe that norms of human behaviour can and do change, and that together we can change these patterns of domination as well, applying the patterns of holistic thinking to one another. Disarming our hearts and our minds!

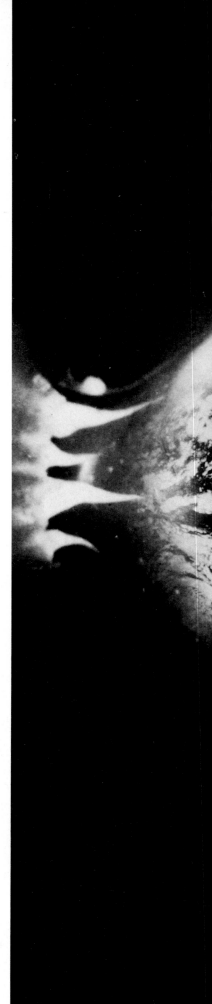

"We have flown the air like birds and swum the sea like fishes, but have yet to learn the simple act of walking the earth as brothers." Martin Luther King 1967

In the modern world, we live not at peace but in an armed state of readiness for war – and though no war is declared, at any one time many parts of the world are experiencing devastating conflict. This situation is perpetuated by the pursuit of sovereignty, and by our signal failure to develop the means of collective security and accept the rule of law.

The acceptance of war in our midst distorts our social values, so that from birth we grow into unbalanced human beings, our gentler side suppressed in favour of competition, violence and greed. This "dominance mode" of modern society – dominance of nature, and of each other – brings human injustice and ecological damage, which provoke further conflict in a spiral of mounting suffering and despair.

The origins of warfare

It is widely believed that "war is a part of human nature". This is simply not true. While aggression is an innate drive, it does not necessarily follow that warfare is its inevitable expression. Neither is it true that warfare is an inevitable concomitant of the development of civilization, with large hierarchical societies needing more resources. Rather, warfare, in the form of open hostilities between two groups, can be regarded as a social institution, in much the same way as we view others in our culture – marriage, funeral rites, trial by jury, and so on. The difference is that, though this institution has grown increasingly savage over the course of history, so universal is its acceptance that we think of it, not as a social construct, but as an attribute of humanity itself.

We only have to look at peoples of today to find evidence to the contrary. Eskimos are an aggressive and passionate people – yet have never practised warfare. It might be argued that this is because they are nomadic and lack material wealth. But one can easily point to nomadic peoples who do practise war – the Australian aborigines, for instance.

War, then, is a social construct. It is also quite recent. Prior to about 10,000 BC, there is evidence that human beings engaged in ritual conflict, but not in actual inter-group warfare. There is a possibility that early agricultural settlements may have been raided by "marauding nomads", but the evidence for this is very tenuous. The first walled settlement, Jericho, dates from around 7000 BC, though most are several thousand years later. But not until 3000 BC did resource and territorial competition become warlike, with the first recorded "war" between Upper and Lower Egypt occurring around 3200 BC.

With the emergence of secular power élites, and rivalry for dominance, war became established as a social institution. Autocrats were able to accumulate power and wealth by encouraging its use, and for some, their armies provided an opportunity for enhancing

Roots of war

War is not a part of human nature. There is no evidence to suggest that humanity engaged in any inter-group violence until about 12,000 years ago. The first recorded "war" was not until 3200BC. It was between Upper and Lower Egypt and concerned the acquisition of land. In hunter/gatherer societies today, aggressive behaviour is generally ritualized, and if there is violence, injuries are few; there is no reason to believe that early societies were different. War is, historically speaking, a social construct, a culturally determined phenomenon. It is "civilized" people who kill each other with ever greater violence as our technology and numbers increase. We are faced with a paradox. Our very co-operative and social nature, which provides the impetus for civilization, can also lead to war – through a deep-rooted distortion of our society, and thus of our nature.

When the prerequisites for sustainable peace are not fulfilled, a society is unstable and prone to violence – either civil conflict or external wars. These underlying causes are aggravated by establishment control of the way in which we view "outsiders", and by our tendency to blame an external agency for the problems that beset our own society.

Lack of consensus
A government that holds power without the general consensus of the people can do so only by force, and/or by the "threat" of outside enemies. Repressive measures to try and maintain "law and order" may succeed for a while, but eventually produce an often violent social backlash.

Unsustainable ecology
A breakdown in a society's relationship with the environment can lead to social unrest and civil war. To avoid this, those in power often widen their resource base by territorial expansion, or support other unstable regimes in order to protect sources of raw materials.

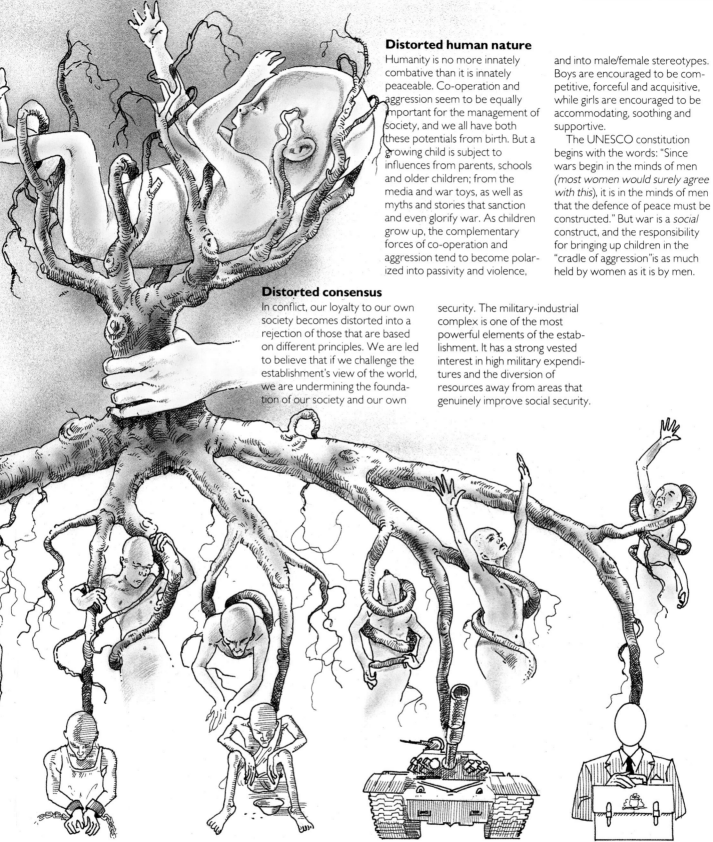

Distorted human nature

Humanity is no more innately combative than it is innately peaceable. Co-operation and aggression seem to be equally important for the management of society, and we all have both these potentials from birth. But a growing child is subject to influences from parents, schools and older children; from the media and war toys, as well as myths and stories that sanction and even glorify war. As children grow up, the complementary forces of co-operation and aggression tend to become polarized into passivity and violence, and into male/female stereotypes. Boys are encouraged to be competitive, forceful and acquisitive, while girls are encouraged to be accommodating, soothing and supportive.

The UNESCO constitution begins with the words: "Since wars begin in the minds of men (*most women would surely agree with this*), it is in the minds of men that the defence of peace must be constructed." But war is a *social* construct, and the responsibility for bringing up children in the "cradle of aggression" is as much held by women as it is by men.

Distorted consensus

In conflict, our loyalty to our own society becomes distorted into a rejection of those that are based on different principles. We are led to believe that if we challenge the establishment's view of the world, we are undermining the foundation of our society and our own security. The military-industrial complex is one of the most powerful elements of the establishment. It has a strong vested interest in high military expenditures and the diversion of resources away from areas that genuinely improve social security.

Injustice

Martial law, military rule, dictatorship and human rights violations are the likely results when the law lacks justice or when legal sanctions are unacceptable. Then the society is prone to violence from within, just as it is likely to be attacked if it acts illegally towards its neighbours.

Poverty

One billion people today live in absolute poverty, in hunger and despair. This failure of global society to provide for the most basic needs of humanity is producing a tremendous pressure for change. Poverty and suffering are major factors in civil and local wars and in growing North-South tension.

Militarism

High military expenditures and the consequent diversion of resources away from *real* security needs are raising domestic tension and conflict to dangerous levels. Military proliferation via the arms trade is also culpable in the escalation of Third World conflicts into all-out wars.

Political élite

When society hands the functions of governance over to a ruling group, it risks creating a political élite that is primarily concerned with maintaining power. When this power is abused nationally, revolution is sometimes the only recourse; when it leads to international adventurism, war is likely.

prestige, particularly for young men anxious to prove themselves. Many societies since have made much of the link between manliness and organized killing.

Today, some 3000 years on, we are still using the same institution as the ultimate means of settling a dispute. Warfare has become so ingrained in our culture that few nations even question its legitimacy, let alone consider other alternatives.

We have become addicted to war and, like any addict, feel helpless to defy its grip. Yet the fact remains that the institution is a defective one, and one that has become seriously outmoded in the light of recent developments in modern weaponry. We must unmake what we have made. For warfare could now mark the end, not only of civilization but of humanity.

Follow my leader

The vast majority of people yearn for peace. Yet wars are increasingly frequent and violent, and the risk of a nuclear world war grows constantly greater. This paradox arises from the nature both of today's leaders and of the people they lead.

All complex societies tend towards hierarchy, and create governing élites that become distanced from the society whose wellbeing they should serve. But modern political systems – capitalist, communist, democratic or autocratic – have in common the tendency to throw up leaders with characteristics psychiatrists regard as symptomatic of psychopathy – an extraordinary desire to control other people, megalomania, arrogance, unwillingness to listen to criticism and a reluctance to relinquish any control. Such are the people who rule us in the nuclear age.

This is not to deny that many ordinary politicians are motivated by the wish to contribute to the common good. But they are seldom prepared to go through the processes needed to become leaders. Only those with undesirable traits strive for supreme power.

Global problems – particularly those related to the nuclear arms race – persist largely due to the lack of political will on the part of leaders to set up the, often supranational, institutions needed to solve them. Political leaders know that there are powerful vested interests in the *status quo*, whether in arms industries or financial establishments, that can be strong enough to remove them from power or prevent their re-election. Obsessed with power, they cave in to such pressure in the name of political expediency. The problems remain unsolved.

Many political leaders would, in their hearts, like to be autocrats – but are constrained, to a greater or lesser extent, by the people they lead. Nevertheless, many of the led respond to strong leadership – they prefer to be directed rather than managed. Feelings of patriotism, loyalty and an instinct to defend the group are also easily aroused and manipulated. The led, therefore, often tolerate unreasonable and destructive power in their leaders. Distorted values at the top of the pyramid – such as the fear and coercive violence implied by sanction of nuclear weapons – filter down

Leaders and led

The hierarchical, pyramidal nature of society arose with complex civilization, and though often challenged, is now the norm. In the past, leaders were chosen for religious or military ability, or royal descent. But today, party machines create leaders intent on survival and power, with forceful media personalities able to mould public opinion to political ends. Just how persuasive such leadership can be is shown by its power to distort social values, such as loyalty, and exploit human weakness and fears to create enemy images and a readiness to go to war. In Aldous Huxley's words:

"So far from discouraging nationalistic hatred and vanity, all governments directly or indirectly foment them . . . War strengthens all the ties that bind the individual to the group and heightens his sense of group solidarity to the pitch of intoxication . . . War justifies hatred, hallows violence, sanctifies delight in destruction, baptises with the sacred name of patriotism all the antisocial tendencies we have been so carefully trained to suppress."

Until WW I, with the exception of the standing Soviet peasant armies, soldiers were either professionals and/or mercenaries. With the introduction of conscription, however, mass armies became usual in war. But citizens have to be persuaded, by jingoistic appeals to fight. As a rule, conscripts go to war with enthusiasm, but once they have experienced the full horror, become "reluctant heroes".

From band to theocracy
The oldest form of society is the small egalitarian band, choosing occasional "charismatic" leaders. As these evolve into tribes related by kinship, decisions are made by chiefs, wise elders and spiritual shamans. Religion and bureaucracy slowly develop hierarchies of civil power or theocratic rule.

The warrior king
Secular kingship sanctioned by the gods brings militarism and war. Intent on accumulating wealth and power, warrior kings become empire builders. Alexander the Great (356-323 BC), convinced of his divine calling to conquer and civilize, extended his Macedonian empire to the limits of the known world.

The just king
Justice and protection are ancient leadership roles, absorbed into the ideal of the "just king". Alfred the Great (871-99 AD), "the most glorious and Christian king of the English" was both warrior and legislator, uniting resistance to invasion, reforming legal codes and introducing literacy and learning.

Princely polities
Councils and advisers are as old as kingship. Renaissance Italian cities, with "enlightened" despots such as Francesco of Milan (left) and powerful Councils, bred the archetypal political expediency of Macchiavelli, who advised that all means were justifiable to a prince if the ends were desirable.

The dictator
States suffering from economic and civil turmoil are prey to absolute dictators. The 20th century saw the rise of fascism, feeding on failure and disaffection and the dream of national or racial superiority. It concentrated power in the hands of cult figures such as Benito Mussolini.

Media world leader
The post-1945 emergence of the nuclear superpowers has elevated political leaders to positions of immense military and economic influence, wielding the power to destroy civilization, even humanity itself. In the electronic age, a media "image" is an essential pre-requisite for such power.

Pyramids of power
Not only are political and economical power, social prestige and honours perceived to be greater at the top of the pyramid, but national leaders have for many centuries been expected to set the moral tone of the state. The myth that the leader, merely by virtue of being the leader, is good and that all his/her decisions are morally right is deeply imprinted. A willingness to commit absolute violence is now the moral standard set at the top of the pyramid by all states supporting a policy of "deterrence" involving massive and indiscriminate nuclear retaliation. The morally corrosive effect this has at the bottom of the pyramid is incalculable.

Examples of pyramids of power through history are shown above, with leaders being pushed up from society. The explosion signifying the first use of nuclear weapons marks the break between modern leaders and those of the past. Today's "media leaders" head massive military and economic machines and have the power to destroy totally all life on the planet.

through society, weakening its moral foundations. In time, the process contributes to societal decay and even collapse – or to war.

The concept of "security"

In the eyes of the military strategist, "security" involves three major concerns: the defence of one's territory from occupation and invasion; the defence of strategic raw materials and markets; and the defence of the society's political and social values.

These military threats have been recognized for a long time and have roots in our social evolution. In particular, a perceived need to defend territory is instinctive. Territorial behaviour is common among animals to balance food supplies and population.

Human societies that live by hunting and gathering do not own land and resources, but believe that they belong to nature and are held by humans in trust. Traditional hunting grounds are usually defended by ritual and agreement. It is the idea of "ownership", established in most settled civilizations by at least 3000 BC, and the accumulation of individual and state wealth, that have led to concepts of security and to military defence of territory and resources.

Wars were, and sometimes still are, fought to expand territory and, more often, to defend resources or ideologies. But it is increasingly realized that there are a number of non-military threats to security and these may be, or will soon become, more serious than the military threats (*see pp. 110-26*).

The "need" to defend territory and resources

The perceived threat of invasion and occupation of one's territory varies considerably from one country to another. The Israelis, for example, are, perhaps with good reason, much more afraid that they will see their country, or part of it, invaded and occupied by foreign armies than the Western Europeans. Although NATO strategists may propagate fears that Warsaw Pact forces will invade Western Europe, NATO citizens generally recognize that this danger is small. And, many Warsaw Pact citizens feel rather the same about the threat from NATO. In other words, whereas the average Israeli assesses the threat of invasion to be high, the average European is much less concerned – indeed, more worried by nuclear "defence".

More pressing is the perceived need to defend sources of vital raw materials and strategic markets. The shock of the 1973 oil crisis, when Arab states cut off supplies during the Arab-Israeli war, and the increasing dependence of NATO European countries and Japan – and, in future, East European countries – on Middle East oil, are among the factors that are exacerbating this aspect of security.

How do politicians calculate the military budget required to provide "security"? Not by any reasoned assessment of the changing need to defend national boundaries and secure access to vital raw materials. If objective analysis were the norm, budgets would go up

Territory and resources

Territory and resource conflicts have changed in nature. Empire building is no longer a problem since the world is now "full". The struggle is, instead, for dominance and ideological influence.

Apart from the poles and the high seas outside the exclusive economic zones (EEZ), almost all territory and resources are owned by somebody. But it is in these areas that tensions are at a peak and the exploitation of mineral resources is an unsolved issue. Many believe these should be part of the heritage of humankind. Similarly, outer space should not be monopolized nor militarily dominated by the superpowers.

The map, *right*, shows how competition for territorial and resource "security" is a continuing cause of tension. Because of the emphasis on economic growth, resources and raw materials are of strategic importance, the defence of which is seen to justify the use of force. Moreover, growth is perceived to be so vital that environmental damage is regarded as being of secondary importance. Resource problems now represent transnational threats to human security (*see pp. 146-7*).

 Territorial and resource disputes, 1975-87

 Major maritime demarcation disputes, early 1980s

 "Residues of empire"

 Proposed 200-mile EEZ territorial limits

Antarctic claimants

The United Kingdom, New Zealand, France, Australia, Norway, Chile and Argentina currently claim territorial rights in Antarctica. The claims of the latter two are based on geographical proximity, Argentina and Chile disputing the rights of the British.

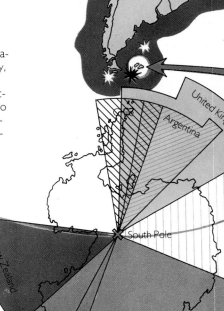

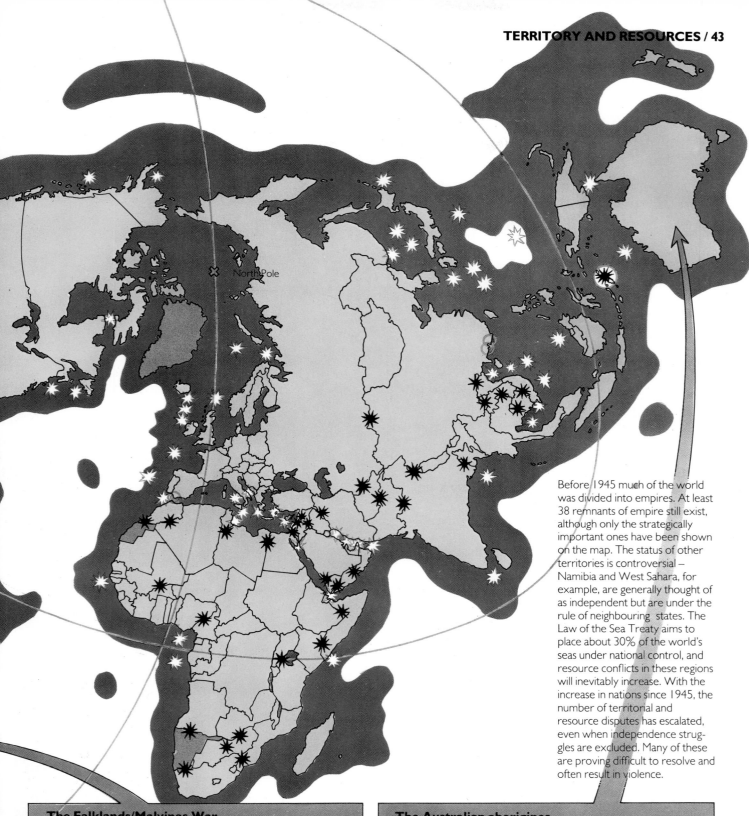

North Pole

Before 1945 much of the world was divided into empires. At least 38 remnants of empire still exist, although only the strategically important ones have been shown on the map. The status of other territories is controversial – Namibia and West Sahara, for example, are generally thought of as independent but are under the rule of neighbouring states. The Law of the Sea Treaty aims to place about 30% of the world's seas under national control, and resource conflicts in these regions will inevitably increase. With the increase in nations since 1945, the number of territorial and resource disputes has escalated, even when independence struggles are excluded. Many of these are proving difficult to resolve and often result in violence.

The Falklands/Malvinas War

For the Argentinians, sovereignty was the main issue in the Falklands/Malvinas conflict. For years, Argentinians have been told that the islands are part of Argentina. British leaders also emphasize sovereignty when they talk about the conflict. But the islands are of considerable geopolitical importance as a staging post for access to the mineral resources of the Antarctic. Positioned in the middle of the South Atlantic, they also have immense naval strategic value. That the British government recognizes the importance of the islands is shown by the fact that it is prepared to spend hundreds of millions of dollars a year to defend about 2000 islanders.

The Australian aborigines

At a subnational level, territory and resources are major causes of social unrest in many regions. For example, the Australian aborigines regard some land as sacred and, therefore, of special importance. But they were only recognized as citizens in 1967 and even now land rights legislation is determined by individual states. In Western Australia and Queensland, where the majority of aborigines live, there is no effective land rights legislation and aborigines are offered title to land only when there are no competing claims from whites, particularly from mining interests. The vested interests in mining for minerals have prevented the effective safeguarding of aboriginal territorial rights.

and down with the levels of external threat. But in most countries, military budgets as a percentage of GNP now remain remarkably constant, year after year.

Politicians know from experience that a certain level of military spending is acceptable to the people. Any who suggest that less should be spent are accused of "weakening the defences of their country", and are either not elected or removed from power. Any who argue that more should be spent are accused of "wanting to waste money on the military" and are also not elected.

Allocation of the military budget between the armed services is also a less than rational process. The service with the greatest lobbying power normally gets the biggest share of the cake. Real security needs do not determine the weapons we buy. This is decided by inter-service rivalry – witness the US Chiefs of Staff insistence that each service – air, land and sea – must develop its own nuclear capability.

Citizens seem to demand that governments provide "security" as another service – like education, health and social benefits – and to feel instinctively what level of expenditure is about right. Military budgets are, in other words, based on our primitive feelings – feelings that can be deliberately manipulated.

The defence of political and social values

This third role for the military forces is as much concerned with threats from internal sources ("the enemy within") as from those outside. The values to be defended are usually those defined by "the establishment". Many argue, of course, that what the establishment really wants to defend is its power and wealth. In many Western European countries, for example, the establishment believes that its interests are threatened by communism and that it would lose its power and wealth under that system. Consequently, with all the manipulations of modern technology, television, newspapers and state propaganda at its disposal, the establishment deliberately fosters demonic images of the enemy (in this case, the Russians), projecting all its own frustrations and tensions outwards on to a handy scapegoat figure.

But the Russians have not always been the "evil enemy". In 1942, among the adjectives chosen in a UK poll to describe the Germans and Japanese, were "warlike", "treacherous" and "cruel". The Russians were described in friendly terms, being Britain's allies at the time. By 1966 a similar poll revealed the situation was reversed, and it was the Russians who were described in venomous terms. Our perception of who is an enemy and who is a friend is based more on political expediency than reality.

The British physicist and former naval officer, P.M.S. Blackett, was one of the first to predict that immense nuclear stockpiles would be tolerated only by people if they were convinced they were protecting themselves from a truly demonic opponent: "Once a nation bases its security on an absolute weapon, such as the atom bomb, it becomes psychologically necessary

Ideology

Differences in religious, political and social values are, in themselves, a source of conflict, both within and between societies. But genuine differences are exaggerated by the vested interests (the "establishment") in each society. The people who are in a position to control the public images of who is a "friend" and who is an "enemy" of society have a strong incentive to maintain the *status quo*, since they are the very same people who hold the power and wealth in the society under the current system. In an attempt to justify its position, the establishment often tries to turn the public against dissident groups or those who hold different views, describing them as "subversive" or "traitorous". This behaviour can create even greater pressure for change if there is a genuine undercurrent of dissatisfaction in society. Unless this is the case, however, the establishment generally retains the implicit support of the population.

Capitalism and communism

Egalitarian societies based on a system of sharing communal wealth are at least as old as hierarchical societies based on private wealth, enterprise and power. The current ideological differences between communism and capitalism can be regarded as a natural evolution of that split, taken to extremes in a world that encourages polarization. If we consider communism a distortion of the desire for social equality, and capitalism as a distortion of the desire for individual freedom, neither is as inherently "evil" as the ideologues and politicians would have us believe.

Religion

Arising from humanity's spirituality and attempts at comprehension, one might expect religion to be a unifying force in the world. But as any religion becomes more established, it tends either to become a temporal power or else to be absorbed by the existing secular authorities, as happened to Christianity in the Roman Empire. Having a common religion helps to bind a society together. But once the religion is inextricably linked with social mores, it also tends to reflect the prejudices against "outsiders" and the other distortions of the secular power.

Prejudice

Group loyalty is considered a virtue in every society of the world. Unfortunately, it goes hand in hand with prejudice and intolerance. Diversity of opinion is actually a valuable human trait, part of the dynamic that allows a society to grow and mature. But there is a tendency to regard ideas that challenge those of the larger establishment group as a threat to social cohesion, ignoring any positive aspects. Prejudice involves a self-fulfilling prophecy: if we expect the worst from some other group we can always find it, even if we overlook reality in the process.

ENEMIES

FRIENDS

Individual perception

Lying between the images of friends and enemies is a grey area in which the establishment projections do not always conform to the public's perception of what is good and bad. Some groups that are portrayed as undermining establishment values, such as peace campaigners, are also striving for a better society. It is in this grey area that individuals begin to develop values that differ from the establishment mores.

The only way to find a more honest reality is actively to seek alternative sources of information. But the notion of challenging establishment images is strongly discouraged by schools, the media, courts and peer group pressure. Individuals disagreeing with these establishment images of who is a friend and who is an enemy risk being cast as outsiders themselves. This creates a powerful incentive to conform. If you do not, your own security is at risk.

Organs of the establishment

1 The state is the ultimate authority in the land and has considerable power over the other organs and the images they project. Career politicians also have reason to maintain the friendly image of the establishment, which helps to keep them in power.

2 Religion attempts to make sense of people's lives with sets of rules. Most people see things in terms of right and wrong and do not allow individual differences.

3 The law is partly responsible for maintaining the cohesion of society and defining acceptable behaviour. Any group that challenges the authority of the law is seen as an "enemy".

4 Finance, the world's money wealth, is largely created by that elusive thing known as "business confidence", in which image is at least as important as reality. Indeed, reality is obscured to maintain "stability".

5 The media (press and broadcasting institutions) is more controlled in some countries than in others; but all media institutions tend to present a narrow, "conservative" view of the world.

6 The military only exists because there is a generally held fear of attack from outside. The size of the military's budget is often directly linked to the extent of that fear, so there is a vested interest in creating an image of a powerful enemy.

Other organs are less obvious. These bodies include the education system, civil bureaucracies and the intelligence agencies that control the dissemination of "sensitive" information.

to believe in an absolute enemy." The rise of these "absolute enemies" has coloured the whole history of our times.

Absolute enemies

On 26 June 1945, seven weeks after the defeat of Hitler's Germany, 50 nations met in San Francisco to found the United Nations – their lofty vision to eradicate war forever as the five victorious powers combined their strength to establish and enforce world peace. Six weeks later – on 6 and 9 August 1945, Hiroshima and Nagasaki were destroyed by nuclear weapons. And so the nuclear age began.

The power of the UN to create and maintain peace has been overshadowed from the start. It soon became clear that its vision was far from reality. The suspicion and rivalry are revealed in a telegram sent on 12 May 1945 – while the UK, the USA, and Russia were still fighting "shoulder to shoulder" – by Winston Churchill to Harry Truman: "What will be the position in a year or two when the British and American armies have melted, and the French have not yet been formed on any major scale, and when Russia may choose to keep 200 or 300 divisions on active service? An iron curtain is drawn down upon their front. We do not know what is going on behind."

Within four years, 12 Western countries – Belgium, Canada, Denmark, France, Iceland, Italy, Luxembourg, the Netherlands, Norway, Portugal, the UK and the USA signed the North Atlantic Treaty to form NATO. They feared, mistakenly, Soviet expansionism. The Soviets, also mistakenly, interpreted NATO as part of an aggressive intent to encircle the USSR, backed by the West's nuclear advantage. Plans to internationalize nuclear weapons foundered on the same suspicion and rivalry. Wiser leaders could have avoided the cold war and nuclear arms race, and all they have entailed.

Instead, the ideological differences between East and West have been projected and amplified into nightmare enemy images, to justify the struggle for global influence, both political and economic.

If we are to abolish war, we must learn to recognize such projections for what they are, and dismantle them through rigorous analysis. "Defending freedom" and "supporting revolution" have become slogans to disguise interference, including military intervention, in other countries' affairs.

A militarized world

In the past 40 years, we have militarized the planet. Compared with the 1930s, when few countries had significant armed forces, the whole world today seems armed and ready for war. Out of nearly 200 nations, only two – Costa Rica and Iceland – have no military forces. Over two million troops are deployed overseas, and military bases ring the globe. Submarines that can destroy cities haunt the oceans, no national boundary is secure against the world reach of missiles and planes. We are even planning to militarize space. And the two superpowers – who together accounted in 1985 for 23

Armed camps

World politics is dominated and distorted by superpower rivalry and projected images of opposing armed camps. The situation began with the formation, on 24 August 1949, of the North Atlantic Treaty Organization (NATO). The USSR, from the outset, opposed the formation of NATO, and Stalin sent a memorandum to each of the 12 original signatories describing their intentions as hostile to the USSR. On 14 May 1955 the Warsaw Pact came into being.

NATO and the Warsaw Pact divide Europe into two heavily armed camps confronting each other across the East-West German border. On both sides sits a total of some 12,000 nuclear weapons and large arsenals of chemical weapons. Vast conventional armies – 2,700,000 strong in the Warsaw Pact and 1,900,000 in NATO – equipped with battle tanks, combat aircraft, missiles and warships, are poised to strike. The military budgets of NATO and Warsaw Pact countries add up to some 75% of world arms expenditure.

Images of the other side

Members of both NATO and the Warsaw Pact have serious economic problems. In many European countries, governments are under pressure to increase expenditure on social welfare systems. The USA has a massive budget deficit; the USSR needs to divert some of its military budget to pay for new and ambitious economic plans. But there is also internal pressure to maintain, and even increase, military budgets. The leaders attempt to resolve this dilemma by claiming that there is a large military threat and by building up a frightening image of the other side. Western propagandists argue that the Warsaw Pact is intent on destroying their freedoms. Their Warsaw Pact equivalents accuse the West of trying to undermine their social and political systems. The result is that each believes the other is poised to strike, while claiming that it is itself defensive.

Can either side win?
NATO leaders claim that Warsaw Pact conventional forces are so superior that they would quickly defeat NATO in a conventional war. The International Institute for Strategic Studies, however, writes in *The Military Balance 1986-1987*:

"Our conclusion remains that the conventional military balance is still such as to make general military aggression a highly risky undertaking for either side. Though possession of the initiative in war will always permit an aggressor to achieve a local advantage in numbers (sufficient perhaps to allow him to believe that he might achieve limited tactical success in some areas), there would still appear to be insufficient overall strength on either side to guarantee victory. The consequences for an attacker would still be quite unpredictable, and the risks, particularly of nuclear escalation, remain incalculable."

The European theatre
The superpowers face each other across the East-West German border. Logically, Europe should not be the focus of confrontation. The superpowers may hope, however, that war can be confined to Europe, thus sparing their homelands.

NATO countries

Warsaw Pact bloc

per cent of the world's armed forces, 60 per cent of military expenditures, over 80 per cent of weapons research, and 97 per cent of nuclear weapons – have enough firepower to kill every man, woman and child on Earth several times over.

This deepening sickness has taken hold of us mainly since World War II, when large resources were for the first time devoted to military science and technology. The momentum of this technology continued in the post-war period, spawning huge arms industries. Today, half a million military scientists invent and develop ever-more complex weapon systems, which arms manufacturers then produce in great numbers. To maximize profits, arms merchants sell huge quantities of these weapons abroad. And there are ready and expanding markets: about the first thing a new country does after independence is to form a national army – the main symbol of nationhood.

The quest for political stability

Growing up under the shadow of the cold war, the world has seen huge political changes. Decolonization has created a plethora of young and politically sensitive states concerned to achieve some measure of stability and establish their sovereign rights.

Even older nations can find stability threatened by such factors as conflicting allegiances, religious intolerance, different languages, and territorial and regional disputes. Such pressures often lead to the birth of separatist movements and to violence and war. Examples include Northern Ireland, the Basques, the dispute between Flemish- and French-speaking Belgium, the Corsican separatist movement – to name but a few. It is hardly surprising, then, that many of the young countries born since 1945 have serious problems.

The territorial borders of the new states were in many cases drawn arbitrarily – often with straight lines on a map – to carve out parts of old empires. No effort was made to include only people of common descent, language, tribe, and culture. Thus many contained, from their birth, divided resources and peoples. They also faced the difficulties of breaking up old trading patterns and financial arrangements made by an imperial power, and forging new ones. Rarely did the colonists leave behind an educated population, a trained local bureaucracy or an adequate infrastructure to form the new state. Where imperial powers were driven out by liberation movements, some deliberately destroyed the country's infrastructure, including the telephone and transport systems.

The judicial and political systems inherited from the out-going power were frequently unsuitable for the new country, and had to be rapidly and drastically read-justed. Political ideologies – sometimes designed more to curry favour with actual or potential donors of development and military aid than to reflect public welfare – were often imposed from above by newborn élites. This imposition provoked nationalistic and fundamentalist fervour, forces then exploited by competing élites in their power struggles. Attempts to forge

New identities, old ties

In the last 40 years the number of countries has increased from about 50 to nearly 200. This represents a new country every three months. All states – new and old – have one thing in common – an obsession with national sovereignty. This sometimes shows itself in strange ways, such as the maintenance of a national airline, whether or not the amount of air traffic justifies it. Similarly, costly weapons and armed forces are seen as essential elements of sovereignty.

States are unwilling to give up elements of sovereignty unless there are considerable advantages to be gained. The main problem is that when national and international interests clash, the former generally takes preference. Sovereignty is, therefore, a main obstacle to the solution of global problems.

Meantime, the health of the new states is impaired by economic patterns and ethnic divisions – a legacy of the past that also challenges the states' sovereign power.

A square flag in a round hole

Former colonies were often delineated simply by drawing arbitrary lines on a map, cutting right through tribal lands. Nomads usually ignored the borders – something the colonial power was prepared to accept, but not the newly formed state.

In general, colonial powers failed to make adequate preparation locally for statehood. Thus, former colonies had to set up

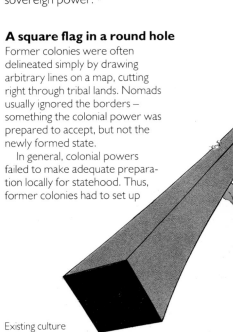

Flag of new nation

Old colonial power

New government

Existing culture

History

Common descent

Religion

Language

Customs

bureaucracies, often using as a model the home government of the former colonial power – structures that often did not suit the new states. It is hardly surprising that civil wars became rife as tribal, religious and other minority groups came into conflict. A lack of mature and stable government made conflicts all the more difficult to control.

The colonial legacy

In 1914, the South was mainly colonized by European powers. And the colonial empires were themselves a major cause of conflict between European countries. In the 1930s, for example, Hitler and Mussolini looked to expand their own territorial holdings through the acquisition of colonies, but most of the available territory was already colonized by others. This led the Fascist leaders to claim unfair treatment and, in Hitler's case, to justify arguments for the annexation of the Sudetenland in 1938 and for attacking the USSR to acquire "living space" and resources.

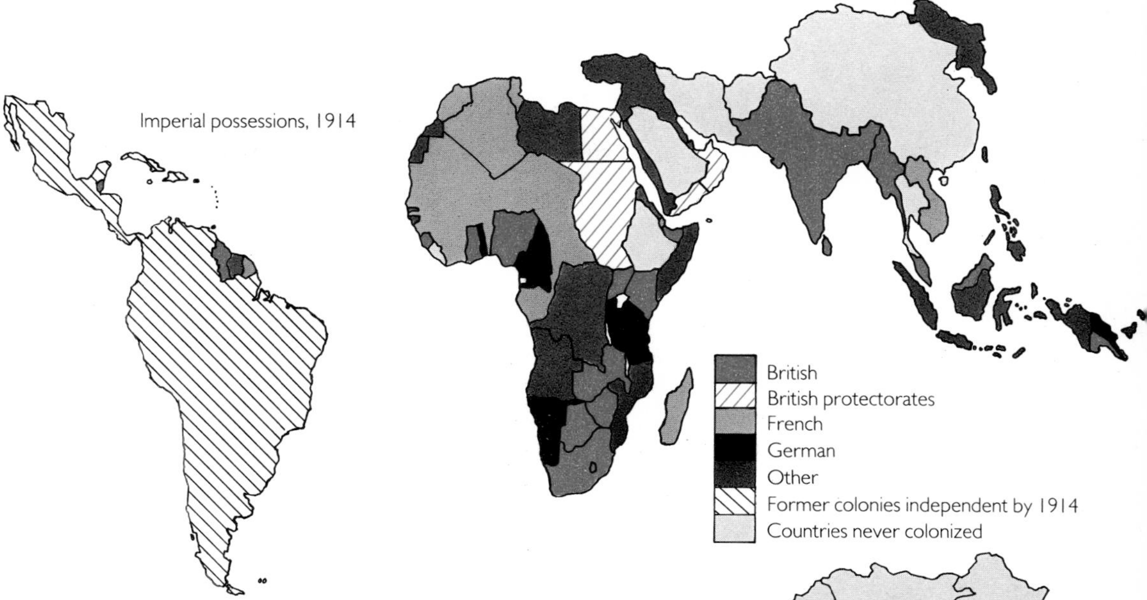

Imperial possessions, 1914

British
British protectorates
French
German
Other
Former colonies independent by 1914
Countries never colonized

The new nations

After 1945, many countries began claiming, and if necessary fighting for, their independence. The decolonization process dramatically increased the number of sovereign states, as can be seen on the map, *right*, which shows the approximate 150 new states that have been created in the last 40 years.

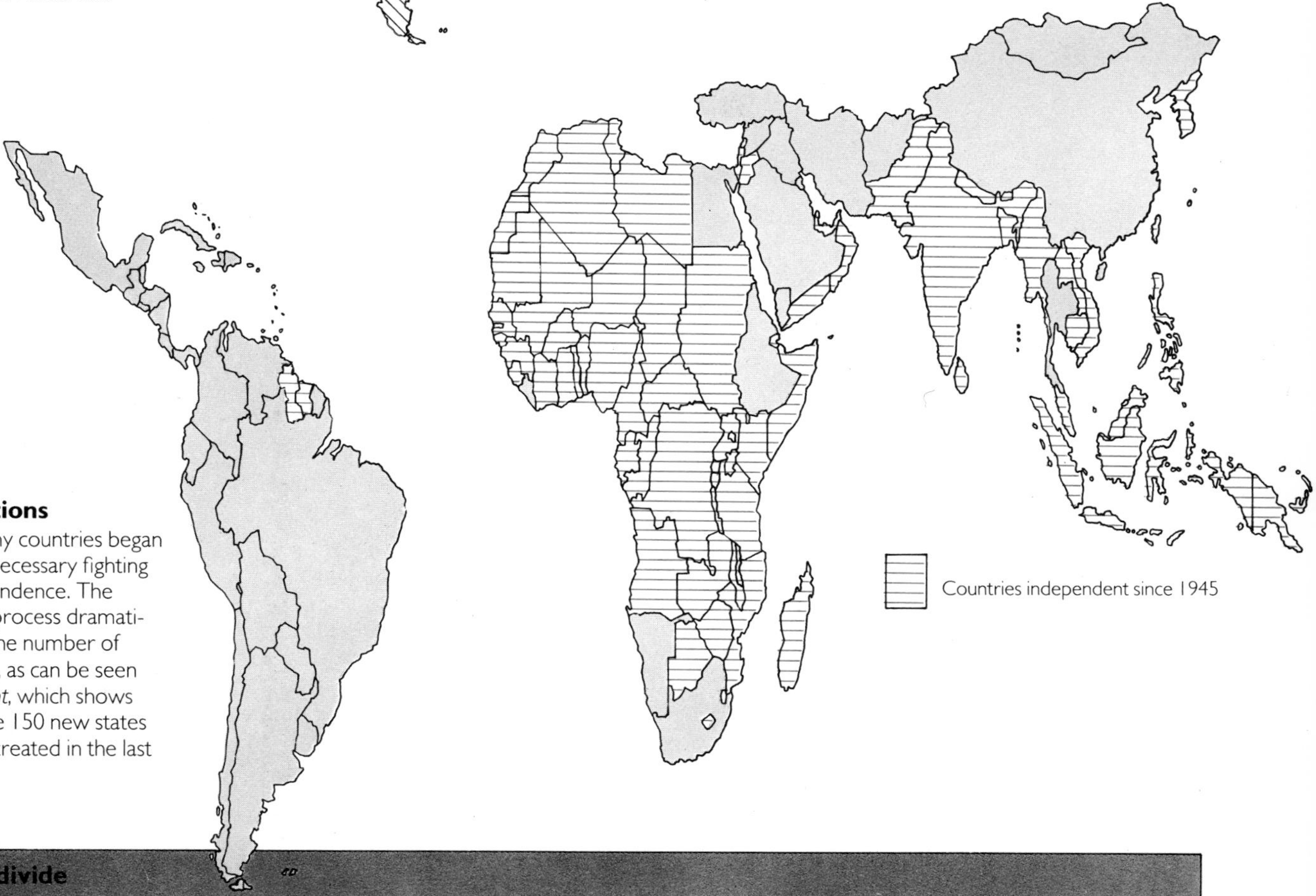

Countries independent since 1945

The great divide

The colonial powers divided up Africa in a very arbitrary way, with the result that many of today's states are not bounded by traditional ethnic frontiers. The notion of a nation-state uniting a people of mainly common descent, language and customs makes no sense in much of Africa. Rather, these states are often ethnically and linguistically pluralist with little hope of achieving a common culture.

Ethnic pluralism has been a major source of conflict in new African states – for example, in Nigeria, Kenya and Uganda. The map, *right*, shows the plurality of ethnic groups in Tanzania and Kenya as well as Uganda, one of the least homogeneous countries in the world. The conflicts that still rage in Uganda are mainly due to ethnic hostilities.

Equally disuniting are the legacies of the colonial bisections of ethnic homelands. The territories of the 200,000 Masai, for example, are split by the Kenya-Tanzania border.

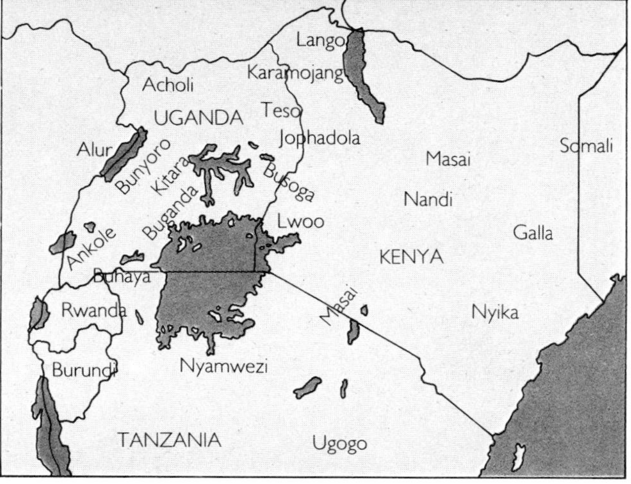

Langor
Acholi
Karamojang
UGANDA
Teso
Alur
Bunyoro
Jophadola
Masai
Somali
Kitara
Buganda
Busoga
Nandi
Galla
Ankole
Lwoo
KENYA
Buhaya
Masai
Rwanda
Nyika
Burundi
Nyamwezi
TANZANIA
Ugogo

new economic trade and financial links soon became enmeshed in superpower rivalry, with countries switching allegiance from one side to the other as it suited them. This rivalry is a continuing and pervasive feature in the South, as the USA and USSR use economic and military aid to manipulate states to their liking and vie for global power.

If a state feels directly threatened, or its leaders pursue aggressive policies, high military spending is likely, often provoking an arms race in the region, and so increasing the chance of war. Such tensions are worst under military dictatorships – half the developing countries now have military rule; but even elected governments often rely on the support of the military to stay in power. The price is large arsenals of the most modern and "glamorous" weapons. A political leader striving for hegemony may devote considerable resources to the military purely to satisy its desire for status and prestige.

The military sickness – out of control?

The world spends on the military more than the poorer half of humankind earns. Why do political leaders tolerate this waste? Because they fear loss of office, if they try to stop it.

Soviet and American political leaders lost control of the East-West arms race years ago. The economies of the USA and the USSR have been kept on a war footing since World War II; industry and agriculture are thus organized, not in the most economical way, but to support strategic objectives and survival in wartime. Indeed, militarization reaches right down to the very roots of society.

People of all ages are affected. The population must be convinced that the high military spending is justified: that "freedom" and security are synonymous with military might, and resources should be spent on the unproductive military sector rather than health, education and other social services. Adaptation to this view begins in school, even in kindergarten. History, geography, social studies, current affairs are taught in ways that generate stereotyped images, and the media repeat the lesson. "The other side", we are told, "is poised to invade us. We will escape subjection only if we are militarily very strong."

This schooling makes us hostile, suspicious and mistrustful of our potential "enemies". To be otherwise is "unpatriotic". Teaching that questions official wisdom about the size of the military threat, the balance of military forces, and the elements of national security, is therefore "subversive".

Almost all political and social systems now behave like this – the disease is entrenched. The perceived "enemy" may be NATO or the Warsaw Pact, the UK or Argentina, Iran or Iraq, Israel or the Arab countries, India or Pakistan. Each side uses the other to generate its image of the "enemy", and so legitimize continuing arms races and militarization.

In a militarized society, a large percentage of scientists, engineers and technologists work full-time

Shackled politicians

"This conjunction of an immense military establishment and a large arms industry is new in the American experience. The total influence – economic, political, even spiritual – is felt in every city, every State house, every office of the Federal government. We recognize the imperative need for the development. Yet we must not fail to comprehend its grave implications. Our toil, resources and livelihood are all involved: so is the very structure of our society.

"In the councils of government, we must guard against the acquisition of unwarranted influence, whether sought or unsought, by the military-industrial complex. The potential for the disastrous rise of misplaced power exists and will persist.

"We must never let the weight of this combination endanger our liberties or democratic processes. We should take nothing for granted. Only an alert and knowledgeable citizenry can compel the proper meshing of the huge industrial and military machinery of defense with our peaceful methods and goals, so that security and liberty may prosper together."
Dwight D. Eisenhower, 1961
Are the politicians in control of the arms race?

Unwarranted influences

Some people believe that US President John F. Kennedy was not killed by Lee Harvey Oswald acting alone, but that a group conspired to assassinate him. Conspiracy theorists include those who argue that the President was killed by those convinced that he was anti-militarist and would cut back military expenditure. This theory is used as an example of the lengths to which the military-industrial complex will go to achieve its objectives.

More recently, President Carter took a number of decisions while in office, cancelling the B-1 strategic bomber, for example, that threatened the military-industrial complex. Some theorists believe that the complex was instrumental in preventing his re-election and in ensuring the successful candidacy of Ronald Reagan, a friend of the complex.

Links in the chain

There are six main groups with vested interests in the arms race:

1. The military
With an annual budget of $1000 billion a year, the military has enormous political lobbying power.

2. The defence industry
With military orders of $250 billion annually, the weapons industry is the second biggest in the world, after oil.

3. Academics
About 500,000 scientists and engineers work full time developing new weapons and improving old ones.

4. Bureaucrats
The 27 million civilians administering military and defence establishments are able to frustrate political decisions that go against their interests.

5. Ordinary industry
Many businesses benefit from the day-to-day products needed by the military.

6. Diplomats
Arms control diplomats see their career as managing rather than stopping the arms race.

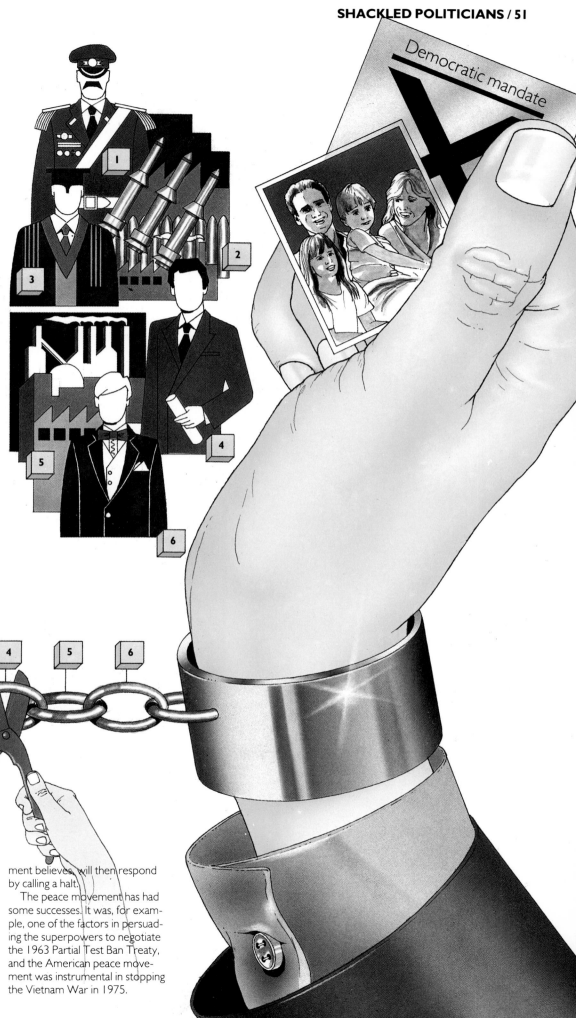

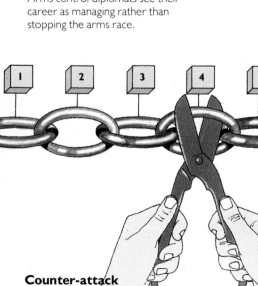

Counter-attack

The aim of the peace movement is to mobilize public opinion against the arms race, particularly the nuclear arms race. If enough people resist, the pressure of public opinion against militarization can be made to exceed that brought by those with vested interests in keeping the arms race going. Politicians, the peace move-ment believes, will then respond by calling a halt.

The peace movement has had some successes. It was, for example, one of the factors in persuading the superpowers to negotiate the 1963 Partial Test Ban Treaty, and the American peace movement was instrumental in stopping the Vietnam War in 1975.

developing weapons and improving old ones. Their motives are not warlike, but a wish for a good career, a desire for profit and personal success, an interest in high technology – and the easy rationalization of patriotism. Given so many scientists and financial resources, military science is bound, in time, to revolutionize weaponry and transform warfare. New weapons and their supporting technologies become ever-more dangerous. Nuclear weapons technology changes, in particular (*see pp. 132-3*), are bringing ever nearer the risk of global war.

Exporting war via the arms trade

The vast majority of the weapons used in wars in developing countries have been imported from the North. This global trade in weapons is vicious, immoral and potentially self-destructive. It is vicious because countries often sell arms indiscriminately. More than 40 countries have, for example, supplied weapons to the combatants in the Iran/Iraq War. Some 15 countries have, with the utmost cynicism, supplied weapons to both sides. It is immoral because the foreign arms used in the 200 or so developing country wars have killed 20 million people, injured many more, and produced millions of refugees. The countries supplying the weapons for these wars must take a large part of the responsibility for the death and destruction caused by them. The arms trade is also potentially self-destructive because the weapons may be turned against the supplier. Two Argentinian warships, for example, were electronically re-fitted in Portsmouth three weeks before the Falklands/Malvinas War. And the Exocet missile that sank *HMS Sheffield* contained many British-made components.

Estimates indicate that the value of the global arms trade is running at about $50 billion a year. Three-quarters of this trade is with the developing countries. And it has created more than a quarter of the South's unmanageable debt burden, now standing at a thousand billion dollars. Channelling expenditure into weapons instead of economic development aggravates domestic tensions and is potentially threatening to a country's internal stability. Yet the governments in the South continue to import arms. Why?

The reasons typically reinforce each other. Arms bought for perceived security needs increase the risk of conflict; this strengthens national unity and the armed forces; this, in turn increases the influence of the armed forces; and stronger armed forces demand more arms. This vicious circle is fuelled by the major weapons suppliers in the North, and cannot be fully understood without examining their motives.

The USA and the USSR sell arms to developing countries mainly to gain political and economic influence or military bases in strategic locations. Other countries – like the UK, France, West Germany, and Italy – believe, mistakenly (*see pp. 106-7*), that selling weapons helps their economies. Some seek the savings to be had from long production runs. Others want to recover part of the large research and development

The arms trade

The world arms trade is worth in the region of $50 billion a year. It is a commercial business conducted without reference to the moral issues involved. Worse still, the North is involved in fuelling conflict in the South for reasons of straight financial gain.

The South is now importing three times as many weapons as the North with most of their major weapons coming from the industrialized countries, in particular the USA and the USSR. Modern wars use munitions so rapidly, particularly missiles, that developing countries at war need new supplies of weapons very quickly. The superpower suppliers therefore become intimately involved through their client states with the conflict, with a grave risk that some future war in the South will escalate into nuclear world war.

1973 Middle East war

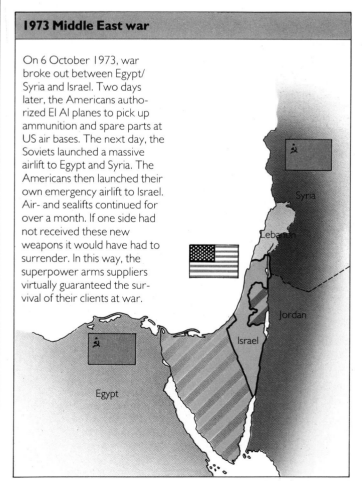

On 6 October 1973, war broke out between Egypt/Syria and Israel. Two days later, the Americans authorized El Al planes to pick up ammunition and spare parts at US air bases. The next day, the Soviets launched a massive airlift to Egypt and Syria. The Americans then launched their own emergency airlift to Israel. Air- and sealifts continued for over a month. If one side had not received these new weapons it would have had to surrender. In this way, the superpower arms suppliers virtually guaranteed the survival of their clients at war.

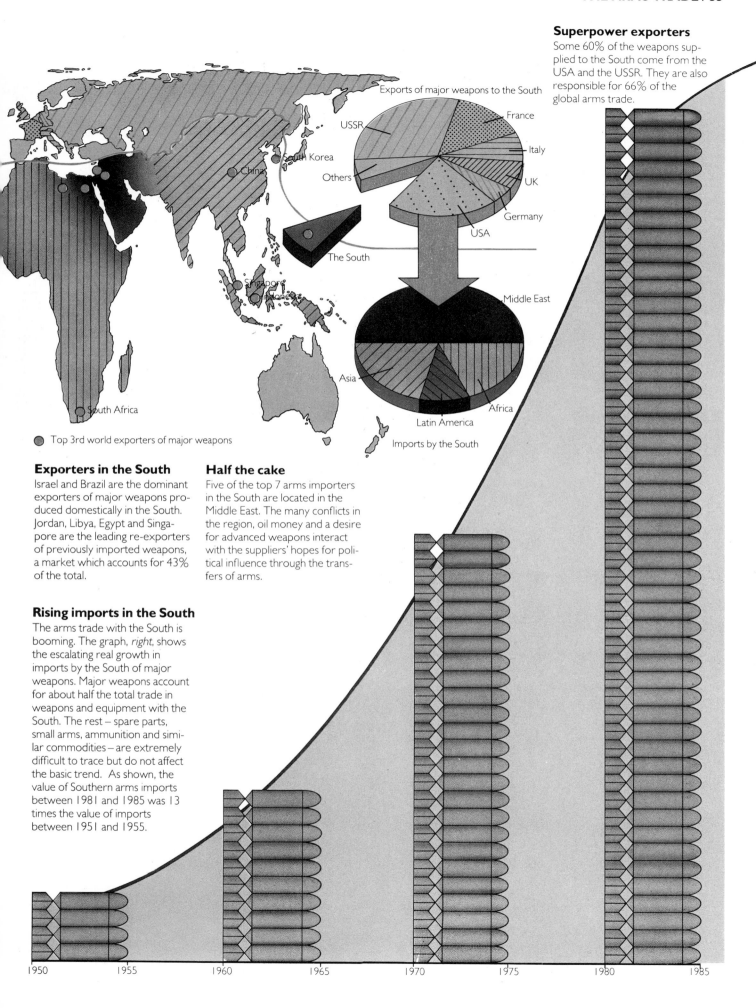

Superpower exporters
Some 60% of the weapons supplied to the South come from the USA and the USSR. They are also responsible for 66% of the global arms trade.

Exports of major weapons to the South

USSR

France

Italy

Others

UK

Germany

USA

The South

Middle East

Asia

Africa

Latin America

Imports by the South

South Korea

China

Singapore

Indonesia

South Africa

● Top 3rd world exporters of major weapons

Exporters in the South
Israel and Brazil are the dominant exporters of major weapons produced domestically in the South. Jordan, Libya, Egypt and Singapore are the leading re-exporters of previously imported weapons, a market which accounts for 43% of the total.

Half the cake
Five of the top 7 arms importers in the South are located in the Middle East. The many conflicts in the region, oil money and a desire for advanced weapons interact with the suppliers' hopes for political influence through the transfers of arms.

Rising imports in the South
The arms trade with the South is booming. The graph, *right*, shows the escalating real growth in imports by the South of major weapons. Major weapons account for about half the total trade in weapons and equipment with the South. The rest – spare parts, small arms, ammunition and similar commodities – are extremely difficult to trace but do not affect the basic trend. As shown, the value of Southern arms imports between 1981 and 1985 was 13 times the value of imports between 1951 and 1955.

1950   1955   1960   1965   1970   1975   1980   1985

costs involved in modern weapons design. In many cases, producers could not afford to develop and manufacture new weapons for their own arsenals unless they sold weapons abroad.

A new development in the global arms trade is the small but increasing share of the market taken by exporters in the South. Due to lower production costs, major weapons produced in developing countries are particularly attractive to other developing countries. They are also beginning to gain export contracts with the North. In 1985, for example, Brazil won the British order for a new basic trainer for the Royal Air Force after fierce competition with Australian, British and Swedish designs. More than 30 developing countries are now producing arms. In addition to major weapons, many of them export small arms, ammunition and services such as the modernization of old weapons. Production and export of arms in the South are continuing to rise. With more and more suppliers in the global market, competition will become even more cut-throat and the arms trade even more difficult to control – and the frequency, destruction and savagery of wars even greater.

The causes of conflicts

About 85 per cent of the armed conflicts since 1945 have begun at the civil level – in efforts to overthrow a ruling regime, or disputes over tribal, religious, or ethnic minority issues. Only 15 per cent have involved the armies of two or more countries fighting each other across borders. Occasionally, wars have also been pursued to divert the attention of populations from domestic political or economic difficulties. The Falklands/Malvinas War, for example, provided a distraction from domestic problems facing the leaderships of both the combatants.

Local conflicts attract superpower involvement. Frequent in wars in the South, it only exacerbates the conflict and makes it more difficult to resolve. It also ensures that local ideological disputes get drawn into the quite different ideological conflict between the superpowers. Tensions in the South unnecessarily become part of the East-West rivalry, and ideological differences increasingly and artificially polarized.

The Iran/Iraq War began because of the traditional enmity between Arabs and Iranians. But another major reason was that each country has an authoritarian leader who needs, for domestic political reasons, to prove to his people that his country dominates the Gulf region. The Gulf region produces 40 per cent of the world's oil. Superpower rivalry in the area is intense, with the Americans keen to prevent the Soviets from increasing their influence. The Americans are also intent on preventing the Iranians from winning the war – an ambition that prolongs the conflict.

In the Middle East, the USA guarantees the continual existence of Israel, and the USSR is a close ally of Syria. The determination of each to maintain its influence in the region, as part of a global power struggle, makes inevitable superpower involvement in

Multiplying conflict points

The superpowers are involved in virtually all wars in the South, since they are responsible for the bulk of the weapons manufactured, sold and ultimately used (*see pp. 52-3*).

Sometimes, a superpower may involve itself directly by sending its own troops to fight. More commonly, however, troops of regional allies are used. In this way the superpowers can be likened to puppet masters manipulating and controlling the actions of their client states, and jostling for influence in strategically important regions by fuelling external as well as internal conflicts.

That the superpowers intend to involve themselves in future wars in the South as part of a deliberate policy is shown by the fact that they are maintaining on alert rapid deployment forces and have arranged to use foreign air bases to make easier the use of such forces. The USSR, for example, maintains a forward deployment base at Cam Ranh Bay in Vietnam, while the USA has a base at Diego Garcia in the Indian Ocean, amongst others.

Often, regional superpowers ape their global counterparts in their perception that they can maintain their status only by becoming involved in local conflicts. Thus, India feels obliged to send armed forces to intervene in the civil war in Sri Lanka and Vietnam has 160,000 troops in Kampuchea.

US in Nicaragua

When the Sandinista National Liberation Front took power in Nicaragua in 1979 it ousted the pro-US Somoza dictatorship that had ruled for 43 years. The present Nicaraguan government has links with the USSR and the Reagan administration accuses the USSR of supplying arms and support to the Nicaraguans in an attempt to set up a "second Cuba" in Central America. The US is, therefore, backing the anti-Sandinista Contras organized by right-wing Nicaraguans based in Miami.

About 4000 Contras are active in Nicaragua but they are unable to control a significant amount of territory. If it were not for American support of the Contras they would not be able to sustain the conflict and the Sandinistas would be firmly in control.

Civil/international conflict

Before 1945 most wars were between nations – declared wars. Since 1945 civil wars have become the norm – these are not declared. Civil wars can be the most brutal in El Salvador some 70,000 have died.

The superpower factor

Because of the danger of escalation to a nuclear war, the superpowers are unprepared to confront each other militarily. They are, therefore, fighting wars in the South by proxy. They are also using these wars to test new weapons under operational conditions.

USSR in Afghanistan

The USSR invaded Afghanistan in 1979 to maintain the pro-Soviet government against the Mojaheddin rebels, and now has about 118,000 troops stationed there. The perceived Soviet need to maintain a friendly regime in Afghanistan is related to Soviet policy of surrounding itself by a ring of buffer states.

The conflict, which seems set to end by the withdrawal of Soviet troops, has cost about 12,000 Soviet and 100,000 Afghan lives. It has been exacerbated by the support given by the USA to the Afghan guerillas – a symbol of the power struggle between the two superpowers.

The Gulf war

This war has its roots in the historical enmity between Arabs and Iranians. Also important, however, are the personalities of the countries' two leaders – Iran's Shiite fundamentalist Ayatollah Khoumeni and Iraq's secular President Hussein. The Ayatollah is disinclined to end present hostilities until Iraq admits responsibility for the initial aggression. Also, the Ayatollah sees himself as having a mission to spread the Islamic revolution to a country such as Iraq, which has a Shiite majority but a Sunni leader.

A major factor of a global nature central to the Gulf war is control of the vitally important oil routes in and out of the Persian Gulf. This, plus the sale of strategic weapons by both the USA and USSR to both countries, makes direct superpower confrontation a dangerous possibility.

Standing armies

In an effort to increase their influence and safeguard security, many countries station troops and/or military advisers overseas, especially in the South *see left*. Ironically, this has the opposite effect, increasing the chance of international conflict.

Only two – Iceland and Costa Rica – have no standing armies or significant military expenditure. Costa Rica does have a paramilitary force organized into the Presidential Guard, and Iceland, a NATO member, hosts a US base.

The Tamils

The civil war in Sri Lanka is a conflict between the Buddhist Sinhalese majority (77%) and the Hindu Tamil minority (17%). India initially supported the Tamils because of the large Tamil population in the south of India, and also to show that India dominates the Indian Ocean as regional superpower. In an effort to enforce the peace accord signed between Sri Lanka's president and the Tamil guerillas, India sent an 8000-strong peacekeeping force to the island. The Indian troops tried to disarm the Tamils but soon became involved in bloody fighting.

all Middle East conflicts. Superpower involvement is perhaps most obvious in, and directly responsible for, the Nicaraguan and Afghan conflicts. If it were not for American support for the Contras there would not be a conflict in Nicaragua; the Sandinistas would be firmly in control of the country. The Soviets invaded Afghanistan to put in power a regime sympathetic to Soviet interests. The perceived need to maintain this government accounts for the continuing conflict there – conflict that is exacerbated by the support given by the Americans to the Afghan guerillas.

The undeclared wars

Before 1945 it was usual for countries involved in such armed conflicts to declare war on each other. War, in other words, was legally defined. But since 1945 no war has been declared – although very many wars have taken place. The United Nations Charter declares wars of aggression illegal – hence the reluctance of governments to label conflicts as wars, their efforts to prove themselves the "innocent party", or to show that they have been "invited" to send in military forces by a beleaguered friendly regime. Hence, too, the numerous "proxy" wars in which a major power supplies armaments, funding, and "advisers" to so-called freedom fighters. (It would also, of course, cease to be possible to sell arms to both sides in conflict if one admitted to being "at war".)

Such absurdities obscure the sad truth that, in the 40 years since World War II, there has been no peace. By any reasonable definition, a conflict is a war if: the armed forces of a government in power engage the armed forces of an opposition (whether a rebel group trying to overthrow the establishment, a religious or other minority, or another country); the fighting between the opposing forces takes place over a significant period of time, even if sporadic; and, in a civil war, the forces opposing the government occupy significant areas of the country.

By this definition, there have been about 200 wars since 1945. There are 38 going on at this moment, involving a quarter of the countries around the globe. Some have been waged for a long time. The Burmese government, for instance, has been fighting the communist resistance almost continuously since 1945.

Although the majority of these wars have been in the South, it should not be thought that Europe is a continent at peace. There has been fighting in Czechoslovakia, Hungary and Poland. Currently, the British government is fighting in Northern Ireland, Basque guerillas are fighting in Spain, and Corsican rebels are fighting the French government.

On average, a new war begins somewhere in the world every three months. In the 40 years since World War II, the territory of some 80 countries and the armed forces of about 90 states have been involved in war. There has not been a single day since September 1945 when the world was free of war. On a typical day, 12 wars are being fought. We live in an age of violence in which the level of conflict is steadily rising.

WORLD

3rd World

"The ending of colonialism does not automatically inaugurate an era of peace and prosperity for liberated peoples. It could equally be the prelude to fraternal wars and new inhumanities . . . It is my considered opinion that the third world war has already begun – in the Third World. The new war is likely to be a cumulation of little wars rather than one big war. Though the form is new, it is basically a war between the great powers and one fought for the realization of their ambitions and the promotion of their national interests. However, this is not obvious because in this new world war, the great powers are invisible."
Sinathamby Rajaratnam, Singapore's senior minister and veteran delegate to the Non-aligned Movement (NaM).

Since September 1945 there have been 120 wars in which deaths have averaged more than 1000 per year. Twenty million people have died in these "major wars" alone. Many more have been injured and there are currently at least 8 million refugees from conflicts worldwide.

The map, *right*, shows the location of these major wars and who has been involved in them, including foreign intervention.

Intervention has been defined as the use of uniformed military personnel from a foreign country. It does not include members of UN peacekeeping forces. Nor does it include countries which have sent advisers to provide "technical military assistance".

EWS

War?

The chart, *right*, lists the 60 countries that have seen at least one major war since 1945. One disturbing trend is the rise in civilian deaths. In WWI 95% of the casualties were military; in modern wars, 60% of the casualties are civilian. In the North, overall casualty rates are generally lower, but it is worth remembering that several hundred people have died as a result of the Basque separatist fighting in Spain, and 2500 in Northern Ireland.

Country/REGION	Deaths Thousands			Country/REGION	Deaths Thousands		
	Civilian	Military	Total		Civilian	Military	Total
LATIN AMERICA				**MIDDLE EAST**			
◐ Argentina	14	5	19	● Israeli/Arab	58	69	127
○ Bolivia	1	1	2	◐ Cyprus	3	2	5
○ Brazil	★	★	1	◐ Iran	17	500	517
○ Chile	★	★	25	◐ Iraq	101	6	107
○ Colombia	200	100	300	○ Jordan	1	1	2
○ Costa Rica	1	1	2	◐ Lebanon	76	26	102
○ Cuba	2	3	5	○ Syria	10	-	10
◐ Dominican Republic	1	2	3	◐ Yemen	(2)	(2)	108
○ El Salvador	40	15	55	**AFRICA**			
○ Guatemala	(43)	(2)	46	◐ Algeria	163	161	324
◐ Honduras	-	2	2	◐ Angola	(30)	(25)	67
○ Jamaica	1	-	1	○ Burundi	80	20	100
○ Nicaragua	43	19	62	● Cameroon	★	★	32
○ Paraguay	-	-	1	○ Chad	★	★	1
○ Peru	2	1	3	◐ Ethiopia	515	66	581
ASIA				○ Ghana	★	★	1
◐ Afghanistan	150	150	300	● Guinea Bissau	5	10	15
◐ Bangladesh	1000	500	1500	● Kenya	3	12	15
○ Burma	-	-	13	● Madagascar	3	2	5
◐ China	(1067)	(41)	2163	◐ Mozambique	(100)	★	130
◐ India	822	11	833	○ Nigeria	(1000)	(1000)	2006
◐ Indonesia	(4)	(1)	841	○ Rwanda	105	3	108
◐ Kampuchea	(2514)	(510)	3180	○ Sudan	51	250	301
◐ Korea	1000	1890	2890	○ Tunisia	3	-	3
◐ Laos	(10)	(9)	24	◐ Uganda	(301)	(4)	555
● Malaysia	★	★	13	● Western Sahara	3	7	10
◐ Pakistan	6	3	9	◐ Zaire	★	★	101
○ Philippines	20	23	43	○ Zambia	★	★	1
○ Sri Lanka	6	1	7	○ Zimbabwe	(2)	★	14
◐ Vietnam	1509	1479	2988	**EUROPE**			
				◐ Greece	★	★	160
				◐ Hungary	★	10	10
				○ Turkey	★	★	5

Conflicts have been:
● International   ( ) Incomplete data
○ Civil   ★ Figures not known
◐ Both   - Less than 1000 deaths

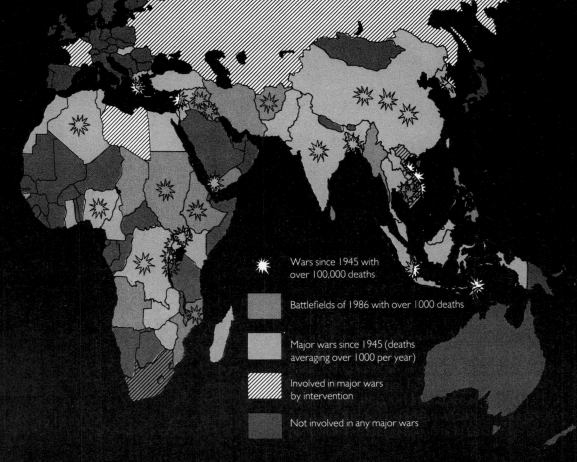

✳ Wars since 1945 with over 100,000 deaths

▨ Battlefields of 1986 with over 1000 deaths

▨ Major wars since 1945 (deaths averaging over 1000 per year)

▨ Involved in major wars by intervention

▨ Not involved in any major wars

3 Keeping the peace

Introduced by Sir Brian Urquhart

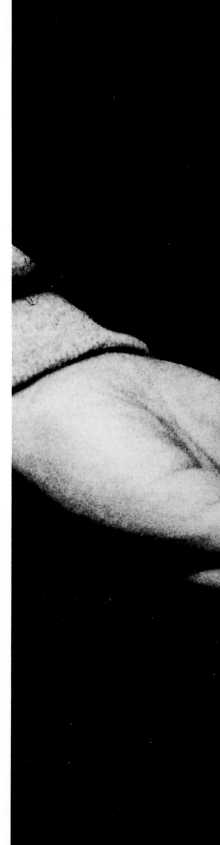

In 1945, after six years of war, the world seemed to have learned an important lesson. That lesson was distilled in the Charter of the UN. The Charter stipulates that armed force shall not be used save in the common interest; that member states shall settle their disputes by peaceful means and refrain from the threat or the use of force; that the UN will take collective measures to deal with threats to the peace or acts of aggression.

These were the assumptions on which it was believed that the UN would encompass a scheme of collective security, administered by the Security Council. With this in place, national security arrangements could be relaxed, the arms race would stop and disarmament would become a reality.

It soon became clear that the conditions for implementing the Charter were not present. The great powers that had won the war, now the permanent members of the Security Council, were supposed to stick together to guard, and if need be enforce, the peace. Instead, the deep and perennial disagreements of the permanent members hobbled the Security Council from the outset.

In addition, the world experienced a series of revolutionary events which were not foreseen by the authors of the Charter. The emergence of nuclear weapons heralded a radical change in great power relations and international affairs. Rapid decolonization rewrote the map of the world and gave rise to a vast new international constituency. Population doubled, while technological revolution radically changed the conditions of human life and contributed to the growing interdependence of nations. The list of global problems which no country, however powerful, can tackle alone, grows longer.

The UN, which, for all its shortcomings, is the only global design we have for trying to master the complexity of our situation, has for more than forty years tried to respond by improvization to this unforeseen world. Instead of the collective security system described in the Charter, it has provided a forum for disagreement and compromise, a last resort when confrontation threatens, a safety net for the superpowers, a capacity for honest brokerage and mediation, and the beginnings of a new system of conflict control – peacekeeping. It remains to be seen whether current developments in superpower relations and co-operation elsewhere will allow the Security Council to fulfil its aim of a permanent system of international peace and security.

In the process of decolonization and the frictions and adjustments it has entailed, the UN has undoubtedly been an indispensable catalyst and facilitator. As for the new generation of global crises, engendered by haphazard evolution from the colonial/ imperial world, only a beginning has been made. An immense amount needs to be done – and with a heightened urgency. Peace, security, trade, finance, social change, poverty, resources, ecological and environmental threats cannot be dealt with in isolation. Effective approaches must be based on common aims and at least a reasonable degree of political consensus.

Efforts to "keep the peace" have not, so far, been widely based on such a consensus. Yet it is vitally necessary. In its absence, international conflicts and disputes, not to mention ideological rivalries, will continue to devour the energy, resources, and international attention urgently needed elsewhere. We must *use* and adapt the international institutions we set up and realize the objectives we so confidently proclaimed in the Charter forty years ago, not only to maintain a level of peace in our dangerous world, but also to free ourselves to tackle the real problems which can radically affect our future.

"If the world could live for a few generations without war, war would come to seem as absurd as duelling has come to seem to us. No doubt there would still be some homicidal maniacs, but they would no longer be heads of Governments." Bertrand Russell

Human communities have had many hundreds of thousand years of experience in handling disputes at the local level, compared with a mere seven or eight thousand at citizen-state level and half this at interstate level. The less our experience, and the higher the level of power involved, the more we still rely on force or threats if our interests are challenged. We need time to learn. But events have overtaken us: in the nuclear age, war is obsolete; yet we have had less than fifty years to unlearn war and develop means of global co-existence. The world moreover is full of young states and power groups larger than any we have known. We must learn fast, or perish.

Conflict in society: laws and procedures

In the words of Catharine Perry of the Quaker Peace and Service: "Conflict resolution is actually very simple. All you have to do is to get the people involved in a dispute to sit down together and discuss the problem rationally. Once they see the point at issue as a shared problem to be solved jointly, rather than viewing the other side as an obstacle to be overcome, you are practically home and dry."

As we all know from experience, this simple truth can prove very difficult in practice. When there is a conflict, people's emotions – fear, prejudice, hate, greed – and their needs, beliefs and personal and family interests determine attitudes much more than any rational assessment of the problem. Approaches are usually so irrational that conflict resolution is a very slow and complicated business.

This is true even for primitive societies, which often recognize it in rituals and hospitable ceremony associated with negotiation procedures. It is even more so for complex ones, in which social structures are more rigid and the inertia of bureaucracies an increasing barrier. But the problems are greatest in societies, like South Africa, with a perceived lack of social justice. And in any society, the élites will manipulate conflicts to maximize and maintain power.

All types of conflict – from individual to international – tend to evolve the same way. It is at the point where communication breaks down, the main parties having become polarized, that the potential for violence is greatest. If they do not fight it out at this stage, the conflict will spread. Each will form alliances and propagate "images of the enemy" to dehumanize the other side. Soon, the original causes and objectives are forgotten. Winning at any cost is the goal. The conflict becomes more hysterical, leaders more fanatical; crisis psychology takes over.

The conflict can end only when one side defeats the other and imposes its will, or when some third party intervenes to de-escalate the crisis and impose a

Conflict resolution

All types of political and social systems have institutions for resolving conflicts. Disputes are settled in civil and criminal courts, both of which can impose sanctions. Civil courts can impose damages; criminal courts penalties such as fines, imprisonment and even death.

In some industrialized nations, negotiation and arbitration to avoid legal confrontation have been developed to a sophisticated level, mainly by trade unions. If negotiations fail, an arbitration is set up, either involving a single arbitrator, respected by both sides, or with a council of arbitration. Thus, third-party initia-

National
At the national level, there are clearly defined pathways once disputes or anti-social behaviour occur (indicated, *right*, by thin arrows).

Negotiation and arbitration
Negotiation is the simplest and most common form of conflict resolution, because a third party is not involved. Arbitration involves the use of an objective third party to hear the arguments of those in dispute and work out a solution.

Resolution or courts
If conflicts are not resolved by negotiation or arbitration they may go to a court. Most legal systems use an array of courts, arranged in a hierarchy. Generally, a lower court must base its decisions on those of higher courts. A court's judgment is normally enforceable by sanctions. The law is effective, however, only if it is "legitimized" – that is, most people respect and intend to obey it, even without the threat of sanctions.

Policing, law enforcement and intervention
When laws and social norms are accepted as reasonable they are effective; when they are not, a police presence is increasingly necessary. Gross inequalities in wealth or opportunity, high unemployment, an absence of minority rights, and discrimination lead to a loss of consensus on moral norms. And if conflict-management institutions are not legitimized in the eyes of significant groups, law and order breaks down. Behaviour is then constrained only by sanctions.

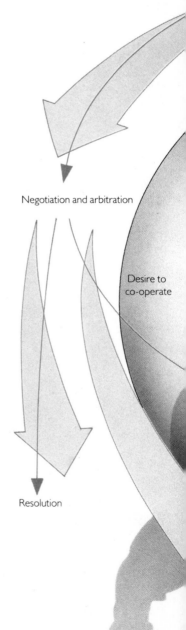

Negotiation and arbitration

Desire to co-operate

Resolution

tives have become an important, and increasingly developed, method of conflict resolution.

Most people follow the moral norms of the society they live in and actively co-operate with others to avoid conflict. To a lesser extent, conflict avoidance also results from a fear of sanctions or of social rejection. The majority of disputes are civil, between individuals or groups within society. However, a minority of people act criminally, in conflict with law and society itself, because they feel rejected, alienated or disadvantaged.

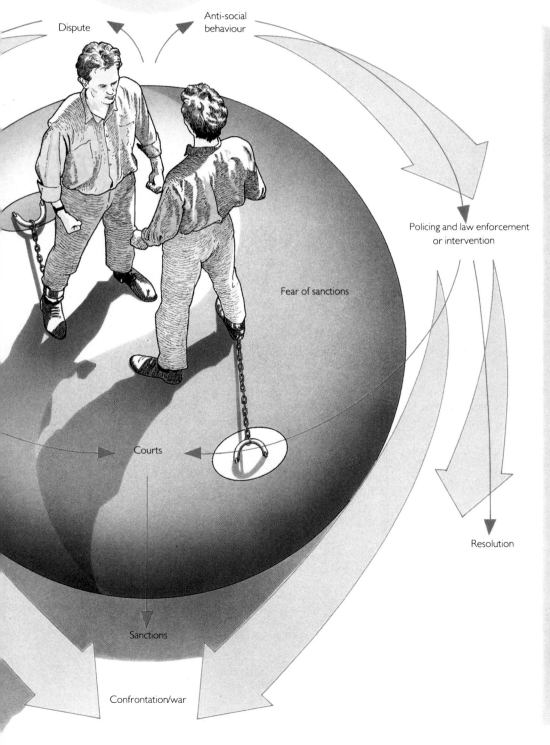

Dispute

Anti-social behaviour

Policing and law enforcement or intervention

Fear of sanctions

Courts

Resolution

Sanctions

Confrontation/war

International

The dynamics of conflict between nations (represented here by broad arrows) are roughly similar to those described opposite. The major difference is that, in international disputes, if negotiation and/ or arbitration fail then war will break out. Initially, diplomacy may be used. If this fails, the parties polarize and diplomatic relations may be broken off completely.

International law enforcement

The major weakness in resolving international conflict is the absence of consensus support for supranational codes of behaviour. This is reflected in the absence of an international police force capable of effective intervention, and the lack of a truly effective international court to impose meaningful sanctions. In this sense, international society is only half evolved, little different from warring barons of the Middle Ages. Sometimes, part of the international community will introduce economic and arms embargoes on the combatants. Historically, however, these have proved ineffectual. Similarly, UN resolutions are unlikely to restrain the combatants until they themselves desire a ceasefire.

War

Violence may first break out locally, but allies are soon sought and the conflict becomes increasingly less containable. We have few mechanisms to prevent relatively low-level violence developing into full-scale war. When war does break out, beating the "enemy" becomes the goal, the original issues forgotten as emotions rise with the escalation of conflict.

settlement. But unless the underlying problem is then tackled, and solved, the row is likely to flare again once the parties have recovered strength.

As societies develop, they set up ways of resolving conflicts peacefully before the main parties become too polarized. All social and political systems have institutions for this purpose. Disputes are settled by peer groups or by negotiation and arbitration, and ultimately by courts of law and sanctions. At the international level, treaties and trade agreements, balance of power and diplomacy, have a history going back to Egyptian times. But to date, war – rather than law – has remained the final arbiter.

Codes, laws and sanctions succeed only to the extent that they are "legitimized" (ie. accepted) by all parties. Over time, a consensus grows within society and moral norms are established that become the basis of conflict resolution. The tragedy of the international order is our inability to establish a full consensus that would legitimize peace. Inequity and structural violence in many sectors of the global community make such a goal even more difficult. When individuals, groups, or states, perceive themselves to be at odds with society they will break moral norms. For them, no method of conflict resolution is legitimized: they are in permanent conflict with society.

Pressures for change

Societies are dynamic – they either develop or decay. This is not only a matter of economics; it involves changing value systems and moral norms. Since 1945, society has been changing at a great rate, driven on by technological revolution and the growing "knowledge sphere" of the modern world.

The pace of change is accelerating. So much change takes place during a lifetime that we become confused and disorientated, and generation gaps grow. Some religious groups, particularly Islamic ones, believe that modernization is a major threat to the stability and culture of their societies and should be resisted. Others recognize that we live at a great turning point of human history, where the ability of societies to change without violence is critical to our survival.

Pressures for social and political change come from many sources – intellectuals, professionals, writers and artists, the media, the labour force, minority groups, special interest groups, and non-governmental organizations (NGOs). Change is resisted by those who wish to maintain the *status quo*, notably the finance establishment, the military, intelligence services, police, industry and the civil service. Interaction between these forces produces a "cyclical flow" of pressure for change into a country's legislative process. New laws result, reflecting a new consensus within the society. The cycle then continues with new forces for change, new reactionary resistance and new legislation. Thus moral norms are slowly modified.

The process is not a smooth, unidirectional one. The 1960s, for example, produced a new tolerance for homosexuality, expressed in laws in various Western

Mechanisms for change

If pressures for change within society are to be accommodated peacefully, they normally must lead to a modification of the law – to take account of a new consensus on the widely accepted moral norms. This consensus is formed by the interaction of the views of many groups within society. Some of these become permanent lobbying groups, with expertise on the methods of agitating for change and with good contacts with the media and influential politicians.

Labour
Trade unions are an important pressure group. Recently, the activities of Poland's Solidarity demonstrated the power of labour to change conditions. Also, in South Africa black trade unionists are rapidly increasing their power.

Education
An education system independent of establishment values is vital to peaceful change. Teachers are helping break the link between the arms race and security by showing the new generation that threats to society are not solely military.

The media
A free media is perhaps the single most important mechanism for change today, in all types of society. As the Watergate affair demonstrated, investigative journalism can change the course of history.

The intelligentsia
Generally this group is in the vanguard of change – whether the political revolutions in France and Russia or the cultural revolution in China. Likewise, the post-1945 peace and ecology movements have been led by intellectuals.

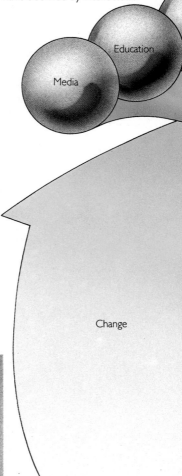

National powers
National establishments resist change. Bureaucratic inertia, for example, tends to be worse in centralized states; vested financial and commercial interests can be equally paralysing in democracies. But sometimes government reform sets the political agenda for a long time as with the UK post-WWII Attlee government, whose social welfare programme did not come under serious threat until the late 1980s.

If social institutions that allow this public voice to influence the law are absent, or obstructed by official systems or autocracy, civil violence and oppression, and ultimately revolution, may ensue. Most societies recognize this and, though the mechanisms differ, do accommodate a changing consensus. The rate of change depends on the balance of conservative and radical forces. Decision-makers are influenced by pressure groups, but restrained by those with a vested interest in maintaining the *status quo*, by establishment bureaucracy and by concern for their own careers.

But in a period of rapid technological advance, reluctant political leaders often feel obliged to agree to social change to take into account the consequences of new technologies. Advances in medical technology, genetic engineering and biotechnology, for example, encourage changes in attitudes to such things as test tube births and euthanasia.

The professions
Because of the respect afforded the professions, their warnings are taken seriously. International organizations of doctors, for example, have had success in educating the public about the consequences of nuclear war.

Public protest
In nearly all societies, public opinion influences politicians and, hence, policy making. Public protest hastened the withdrawal of Israeli troops from Lebanon in 1982, for example.

Alternative views
The views of those arguing for alternative societies can, sometimes, hold considerable sway. The Green movement, for example, was started by those arguing for a new way of thinking about economic growth.

Religion
Religious leaders were actively involved in deposing Marcos in the Philippines. Islamic fundamentalists have transformed international relations and some Catholic leaders are actively opposing the arms race.

Passive resistance
The potential for passive resistance was well demonstrated in 1968. The non-violent resistance of the Czech people to the Warsaw Pact troops greatly complicated the task of the invading forces.

Oppressed and minority groups
Gandhi demonstrated the power of oppressed groups to outface their oppressors. Few regimes today are prepared to go to the most extreme lengths to put down minorities in the full glare of publicity.

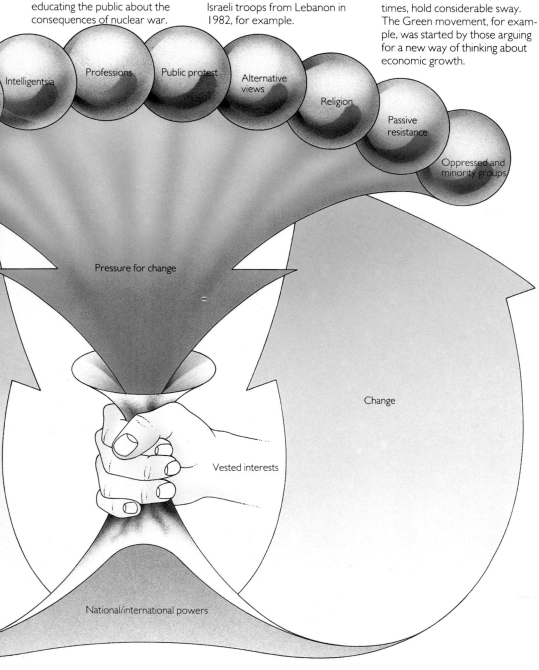

International powers
Efforts to achieve change peacefully at the international level are frustrated both by the sovereign power of states to ignore the wider consensus, and by the lack of developed mechanisms for a public voice in international bodies. Once again, there are bodies that actively resist change. The CIA activity in Italy and France after WWII to prevent election of communist governments is a classic example.

states. The AIDS epidemic has, however, produced a renewed hostility to homosexuals, notably in the UK, and demands for new moral norms. Compassion and tolerance to minorities are a test of the maturity of a society; we should be ashamed to fail it.

Modern societies employ differing mechanisms for change. Democracies rely on free elections and an effective opposition, and politicians responsive to public opinion. (But they can be ahead of it, too – the British Parliament, for example, has eliminated capital punishment, except for treason, even though opinion polls show a majority in favour of it for a range of crimes.) They also aim to have a free media, without monopolies. But they do not often have it. The media is typically more reactionary than radical and tends to be concentrated in the hands of a few press barons who become politically very powerful.

In communist countries, by contrast, the party is supreme. If there are elections, the bulk of the candidates are members of, and chosen by, the party, which also strictly controls the government, legal system and media. The main pressure for change comes from demands by the workers and the need to modernize for economic reasons – or from reforming leadership responsive to world opinion.

At the international level, just as we lack an effective, legitimized system of conflict resolution, so we have not achieved a system to enact changes in moral norms. The United Nations may pass resolutions on needed world reforms, but until we accept global law by consensus these are empty words.

Civil peacekeeping and crisis management

A healthy society is an open one, with few secrets and minimum policing and official violence. Sadly, such cases are increasingly rare – both secrecy and state reliance on armed police are on the increase in many countries. Crime and terrorism may be blamed (*see pp. 122-3 and 148-9*), but these themselves are symptoms of a deeper malaise. A society that elevates material wealth and sovereign rights to its highest gods, and then proceeds to withhold these from a large sector, cannot expect to lie easy.

Establishments everywhere generally believe they know what is best, and see maintaining their own power as synonymous with protecting the well-being and security of the nation. Agitating for change is thus, by definition, "subversive" – and subversives must be watched, their telephones tapped, their offices and homes bugged, their mail censored. When evidence of surveillance emerges, pressure groups become paranoic and a vicious circle of suspicion and enmity builds up. If the establishment perceives a serious threat to itself – and so the nation – violence may escalate to the use of the military, and eventually to civil war.

Even in countries with a long history of democracy, extra-parliamentary, clandestine groups exist that are prepared to act if they believe the existing structure and power of the establishment are threatened. It is

Civil peacekeeping

Ideally within societies, pressures for change and the conservative forces of the establishment are roughly in equilibrium. Change, therefore, when it occurs does so with the general consensus of opinion that the change is desirable. If establishment resistance is too strong, or the aims of a society too divided, pressures for change may break out as civil disturbances. In an unhealthy society, such responses escalate all too rapidly. Police are first armed, then trained in tougher techniques and finally permanent groups of riot squads and paramilitary forces are established, creating a generally tenser society.

The use of the military for civil peacekeeping is a major escalation. The military believes in the immediate deployment of forces to subdue the other side. This alienates the population and broadens the conflict. Also, military leaders, once brought into a civil conflict, are likely to want a say in its political solution.

The military now have a dominant position in about half the governments of the developing countries. Military-dominated governments are the most likely to resist change, thereby fostering future civil violence and rebellion. Countries ruled by the military are the most repressive, with little political freedom and no free press. Military power coupled with political control is the most unenlightened form of government.

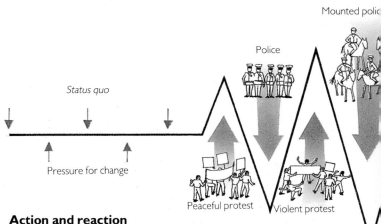

Status quo

Pressure for change

Mounted police

Police

Peaceful protest

Violent protest

Action and reaction

All too often, the evolutionary process of peaceful change is thrown out of balance, and an escalating see-saw of action and reaction is created. The first use of force polarizes the conflict, hardening attitudes, both of those agitating for change and of those opposing it. The original objectives of the protesters become lost and the sole goal is winning the "battle". Depending on the circumstances, paramilitary and then military forces can be drawn into the conflict, threatening the stability of sensitive regions of the world. At this point, the danger is of international intervention, as world or regional superpowers strive to safeguard their own vested interests.

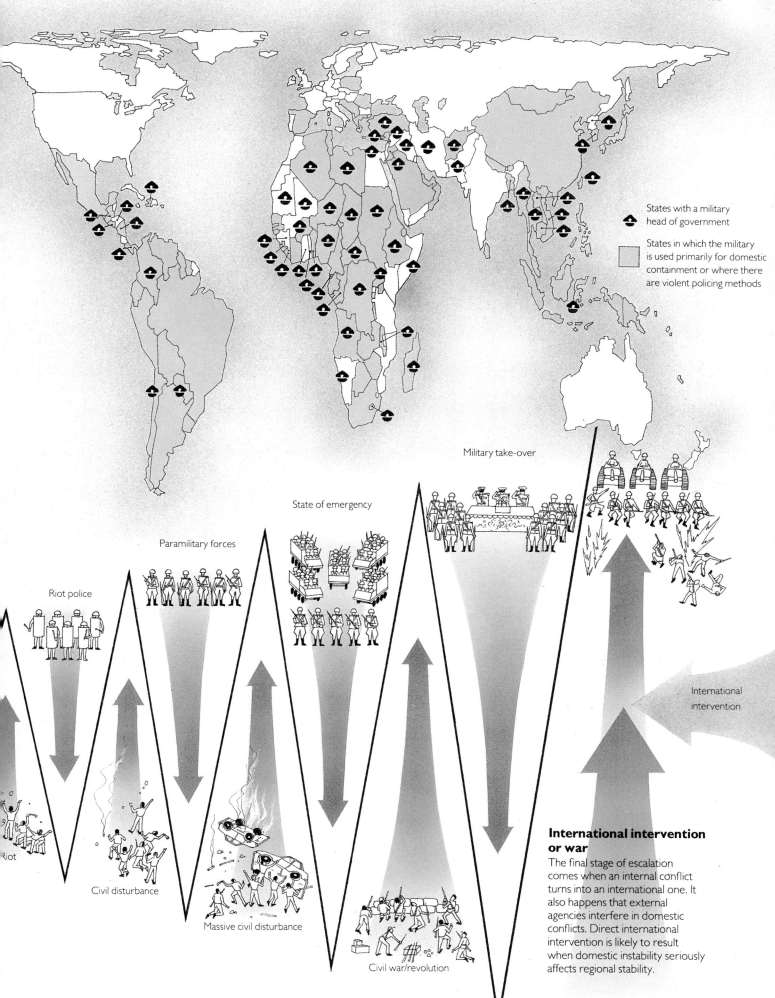

States with a military head of government

States in which the military is used primarily for domestic containment or where there are violent policing methods

Military take-over

State of emergency

Paramilitary forces

Riot police

International intervention

Riot

Civil disturbance

Massive civil disturbance

Civil war/revolution

International intervention or war

The final stage of escalation comes when an internal conflict turns into an international one. It also happens that external agencies interfere in domestic conflicts. Direct international intervention is likely to result when domestic instability seriously affects regional stability.

said, for example, that the Gough Whitlam government in Australia was put out of office by the activities of an extra-parliamentary group; there was suspicion of behind-the-scenes power in the two Kennedy assassinations, and recent reports suggest that there were secret attempts to de-stabilize the governments of British Prime Ministers Wilson and Heath.

The spiral of violence set up when determined pressure for change is continuously resisted can be broken by resort to the established mechanisms for conflict resolution, or by changing the law. Both are more likely to happen if the power élite believes that the consequences to it of escalating the conflict are greater than those of compromise. Where such a choice is in the balance, world opinion can have considerable force in persuading governments to make conciliatory gestures – such as amnesties to political prisoners.

Compromise is often hampered, however, because the political leaders feel that their reputations are at stake if they are seen to be giving in, while on the other side, originally moderate leaders of strikes or protests soon become replaced by more radical ones. And compromise is, itself, seldom a lasting solution – problem solving and real agreement are necessary.

If violence escalates to a level that the civil police cannot handle, paramilitary forces may be used first in an attempt to avoid involving the military. Because the military are not trained for police work and are not happy doing it, the use of military forces to contain civil unrest often rapidly leads to a coup and takeover by a military government. But if those agitating for change can persuade the army to support them, the uprising becomes a revolution and the establishment is replaced. Before this happens, however, outside powers have usually become involved.

The majority of international crises start at civil level, and soon escalate to proxy superpower struggles over ideology, resources and spheres of influence. Increasingly, such conflicts have no end in sight; their object is rather a perpetuation of "low-intensity conflict" (LIC) – an American phrase for a permanent battle of wills. And attempts by the wider global community to end the suffering are increasingly balked by the weakness of the organization we have framed to keep the peace – the United Nations.

The United Nations – humanity's greatest achievement?

Visions of a peaceable world order are almost as old as civilisation. In this century, human efforts for this goal have been greatest after the two world wars. The founding of the United Nations marked the most radical change of all. Global peace would be kept under UN auspices by its peacekeeping forces. And war, other than in self-defence, became illegal.

Comprised of six principal organs (the General Assembly, the Security Council, the Secretariat, the Economic and Social Council, the Trusteeship Council, and the International Court of Justice), the UN offers a mechanism for instant consultation in emergencies, as

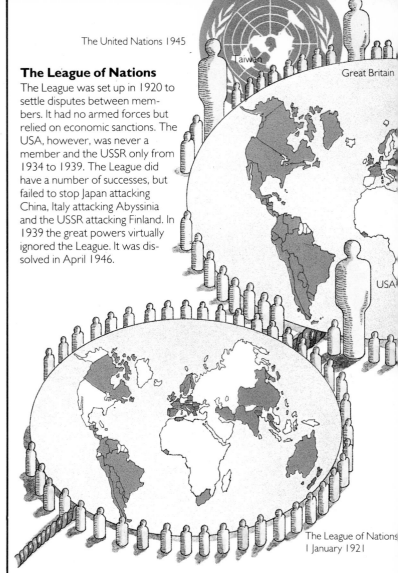

The United Nations 1945

The League of Nations

The League was set up in 1920 to settle disputes between members. It had no armed forces but relied on economic sanctions. The USA, however, was never a member and the USSR only from 1934 to 1939. The League did have a number of successes, but failed to stop Japan attacking China, Italy attacking Abyssinia and the USSR attacking Finland. In 1939 the great powers virtually ignored the League. It was dissolved in April 1946.

The League of Nations
1 January 1921

DisUnited Nations

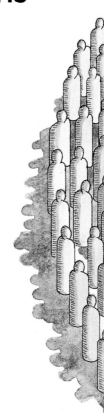

The basic assumption of the founders of the United Nations was that the great powers – the USA, the USSR, the UK, France and China – would work together to keep the global peace. If conflicts could not be resolved by regional peaceful diplomacy, and an international "police" action was necessary to keep the sides apart while the UN mediated, it was assumed that the great powers would contribute units of their own armed forces to a UN international police force.

It was also assumed that the great powers would co-operate to improve social and economic justice within and between countries. Hopes for such co-operation soon died as good intentions were replaced by East-West confrontation and the Cold War.

Another blow to the UN vision was increasing North-South tension. Since 1945, membership of the UN has increased from 50 states to a total of 159 states. The UN's contribution to the decolonization process was considerable, but the organization's failure to close the poverty gap between the rich and poor countries is a major disuniting factor. Increasingly, UN meetings are arenas of confrontation rather than co-operation.

France

USSR

NATO

The UN Security Council

The Security Council is the most important decision-making organ of the UN, especially in regard to peacekeeping operations. There are five permanent members and ten non-permanent members elected by the General Assembly.

Each permanent member has the power to veto Council decisions. The frequent use of the veto weakens the UN and demonstrates that the great powers are not prepared to subordinate national interests.

Western bloc

Eastern bloc

The veto

Barriers to unity

Today's "United" Nations is organized politically into groups that usually take common positions on important issues. The groups are: the so-called group of 77 (now contains about 130 developing countries); the non-aligned movement (100 or so strong); the Western European groups; and a number of sub-groups. The group system has become very rigid, a barrier to consensus and a major disunifying factor.

Warsaw Pact

▬ Permanent member states of UN Security Council

▬ Member states of UN 1987

well as a forum for debate of long-term problems. In cases where international relations are in crisis, it offers the services of the Secretary-General as an impartial third party, and peacekeeping forces.

The UN's weakness lies in the fact that it cannot transcend the sovereign power of states. It is unable to legislate laws that nations must abide by, and its 15-member Security Council is often paralyzed by the veto rights of superpowers. Consequently, no true international peace force has ever been established, and the UN's capability in the peaceful resolution of disputes is increasingly ignored and side-stepped.

It is also in the throes of a potentially crippling financial crisis. An important, and growing, group of member states has been withholding dues, objecting with some justification to UN inefficiency, overstaffing and waste. Financial reform is in progress, and funds may flow again. But many complain also that it has become politicized – the US resents what it sees as use of the UN as a platform for blatant anti-Americanism.

Developing countries, also with justification, are deeply disillusioned by the UN's failure to solve the poorer states' social and economic problems and, in particular, move towards a New International Economic Order. They see too much neo-colonialism and economic self-interest by rich states at the UN and a refusal to grapple fairly with the problems in developing regions, such as the Middle East and southern Africa. Even when measures, such as economic sanctions or arms embargoes, are pushed through, often after bitter battles, some rich members will do all that they can to frustrate them.

All countries pay lip service to the UN Charter. But there is serious disagreement about the nature of the political and social problems we face, the solutions to these problems and the role of the UN in implementing them. The UN cannot operate effectively unless its members agree on a specific and detailed programme of action that each state will enact. Nor can it, without a consensus and agreed mechanisms, operate effectively in crisis management, regional problem solving, and peaceful settlement of conflicts. The intransigence of nations is such that only the global constituency of ordinary people, expressing the wider desire for peace, can save the United Nations and build it anew (see Chapter 9).

When is war legal?

The UN Charter defines the principles governing the legality of war. According to Articles 2 and 51, the use of force by one state against another is regarded as illegal except in defined cases. This makes the unprovoked use of any weapon illegal. Even when the use of armed force is legitimate, not every weapon may be used, and not all methods of warfare are legal. Article 22 of the 1907 Hague Convention states that "the right of belligerents to adopt means of injuring the enemy is not unlimited." Article 23 goes on to forbid the combatants to "employ arms, projectiles, or material calculated to cause unnecessary suffering." Two

The law of war and peace

The international law of armed combat is an attempt to constrain conflict. The Charter of the United Nations says, "All members shall refrain from the threat or use of force against the territorial integrity or political independence of any state". Under Article 51, however, armed force may be used for self-defence. But this is the only legal reason for waging war. Before this stage is reached every possible means of peaceful settlement must be exhausted.

Policy makers who start and wage an illegal war commit a crime against peace and can be punished as war criminals. Those that can be prosecuted range from the political leaders to individual soldiers. (As yet, however, only the losers have been tried – not the victors.)

There are those who argue the case for a "just" war. But usually people who advocate this type of war believe that it is permissible only to confront a real and certain danger. Even then, the enormous destructive power of modern weapons negates such justification.

The "just war" tradition is giving way to the "just revolution" argument – that an oppressive government may lose its claim to legitimacy, when oppression becomes intolerable, and violence justified.

War crimes trials

The Nuremberg Tribunals made some acts against the law of war punishable judicially. Such crimes include:

Crimes against peace
These include the planning, preparation, initiation or waging of a war of aggression.

War crimes These are violations of the laws or customs of war which include murder, ill treatment, or deportation to slave labour or for any other purpose of civilian population of or in occupied territory, murder or ill treatment of prisoners of war, killing of hostages, plunder of public or private property, wanton destruction of cities, towns or villages, or devastation not justified by military necessity.

Crimes against humanity
These include murder, extermination, enslavement, deportation and other inhuman acts done against any civilian population, or persecution on political, racial or religious grounds, when such acts are done or such persecutions are carried on in execution of or in connection with any crime against peace.

Dresden: was this immoral?

The bombing of Dresden occurred in February 1945 at a time when the city was crowded with refugees. The raid was specifically intended to induce civilian terror.

The strategy of "coercive terror", whereby civilians are attacked in war to make life so unbearable that their govern-ment is forced to capitulate, was commonplace in WW II. The heaviest explosives were dropped on civilians in cities.

The wars in Vietnam and Afghanistan have followed the same pattern, civilians often being the primary targets – surely an immoral action.

Hiroshima: was this illegal?

The bombing of Hiroshima on 6 August 1945 produced 130,000 immediate casualties and razed 90% of the city. The atomic bomb did not distinguish between civilians and soldiers; it inflicted unnecessary suffering out of all proportion to the object of the attack; it infringed the Hague Convention because it produced radioactivity, which is poisonous; its effects were not limited in scope or in duration. On all these grounds, the bombing was illegal.

WHAT ARE THE CONSTRAINTS ON WAR?

CAN WAR EVER BE JUSTIFIED?

IS WAR LEGAL?

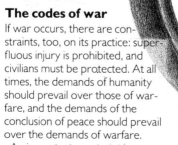

Can war be justified?
Today's concept of the "just" war is normally confined to the pro-tection of innocent lives, the pre-servation of a decent existence and securing basic human rights.

The codes of war
If war occurs, there are con-straints, too, on its practice: super-fluous injury is prohibited, and civilians must be protected. At all times, the demands of humanity should prevail over those of war-fare, and the demands of the conclusion of peace should prevail over the demands of warfare.

An important constraint is prop-ortionality – that the damage to be inflicted and the costs incurred by war must be proportionate to the good expected to come from it. In the nuclear age this principle constrains war totally.

Is war legal?
Since 1625, attempts have been made to formulate a legal code for war. But generally, agreements have only mitigated conditions, and failed to control weaponry.

The only legal reason for con-flict is self-defence. Acts of vio-lence that are unnecessary to the conduct of war are not permitted. Indiscriminate weapons that harm both combatants and non-com-batants, and cause disproportion-ate suffering, are also illegal.

The growth of liberation armies, terrorists, guerillas, has given rise to groups not legally regarded as belligerents and so not covered by the law of war.

Geneva Protocols of 1977 prohibit "methods or means of warfare which are intended, or may be expected, to cause widespread, long-term and severe damage to the natural environment."

The principles governing the laws of war are:
*prohibition of unnecessary injury – and hence, of weapons that cause unnecessary suffering and weapons which cause disproportionate suffering (relative to the provocation, or military objective)
*distinction between civilians and soldiers – and hence, prohibition of direct attacks on civilians, and of indiscriminate weapons
*recognition that the demands of humanity should prevail over the demands of warfare.

The use of nuclear weapons is thus illegal because it violates all these principles. There is also a strong legal case for maintaining that planning and preparing for nuclear war is illegal. The 1950 Nuremberg Principles justify this view. Principle VI states that "planning, preparation, initiation or waging of a war of aggression or a war in violation of international treaties, agreements or assurances" is a crime against peace, punishable in international law.

Forty years on, war has not ended. And we certainly cannot wait for another holocaust to prompt renewed idealism – the next will certainly end all wars, but not in a way we would wish. As a first step, we must at least abide by the rules we have already affirmed – most of the world's sovereign states are bound by adherence to the Charter. Let them observe it.

The UN peace police

The original intention of the UN, as set out in 1945, was that the big five, the permanent members of the Security Council, would be the world's peacekeepers, using their conventional military forces as police forces to intervene when necessary in conflicts. When it became obvious, however, that this system, based on superpower consensus, was pie in the sky, a substitute had to be found. What evolved, more or less by trial and error and in desperation as the frequency of wars escalated, was the setting up of multinational bodies, under the auspices of the UN, of military personnel. Their activities became known as "peacekeeping".

UN peacekeeping forces usually go into operation once combatants have been persuaded to stop fighting, typically by pressure from one or both superpowers. The fact that UN peacekeeping forces are needed is, of course, an admission that the peace imposed is not genuine and that the problems that caused the war in the first place remain unsolved.

The 1956 Suez War, for example, ended when American and Soviet pressure persuaded the British, French and Israeli governments to stop their attack on Egypt. A UN Emergency Force (UNEF) was then sent to supervise the ceasefire, ensure orderly withdrawal of British, French and Israeli forces and patrol the Egypt-Israel border. Even though the UK and France are permanent members of the Security Council, they could not resist superpower pressure – a testimony to

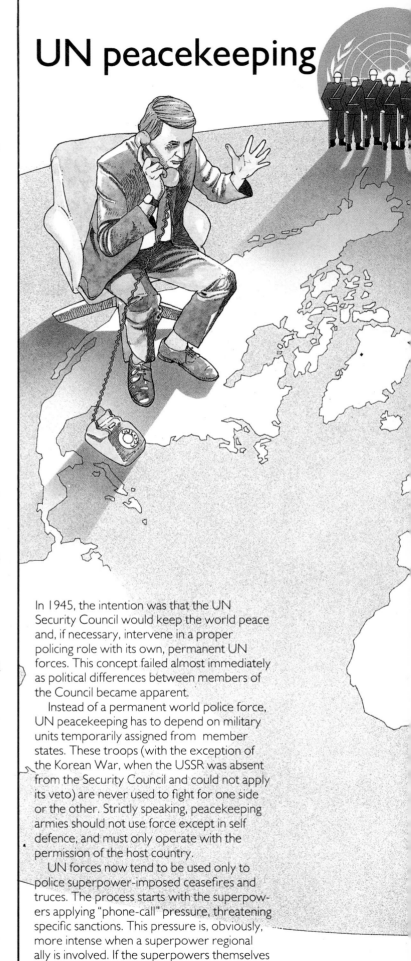

UN peacekeeping

In 1945, the intention was that the UN Security Council would keep the world peace and, if necessary, intervene in a proper policing role with its own, permanent UN forces. This concept failed almost immediately as political differences between members of the Council became apparent.

Instead of a permanent world police force, UN peacekeeping has to depend on military units temporarily assigned from member states. These troops (with the exception of the Korean War, when the USSR was absent from the Security Council and could not apply its veto) are never used to fight for one side or the other. Strictly speaking, peacekeeping armies should not use force except in self defence, and must only operate with the permission of the host country.

UN forces now tend to be used only to police superpower-imposed ceasefires and truces. The process starts with the superpowers applying "phone-call" pressure, threatening specific sanctions. This pressure is, obviously, more intense when a superpower regional ally is involved. If the superpowers themselves are involved, then the veto is applied and the UN cannot operate.

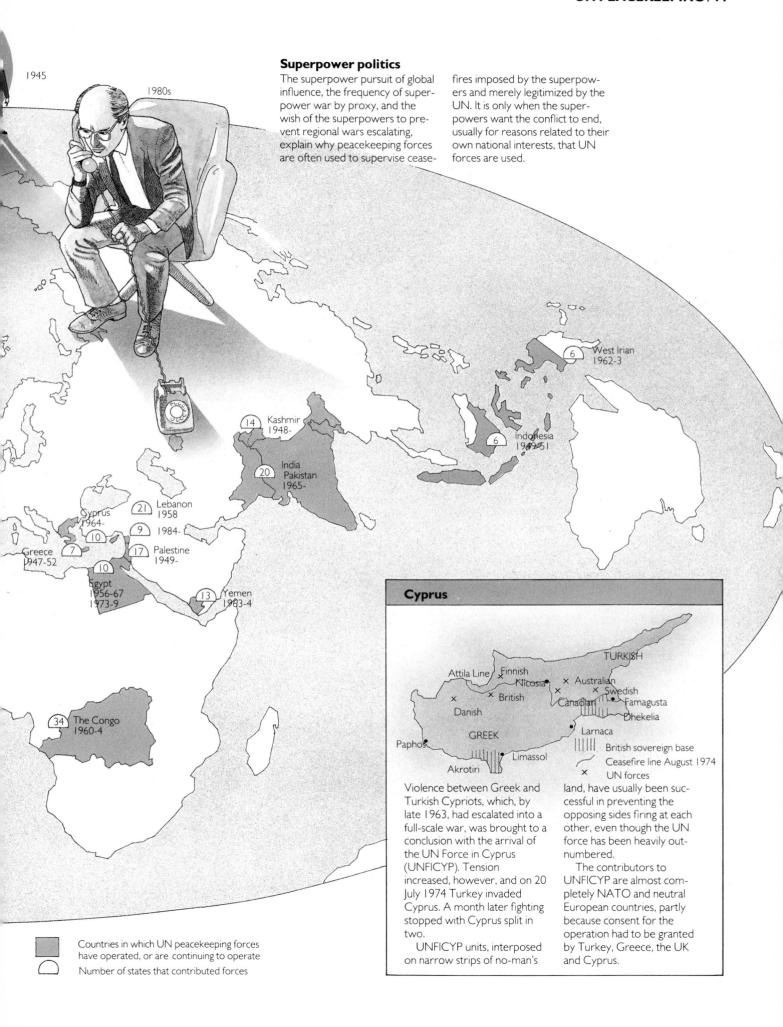

1945

1980s

Superpower politics

The superpower pursuit of global influence, the frequency of superpower war by proxy, and the wish of the superpowers to prevent regional wars escalating, explain why peacekeeping forces are often used to supervise cease-fires imposed by the superpowers and merely legitimized by the UN. It is only when the superpowers want the conflict to end, usually for reasons related to their own national interests, that UN forces are used.

West Irian
1962-3

Kashmir
1948-

India
Pakistan
1965-

Indonesia
1949-51

Lebanon
1958

Cyprus
1964-

1984-

Greece
1947-52

Palestine
1949-

Egypt
1956-67
1973-9

Yemen
1963-4

The Congo
1960-4

Cyprus

Attila Line — Finnish
Nicosia
British
Danish
GREEK
Paphos
Akrotiri
Limassol
Larnaca
TURKISH
Australian
Canadian
Swedish
Famagusta
Dhekelia

British sovereign base
Ceasefire line August 1974
× UN forces

Violence between Greek and Turkish Cypriots, which, by late 1963, had escalated into a full-scale war, was brought to a conclusion with the arrival of the UN Force in Cyprus (UNFICYP). Tension increased, however, and on 20 July 1974 Turkey invaded Cyprus. A month later fighting stopped with Cyprus split in two.

UNFICYP units, interposed on narrow strips of no-man's land, have usually been successful in preventing the opposing sides firing at each other, even though the UN force has been heavily outnumbered.

The contributors to UNFICYP are almost completely NATO and neutral European countries, partly because consent for the operation had to be granted by Turkey, Greece, the UK and Cyprus.

Countries in which UN peacekeeping forces have operated, or are continuing to operate

Number of states that contributed forces

the extent that the UN had become a servant of superpower policies. This is also shown by the impotence of the UN to affect wars in which one or the other superpower is a combatant. The UN was unable to influence Soviet behaviour in Hungary in 1956, or America's war in Vietnam, or Soviet aggression in Afghanistan. It is also currently paralyzed in the Gulf conflict due to multi-power interests.

UN peacekeeping is no substitute for common security. At best confined to keeping combatants apart, it can neither resist nor punish aggression. The only significant sanctions the UN can apply are diplomatic and economic pressures by bigger powers on smaller ones, superpower threats of the use of force, and superpower nuclear blackmail. But these will be used only when it suits the superpower concerned.

If we are to have a future, we must begin to devise the means of global conflict resolution and security.

Living under the bomb

International relations changed qualitatively on 6 August 1945, when an American B-29 bomber dropped an atom bomb on Hiroshima. Warfare was transformed and so was security thinking.

The motives for dropping nuclear weapons on Hiroshima and Nagasaki have been questioned. The two Japanese cities had not been bombed before. A single bomber was sent over the cities to get the people used to it so that they would not bother to go to the shelters. The bombs were dropped in the morning at times when people were in the streets. Hiroshima is flat; Nagasaki hilly. These facts have led to the speculation that the atomic bombs were dropped not only to finish the war against Japan, but to measure the effects of the weapons on people and property, and to signal the extent of American power to the Soviets.

The sinister nature of the beginning of the nuclear age has followed it throughout its history. An early effort, called the Baruch plan, to internationalize nuclear energy failed mainly because of Soviet suspicion of US intentions, and consequent refusal to allow verification inspections on Soviet territory.

As the Cold War developed, the West believed that Stalin intended to invade and occupy western Europe with his vast conventional forces. Western European countries were unwilling to pay for large conventional forces to match the Soviet ones. Nuclear weapons were seen as a cheap alternative and several thousand were deployed in western Europe. In hindsight, it is clear that the Soviets had no serious intention of invading. They were too busy bringing East European countries under control – to provide a ring of buffer states around the USSR in order to prevent invasion from the West.

Once the Soviets acquired nuclear parity, NATO policy shifted to deterrence by "mutual assured destruction" – a policy they assert has kept the peace in Europe for 40 years. The truth of the matter is, though, that peace in Europe has grown despite nuclear deterrence, not because of it. Neither side wishes to attack the other, or has wished to. Nor has the

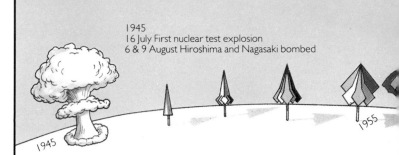

1945
16 July First nuclear test explosion
6 & 9 August Hiroshima and Nagasaki bombed

1945
1955

The nuclear umbrella

The shadow of the "nuclear umbrella" first spread over Europe in the 1950s. Fearing Soviet expansion, the West adopted a policy of relying on US nuclear superiority to threaten massive retaliation in case of Soviet invasion. Once the USSR reached nuclear parity in the early 1960s, however, the threat of massive destruction lost all credibility and was replaced by "flexible response", which means that any aggression by Warsaw Pact forces will first be met with NATO conventional forces; then, if this fails, with tactical nuclear weapons; and, in the last resort, with a long-range US strategic nuclear attack on Soviet sites. This largely discredited escalation threat now provides the so-called "nuclear umbrella" on both sides.

But for more than two decades the "umbrella" has been closing, resembling more and more a missile aimed at the heart of humanity. Nuclear technology is developing smaller, more accurate weapons, suited more to fighting than to preventing a nuclear war. This leads to the perception that nuclear war is "fightable and winnable" (*see pp. 132-3*).

In a speech in 1979, Henry Kissinger said that all nuclear umbrellas are a myth. The USA will not sacrifice American cities to defend any non-US territory. In President de Gaulle's words: "... **no US President will sacrifice Chicago for Paris. Both the USA and the USSR will do their utmost to prevent nuclear weapons exploding on their territories.**" Speech to conference on *NATO, the next 30 years*, 1 to 3 September 1979, Brussels.

Nuclear weapons states

US
US "umbrella" states

USSR
USSR "umbrella" states

Independent nuclear weapons states

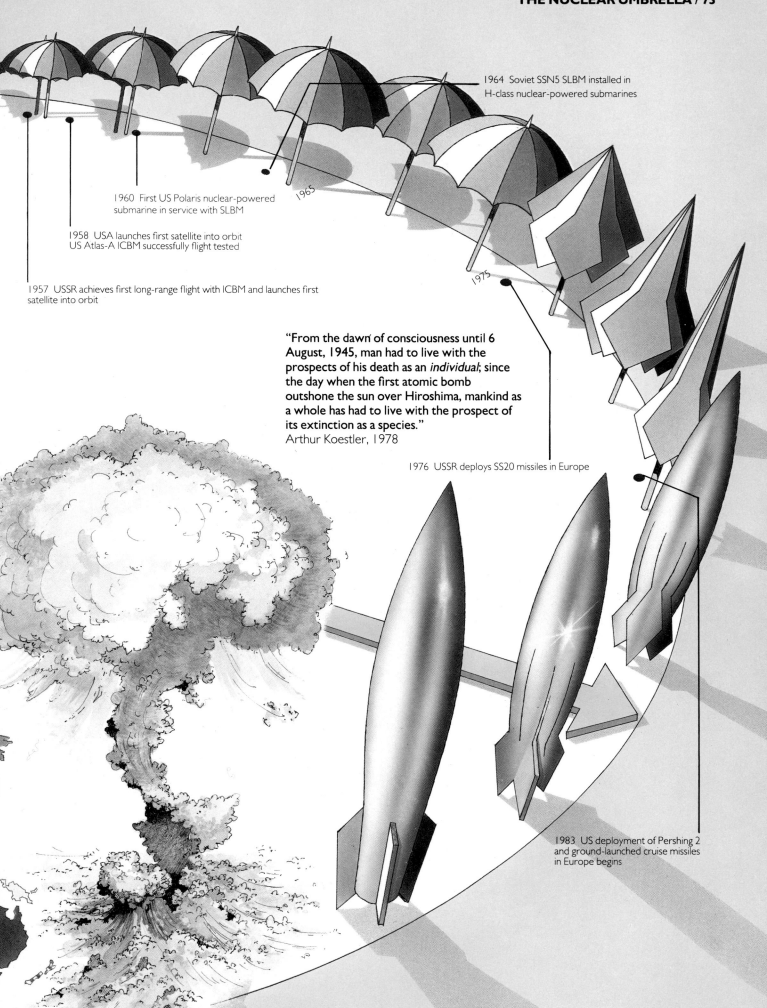

1964 Soviet SSN5 SLBM installed in H-class nuclear-powered submarines

1960 First US Polaris nuclear-powered submarine in service with SLBM

1958 USA launches first satellite into orbit
US Atlas-A ICBM successfully flight tested

1957 USSR achieves first long-range flight with ICBM and launches first satellite into orbit

1965

1975

"From the dawn of consciousness until 6 August, 1945, man had to live with the prospects of his death as an *individual*; since the day when the first atomic bomb outshone the sun over Hiroshima, mankind as a whole has had to live with the prospect of its extinction as a species."
Arthur Koestler, 1978

1976 USSR deploys SS20 missiles in Europe

1983 US deployment of Pershing 2 and ground-launched cruise missiles in Europe begins

existence of nuclear weapons banished war – we have had more deaths in wars since World War II than during it. Those who believe that the destructiveness of nuclear weapons prevents their use are wrong, too. Such an argument only works if neither side believes it can win, or lose less badly than the other. But American and, probably, Soviet nuclear policies are currently moving from deterrence based on mutual targeting of cities, to more flexible policies with smaller, fighting weapons (*see Chapter 5*), and to the perception of "fightable, winnable" nuclear war. Aside from its insanity, the nuclear weapons race is both expensive and increasingly destabilizing, causing Europe to live in permanent fear.

Those who support "deterrence" encourage the spread of nuclear weapons, since arguing that they keep the peace in Europe implies that they will do the same elsewhere. The leaders of the nuclear powers behave as though they believe nuclear weapons have military and political uses. They cannot be surprised if other countries follow suit and acquire them.

The UN – building peace for the world

It is easy to find fault with the UN. It has failed to provide global collective security, or bring about multilateral negotiations on nuclear or conventional disarmament, in spite of great efforts throughout the past 40 years. It has failed to negotiate effective international economic and trade arrangements, and reduce the poverty gap between rich and poor.

But the benefits of the UN to the international community greatly outweigh these criticisms. The fact that the UN is a place where diplomats and political leaders regularly meet and discuss regional and global issues is sufficient to justify its existence. Apart from its vital role in decolonization, the UN has had, through its agencies, great successes in meeting basic human needs – from the eradication of smallpox and other communicable diseases to dramatic increases in food production, and a steady rise in life expectancy.

The UN enacts the conscience of the world. It has had a unique role in helping refugees and children in need, and in its disaster relief operations, has set world humanitarian standards, especially with the 1948 Universal Declaration of Human Rights.

UN agencies co-ordinate and set standards in a wide range of fields, from international air transport to postal services and weather forecasting; many aspects of our daily lives depend on their work. They have been active, too, in protecting the environment, as for instance in the effort to clean up the Mediterranean. The UN, in fact, does much to force governments at least to consider a range of global problems, such as pollution, population, energy and housing.

The issues raised by the UN are brought to public attention by NGOs. UN associations, which are active in a number of countries, specifically exist for this purpose. Many believe that NGOs should play an even greater role in the future United Nations – one where the voice of the world's peoples will be heard at last.

UN peace building

In the narrow sense of peace – the absence of armed conflict – the UN has seen its role via the Security Council gradually weakened and blocked. But in the broader sense of peace, in setting and pursuing global standards of human welfare, justice and equality, and in building a global perspective into national thinking, the UN has a crucial role. The only organizations approaching independent, supranational status are those of the UN, in particular the specialized agencies. We must, therefore, learn from the experiences of the UN – both its failures and successes – in order to build a positive peace.

The UN handles many problems well, particularly those with humanitarian dimensions, such as health, food distribution, disaster relief, refugees and children's welfare. It has much more difficulty with matters that challenge the international *status quo*, such as economic justice. The structures and methods of operation of effective agencies, such as WHO, UNICEF and UNRWA, have much to tell us about which characteristics must be built into future supranational agencies.

Evolving global peace and security is a dynamic process. In spite of the many obvious differences in the world, there are also many areas of common interest and agreement. By building on these, and with a continuous dialogue on the missions and roles of the various agencies, it should be possible to evolve institutions that are capable of overcoming today's deep political divisions and building a consensus for positive peace. The UN is all we have, troubled though it is. Governments should support it strongly and work for its reform on a wider participatory base, with the strength to tackle difficult issues. The original "peoples of the United Nations" mentioned in its Charter still have little say in UN affairs.

IAEA

UNRWA

Main and other sessional committees

Standing committees and ad hoc bodies

Other subsidiary organs and related bodies

The UN structure includes the Economic and Social Council, the Trusteeship Council, the International Court of Justice and a host of specialized agencies. Some international agencies ante-date the UN. That with the longest history is the International Telecommunication Union, formerly the International Telegraph Union, set up in 1865. The Universal Postal Union dates from 1874; the World Meteorological Organization from 1878 and the International Labour Organization from 1919. The World Health Organization was the first specialized agency to be created, in 1946, by the UN itself.

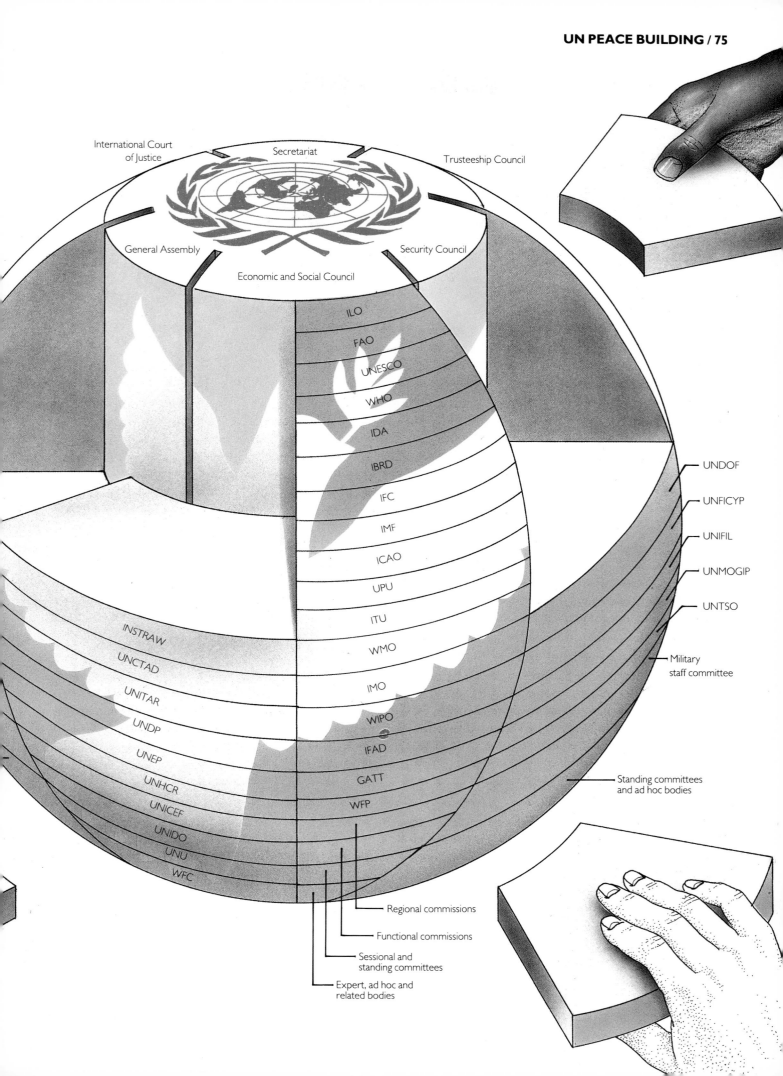

International Court of Justice

Secretariat

Trusteeship Council

General Assembly

Security Council

Economic and Social Council

ILO
FAO
UNESCO
WHO
IDA
IBRD
IFC
IMF
ICAO
UPU
ITU
WMO
IMO
WIPO
IFAD
GATT
WFP

INSTRAW
UNCTAD
UNITAR
UNDP
UNEP
UNHCR
UNICEF
UNIDO
UNU
WFC

UNDOF
UNFICYP
UNIFIL
UNMOGIP
UNTSO

Military staff committee

Standing committees and ad hoc bodies

Regional commissions

Functional commissions

Sessional and standing committees

Expert, ad hoc and related bodies

PART TWO: PRESENT

"We have an economic crisis; we have the crisis of nuclear weapons; and terrorism; inflation; unemployment, and so on, and I have come to see these as manifestations of one and the same crisis, which is essentially a crisis of perception." Fritjof Capra 'Einstein and the Buddha', *The Listener* 1982

The first part of this book has traced the evolution of our institutions of peaceful governance, and of war, and the so-far largely unsuccessful attempts of nations to achieve collective security under the rule of law. This second part is also descriptive (rather than prescriptive). It delineates the predicament of contemporary humanity, caught between the old world and the new. Chapter 4 describes the potential for peace of the half-formed global community; Chapter 5 the multiplying crises that now threaten our future; and Chapter 6, our intensifying struggle to change and adapt, evolve new responses, and so survive.

The hardest age to see is one's own. Certainly, we live at a time of great change. So rapid has the change been, that we forget for how short a time we have been living with access to global communications, with mass media, or with superpower politics and nuclear fear. In such an age, it is easy to lose our sense of history, and of direction: the past begins to seem irrelevant, the future we would rather not concern ourselves with. Yet civilizations of the past have fallen repeatedly through just such a blinkered vision.

In an age of rapid change, old and new approaches can become polarized. Out of the multiple and complex changes in our times, two such battles of the old and the new have emerged sharply. First, there is the geopolitical one. The older industrialized North, with less than a quarter of world peoples, consumes nearly four-fifths of all resources, and dominates world political, military and financial institutions, as well as ideology and culture and technology. The developing nations, with most of the population and one-fifth of the consumption, are challenging this dominion – in philosophy as well as in share of wealth and power. The persistence of conflict and economic disadvantage in the South is the result not merely of history, but of a deep struggle by the richer nations to preserve the *status quo* and Northern advantage – a struggle embittered by the two superpowers, who are engaged in a "war" of dominance in the South.

Second, there is the struggle between old and new ideas across the whole field of human endeavour. Alvin Toffler wrote of the emergence of a "Third Wave" of civilization, post-industrial and information based, and of the intensifying conflict with the declining old guard of the second, or industrial wave; Fritjof Capra wrote of a "turning point" towards a holistic, decentralized and spiritual society, and many others have echoed these themes. Most of the new ideas are arising from non-governmental organizations, green and peace movements, intellectuals and alternative groups, both in the North and latterly in the South, too; the old ideas are concentrated in national governments, banks, corporations, and the military. This polarization is creating a growing impatience in ordinary people, and all those tackling the world's problems "at the coal face", with our bureaucracies and institutions of power – whatever their political flavour or creed.

We live, too, in an age of frightening contrasts. Acquisitive materialism, and the pursuit of economic growth and high expectations of life, persist alongside a daily awareness of previously unthinkable savagery in war, and poverty, famine and suffering on a terrible scale. This seems to blunt both our understanding and our moral sense: we become unable to repond with heart and mind to our situation.

Yet we are seeking to build a global community. At the level of everyday management of affairs, this global community is increasingly a reality – trade, communications, culture, language, financial markets, all operate with international co-operation. We can also see emerging ideas of supranationalism, of regional co-operation, of trans-national groupings and new concerns for human rights, for the environment, for collective security and peace,

BETWEEN TWO WORLDS

reflected in hugely growing grass roots activity. But what we have created is, so far, neither an equitable nor a sustainable community.

The modern world, with its nearly 200 states, its territorial seas, its great business corporations and globe-wide travel, is becoming full. There is nowhere free of human claim, save the deep oceans, Antarctica and space – and towards these we are looking with eager eyes. There is no new frontier to develop or sudden flood of new resources to enrich us. Yet our numbers continue to grow fast, and our demands faster. We have seen a twenty-fold rise in production and consumption this century already.

If this were more evenly distributed, we would have less to fear. But instead, consuming wealth and grinding poverty provide twin engines of environmental destruction. Militarism exacerbates the problem, its cost reaching far beyond the immediate tragedy of war. While nations waste resources and lives in military escalation, problems left to fester unattended have created new threats which no nation can tackle alone – of land failure, climate change, and conflict over declining resources. As human numbers rise, such threats can only worsen, unless a will to solve them is found in time. And the interaction of these rising pressures with an uncontrolled technological arms race will gravely raise the risk of nuclear war.

Despite recent moves by the superpowers to cut the numbers of nuclear warheads, neither the pace of weapons design technology nor the spiral of militarism shows any sign of slackening. The race for "nuclear strategic superiority" is only obscured, not halted, by words of peace. Half the developing nations are under military rule, and among Western democracies aggressively materialist policies at home, and export of ever more lethal weaponry overseas, are increasingly the norm. Forty years of arms talks and peace movements, of environment movements and major world reports on needed reforms, barely touch the dogmatic institutions of power. Ours may indeed, as US President Ronald Reagan remarked, be the generation which sees armageddon.

Our civilization is in crisis, suffering a loss of meaning and of understanding in face of threats whose cure it seems we cannot grasp. The truth is that no small adjustment or "more of the same" will serve. The absurdity of piling weapon on weapon in a race none can win; of crying out against the depletion of the environment while persisting in the very policies that force it on; of bewailing terrorism and unrest while tolerating injustice; of "sovereign" states seeking "security" from each other, while all our security is threatened – must surely come home to us. It cannot be our fate to go down, locked in battle over what appear to be our rights and resources, into a new Dark Age.

The Industrial Age brought many benefits; but it also brought the seeds of competitive materialism, and the Descartian view of nature as machine. The Nuclear Age has brought weapons of absolute violence, and with them a rising wave of power, dominance and fear. The Information Age may bring us hope. There are many new voices in the world. A global constituency is arising, of those who seek peace, non-violent change, and a new relationship with each other and with Gaia. They speak of a new perception, and a new ethic; of an age of spiritual concern, of understanding, and of democracy and justice. But before these voices can be heard, the world has much to unlearn. We have to unlearn reliance on war, and on materialism and competition; we have to unlearn our belief that we are masters of nature. And we have to unlearn fear and sovereign pride.

4 The emerging global community

Introduced by Mwalimu Julius K. Nyerere

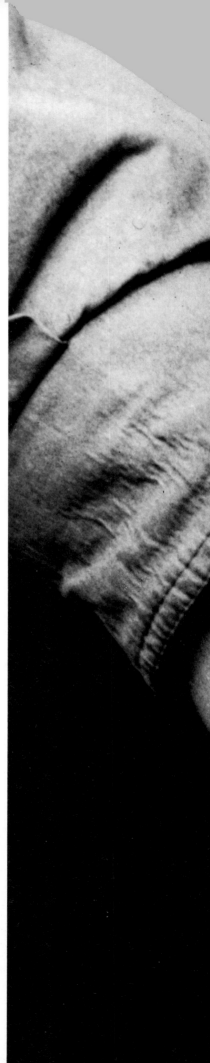

In the modern world, peace is indivisible. Technology has made it so. A war in which just a fraction of nuclear weapons were used would cause a nuclear winter and make life impossible throughout the Earth. All life would cease in Tanzania, Sweden, Argentina, Mexico and Greece – none of which possess nuclear weapons – just as it would in the states which do hold nuclear weapons.

Abolition of all nuclear weapons is vital for humankind's security. But this is not enough, by itself, to bring peace to the world. War is not caused by weapons; these are simply implements used in war. Real and sustainable peace is therefore not obtained simply by abolishing armaments. For the basis of war is injustice; and the foundation of real peace is justice and equality.

It is not justice when a person is denied the power to participate in the government of his own community, his own nation, and the world at large because of his colour, his race, or his religion. It is not justice when speculation on the stock exchange in one continent can destroy the livelihood of a peasant producer in another. Under these circumstances there will be no peace.

The promotion of disarmament, basic human rights, and economic justice, are all essential to the struggle for peace. All of them concern us all, for they are all interlinked.

The people of the economic North have an understanding of the threat to life which comes from nuclear weapons. When they talk about working for peace, they mean working for disarmament, particularly nuclear disarmament. Very few people in the South see that as a major concern. Nuclear weapons are seen as a problem for the North; our problem in the South is hunger and poverty. But the reality is still there. If a nuclear war starts in the North, our problems of hunger and poverty will have been wiped out – because the people suffering from them will have been wiped out.

Conversely, the vast majority of people and governments of the economic North now regard international economic injustice and institutionalized racism as being irrelevant to their own future and completely separate from issues of peace. Those in power in the North deny the connection between the ever-fluctuating prices of commodities, and high interest rate debt, and the lack of peace within and between Third World countries which jeopardize relations between the big powers. The millions of compassionate people in the North who send aid to famine victims, fail to perceive the connection between hunger, disease and poverty on the one hand, and apartheid, or the present workings of the international economic order, or the wealth of the North, on the other.

The problem is to combine the peace efforts of North and South. But how can one make the Maasai, or the peasants in the Andes, understand what nuclear weapons are and the danger to their own lives? How can one help a factory worker in Europe or America understand the links between the price of the coffee he drinks, and famine in Bangladesh or Ethiopia?

These are the challenges of Peace. Capitalist or socialist, former colonial power or not, possessor of nuclear weapons or not; all nations are involved in the world financial systems and benefit or suffer from their present workings. Black, white or brown in skin colour, all of us are affected by the struggle against racism. Economic North or economic South, Western bloc, Eastern bloc or Non-aligned: all of our peoples would be wiped out by a nuclear disaster.

Peace in the world requires Justice in the world. None of us can escape the responsibility to act for our own future.

"We must live in an absolutely inter-dependent planet; we must work to bring this about or the bright day will be done and there will be dark."
Barbara Ward

We are headed on the road to a global society – carried, whether we will or no, into growing mutual inter-dependence. Yet we are also ever more divided – in politics, economic well-being, and world view. And though we can devise codes for peace, human rights, and sustainable living, we have not found the will to live under such laws by common consent. But we must. We must make a united world. We have no other choice.

Unity and diversity

The post-war powers of 1945 envisioned a new era, one world forever free of war, poverty and famine. The dream faded rapidly, however, as the world became not one, but two, when the suspicion and rivalry between East and West surfaced. This bipolar world, Atlantist and Eurocentric, was soon troubled by the emerging Third World of younger nations, adding new arenas for the superpower struggle. A wealth gap opened between Northern First and Second Worlds and Southern Third World, deepening into the North-South divide.

Instead of the "one world" dreamed of in the United Nations Charter, we now perceive at least five: the Western group of industrial market economies, the communist bloc with non-market economies, the newly rich oil-exporting countries, states industrializing and entering world markets, and the "underdeveloped" nations. Even this picture is oversimplified – the underdeveloped nations actually comprise at least two groups: those slowly developing, and those which may never reach the "take-off point" where development can start. The Chinese centrally planned economy is wholly different from the Soviet; emerging Third World ones different again. The rise of Islam is another new factor, while minority movements for self-governance and secession, from Basques to Sikhs, are multiplying.

Not only is our world divided, but it is undergoing a major geopolitical shift. We are witnessing the dawn of the Asio-Pacific Age. The economic power of Japan, for example, will soon exceed that of the USSR, while a huge market for its goods waits to be tapped in nearby China. The circum-Pacific centres, from Tokyo and Sydney to Los Angeles, are cultural leaders – pioneering a shift from the mechanistic, competitive ethos of the Industrial Age to the co-operative, holistic and spiritual values of the Information Age.

Such a fragmented, imbalanced and fast-changing world, with its enormously increased number of states – all obsessed with sovereignty – cannot help but be fraught with tension. The more pluralistic the world becomes, the harder it is to govern by existing institutions and outmoded models of "central" authority. The continuing image of a bipolar world perpetuated by the superpower struggle only makes adjustment to the real situation more difficult, and the cries of the

One world?

"The Earth is one but the world is not. We all depend on one biosphere for sustaining our lives. Yet each community, each country, strives for survival and prosperity with little regard for its impact on others."
WCED, *Our Common Future*

Although decolonization after World War II saw the emergence of many new states, they have failed to make much impression on the international balance of power. Deeply divided by ideology, wealth, location, size, culture and type of colonial legacy, they have been used as pawns by the superpowers in their political manoeuvrings.

Yet even though superpower relations still dominate world affairs, the focus of their attention is shifting away from the Atlantic seaboard. With the dawn of the information age, and the growth of the microelectronics industry, the Asian Pacific is enjoying an economic boom even at a time when other developed economies are stagnating. The much-heralded Pacific century is already here.

Five worlds

Dividing the world into neat categories is always misleading. For example, the North-South divide, while geographically only partially correct, is supposed to provide a convenient means of distinguishing rich from poor nations. Yet if we look at the "South" more closely, we see that it contains important subgroups such as the oil-exporting and the newly industrialized countries, many of which have more in common with the developed nations of the North.

Today most people are aware of the divisions within our world because of better communications. This in itself can be a source of tension between North and South as the poorer nations, through access to television, are exposed to the high-consumer Western lifestyles portrayed by the media.

Industrial market economies

Non-market economies

Oil-exporting countries

Newly industrialized countries

All the rest

Culture moving East

No other person did more to shatter the Western view of reality than Albert Einstein (1879-1955). His revolutionary theory of relativity necessitated profound changes in concepts of space, time and matter – changes so fundamental to the Cartesian mechanistic view of the world that physicists trained in Western ways of thinking found them difficult.

The world view emerging from modern physics is a systems view. The world is no longer seen as a machine, made up of a host of objects, but as one, indivisible, dynamic whole. This view is more in keeping with Eastern philosophies and religions, which tend to explain our relationship *to* the world, rather than trying to explain *how* the world works. The logic of Eastern thought is that because it is impossible to understand the way the world is, it is futile to try to control it. The notion of complementarity, as reflected in the yin and yang opposites of ancient Chinese thought, has become an essential part of the way physicists now think about nature.

$$E = mc^2$$

The Pacific shift

The traditional industrial culture of Europe and the American East Coast is on the decline. The growing economic strength and cultural importance of the nations on the Pacific rim are leading the superpowers to strengthen their ties with, in particular, China and Japan. We can only hope that these new alliances will provide a fulcrum for overcoming the US-Soviet stalemate that has paralysed world politics for over forty years.

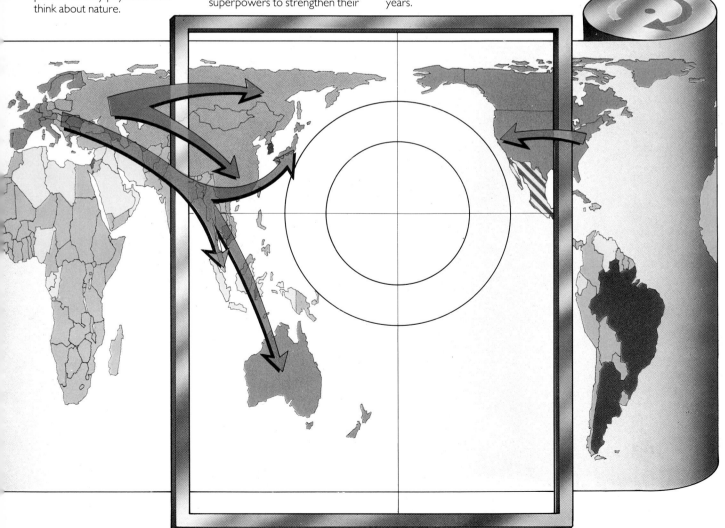

"other" worlds shriller and more violent. We have to recognize that there is strength in diversity – only this way lies peace. We have to learn to respect the views and aims of differing cultures, and move towards greater economic and social justice between them. We need new models of shared governance.

And if an effective system of self-governance is to be developed for this united global community, all states will have to accept some limitations on sovereignty – some redefinition of its function and jurisdiction. Our future depends on political acceptance of and support for supranational thinking.

"Supranational" literally means *above* the state; it describes issues which override national aims and institutions and which subordinate national authority to the interests of many nations, all humanity, or the planet itself. "International", by contrast, refers to activities *between* nations, and "transnational" to activities that *cross* national boundaries, from peace movements to commerce. All three levels can help to counter nationalism and build an integrated community.

The international fabric of life

The number of issues currently served by some form of international legislation is legion. Imagine, for example, how many agreements are involved in getting food to your table: on finance, trade, air and sea transportation, weather, customs, pollution and health control, and so on. Typically, states that ratify these agreements incorporate the obligations in their domestic law, and in so doing may cede a fraction of sovereignty. Transnational and subnational activity, too, is woven into all levels of society. Greenpeace and the anti-nuclear movement, WWF and OXFAM are explicitly transnational organizations fostering wide loyalties that ignore sovereignty; subnational groups promote cultural and ethnic diversity within society, and pay scant regard to national boundaries.

International agreements work only if states freely give their consent, perceiving them to be in their immediate interest. But they do provide useful clues to the conditions for successful supranational ones. They teach us that the most important factor is the political will to succeed. And that this will is easier to achieve if: there is genuine agreement between states on the need and scope of the activity; a well-defined plan; and a competent bureaucracy to see the work through.

Emerging regionalism

Europe provides the example, *par excellence*, of the subordination of old enmities to a wider concern. The Council of Europe, founded in 1949, was the brain-child of Winston Churchill, who believed that regional councils could ease problems and exploit opportunities in the future. Representing 21 European countries with 400 million people, it works via two main organs – the Committee of Ministers, and the Assembly. Though limited to democratic states, it has successfully added a parliamentary dimension to international relations. However, the states involved have not conceded

Networks of agreement

Over the last hundred years, a vast network of international and regional agreements has been thrown across the globe. Covering a wide variety of issues and activities, these agreements serve as instruments of peace, fostering co-operation and goodwill.

The stumbling block, as ever, to peaceful international relations is sovereignty. Not only is it a barrier to understanding between countries, but it can also be a problem within countries, destroying opportunities for cultural diversity, and causing conflicts of loyalty for members of professional, religious and ethnic groups.

Non-governmental organizations with transnational networks frequently breach sovereignty. The peace movement is a classic example of such an NGO, with its ideas, activities and personnel infiltrating all sectors of society. The strength of its support has been dramatically demonstrated in numerous frontier-defying actions, including marches, border crossings and voyages.

The network, *right*, depicts just eight classes of international agreement which link every country of the world together.

Czechoslovakia

Czechoslovakia is bound by numerous arms control agreements, including the Geneva Protocol and the Partial Test Ban Treaty. In trade, it is subject to the terms of GATT, and large corporations such as Tovarny Strojirenske Technicky have co-production agreements with Western factories. NGOs also play a part: the IPPNW has a branch in

Prague and the jazz section of the Czech Musicians' Union (affiliated to both END and the International Jazz Federation) promotes local culture as well as providing a voice for the peace movement. At the local level, twinning agreements with cities in the West, and even community health schemes, all help circumvent the state's sovereign power.

Environment

Organizations concerned with environmental issues are major links between countries. Particularly important are the regional organizations and agreements dealing with the Baltic Sea, North Sea, Mediterranean, Persian Gulf, Red Sea and Gulf of Aden, West and Central Africa, East Africa, Asia, the Pacific and the Caribbean Sea.

Arms control

International agreements on the conduct of war, the prohibition of weapons and the banning of certain military activities date back to the 19th century. The new Intermediate Nuclear Force Treaty, for example, will probably start a process re-establishing détente between East and West.

Human rights

Apart from the 1948 Universal Declaration of Human Rights, the first international bill of rights in history, treaties on human rights include the 1953 European Convention for the Protection of Human Rights and Fundamental Freedoms and the 1978 Latin American Convention on Human Rights.

Health

As the success of the World Health Organization shows, agreements on health are extremely effective. In fact, only the Universal Postal Union has more members than WHO. Clearly, the continuous exchange of information on health issues produces a web of links between nations.

Labour

The International Labour Organization was founded in 1919 and became the first specialized agency of the UN in 1946. The 150-country ILO has approved many conventions that form an international code of labour. Also important are regional organizations, such as the European Trade Union Institute.

Legal

There is a large number of agreements between nations on issues such as the Prevention and Punishment of the Crime of Genocide and a multitude of treaties on extradition. Regional and international courts are often courts of last resort to which individuals can submit their complaints.

Communications

Agreements on communications form crucial bonds between countries. The International Telecommunications Satellite Organization, for example, has a membership of 110 governments. Also important are regional organizations, such as the Asia-Pacific Telecommunity and the African Postal and Telecommunications Union.

Economic

The need for international co-operation, particularly to reduce the gap between rich and poor countries, has motivated the establishment of bodies such as the Organization of Economic Co-operation and Development, the Customs Co-operation Council and the UN Conference on Trade and Development.

their sovereign right to go their own way in the last resort. In this respect the younger European Economic Community is stronger, the majority vote having the power to overrule individual members. The Council's real success is in the legal field, particularly human rights. The 1950 European Convention on Human Rights (*see pp. 86-7*) guarantees certain rights and freedoms. Complaints of violations may be brought against a state by another state, an organization, or even an individual. Cases are tried by the European Court of Human Rights; 19 of the 21 member states have accepted the Court's jurisdiction as compulsory.

Regional organizations are growing. They provide permanent forums for neighbours to tackle problems, resolve crises between states at an early stage, and manage co-operative schemes like UNEP's Regional Seas Program. But attempts to extend these efforts at unity *within* cultural regions, to better relations *between* differing regions, are more difficult.

Successes – and failures

One outstanding example of an international agreement with supranational intentions to safeguard our global heritage is the Law of the Sea – surely our most ambitious effort yet to create an international regime for ocean management. But it has also been a salutary lesson in our weakness. Not all states have ratified the treaty, and "common heritage" status for deep sea bed minerals was rejected by three leading countries. The new 200-mile limit to offshore Exclusive Economic Zones is, however, a major incentive for states to safeguard their fisheries and combat overfishing.

Hopeful, too, is the example of the World Health Organization. The almost supranational activities of WHO, from smallpox control to sanitation, are based simply on national governmental co-operation – and are very successful. All countries agree the need to improve health; the programme is well defined, the WHO secretariat competent, the objectives clear.

It is when political objectives or vested interests clash that supranational agreements become exceedingly difficult to negotiate. The fact that many global issues are confined to restricted or bilateral talks between a small group of dominant states only makes things worse, hampering development of international, let alone supranational, consensus. For years the USA and the USSR have for example conducted nuclear arms control talks bilaterally, despite the existence of a permanent multilateral forum for arms control and disarmament in Geneva. Talks in Geneva are stymied while the superpowers seek private agreement.

The larger powers often behave as though they hold the smaller ones in contempt – provoking a similar attitude in response. This *must* change. Our future hope lies in the common will of all humanity, and a first step in this direction is for the great powers to stop monopolizing discussion of vital international issues, and open their debate to multinational forums.

We do now have large regional and international bureaucracies, set up to handle many fields, and a great

International or supranational?

Essentially, the difference between an international and a supranational activity is that the former concerns the interests between nations, whereas the latter concerns matters of wider interest that may subordinate sovereignty.

Given this definition, it is clear that although we have many international agencies, there are few that could be called truly supranational despite the supranational issues they confront. Those that do work do so because:

- Their goals are specific.
- Their activities receive public support.
- The agencies engage specific professionals.
- Their activities can be verified with legal sanction/support.
- Their activities enjoy the full support of all governments, and do not conflict with "vital" sovereignty issues.

These five criteria must be met if a successful supranational institution is to be built.

A supportive network

The globe, *right*, supported by the network of international and regional agencies, is in danger of rolling out of the net because of the failure of political will to endorse supranational action. There is also the marked absence of a balanced input from the South. All but one (Nairobi) of the UN agency headquarters are located in the North.

The EEC

The EEC is not only the most sophisticated regional institution ever created, it is also a curious political anomaly. A dozen states, some of them old enemies, have agreed to relinquish to a higher authority their sovereign rights on a number of important issues. Decisions on common tariffs, the mobility of labour, agriculture and investment policy are made by the Council of Ministers or the European Commission. In the Commission, the majority vote has the power to overrule individual member states. Although it has its limitations, the EEC provides the most successful working model we have for future supranational organizations.

Specific skills

Agencies that employ mainly specific professionals, particularly medical or natural scientists, are often the most successful. Examples include WHO, UNCTAD and the World Weather Watch.

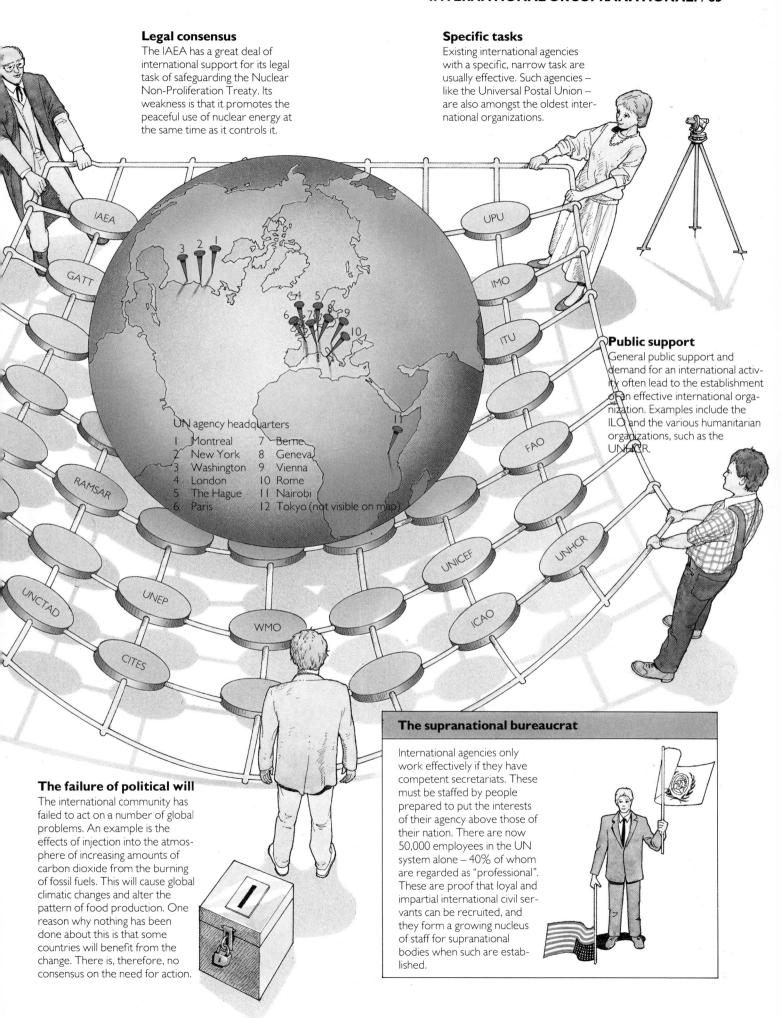

Legal consensus
The IAEA has a great deal of international support for its legal task of safeguarding the Nuclear Non-Proliferation Treaty. Its weakness is that it promotes the peaceful use of nuclear energy at the same time as it controls it.

Specific tasks
Existing international agencies with a specific, narrow task are usually effective. Such agencies – like the Universal Postal Union – are also amongst the oldest international organizations.

Public support
General public support and demand for an international activity often lead to the establishment of an effective international organization. Examples include the ILO and the various humanitarian organizations, such as the UNHCR.

UN agency headquarters

1	Montreal	7	Berne
2	New York	8	Geneva
3	Washington	9	Vienna
4	London	10	Rome
5	The Hague	11	Nairobi
6	Paris	12	Tokyo (not visible on map)

The failure of political will
The international community has failed to act on a number of global problems. An example is the effects of injection into the atmosphere of increasing amounts of carbon dioxide from the burning of fossil fuels. This will cause global climatic changes and alter the pattern of food production. One reason why nothing has been done about this is that some countries will benefit from the change. There is, therefore, no consensus on the need for action.

The supranational bureaucrat
International agencies only work effectively if they have competent secretariats. These must be staffed by people prepared to put the interests of their agency above those of their nation. There are now 50,000 employees in the UN system alone – 40% of whom are regarded as "professional". These are proof that loyal and impartial international civil servants can be recruited, and they form a growing nucleus of staff for supranational bodies when such are established.

many experienced international civil servants, able and willing to subordinate national loyalties to supranational service. Both the bureaucracies and the bureaucrats have faults. But if we can shape the social and political institutions for effective global governance, and the leaders with the will and strength to make them work, there will be at least a nucleus of able supranational civil servants to staff them.

Global unity must be built on public support for crucial and controversial issues. This, and the political will to act, cannot be imposed. They must come by discussion, understanding and consensus. The time and forums for such debate must be appropriate, too – we need institutions in which consensus can be achieved. For some issues, the United Nations is an appropriate institution. But it is proving not to be so for issues where common human or planetary welfare is at odds with immediate political interests. New institutions are essential, if those tasks which we are now failing to tackle internationally are to be successfully handled as supranational concerns.

The rise of human rights

There can be no peace without fundamental human rights and a recognition of "the dignity and worth of the human person" – as the United Nations Charter affirms. But in the 40 years since the UN set global standards in The Universal Declaration of Human Rights, we have not succeeded in implementing those rights world-wide.

One fundamental obstacle is that there is still no international consensus on their definition. Genuine value differences between East and West are obscured by ideological intransigence that blocks discussion. The US, leading "the free world", symbolizes both the ideal of democracy, based on respect for the rights and liberties of individual citizens, and the West's belief in its own superiority in this respect to "non-democratic" or "totalitarian" states. The USSR argues that social equity and freedom from exploitation are also basic human rights, denied in many "capitalist" countries. A new element is the rise of Islamic fundamentalism – states under religious rule determine human rights via their religious precepts.

Ideology only exacerbates another basic obstacle to implementation – national jurisdiction. Sovereign states are notoriously touchy about outside interference, and unlikely to implement voluntarily codes which conflict with their perceived self-interest.

A concern for human rights depends on public will; but unless the rights are protected by law, they are not worth much. In most states, rights protected by national laws are minimal, with children, old people, and minorities getting short shrift, and international codes are non-enforceable. Once such states run into domestic troubles, their willingness to listen to the international community, and their sanctions on human rights, is likely to be quickly suspended.

Public opinion, however, is a powerful weapon in the long run. In Europe, the overall jurisdiction of the Court of Human Rights is at last being accepted, nearly 40

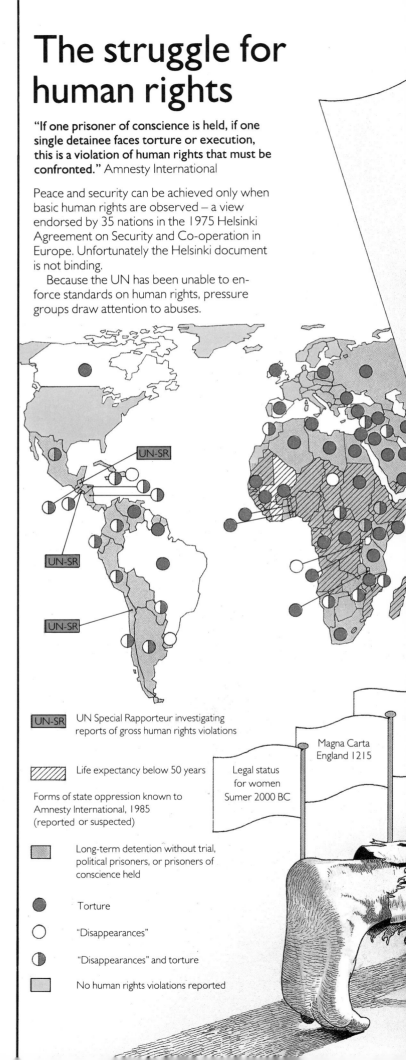

The struggle for human rights

"If one prisoner of conscience is held, if one single detainee faces torture or execution, this is a violation of human rights that must be confronted." Amnesty International

Peace and security can be achieved only when basic human rights are observed – a view endorsed by 35 nations in the 1975 Helsinki Agreement on Security and Co-operation in Europe. Unfortunately the Helsinki document is not binding.

Because the UN has been unable to enforce standards on human rights, pressure groups draw attention to abuses.

UN-SR   UN Special Rapporteur investigating reports of gross human rights violations

/////   Life expectancy below 50 years

Forms of state oppression known to Amnesty International, 1985 (reported or suspected)

Long-term detention without trial, political prisoners, or prisoners of conscience held

●   Torture

○   "Disappearances"

◐   "Disappearances" and torture

No human rights violations reported

Magna Carta England 1215

Legal status for women Sumer 2000 BC

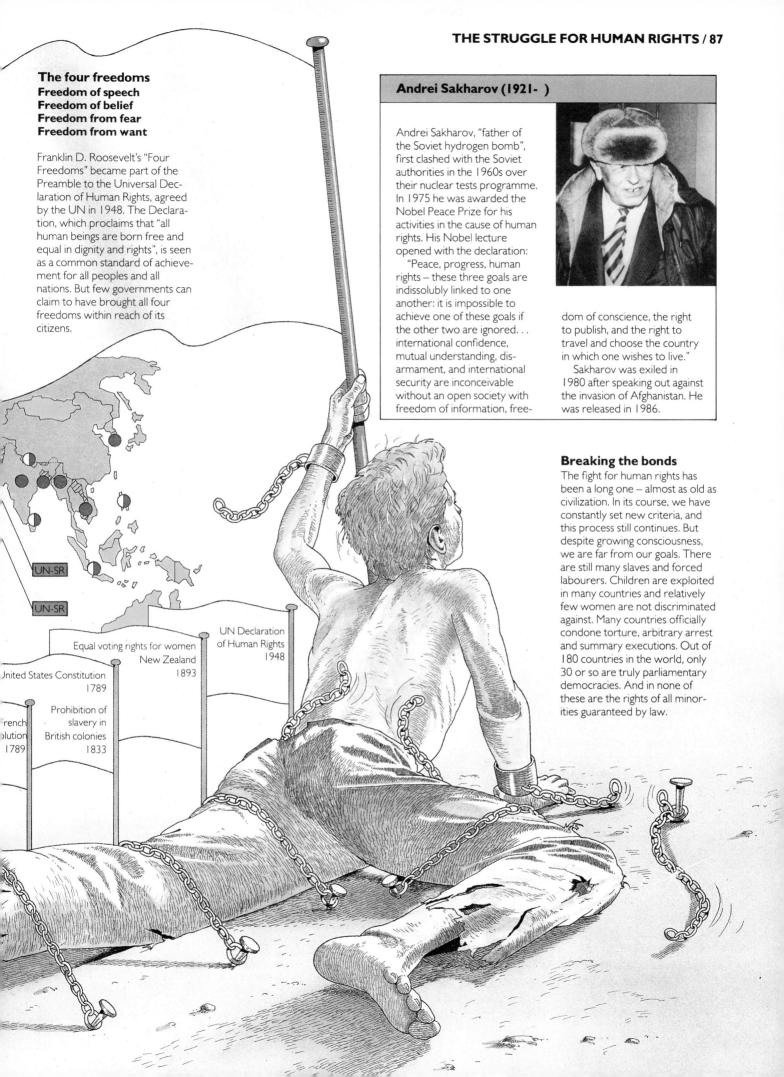

The four freedoms
Freedom of speech
Freedom of belief
Freedom from fear
Freedom from want

Franklin D. Roosevelt's "Four Freedoms" became part of the Preamble to the Universal Declaration of Human Rights, agreed by the UN in 1948. The Declaration, which proclaims that "all human beings are born free and equal in dignity and rights", is seen as a common standard of achievement for all peoples and all nations. But few governments can claim to have brought all four freedoms within reach of its citizens.

Andrei Sakharov (1921-)

Andrei Sakharov, "father of the Soviet hydrogen bomb", first clashed with the Soviet authorities in the 1960s over their nuclear tests programme. In 1975 he was awarded the Nobel Peace Prize for his activities in the cause of human rights. His Nobel lecture opened with the declaration:
  "Peace, progress, human rights – these three goals are indissolubly linked to one another: it is impossible to achieve one of these goals if the other two are ignored. . . international confidence, mutual understanding, disarmament, and international security are inconceivable without an open society with freedom of information, free-dom of conscience, the right to publish, and the right to travel and choose the country in which one wishes to live."
  Sakharov was exiled in 1980 after speaking out against the invasion of Afghanistan. He was released in 1986.

UN-SR

UN-SR

Equal voting rights for women
New Zealand
1893

UN Declaration
of Human Rights
1948

United States Constitution
1789

Prohibition of
slavery in
British colonies
1833

French
Revolution
1789

Breaking the bonds
The fight for human rights has been a long one – almost as old as civilization. In its course, we have constantly set new criteria, and this process still continues. But despite growing consciousness, we are far from our goals. There are still many slaves and forced labourers. Children are exploited in many countries and relatively few women are not discriminated against. Many countries officially condone torture, arbitrary arrest and summary executions. Out of 180 countries in the world, only 30 or so are truly parliamentary democracies. And in none of these are the rights of all minorities guaranteed by law.

years after the European Convention on Human Rights was drawn up. Even close neighbours take a long time to yield legal sovereignty. Where rights are backed by law, they are narrower than in declarations which are not legally enforceable. The European Convention, the most comprehensive legal guarantee, includes what one would regard as the basic rights in a reasonably civilized society – life, liberty and security; fair trial; privacy; enjoyment of possessions; education; freedom of domestic travel and residence; freedom of thought and religion; freedom of speech and assembly, including joining a union. And it prohibits torture, inhuman treatment, slavery, retroactive criminal laws, discrimination, and (recently) the use of the death penalty.

But it excludes the more far-reaching provisions of the typically non-enforceable UN Declaration – the right to work, or to protection against unemployment, for example. Yet more far-reaching ideas – the right to a sustainable livelihood and quality of life, denied to the world's poor, or the inclusion of human rights in definitions of détente – are now being raised by peace and environment movements.

A new environmentalism

Thirty years ago, there was virtually no political awareness of environmental decline – and few people had even heard of ecology. Now there is large and growing public concern about a variety of potential eco-disasters. We have begun to perceive the dangers, and we have the know-how and means to tackle many of them – whether to halt deforestation and the spread of deserts, or to control the rise of human numbers, poverty and maldistribution of resources. But we do not know how to create the *common will* to tackle such global problems as a united community.

There are many reasons for this failure. Solutions can threaten large commercial interests, and challenge long-established patterns of society – whether global interaction in finance and trade, or our own ordinary consumer habits. A very large pressure from public opinion must then be mobilized to overcome the political power of the vested interests concerned, while time is needed to delink our own behaviour.

Another block is the lack of a sense of urgency among decision makers. The environment does not seem to them visibly to deteriorate from day to day, and poverty is far away. There is a feeling that, though a problem may be getting steadily worse, we will have sufficient warning before disaster really strikes.

The myth that time is on our side will persist until more people – academics, politicians or public – take a broad view of the globe's many problems and the interactions between them. Politicians tend to react rather than act, and do the minimum needed to keep electoral support. Issues such as ozone depletion and species loss are rarely vote-catchers! And because people find it psychologically paralyzing to dwell on global disasters for long, the media are perhaps rightly unwilling to cover them very often. But if an issue is not news, politicians don't feel under much pressure to take

Perceiving the dangers

Peace, security and the environment are inextricably linked. That we have only just become aware of this fact in the last 20 years is an indictment of our nation state system. As individual countries blindly pursue unsustainable forms of development, key environmental resources are being squeezed, and competition for them between countries increases.

The very security that the nuclear arms race promises to countries is in reality the major threat to environmental security. Arms production not only has the potential for environmental destruction, but also makes huge claims on human resources and wealth that could be used to combat the collapse of our fragile ecosystems. Fortunately for the planet, public sensitivity to environmental issues is growing. We have at last begun to perceive the dangers.

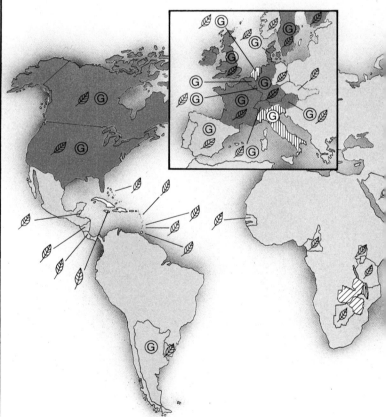

Greening the world

Five governments have to date endorsed National Conservation Strategies based on IUCN guidelines, and a further 7 are about to. Many more are busily establishing their own. It can take several years for an NCS to achieve political consensus, but this in itself can be a valuable educative process, since it involves raising the environmental awareness of all government officials.

Political intolerance may explain the absence of any Green parties in the developing world. Public interest certainly exists – the majority of the 45 countries with an active ecological movement in 1984 were located in the South.

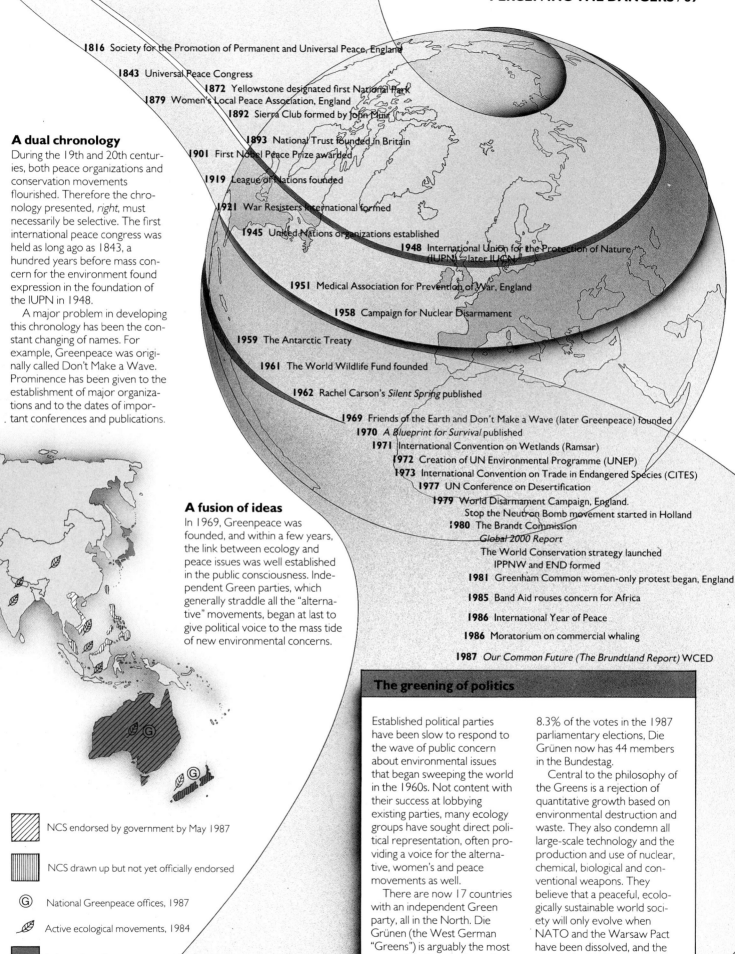

A dual chronology

During the 19th and 20th centuries, both peace organizations and conservation movements flourished. Therefore the chronology presented, *right*, must necessarily be selective. The first international peace congress was held as long ago as 1843, a hundred years before mass concern for the environment found expression in the foundation of the IUPN in 1948.

A major problem in developing this chronology has been the constant changing of names. For example, Greenpeace was originally called Don't Make a Wave. Prominence has been given to the establishment of major organizations and to the dates of important conferences and publications.

1816 Society for the Promotion of Permanent and Universal Peace, England
1843 Universal Peace Congress
1872 Yellowstone designated first National Park
1879 Women's Local Peace Association, England
1892 Sierra Club formed by John Muir
1893 National Trust founded in Britain
1901 First Nobel Peace Prize awarded
1919 League of Nations founded
1921 War Resisters International formed
1945 United Nations organizations established
1948 International Union for the Protection of Nature (IUPN), later IUCN
1951 Medical Association for Prevention of War, England
1958 Campaign for Nuclear Disarmament
1959 The Antarctic Treaty
1961 The World Wildlife Fund founded
1962 Rachel Carson's *Silent Spring* published
1969 Friends of the Earth and Don't Make a Wave (later Greenpeace) founded
1970 *A Blueprint for Survival* published
1971 International Convention on Wetlands (Ramsar)
1972 Creation of UN Environmental Programme (UNEP)
1973 International Convention on Trade in Endangered Species (CITES)
1977 UN Conference on Desertification
1979 World Disarmament Campaign, England.
Stop the Neutron Bomb movement started in Holland
1980 The Brandt Commission
Global 2000 Report
The World Conservation strategy launched
IPPNW and END formed
1981 Greenham Common women-only protest began, England
1985 Band Aid rouses concern for Africa
1986 International Year of Peace
1986 Moratorium on commercial whaling
1987 *Our Common Future (The Brundtland Report)* WCED

A fusion of ideas

In 1969, Greenpeace was founded, and within a few years, the link between ecology and peace issues was well established in the public consciousness. Independent Green parties, which generally straddle all the "alternative" movements, began at last to give political voice to the mass tide of new environmental concerns.

NCS endorsed by government by May 1987

NCS drawn up but not yet officially endorsed

Ⓖ National Greenpeace offices, 1987

Active ecological movements, 1984

Independent Green party in existence, 1987

The greening of politics

Established political parties have been slow to respond to the wave of public concern about environmental issues that began sweeping the world in the 1960s. Not content with their success at lobbying existing parties, many ecology groups have sought direct political representation, often providing a voice for the alternative, women's and peace movements as well.

There are now 17 countries with an independent Green party, all in the North. Die Grünen (the West German "Greens") is arguably the most successful of these. Capturing 8.3% of the votes in the 1987 parliamentary elections, Die Grünen now has 44 members in the Bundestag.

Central to the philosophy of the Greens is a rejection of quantitative growth based on environmental destruction and waste. They also condemn all large-scale technology and the production and use of nuclear, chemical, biological and conventional weapons. They believe that a peaceful, ecologically sustainable world society will only evolve when NATO and the Warsaw Pact have been dissolved, and the arms industry dismantled.

action on it. What the media *could* do is show the good news more often – if we were more aware of how successful human initiative can be, we might be able to turn despair into a commitment to a better future. The individual often feels powerless in the face of huge problems and growing bureaucracies. But many individuals do act, and they can also be successful – witness our on-going efforts to ban whaling, raise money for famine relief, or halt nuclear atmospheric testing.

There is much we can do, and the most urgent need for us to do it. Successes so far have barely dented the encroaching crises. To avert disasters, we must anticipate them – and commit our governments to prevention on a global scale. Macro-planning however is bedevilled by lack of agreement: about the need for it; the nature, scale and urgency of problems; and on the political will to act. Such division and vacillation can be overcome only by public consensus. It is up to us.

Grass roots activity

If and when consensus on tackling global problems does arrive, it will be largely due to ordinary men and women at grass roots level. The political scene today is very different from thirty or forty years ago. Millions of individuals are now actively involved in a great range of issues – a phenomenon that may change the world.

The sudden uprise of public interest in a global problem sometimes seems to suggest that human society instinctively knows when its survival is threatened. One example is the recent success of Green politics. Another is the surge of public concern in the early 1980s about the risk of a nuclear world war. Rapidly deteriorating relations between the USA and the USSR, the development of destabilizing nuclear weapons, and talk by President Reagan's administration about preparing for "limited" or "protracted" nuclear war all greatly increased public concern.

But it was the plans to deploy "enhanced radiation" warheads (neutron bombs) in Europe that finally sparked an explosion of public protest. This protest, and subsequent resistance to the deployment of Cruise and Pershing II missiles, was so strong that Western politicians have never since been able to ignore public reaction to military policy. For the first time in recent Western European history, armament policies have to be publicly justified.

Grass roots activity was a major factor in the USA in stopping the Vietnam War and, earlier, in 1963, in pressing President Kennedy to negotiate a Partial Test Ban Treaty. Successful protest campaigns, in fact, have an increasingly impressive record world-wide.

Public pressure on specific issues is often organized through voluntary or "non-governmental" organizations (NGOs). There is now a very large family of NGOs, from OXFAM or CND to the Indian Chipko tree-savers. Over 5000 operate in more than one country, with many transnational contacts, and some form joint campaigns with other NGOs, a notable example being the Antarctic Coalition of more than 150 conservation groups. NGOs speak for millions, and form a global

Redressing the balance

All over the world, ordinary people are challenging the establishment. They are criticizing failures to tackle fundamental human security issues and the high levels of military spending. And they are also questioning one of its fundamental beliefs – that natural resources are inexhaustible, are there for the taking, and can sustain any amount of abuse. As more people become involved in development and peace activities, new solutions are emerging with new voices to champion them. Governments at last are having to sit up and listen.

"People want peace so much that one of these days governments had better get out of their way and let them have it." Dwight D. Eisenhower

Imaging the future

Except in times of deep crisis (such as a great depression or war) governments are too responsible for "peace" (seen as maintaining the *status quo*) to take the responsibility for change. Constrained by a detailed knowledge of the practicalities and caught within the confines of the day-to-day problems, the only change governments perceive is in terms of gradual adjustments to existing institutions.

Most of the existing international structures were created in the 1940s and have not kept up with the pace of change. A peaceful, sustainable world will not be achieved merely by extrapolating from present experience. Something new must be the objective. But in order to bring about a better future it must first be created in your imagination.

This is one of the great strengths of the voluntary organizations – they are able to think laterally and optimistically about a future without war, a future without weapons. By first creating positive images of the future, NGOs are able to develop action plans that are more far-sighted than those of the establishment.

The rise of the NGOs

Worldwide, there are now nearly 5000 international non-governmental organizations (NGOs), representing millions of supporters and working on a huge range of issues. Broadly, their aims are to counter vested interests in the arms race; to counter the influence of those who oppose the transfer of resources from North to South; and to protect the environment. The oldest NGOs are those dealing with peace and security issues, some of which date back nearly 200 years, having their roots in Quakerism. Most NGOs, however, are post-1945 movements, formed out of concern for the environment. The developing countries in particular have witnessed a dramatic increase in the number of NGOs formed in the last 20 years.

Politicians can no longer ignore NGOs. In fact, some modern political parties, like the European Greens and the Nuclear Disarmament Party in Australia, evolved from NGO activities. Political parties in most developed countries now have to include in their manifestos promises of action on peace, development and environmental issues.

Thousands of NGOs

1900 05 10   35 40 45 50 55 60 65 70 75 80 85

2   4

The Green Belt Movement

Because of the problems associated with hunger, poverty and disease, many of the NGOs in developing countries are qualitatively different from their counterparts in developed countries. Often they are concerned directly with combating local deprivation and preserving scarce natural resources. An example is the Green Belt Movement in Kenya. Managed and led mainly by women, it organizes local efforts to manage local resources and works for the preservation of the topsoil, stabilization of climate and the sustainable use of tree products. A tree project, involving local people in planting and caring for native trees, has proved so successful that it is now supported by the United Nations and the US National Council of Negro Women. Under the guidance of foresters, local people learn to recognize and find the seeds of native trees, germinate them in nursery conditions and then transplant them into the open. As an incentive, a small remuneration is paid for each surviving tree. So far, several million trees have been nurtured in village nurseries.

"On the ground" movements such as these challenge the solutions proposed by distant bureaucrats, but they need support for their own, more appropriate, methods.

The Partial Test Ban Treaty

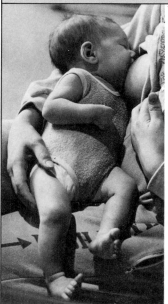

The 1963 Partial Test Ban Treaty is a particularly important treaty, serving as the starting point for limiting nuclear tests. Endorsed by 106 states, it prohibits nuclear-weapon tests in the atmosphere, in outer space and under water. Until 1963, nuclear weapons were frequently exploded in the atmosphere and under water, thereby injecting a great deal of radioactivity into the atmosphere (which subsequently entered the food chain).

One consequence of this action was publicized by a group of American doctors who analysed babies' teeth and found that they contained radioactive strontium. Clearly, this substance was being ingested in food and laid down in bone.

World pressures increased for an end to the radioactive contamination of the atmosphere. Fears and protests were widespread – coming from the West, the East and the non-aligned countries. But the most effective pressure came from women in the USA, the USSR and the UK. This, together with the experience of the 1961 Cuban missile crisis, which brought the USA and the USSR to the brink of nuclear war, persuaded the political leaders to negotiate the Partial Test Ban Treaty.

network through which public pressure can be brought to bear on decision-makers. A significant constraint on political leaders, they undercut sovereignty and help to bypass bureaucratic inertia and get things done. The NGO route is cost-effective and successful in transferring appropriate strategies upwards, from the village where local understanding is greatest, to the government level where far-reaching decisions occur.

NGO activity is rapidly spreading in developing countries, with increasing membership in local groups and branches of organizations like Friends of the Earth and Greenpeace. It may well be that in this struggle toward local self-determination and grass roots power lies their greatest hope of future well-being.

Building a global community

Global moves to peace and security will require united action. Such action will only be possible if our global understanding, our sense of single community, evolve to become a majority view. But will this unity demand a loss or homogenization of cultures?

Not necessarily. Most people believe that diversity within and between societies strengthens civilizations. A healthy and lively global community will surely draw some of its vigour from a pluralist society, one that guards the diversity of human heritage and skills.

As countries become ever more dependent on each other for trade, financial dealings, and a wide range of cultural activities – sport, music, theatre, art exhibitions, literature – the evolution of a global culture seems less distant. The recent Geldof Food Aid campaign could not have been so successful had it not been for the global reach of Western pop music.

Many professions, too, are transnational, and can do much for global society. Outstanding examples are the International Physicians for the Prevention of Nuclear War (IPPNW), founded in 1980, and Pugwash.

The IPPNW has succeeded in making it understood just how catastrophic a nuclear world war would be – and how utterly helpless the medical services. If we do avoid a nuclear war, we will owe much to IPPNW for mobilizing opinion against the nuclear arms race.

Pugwash is quite different. Set up 30 years ago at the height of the Cold War, to establish behind-the-scenes contacts with military and political power, it shuns publicity. But through personal influence its eminent scientists facilitated the 1963 Partial Test Ban Treaty, the 1970 Nuclear Non-Proliferation Treaty, the 1972 ABM Treaty, and negotiations to end the Vietnam War.

Today, the peace movement prefers public protest to private persuasion of leaders. Perhaps this reflects a growing public impatience with politics and politicians of all kinds – a sense that the political process itself is bankrupt. There is certainly a swing to direct, non-governmental action, circumventing the barriers of bureaucracy and vested establishments.

If there is to be "one world", it will have to be born of a massive, world-wide, local and general public rejection of the "can't be done" mentality, and a firm majority intention that it can, and will, be done.

A global culture?

In many cultures around the world, peace is a central theme. Hinduism, Buddhism, Christianity and many African cultures all have peace as a basic value. Why, then, has humanity consistently overthrown peace with war and conflict throughout history?

Where competition is the economic norm, and where technology – particularly weapons technology – is turned against both nature and humanity, it is not surprising to find that we have adopted a war culture. But if we are to survive into the next millennium, it is essential that we learn, within the diversity of many cultures, to cultivate a single global culture of peace.

Such a culture is most likely to be built on the foundations of our present non-violent cultural activities. Literature, science, music, art and the media – all serve to reduce tensions between nations and spread common understanding. Already English is being adopted as a global *lingua franca*, with almost a billion speakers worldwide.

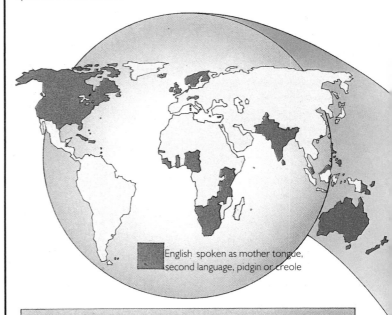

English spoken as mother tongue, second language, pidgin or creole

English – the global language

Today, about 330 million people speak English as a mother tongue, with about the same number using it as a second language, and about the same number again using it with reasonable competence as a foreign language. It is one of the two working languages of the UN, and has become the language of both international youth culture and science.

English is now officially spoken in more than 40 countries. Relatively easy to pronounce, and with fairly straightforward syntax and no confusing gender system,

the English language in some ways fits its role well – although its huge vocabulary and peculiar idioms have been seen as serious drawbacks. Spelling, which, for historical reasons, does not always follow pronunciation, can also be a problem. But whether or not English is the most suitable language, the value of a common means of communication for peace is indisputable. The main disadvantage of this seems to be its effect on reducing diversity among small, indigenous cultures.

The case for religious diversity

Religious differences have often been a cause of war. This reflects not only humanity's failure to comprehend its fundamental interdependence, but also our failure to perceive the value of diversity. The Taoist view of reality is currently illuminating many of the problems on which Western thinking has reached an impasse, while Buddhism, which views all life as sacred, is influencing developments in conservation.

The different cultural values embodied in the various religions may also provide a glimpse of how a future global society might operate. While modern economists regard human labour as little more than a necessary evil, Buddhists view work as an opportunity to develop their faculties, to overcome ego-centredness, and to bring forth the goods and services needed for a comfortable existence.

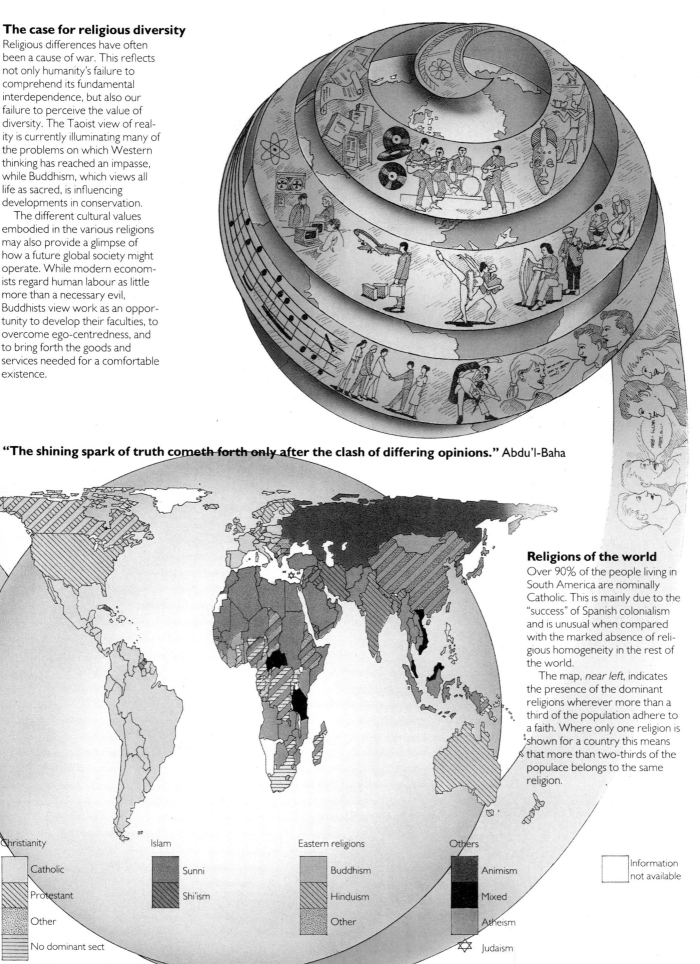

"The shining spark of truth cometh forth only after the clash of differing opinions." Abdu'l-Baha

Religions of the world

Over 90% of the people living in South America are nominally Catholic. This is mainly due to the "success" of Spanish colonialism and is unusual when compared with the marked absence of religious homogeneity in the rest of the world.

The map, *near left*, indicates the presence of the dominant religions wherever more than a third of the population adhere to a faith. Where only one religion is shown for a country this means that more than two-thirds of the populace belongs to the same religion.

Christianity
- Catholic
- Protestant
- Other
- No dominant sect

Islam
- Sunni
- Shi'ism

Eastern religions
- Buddhism
- Hinduism
- Other

Others
- Animism
- Mixed
- Atheism
- Judaism

Information not available

5 Civilization in crisis

Introduced by Gro Harlem Brundtland

The World Commission on Environment and Development was given a challenging mandate. We were asked to take a fresh look at the interrelated issues of environment and development and to define shared perceptions on long-term environmental issues and aspirational goals of the world community to the year 2000 and beyond. And the call from the General Assembly was an urgent one. Our report, carrying the consensus signature of Commissioners from 21 countries, most from the developing world, contains a strong message of warning.

Present trends and policies cannot continue. They will destroy the resource base on which we all depend. We are not winning the battle against poverty, which continues to tie hundreds of millions to an existence irreconcilable with human dignity, and is the main cause, and effect, of environmental degradation in many developing countries. Severe threats to the global environment also come from excesses of affluence in many countries in the North, which consume the Earth's resources at rates that can lead to their rapid depletion. Environmental degradation and the unequal distribution of wealth and power are in reality different aspects of the same set of problems.

Threats to the environment are becoming global in scope and devastating in scale. The grim statistics are now all too familiar. The atmosphere is not a limitless garbage sink for by-products of industrialization. Global heating, and the threat of climate change, risk rising sea levels and severe impacts on food production and settlement patterns. Acidification, hitherto a disease of the rich countries, is moving into the developing world. Deforestation and erosion are major problems: 6 million hectares of productive dryland turn into desert each year; forests the size of Denmark are lost every 12 weeks.

International economic inequalities are one root cause of the environment-development stalemate. The environment and resources of developing countries, the capital on which they depend, have become the victims in a troubled world economy. Debilitating debts, soaring interest rates, interrupted financial flows, and adverse terms of trade offer them few options but to overuse their resource base, while their capacity to address environmental issues remains low.

While the possibility of nuclear war, or conflict involving any weapons of mass destruction, is undoubtedly the gravest threat to the environment and humanity, peace and security issues are central to all development problems. Environmental stress is both a cause, and an effect, of political tension and military conflict. And the coexistence of substantial military spending with unmet human needs evokes grave concern.

All nations will ultimately share the same destiny. Our environment and economies have become so intertwined that we may no longer choose to remain apart. The environment respects no national boundaries. We cannot act as if it did. Nations must turn away from the destructive logic of an "arms culture" and focus instead on our common future.

The overriding concept on which this future depends is that of sustainable development – meeting the needs of present generations without compromising those yet to come. The time and the opportunity has come to break out of the negative trends of the past. Never before in our history have we had similar capacities. But we need a new vision, a new courage, and a stronger political will and determination. We need a new global ethic. I believe very strongly that such change is not only necessary, it is also possible. Our report is not a prophecy of doom, but a positive vision of the future.

Gro H. Brundtland

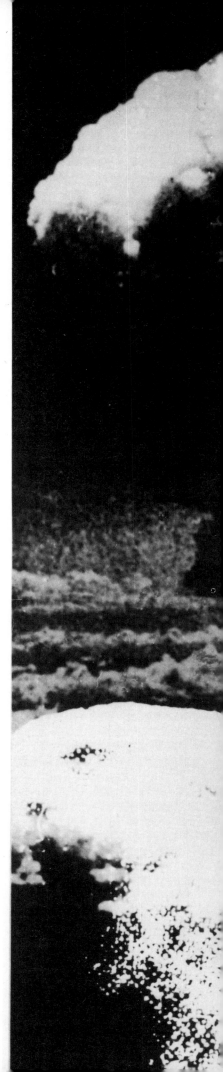

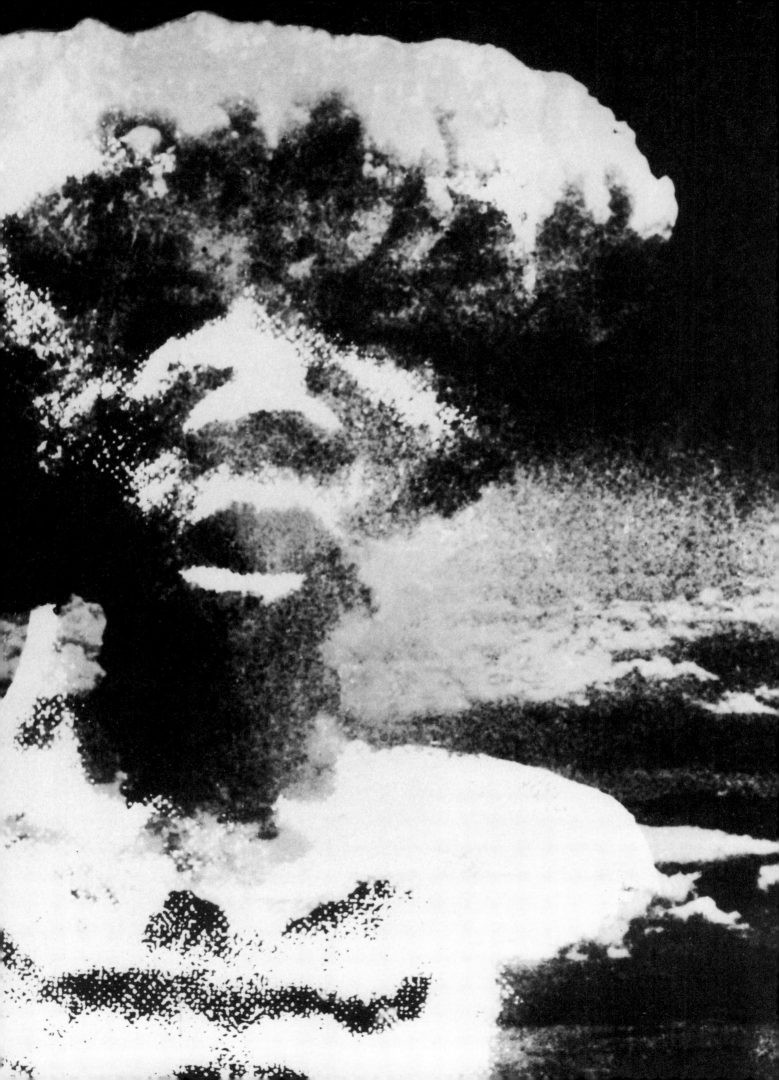

"It was a wise physician who reminded us that statistics are just people with the tears wiped off . . . Behind the numbers is the pain of millions of lives lost to neglect as well as to violence." Ruth Sivard *World Military and Social Expenditures.*

The world is sick, and the crisis stage of the illness is upon us. The symptoms are plain: first, the fever of militarism and violence that wastes our strength; second, the tremors in the overstrained world system and mounting damage to life support mechanisms brought on by our neglect; third, the growing risk of final insanity, in unleashing nuclear war. We see the symptoms; we document them. But when it comes to diagnosing the disease itself, and seeking the cure, the world community is in disarray. We are suffering from a failure of perception.

The cost of military solutions

Wars have always been expensive. But, in the past, military spending has shrunk back afterwards to peace-time levels. Since World War II, however, no such "shrink-back" has occurred. World military spending has continued to rise. By 1960, the world was spending five times as much on the military, in real terms, as in the inter-war years; by 1986, in the "Year of Peace", more than 12 times – or $900 billion. Wars, from Vietnam to the Gulf, merely have a ratchet effect on this relentless upward trend.

The cost to all other sectors of the economy is huge. The rise has negated all world economic growth. The annual GNP increments from 1960 to 1985 totalled $8.6 trillion, for instance, while military spending in the same period was $14 trillion. Like the proverbial cuckoo in the nest, the military sector has grown fat, while the rest of humanity and the environment grow lean.

In part, the cause is our tacit acceptance of the military establishment as a permanent fixture in our society, irrespective of any current "threat" to national security. After World War II, and even more so after the Korean War, both the USA and the USSR retained huge military establishments. This led to the emergence of increasingly powerful economic and bureaucratic interests that resisted any decline in military powers and continually promoted their expansion. Over time, these have become extremely difficult to resist. With the growth of the military machine has come a concomitant rise in the arms industry. Together, these two spheres of influence present a formidable, self-perpetuating force. National security is increasingly identified with military security, and a large military capacity seen as the means of furthering foreign policy.

Driven on by rapid technological change, these factors have triggered off an East-West arms race where superiority is measured mainly in terms of sophistication in weaponry – the "shiny new toy" syndrome. This competition causes the arms race to follow a characteristic pattern of action and reaction or, often, overreaction. Soviet military activities, for

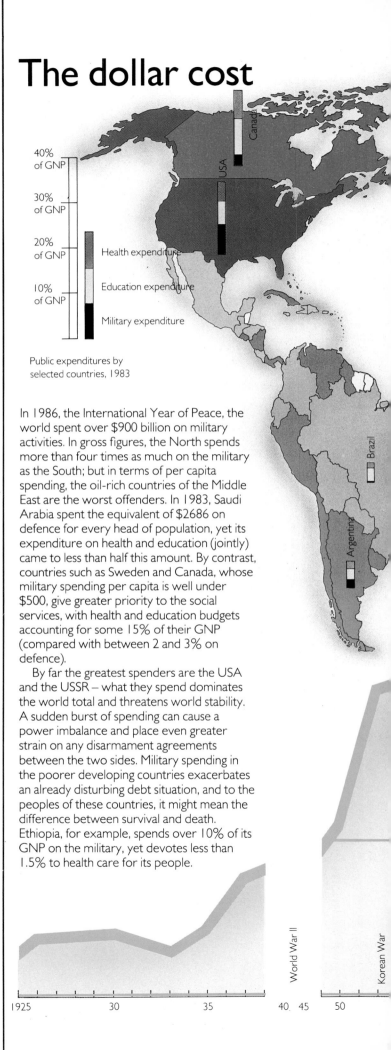

The dollar cost

Public expenditures by selected countries, 1983

In 1986, the International Year of Peace, the world spent over $900 billion on military activities. In gross figures, the North spends more than four times as much on the military as the South; but in terms of per capita spending, the oil-rich countries of the Middle East are the worst offenders. In 1983, Saudi Arabia spent the equivalent of $2686 on defence for every head of population, yet its expenditure on health and education (jointly) came to less than half this amount. By contrast, countries such as Sweden and Canada, whose military spending per capita is well under $500, give greater priority to the social services, with health and education budgets accounting for some 15% of their GNP (compared with between 2 and 3% on defence).

By far the greatest spenders are the USA and the USSR – what they spend dominates the world total and threatens world stability. A sudden burst of spending can cause a power imbalance and place even greater strain on any disarmament agreements between the two sides. Military spending in the poorer developing countries exacerbates an already disturbing debt situation, and to the peoples of these countries, it might mean the difference between survival and death. Ethiopia, for example, spends over 10% of its GNP on the military, yet devotes less than 1.5% to health care for its people.

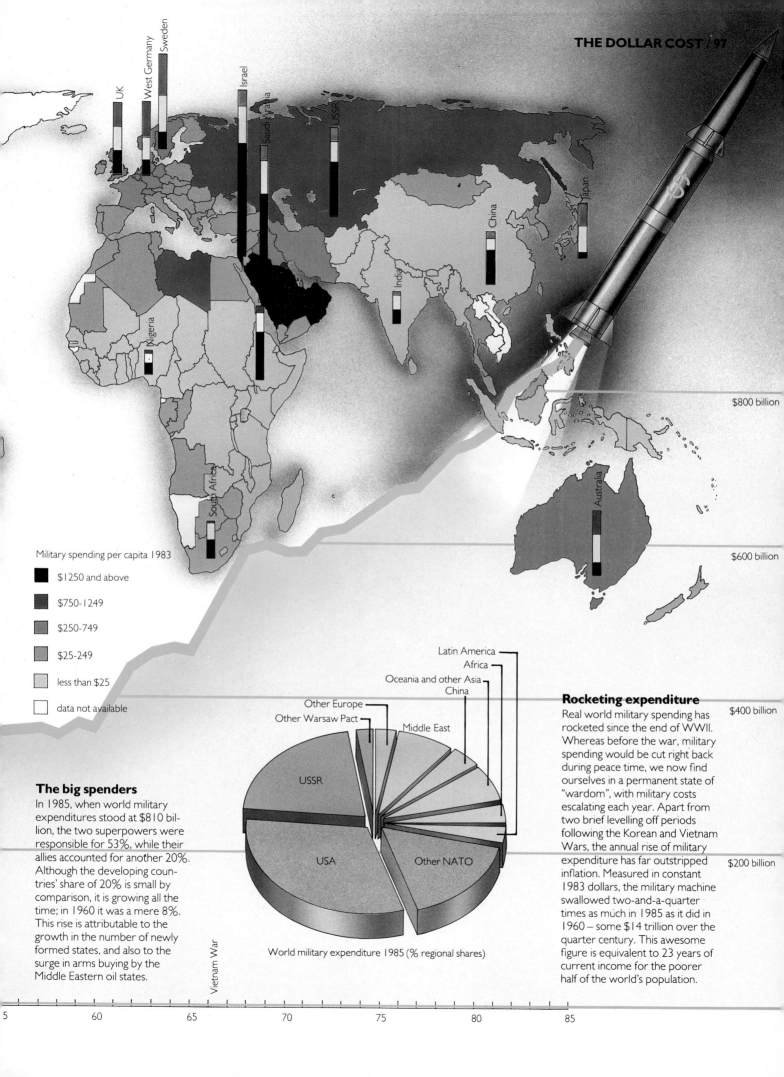

$800 billion

$600 billion

Military spending per capita 1983

- $1250 and above
- $750-1249
- $250-749
- $25-249
- less than $25
- data not available

Latin America

Africa

Oceania and other Asia

China

Other Europe

Other Warsaw Pact

Middle East

USSR

$400 billion

Rocketing expenditure

Real world military spending has rocketed since the end of WWII. Whereas before the war, military spending would be cut right back during peace time, we now find ourselves in a permanent state of "wardom", with military costs escalating each year. Apart from two brief levelling off periods following the Korean and Vietnam Wars, the annual rise of military expenditure has far outstripped inflation. Measured in constant 1983 dollars, the military machine swallowed two-and-a-quarter times as much in 1985 as it did in 1960 – some $14 trillion over the quarter century. This awesome figure is equivalent to 23 years of current income for the poorer half of the world's population.

$200 billion

The big spenders

In 1985, when world military expenditures stood at $810 billion, the two superpowers were responsible for 53%, while their allies accounted for another 20%. Although the developing countries' share of 20% is small by comparison, it is growing all the time; in 1960 it was a mere 8%. This rise is attributable to the growth in the number of newly formed states, and also to the surge in arms buying by the Middle Eastern oil states.

USA

Other NATO

Vietnam War

World military expenditure 1985 (% regional shares)

5   60   65   70   75   80   85

example, are determined almost exclusively by those of the USA, and vice versa. Overreaction occurs because there is no consensus on how much military capability is "enough". Uncertainty typically leads to decisions to procure too much weaponry rather than too little.

This technological arms race proceeds on a global scale. Once a country gets involved, its military spending will increase in leaps and bounds. Many believe that arms races themselves lead to wars. Whether they do or not, we can be certain that they perpetuate them, and increase the level of death and destruction once war breaks out.

As long as politicians remain willing partners in this murderous game, then military expenditure will continue to rise. Enormous resources will continue to be wasted in a world where resources are finite. Development activities will be postponed, increasing international tensions, environmental pressures will be increased, causing irreparable damage, and social needs will be neglected, creating human misery and the internal instability that leads to wars.

The world's annual military bill now equals the gross income of the poorer half of humanity. The prognosis for the 1990s looks bleak.

Man's inhumanity to man

When wars were fought with swords and spears, the number of soldiers involved was small, the times and places of battles were predetermined, and the total number of dead and injured was generally small. When firearms replaced hand weapons, casualties increased but not dramatically. The Industrial Revolution led to mass production of artillery and explosive shells, and this increased the numbers killed and wounded. Machine guns, hand grenades, bombers, tanks and automatic weapons made wars increasingly destructive; the number of casualties soared.

But with modern technology, particularly during and since World War II, weapons have become exceedingly destructive. With conventional warheads, from fuel air explosives to fragmentation bombs, all humans in large areas can be killed or very seriously wounded. Populations can also be wiped out with chemical and biological weapons. And with nuclear weapons, whole cities can be obliterated by a single warhead.

The horror caused by the dreadful slaughter of soldiers in World War I, in which at least 19 million men were killed, led to the General Treaty for the Renunciation of War, signed in 1928. This Treaty effectively outlawed war but it did not prevent the outbreak of World War II. This war killed over 40 million people, more than half of them civilians.

World War II was a watershed in the human costs of war. Virtually all standards of morality and decency collapsed, as did the humanitarian laws of war. The genocide of six million Jews and a considerable number of gypsies and other minorities in the gas chambers of German concentration camps; the use of human guinea pigs for medical experiments; the devastation of whole cities by aerial bombardment, culminating in the

The human cost

This century, around 100 million people have already been killed in war. In World War I, about 95% of those killed were soldiers. In World War II, over 50% were civilians. In the 1982 Lebanese war, about 90% were civilians, mostly women and children.

But the human cost of war does not stop with death statistics. Huge numbers of refugees are among the casualties. For example, more than half the population of Afghanistan have become refugees since the Soviet occupation in 1979. Forced to flee their homes, these people are often the victims of malnutrition and disease, compounded by lack of food and poor health care facilities.

Modern war produces large numbers of seriously disabled people. Some weapons, such as fragmentation munitions, are deliberately designed to produce multiple injuries, while others, such as tumbling and high speed bullets, inflict gaping wounds. Other weapons use plastic, so that fragments do not show up on X-rays, making treatment difficult.

Some of the costs are unquantifiable. How can a figure be attached to the psychological damage suffered by women raped, or children who have grown up in an environment of war, their parents killed before their eyes? Nearly half the women fleeing Vietnam by boat in 1980 were raped in passage. Many US and Australian veterans of the Vietnam War suffer high rates of mental instability.

The suffering does not stop when the war ends. Huge numbers of unexploded munitions have to be disposed of, creating a hazard for decades. For example, in Libya, since World War II, about 4000 people have been killed by explosive remnants.

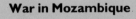

War in Mozambique

Since achieving independence from Portugal in 1975, Mozambique has suffered almost continuous civil conflict between the regular army and rival guerilla groups, one of which, the MNR, has South African backing.

Mass terrorism has taken a heavy toll on the populace. Over 100,000 have died as a direct result of military action in the last decade. The MNR has intentionally disrupted food production, causing the 1983 famine in which at least another 100,000 died. The largest toll, however, has been amongst children caught in a spiral of malnutrition, disease, lack of access to clean water

and a breakdown of rural health services. Between 1980 and 1986, there were more than 300,000 conflict-related deaths amongst children under 5 – deaths which could have been avoided if the country had not been in a war in which one of the protagonists has sworn to undermine the economy and administration.

As well as a 35% child mortality rate – the highest in the world – 42% of Mozambique's health posts and 40% of its schools have been destroyed. Half the rural population have been driven off their land. Wells have been deliberately poisoned and entire villages burned.

Lebanon 90%

Women and war: the real victims

Since modern wars are no longer fought "on the battlefield" but in towns and villages, civilians have borne the brunt of the killing. Women in particular are vulnerable – not only are they tortured and killed because of their relationship to the combatants, but they are also commonly raped. Rape and other acts of violence against women, however, frequently go unreported (or are ignored if the act has been a prelude to murder), except when they are committed by "the other side".

War seems to aggravate the fundamental inequalities ingrained in male-female relations. As refugees, women are regularly subjected to sexual exploitation and intimidation in the absence of any social infrastructure. The UNHCR has also observed that, even when food supplies have been adequate, the men still eat first, resulting in gaunt women and children alongside well-fed men.

WWII 50%

Southern Africa: 750,000 child deaths due to war in the 1980s

Countries with over a million war deaths since 1945:

Bangladesh
Kampuchea
China
Vietnam
Korea
Nigeria
Iran/Iraq

Countries with over 500,000 war deaths since 1945:

Afghanistan
India
Indonesia
Ethiopia

Civilian casualties: WWI 5%

20 million dead in wars since 1945 mostly women and children

12-14 million international refugees

Nicaragua: destruction of health facilities 1981-5: $70 million

Rape: reported by 48% of Vietnamese boat people, 1980

Lebanon: 40% of population homeless

Bangladesh war: 250,000 cases of smallpox

destruction of Hiroshima and Nagasaki by atomic bombs; wholesale and horrific atrocities on civilians; and the inhuman treatment of hundreds of thousands of prisoners of war, including systematic starvation, were among the acts that would have been unthinkable before 1939.

In World War II, for the first time in modern history, the number of civilians killed exceeded the number of soldiers. In fact, a characteristic of modern war is that civilian deaths are likely to be higher than those of the military. The traditional distinction between soldiers and civilians has been eroded, mainly because the military now perceive civilians as legitimate targets for the purposes of undermining a hostile regime. This strategy, under which civilians are deliberately attacked to make the war so unbearable for them that they put pressure on their government to surrender, is known as coercive warfare.

World War II confirmed coercive warfare as the military practice of the major nations, even though the strategy had failed to demoralize the civilian populations. The example has been followed by the Americans in Vietnam, the Soviets in Afghanistan, and the anti-government forces in Mozambique and Angola, to name just a few. In all three cases, civilians were not only deliberately targeted but were the major targets. In Mozambique and Angola, UNICEF reported in 1987 that: "health workers, as well as clinics and health posts, schools, teachers and pupils, foreign aid personnel and vehicles transporting health and relief supplies, [were] all deliberately chosen as targets of the war for the purpose of causing a breakdown in civil administration and making large areas of both countries ungovernable." Terrible suffering was inflicted on large numbers of civilians but again, coercive warfare failed in its objective. North Vietnam, for example, did not capitulate even though it was bombed for years with an intensity that exceeded the bombing of Germany during World War II.

Nuclear deterrence based on mutual assured destruction takes the strategy of coercive warfare into another realm. Whole populations in enemy cities are held hostage to nuclear deterrence (see p. 130). And weapons have become so destructive that war now threatens the very existence of humankind. When we live continually under threat of total destruction, all humanitarian constraints on warfare and all respect for international law disappear.

No wonder if we fail to be moved by the deliberate massacres and mass starvation of thousands of women and children in Palestinian camps in Beirut or the massacre of two million civilians in Cambodia by the Pol Pot regime.

No wonder, too, if we even countenance the use of children to fight wars. Several countries, including Britain and the United States, have refused to ratify the 1977 Protocols to the Geneva Conventions which stipulate that children under the age of 15 should not carry guns. Child soldiers are used in over 50 countries.

The nuclear age is an age of barbarism.

Children and war

It is impossible to get even a rough estimate of how many children are currently involved in armed conflict around the world. We know that child soldiers are recruited in some 50 countries, and that a high proportion of the victims are children.

Children living in war zones suffer from traumas, poor educational ability, aggressive outbursts, and general insecurity. In the Lebanon, at war since 1975, at least 70% of the children have never known peace.

Even in those countries not at war, children are being taught to accept war and violence as an integral part of life. Images in the media desensitize children to violence, while toy manufacturers foster violent play, and the "macho" virtue of the warrior hero, thus helping to "legitimize" the act of war. At school, children are taught about patriotic wars often from a one-sided view, and encouraged to respect and honour soldiers of war. Yet surely children should also be made aware of the awesome destructive power now in the hands of the military, and of the evils of war – otherwise what kind of future society can we expect them to create?

Image and reality

There seems little doubt that violence in the media, by desensitizing people, leads to real life violence. Young children in particular are vulnerable to this. Just as behavioural therapists commonly desensitize people with irrational phobias by slowly increasing contact with the very thing they are afraid of, so inhibitions about the use of violence in real life are gradually reduced by letting people watch violence in the safe atmosphere of their own homes. This process is aided by showing the act of aggression but not the consequences of the act. We are led to believe that violence is excitement, not primarily suffering and pain. It is strange that it should be necessary to prove the effect of media violence. We normally accept that what one reads and watches has influence – an assumption fundamental to both advertising and the whole educational system.

Child soldiers

Iranian children have been used to clear mine fields, accepting death as religious martyrdom. During offensives, draftees and volunteers alike are sent out by the thousands, just to deplete the Iraqi stock of ammunition. In Nicaragua, both the Sandinistas and the Contras have admitted dependence on child soldiers.

In Uganda, 3000 out of Presi-dent Museveni's 20,000-strong National Resistance Army are children under the age of 15. Many of them were orphaned during former President Obote's attempts to wipe out the Buganda tribe living in the Luwero triangle: 300,000 people were slaughtered. The children who survived were taken in by the NRA, given shelter, food, clothing and military training. Museveni acknowledged that children as young as 5 were trained, and that 8-year-olds were involved in the fighting.

Many of these children have become hardened to violence. Now that the fighting seems at last to be over, the new government is having great difficulties resettling the children, most of whom have never been to school, and cannot remember a time when their purpose in life was not revenge.

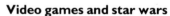

Video games and star wars

In this age of microelectronics, killing and destruction have become increasingly removed from the aggressors. Targets can be obliterated from great distances, absolving the attacker from the moral implications of his actions. It is this same technology which has made violent video games, via home computers, available to children. According to Ariel Dorfman, those who play video games "do so in the same society which contemplates mass murder as deterrence, corpses as statistics, 40 million dead as victory, permanent escalation as peace. Their remoteness from what their fingers are pressing . . . is just a minor product and prolongation of the general remoteness of a system that has lost its capacity for caring about, or even believing in the reality of, other human beings."

Pressures on the environment

Even in peace time, technological developments and larger standing armies have led to greater military demands on land and resources. The testing of nuclear weapons, missiles and other modern munitions requires large areas of land. Nuclear testing especially, as in the Pacific renders the land uninhabitable for many species, and many generations. And the disposal, often at sea, of large quantities of redundant munitions, frequently containing toxic chemicals, has severe effects on the marine environment.

The military is a heavy user of some raw materials. According to two Norwegian researchers, H. Hveem and R. Malnes: "In certain years the military accounted for more than 40 per cent of the US consumption of titanium and thallium, more than 30 per cent of germanium and thorium, and more than 20 per cent of garnet, cobalt and copper." In addition, the military accounts for about 6 per cent of global petroleum consumption – a waste equivalent to over half of all commercial energy used in world agriculture.

The direct environmental impact of the military in peace time is trivial compared with the carnage and destruction done during war. Vietnam, Afghanistan and the Lebanon are dramatic examples of the devastation modern warfare brings, not only to the infrastructure of civilization but also to agriculture, the natural environment and the livestock and wildlife associated with them. The economy and farming base of war zones are utterly wrecked, disease spreads, and any efforts at environmental repair become impossible.

The damage spreads outward. War generates refugees, and as people flee they often unwittingly export an added cost to the environment. Large numbers of displaced people struggling to survive put pressure on fragile ecosystems – a phenomenon that has been seen at its most graphic in north-west Pakistan. Trees have almost entirely disappeared, cut down for firewood, and the refugees' flocks of animals have overgrazed marginal lands – accelerating the soil erosion and general ecological degradation already in process. Where refugees have sought shelter in cities, they have heightened the already serious problems of explosive urban growth – crowding, poverty, pollution and the breakdown of public services.

Environmental damage itself is a cause of conflict. In key areas of superpower tension – Central America, the Horn of Africa, Iran and Afghanistan – political instability can be indirectly linked with soil erosion and reduced crop yields. A report on the state of the environment in El Salvador, prepared by USAID in 1982, declared that the "fundamental causes of the present conflict are as much environmental as political, stemming from problems of resource distribution in an overcrowded land". Inequitable land distribution, and loss of livelihood through erosion and deforestation, create ideal breeding grounds for conflict and strife. Environmental refugees now outnumber those fleeing persecution and war; their rising tide spreads land pressure and instability further and further afield.

The environmental cost

Environmental degradation, and arguments over "ownership" of shared renewable resources, are becoming increasingly important causes of civil and international tension. When tensions escalate into conflict, the environment is put under even greater pressure. This leads to more conflict, and so the circle continues. . .

Yet measures to protect the environment usually have a lower budgetary priority than military expenditure. Governments caught in this cycle find themselves having to cope with food riots as well as hosting huge numbers of refugees and migrant workers.

War is not only waged against all humanity. From a Gaian perspective, war is environmental rape. Local ecosystems are, at best disregarded victims or, at worst, outright military targets of our hostilities.

4 War

Peace time costs: testing in the Pacific

During the period 1945 to 1984, no fewer than 1522 nuclear test explosions were conducted, of which 461 were above ground. The Pacific Ocean, often called the backyard of the nuclear arms race, is a favourite weapons testing site. Not only is it huge and remote, but it is a highly strategic area, housing many military bases. The true effects of nuclear testing on both the environment and the local population have only recently become public knowledge, and in some cases it has taken years for the symptoms of radiation-linked illnesses to become apparent. A 1976 report showed that 69% of children in Rongelap in the Marshall Islands who were under 10 at the time of the 1954 Bravo tests have since developed thyroid tumours. Other people have been forcibly relocated from their islands, to avoid contamination. Unfortunately, wildlife has not had that opportunity: the Pacific region has the highest rate of species extinction per capita in the world.

Ethiopia and the Sahel

Ever since the early 1970s, the inhabitants of the wide belt of African states in the Sahel have been the victims of periodic drought, hunger, desertification and social unrest. Forced to migrate southwards because of the failure of the land to support their growing numbers, throngs of nomadic pastoralists, with their herds and flocks, have come into conflict with farmers in the south. Often these "environmental refugees" cross national borders in search of a livelihood. Well-supported speculation suggests that such migrations, often triggered by population increase and environmental decline, have contributed to much civil unrest. Inside Ethiopia itself, evidence of such a link is strong. Researchers noted that the loss of soil in the country's highland farming areas in the early 1970s led to food shortages, provoking riots in cities, and bringing about the downfall of the Emperor Haile Selassie. Since then ecological damage has increased, especially in rebel strongholds in the north.

1 Environmental depletion and damage

2 Tension

3 Conflict

The Gulf war

The Gulf war between Iran and Iraq, in the 7 years up to 1987, has caused severe environmental damage. Quite apart from the physical destruction at the front, the war has led to the disruption of the unique lifestyle of the Marsh Arabs in southern Iraq, a community that had lived in harmony with wildlife and its aquatic environment for countless generations. Even more injurious has been the deprivation caused in rural Iran by the call-up of millions of young men, thus robbing farms of labour. In the waters of the Persian Gulf itself, devastation has mainly been caused by huge oil spills from damaged wells. Most commercial fishing in the area has been suspended. Dead fish, birds, turtles and dolphins have been washed up on to beaches; almost the entire Gulf population of the dugong has been wiped out. The whole Gulf community is now at risk.

Vietnam – ravaged by war

During the Vietnam War, the US used about 14 million tons of high explosives in aircraft bombs, artillery shells and other weapons. Between 10 and 15 million large bomb craters were created in South Vietnam alone, pockmarking the landscape and disrupting agriculture and forestry. These craters, which covered about 100,000 ha, became filled with stagnant rain water, forming ideal breeding sites for malarial mosquitoes.

In addition, about 100,000 tons of chemical warfare agents, such as defoliants and CS gas, were used in Vietnam. Anti-plant agents were deposited over an estimated 1.7 million ha. This was partly to kill off food crops, and partly to destroy the forest cover in which the Viet Cong forces could hide. The total cost to South Vietnam's forests has been put at 15 million cubic metres of marketable timber, worth $150 million. But the overall cost to the Vietnamese people, in economic, social and health terms, is incalculable.

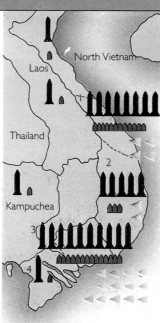

1-4 Military zones in South Vietnam

Bomb and shell duds (in 100,000s)

Munitions fired (100 kg/ha)

Herbicides sprayed (litres/ha)

The Lebanon

Years of civil war in the Lebanon have reduced what used to be one of the most beautiful countries of the Mediterranean to a pale shadow of its former self. Sustained bombardment of Beirut, and street fighting, have shattered what was once the most prosperous centre in the Middle East. Some 40% of the Lebanese population are homeless, and inflation is now running in excess of 100%. Only the black market thrives, which has put control of the economy into the hands of the war profiteers and militias, who smuggle what the central authorities provide.

The majority of the Lebanese people have been reduced to unprecedented hardship. The 1987 minimum wage has only 5% of the purchasing power of its 1983 value. Reconstruction of the economy could cost up to $50 billion. The government has little time or money to address the problems of protecting the environment.

The vicious circle of decline and conflict is fuelled by the gravest environmental cost of military spending – the waste of funds, skills and attention that are desperately needed elsewhere, and the neglect of human and environmental security.

Lost opportunities – gone forever?

Resources spent by the military are lost to civilian use. In the past forty years, we have missed chance after chance in favour of this unproductive expense, with serious consequences to the social and economic wellbeing for all of us – especially the poor.

The developed countries spend more on the military than on either health or education. Huge military expenditures have adverse consequences on domestic economies – employment, productivity, inflation – and also eat into the amount of money that is available for foreign economic aid. The diversion of a mere 5 per cent of the military budget of these richer nations would more than double annual overseas aid.

In developing countries, the use of scarce foreign currency reserves to buy weapons is an even worse waste. It fuels debt, leads to adverse balances of payment, and so seriously hampers development. And the trend is accelerating, with many poor countries devoting a substantial and increasing fraction of their budgets to the military. The military spending of developing countries with per capita GNPs of less than $1000 is now more than two and a half times all the money they receive in development aid. Overall, developing countries spend more on the military sector than on health and education combined – despite the desperate need for both. Obviously, it is the poorest countries that can least afford to waste money on the military and whose people suffer most.

But even the superpowers cannot afford to spend year after year significant percentages of their annual GNPs (about 6 per cent in the USA and about 12 per cent in the USSR) on the military. High military budgets in the USSR are threatening Secretary-General Gorbachev's ambitious short-term and, even more, his long-term economic reform plans. In America, the huge budget deficit, now running at about $200 billion a year, is risking the stability of the world economy.

Deepened by military spending, the US deficit contributes to high interest rates that have direct consequences both for its own economy and for debtor countries in the South. But the debt crisis also has more direct links with the arms race (*see pp. 112-13*). Between 1974 and 1985, developing countries increased their external debt by some $580 billion; in the same period, over 40 per cent of this went to import $250 billions worth of armaments.

Military spending is a powerful stimulus to inflation, too, and this causes economic disruption and political instability, triggering further arms purchases. Inflation, debts, and economic instability can be exported. The world economy is interdependent and it is hard for trading countries to prevent ills elsewhere from spreading to their own economies.

Lost opportunities 1: Then and now

As World War II drew to its close, a group of world leaders sketched out a vision: a phoenix rising out of the ashes of conflict, that would be the United Nations of all peoples working in co-operation to further peace.

Now, 40 years on, the dream has been clouded by reality. Far from disarming, we have built up nuclear arsenals that threaten global destruction. The population has more than doubled, and the gap between rich and poor has worsened. Tension and conflict are rife in a world where, despite much advance, millions still die unnecessarily of hunger and disease. And in the vortex of all this turbulence, faced with a seemingly impossible task, is the United Nations. How have we lost the opportunities of these 40 years, and what now is our hope for the future?

The UN: noble aims

The preamble to the Charter of the UN begins: "We the peoples of the United Nations, determined to save succeeding generations from the scourge of war . . . and to promote social progress and better standards of life in larger freedom." From the start, the twin goals of disarmament and development were there. Yet the arms race grew and development languished. In the 1980s, the UN worked on disarmament and development links. In August 1987, the US boycotted a UN conference on those links, saying they were based on a false premise. But over a hundred other countries agreed with the UN, that until the world proceeds more resolutely towards disarmament, sustainable development cannot be achieved.

THEN 1947	Military cost – steps down 1-5
Forty years ago, most of today's "developing countries" were still under colonial rule. Although considerably poorer than the rich world, they were fairly self-sufficient, and unencumbered by debt. As new countries, led by India, began to win independence, expectations grew. But economic aid was channelled instead to the battered nations of Western Europe and subsequently Japan, to build a strong counterweight to the Soviet bloc as the Cold War set in. As the new countries began to acquire armies, loans turned	1 Current military spending is equivalent to the current GNPs of all the countries where the poorest half of the world's population lives.
into a nightmare debt and the economic gap widened. In 1900, the average person in the North owned 4 times as much as a person in the South. By 1970 the ratio of wealth had become 40:1.	

Missed credit – steps up 1-5

5 As many as 700 million people are chronically hungry. Their plight could be eliminated if more money was spent on adequate and equitable distribution of food.

4 Nearly 1 billion adults, 60% women, are still illiterate. In developing countries, 30% of children aged 6 to 11, and 60% aged 12 to 17, do not attend school.

3 In an industrialized society, every billion dollars invested in the service industries would create about 51,000 more jobs than it would in the defence sector.

2 Poor countries now spend 3 times as much on arms as would be needed to provide health care, clean water and sanitation.

1 Every year, 13 million children die unnecessarily from hunger and disease. Their deaths could be avoided if primary health care was adequately funded, and dietary supplements were made available.

What could have been achieved?

It is difficult to visualize the world we might be living in now had not so many opportunities been lost to military spending. But we know for sure that the unmet needs of the developing world need never have arisen. At a mere fraction of what we spend on arms we could afford to: eliminate hunger; provide basic primary health care, including immunization of all children against the 6 most common contagious diseases; eradicate diseases such as malaria; supply clean water to every household; halt the spread of deserts; make contraceptives freely available to all; reduce unemployment; and meet the educational needs of all.

These are just some of the goals we have forsaken in the name of national security. The final irony is that the more we spend on defence, the greater the risk of annihilation.

Weighing the costs

The costs of the enormous expansion in military power extend far beyond dollars or war deaths. In terms of opportunities lost, of sheer human misery and wastage, they are incalculable. Consider the one billion people who live in absolute poverty, the thousands engaged in useless military pursuits, the wastage of the Earth's reserves, and the environmental degradation that continues. Yet when we look for the political will to implement change, we see that democracy itself is threatened by militarism. Half the governments in the South are controlled by the military, and 90% of their people do not have full voting rights.

NOW 1987

There are now almost 160 members of the UN – 3 times its 1945 level. But the gulf between rich and poor continues to grow. About 800 million people are starving or malnourished; 800 million are also without minimal health care. In developing countries, only 2 out of every 5 people have easy access to safe water, and 1 in 4 to proper sanitation. In the worst cases, such as Afghanistan and Burkina Faso, 1 in 5 babies die before reaching their first birthday. Yet the birth rate is still extremely high, especially in Africa and South Asia, adding new pressures in a world whose population has already topped 5 billion. Meanwhile the escalation in military spending goes on, devouring resources that could otherwise be spent on improving the quality of life. Though superpower dominance of the arms race is as strong as ever, the developing world is taking up a growing share of total spending. Almost all the wars since 1945 have been in developing countries; nearly 20 million have been killed. Yet as many as 20 times that number have died from neglect, the victims of starvation and/or disease. Less easy to quantify are the many millions who are debilitated or damaged, not only from wars but also from disease, hunger and poverty.

2 At present levels of military expenditure, the average person can expect to give up 3-4 years of his/her working life to pay for it.

3 Since 1960, military spending in the developing world has increased 6-fold, in constant prices, while unemployment has risen 8-fold.

4 Developed countries now spend on average about 5.4% of their GNP for military purposes, as opposed to giving 0.3% in aid to the developing countries.

5 Over 100 million people are working for various war ministries around the world – almost the same as Europe's working population.

Unemployment, poverty and militarism

High military expenditure is often justified by claims that it creates jobs and stimulates economies. But there is unequivocal research evidence that, in fact, it does neither. A whole series of conversion studies in the US, Britain and elsewhere have shown that, dollar for dollar, government spending on the military creates far *fewer* jobs than would equivalent public money spent on, say, health and services. According to the US Bureau of Labor Statistics, one billion dollars spent in education rather than on the military would create 111,000 more jobs. The military industry is capital intensive and becoming ever more so, offering less and less employment.

Military ambitions have produced a certain level of schizophrenia among Western politicians, particularly those who espouse a monetarist economic doctrine. On the one hand they blame inflation and unemployment on excessive public deficits, and on the other they press for higher military expenditure (which increases public sector deficits), saying that it will help to *reduce* unemployment. Military industries are able to exploit this warped logic to their own advantage.

According to Ruth Sivard, unemployment since 1960 has increased about fourfold in developed countries and eightfold in poorer ones. ILO estimates of world unemployment run at 90 million people, with a further 300 million underemployed. Lack of work is the major cause of poverty, which itself is the root of the problems of the environment and human need. Unless governments recognize that militarism will only exacerbate this socially explosive problem, worse is likely to follow.

Military spending is also sometimes justified on the grounds of the so-called "spin-off" from military research and development (R and D). In the past there has been some significant spin-off to the civilian sector. But today, this is small in terms of the amount of resources devoted to military R and D, and is diminishing as the gap between military and civilian technology grows wider. It is becoming increasingly difficult to adapt military technologies to civilian use: modern weapons use specialist and complex technologies, and much more expensive raw materials and workmanship than civilian products, for which cost is a crucial factor.

The resources devoted to military R and D are then, by and large, of no value to civilian production. These resources are huge. The world's governments give about $100 billion a year to military science, much more than they give to civilian science. Britain, for example, devotes 55 per cent of government R and D spending to the military. But even more damaging is the waste of the world's most skilled scientists.

The number of research scientists and engineers in the world is about 2.5 million. A half million, or 20 per cent, of these are employed in military science. In addition, about half of an estimated 850,000 people working on space activities are engaged in military work. The use of so many skilled people by military

Lost opportunities 2: Fulfilling basic needs

Every 6 seconds, at least one child dies and another is severely disabled by disease. Yet for the equivalent of what the world spends in 6 hours on defence, this could be avoided.

Though often stated, the facts are plain. Governments in the South give higher priority to arms than to health and education combined. In 1984, a year of famine and drought, Africa spent more on importing arms than importing food. These arms purchases eat into scarce foreign currency reserves, increasing the burden of debt and depriving millions of the basic necessities of life.

It is the rural poor who suffer most. In some developing countries, health care scarcely exists. Infant mortality rates are nearly 10 times higher than in the North, and life expectancy at birth is almost 30 years shorter. Literacy too is a serious problem, especially for women who do not have the same educational opportunities as men.

Unfortunately, statistics quantifying the scale of neglect could easily fill these pages. But behind the statistics we must not forget the millions of people they represent – people living in desperate poverty, denied the richness of life through illiteracy and ill health.

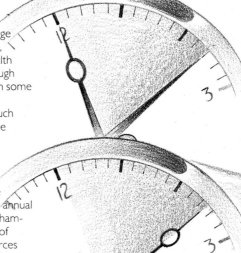

35 seconds
For a million dollars, 1000 classrooms could be provided for 30,000 children. Or storage facilities could be improved to save an extra 4000 tons of rice a year – enough to feed 22,000 people over the same period.

12 minutes
For $20 million, 40,000 village pharmacies could be set up, revolutionizing primary health care in the rural areas. Though this has already happened in some countries like China, most developing countries lack such facilities, let alone preventive medicine.

2½ hours
That's how long it takes the military to spend the entire annual budget of WHO. WHO is hampered in its work by a lack of adequate funds. If its resources were doubled, the organization could increase its co-ordinating work not only in controlling the effects of specific diseases but, more importantly, in preventive care and research, including giving AIDS the attention it deserves.

3 weeks

The cost of 3 weeks' arms spending would pay for primary health care for all children in the developing world, including full immunization against the 6 most common infectious diseases (at $5 per child) and access to safe water. This would be a sound investment, guaranteeing a far healthier future working population, in a better position to help its country's development.

12 days

WHO says that the number of water taps per 1000 persons is a better indication of health than the number of hospital beds. At the beginning of the 1980s, 71% of people living in rural areas of the South were without clean water. For $30 billion a year they could have it.

7 days

Hunger is still a killer for children in the developing world. Even those who survive may be permanently impaired by malnutrition. Yet for just the equivalent of a week's military spending, we could supply basic food needs for every child.

12 hours

One half-day's worth of world arms spending would be enough to finance the whole malaria eradication programme of WHO. Much less would be needed to wipe out river blindness.

10 hours

A billion dollars is approximately what it would take to reduce the projected global population peak by 1 billion people – simply by making contraception available to the estimated 80 million women who want it, but cannot obtain it.

6 hours

The death of 5 million children from diarrhoea could be avoided each year if $700 million was spent on bringing oral rehydration therapy to the developing world.

Defusing the bomb

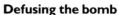

World military spending is running currently at about $1.7 million a minute. But whereas time is constant, arms spending is on the increase. So too are the problems which are not being properly tackled, partly because resources are not available: health care and the meeting of other basic needs being the most obvious. The bomb illustrated, *centre*, represents just over 10% (41 days) of annual world military expenditure, i.e. $100 billion. Segments of the bomb have been pulled out to highlight just how much could be achieved from the diversion of comparatively small fractions of military expenditure. The clockface represents 12 hours' spending – as a segment of the bomb it occupies about 1%.

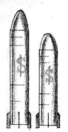

2½ months

Given the current level of the world's population, and the improved farming methods available, we should not have to accept the situation where 20% of the world's people go consistently hungry. Hunger could be ended by the year 2000 if sufficient action was taken now in helping developing countries to restructure their own agricultural production, as well as improving storage and transport facilities. There are many obstacles but, as usual, a lack of financial resources is the key impediment. Properly spent, $200 billion could wipe hunger off the face of the Earth.

science is one reason why development in the South is so slow. The loss of human skill may well have a more serious impact on the ambitions of developing nations than the loss of money spent on the military.

Wasting human skills

Developed countries that lock up much innovative talent in military science also seriously damage their own economies. Professor Lloyd J. Dumas, the American expert on this subject, blames America's poor economic performance, compared with, for example, that of Japan, on this diversion. He points out that as the USA spent more on military R and D, there was a rapid decline in the number of American innovations. This is reflected in a very low rate of annual growth in manufacturing productivity. Between 1960 and 1980, the rate in the USA was 2.5 per cent; in Japan it was 9 per cent. The percentage of government R and D funds given to the military is in inverse proportion: in Japan it was 2 per cent; in the USA, 60 per cent.

The contrast is stark. And Dumas is in no doubt about the reasons for it. "It is not the failure of technology as a whole that produced our present productivity problems – the [American] scientific and engineering community is not becoming less ingenious or less productive. Rather the collapse is a direct, inevitable, though long-term, result of the decades-long diversion of a large fraction of the nation's critical scientific and engineering effort from productive civilian technological development to military research and development." But the major and urgent needs of the South – to deal with food crises, disasters, pollution, and the effects of war and urbanization; to develop new sources of energy and raw materials while preserving current resources and the environment; and to reduce poverty, improve health standards, diet, education and housing – are in immediate competition with the military for claims on capital investment, research and development skills.

Development experts now agree that the developing world would be unwise to adopt the route followed by older industrial nations. Research into and the development of suitable technologies for use in the South may be the most useful single contribution that could be made to development there. Many of these innovations – such as the improvement of food supplies and their preservation, the design of more appropriate cheap energy sources, the control of pollution, the creation of cheap but adequate housing, and the wide-scale prevention of disease – involve the systematic, large-scale and purpose-orientated approaches that military scientists are renowned for.

Many of the opportunities we have lost to militarism are quantifiable, in clear economic and environmental deficits. But the fear and hostility, the damage to democracy and human rights, and the sheer human suffering of the estimated one billion people left in absolute poverty, who are the legacy of a wasteful and uncontrolled arms race, cannot be measured.

Lost opportunities 3: Environment and development

Degradation of the biosphere is one of the few things keeping up with or even outstripping the rate of increase in arms expenditure. Together they threaten the very existence of human life and civilization on Earth. But the likelihood of sufficient resources being made available for both environmental protection and development in the South is remote, so long as the growing demands of the military are satisfied. This is a fundamental problem to be faced both by the rich North – which must choose between the arms race and sustainable development – and by the poor South – which must evaluate its own spending priorities. As long as all our finances and best expertise are drained by militarism, we cannot even begin to plan for an environmentally sustainable future.

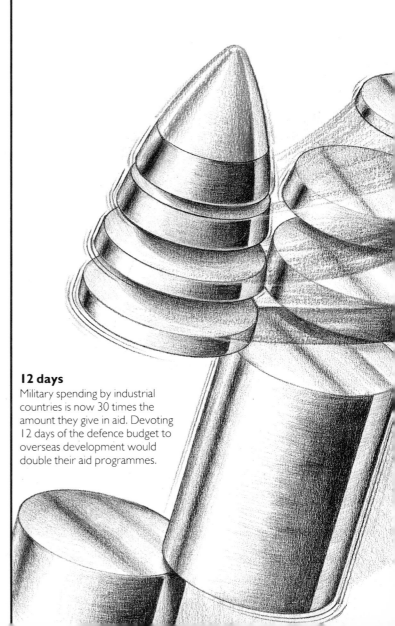

12 days
Military spending by industrial countries is now 30 times the amount they give in aid. Devoting 12 days of the defence budget to overseas development would double their aid programmes.

1 min = $1.7 million

1 min 10 sec = $2 million – enough to double the WWF's annual contribution to the IUCN's environmental programmes

1 min 32 sec = $2.6 million – enough for UNEP's Oceans and Coastal Areas Programme to combat pollution

1 min 46 sec = $3 million – the cost of co-ordinating the international CITES programme

5 minutes

The cost of protecting endangered species from illegal trade and funding additional field projects is $5 million a year. The UNEP budget for combating pollution in the oceans is $2.6 million a year. All this could be achieved for $8 million, 5 minutes' worth of arms spending.

Half an hour

The environmental breakdown and food shortages in Ethiopia and Somalia could have been avoided for $50 million a year (10% of the annual cost of relief measures) as part of the UN Anti-Desertification Plan in the late 1970s.

12 hours

The World Bank has come up with an Action Plan for Tropical Forests, budgeted at $1.3 billion a year (half a day's military spending) over 5 years.

1 day 20 hours

The Brandt Commission estimated that 0.5% of arms spending would pay for all the farm equipment needed to enable low-income, food-deficit countries to achieve self-sufficiency.

Militarism vs manufacturing

"Guns or butter" is a choice many governments have had to make, but as the graph, *right*, shows, high defence spending also corresponds to low growth in manufacturing productivity. The arms industry is capital-intensive, but creates relatively few jobs.

2 days

Deserts are encroaching on to marginal lands, causing some people to move to the cities. The UN plan to counter this would cost $4.5 billion a year, or 2 days of military expenditure.

Global R and D expenditure

The globe, *below*, represents world expenditure on research and development. The sums devoted to military R and D far exceed those for any other civilian research objective. In 1985 it stood at about $80 billion – about 24% of global R and D spending. World military R and D expenditure is dominated by the two superpowers.

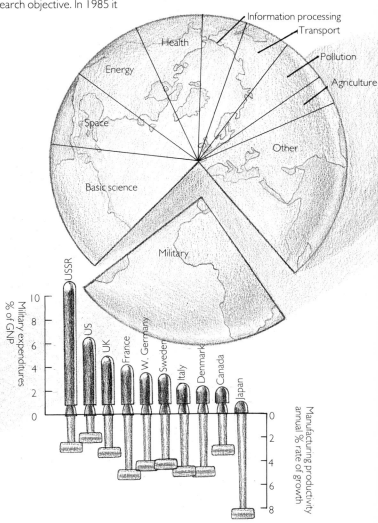

Environmental decline

The UN Environment Programme (UNEP), based in Nairobi, has a limited budget to help combat environmental decline. But it is prepared to set up new projects if individual nations divert some of their military expenditure to environmental protection. Eligible countries include China, Peru and Argentina, which have all cut back on military activities.

Agricultural resource base

Farming and livestock-rearing areas in many countries are being destroyed or severely damaged through bad management, overgrazing and environmental abuse. Unfettered, such action renders fragile lands useless. Preventive action is a good investment. It would have cost just one-tenth of the amount spent on relief in the Sahel to have averted the disaster.

Pollution

About 85% of West Germany's forests are damaged by acid rain. Oxides of sulphur and nitrogen, mainly from power stations, and hydrocarbons emitted in car exhaust fumes, are the chief culprits. But countries accused of creating pollution from their power stations plead an inability to pay the huge costs of controls. Pollution controls are almost non-existent in the South.

Debt

Annual global military expenditure is almost exactly equal to the whole foreign debt of the South (*see also pp. 112-13*). That debt threatens the world's economic system and general security, but could be cleared in 20 years by devoting 10% of arms spending to debt relief. Meanwhile, arms imports by developing countries increased their burden of debt: by 40% between 1975 and 1985.

Transnational threats to security

"We travel together, passengers on a little spaceship, dependent upon its vulnerable reserves of air and soil, committed for our safety to its security and peace . . . We cannot maintain it half-fortunate, half miserable, half confident, half despairing, half free in a liberation of resources undreamed of until this day, half slave to the ancient enemies of man. No craft, no crew, can travel safely with such vast contradictions. On their resolution depends the survival of us all." Adlai Stevenson, 1965.

Nations perceive it as their sovereign right and duty to defend their peoples. But in the pursuit of this "security" we have neglected wider, and growing threats that are not amenable to military, nor to national, solutions. We cannot shoot a cloud of acid pollution; nor can one nation prevent the climate change that will damage world agriculture. It will take a fundamental shift to a more co-operative, caring and equitable global society for us to address such trans-national threats to our security.

The demographic trap

Many of the worsening non-military threats to security are linked to the rapidly increasing world population. It is not that we lack enough food to feed the people or the technology to develop cheap energy, supply safe water, or provide health services and housing. The problem is that consumption, and the distribution of wealth, are inequitable, and the bulk of population growth is afflicting countries least able to cope with it – in the world's most impoverished regions.

In the North, population growth is slow or almost non-existent. With rising living standards, higher per capita incomes and lower infant mortality rates, the desire for large families is reduced. We can say that a state of demographic equilibrium (ie. births in equilibrium with deaths) has been reached.

But in the South, many countries find themselves caught in a demographic trap, unable to achieve a state of equilibrium. With low living standards, high infant mortality, and lack of any social security, high birth rates persist. Poverty and rising numbers put great strain on the carrying capacity of the land, leading to environmental degradation and a fall in food production per capita. Population growth and environmental decline reinforce each other, and the country becomes locked in a downward spiral.

Sheer population pressure *per se* has not yet caused significant violence in or between countries. But violence has come from factors affected by rising numbers – intensified competition for resources, for example, and breakdown of social infrastructure, economic stress and associated unemployment – problems greatly compounded by inequitable distribution of wealth and land.

A characteristic of rapidly expanding populations is the preponderance of the young. This alone puts

Population insecurity

The world's human population increased from 1.6 billion in 1900 to 2.5 billion in 1950 and 5 billion in 1987. The median forecast for 2025 is 8.2 billion. Most of the increase is anticipated in the South, which could almost double its population in the next 40 years from 3.8 billion to 7 billion. Such scenarios assume, of course, that life-support systems do not collapse, that we avoid a nuclear world war, and that no unforeseen disease occurs – the advent of AIDS, alone, could decimate humanity.

Rapid population increase is extremely destabilizing, while cross-border population pressures pose wider security threats. Globally, the impact on ecosystems is profound. Even with a relatively optimistic view of natural resources and technology, it is obvious that either the world birth rate has to go down, or the death rate will go up.

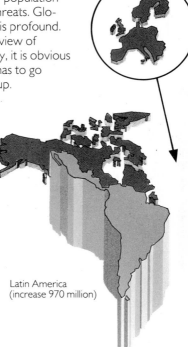

Europe
(increase 113 million)

USA and Canada
(increase 97 million)

The age factor

In 1980, only 23% of the population in the North, but 39% in the South, were under 15 – approaching child-bearing and working age. The youth bulge in the South means faster population growth, and huge numbers of youngsters flooding the labour market. Providing jobs will require major revisions in government policies and huge costs (an estimate of $1 trillion for the Caribbean for 1985-2000). In the North, a smaller working-age group will have to support large numbers of old people.

Latin America
(increase 970 million)

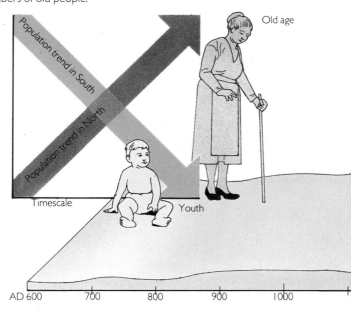

Population trend in South

Population trend in North

Old age

Youth

Timescale

AD 600   700   800   900   1000

Shifting population pressures

Percentage increases in population will vary considerably between regions, and even between ethnic sectors within states. Particular tensions may arise where developed countries border on developing countries. The strategic consequences to the USSR, for example, of having a national population expected to stabilize at only 377 million, up to 40% of them Muslim, while perhaps 3 billion people press its southern and eastern borders, will become greater than the perceived threat from NATO.

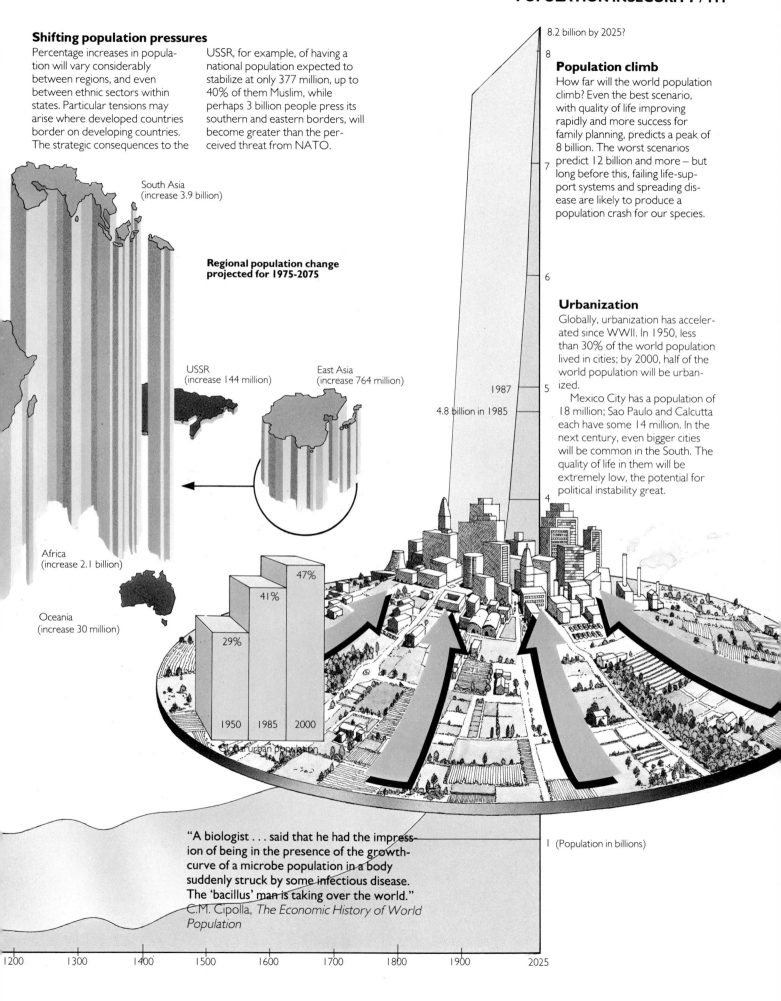

8.2 billion by 2025?

South Asia
(increase 3.9 billion)

Regional population change projected for 1975-2075

USSR
(increase 144 million)

East Asia
(increase 764 million)

Africa
(increase 2.1 billion)

Oceania
(increase 30 million)

47%

41%

29%

1950   1985   2000

Global urban population

1987

4.8 billion in 1985

Population climb

How far will the world population climb? Even the best scenario, with quality of life improving rapidly and more success for family planning, predicts a peak of 8 billion. The worst scenarios predict 12 billion and more – but long before this, failing life-support systems and spreading disease are likely to produce a population crash for our species.

Urbanization

Globally, urbanization has accelerated since WWII. In 1950, less than 30% of the world population lived in cities; by 2000, half of the world population will be urbanized.

Mexico City has a population of 18 million; Sao Paulo and Calcutta each have some 14 million. In the next century, even bigger cities will be common in the South. The quality of life in them will be extremely low, the potential for political instability great.

1 (Population in billions)

"A biologist . . . said that he had the impression of being in the presence of the growth-curve of a microbe population in a body suddenly struck by some infectious disease. The 'bacillus' man is taking over the world."
C.M. Cipolla, *The Economic History of World Population*

1200   1300   1400   1500   1600   1700   1800   1900   2025

marked strain on social institutions such as schools, making a mockery of education systems. When population growth outstrips local economic growth (for whatever reason), a steady decline in living standards is accompanied by mass youth unemployment. Large numbers of disaffected youths make ideal recruits for subnational groups, bent on directing violence at those they hold responsible for their plight.

Future populations may be so large in some areas that population pressure itself could be the cause of violence. Religious, ethnic and cultural differences are less likely to be tolerated in overcrowded conditions. Mass migrations from poorer to richer regions may be attempted, with security implications for nations in the North. Already about a million illegal Mexican migrants are believed to enter the USA each year in search of work and a better living.

A higher standard of living is also the reason for mass internal migrations in the South, from the rural areas to the cities. Whether environmental refugees from degraded areas, or dispossessed farmers forced off the land by powerful interests in agriculture, the migrants exacerbate the growing urban problems.

Imagination balks at the size of the metropolises of the 21st century. According to the UN, cities with populations several times greater than that of a small European country will be commonplace in the South. Some demographers contest these projections on the grounds that intolerable conditions will halt the influx. Certainly, until we supply basic services most inhabitants will live in shanty towns in severe poverty. The potential for violence is obvious.

The growing gap

While the world population has tripled since 1900, the gross world product has gone up 20 times. Measured in constant 1980 dollars, the gross product rose from $600 billion in 1900 (about the same as France's GNP today) to about $13 thousand billion in 1986.

This large increase in output of goods and services has been created by technological advance and abundant cheap energy. Though military spending absorbs more and more, the world is undoubtedly richer overall. The problem is that the wealth is unevenly shared. Today, 80 per cent of the gross world product is consumed by the richest 20 per cent of the population.

One in five people in the world live in absolute poverty. Without income to buy fuel, they must scour the land to gather it, or remain cold and ill fed. Without income, they may starve, though food may be on sale. Without income, they may have to watch a sick child die, though doctors and medicines are available. And without a sustainable livelihood, they are forced to exhaust the land on which their survival depends.

An economic gap between North and South is not a new phenomenon – it has been with us ever since the European nations first began to industrialize. But the gap has grown wider since the mid-1970s. Up until then, incomes had been rising significantly in nearly all countries. Continual economic growth and ever-impro-

Economic insecurity

Despite advances in newly industrialized countries, the economic gap between North and South is widening and may soon overtake East-West tension as a major threat to global security. Crippling debt repayments, trade imbalances and protectionism all serve to increase tension – and the situation is exacerbated by a gross inequality of consumption of the world's resources and energy by North and South.

Perceived inequalities within nations also produce economic insecurity. In many poor countries, a powerful elite increases its share of the national wealth at the expense of other sections of society. In rich countries, a growing underclass of unemployed and low-paid unskilled workers exists alongside skilled and increasingly affluent workers. A divided society is not a happy one – a large, alienated underclass may lead to societal upheaval.

The north-south divide in the UK

The United Kingdom is a seriously divided developed society, with old people, unemployed and many low-paid workers living in poverty. A growing degree of inequality in income, wealth, power and opportunity now characterizes British life.

By and large, the south of the country is more affluent than the north. The richer southern regions of the country are alienating those areas that are economically disadvantaged. This trend was reflected in the 1987 General Election result, in which the Conservative government gained a landslide victory in the south, but received virtually no mandate in the north. From this, it becomes increasingly difficult to see Great Britain as a truly "United Kingdom". Government policies that are popular in the wealthier parts of the country do not necessarily reflect the needs of those people living in the more depressed areas. The gap between the rich and poor is widening.

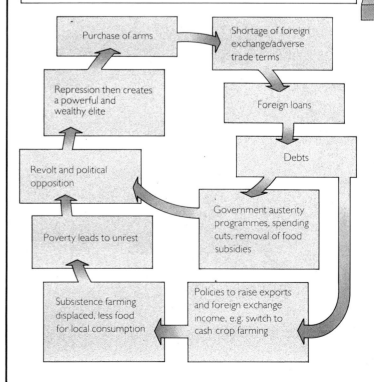

The global financial system

In total, the South owes about a trillion dollars – or roughly what the world now spends on the military in a year. The cost of servicing this debt is becoming increasingly onerous, causing economic stagnation, spreading poverty and ecological decline.

The situation is complicated by the fact that many rich countries also have large debts. The US budget deficit (then about $220 billion a year) was a major factor in the stockmarket crash of 1987. Trade imbalances with Japan and West Germany (which have large trade surpluses) are increasing world economic instability. The pressure of debts in the South, and the spectre of a Northern recession, are threatening financial chaos and profound social disorder. World economic reform is urgently needed.

Commercial energy consumption: North (% of world total)

USA

Other Japan

USSR

Europe

Belgium

USA

Japan

ASIA
Regional debt (1984)
$171 billion

Debt per capita $130
= 34% of GNP per ca

Sri Lanka

LATIN AMERICA
Regional debt (1984) $371 billion

Debt per capita $986
= 52% of GNP per capita

Brazil

AFRICA
Regional debt (1984)
$88 billion

Debt per capita $237
= 35% of GNP per capita

Kenya

Other & Asia

China

Latin America

Africa

Percentage share of household income by poorest 20% and richest 20%

Poorest 20%
Richest 20%
(data 1970 or later)

Commercial energy consumption: South (% of world total)

GNP per capita 1984

$12,501 +

$10,001-12,500

$7501-10,000

$5001-7500

$2501-5000

$1001-2500

$501-1000

$0-500

Total accumulated debt of developing countries = $1035 billion

North/South trade imbalance

Over the last decade, the price of raw materials from the South has fallen significantly. We effectively "undervalue" these goods, compared with manufactured exports from the North (as the arrows notionally show).

Income distribution

The gap between the richest and poorest fifth of population is some measure of a country's concern. In Brazil the poorest 20% command 2% of total income; in wealthy Japan their share is still less than 10%.

Servicing debts

Some countries must use a large fraction of their export earnings just to pay the interest on their external debts. Brazil owes $112 billion; the annual interest on this debt amounts to about 40% of her export earnings.

ving living standards had become the goal of all governments, from the very rich to the very poor. The 1973 rise in oil prices, however, led to a dramatic fall in the rate of expansion of the world economy.

The least stable governments often come under the greatest pressure when living standards are threatened, because other dissatisfactions then surface and cause unrest. This is particularly true for countries with extremes of wealth and poverty. To try to contain this unrest, many governments of developing countries borrowed large sums from foreign banks.

In many cases this strategy succeeded for a time. But escalating interest rates and the sluggishness of the global economy have meant that some countries face great difficulty in meeting their interest payments, let alone their debt repayments. Little of the money was used to protect the land or alleviate rural poverty, and environmental degradation began to take its toll on agriculture, forcing countries to import food – which also contributed to external debt. By the 1980s, many developing countries were increasingly less self-sufficient, more dependent on aid – and, though some resisted, more constrained and controlled by international financiers and more susceptible to manipulation by the rich countries, particularly the superpowers. The resentment caused by the increasing dependence of the poor countries on the rich merely exacerbates North-South tensions.

The debt crisis

The mountain of debt owed by the developing countries threatens the stability of the world's financial system. Since 1975, this debt has increased more than four times; in relation to their overall GNP, it has risen from 9 per cent to a crippling 27 per cent.

The burden of debt is most keenly felt in Africa and Latin America. Sub-Saharan Africa has been badly affected by fluctuating commodity prices in the last decade, compounded by rising debt repayments and interest charges. The industrial world is reluctant to invest in the region, with the result that more capital (ie. resources) is flowing out of the poverty-stricken continent than in.

In Latin America, the scale of the problem is much greater. Of the total world debt of some $1 trillion, about one-third is owed by four countries: Brazil, Mexico, Argentina and Venezuela. These countries have been forced to devote land to cash exports to earn the money to service their debts. Pressures on the environment have increased – not for development, but to meet financial obligations overseas.

Debt is acting like a pump, extracting wealth from the South and transferring it to the Northern banks. Those who pay are the poor, to whom stringencies imposed by indebted governments bring growing despair. As Susan George, in *A Fate Worse than Debt*, comments: "Economic policies are not neutral. Contrary to received opinion, they can even kill."

Creditor banks, increasingly aware of the debtors' predicament, have begun to make provisions – such as

Human insecurity

"An adequate food supply is no longer the source of the problem . . . from among the many forces that conspire to leave almost one person in five in today's world underfed, one stands out above all others: poverty"
World Bank

Poverty today is a major global scourge. It forces people to destroy their immediate environment in order to survive, by cutting down forests, overgrazing pastureland, polluting rivers and overcrowding cities.

The seeds of tomorrow's disasters are already sown. As the rich get richer, the poor get poorer, and the rapid depletion of the Earth's resources by both deprives future generations of their inheritance. We are creating problems to which we have no solutions. The "greenhouse effect", for example, caused by increased carbon dioxide and other greenhouse gases, will not only disrupt agricultural patterns, but also raise sea levels enough to inundate many major low-lying coastal cities.

Human insecurity cannot be solved by a technological "fix". At the heart of the problem are people, ordinary people. Poor people need land that can grow food; employment so that they can climb out of poverty; welfare schemes to fall back on; and a greater say in decisions that affect them. Rich and poor, we need governments that will tackle the roots of poverty before it is too late.

The plight of the refugee

According to the UN, between 12 and 14 million people are international refugees, tragic and forgotten people who have fled, or been expelled from, their home countries. An additional 13 to 16 million are refugees in their own countries. An estimated 2000 people a day become refugees. The bulk of them move between developing countries; the doors of virtually all rich countries are firmly closed. So little attention is paid to these unfortunates that we do not know who or how many they are.

Most refugees are victims either of war or of ecological disaster. Iran has reported that in its war with Iraq about 2 million people have fled from their homes in the battle zone. Some 5 million Ethiopians are believed to have been displaced since 1970 – many because of environmental degradation.

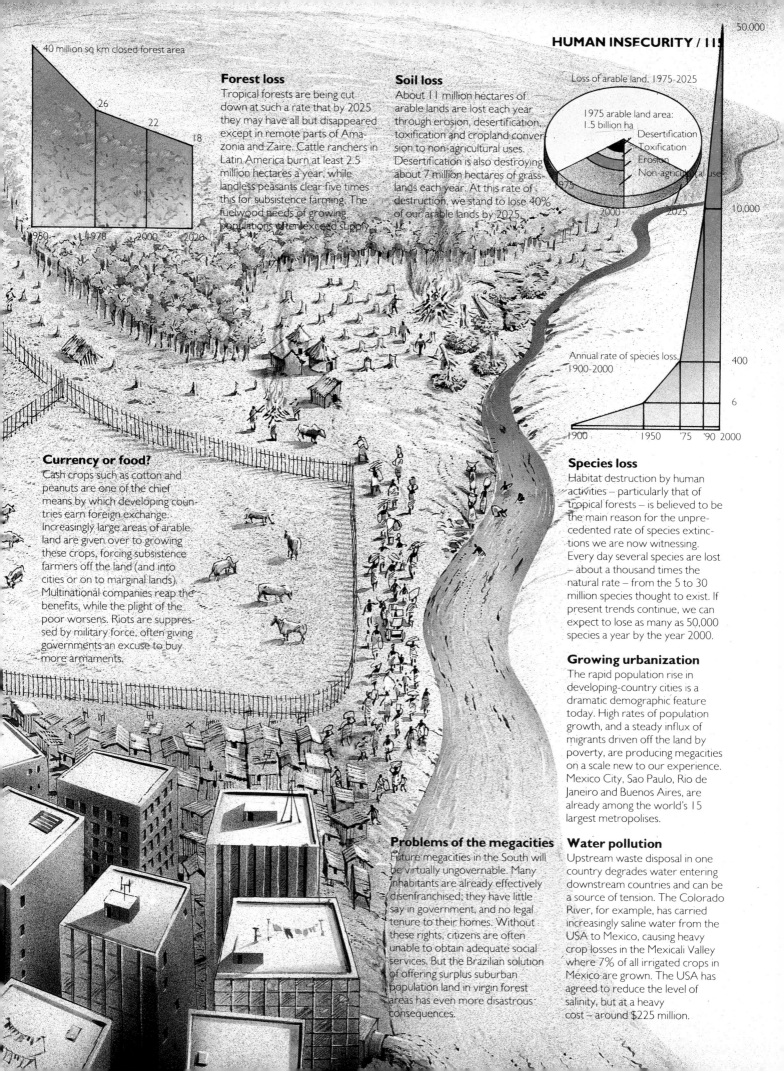

40 million sq km closed forest area

26
22
18

1950   1978   2000   2020

Forest loss

Tropical forests are being cut down at such a rate that by 2025 they may have all but disappeared except in remote parts of Amazonia and Zaire. Cattle ranchers in Latin America burn at least 2.5 million hectares a year, while landless peasants clear five times this for subsistence farming. The fuelwood needs of growing populations often exceed supply.

Soil loss

About 11 million hectares of arable lands are lost each year through erosion, desertification, toxification and cropland conversion to non-agricultural uses. Desertification is also destroying about 7 million hectares of grasslands each year. At this rate of destruction, we stand to lose 40% of our arable lands by 2025.

Loss of arable land, 1975-2025

1975 arable land area:
1.5 billion ha

Desertification
Toxification
Erosion
Non-agricultural use

1975   2000   2025

Currency or food?

Cash crops such as cotton and peanuts are one of the chief means by which developing countries earn foreign exchange. Increasingly large areas of arable land are given over to growing these crops, forcing subsistence farmers off the land (and into cities or on to marginal lands). Multinational companies reap the benefits, while the plight of the poor worsens. Riots are suppressed by military force, often giving governments an excuse to buy more armaments.

50,000

10,000

Annual rate of species loss, 1900-2000

400

6

1900   1950   '75   '90   2000

Species loss

Habitat destruction by human activities – particularly that of tropical forests – is believed to be the main reason for the unprecedented rate of species extinctions we are now witnessing. Every day several species are lost – about a thousand times the natural rate – from the 5 to 30 million species thought to exist. If present trends continue, we can expect to lose as many as 50,000 species a year by the year 2000.

Growing urbanization

The rapid population rise in developing-country cities is a dramatic demographic feature today. High rates of population growth, and a steady influx of migrants driven off the land by poverty, are producing megacities on a scale new to our experience. Mexico City, Sao Paulo, Rio de Janeiro and Buenos Aires, are already among the world's 15 largest metropolises.

Problems of the megacities

Future megacities in the South will be virtually ungovernable. Many inhabitants are already effectively disenfranchised; they have little say in government, and no legal tenure to their homes. Without these rights, citizens are often unable to obtain adequate social services. But the Brazilian solution of offering surplus suburban population land in virgin forest areas has even more disastrous consequences.

Water pollution

Upstream waste disposal in one country degrades water entering downstream countries and can be a source of tension. The Colorado River, for example, has carried increasingly saline water from the USA to Mexico, causing heavy crop losses in the Mexicali Valley where 7% of all irrigated crops in Mexico are grown. The USA has agreed to reduce the level of salinity, but at a heavy cost – around $225 million.

strategic capital restructuring – so that the funds of depositors remain relatively secure. But in 1987, shocks ran through the world economy. In early 1988, one big bank, Barclays, declared a loss. The option of debt rescheduling (basically the postponement of interest payments) is only a short-term palliative. The main official Western solution is the proposal put forward in 1985 by US Secretary of the Treasury, James Baker.

The Baker plan requires: faster growth of OECD markets to take in more exports from the South; more structural adjustment of developing country economies, particularly encouraging private enterprise; and additional lending to developing countries by official (mainly World Bank) and private sources. But critics point out that the Baker policy will lead to a glut of many developing country products (and so deteriorating terms of trade), plus increased exports of agricultural commodities from the South, with grave environmental consequences. The dogma that higher output in the North brings higher output in the South is being increasingly challenged.

The debt crisis goes very deep. Some regard it as a new form of colonialism, enabling the North to control the resources of the South. But rich nations, too, have large debts. And indebtedness permeates all levels of society, from poor farmers to large corporations.

The links with militarism are plain (*see p. 106*). Reductions in military budgets are essential as a first step. Less obvious, but crucial, is the link with our neglect of the environment and of social welfare. Only by investment in the land, or in human potential, can debt be removed long term (*see p. 204-5*). Solutions based on higher growth in *output* only place more pressure on a deteriorating resource base. The "buy now, pay later" attitude will leave a debt for future generations that none can repay.

Resource depletion and environmental stress

Standards of living and, indeed, human survival itself depend on "resources" from the environment. Access to these is a primary security issue. Countries will use force to guarantee it; civil wars arise over it.

Natural resources are conventionally divided into non-renewables (such as soil, water and minerals) and renewables (such as forests, crops and fish). But this distinction is misleading. Soil is a complex life community; water flows are mediated by living plant cover. If the health of the environment is preserved, both are self-renewing. Forests, crops and fish are *not* renewable if over-used. All are subject to the pressures of human exploitation. The very term "resources" shows our misunderstanding of the living world of which we are part.

Conflicts over resources arise when the "carrying capacity" of a given area is exceeded – because human populations grow too large, consumption increases too fast, or we misuse the environment and create, for example, soil degradation and erosion, depletion of

Resource insecurity

We are living beyond our resources, running up a debt to the environment that may bankrupt our children, and is a growing source of conflict.

Land is a fundamental resource. As populations increase, the amount of land per person decreases. At the beginning of this century, there were nine hectares of land per person. By 2000 AD, there will be only two.

Yet in almost every region of the world we are degrading our means of producing food: through erosion in North America, soil acidification in Europe, and deforestation and desertification in Asia, Africa and Latin America. In Central America, an eroded agricultural resource base has contributed to political instability and civil strife.

Another crucial resource is water. Where more than one country depends on the same river, or ground water reserves, supply can be a contentious issue. At least 40% of the world's population live in multinational river basins, and their access to reliable and unpolluted water is central to their security. Transnational water disputes affect the polluted industrial heartlands serviced by the Rhine as much as the populous rural economies supplied by the Nile.

Large holdings as a percentage of:

Total no. of holdings   Total area

Land distribution

Land hunger is caused not by shortage of land, but by inequality of distribution. Large, inefficient estates are frequently situated next to small, overcropped peasant holdings. For Latin America, a large holding is defined as 100 ha or more; for Africa and the Far East, 10 ha or more.

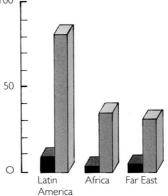

Strategic resources

A prerequisite to national security is self-sufficiency in, or at least minimum dependence on, imported energy sources – notably oil and, increasingly, uranium. Tensions are heightened when potentially hostile or politically unstable regions control supply. Even "contained" disputes between neighbouring countries, such as Iran and Iraq, have wider implications for the superpowers, both of which have keen interests in the region's oil supplies. Even though the US has vast proven reserves of oil, the cost of recovery is such that its interest in the Middle East will remain high.

Oil production is expected to fall off from 2025 as supplies run out. Already states see the need to secure supplies of substitute resources. Namibia, a *de facto* territory of South Africa, is one of the top five uranium-producing states and seen as vital to South Africa's security. It is to this end that the South African army is fighting SWAPO, the Namibian liberation movement, which in turn is supported by Angola, an ally of Cuba and the USSR.

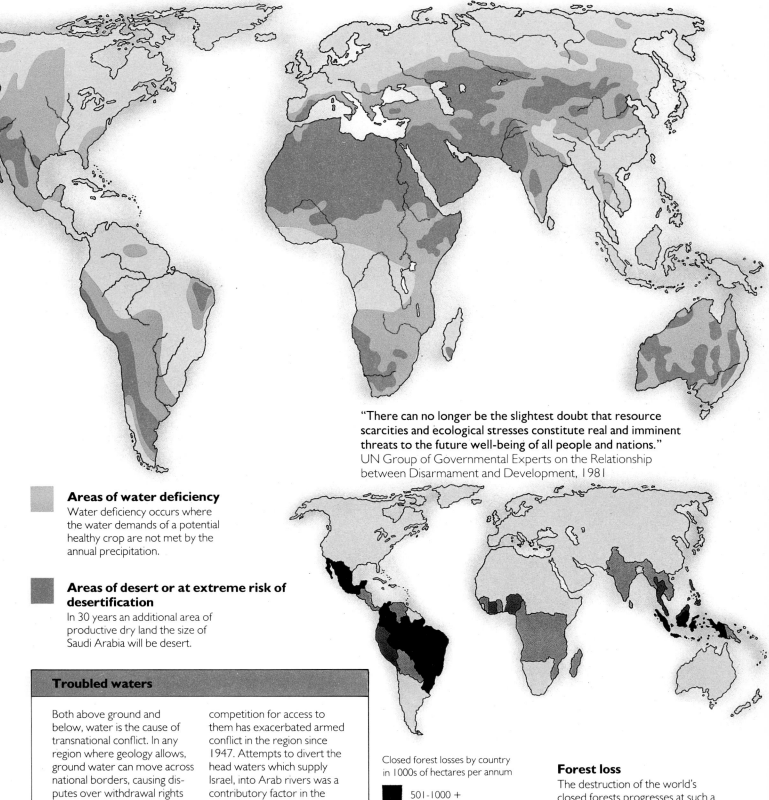

"There can no longer be the slightest doubt that resource scarcities and ecological stresses constitute real and imminent threats to the future well-being of all people and nations."
UN Group of Governmental Experts on the Relationship between Disarmament and Development, 1981

Areas of water deficiency
Water deficiency occurs where the water demands of a potential healthy crop are not met by the annual precipitation.

Areas of desert or at extreme risk of desertification
In 30 years an additional area of productive dry land the size of Saudi Arabia will be desert.

Troubled waters

Both above ground and below, water is the cause of transnational conflict. In any region where geology allows, ground water can move across national borders, causing disputes over withdrawal rights even between friendly states, such as France and West Germany. Of greater magnitude are water disputes between countries sharing the same river system, especially in arid regions where water competition is exacerbated by water scarcity. The waters of the Jordan are shared by Israel, Lebanon, Syria and Jordan, and competition for access to them has exacerbated armed conflict in the region since 1947. Attempts to divert the head waters which supply Israel, into Arab rivers was a contributory factor in the 1967 Arab-Israeli war. Water is still fuelling tension between Israel and the Palestinians in the West Bank and Gaza, where Israel draws about half its supplies. According to a military order, Palestinian wells are restricted to a maximum depth of 100 metres, while settlers' wells are dug to a depth of 700 metres.

Closed forest losses by country in 1000s of hectares per annum

- 501-1000 +
- 201-500
- 10-200
- Generally stable

Forest loss
The destruction of the world's closed forests progresses at such a rate that in 30 years an area of land the size of India will have been stripped of trees. Brazil alone lost some 1.5 million ha from 1981 to 1985. Deforestation disrupts life-support systems, threatening local and global climate change. Yet only a tiny percentage of the cleared land is suitable for sustained farming; most is abandoned after a few years.

fishing stocks, or disturbed water flows through deforestation. Increasingly, these problems cross borders or even afflict far distant nations, and the human disturbances caused provoke further problems.

Nations are not equally endowed with resources inside their own borders. Sheer size has much to do with this. The division of Vietnam, for instance, left neither half self-sufficient – minerals were located in the North, agricultural lands in the South. Generally, large countries are more self-sufficient in natural resources and so much more powerful in international relations than small countries, which may be dependent on others, and even vulnerable to resource "blackmail" by big suppliers.

Conflicts also arise over "strategic" raw materials specifically required for military use. Titanium, for example, is sought after for military aircraft and submarines. It is not always an advantage to own such resources. The uranium of Namibia make that country prey to great power rivalry and violent conflict.

The resource most often linked with security is oil. Continuous supplies of oil are essential in war. European NATO countries (excluding the UK) and Japan are dependent on the Middle East – they are hostages to Arab oil. This determines their bilateral relations with Arab states. Thus France is prepared to supply nuclear facilities and major weapons to Iraq in return for guaranteed oil supplies. The USSR, self-sufficient in oil itself, is becoming less able to supply its East European allies and these countries, too, are increasingly looking to the Arab countries to make up the short-fall. East-West competition for Middle East oil will have growing security consequences for us all in future (*see also pp. 202-3*).

Competition for resources everywhere is turning attention to the wealth of the oceans, Antarctica, and even outer space. This has led to the concept of the Heritage of Mankind, in which such resources would be shared by all, not just those with power to exploit them. Many conservationists would prefer to see these regions protected against all exploitation, fearing a new and greater "tragedy of the commons".

Disputes over resources will inevitably increase in the decades to come. It will be extremely difficult to prevent many of these disputes becoming wars.

Pollution as a threat to security

Pollution comes in many guises. It can be injected into the atmosphere as a noxious cocktail of sulphur dioxide, nitrogen oxides, hydrocarbons, heavy metals and ozone; it can be dumped directly into landfill sites as any number of toxic compounds; and it can be flushed into the sea, either as industrial effluent or as agricultural run-off (fertilizers and pesticides). Whatever the route, the hard facts remain: pollution rarely stays put, and it does not go away. Slowly and insidiously, persistent toxins are entering into our food chains, accumulating in fatty tissues of animals, contaminating the air we breathe and posing unknown health risks both for us and future generations.

Pollution

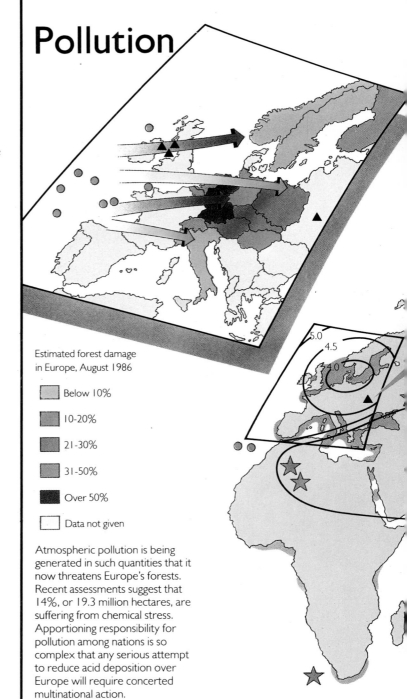

Estimated forest damage in Europe, August 1986

- Below 10%
- 10-20%
- 21-30%
- 31-50%
- Over 50%
- Data not given

Atmospheric pollution is being generated in such quantities that it now threatens Europe's forests. Recent assessments suggest that 14%, or 19.3 million hectares, are suffering from chemical stress. Apportioning responsibility for pollution among nations is so complex that any serious attempt to reduce acid deposition over Europe will require concerted multinational action.

Pollution knows no borders. What one country does in its own backyard affects not only its neighbours, but the global community. While people in the North are waking up to this fact, people in the South have more urgent priorities. Pollution controls are more likely to come *after* a certain living standard has been reached.

As industries in the North face more stringent pollution controls, they become more likely to export pollution to the South. This may be in the form of toxic wastes, pesticides, or actual production plants which discharge wastes unacceptable in the North. Exported pollution eventually comes home, either indirectly via food chains, or directly in imported produce.

Chernobyl: a lesson learned?

On 23 April 1986, two large explosions destroyed one of four nuclear reactors at Chernobyl in the USSR. Dust and smoke from the burning reactor were blown all over Europe. People were exposed to radioactive materials deposited by rain, inhaled from the air or ingested in food.

An official Soviet report indicated that up to 40,000 may eventually die from radioactive contamination of the food supply. But some scientists place the figure even higher. John Gofman, an American biophysicist, has calculated that more than a million people will develop cancer, and that about half these will die.

Ironically, Chernobyl could finally resolve the controversy about the risks of radiation. Epidemiological studies will be required, and international collaboration could pave the way for global action in dealing with such disasters.

Pollution in the US

Pollution is as great a problem in the US as it is in Europe. Every year millions of tons of pollutants are released into the atmosphere, discharged into rivers, or buried in the soil. About 24 million tons of sulphur dioxide – just one of the constituents of acid rain – are generated each year by the US, causing $7 billion worth of corrosion damage alone. Yet the cost of reducing these emissions by half would be around $5 billion a year, increasing electricity rates by a mere 2-3%.

Estimates of the total amount of hazardous waste produced in the US vary greatly, but we can safely say that at least one ton is produced for every American citizen each year. Two-thirds of this is disposed of in or on the land through injection wells, pits, ponds or landfills, at the risk of contaminating groundwater reserves.

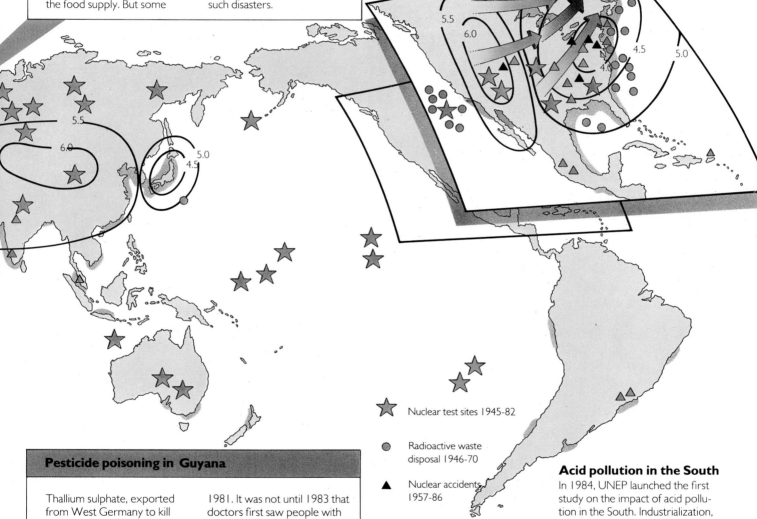

★ Nuclear test sites 1945-82

● Radioactive waste disposal 1946-70

▲ Nuclear accidents 1957-86

△ Chemical and fuel accidents 1980-5

Moderate/severe sea pollution

5.0 / 4.5 Estimated pH distribution in northern hemisphere for late 1970s

➤ Winter winds

➤ Summer winds

Pesticide poisoning in Guyana

Thallium sulphate, exported from West Germany to kill sugar cane rats in Guyana, is causing alarm. Already hundreds of people have died, and it is feared that many of Guyana's 800,000 population have been affected. Less than 1 gram of thallium sulphate is all that is needed to produce delirium, coma, convulsions and haemorrhage.

The poison, whose use has been banned in the North, was imported in quantity from 1981. It was not until 1983 that doctors first saw people with thallium poisoning – by which time, the toxin was already in the food chain.

The poison could boomerang back on the North. Poor farmers were using it as fertilizer – thallium makes plants grow greener and stronger – so many crops other than sugar cane could be contaminated. Many Western countries are now screening all Guyanan produce.

Acid pollution in the South

In 1984, UNEP launched the first study on the impact of acid pollution in the South. Industrialization, particularly in the NICs, is increasing the emissions of potential pollutants with scant regard for the environment. Besides which, emission controls are costly – and the South has other priorities.

The red laterite soils of tropical South America, Africa and South Asia are especially vulnerable to acid pollution because they are thin and poor. The prospect of *Waldsterben* or forest death affecting tropical forests could have serious repercussions.

Not surprisingly, pollution can be a significant security issue. It is, for example, a major cause of tension between Canada and the USA. Acid rain originating chiefly from the US is destroying life in many of Canada's acid-sensitive lakes and damaging its buildings. Similarly, acid rain caused by British pollution is adversely affecting Scandinavian inland waters. And air pollution from East Germany and Czechoslovakia is killing trees in West Germany.

The accident on 23 April 1986 at the Soviet reactor at Chernobyl was a stark reminder that pollution does not stop at national boundaries. Within days radioactive fall-out from Chernobyl spread right across Europe. Nuclear power is now an important bilateral issue between European countries, especially when nuclear power plants are sited with little regard for population density in the neighbouring state. The French plant at Cattenom is a classic example: built 10 kilometres from both Luxembourg and West Germany, this large power complex stands within 50 kilometres of the homes of 1.5 million people. Radioactivity is also a concern in relations between the UK and Eire. The reprocessing plant at Sellafield, England, discharges radioactive waste into the Irish Sea, which has become the world's most radioactive sea.

Pollutants such as pesticides, sewage, oil and radioactivity can be a hazard both to groundwater reserves and to coastal fishing. Tensions also arise between nuclear and non-nuclear states over the matter of dumping radioactive waste in the oceans. As populations increase, pollution of all types may too, unless controls or cleaner technologies are adopted. This is bound to increase international tensions.

Food power and climate change

Food is a political weapon. Major food exporters, such as the USA, use food as a means of furthering their own foreign policy goals. Yet the production of food is extremely sensitive to climate. Any alteration in climate could disrupt patterns of production and have serious security implications for many nations.

Human activities are increasing the load of carbon dioxide, methane and other "greenhouse gases" in the atmosphere. As their concentrations increase, so the Earth's temperature is gradually rising. A general global warming of the Earth's surface will bring shifts in rainfall patterns and raised sea levels. There will be benefits to some countries, while others will suffer. We do not understand what the full effects of long-term climatic change will be, especially on food production, but we do know that the consequences could be both severe and irreversible. The prudent course under these circumstances would be to proceed with great caution and to adopt policies that reduce the possibilities of destabilizing global climate.

All nations stand to lose when international relations become seriously destabilized. The pursuit of potentially small national or commercial gains and of uncertain short-term military and foreign policy advantages, at the expense of global common security, is supreme

Food power and climate change

"Food is a weapon. It is now one of the principal weapons in our negotiating kit."
Earl Butz, former US Secretary of State for Agriculture

Climate change *is* avoidable, but once it has happened, it is irreversible. At present, we seem determined to change it. By continuing to discharge 5.5 billion tons of carbon dioxide into the atmosphere each year from the burning of fossil fuels, we will double the concentration of atmospheric carbon dioxide over pre-industrial levels by the 2030s.

The initial consequence of such an increase will be a global warming of about 1°C, caused by solar radiation being "trapped" near the ground (the "greenhouse effect"). Warming will be more pronounced at higher latitudes than at the equator, with the poles experiencing about double the mean. This will severely affect agriculture, and shift the balance of food power: it could also cause a rise in sea level of 25-140 centimetres, inundating large areas.

The costs of accommodating such a change could be astronomic. Irrigation adjustments alone could cost $200 billion – a price that many countries will be unable to afford.

The ozone hole

1979

1982

Like a shield positioned 25-40 km above the Earth, the ozone layer protects surface life from excessive exposure to UV radiation. But the shield is showing signs of wear. Most believe the cause to be CFCs, in refrigerators, air conditioners and aerosols; filtering into the stratosphere, these are reacting with light, and releasing chlorine atoms which cause ozone to be destroyed. Ozone is declining in the northern hemisphere; but the worst problem is in the Antarctic, where a growing "hole" has developed.

1984

 Ozone-depleted area

Severely ozone-depleted area

Climate change

The effects of climate change will show geographical variation. Wet areas will get wetter and warmer, while dry areas will get hotter and drier. Since a warmer atmosphere will hold more moisture, we can expect average rainfall to increase by 7-11% (based on the equivalent of a doubling of CO_2 levels). This may be offset, however, by higher evaporation, causing soil moisture to decrease. Rainfall regimes may also be disrupted by a slowing of the "atmospheric heat engine", which is driven by the differences between equatorial and polar temperatures.

Food power

Together, the USA and Canada dominate the world cereal market – a fact which allows them to influence the development of food-deficit states. A significant warming of the Earth's surface, however, could change all this, by drying out the traditional grain belts and cutting their yields.

While some regions stand to "lose" from a shift in climate, others will gain. Warmer and wetter conditions in India and southeast Asia may boost rice production, although fertile delta regions may be threatened by rising sea levels. In more northerly areas, nutrient-poor soils could be a bar to agricultural expansion.

Upward trends

In 1860, the concentration of CO_2 in the atmosphere was 260 ppm. Today it is around 350 ppm. In just 125 years, human activities have increased the concentration of CO_2 by 30%. We have influenced some of the other greenhouse gases, too, which are equally important in accelerating the rate of global warming: methane, CFCs, nitrous oxide and ozone. Projections are estimates based on current trends.

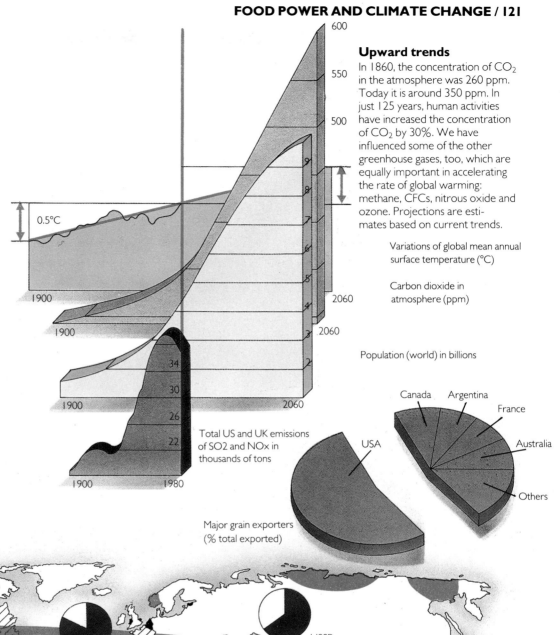

Variations of global mean annual surface temperature (°C)

Carbon dioxide in atmosphere (ppm)

Population (world) in billions

Total US and UK emissions of SO2 and NOx in thousands of tons

Major grain exporters (% total exported)

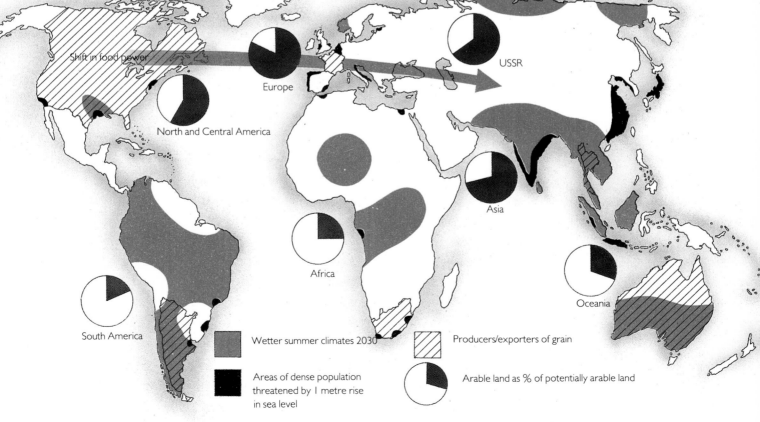

Shift in food power

North and Central America

Europe

USSR

Africa

Asia

South America

Oceania

Wetter summer climates 2030

Areas of dense population threatened by 1 metre rise in sea level

Producers/exporters of grain

Arable land as % of potentially arable land

folly. When it comes to caring for the environment, governments are dragging their feet. But millions of ordinary people are voicing their concern. Surely this should encourage politicians to believe that, even if the medicine is painful, public support would be found for actions to reduce the climatic impacts of human activities – before their potentially catastrophic consequences become reality.

International crime: drugs and arms

Crime is big business. Profits from the international drugs trade, second only to those from the arms trade, run into tens of billions of dollars annually. In the US alone, drugs traffic is worth $80 billion a year.

Unlike the trade in arms, however, the drugs trade is from South to North, and is opposed by most governments. With huge profits accruing to just a few big criminal dealers (who are then able to infiltrate social and political institutions and wield tremendous influence), drugs are not regarded as beneficial to the state. But the two trades are linked, and the combination is a volatile one. Profits from drugs are often used to buy weapons – a fact that has become an acute source of embarrassment to the US, which is at the forefront of the movement to combat the drugs problem. The rebels in Afghanistan are in part funded by the heroin trade; similarly, pro-US Contra rebels in Nicaragua are partly financed by profits made from drugs smuggled from Colombia for sale in the US.

Apart from the obvious security risks of acquiring weapons from illicit drug dealing, there are the effects of drug abuse on society to consider. Drug abuse on a significant scale seriously undermines the moral fibre of society and threatens its political and social values. The defence of these values is generally considered to be an important element of national security. Violent crime is also exacerbated by large-scale drug dealing because of the weapons connection. Los Angeles youth gangs dealing in the cocaine derivative "crack" – a billion-dollar trade – use handguns and even Soviet-made assault rifles, which are gained from transactions with arms smugglers.

The international drug trade has long been out of control. Even the most sophisticated police forces can do little more than prevent a rapid increase in the amount of drugs sold. Controlling the trade requires transnational action. Yet this has been slow to emerge, despite the fact that many nations are now very concerned about drug abuse.

One difficulty is that drug trading provides some developing countries with a significant fraction of their GNP, and the livelihood of many communities, though governments may not be directly involved. It is extremely hard to effect transnational control of an activity that benefits some of the parties.

There are international treaties controlling drugs – for example, the 1961 Single Convention on Narcotic Drugs, designed to control stimulants, depressants and certain hallucinogens. But although many countries have ratified these treaties, there is surprisingly little

Crime

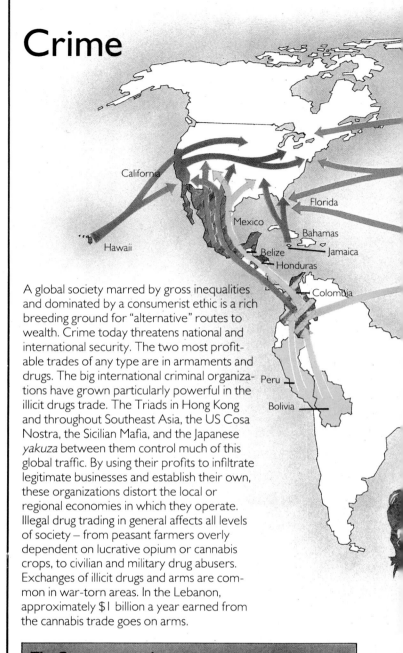

California
Florida
Mexico
Bahamas
Hawaii
Belize
Jamaica
Honduras
Colombia
Peru
Bolivia

A global society marred by gross inequalities and dominated by a consumerist ethic is a rich breeding ground for "alternative" routes to wealth. Crime today threatens national and international security. The two most profitable trades of any type are in armaments and drugs. The big international criminal organizations have grown particularly powerful in the illicit drugs trade. The Triads in Hong Kong and throughout Southeast Asia, the US Cosa Nostra, the Sicilian Mafia, and the Japanese *yakuza* between them control much of this global traffic. By using their profits to infiltrate legitimate businesses and establish their own, these organizations distort the local or regional economies in which they operate. Illegal drug trading in general affects all levels of society – from peasant farmers overly dependent on lucrative opium or cannabis crops, to civilian and military drug abusers. Exchanges of illicit drugs and arms are common in war-torn areas. In the Lebanon, approximately $1 billion a year earned from the cannabis trade goes on arms.

The Contra connection

Sheltering under Project Democracy – the covert umbrella organization of the Iran/Contra affair – lay another secret network: the Contra connection. This private-aid network of Contra bases, bank accounts, airplanes, pilots and landing strips was used by arms and drug traffickers as well as Contras and their supporters. According to an October 1986 report by US Senator John Kerry, members of the network not only violated several Congressional acts prohibiting aid to the Contras, but also participated in other illicit activities. An American rancher in northern Costa Rica was alleged in the report to have engaged in activities connected with drug traffickers. Reported to be working for the CIA, he was accused of allowing Colombian drug dealers to refuel their planes on his strategically placed airstrips and of buying arms for the Contras with the proceeds. The US National Security Council was reported to have paid him $10,000 a month.

He and others were accused of participating in weapons trafficking. As the Contra connection revealed, the war against the Sandinistas was vastly more expensive than the US Congress-approved millions suggested.

Turkey
Sicily
The golden crescent
Afghanistan
Lebanon
Syria
Nepal
Morocco
The golden triangle
Egypt
Pakistan
The Philippines
Senegal
Nigeria
Sri Lanka
Swaziland

Global drug routes

The prime sources of illicit drugs are regions with optimal growing conditions, traditional usage and economic need. Smuggling routes, however, shift in response to police crackdowns, levels of international demand and availability of refineries. Most of the world's opium is grown in Burma, Laos, Thailand, Afghanistan, Iran, Pakistan, Turkey and Mexico. Unprocessed opium from Southeast Asia travels via India to Western Europe and the USA. Southwest Asian opium is increasingly processed within the area. Peru and Bolivia grow the most coca. Processed mainly in Colombia to produce 80% of the world's cocaine, it is then flown to the USA and Europe.

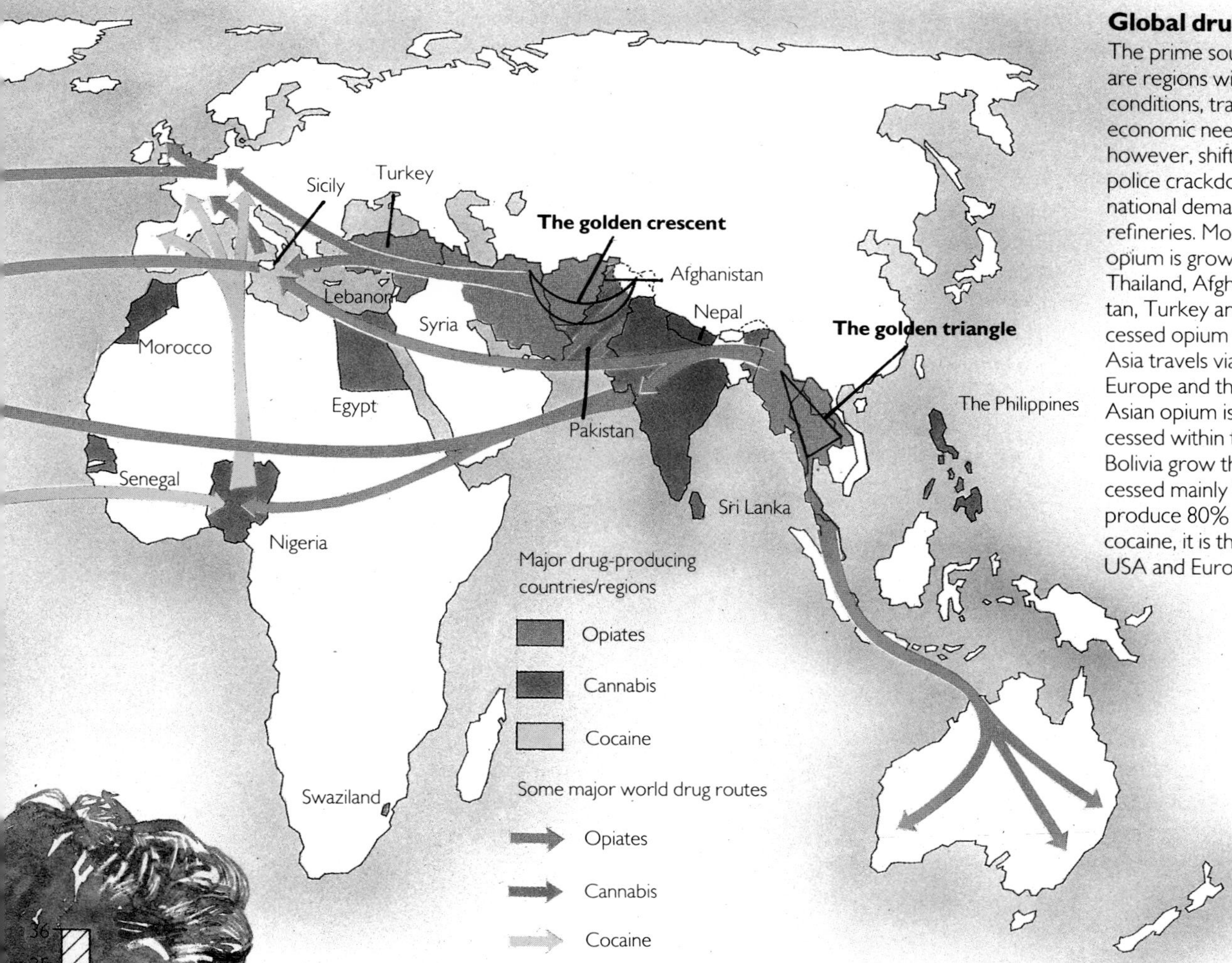

Major drug-producing countries/regions

- Opiates
- Cannabis
- Cocaine

Some major world drug routes

- Opiates
- Cannabis
- Cocaine

Drugs: not a new problem

We are more aware of drugs as a problem now than we were in 1967. The reason why most countries recorded few drug offences in the 1960s was not because it wasn't as big a problem; rather, the level of concern – both from the public and the police – was lower.

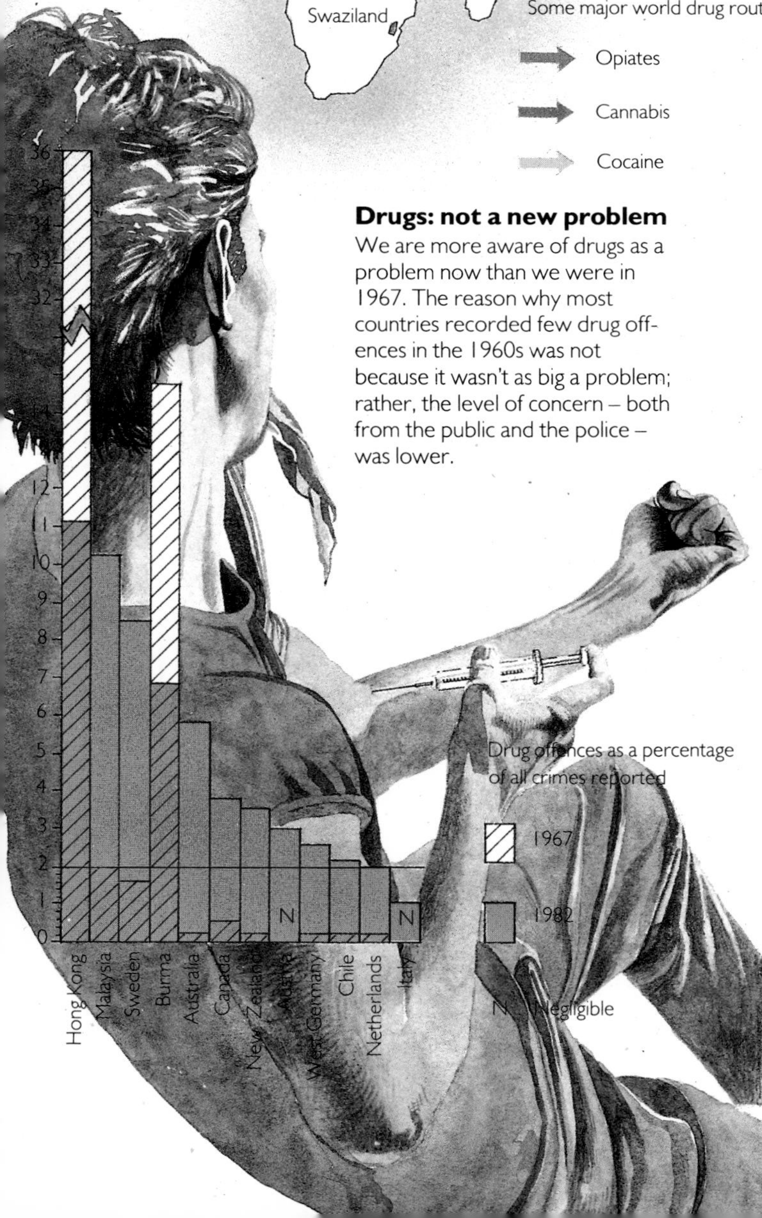

Drug offences as a percentage of all crimes reported

- 1967
- 1982

N Negligible

Hong Kong
Malaysia
Sweden
Burma
Australia
Canada
New Zealand
Japan
West Germany
Chile
Netherlands
Italy

The Mafia: WWII and after

The Mafia's role in WWII amply illustrates the power of organized crime. The Sicilian Mafia and its American offshoot, the Cosa Nostra, were both instrumental in the Allied invasion of Sicily. When the Americans entered Sicily in July 1943, they met with the full co-operation of the capo-mafia, Don Calogero Vizzini. At this time, the Mafia was unconnected with the drugs trade, and was weakened by Mussolini's anti-Mafia campaign. But it still retained its traditional position as a feudal organization reliant upon exploitation of the poor for its power. The Allies, out of interest in Sicily's strategic location, unwittingly approved schemes which gave the Mafia a foothold in a new phase of power: Don Calo's bodyguards were re-armed, and Mafia mayors were installed throughout western Sicily. In the post-war period the Mafia evaded the government's attempts to eradicate it. Mafiosi "punished" by exile to Italy simply succeeded in establishing power bases there. Their operations soon spread to neighbouring countries. Through the processing and sale of narcotics, the Mafia has now gained tremendous purchasing power. Sicily's heroin refineries can, for example, produce $500 million worth of the drug (at street prices) per week. The Mafia's rule by violence continues to disrupt Italian society while its interests in banking and business continue to expand. With an economic status comparable to that of a multinational corporation, and a growing network of operators and supporters, the Mafia is more than ever a force to be reckoned with – a parallel government controlling an "invisible" economy.

co-ordination of the activities of national police forces and enforcement agencies. There is, moreover, insufficient sharing of intelligence data by national authorities, and no international clearing house for this data.

The control of terrorism

Terrorism is the killing or kidnapping of people or the destruction of property for political reasons. Terrorist actions are distinct from those carried out purely for vengeance or by criminals for gain.

Terrorism can succeed in its purpose in politics, and violence can be made to pay. For example, after World War II, Jewish terrorists in Palestine, including the Irgun and Stern organizations, successfully drove out the British and contributed to the establishment in 1948 of the state of Israel. Some Jewish ex-terrorists became political leaders – M. Begin, for example, became Prime Minister of Israel. Similarly, the Mau-Mau organization contributed to the independence of Kenya, and ex-terrorist leader Kenyatta became President of Kenya.

Many contemporary so-called terrorists begin their careers with motives we can understand, sympathize with and often support – a desire for social justice, a concern for the environment, a desire for national liberation, an abhorrence for a racialist regime, and so on. But violence corrupts. And impatience, and the knowledge of wide support for their values, leads to the belief that they can defy the rule of law to gain their ends. The result is the indiscriminate, and often large-scale, killing of innocent people that is the hallmark of modern terrorism.

Ezekiel Drorr, an Israeli expert on terrorism, sees today's terrorist as an "idealist who despairs of achieving his values by normal means and, therefore, becomes a fanatic who we define as an idealist whom we don't like, someone who uses tools and instruments we regard as immoral. Modern society provides very few legitimate roles for persons who centuries ago would have become saints, explorers, or adventurers."

The activities of terrorism include kidnapping, hostage taking, barricading, bombing, armed attack, hijacking, arson and shootings. They are classed as international terrorism if they involve foreigners or occur on foreign aircraft, ships or territory.

So far, terrorists have been unimaginative in their actions. Their operations have been contained and they have confined themselves to the use of conventional weapons. But we can expect this pattern to change in the future. Existing terrorist groups are rather small, their scientific and technical skills are limited. How long will it be before some groups combine to produce weapons of mass destruction, such as nerve gases, biological weapons or nuclear explosives? Or extremist terrorist groups are given such weapons by extremist governments?

Leaders of terrorist groups have certainly already thought about these possibilities. Presumably, they have until now decided that killing, or threatening to kill, large numbers of people indiscriminately in a single

Terrorist or freedom fighter?

"Various kinds of belligerence fit uneasily into an international state system. With the growth of the power of the state it has become common to label as war only those kinds of organised violence which are conducted by a state . . . but there remain further kinds of belligerence, commonly disparaged as terrorism. This is a word to beware of. It has become a term of abuse, used to excite prejudice and fuel unthinking reactions – which is all the more deplorable since terrorism does exist and has to be countered."
Peter Calvocoressi. *A Time For Peace*

One person's terrorist is another's freedom fighter. Terrorism is defined as criminal violence – bombing, murder, kidnapping and hijacking – by minorities using "coercive terror" for political ends. But gangs such as Bader-Meinhof cannot be grouped with organizations such as the ANC in South Africa, which has genuine reason to despair of the political process.

Terrorism achieves little; yet it continues. Liberation, separatist or human rights movements lacking legitimized national status are neither protected by nor subject to international codes of behaviour and law. This breeds support for the methods of the terrorist – from illegal arms buying to secret deals with friendly states. And when we turn on the television to learn of the latest publicity-seeking atrocity, we justify its credo: only violence is newsworthy.

Terrorism on the increase
Between 1968 and 1980, the total number of international terrorist incidents resulting in casualties was 1435. During this 13-year period, bombings were the preferred mode of attack, accounting for nearly half of all incidents. During the same period, over 400 kidnappings, 450 assassinations and over 100 barricade and hostage situations took place.

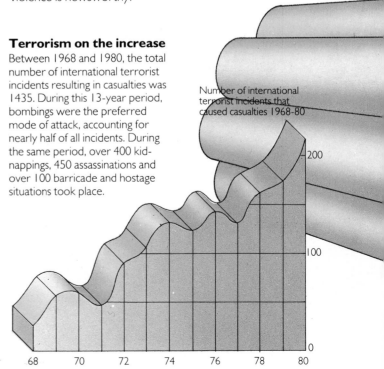

Number of international terrorist incidents that caused casualties 1968-80

200

100

0

68   70   72   74   76   78   80

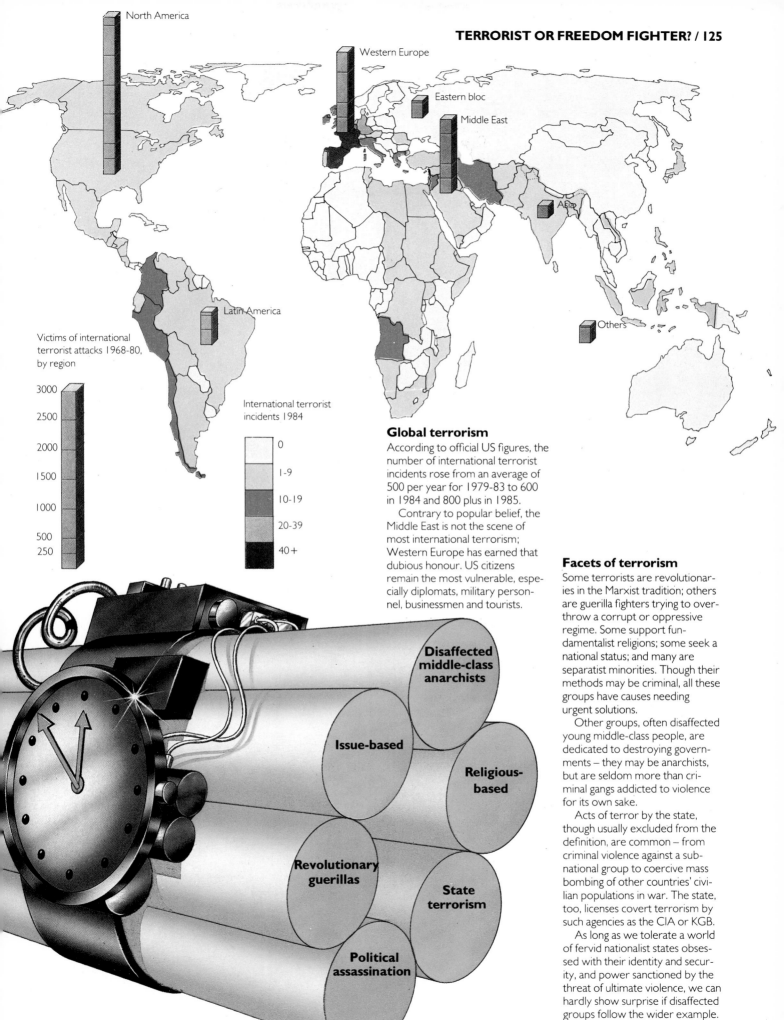

North America

Western Europe

Eastern bloc

Middle East

Asia

Latin America

Others

Victims of international
terrorist attacks 1968-80,
by region

3000
2500
2000
1500
1000
500
250

International terrorist
incidents 1984

0

1-9

10-19

20-39

40+

Global terrorism

According to official US figures, the
number of international terrorist
incidents rose from an average of
500 per year for 1979-83 to 600
in 1984 and 800 plus in 1985.

Contrary to popular belief, the
Middle East is not the scene of
most international terrorism;
Western Europe has earned that
dubious honour. US citizens
remain the most vulnerable, especially diplomats, military personnel, businessmen and tourists.

Facets of terrorism

Some terrorists are revolutionar-
ies in the Marxist tradition; others
are guerilla fighters trying to overthrow a corrupt or oppressive
regime. Some support fun-
damentalist religions; some seek a
national status; and many are
separatist minorities. Though their
methods may be criminal, all these
groups have causes needing
urgent solutions.

Other groups, often disaffected
young middle-class people, are
dedicated to destroying governments – they may be anarchists,
but are seldom more than criminal gangs addicted to violence
for its own sake.

Acts of terror by the state,
though usually excluded from the
definition, are common – from
criminal violence against a subnational group to coercive mass
bombing of other countries' civilian populations in war. The state,
too, licenses covert terrorism by
such agencies as the CIA or KGB.

As long as we tolerate a world
of fervid nationalist states obsessed with their identity and security, and power sanctioned by the
threat of ultimate violence, we can
hardly show surprise if disaffected
groups follow the wider example.

Disaffected
middle-class
anarchists

Issue-based

Religious-
based

Revolutionary
guerillas

State
terrorism

Political
assassination

incident would not further their political goals. But, as access to weapons of mass destruction becomes easier, this attitude may well change. And as wars, and society itself, become more violent, moral constraints on mass killing weaken.

In the coming years, terrorism will be more violent and the extent and frequency of incidents will rise. A major reason will be the combination of increasing world population, urbanization and poverty. Unless we tackle these, the control of terrorism may challenge our democratic freedoms, already severely limited by the secrecy of government.

Official secrecy – necessary to national security?

Though national security is the usual excuse, there are other reasons why governments like to control the information available to their citizens. Few regimes welcome anyone questioning their own legitimacy, whether power be in the hands of a military dictator, or a political system – such as communism – which does not countenance the possibility (let alone the desirability) of being replaced. Survival is the name of the game, and too free access to information is a "danger" that is recognized across the political spectrum, from far left to far right. In principle, only liberal democracies acknowledge the concept of an overriding right to know as much as possible about anything. But even then, there are constraints – especially in those countries that have nuclear weapons or other sophisticated technologies which they do not wish to see fully known or shared.

The nuclear state prefers to keep in ignorance not only the general public, but often their elected representatives, too. The British Chevaline warhead, for example, was under development for seven years before the full British Cabinet was told and for 13 years, including four changes of government, before the British Parliament learned of it. The design and testing of the Chevaline was virtually complete before the public was even aware of its inception. The government's aim was to prevent public discussion and debate. This is how most governments would like the nuclear state to operate. The people are not supposed to affect decisions about nuclear matters, though they crucially affect their security.

On top of domestic considerations, there is the desire to save face in the world. Most countries would like to vet what other nations know about them, not only in the field of defence, but also in such areas as the abuse of the environment (such as Brazilian Amazonia) or the suppression of minority rights (as in East Timor, under Indonesian occupation). When potential threats to international security are covered up, and thus left to fester, it makes them all the more dangerous.

As transnational threats to security – from human suffering to world climate change – multiply and interact with effects beyond national control, what we have most to fear is a growing intransigence by hard-pressed governments, with risks of civil oppression and rapid escalation of conflicts to a global scale.

Media and the secret state

Information is power, as governments, businesses and an increasing number of ordinary people are beginning to realize. One of the great paradoxes of the modern world is that while computer technology and telecommunications have made spreading news and information easier, most governments have clamped down harder on people's right to know. In several countries of Eastern Europe, there are tight controls over the methods of dissemination. In other places, the restrictions are more subtle, as newspaper publishers and broadcasters co-operate with governments to limit what is made public. Only a handful of nations, most notably the USA, have Freedom of Information legislation, which gives people the right of access to data that may deeply affect their lives. And just about everywhere, secrecy shrouds defence matters – especially where nuclear weapons are concerned. Governments justify this on grounds of national security. But obsessive government secrecy is itself a barrier to peace between nations. Equally, domination and control of media coverage by any large power group is a barrier to understanding and peace between all peoples.

Israeli nuclear secrets

For years there have been fears that the protracted Middle East conflict might take on a nuclear dimension – with Israel being the state most likely to be able to develop nuclear weapons first. Rumours have abounded about the exchange of nuclear know-how between Israel and South Africa. But in October 1986, a British newspaper, *The Sunday Times*, printed a startling account by an Israeli nuclear technician, Mordechai Vanunu, who had spent nearly 10 years working in a top-secret bunker making components for atomic warheads. Convinced that this work was morally wrong, he left Israel. After his story was published, Vanunu was lured to Rome, where he was abducted by the Israeli secret service Mossad. He was taken back to Israel to stand trial for treason and convicted in 1988. Vanunu said he knew the risks he had taken, but wanted the world to have the information. A scrawled message on his palm gives brief details of his abduction.

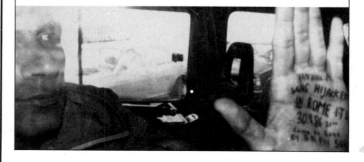

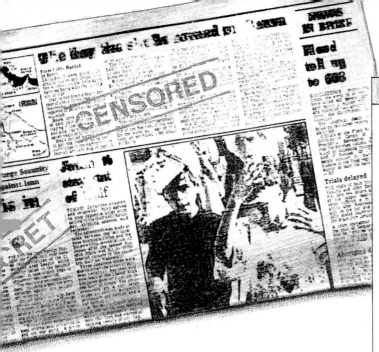

The secret state and the BBC

Snooping into defence or other state secrets – even in the name of investigative journalism – can land people in trouble, perhaps in jail. One man who has discovered this to his cost is the reporter Duncan Campbell. In 1978, he was put on trial for offences under the Official Secrets Act – for collecting information about defence communications. Undeterred, he kept up his activities and in 1987 was in the news again, for revealing secret government plans to commission an expensive new satellite system, Zircon. British Broadcasting Corporation television in Scotland asked Campbell to make a series of programmes to illustrate such issues, but pressure was put on the BBC not to show them. Police even raided BBC offices in Glasgow, to seize copies of the material, and Campbell's own home in London was searched. Protests by BBC employees and opposition MPs in the House of Commons were brushed aside on the grounds of national security and, as a result, the BBC's cherished reputation for independence was damaged. Months later, Zircon was abandoned as "out of date".

The media and the establishment

Censorship is an inevitable feature of the printed and broadcasting media, in the many countries where these belong to the state or the ruling party. But even where the media is private or "independent", it can fall foul of measures designed to restrict its freedom to report. Such censorship can happen anywhere:

Britain provided a noteworthy example in 1987, when a former intelligence operative, Peter Wright, published his memoirs in the US. The British government acted not only to stop extracts appearing in the British press, but tried to do the same elsewhere, including such countries as Australia and New Zealand.

The North's domination of the information network

Colonialism left many legacies in developing countries that have proved to be mixed blessings, not least the control industrial powers still have over news and communication. Huge news agencies, such as Reuters and Associated Press, dominate the news and features world wide, gearing their material to the tastes and interests of their main target audiences in North America and Western Europe. Both the subjects and the style are often of dubious relevance to people in the South. Similarly, the interpretation of events in developing countries themselves can be inappropriate. As the late Kenyan Minister for Economic Planning and Development, Tom Mboya, said: "The news coming out of Africa is often, if not always, related to the already biased and prejudiced mind that keeps asking such questions as 'Is this pro-East or pro-West?' Very few, if any, of the world's press ask such logical, in one view simple, questions as 'Is this pro-African?'"

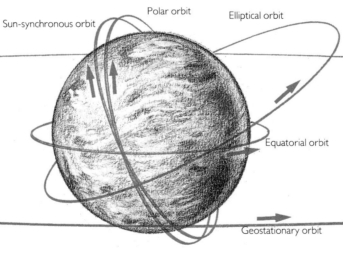

Sun-synchronous orbit · Polar orbit · Elliptical orbit · Equatorial orbit · Geostationary orbit

Satellite power

Access to communications satellites in geostationary orbit has become an increasingly important element of media power. The North has traditionally dominated outer space, with the US and USSR accounting for 98% of all satellite launches up to 1982. Since that time, however, more developing countries have put their own satellites into space, and there are now fears that the geostationary orbit may become overcrowded. With only a limited number of slots available, many African and South American countries – which have yet to launch satellites – may be unable to find room for their craft.

	USA	USSR	Others*
Payloads launched since 1957:	997	2069	59
Still functioning in 1982:	183	102	7

*European Space Agency, Japan, France, China, Italy, India, Australia, UK

Fear of armageddon

"The sky was dark as pitch, covered with dense clouds of smoke: under that blackness, over the earth, hung a yellow-brown fog . . . All the buildings I could see were on fire . . . it seemed like the end of the world."
T. Akizuki, Nagasaki 1945

There are now enough nuclear weapons for a million Nagasakis; enough to wipe out the future. How can one explain to a child what is their purpose? Or why we have countenanced a world in which that child must grow up under the shadow of despair? To a child, the very words we use to explain must seem the language of madness. And so they will seem to future genera-tions too – if such generations are ever born.

The road to nowhere

The greatest single threat to humanity is an all-out nuclear war. Despite recent moves towards disarma-ment, the risk of such a war is increasing, month by month, hour by hour. Nuclear weapons technology is spreading to regions where political instability is high. New and unpredicted conflicts are continuously arising in the world. The military strategists still cling to their belief that "for the foreseeable future" defence will depend on nuclear weapons. And new weapons are being introduced whose design is more useful, not for deterring a nuclear war, but for "winning" one.

This technological impetus is upsetting the nuclear strategic balance between the superpowers. Neither is likely to start a nuclear war by attacking the other out of the blue. But a conflict between their client states could rapidly escalate to global conflagration. The most likely flash points are the Middle East and the Gulf, with their vast reserves of oil; others are southern Africa, Korea and Central America.

The dangers of escalation stem from the superpow-ers' involvement in the developing world. The two giants of the North are locked in battle in the South, in a war of wills over control of secure supplies of strategic raw materials; over defence and expansion of markets; over political and economic influence and spheres of ideological dominance.

The arms trade is a direct result of this "Third World War" – most of the weapons used in conflicts in the South are supplied by the USA and the USSR. Modern war uses weapons, particularly missiles, at a great rate, and supplies must flow continually, as was shown dramatically in the October 1973 Middle East war (*see p. 52*). Moshe Dayan, former Israeli Defence Minister, describing how weapons supply affected the situation in this war, put it succinctly: "The dependence on outside sources – the Soviet Union and the United States as suppliers of arms – was so great in this war that it would have been impossible for the fighting to continue in defiance of the decisions of Washington and Moscow. The troops of these Super Powers did not take part in the campaign, but Israel and the Arabs were dependent on their will. They were not their own masters, neither

(see p. 52)

Use by terrorists

Nuclear fuel produced in nuclear power plants is going astray. The IAEA have developed a system based on accountancy and mate-rials control to safeguard enriched fuel, but examples of losses abound. The US alone is unable to account for 4500 kg of enriched uranium produced since 1950. The risk of terrorists acquiring weapons-grade plutonium and uranium and manufacturing their own nuclear weapons is a major area of concern.

Deliberate decision

Every US president, from Truman to Reagan (with the possible exception of Ford), has at some time considered using, or threatened to use, strategic or tactical nuclear weapons. When the US achieves a "first-strike capability" (as it seems set to do in the near future), the temptation to launch a nuclear strike before the USSR "catches up" may be difficult to resist.

Nuclear war: Likely causes

An all-out nuclear world war between the USA and the USSR could start for any one of the following reasons:
- a deliberate nuclear first-strike or a pre-emptive nuclear attack by one superpower on the other;
- the escalation of a conventional war;
- a mechanical failure or malfunction of a nuclear-weapons system;
- an error by humans or computers controll-ing the nuclear alert and firing systems;
- irrational behaviour by those controlling nuclear weapons;
- the acquisition and use of nuclear weapons by irresponsible governments;
- the acquisition and use of nuclear weapons by terrorists or other subnational groups.

A future world war would probably be the result of a combination of several of these factors. A conventional war in a region such as the Middle East could easily escalate to a local nuclear war in which nuclear weapons pro-duced by the local powers are used. Super-power involvement would become likely, mainly because of their links with these countries through the arms trade (*see pp. 52-3*), and also because of their keen interest in the region's oil resources.

(see pp. 52-3)

Irresponsible governments

At least 33 non-nuclear states now appear technically capable of making nuclear weapons within the next decade. This increases the chances of their weapons being used in a regional conflict.

With more countries possessing nuclear weapons, possibly with less-stringent safeguards, we must expect an increase in the number of accidents that could inadvertently cause a nuclear war.

Irrational behaviour

Drug abuse is a problem among those who handle nuclear weapons. About 112,000 people are entrusted with this work in the US alone, and of these some 5000 are removed each year, usually because of drug abuse or psychiatric problems. This means that at any time potentially unstable people have access to nuclear weapons.

Some weapon systems are very prone to mis-use. For example, on a strategic nuclear submarine, just two people behaving irrationally – the radio operator and the captain – could launch the submarine's ballistic missiles.

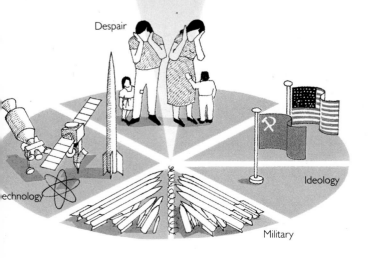

Escalation

Of all the possible causes of a nuclear world war, the most likely is the escalation of a conflict in the developing world. There are many such conflicts – on average, a new one begins every 3 months. The war could then spread to Europe, as a conventional war, escalating to a tactical nuclear war and finally to an all-out strategic nuclear war between the superpowers.

Malfunction or human error

The probability of accidental nuclear war increases with the complexity of nuclear-weapon systems. This is particularly true when nuclear decision-making is computerized. When very accurate missiles with short flight times are deployed, a country may feel compelled to make a pre-emptive attack. If these weapons were not deployed the country would wait and the crisis would pass.

"You can't sample (marijuana) on a sub, they'd smell it. I do uppers most of the time, but as a special treat, like when I'm on watch, I'll do a little mescalin. It's really a buzz to know that you're cruising the Arctic with Polaris missiles that could wipe out half of Russia – man, that's a real trip."
US nuclear submarine crewman

Fundamental causes

A combination of technological, political, military and psychological factors are increasing the risk of a nuclear world war. The technical characteristics of the weapons themselves are partly to blame, forcing political leaders to adopt policies they would rather avoid. Conflicting ideologies lead to feelings of insecurity. These may be deliberately fostered to justify high military budgets. The risk of war is increased by the ingrained linkage of security with military force. Military action is still seen to be a solution to international problems, even in today's world in which war is national suicide. When people feel incapable of influencing crucial decisions in a nuclear and violent age they come to believe that nuclear war is inevitable. In fact, an aroused public is the best way of persuading political leaders to move back from the brink of nuclear war.

in the opening stage of the war, nor in its conduct, nor, above all, in determining its end."

Escalation of a conflict in the South to nuclear world war is most likely if one of the belligerents resorts to its own nuclear weapons. Proliferation of nuclear technology may soon give nuclear weapons not only to unstable regions or oppressive regimes – in the Middle East, for instance, Israel has nuclear capacity, and so, too, it is suspected, has South Africa – but to sub-national or terrorist groups. What if Libya's present leadership, or one of the Middle East related terrorist organizations, acquire them?

Such a local nuclear war may well spread, say, to Europe, and escalate to a tactical nuclear war between the superpowers or their military alliances. This would very probably escalate rapidly to an all-out strategic nuclear war between the USA and the USSR.

The probability of this final escalation is being increased by current developments in the Soviet and American nuclear arsenals. Planning in the USA, for example, may involve the production, during the 1980s and up to the mid-1990s, of some 24,000 new warheads. These weapons will incorporate new technologies and be qualitatively different from those they replace. About 17,000 nuclear warheads will be withdrawn or replaced in the same period. The American nuclear stockpile will then contain about 32,000 nuclear warheads, compared with today's figure of 25,000.

We must expect the Soviets to increase their arsenal to a similar extent. By and large, Soviet nuclear activities tend to follow those of the USA, although with a time delay of a few years. Today's Soviet nuclear arsenal contains about the same number of nuclear warheads as the American, ie. 25,000.

From MAD to NUTS

For a credible policy of nuclear deterrence based on mutual assured destruction (MAD), only a small number of nuclear warheads is needed. There are at most 200 cities in each superpower with populations greater than 100,000 people. Assuming that two warheads are needed to destroy a large city, about 400 each would be more than enough deterrence – promising to kill promptly roughly 100 million people on either side and destroy about half its industrial capacity.

For a policy of minimum nuclear deterrence there is, therefore, an absurd amount of overkill in the superpower arsenals. Instead of 400, they each have some 10,000 strategic nuclear warheads.

There are so many nuclear weapons in both arsenals that improvements in design and performance are much more significant than adjustments in numbers. Advances in military nuclear technology rapidly outdate strategic thinking and provoke changes of policy that increase the risk of nuclear war.

In particular, new developments in nuclear weapons are making MAD impossible to implement. MAD depends on the belief that the enemy will not attack suddenly and pre-emptively, because most of its own cities and industry would be destroyed in retaliation. A

Nuclear proliferation

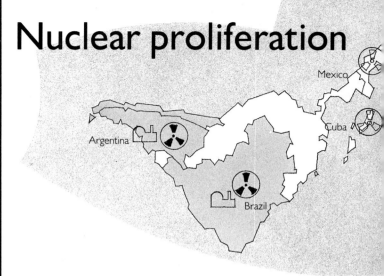

The design of nuclear weapons is no longer secret. Plutonium, the essential ingredient, is produced in abundance in nuclear reactors. Any country which generates its own nuclear power also has the potential means to manufacture its own nuclear weapons. In the words of Nobel Prize winning physicist Hannes Alfven: "The peaceful atom and the military atom are Siamese twins."

Although there are still only five declared nuclear powers, at least 12 non-nuclear states have the technical ability now to make nuclear weapons, and another 21 or so could achieve nuclear status within the next 10 years. Should nuclear proliferation occur, international tensions will rise. Regional conflicts will be more likely to escalate into nuclear war, while the risks of a war being caused inadvertently through fewer safeguards will multiply. There is also the real danger that, as the amount of plutonium in circulation increases, some of it may fall into the hands of a terrorist organization. The measures needed to ensure satisfactory protection of this plutonium would be little short of Draconian. Could democracy survive in the plutonium age?

Plutonium production

There are no official figures on the amount of plutonium in the world. But currently, the world's reactors are producing about 75 tons a year; by the year 2000 they will be producing twice this amount, giving rise to a cumulative total of about 1700 tons in the non-communist world alone.

Not all nuclear energy countries have reprocessing plants. France, the UK, Germany and Japan will probably separate most plutonium in the near future, involving the transport of plutonium by road, rail, air and sea. The scope for the theft of some of this plutonium will be considerable.

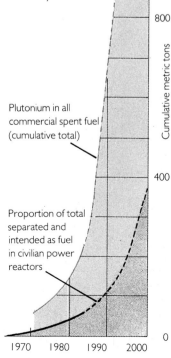

Plutonium in all commercial spent fuel (cumulative total)

Proportion of total separated and intended as fuel in civilian power reactors

Cumulative metric tons

1700
1600
1200
800
400
0

1970   1980   1990   2000

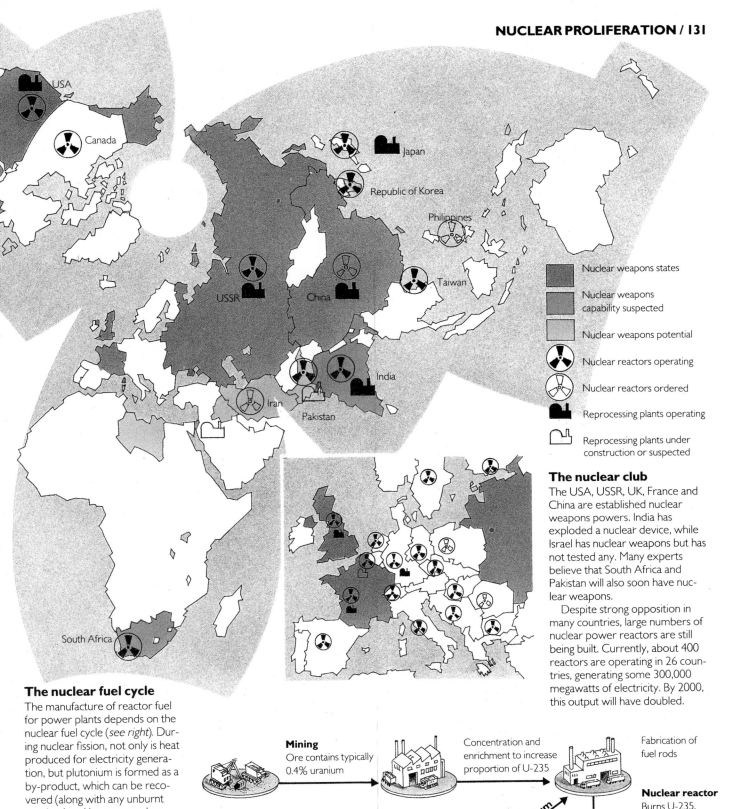

The nuclear club

The USA, USSR, UK, France and China are established nuclear weapons powers. India has exploded a nuclear device, while Israel has nuclear weapons but has not tested any. Many experts believe that South Africa and Pakistan will also soon have nuclear weapons.

Despite strong opposition in many countries, large numbers of nuclear power reactors are still being built. Currently, about 400 reactors are operating in 26 countries, generating some 300,000 megawatts of electricity. By 2000, this output will have doubled.

Legend:
- Nuclear weapons states
- Nuclear weapons capability suspected
- Nuclear weapons potential
- Nuclear reactors operating
- Nuclear reactors ordered
- Reprocessing plants operating
- Reprocessing plants under construction or suspected

The nuclear fuel cycle

The manufacture of reactor fuel for power plants depends on the nuclear fuel cycle (*see right*). During nuclear fission, not only is heat produced for electricity generation, but plutonium is formed as a by-product, which can be recovered (along with any unburnt uranium) and later re-used as reactor fuel. Plutonium is an extremely dangerous material, with both civil and military applications. If fast breeder reactors are ever developed commercially (attractive because they produce more plutonium than they consume), then there will be strong economic pressures to separate more of this plutonium in reprocessing plants. But this very same plutonium can also be used to make nuclear explosives — just 10 kg is required to make a nuclear device.

Mining
Ore contains typically 0.4% uranium

Concentration and enrichment to increase proportion of U-235

Fabrication of fuel rods

Nuclear reactor
Burns U-235, generates heat for electricity, and plutonium as a by-product. Fuel rods removed when half fissionable atoms gone.

Uranium

Plutonium

Waste

Breeder reactor
Makes plutonium for itself and other reactors

Fuel fabrication
Plutonium made into breeder fuel

Reprocessing plant
Recovers unused uranium and plutonium

Radioactive waste
Includes spent fuel rods, caesium, strontium and a variety of other radioactive fission products.

Manufacture of weapons-grade plutonium possible

paradox of the nuclear age is that MAD only works when nuclear weapons are inaccurate, requiring large targets, such as cities. When accurate weapons capable of hitting a single installation are deployed, the enemy assumes that the other side's warheads are targeted not on its cities but on its military forces. The cities then cease to be the hostages. And if the enemy no longer fears that its cities are at risk, MAD fails.

Competition between the nuclear weapons scientists of both sides leads to increasing accuracy – and this negates deterrence by mutually assured destruction. The accurate nuclear weapons are therefore given new justifications. They are "counterforce" rather than "countercity" – more useful to fight a nuclear war than deter it. With accurate nuclear weapons, nuclear war-fighting based on destruction of hostile forces becomes the preferred strategy. Thus, the impetus of technology forces a change in nuclear policies whether the politicians want it or not.

A nuclear war-fighting policy is also known as nuclear utilization targeting strategy, or NUTS. Current American and, presumably, Soviet, policy is a confusing mixture of MAD and NUTS. While submarine-launched ballistic missiles (SLBMs) provide a MAD element, being still inaccurate enough to be targeted on cities, the land-based intercontinental ballistic missiles (ICBMs) are accurate, nuclear-war-fighting weapons to be directed against enemy strategic nuclear forces. Within a few years, however, SLBMs will also be accurate enough for military targets. Then nuclear policies will become totally NUTS.

A "fightable, winnable" nuclear war

Very accurate tactical weapons are being deployed in Europe and will become part of nuclear-war-fighting policies. When large numbers of tactical nuclear-war-fighting weapons are integrated into military tactics at low levels of command, the military come to believe that a nuclear war is "fightable and winnable" and that "limited and protracted nuclear war" is possible. Such beliefs make such a war more likely.

But things will not stop here. Newer technologies on the way will strengthen the belief that an all-out nuclear war can be won. Two such believers, the well-known and influential US strategists Colin Gray and Keith Payne, have argued that: "the United States should plan to defeat the Soviet Union and to do so at a cost that would not prohibit US recovery. A combination of counterforce offensive targeting (ie. attacking military targets), civil defense, and ballistic missile and air defense should hold US casualties down to a level compatible with national survival and recovery."

The most important "war-winning" technologies now under development are those related to anti-submarine warfare (ASW), anti-ballistic missile (ABM) systems and anti-satellite (ASAT) weapons. The aim of ASW is to detect and destroy within a short time all enemy strategic nuclear submarines within range of one's homeland. Currently, strategic nuclear submarines carrying SLBMs are much less vulnerable than ICBMs

The infernal machine

The most crucial qualitative advance in nuclear weapons is the improvement of delivery systems. Accuracy is normally measured by the circular error probability (CEP), defined as the radius of the circle centred on the target within which more than 50% of warheads will land. The US, for example, has reduced the CEP of the Minuteman ICBM from about 400 to 200 metres. At the same time, its warhead was improved so that, for the same weight and volume, its explosive power has increased from 170,000 to 330,000 tons of TNT.

Yet qualitative improvements in nuclear weapons are, in fact, increasing the risk of nuclear world war. The policy of "mutually assured destruction" (MAD) is no longer seen to work when the main targets are not the cities, but the weapons silos. If a country believes that it has a good chance of knocking out most of the enemy's nuclear forces before they can be fired, the incentive to make a pre-emptive first strike increases. Such a nuclear war-fighting policy is known as "nuclear utilization targeting strategy" (NUTS).

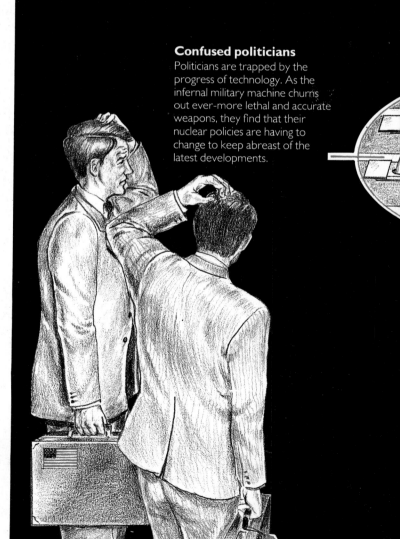

Confused politicians
Politicians are trapped by the progress of technology. As the infernal military machine churns out ever-more lethal and accurate weapons, they find that their nuclear policies are having to change to keep abreast of the latest developments.

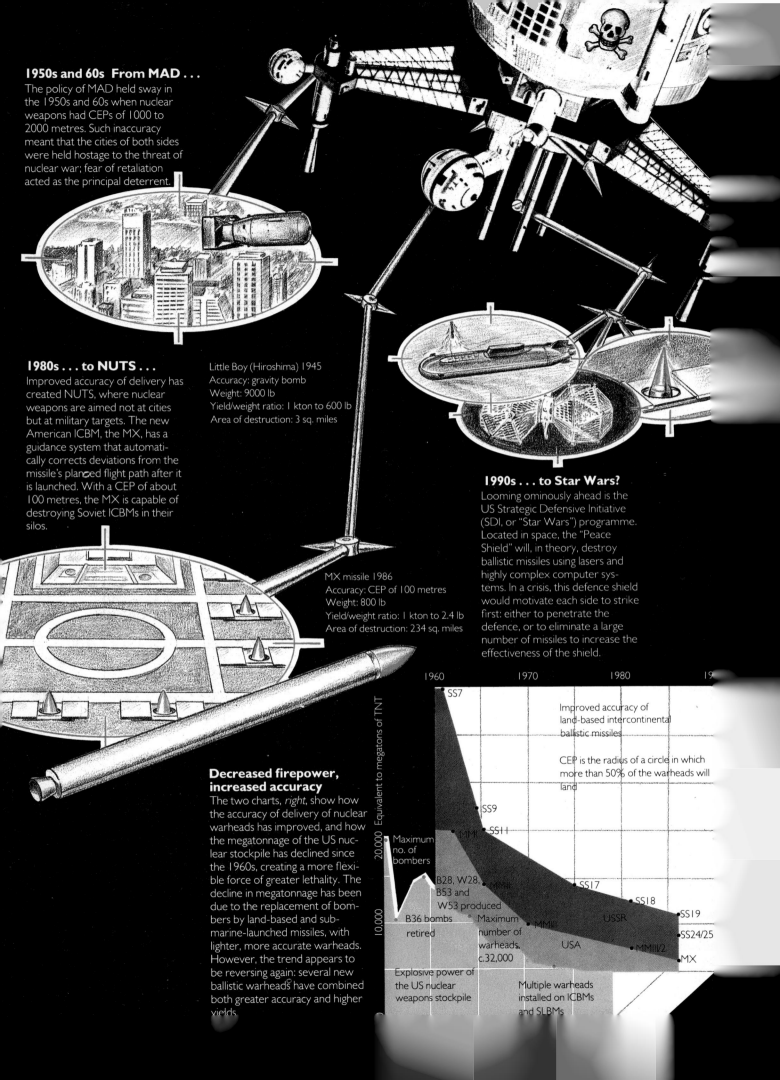

1950s and 60s From MAD . . .

The policy of MAD held sway in the 1950s and 60s when nuclear weapons had CEPs of 1000 to 2000 metres. Such inaccuracy meant that the cities of both sides were held hostage to the threat of nuclear war; fear of retaliation acted as the principal deterrent.

1980s . . . to NUTS . . .

Improved accuracy of delivery has created NUTS, where nuclear weapons are aimed not at cities but at military targets. The new American ICBM, the MX, has a guidance system that automatically corrects deviations from the missile's planned flight path after it is launched. With a CEP of about 100 metres, the MX is capable of destroying Soviet ICBMs in their silos.

Little Boy (Hiroshima) 1945
Accuracy: gravity bomb
Weight: 9000 lb
Yield/weight ratio: 1 kton to 600 lb
Area of destruction: 3 sq. miles

MX missile 1986
Accuracy: CEP of 100 metres
Weight: 800 lb
Yield/weight ratio: 1 kton to 2.4 lb
Area of destruction: 234 sq. miles

1990s . . . to Star Wars?

Looming ominously ahead is the US Strategic Defensive Initiative (SDI, or "Star Wars") programme. Located in space, the "Peace Shield" will, in theory, destroy ballistic missiles using lasers and highly complex computer systems. In a crisis, this defence shield would motivate each side to strike first: either to penetrate the defence, or to eliminate a large number of missiles to increase the effectiveness of the shield.

Decreased firepower, increased accuracy

The two charts, *right*, show how the accuracy of delivery of nuclear warheads has improved, and how the megatonnage of the US nuclear stockpile has declined since the 1960s, creating a more flexible force of greater lethality. The decline in megatonnage has been due to the replacement of bombers by land-based and submarine-launched missiles, with lighter, more accurate warheads. However, the trend appears to be reversing again: several new ballistic warheads have combined both greater accuracy and higher yields.

1960   1970   1980   19

Equivalent to megatons of TNT

Improved accuracy of land-based intercontinental ballistic missiles

CEP is the radius of a circle in which more than 50% of the warheads will land

SS7

SS9

MMI   SS11

20,000

Maximum no. of bombers

B28, W28, B53 and W53 produced

MMII   SS17

SS18

SS19

USSR   SS24/25

10,000

B36 bombs retired

Maximum number of warheads, c.32,000

MMIII

USA   MMIII/2   MX

Explosive power of the US nuclear weapons stockpile

Multiple warheads installed on ICBMs and SLBMs

to a pre-emptive strike – and so could retaliate. But when one side has effective ASW systems, can limit the retaliatory damage by the other side's strategic forces, and believes its ballistic missile defences would destroy any enemy warheads surviving a surprise attack, then the temptation to make an all-out nuclear first strike may become hard to resist.

The first action in a nuclear surprise attack would be to destroy the other side's military satellites, the "eyes and ears" of the military in space – hence the efforts to develop effective ASAT weapons.

The combination of accurate nuclear weapons with effective ASW, ABM and ASAT technologies, by raising perception of a nuclear first-strike capability, will again considerably increase the risk of nuclear world war. In fact, the risk of nuclear catastrophe would become too high to be acceptable to rational people.

Nevertheless, there are those in influential positions – groups within the Pentagon, for example, and within the Soviet military – who argue that all efforts should be made to develop technologies to achieve a strategic nuclear superiority. The main motive is not necessarily to wage nuclear war, but to gain the advantage in the superpower struggle for global influence and domination. Strategic nuclear superiority would give a superpower great scope for adventurism, knowing that the other side would not dare oppose it.

Conventional war – a "safer" alternative?

New military technologies are making available conventional offensive weapons of great destructive power – artillery, missiles, incendiary weapons, aerial bombs, and so on – and modern chemical and biological weapons of exceeding lethality.

One example, of many, of a conventional weapon with a large fire-power is the multi-launch rocket system that fires a salvo of 12 rockets in less than one minute. The rockets release about 8000 grenade-like munitions. When these explode they scatter razor-sharp and hot metal fragments at very high velocity over an area equal to six football fields. The cloud of fragments is highly lethal to people in that area. So lethal, in fact, that the destructive power of *each salvo* is similar to a low-yield nuclear weapon.

Another very destructive conventional weapon is the fuel air explosive in which an aerosol cloud of an explosive mixture is ignited to produce a high blast pressure. Aerosol clouds can be joined together to produce huge explosions over very large areas.

Many of the new conventional weapons produce horrific effects. Some fragmentation weapons cause multiple injuries in many casualties. Treatment is then required by several doctors, each with a different medical speciality. The chances of such sophisticated medical services being available near a war zone are slim. And they would soon be swamped by the large number of casualties these weapons produce. Fragmentation weapons are, in fact, deliberately designed to prevent the lives of casualties being saved.

Conventional war: Horrors of today

Central Europe, where East and West face each other across the East German-West German border, is the most heavily armed region in the world. Not only are thousands of nuclear weapons deployed there, but large numbers of troops and huge arsenals of conventional weapons sit waiting in the wings. Today's conventional weapons are so destructive that a conventional war in Europe would destroy central Europe almost as thoroughly as would a nuclear one. The choice for Europe is not nuclear or conventional war, but war or no war. This is not to equate conventional and nuclear war in general but to emphasize that *locally* conventional war with modern weaponry is extremely destructive.

The map (*right*) shows the numerical strength of the opposing conventional forces in Europe. While this information is useful, it is also misleading: it fails to take into account the considerable technical superiority of the NATO forces, which offsets their numerical inferiority in some categories. The sites of nuclear power stations are also depicted; such is their profusion that the likelihood of one being hit during a conventional war (and thus creating a nuclear war) is too real to ignore.

Chemical warfare

Nuclear weapons are not the only weapons of mass destruction – chemical weapons, too, are indiscriminate killers. Chemical weapons were first used in WWI, in which more than 100 million kg of chemicals – mainly chlorine, phosgene and mustard gas – were released to kill 100,000 people and injure another million. But compared with today's chemical weapons, these early ones were primitive.

The most advanced chemical warfare agent is the binary nerve gas. A binary chemical weapon consists of two chemicals of relatively low toxicity stored separately in a chemical munition. They mix when the munition is fired or when it reaches its target. When they mix, a nerve gas – such as sarin – is produced which is normally lethal instantaneously.

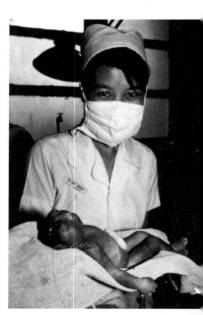

Agent Orange, a chemical used by the USA in Vietnam, caused this child's deformities.

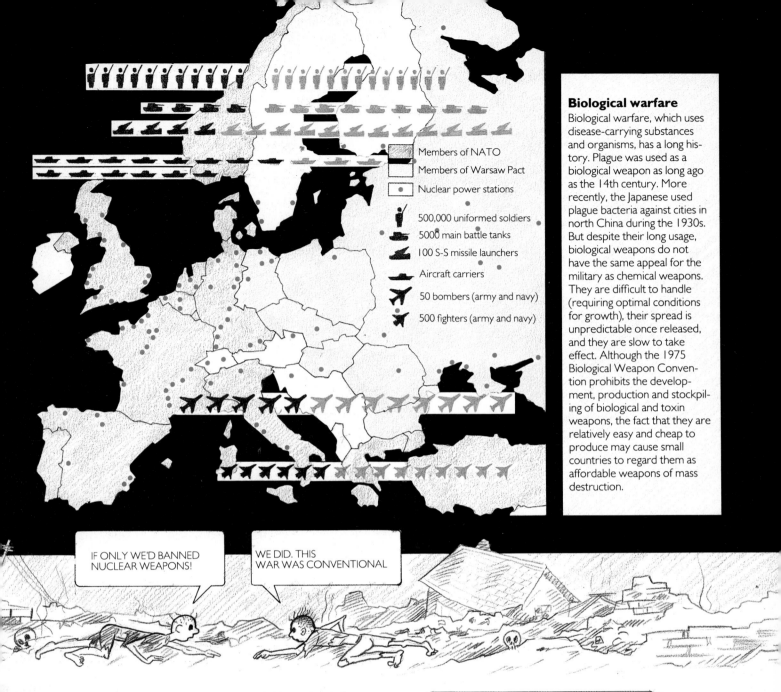

Biological warfare

Biological warfare, which uses disease-carrying substances and organisms, has a long history. Plague was used as a biological weapon as long ago as the 14th century. More recently, the Japanese used plague bacteria against cities in north China during the 1930s. But despite their long usage, biological weapons do not have the same appeal for the military as chemical weapons. They are difficult to handle (requiring optimal conditions for growth), their spread is unpredictable once released, and they are slow to take effect. Although the 1975 Biological Weapon Convention prohibits the development, production and stockpiling of biological and toxin weapons, the fact that they are relatively easy and cheap to produce may cause small countries to regard them as affordable weapons of mass destruction.

Members of NATO	
Members of Warsaw Pact	
Nuclear power stations	
500,000 uniformed soldiers	
5000 main battle tanks	
100 S-S missile launchers	
Aircraft carriers	
50 bombers (army and navy)	
500 fighters (army and navy)	

IF ONLY WE'D BANNED NUCLEAR WEAPONS!

WE DID. THIS WAR WAS CONVENTIONAL

Exposure to even extremely low concentrations produces sweating and vomiting, followed by paralysis, respiratory failure and death.

Even more toxic agents are under development. We can foresee the development of synthetic peptides with relatively low molecular weights which will have especially high lethality – maybe a hundred times greater than that of today's nerve gases.

The USA, the USSR and France have chemical weapons in strategic quantities. The USA probably has about 38,000 tons of chemical warfare agents. About half are the lethal dermal agent mustard gas and the rest nerve gases (VX and sarin). Of these, between 500 and 1000 tons of nerve gas are thought to be deployed in West Germany. France probably has the same amount. The USSR is thought to have a much bigger chemical arsenal than the USA, although much of it is probably old agents, such as mustard gas. It seems reasonable to assume that NATO and the Warsaw Pact have comparable chemical warfare capabilities.

In a war in Europe, chemical weapons could be used against large military targets or centres of population. But it is likely that a significant chemical attack would be answered by nuclear weapons.

Iraq is said to be producing on average about 60 tons of mustard gas a month, as well as 4 tons a month of each of the nerve agents sarin and tabun. Iraq's chemical weapon capability has focused attention on the proliferation of chemical weapons in developing countries. Chemical weapons have become known as "the poor countries' nuclear weapons".

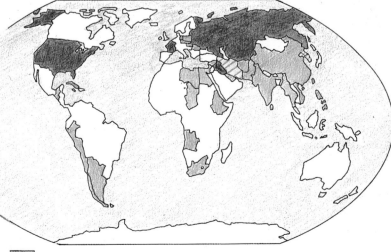

	Countries known to possess chemical weapons
	Countries thought to possess chemical weapons
	Countries thought to be seeking possession of chemical weapons

Incendiary weapons are still being refined. Modern ones scatter highly inflammable chemicals over large areas, chemicals that can cause exceptionally severe burns over much of the body. And there are battlefield lasers that, although designed to "blind" optical sensors in enemy weapon systems, can also blind people who are in the battle area.

Modern chemical weapons are much more lethal than their predecessors. Like biological weapons, they are potential weapons of mass destruction that can be produced by small nations rather easily and cheaply in amounts that, in their regions, are strategically significant. The ease of proliferation of these weapons makes them all the more dangerous.

The shadow of nuclear war should not blind us to the horror of modern conventional weapons. Their very violence could, moreover, in future blur the distinction between conventional bombardment and small, "fighting" tactical nuclear weapons – making the risk of escalation from one to the other, and thence to all-out nuclear war, all the greater.

Nuclear war – what would happen

Soviet and American nuclear arsenals together contained in late 1987 some 50,000 nuclear warheads. Their total explosive power of about 15 billion tons of TNT, or three tons of TNT for every man, woman and child on Earth, is 750 times all the explosives ever used in war. This destructive power is equivalent to approximately 1,250,000 Hiroshimas. The world has stockpiled more explosive power than food!

There have been several attempts to model the outcome of a nuclear war. Most presume that any use of nuclear weapons will inevitably escalate into a war in which many of the warheads in the arsenals are used. In the highly charged atmosphere of a major war, countries do not surrender while they still have firepower left – rather, they fight to the bitter end though the nation is destroyed in the process. Nor are the original objectives of the war long remembered once it has begun. Many alive today have experienced this "war mentality". We would do well not to forget it.

Any talk, as by for example the US Secretary of Defense, of "limited" nuclear war or "protracted but controlled" nuclear war, is simply unrealistic. In a nuclear war, political and military leadership command, control and communications centres would be priority targets. Once it had begun, a nuclear war would be impossible to control – very soon, there would be nobody left to control it.

Given the types of weapons deployed in Europe, any war on the continent is particularly likely to escalate rapidly to an all-out strategic war between the USA and the USSR. A conventional war in Europe would probably become nuclear as soon as one side penetrated the other's territory – NATO's "flexible response" policy (see p. 60) assumes that a major Warsaw Pact breakthrough with conventional forces would be stopped with tactical nuclear weapons. Any nuclear arsenals in danger of being overrun by the

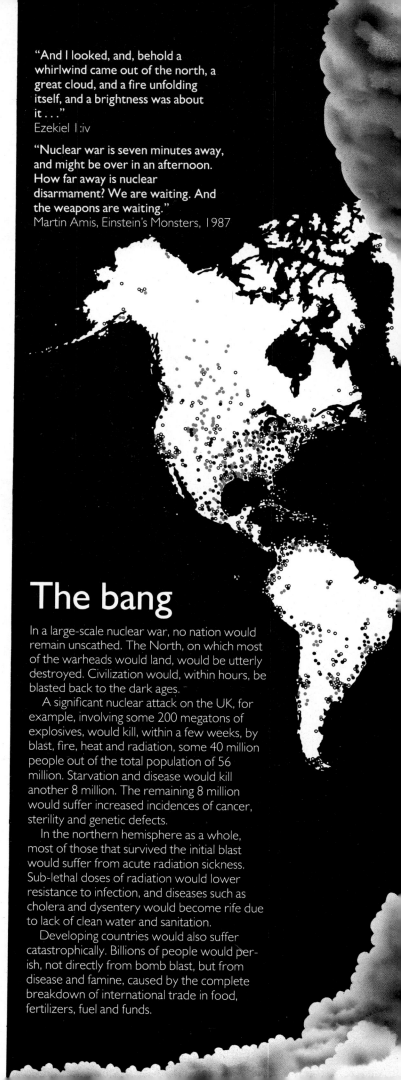

"And I looked, and, behold a whirlwind came out of the north, a great cloud, and a fire unfolding itself, and a brightness was about it . . ."
Ezekiel I:iv

"Nuclear war is seven minutes away, and might be over in an afternoon. How far away is nuclear disarmament? We are waiting. And the weapons are waiting."
Martin Amis, Einstein's Monsters, 1987

The bang

In a large-scale nuclear war, no nation would remain unscathed. The North, on which most of the warheads would land, would be utterly destroyed. Civilization would, within hours, be blasted back to the dark ages.

A significant nuclear attack on the UK, for example, involving some 200 megatons of explosives, would kill, within a few weeks, by blast, fire, heat and radiation, some 40 million people out of the total population of 56 million. Starvation and disease would kill another 8 million. The remaining 8 million would suffer increased incidences of cancer, sterility and genetic defects.

In the northern hemisphere as a whole, most of those that survived the initial blast would suffer from acute radiation sickness. Sub-lethal doses of radiation would lower resistance to infection, and diseases such as cholera and dysentery would become rife due to lack of clean water and sanitation.

Developing countries would also suffer catastrophically. Billions of people would perish, not directly from bomb blast, but from disease and famine, caused by the complete breakdown of international trade in food, fertilizers, fuel and funds.

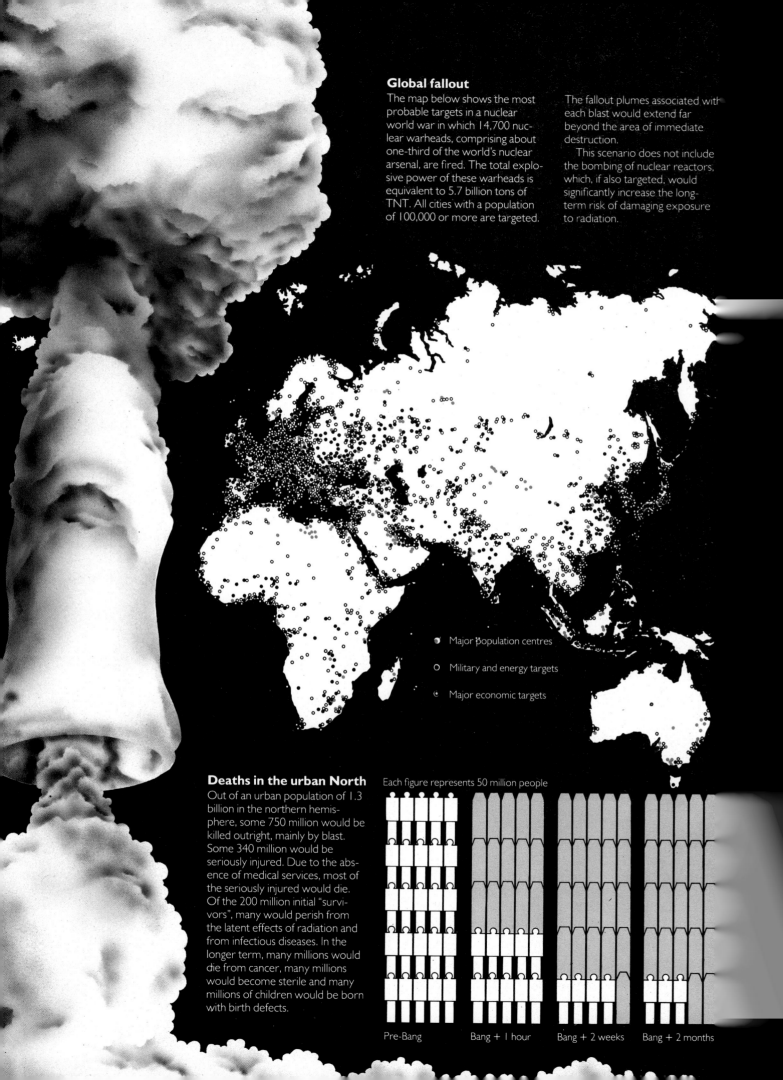

Global fallout

The map below shows the most probable targets in a nuclear world war in which 14,700 nuclear warheads, comprising about one-third of the world's nuclear arsenal, are fired. The total explosive power of these warheads is equivalent to 5.7 billion tons of TNT. All cities with a population of 100,000 or more are targeted.

The fallout plumes associated with each blast would extend far beyond the area of immediate destruction.

This scenario does not include the bombing of nuclear reactors, which, if also targeted, would significantly increase the long-term risk of damaging exposure to radiation.

● Major population centres

○ Military and energy targets

◔ Major economic targets

Deaths in the urban North

Out of an urban population of 1.3 billion in the northern hemisphere, some 750 million would be killed outright, mainly by blast. Some 340 million would be seriously injured. Due to the absence of medical services, most of the seriously injured would die. Of the 200 million initial "survivors", many would perish from the latent effects of radiation and from infectious diseases. In the longer term, many millions would die from cancer, many millions would become sterile and many millions of children would be born with birth defects.

Each figure represents 50 million people

Pre-Bang   Bang + 1 hour   Bang + 2 weeks   Bang + 2 months

advance would certainly be used, and since nuclear artillery is deployed near the front line, escalation could be rapid.

A nuclear war in which even half of the existing warheads were used would be utterly catastrophic. Over 60 per cent of people in urban centres in the northern hemisphere would be killed outright, and over 25 per cent more seriously injured and unlikely to live. The medical profession, and especially the International Physicians for Prevention of Nuclear War, have repeatedly warned that, in the conditions after a nuclear attack, treatment of the seriously injured would not be possible; they could, at best, only ease their death.

Of the scattered "survivors", many would perish from radiation exposure or infectious diseases such as cholera. A large fraction would be rendered sterile.

And then would come the nuclear winter.

Nuclear winter: the aftermath

The term "nuclear winter" is used to describe the state of the world after a major nuclear war, particularly the cold and dark caused by the smoke, dust and debris. A nuclear war in which about half of the nuclear arsenals were used could inject into the atmosphere roughly 40 million tons of fine dust and up to 200 million tons of smoke particles. The dust and smoke could block up to 90 per cent of sunlight.

The Earth's surface would cool quickly; surface temperature in the northern hemisphere could drop by 10-15 degrees centigrade or more. Light levels could drop drastically – to well below 50 per cent of normal. There would be a permanent dusk.

The effects on food production would be catastrophic. Temperature drops of less than five degrees could destroy, for example, Canadian and Soviet cereal crops. The world's people, many of them dependent on the Northern "grain basket", would face starvation as food production ceased. All countries, whether or not they are directly involved in the war, would risk famine.

The smoke produced by nuclear detonations would rise to high altitudes and become trapped in the stratosphere. The normal global weather circulation patterns would change dramatically. Climatic stress would be greatest in northern middle latitudes, the northern subtropics and the equatorial zone, areas in which about 85 per cent of the world's population lives. The climatic effects could last for a year or more.

In continental areas of the northern hemisphere and Australia, usual rainfall could cease for several months over large areas. In Africa, Asia and the Pacific, the monsoon rains might disappear. As the smoke and dust clouds cleared, the climate would slowly return to normal. But there would be more death to come. The depletion of the ozone layer in the stratosphere would cause considerably increased levels of ultraviolet radiation that would be extremely damaging to all surviving life on Earth.

Overall, the southern hemisphere would be affected less by climatic disruption. But countries dependent on imported grains, pesticides, fuels and farm machinery

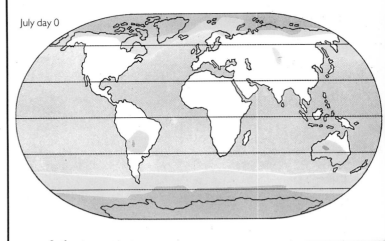

July day 0

Surface temperature
- Below 10°C
- Below 0°C

Light levels, % of normal
- 1%
- 15%
- 50%

30°N

0°

30°S

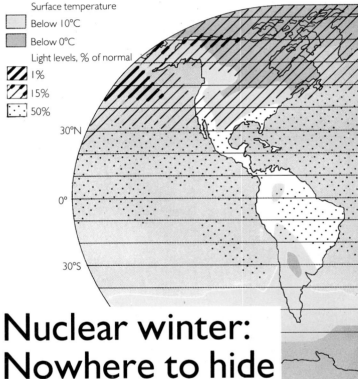

Nuclear winter: Nowhere to hide

"2,500 million people, about 60 per cent of the world's population, could die of starvation alone after a nuclear war . . . in which just one half of today's nuclear arsenals is used."

This is the alarming conclusion of the Scientific Committee on Problems of the Environment (SCOPE) on the effects of a nuclear winter. Starvation would arise mainly from the effects of climate change on food production and from the lack of fertilizers, pesticides and fuels. The smoke pall from the combat zone would block so much sunlight that temperatures could drop to below freezing over much of the northern hemisphere. In parts of the northern hemisphere and Australia, regular rainfall could cease for months.

Developing countries dependent on imports would suffer hardship even if they totally avoided nuclear attack. Within a hundred days of the attack, up to 450 million Africans, for example, would starve.

The cold and the dark

The likely effects of a nuclear winter have been calculated using models of the world's climate, such as the Community Climate Model, a general air-circulation model. On a typical July day, before the war, as can be seen on the map, *left*, areas of the planet below freezing are confined to the polar regions and high altitudes. With the onset of war, tremendous fires in the combat zone would start that would rage, uncontrolled and uncontrollable, for weeks, injecting a thick smoke layer into the atmosphere. This would drastically reduce the amount of sunlight reaching the Earth's surface, causing surface cooling and darkness. Any agricultural activity in the northern hemisphere would grind to a halt.

The larger map, *below*, shows the extent of the climatic disruption 20 days after the summer outbreak of war. If the war occurred during another season, then temperature changes would be different, and the effects would probably be less severe.

More deaths from starvation than blast

It seems difficult to believe that the principal threat to life in the event of a nuclear world war is not the direct effects of the blast but starvation. Only a small percentage of the world's population could possibly be fed in the nuclear aftermath, putting those people living in the non-combatant countries at just as much risk. With large-scale climatic disruption brought on by the nuclear winter, food production would be drastically reduced. Those countries not able to produce enough food to feed their teeming populations would suddenly find their food imports cut off, and their supplies of fertilizers, pesticides, heavy machinery and fuel removed. Malnutrition and starvation would inevitably result.

The bar chart, *below*, shows the impact of the nuclear winter on the world's population 365 days after the holocaust. The number of survivors are calculated assuming that food stocks are at typical levels when war occurs.

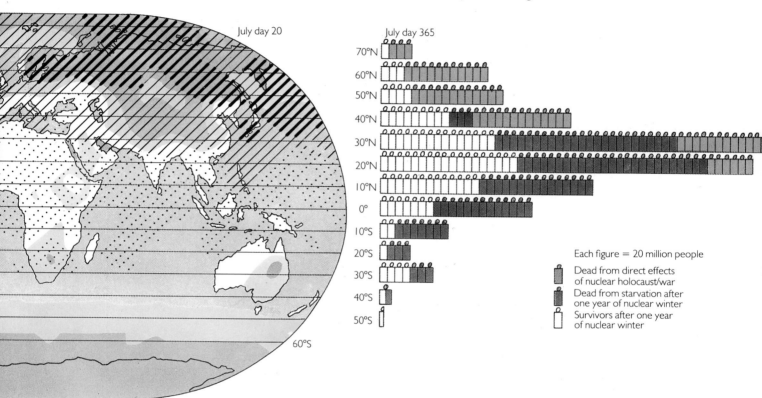

July day 20

July day 365

Each figure = 20 million people

Dead from direct effects of nuclear holocaust/war

Dead from starvation after one year of nuclear winter

Survivors after one year of nuclear winter

Small climatic change – huge drop in rice yields

Rice is one of the world's principal staples, and would become the main food source to a disproportionate fraction of the survivors of a nuclear war. But rice is extremely sensitive to climatic fluctuations. As the diagram *below* shows, a temperature drop of a mere 2°C and a reduction in rainfall of some 15% can reduce rice yields by as much as 20%. More extreme variations, as would be likely in a nuclear winter, could completely wipe out rice production in the northern hemisphere.

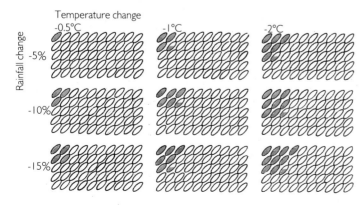

USA: 3000 years after the holocaust

If survivors were to set foot on the devastated land that was once the USA some 3000 years after a nuclear holocaust, they would find a strange and unstable land. While the forests, grasslands and deserts would exhibit a depressingly low diversity of life forms, some organisms would thrive in abundance. Cockroaches, rats and houseflies would exist in huge populations, as would other generalized feeders, such as crickets and grasshoppers. In the absence of predatory insects (the impact of the war would have been similar to spraying the entire land with insecticides), there would be wild fluctuations in the insect populations.

In the cooler parts, many seeds would have survived the cold and radiation, and weeds, grasses and scrubby plants would gradually have recolonized the blackened land. In the subtropical and tropical zones, however, recovery would have been hampered by the plants' and animals' intolerance to cold.

Should human survivors from the southern hemisphere ever manage to repopulate North America, their mode of existence would be primitive. With the exhaustion of Earth resources, advancement from the post-war Stone Age would be unlikely.

would be hard hit, even without the effects of the nuclear winter. Continents such as Africa would suffer massive death rates from starvation. There would be literally no place to hide.

Whether or not the survivors (mainly from the southern hemisphere) could establish viable societies is an open question. Given the loss of fertility and genetic effects due to radiation, a major nuclear war could, in the long term, wipe out humankind.

But not Gaia – though the shock would be severe. The post-nuclear-war conditions would favour insects and animals that breed fast and are relatively resistant to radiation. Cockroaches, rats and mice would flourish; larger animals and birds would perish. A nuclear war between the superpowers would give the Earth back to the insects.

Despair in the nuclear age

"The 'defensive' preparations to counter aggression in which both sides in an arms race engage must create unstable fear". This is how psychologist Hanna Segal describes the mental effects of the nuclear arms race. In the past few years, knowledge of the catastrophic effects of nuclear war has become widespread. Many people deal with this knowledge by denial, the normal psychological reaction. Others accept the fiction that nuclear weapons are "necessary". A few even take steps to survive a nuclear war. But most people, if they think about nuclear holocaust, feel terror.

This terror goes deeper than fear of the weapons themselves. The psychologist C. A. Meier has said, for instance, that in denying and destroying the natural world or "outer wilderness", humankind risks that it will "resurrect powerfully from within, whereupon it would be immediately projected. Enemies would be created, and its terrifying aspects would take revenge for our neglect, our lack of reverence, our ruthless interference with that beautiful order of things. " Fear of nuclear violence as a projection of violence done to our own nature is not uncommon, encouraging some fundamentalist religious beliefs that nuclear armageddon is the "wrath of God".

Fear is paralyzing. Public opinion polls in Europe, the US and Canada show that many people, in some countries the majority, think that a nuclear war is inevitable and there will be no survivors. Not very surprisingly, living for decades under this shadow, in a world dominated by an irrational pursuit of the technology of death, has produced widespread apathy and despair.

The sense of helplessness is deepened by the fact that even when the majority is strongly opposed to certain weapons, political leaders go ahead with their deployment. So great are the vested interests in nuclear weapons, that military affairs are simply not dealt with in a democratic manner.

Nevertheless, there is hope. Human instincts for survival are strong, and we can learn. Millions of people are now actively seeking an end to fear and a new world order, at peace with Gaia and ourselves.

Despair and hope

Before the nuclear age, all generations knew that others would follow. That certainty is now lost forever. We live with the knowledge that war could obliterate our world in an afternoon. People avoid thinking about nuclear war. If they do, feelings of deep terror and anxiety are reported. The image of holocaust represents all that is dark in our own nature, the very face of evil. Unable to handle such feelings, most of us repress them, and do nothing. Thus we drift towards armageddon.

Some of the worst effects are on children, who feel cheated of their future. Surveys in various countries reveal that they know rather accurately what a nuclear war would be like, and believe they and their families will not survive. US high school seniors believing that "nuclear or biological annihilation will be the fate of all humanity in my lifetime", rose from 22% in 1975 to 36% in 1982, for example.

How can we deal with this sense of despair and helplessness? Chiefly, by confronting fear. People who join groups, demonstrate, and demand that the future be given back to them, show they believe we still have the power to choose.

Hope

Since the start of the nuclear age, there have been those with courage to face up to the fear of armageddon and campaign for a future. The tide of opposition has at its forefront doctors, scientists, historians, teachers and lawyers – people used to looking at facts objectively. With the rise of a new style of leadership in the USSR, and the first treaty ever to reduce nuclear weapons, hope has begun to seem real. But it is our children, most of all, who hold the key. Asked if governments were doing enough to prevent nuclear war, 80% of British children surveyed said "No". Asked if it could be prevented, 93% of Soviet children (compared with 65% in the US and 45% in Sweden) replied "Yes". The greater optimism of these Soviet children can perhaps be related to the participation of nearly all in peace activities. Involving children in peace education and conservation projects, and in caring for their own future, could help to make that future possible.

"Pacifism could have worked in Germany if only the church had given a lead, but it didn't. If you have sufficient resolve, you can prevail. Take Norway. Hitler put in a Quisling government and attempted to change the whole school system to teach the philosophy of Aryan supremacy. But 12,000 unarmed school teachers refused to co-operate and the government had to capitulate. In Denmark when the Jews were ordered to wear the Star of David so they could be identified and shipped to concentration camps, the King put on the Star and so did the rest of the citizens and the plan failed. Non-violent, passive resistance can work." Bishop Thomas Gumbleton

Despair

One survey of Canadian children revealed that over two-thirds believed nuclear war would occur in their lifetime, as this poem by a 14 year-old reflects.

Why even try;
the striving and struggle
to be our best,
would be in vain.

Why even try;
all our technology
and advancements
will destroy us,
someday soon.

Why even try;
our family, our friends
our language
and culture,
gone with the push of a button.

Why even try;
if we have to live
in fear of the end,
of everything.

Why even try;
if we are probably going to die,
anyway.

6 The struggle for peace

Introduced by Archbishop Desmond Tutu

All the great religions set store by this elusive thing, peace. Almost invariably their stories tell of a golden past when all the inhabitants of the universe, divine, human and animal, dwelt in an undisturbed harmony, or point to a time in the future when such an idyllic period would once more be restored, whether in a heaven or in a reordered and transfigured world. Such memories of a paradise lost and burning desire for paradise regained cannot be illusory, the insubstantial stuff of which dreams are made. They seem more properly to say that we know in our very bones that we were made for something better than what we experience as harsh realities. We were not meant for such things as Cain slaying his brother Abel and forever having his blood crying out from the earth for revenge. How can we ever not bow our heads in shame when we think of the Auschwitzes, of the Hiroshimas and the Nagasakis?

No it is not a quest after a chimera, an illusion, this noble quest after peace. It is to look for something which will enable us to be truly human. For Christians it is a humanity measured by nothing less than the humanity of Jesus Christ himself, and other great religions have their ideals which are greatly sought after and often embodied in the life of a great teacher or founder.

In Africa we say: "A person is a person through other persons." A solitary human being is a contradiction in terms. I do not come into the world a fully formed person, I would not know how to eat, walk, think, speak or behave at all as a human being unless I learned these things in human community. We need one another to complement one another.

We find that we are placed in a delicate network of vital relationships with the divine, with fellow human beings, and with the rest of creation. We violate nature only at our peril, and are meant to live as members of one family. This is the law of our being, and when we break this law things go disastrously wrong. We know the consequences of our wanton destruction of natural resources, the ecological misadventures that follow in the train of our pollution of the biosphere. We are perhaps more aware of the threats to peace and to human survival posed by the reckless arms race. Nations spend obscenely large amounts of public funds on instruments of death and destruction. We know that a very minute fraction of that budget of death would ensure that God's children everywhere would have a clean supply of water, would have enough to eat, would have a reasonable chance of survival.

Peace is more than the absence of war. The peace we want is something positive and dynamic. In the Hebrew it is called shalom – wholeness, integrity; it means wellbeing, physical and spiritual. It means the abundance of life which Jesus Christ promised he had brought. It has all to do with an harmonious coexistence with one's neighbours in a wholesome environment allowing persons to become more and more fully human.

In South Africa, apartheid has brought the East/West cold war into our region: we can rightly assert that apartheid is a threat to world peace. Until the system is done away with we will never have true peace and stability which have to be founded on justice, on the rule of law and the recognition of fundamental human rights.

We can translate this into a global scale. The world will know no peace until there is global justice, when nations will be ready to share their resources more equitably; when nations don't need to envy one another, but will behave as though they did indeed belong to one family, God's family, the human family.

+Desmond Cape

"Mankind must put an end to war, or war will put an end to mankind." John F. Kennedy

Since war began, philosophers have decried its folly, individuals sought to resist it, and leaders tried to tame it with codes of honour or bans on weapons. But this century has seen a new phenomenon: shocked by the atrocities of two world wars, and in fear of nuclear holocaust, humanity has set out to abolish war itself. The outlawing of war, years of effort at disarmament, and mass movements for peace all reflect this intent. We have also tried to address transnational security issues and seek non-violent means for change. Mostly, we have failed, so far. But at least we have begun.

Disarmament efforts

In 1868, the St Petersburg Conference considered "forbidding the use of certain projectiles in time of war among civilised nations". In 1907, the Hague Convention Respecting the Laws and Customs of War on Land was signed, followed in 1925 by the Protocols for the Prohibition of the Use in War of Asphyxiating, Poisonous or other Gases, and Bacteriological Methods of Warfare. These treaties, however, did little to modify behaviour in the two subsequent world wars.

The birth of atomic weapons and demonstration of their terrible destruction at Hiroshima triggered efforts to prevent a nuclear arms race and establish nuclear and general disarmament. Since 1945, hundreds of international meetings have taken place to achieve these objectives. But instead, arms have multiplied, and negotiations have become institutions where politicians "talk peace but plan for war".

Within weeks of its founding, the United Nations set up an Atomic Energy Commission to consider plans for eliminating nuclear weapons and ensuring the peaceful use of atomic power. The AEC initially endorsed the Baruch Plan to internationalize nuclear energy and nuclear disarmament, until fears that the plan would perpetuate a US monopoly of nuclear technology brought US/USSR differences to the surface.

But the major failure was the decision in the early 1960s to abandon general and complete disarmament in favour of "arms control" – even though American President Kennedy, Soviet Secretary-General Khrushchev and British Foreign Minister Selwyn Lloyd had each tabled treaties on general and complete disarmament. Indeed, the powers were then close to agreement on a timetable for far-reaching disarmament. This is bound to raise suspicions that vested interests in the arms race in both superpowers sabotaged negotiations.

Disarmament means ridding ourselves of weapons; arms control means managing the arms race. Its advocates argue that, in a world of security-obsessed states, the only practicable approach is to take small steps and work up to bigger ones as confidence grows. But the record of 25 years of arms control is dismal.

The only disarmament that had taken place by 1987 was destruction of stockpiles of biological weapons under the 1972 Convention – the military had little

Disarmament talks

The years since 1945 have witnessed a relentless increase in the lethality of global arsenals. Although disarmament and arms control talks have multiplied correspondingly (*see below*), the arms race has continued unabated, while negotiators have concentrated on limited "control" measures.

But there is now hope that we have reached the peak in weapon lethality, and that the curve may even be descending. There are twin grounds for optimism: radical leadership and economic necessity. The USA must cut its huge budget deficit; Gorbachev must cut military spending to pay for his economic reforms.

Moon
Sea bed
Antarctica

Nuclear-free environments
Arms control treaties have banned nuclear weapons from various remote regions outside national control. The Outer Space Treaty prohibits the placing of nuclear weapons in space. The Sea Bed Treaty prohibits nuclear weapons on the sea bed, the ocean floor and in its sub-soil. The Antarctic Treaty prohibits deployment of such weapons on the Antarctic continent.

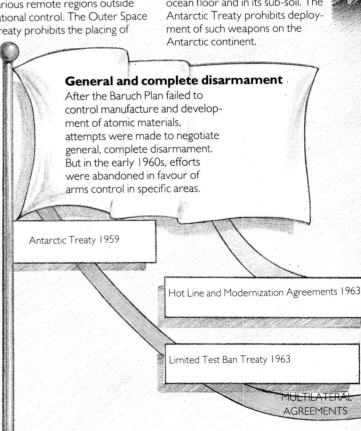

General and complete disarmament
After the Baruch Plan failed to control manufacture and development of atomic materials, attempts were made to negotiate general, complete disarmament. But in the early 1960s, efforts were abandoned in favour of arms control in specific areas.

Antarctic Treaty 1959

Hot Line and Modernization Agreements 1963

Limited Test Ban Treaty 1963

MULTILATERAL AGREEMENTS

Gorbachev's initiative

Since Gorbachev came to power in 1985, there has been a mood of hope generated by his oft-repeated wish to halt the nuclear arms race, end the militarization of space, achieve nuclear disarmament and reduce conventional weapons. The Reagan-Gorbachev summits do much to fuel this new mood of optimism.

It is certainly in Gorbachev's interests to reduce the Soviet military budget in order to finance his economic reforms. But to retain military backing he must achieve arms control treaties. If not, the military hawks, and others, will make it impossible for him to push through his reforms.

The vast budget and trade deficits in the USA may help Gorbachev achieve his goals. The USA can substantially reduce its budget deficit only by cutting military spending. Economic restraints may, in the end, produce widespread acceptance of disarmament.

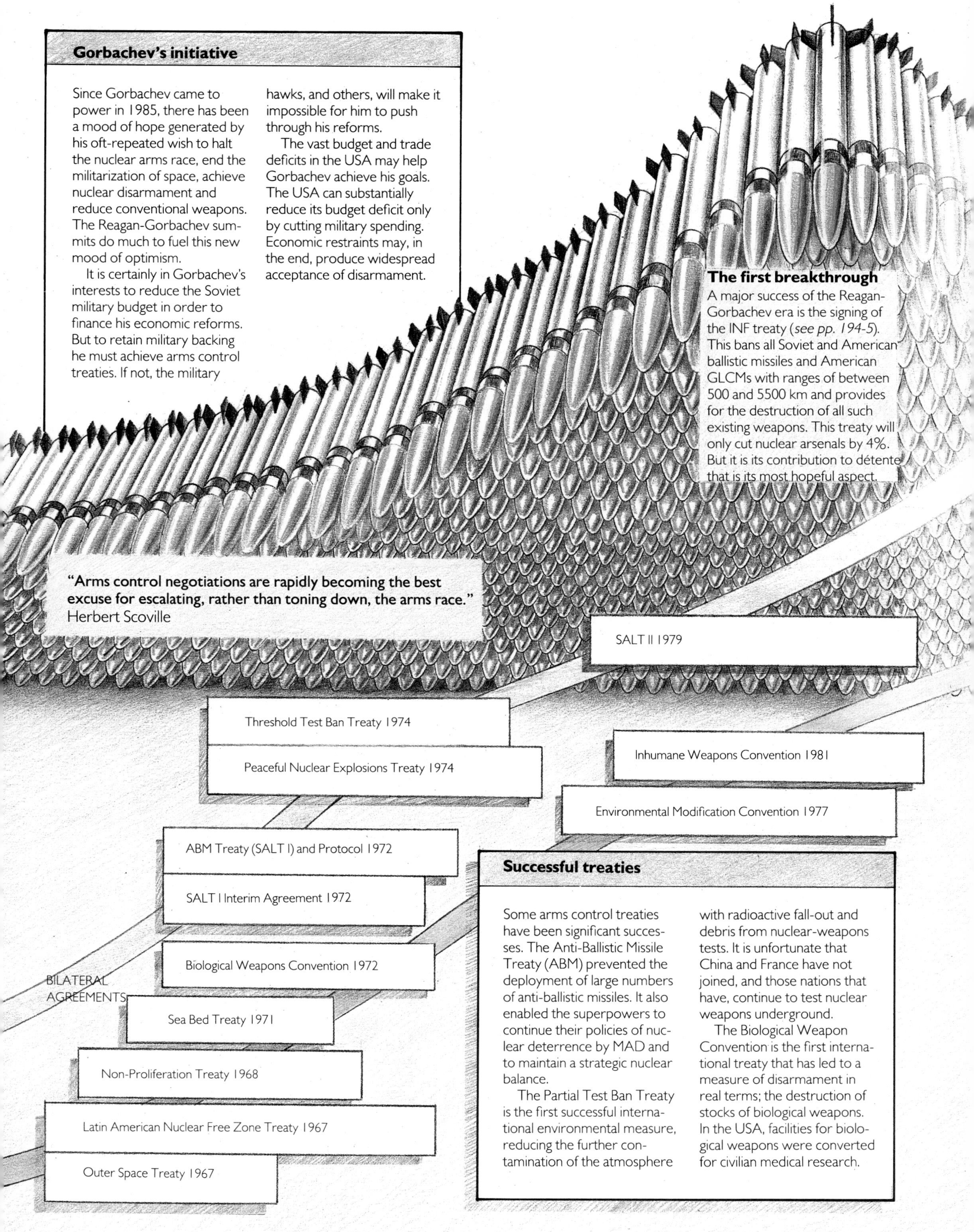

The first breakthrough

A major success of the Reagan-Gorbachev era is the signing of the INF treaty (*see pp. 194-5*). This bans all Soviet and American ballistic missiles and American GLCMs with ranges of between 500 and 5500 km and provides for the destruction of all such existing weapons. This treaty will only cut nuclear arsenals by 4%. But it is its contribution to détente that is its most hopeful aspect.

"Arms control negotiations are rapidly becoming the best excuse for escalating, rather than toning down, the arms race."
Herbert Scoville

SALT II 1979

Threshold Test Ban Treaty 1974

Peaceful Nuclear Explosions Treaty 1974

Inhumane Weapons Convention 1981

Environmental Modification Convention 1977

ABM Treaty (SALT I) and Protocol 1972

SALT I Interim Agreement 1972

Biological Weapons Convention 1972

BILATERAL AGREEMENTS

Sea Bed Treaty 1971

Non-Proliferation Treaty 1968

Latin American Nuclear Free Zone Treaty 1967

Outer Space Treaty 1967

Successful treaties

Some arms control treaties have been significant successes. The Anti-Ballistic Missile Treaty (ABM) prevented the deployment of large numbers of anti-ballistic missiles. It also enabled the superpowers to continue their policies of nuclear deterrence by MAD and to maintain a strategic nuclear balance.

The Partial Test Ban Treaty is the first successful international environmental measure, reducing the further contamination of the atmosphere with radioactive fall-out and debris from nuclear-weapons tests. It is unfortunate that China and France have not joined, and those nations that have, continue to test nuclear weapons underground.

The Biological Weapon Convention is the first international treaty that has led to a measure of disarmament in real terms; the destruction of stocks of biological weapons. In the USA, facilities for biological weapons were converted for civilian medical research.

interest in these weapons. Similar reasons enabled the 1972 Anti-Ballistic Missile Treaty, the 1977 Environmental Modification Convention, bans on weaponry in space, and so on. The 1963 Partial Test Ban Treaty has been valuable, but only a comprehensive test ban treaty will halt the nuclear arms race.

Meantime, vast numbers of new weapons have been developed and deployed. Few efforts have been made to control or reduce conventional weapons, which account for the greater part of military budgets and are ever more destructive – some now boast similar explosive power to low-yield nuclear warheads. Nor have any serious attempts been made to control the arms trade, which fuels wars and debt in the South.

But a breakthrough has begun: the Stockholm Accord (1986) agreed East/West notification and verification of all troop movements, so largely removing fears of surprise attack. An even greater openness is built into the historic 1987 INF Treaty – the first ever to remove existing nuclear weapons (*see pp. 194-5*).

There is, at last, some hope. Secretary-General Mikhail Gorbachev seems genuinely to want far-reaching disarmament. And his ambitious plans for the Soviet economy will depend on money taken from the Soviet military budget. The US, too, is feeling the pinch. In the final analysis, economic constraints may force disarmament on a reluctant establishment. But if leaders are to succeed against strong vested interest in armaments, we must create public pressure.

Tackling transnational problems

Forty years of failure to deal with the threat of nuclear world war has been matched by an equal failure to tackle other global threats to peace and security – particularly poverty, environmental stress and the unjust and unstable world economic order.

There have been successes: life expectancy has risen, and humanitarian issues – refugee and child relief, and disease control – are now dealt with more effectively. Environmental reclamation measures too are growing, at both local and regional levels.

But all these are "repair" efforts, rather than a correction of the root causes in the economic and power structures of society. For such true reforms, political consensus is not forthcoming. Any solution that even hints at loss of sovereignty rarely reaches the negotiating table, let alone the draft treaty stage. And in an era where government policies are dominated by market-force economics, all recommendations for reform are largely ignored.

The irony is that we *do* know the root causes – and some solutions too. Hundreds of conferences have taken place, discussing and documenting all manner of global problems, their nature, extent and proposals to tackle them. Schemes for a New International Economic Order, for a World Conservation Strategy, for tackling poverty and debt, all have been "on the books" for years. They are promoted by NGOs, pressure groups, development agencies, and the UN Assembly – but to little avail.

Transnational efforts

Our transnational problems are worsening steadily (as the conceptual graph on the right shows), while we fail to evolve and implement solutions. Deforestation, climate change and environmental decline; inequalities in world finance and trade; human poverty and population pressure – all are issues where there is no ready international political consensus, and the United Nations consequently fails to act.

As for governments, they largely ignore global issues. Leaders are loath ever to discuss problems if they know that the effective remedy will involve unpopular policies, or worse still, some loss of national sovereignty. So far, what little action has been taken has been stimulated by non-governmental pressure or research groups. But the urgent international agreements, codes and treaties have proved extremely difficult to negotiate.

There are signs of hope – the Montreal Treaty to protect the ozone layer, for example (*see pp. 120-1*). But most transnational problems require specific new institutions and social mechanisms to solve them – a challenge to which the human community must rise.

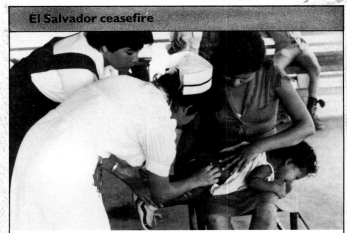

El Salvador ceasefire

In many poor regions of the world, endemic conflict makes the work of aid and development doubly difficult. Sometimes, however, humanitarian considerations do override nationalist ambition. In El Salvador, for example, on three days in 1985, a violent countrywide conflict was halted for a health campaign that saved the lives of thousands of children. For those three days, some 3000 health workers immunized about 250,000 of a target population of 400,000 children against the main killing diseases – polio, measles, diphtheria, tetanus and whooping cough. This unusual event was jointly organized by UNICEF, WHO, the Catholic Church, the international Red Cross and the Salvadorean Red Cross, all of whom worked closely with the national health authorities. The total cost was a mere $609,000, the amount spent by the world's military in less than 30 seconds.

The New International Economic Order (NIEO)

The concept of the NIEO was evolved by the South, specifically countries in the Group of 77 and the Non-aligned Movement (*see pp. 152-3*). Based on ideas of national sovereignty, and the right of states to choose their own methods of economic development, the NIEO opposes foreign exploitation and seeks greater economic "justice" between North and South. The NIEO was put forward at the UN General Assembly in 1974. There was then a period of détente between East and West. When superpower relations changed to confrontation, with the Reagan administration, Western interest evaporated.

The most important feature in the NIEO is the integrated programme on commodities, aimed at normalizing prices. But lack of interest on the part of the rich countries, meant that only 3 out of 18 suggested agreements are in force.

"We have reached a place where it is not a question of 'can we live in the same world and cooperate' but 'we must live in the same world and learn to cooperate'."
Eleanor Roosevelt

Development assistance

In an effort to relieve some of the suffering, the international community responds by giving economic aid. In 1970, the UN set a target of 0.7% of the GNP as the amount of development assistance that each developed country should contribute. Only a handful actually meet this target regularly. Kuwait is the best donor in percentage terms, giving nearly 4% of GNP in 1984. Foreign aid, however, is not a priority in countries that can see only their own escalating problems. As a result, aid often has various "strings" attached, bringing investment opportunities or other benefits to the donor country. Northern governments also find it difficult to justify giving aid to countries that are spending extravagantly on the military while their people are starving. The fact that this is not the fault of the starving themselves is often ignored.

Non-governmental organizations

NGOs are much more active in addressing transnational problems than governments, but they must have government involvement to succeed. Recently, the bodies that have had most impact have been three independent commissions: the Commission on North-South Issues, chaired by Willy Brandt; the Commission on Security and Disarmament Issues, chaired by Olof Palme; and the World Commission on Environment and Development, chaired by Gro Harlem Brundtland. The Brundtland Commission's Report *Our Common Future*, Palme's *Common Security* and Brandt's *Programme for Survival* and *Common Crisis* provide an account of the transnational problems of humanity and contain recommendations that are fair, but there has been no mechanism for implementation.

When it comes to offering solutions, however, governments have consistently failed to heed recommendations. The problem is not just government intransigence. What we need are specific, practicable proposals on how change can be made effective. This depends on new government thinking, on consensus public support and on credible new institutions to carry out actions peaceably.

The 1980 Brandt Commission, for example, recommended an immediate five-year action programme "to avert the most serious dangers": a large-scale transfer of resources to developing countries; an international global food programme; and a start on major reforms in the international economic system. Not one of these recommendations has been taken up by governments.

As with disarmament, talks on world problems soon become institutionalized and lose their urgency. Problems are discussed in isolation, with too little study of the links between them or of new institutions needed to solve them. Professional "optimism" arises, and radical change is discounted.

Consequently, global problems worsen, and the short-term measures frequently proposed to "cure" the symptoms, such as economic and arms embargoes and secret deals on finance and trade, remain cosmetic. They fail to deal with the underlying disease. We tinker with the ship, rather than steering a new course. Governments and establishments proceed with business as usual.

This cannot continue. The 1987 stock market crash has raised world perception of the links between debt, trade, financial instability and militarism. We must go further, recognizing that the debt is owed, not to human institutions, but to the environment, and to the poor. Our models of economic "growth", of "security" and of "sovereignty", are fundamentally mistaken. ·

What we need is a new approach, stepping outside the traditional constraints of sovereignty, military power and competition, to examine *all* the interlinked systems of our society and our environment. We need institutions reflecting a true global consensus, free to act on issues of global concern, to help us build a more workable relationship between societies, and between people and resources. And we need them *now*.

Controlling terrorism: the choices

Terrorism provides a classic demonstration of the challenge to our world of separate states posed by the new transnational security problems. Once again, temporary, separate efforts at control achieve little, where a united approach to root causes could do much.

The surge in terrorism in the past few years has forged a larger consensus on the need for its control. But this is turning out to be a difficult business. A particular obstacle is the role of Middle-East-related terrorism in international incidents. Arab states are seldom directly involved, but they are sensitive to action against Arab sub-nationals. Many countries are unprepared to complicate their relations with Arab nations, thus concerted overt action against Middle-East-related terrorism has been virtually impossible.

Nevertheless, a number of countries are considering measures to improve security. Effective control of terrorist activities depends mainly on collecting and analysing intelligence on groups and activities abroad and sharing this information with other governments. Co-operation between states is, therefore, essential. Many countries now have bilateral arrangements with

Responses to terrorism

Terrorism is a challenge to the moral strength and democratic principles of the global community. Ultimately, the control of terrorism depends on two things: redressing the underlying injustice and oppression which may be causing the violence; and utterly repudiating that violence.

Authorities try to control terrorism in a number of ways. Although attempts are made to prevent terrorist attacks occurring, successful pre-emption requires accurate intelligence, and this in itself provides justification for the "secret" activities of state and police. If pre-emption fails, and attacks, kidnappings or sieges occur, attempts are first made to resolve the incident by third-party mediation or direct negotiating techniques. Ultimately, military force may be used.

To cope with terrorist threats, physical and personal security measures are used, and the co-operation of other governments is enlisted. In the longer term, international efforts are made to mitigate the grievances of terrorists so that their justification for violence is removed.

More and more states realize that national efforts to control terrorism are inadequate. Some progress has been made in international co-operation in aviation and maritime security. But despite these measures, the fact is that the international community has yet to condemn terrorism as unacceptable behaviour.

Northern Ireland

The "Irish problem" is fundamentally an issue of minority rights. All attempts to arrive at a negotiated solution have so far foundered in extremist violence. The community remains ensnared in sectarian politics, effectively disenfranchised from the political life of either parent community. In using troops to control "terrorism", the British give the IRA grounds to declare itself a liberation movement combating an occupying army. Yet actions like that at Enniskillen in 1987 surely earn the IRA the "terrorist" label.

Revulsion may at last give the moderates a chance as the negotiators struggle for a solution. Shortly after Enniskillen, Eire signed the European Convention on the Suppression of Terrorism. The best hope for Ireland may lie within the broader framework of a more united Europe.

The US bombing of Libya

The bombing of a discotheque in West Berlin on 5 April 1986 was blamed on Libya and used to justify the bombing of Tripoli and Benghazi. About 100 civilians were killed.

The official purpose of the bombing was to discourage Palestinian terrorists, but the action has been severely criticized on the grounds that innocent people were killed and international law brought into disrepute without the action having any significant effect on the incidence of terrorism. There is, in fact, little evidence that many Palestinian terrorists are controlled from Libya.

The American attack on Libya was a breach of the UN Charter and contrary to the laws of war (see pp. 68-9), which require that the force used should be proportionate to the action giving rise to it, and that innocent civilians should not be deliberately endangered.

1 Violence with violence

Direct military action is sometimes used in response to terrorism. Two examples are the Israeli commando raid at Entebbe (1976) and the storming of the Iranian embassy in London (1980). This risky "attack" philosophy can have disastrous consequences, leading to such illegal behaviour as the bombing of Libya (left).

Terrorism can also be used by governments to justify the growth of paramilitary forces, invasions of civil liberties and other repressive measures. It would be better for democracy, in the long run, to address the root causes of terrorism instead.

2 Negotiation

Even countries that claim to make no concessions to terrorists negotiate with them from time to time, particularly to gain the release of hostages. This happens despite the general acceptance that "dealing" with one group of terrorists encourages others.

Some argue that sub-national violence would be better controlled if a distinction were made between groups, such as organized freedom armies, and terrorist units. The laws of armed conflict would then be applied to the former, and it would be justifiable to negotiate with them. But groups defined as terrorist would be dealt with by police.

3 No deal

The refusal to deal with, or harbour, terrorists requires support by all nations. President Reagan said on 18 June 1985 that "America will never make concessions to terrorists – to do so would only invite more terrorism – nor will we ask or pressure any other government to do so". But, as the Irangate scandal showed, this policy is not consistently applied. The "no deal" approach is also the basis of the European Convention on the Suppression of Terrorism. The 1978 Bonn declaration provides for concerted action against member countries that do not prosecute or extradite hijackers. Many of these measures are extremely difficult to implement and are largely symbolic. But the convention does have some bite, and is strengthening steadily.

others on counter-terrorist activities. The USA, Canada, the UK and Israel, for example, work closely together to combat terrorism and ties between these countries and Italy, the Netherlands, Turkey and Egypt are being rapidly strengthened. The USA, in fact, has significant agreements with some fifty governments.

Western Europe, too, has made progress towards co-operation, with the signing by 17 states of the 1978 Convention on the Suppression of Terrorism, which aims to facilitate the extradition and prosecution of all perpetrators of terrorist acts. Slow ratification, however, and insertion of a "loophole" permitting a state to withhold extradition for certain "political" offences, indicate a reluctance to accept outside juris-diction and distrust of other countries' politics, which are common barriers to co-operation.

There are a number of options open to a state deciding to adopt a counter-terrorist strategy. It may increase the size and powers of security forces; it may enact laws for greater controls over the public by identity cards, or registration of residence; it may introduce internment without trial and/or restrict the ability of the media to report terrorist acts. This list, while not exhaustive, illustrates the profound effect such measures could have on the society we live in.

In the words of Paul Wilkinson, Professor of International Relations, University of Aberdeen: "Any bloody tyrant can 'solve' the problem of political violence if he is prepared to sacrifice all considerations of humanity, and to trample down all constitutional and judicial rights." We must remember that democracy and the rule of law outweigh even security from terrorism. Their suppression provides fertile ground for violence.

In embarking on a programme of anti-terrorist legislation, governments must avoid falling into the trap of thinking that legal sanctions can solve the terrorist problem. At best they give temporary relief. It is imperative that governments address the deep-rooted social and economic problems that give rise to terror-ism in the first place; containment will never produce understanding – or solution.

Ambassadors in a lawless world

We cannot avoid recognizing in terrorism a "mirror" of global society – with its states obsessed by nationalism and the selfish pursuit of power, its refusal to accept the rule of law, its dependence on armed force. We must seek the same cure for both.

The absence of an effective system of world conflict resolution has left the community of nations to cope as best it can. Traditional diplomacy is still the base line of all efforts to defuse disputes and head off international crises, but there have also been *ad hoc* solutions, from economic and arms sanctions to deals of all kinds.

The *ad hoc* approach has produced a corresponding rise in importance of individual negotiators – from shuttle diplomats, such as Henry Kissinger and Olof Palme, to the UN Secretary-General's mission in the Gulf, and recent efforts by US Secretary of State George Schultz in the Middle East. World church

Individual pressures for peace

The immunity of ambassadors and nego-tiators, and their role in persuading intransi-gent leaders to seek compromise solutions, has a long and honourable history in human affairs. In times when international tensions are not too high, disagreements and minor conflicts between countries are solved by ordinary diplomacy. But when conflicts become serious, influential individuals some-times mediate directly. The 1970s saw the birth of "shuttle diplomacy" by eminent states-men; the 1980s have seen religious leaders and people commanding high moral respect play this role too. The weakness of the UN peace-keeping role and increasing sectarian violence and tension, make mediation even more vital. As communications become more rapid the media provides a "world audience" and the scope for individual mediation increases. New thinking in the peace move-ment, too, means that influential citizens are trying to apply their skills of conflict resolution alongside the official talks, as "second track" diplomacy.

President Jimmy Carter

US President Carter estab-lished himself as a first-class mediator by persuading Egyp-tian President Sadat and Israeli President Begin to sign the Camp David agreements. Car-ter invited Sadat and Begin to meet him at Camp David on 5 September 1979. The agree-ments covered Egyptian-Israeli relations and set out the direc-tion that negotiations on the West Bank and Gaza strip would take. The fact that Begin publicly acknowledged the importance of the Palestinian question was a major step forward.

Henry Kissinger

When he was US Secretary of State, Henry Kissinger invented what became known as "shuttle diplomacy". Within days of the Israeli-Egyptian ceasefire after the 1973 Yom Kippur war, Kissinger orga-nized negotiations for a settle-ment. By repeated travel between Israel and Egypt, Kis-singer evolved the first disen-gagement agreement between the two forces on 18 January 1974. A second agreement was signed on 5 June 1974. Personal diplomacy had suc-ceeded where a multilateral conference could not.

Alfonso Garcia Robles

The ex-Mexican Foreign Minister and Disarmament Ambassador Garcia Robles has had more impact on arms control negotiations than any other individual. He has over many years persistently encouraged the nuclear-weapon powers to achieve some nuclear disarmament and has reminded them of their legal obligations to negotiate such disarmament. His negotiation of the Tlatelolco Treaty (1967) won him the 1982 Nobel Peace Prize.

The Pope

Pope John Paul II's visit to Poland in June 1983 symbolized the important mediating role played by the Roman Catholic Church (the most influential organization in Poland) during the crisis over the Solidarity movement. Shortly after, martial law in Poland was abolished.

Terry Waite

As the special envoy of the Archbishop of Canterbury, Terry Waite was instrumental in arranging the release of several hostages in Beirut. Between 14 and 19 January 1987 he held talks in Lebanon with Muslim leaders, but on 20 January 1987 he was reported missing.

Shridath Ramphal

The Commonwealth Secretary-General made considerable efforts to achieve a Commonwealth consensus on bringing pressure to bear on South Africa to dismantle apartheid. This was opposed only by the UK Prime Minister, Mrs Thatcher. The influential report by the Group of Eminent Persons focused world attention on South Africa.

Alva Myrdal

Although she held numerous ministerial appointments and pioneered works in social philosophy, population control and equality of the sexes, Myrdal's most valuable contribution was as a leader of the bloc of neutral countries at the Conference on Disarmament in Geneva. A persistent critic of the superpowers for passing up opportunities to achieve progress in disarmament, she was joint winner of the 1982 Nobel Peace Prize.

Archbishop Desmond Tutu

Archbishop Tutu has made courageous efforts to reduce violence in South Africa at times when supporting it would have made him more popular. His negotiations on behalf of the black community with the police and security forces have been tireless, and on many occasions he has addressed angry crowds appealing for calm, often putting his life at risk.

Julius Nyerere

Tanzanian President Nyerere played a major role in the diplomatic efforts that led to Zimbabwe's independence in 1980. This experience led him to become the *de facto* leader of the Front Line group of states (Angola, Botswana, Mozambique, Tanzania, Zambia and Zimbabwe) and, as such, he has a great influence in the struggle of the Southern African states against the Pretoria regime.

Pérez de Cuéllar

The United Nations Secretary-General's visit to Iran in September 1987 was a brave attempt to persuade Tehran to accept the Security Council's resolution demanding a ceasefire to end the Iran/Iraq war, which Iraq had already accepted. Pérez de Cuéllar's chances for success were slim; he risked rebuff, but persisted, aware that he represented the only potential multilateral consensus for a ceasefire.

leaders and people of outstanding moral authority, too, are taking a strong stand in condemning violence.

Peace can be a dangerous business. We owe much to the courage of those who work for it in a lawless world. But we should not accept this state of affairs. The community of ordinary citizens must insist that proper collective security and means of peacekeeping under law become the norm.

Initiatives from the wider community

Failure by the nuclear powers to disarm, and their dominance of all world affairs, have led to many initiatives by groups of non-great-power states seeking to denuclearize the planet and defuse risks of war. The Five Continent Initiative, for example, is pressing the superpowers to agree a comprehensive ban on nuclear weapons testing. The Contadora Group seeks to prevent conflict and reduce superpower tension in Central America. The Non-aligned Movement, now representing over 100 states, is concerned to see broad reforms in security and the economic order.

One initiative viewed with ambiguous feelings by the nuclear powers is the creation of nuclear-weapon-free zones. States joining a zone ratify a treaty and, typically, this commits them to not use any nuclear material or facilities under their jurisdiction other than for peaceful purposes; not to produce, acquire or test nuclear weapons; and not to permit the presence of those of any other country.

Only two inhabited regions of the Earth have been declared nuclear weapon free so far – Latin America and the South Pacific. The 1967 Treaty of Tlatelolco prohibits the testing, use, manufacture, production or acquisition, and the receipt, storage, installation, deployment or any form of possession of any nuclear weapons, by Latin American countries. (However, the participants do not include Argentina, Brazil, Cuba or Guyana.) Both superpowers have signed protocols respecting this nuclear-free status. The 1985 Treaty of Rarotonga makes the South Pacific region, including New Zealand, nuclear weapon free, and also contains a non-weapon prohibition – it bans all dumping of radioactive waste in the seas of the South Pacific. A nuclear-free Pacific is less than welcome to the nuclear powers – New Zealand has already clashed with the US over the issue (*see pp. 196-7*).

Many other potential zones have been suggested. The most famous proposal was made as long ago as 1957 by Adam Rapacki, the then Foreign Minister of Poland. Poland offered to ban the production and stockpiling of nuclear weapons on its territory if both East and West Germany would do the same. Czechoslovakia, East Germany and the USSR supported the Rapacki Plan. It might have succeeded but for the opposition of West German Chancellor Konrad Adenauer. Central Europe has since become the most nuclearized region on Earth.

There have been more recent attempts to make parts of Europe nuclear weapon free. The Independent Commission on Disarmament and Security Issues,

New peace initiatives

The escalation of the superpower arms race and ideological intransigence have prompted the formation of several "counter-groupings" of nations. Some are trying to exert influence on the US and USSR to halt the arms race; others are suggesting new solutions to problems of economic and political conflict.

These initiatives are reactions against the superpower domination of international politics – two countries with 10% of the world's population dominating the rest. Superpower response, however, is often one of indifference or outright rejection. But some initiatives, like the nuclear-weapon-free zones, have been successful. Others, such as the Non-aligned Movement, have not yet fulfilled early expectations. Generally, though, these "other voices" are multiplying and they now span the globe (*see right*).

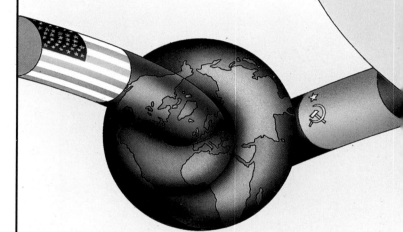

Untying the superpower knot

The East-West superpower struggle between the US and the USSR binds the global community into an ideological deadlock that blocks all change. A desire to dissolve this grip on the world's potential for peaceful development has been the spur for alternative peace initiatives. Not surprisingly, the profile of these is higher at times of greatest tension, or when adverse effects are most keenly felt. The initiatives, however, are proving fruitful in other ways – by creating new forums for détente, in testing "third party" approaches to resolving international conflict, and by building a more truly international community.

The Five Continents Peace Movement

This movement was started by Prime Ministers Andreas Papandreou of Greece, Indira Gandhi of India and Olof Palme of Sweden, and by Presidents Miguel Hurtado of Mexico and Julius Nyerere of Tanzania. Later, President Raul Alfonsine of Argentina joined the Initiative.

The Five Continents Initiative believes that the negotiation of a comprehensive ban on all nuclear-weapon tests is the most urgent arms control measure. Its six leaders are pressing the Americans and the Soviets to negotiate such a ban and have offered to supervise the setting up of an international verification system to ensure compliance.

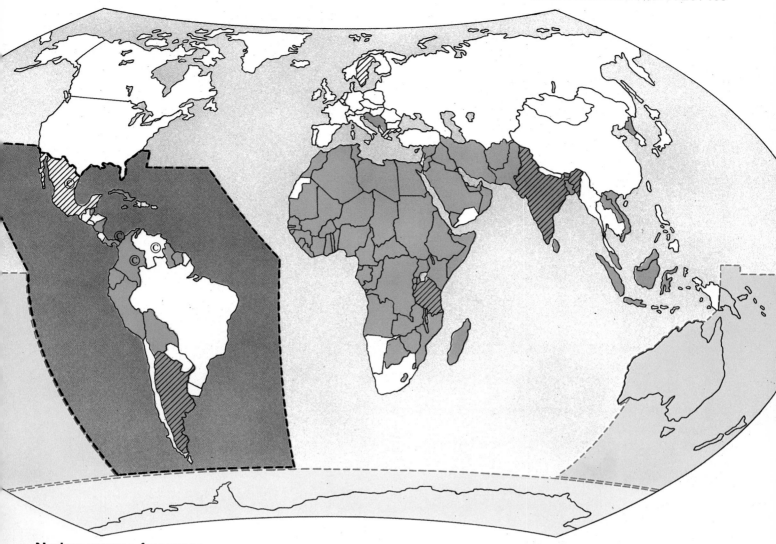

Nuclear-weapon-free zones

These zones are an important arms control measure simply because the superpowers have failed to negotiate disarmament. Also, the zones help to prevent the spread of nuclear weapons to countries that do not possess them. From a global viewpoint, the area most in need of being declared nuclear-weapon-free is Central Europe, where most nuclear weapons are deployed.

The oldest nuclear-weapon-free zone was established by a 1959 treaty, which banned nuclear weapons in the Antarctic. The second oldest, signed at Tlatelolco, Mexico, in 1967, made Latin America nuclear-weapon-free, but not all states ratified it. In 1985, the Treaty of Rarotonga was signed by 8 countries, and the remaining 4 promised to sign at a later date. A major problem here, however, is that France is unlikely to abide by the Treaty's terms.

The map shows the extent of such initiatives around the world.

 97 members at 1986 NaM Conference, Harare

 Members of The Five Continents Initiative

 Contadora Group

 Latin American nuclear-weapon-free zone, Tlatelolco

Antarctica nuclear-weapon-free zone

Proposed nuclear-weapon-free zone, South Pacific

The Contadora movement

Concern about the militarization of and the increasing conflict in the Central American Isthmus led to the Contadora group of countries (Colombia, Mexico, Panama and Venezuela) tabling the Contadora Act (1983), designed to "strengthen peace, co-operation, confidence, democracy and economic and social development among the peoples of the region".

The Act is not yet in force because of tensions between Nicaragua and the USA. Nicaragua insists that the USA should first pledge to stop its support for the Contra rebels and the USA refuses to continue bilateral talks to normalize relations between them. This action by the USA has been criticized by most of the powers in the region and by the Non-aligned Movement.

The Non-aligned Movement

Non-alignment was born from Jawaharlal Nehru's dream of a coalition of developing countries having great influence on world security. Twenty-four states attended the Afro-Asian Conference in 1955 and laid down the "Five Principles of Peaceful Coexistence". Resolutions were passed on world peace, human rights and self-determination, problems of dependent peoples and economic and cultural co-operation.

The Movement now has over 100 member states, but has had little success in countering superpower domination. Nevertheless, this does not detract from its successes in, for example, originating the ideas of a New International Economic Order and a New International Information Order – ideas rejected by aligned powers since they involve demands for the transfer of resources from North to South.

chaired by the late Olof Palme, recommended a nuclear-weapon-free zone 300-kilometres wide along the East-West German border. There is also discussion of a Nordic nuclear-weapon-free zone to include Sweden, Denmark, Norway, Finland and possibly Iceland. The Balkans, too, have been proposed, with support from Bulgaria, Greece, Yugoslavia and Romania.

The UN General Assembly has passed resolutions on nuclear-weapon-free zones in Africa, the Middle East, South Asia and the Indian Ocean. The problem in Africa is South Africa, which probably has nuclear weapons; equally, Israel's suspected possession is an obstacle in the Middle East. Differences between India and Pakistan are a barrier in South Asia. While in the Indian Ocean, the sustained military presence of the two superpowers remains a stumbling block.

Establishment of nuclear-weapon-free zones requires governments with courage to stand outside superpower influence – and this in turn requires public pressure against the nuclear arms race – usually, as in the case of New Zealand, from well-organized peace movements.

The rise of the peace movement

Mass public protests on peace and disarmament are a phenomenon of the nuclear age. They began in the 1950s, and by 1987 there were some 1400 peace groups worldwide, representing many millions of people, with millions more supporting environmental or humanitarian groups of similar aims. Joining peace-oriented groups has been described as the fastest-growing social movement in recent history.

But the roots of the peace movement are older, in 19th-century pacifism and conscientious objection, and in the increasing concern at the savagery of war which produced the great series of Peace Conferences at the Hague from the 1890s onwards. The International Peace Bureau (1892), for instance, grew out of the London Peace Society set up by the Quakers in 1816; it helped to create the League of Nations, and is still active. Its members have won 13 Nobel Peace Prizes, and the Bureau itself was awarded the prize in 1910.

So in 1905 was Bertha von Suttner; a life-long peace campaigner, she was the only woman at the 1899 Hague Conference and had herself suggested that Alfred Nobel create the Prize. The most famous women's group, the Women's International League for Peace and Freedom, was formed at the 1915 Hague congress. Over 1000 women met to protest against World War I and try to end it. The League now has 50,000 members in 26 countries; its Nobel prize winners include Jane Addams (1931), Emily Greene Balch (1946) and Alva Myrdal (1982).

The main aim of the modern peace movement is to stop the nuclear arms race, by exerting more pressure on politicians than those who want it to continue. Activity was first centred on the Campaign for Nuclear Disarmament (CND), until the Partial Test Ban Treaty of 1963 brought a lull. In the late 1970s, protest was

The peace movement

As the technology and scope of war spreads ever greater destruction, more and more consciences are stirred. The 19th-century peace societies were minority voices; the 1915 women's protest against World War I was not much more. World War II brought wider disenchantment. Then, in 1945, the "unleashing of the atom" on Nagasaki and Hiroshima shocked humanity. Fear of weapons of ultimate destructive power provoked the first truly "popular" and sustained protest: the international peace movement.

There have been four major "waves" of action for peace since 1945 (see the graph, below). The first two were based on the fear of a nuclear holocaust, the third centred on Vietnam and the latest has been sparked by the deployment of the neutron bomb and strategic nuclear weapons in Europe. Each has died down in response to partial success – the Test Ban Treaty, the withdrawal from Vietnam – and then risen, stronger than before, to meet new threats. The 1987 INF Treaty is widely seen as a success for the international peace movement. But if further reductions in the global arms race are to be achieved louder voices still will be needed.

On 6 August 1945 the first atomic bomb was used against the people of Hiroshima, and their tragedy became the focus of the peace movement. By the late 1940s, anti-Bomb protest was rising all over the world. Here, in 1947, citizens of Hiroshima witness the unveiling of the monument erected where the bomb exploded over the city.

MARCH FROM
LONDON
TO
ALDERMASTON

With the signing of the Partial Test Ban Treaty in 1963, the anti-Bomb lobby quietened. The mid-1960s saw peace movements shift their concern to foreign involvement in local wars, especially Vietnam. By 1968 the US had half a million troops there. Massive demonstrations at home and abroad, and the birth of civil disobedience and alternative movements, brought great pressure to bear on the US government to withdraw.

The Pentagon decision to deploy "enhanced radiation weapons" – neutron bombs – and the stationing of Cruise and Pershing missiles in Western Europe, sparked the latest anti-nuclear wave in 1980. Unwilling to be the "theatre" for a limited nuclear war between the superpowers, hundreds of thousands of Europeans have supported protests, from Greenham to the 1984 "die-in" at Dam Square, Amsterdam.

As economic recovery began, concern mounted over growing nuclear stockpiles and peacetime testing. Bertrand Russell's 1955 appeal against the H-bomb, and the 1957 Gottinger appeal against nuclear deployment in Germany, triggered organized peace movements. In the UK, CND (1958) began its annual march to Aldermaston, attracting up to 100,000 participants.

rekindled by the Pentagon decision to develop and deploy enhanced radiation weapons – neutron bombs – and soon involved millions. Anxieties were increased by statements made by President Reagan and some of his colleagues about the possibility of "fighting a limited nuclear war" and even "nuclear victory", and by the decision to deploy Cruise and Pershing II missiles. In the last quarter of 1981, roughly two and a half million people demonstrated against nuclear arms in Europe.

Except for Turkey, major demonstrations took place in all NATO countries, including the USA and Canada; and also in Sweden, Finland, Japan, Australia and New Zealand. By the end of 1982, unofficial disarmament movements had sprung up in Hungary, Romania and East Germany. In the USSR, small groups began independent disarmament activities, but these were harassed and suppressed. Harassment is not, however, confined to Warsaw Pact countries. In Turkey, a NATO country, the military regime in 1981 suppressed the Turkish Peace Association, jailing all its leaders.

Current voices

Historians may come to regard the rise of mass movements for change as the most significant factor in the late 20th century. Today's politicians ignore this public concern at their peril.

That many politicians are nervous about the success of protest movements is shown by such incidents as the sinking, in 1985, of the Greenpeace ship *Rainbow Warrior* by French secret-service agents – just before it was about to sail to Muraroa Atoll in French Polynesia to protest against French nuclear testing.

Huge demonstrations, or *causes célèbres*, like that of the women at Greenham Common, have been the most dramatic peace activity. But the movement now covers a wide range of issues, and tactics from political lobbying to direct action, even by small groups. In the US, small numbers of protesters deliberately entered the nuclear weapons testing site in the Nevada Desert. Their forcible removal and arrest drew attention not only to the nuclear testing programme, but to a minority rights issue, for the American Indians were also claiming ownership of the test site. A similar mixture of issues – peace and minority rights – occurred in Australia, where land claimed by the Aborigines was taken for uranium mining. And in Hawaii, the Hawaiians launched a boat blockade to stop the US Navy shelling their sacred island of Kahoolawe.

In using such tactics, the peace movement, and the movements for human rights and conservation, all draw on the philosophy of non-violence pioneered by Mahatma Ghandi, whose "ahimsa", or active love, was a blend of Christian and Hindu teachings of absolute pacificism. Non-violence involves resistance to oppression in all its forms, by non-co-operation and protest techniques developed over a long history of human effort, especially by trades unions and suffragettes.

The movement for non violence has gained great strength from its leaders, people of outstanding moral stature and courage: Martin Luther King in America,

Voices of peace

There are at least 1400 peace groups in the world with a total membership of many millions. Millions more belong to development and environmental groups, which share many of the same fundamental aims as the peace movement.

A number of peace groups have sprung up in the past 10 years. In fact, joining peace-

CND
The Campaign for Nuclear Disarmament, launched in 1958, is the most famous European peace group. CND's general aim is worldwide nuclear disarmament. But it is best known for its aim for unilateral disarmament in the UK and withdrawal from NATO.

Freeze
The Nuclear Freeze movement, which operates in the USA and UK, seeks a comprehensive worldwide freeze on the testing, deployment and production of all types of nuclear weapons. The Freeze campaigns are a first step towards a comprehensive and permanent ban on nuclear weapon tests and a freezing of space weapons programmes. A nuclear freeze would be followed by large reductions in nuclear arsenals.

oriented groups has been described as the fastest-growing social movement in recent history. Since the INF negotiations, peace groups are responding to the new spirit of co-operation between the US and USSR by retargeting their strategies.

The peace movement, at least in Western Europe, has succeeded in making security and military policy decisions a public issue. Consequently, changes in military postures and the deployment of new nuclear weapon systems now need to find a measure of public acceptance. Gone are the days when opposition parties let defence issues go unchallenged. The great number and variety of peace groups around the world show the unity of desire for peace among different cultural, social, religious and political groups.

Countries with an active peace movement, 1984

Location of independent peace actions with over 100,000 participants, 1980-6

"We utterly deny all outward wars and strife, and fightings with outward weapons, for any end, or under any pretence whatever; this is our testimony to the whole world . . ."
Quaker Peace Testimony

This map shows the large number of countries – capitalist, communist and developing – with active peace groups. The list is by no means comprehensive, since data is not available for all countries. These groups express their concern by holding massive demonstrations, common during the early 1980s and still growing. Some 100,000 people from many European countries took part in a peace demonstration in Brussels in October 1987.

UNICEF
The work of UNICEF encourages global co-operation by focusing on a "specific task" which meets with near universal concern – the plight of suffering children. That UNICEF helps to forge links between rich and poor nations was recognized when the organization was awarded the Nobel Peace Prize in 1965.

Society of Friends
The Quakers are a religious sect originating in England in the 1650s, and one of the oldest existing groups to oppose war. Always known for their pacifism, the Quakers are today actively involved in human rights issues. In 1947 they were awarded the Nobel Peace Prize and now have consultative status at the UN.

Women
Women have always played an innovatory role in working for peace. In ancient Greece, women went on sexual strike until their men stopped fighting. In 1915 the International Suffrage Alliance held a women's peace conference. Since then their work has continued through women-only initiatives such as the Greenham Peace Camp.

Generals for Peace
Since 1981, this group of retired senior NATO officers has been using its influence to challenge NATO and Warsaw Pact strategies, particularly the continuing build-up of nuclear weapons. The generals have an effective working dialogue with their counterparts in the Warsaw Pact and are trying to develop structures which can circumvent the East-West stalemate.

"Hands across Scotland"
In 1986 a human chain was formed to stretch across the width of Scotland. The event was organized by Parents for Survival, and was supported by over 70 national groups. The organizers described it as "a symbol of the hand of friendship extended between East and West . . .".

and now Archbishop Desmond Tutu in South Africa. In a world of cynical military power, non-violence and the moral abjuration of war are signs of great hope.

Philosophers and priests

"It is entirely clear that there is only one way in which great wars can be permanently prevented, and that is the establishment of an international government with a monopoly of serious armed force." Thus spoke Bertrand Russell in October 1946.

Virtually all thinkers agree that humanity will only survive in the long term if war is eliminated. And most concur that this requires replacement of the anarchy of today's international system of sovereign states with an organized world community, respecting international law, and with enlightened institutions to resolve conflict. But what kind of "organized world community"?

Russell's liking for world government was shared by Albert Einstein, who said in 1948: "I advocate world government because I am convinced that there is no other possible way of eliminating the most terrible danger in which man has ever found himself." To some, however, talk of a world government with a monopoly of armed force raises Orwellian visions of "Big Brother". Latterly, too, the rise of popular movements and of NGOs worldwide has led to a feeling that all governments tend to excess bureaucracy, power-seeking and inflexible attitudes, and that we have had too much of government already. What this suggests is that we need, not a centralized world *government*, but a system of popular world *governance*, working through a democratized United Nations, with decentralized functions. The spread of communications and information technology could assist the evolution of such a self-governing world community – a true global village.

Government or governance, however, we must have an effective global system empowered to keep the peace. In their famous Pastoral Letter on War and Peace, *The Challenge of Peace*, published 1983, the American Catholic Bishops said: "There *is* a substitute for war. There is negotiation under the supervision of a global body realistically fashioned to do its job. It must be given the equipment to keep constant surveillance on the entire earth. It must have the authority, freely conferred upon it by all the nations, to investigate what seems to be preparations for war by any one of them. It must be empowered by all the nations to enforce its command on every nation . . . is it hoping too much to believe that the genius of humanity, aided by the grace and guidance of God, is able to accomplish it?"

Philosophers and priests alike perceive the great challenge now facing humanity. In the words of Jerome D. Frank: "nations will probably not be able to make the drastic changes in habitual attitudes and behavior necessary for survival in a nuclear world until they come to the brink of disaster. At that moment, though probably not before, enough national leaders may see bottom before they hit it and abandon resort to war as the ultimate recourse for resolving international disputes."

Non-violence

Advocates of non-violence believe that peace depends, ultimately, on abjuration of violence and coercive force by every individual, even in defence of freedom and human rights, and the practice instead of "active love". Nearly all major religions embody this ethic, especially early Christianity, Buddhism and Hinduism, with their "ahimsa", or non harm. But in practice, states (and established religions) sanction all forms of violence. Dissenting voices of conscience, from Anabaptists, Mennonites and Quakers to individual conscientious objection and non-co-operation, have a long history. But in this century, non-violence has been forged into a powerful tool for mass resistance.

Those who object to war and violence as being tools of injustice and coercion and, as such, immoral and ineffectual, have sought and tested alternative means to effect social change. The lessons of the labour and suffragette movements and the leadership of Gandhi and Luther King have taught the peace, civil rights and environment movements to use strikes, marches, sit-ins and civil disobedience to powerful effect. Public campaigns are matched by emphasis on personal non-violence and "Right Livelihood" (*see pp. 226-7*), and education in conflict-resolution techniques.

Judaism
"What is hateful to you, do not to your fellow men. That is the entire Law, all the rest is commentary." The Talmud

Buddhism
"Hurt not others with that which pains yourself." Udana-Varqa

---

The power of example

Prophet, priest or media hero, the lone courage of individuals with vision has the power to move us, and to change the world. Many of these people are religious leaders, who have become involved in civil rights and have roused the public conscience. Martin Luther King and Desmond Tutu have, in a sense, continued the example of non-violent resistance to oppression set by Jesus Christ. Others are intellectual leaders, who, from Tolstoy to Bertrand Russell, decry the folly of war. The most influential of all modern advocates of non-violence was Mohandas ("Mahatma") Gandhi. Integrating the ideas of Christian love and Hindu "ahimsa" he forged them into an active force for political change: "satyagraha", the power of truth. Though he failed to secure peaceable independence for India, Gandhi has inspired millions to adopt non-violence, leaving an indelible mark on our times.

This photograph, taken in 1932, shows Mahatma Gandhi embracing the daughter of the jailed former president of the Indian congress. On his forehead is a caste-mark.

"Non-violence is more powerful than all the armaments in the world. It is mightier than the mightiest weapon of destruction devised by the ingenuity of man." Mohandas Gandhi

Zoroastrianism
"That nature only is good when it shall not do unto another whatever is not good for its own self." Dadistan-i-Dinik

The golden rule
All the major religions have one fundamental precept in common – that we should treat others as we would expect to be treated ourselves.

Christianity
"All things whatsoever ye would that men should do to you, do ye even so to them: for this is the law of the prophets." The Gospel of Matthew

Non-co-operation
Conscientious objection to military service is not the only way that individuals can assert their commitment to peace. In 1984, two Quaker women in the UK sought (unsuccessfully) to withhold the proportion of their taxes attributable to the defence budget. Such "Peace Tax" campaigns are now common. Another example, if we define peace to include structural non-violence, is the burning of government-issued identity papers in South Africa. But the real success of non-co-operation is the publicity gained for the cause of peace and the inconvenience to the state.

Islam
"No one of you is a believer until he desires for his brother that which he desires for himself." Hadith

Hinduism
"This is the sum of duty: do naught to others which if done to thee would cause thee pain." The Mahabharata

PART THREE: FUTURE

"It is more difficult to organize peace than to win a war."
Aristotle
"Most of the things worth doing in the world had been declared impossible before they were done." Louis Brandeis

The first two parts of this Atlas are descriptive – mapping and analysing the roots of peace and war, and the dangers and opportunities of our contemporary world. But this third part is, to an extent, prescriptive – it is concerned with how we should *act* to survive and build sustainable peace. Chapter 7 examines the choices open to humanity and suggests some of the bases on which they might be made. Chapter 8 sets out emergency actions by the global community that could gain us a "breathing space" and deflect immediate crises. And Chapter 9 proposes the fundamental redirection of human attitudes, actions and institutions on which the future of the world may demand.

This was by far the most difficult part of the Atlas. The facts of war, of militarism, and of the threatening environmental crises are now well documented and, with some discrepancies, agreed on by those who are concerned with such issues. But when it comes to "solutions" one finds wide disagreement, a dearth of rigorous analysis and, most of all, a shortage of hope – of belief that the impossible can become possible, before it is too late.

Nonetheless, there is much new thinking, coming from many fields. There are think tanks, institutes and NGOs dealing with a great range of future scenarios and proposals for global reform. There have been major reports, too, most recently that by the World Commission on Environment and Development chaired by Norwegian Prime Minister Gro Harlem Brundtland. The connection between disarmament and development is receiving more attention. And there have been many books published on peace, on world development, and on planetary ecology.

The difficulty is that there is a wide gap between "official" solutions, however forward looking, and the new ideas of the peace and ecology movements. Both tend to consider the other's approach unrealistic: and both are right, at least to some degree.

Underlying this divide is a profound "philosophy gap". Ecologists and green movements see human civilization as out of step with Gaia, and thus unsustainable in both spiritual and material terms. They prescribe a radical change in the world economy – to a decentralized, conserver society – and a reawakening of respect for Gaia and a reintegration within Gaian systems. Peace thinkers also see civilization as materially and spiritually on the wrong course, through its pursuit of dominance, its patriarchal values, its injustice and oppression. Some seek disarmament; some justice and freedom (economic or political); all seek a spiritual change through education and religion – an abjuration of violence and materialism, a reawakening of our sense of common human compassion, and of the divine.

Official approaches, however, are more pragmatic, both in analysis of causes, and in solutions. Thus debt and poverty are seen as a malfunction of economic systems, requiring varying degrees of adjustment; rather than as symptoms of a wholly wrong course needing a radical reversal. Power-seeking, nationalism and sovereignty are decried, yet solutions proposed rest on present governmental systems as main actors, largely unchanged. Militarism is deplored, yet proposals to halt arms sales, divert military funding to civil use, or abandon the nuclear arms race are long-term, with "realistic" allowance for national security needs. Even so, many of the practicable adjustments proposed are major enough themselves to provoke rejection as "unrealistic" by the powers that be.

Between the pragmatic and the idealistic, there is a whole spectrum of ideas and proposals. In an attempt to thrash out this conflicting area of "solutions", the Gaia team itself held a Think Tank *(see p. 5)*, drawing together a cross-disciplinary group with widely differing backgrounds. Their debate began a struggle for synthesis of the varying pragmatic and idealistic approaches whose outcome is reflected in these chapters.

OUR FATE IN OUR HANDS

Humanity stands at the edge of an abyss. Unless we make the right choices, individually and as a global community, we shall go over that edge – irrevocably. There is not much time left for us to choose.

The future challenges us with the unknown and unpredicted. But by projecting present trends we can see some way ahead. Technology is moving very rapidly, bringing the possibility of hope, and of nightmare. Unless we can learn to control this technological impetus, to direct it towards human need and create an environmentally benign science, we face the nightmare, not the dream. And unless we can share such a benign and appropriate technology more equitably than now, it will not save us from calamity.

We also face choices of our economic path, of our future governance, of what value we place on rights and freedoms, even on life itself, and on the living world of Gaia. And with rising numbers and expectations, but declining resources, we may have to choose between affluence for the few and survival of the many. All these are fundamentally moral choices – and we need a clear ethic to make them. It cannot be right to leave the poor in their poverty – we have to recognize that economics itself is a moral issue. It must be time we rejected justifications of violence as morally unacceptable.

We have to start choosing now, all of us, in our everyday lives, and in those we elect to power. And the existing institutions of the world, from the United Nations, to the banks, governments, multinational corporations, and the military-industrial establishment must choose, too. Change takes time, and peace has to grow from within. Yet nuclear war approaches faster and faster, and the environmental crisis is already upon us. We must take emergency measures to gain time, in the short term, even while we begin the long-term redirection of our aims and beliefs.

Such emergency measures will have to be carried out by the institutions we have. Only great pressure from the peoples of the world will achieve this. Today, with international financial systems in disarray, and moves towards arms cuts by the superpowers, there is growing sensitivity to such pressure. We have to seize the hour.

If the world were threatened by an invasion from outside, nations would set aside their petty differences to act together. Our world is indeed invaded, but by a fever mounting from within. Let us at least prevent the death of the patient while we seek a cure, and a restoration of harmony and health.

We have the capacity and the knowledge. And we have institutions whose concern is the security of the world, as we have those whose concern is the security of nations. Such "security" means nothing if we cannot find food to eat or water to drink, if the air we breathe is poisoned, if climate change threatens agriculture, if the gifts of evolution are destroyed. It means nothing when millions die of hunger, and all are threatened by nuclear war, through accident or design. We have to redefine security.

Peace is a process, a gradual change that rises like yeast through all the interactions and institutions of society. To build a positive peace, we must steadily eradicate the roots of war, and in their place seek a sustainable ecological base; a true global consensus and spirit; a just and freedom-loving society; and systems of self-governance that honour the rule of law.

Idealism may be the only true realism for humanity now. We must put an end to war, beat our swords into ploughshares, and seek a balance with nature and a lasting peace – or simply not survive. We must have a dream, a vision of the future, and bring that dream to pass.

The shift from dream to reality may be closer than we think. Change, when it reaches the halfway point in permeating society, can be suddenly upon us in earnest. And there is a great movement for change rising from the global constituency or ordinary people, all around the world, to challenge established power. In the words of Joanna Macy: "Before water turns to ice, it looks just the same as before. Then a few crystals form, and suddenly the whole system undergoes cataclysmic change".

7 The choices for humanity

Introduced by Kenneth E. Boulding

To parody an old saying, we could say: "all statements about the future are wrong, including this one." We have to face the fact, however, that the future has the property of irreducible uncertainty, especially as we move into systems in which information is a large component. It is only in systems where information is a very minor component, like the solar system, that the future is predictable. With the evolution of the human race, we get systems in which information is a larger and larger component. Knowledge and know-how are even less predictable. We cannot predict what we are going to know in, say, the year 2000 or we would know it now. Nevertheless, there is great value in constructing images of the future, simply because the human race has this extraordinary capacity not only of imaging a variety of futures but also of choosing among them. Up to a point, the greater variety of futures that we contemplate, and the greater the probability of these futures, the more likely are we to make good decisions rather than bad ones. The fact that we can make decisions means that we can change the probabilities of various futures, and this is a deep responsibility of all members of the human race.

Probably in the whole history of Planet Earth there has never been another time at which a wider variety of possible futures has been open to it. The range of possible futures includes: first, an irretrievable catastrophe, which would bring the evolutionary process to an end, or at least set evolution back maybe a billion years. Next we have some probability of retrievable catastrophe, like a limited nuclear war, climatic change, mass famine, and so on. Then we have the possibility of a gradual exhaustion of exhaustible resources. Finally, there is also the probability that a better world lies ahead, in which we get rid of war, which has now become the greatest enemy of the human race, we control population while respecting individual freedoms and rights, we move steadily towards the use of renewable resources, we get rid of crippling poverty, and we go on learning to the full capacity of the human organism. Each of us by our decisions and actions will influence to some degree, however small, the probabilities of these various futures. For each one of us there is a moral imperative to increase the probability, by however little, of a better world. The more people accept this moral responsibility, the greater the probability of a better world will become.

The great key to change in these probabilities of the future is the process of human learning. The distribution of this knowledge among the human race is of great importance. If powerful people have illusions about the world, as they frequently do, this is much more dangerous than if ordinary people have such illusions. Knowledge grows partly by research, but mainly by transmission through education, books, the media, and so on. If there is one source of ultimate optimism it is that if we believe something that is true, that is, that corresponds to the real world, we are less likely to change that belief than if we believe something that is not true, that is, is in error and does not correspond to the real world. Errors can persist for a very long time, especially where they are hard to test. Communication, however, may make error more testable and increase what I have sometimes called the "outability of truth". Many statements in this chapter can be challenged, but the very fact that they are being made increases the probability of the better world.

Kenneth E. Boulding

"The human condition can almost be summed up in the observation that, whereas all experiences are of the past, all decisions are about the future. It is the great task of human knowledge to bridge this gap and to find those patterns in the past which can be projected into the future as realistic images. The image of the future is the key to all choice-oriented behaviour."
Elise Boulding

The world is in a catastrophe-prone condition. Technological developments in nuclear arsenals may themselves lead to a nuclear world war and the possible elimination of humankind, despite efforts by political leaders to avoid it. The international security institutions set up with great hopes in 1945 – particularly the United Nations – have lost credibility. The international monetary system is in chaos. The concept that the rich countries would help the poor by supplying capital has been turned on its head. The massive debt borne by the South means that poor countries are transferring billions of dollars worth of resources each year to the rich ones. Ecological destruction is accelerating. Alarming changes in the world's climate are predicted for the 21st century. Rapidly increasing world population and expectations of higher living standards are creating huge pressures on non-renewable resources.

Governments are loath to challenge the view that "growth" and "industrial development" are good, yet the idea that development of poorer countries would "trickle down" from growth in the industrialized countries has proved false. Limited resources and a finite environment mean that today's development processes are unsustainable.

Politicians seem incapable of finding solutions; they are too bound up with short-term national issues. Some of the public are concerned – spasmodic upsurges of the peace and ecological movements show this. But most do not yet realize the far-reaching institutional changes needed to solve global problems.

If we are to avoid catastrophe, it will be because we have a strong vision of the future, and make the correct *moral* choices. Technology, economics, and security are moral issues as well as practical. Only moral vision can determine whether we move towards greater social justice within and between countries; whether we pick the right technologies; and, in particular, whether we finally perceive war as a non-rational way of solving conflicts, and make the "just war" an obsolete concept.

More people and higher expectations

Demands for higher living standards by people in the South are mainly confined to the basics of life, rather than any luxuries. More food, safe water, better health services and educational facilities are immediate needs.

But demands do not stop at the basics, as experience in developed countries shows. Although immediate needs are satisfied for most people in the North, the public demand for consumer goods still grows. In the UK, for example, the GNP per family is about £12,000 ($22,000) a year. After taxes, the average family is left

Moral choices

"We need an essentially new way of thinking if mankind is to survive."
Albert Einstein, 1946

Humanity is adaptable, accustomed to solving problems. It is hard for us to recognize that the crisis we now face is of a wholly new order, and that the usual remedies – new resources, new technologies, new weaponry – may not serve.

What the future demands of us is, rather, a fundamental shift in our relationship to the planet. We need to recognize that resources are finite, technologies usable for good or ill, that weapons are as often a spur to violence as they are a sanction against it. We face hard choices, on both the personal and institutional levels, and need a stronger moral framework in which to achieve our adopted aims. For example, is violence permissible or should governments impose patterns of behaviour on people through strict laws? Totalitarian regimes and both capitalist and socialist systems have implicit priorities and behaviour patterns within them – yet individuals cannot avoid the need to make choices themselves.

Violence or non-violence

Virtually all religions and states consider peace and non-violence desirable; nearly all law systems prohibit acts of aggression (*see pp. 30-1*). But nearly all, too, waive that principle in certain circumstances. Even the UN legitimizes force in self-defence or peace keeping. For pacifists, by contrast, non-violent solutions are the *only* acceptable ones. How soon society chooses to endorse their view may be central to human survival.

The value of life

At the root of many moral choices is the assumption that life is of supreme value. Catholicism speaks of its sanctity; Buddhism extends such notional protection for people to animals. Plant life is less often looked at in the same light, though aboriginal peoples regard all of nature as sacred, and environmental concern is now making all of us rethink our right to over-exploit it. But most societies make respect for life conditional on circumstances. Our laws say it is a crime to murder, yet to kill in battle is blessed. Many states have regulations concerning how and where animals may be humanely slaughtered. But carnage continues unabated elsewhere: human beings in the Iran-Iraq war, in the name of Islam; elephants in Africa, in the name of profit. Most people in industrialized countries are divorced from the direct responsibility for taking life, but cannot escape the indirect responsibility for things done on their behalf.

Restoring the moral balance
Human societies always show a complex mix of attitudes. But in today's world the mix is strongly biased towards dominance, competitiveness and greed, and away from compassion or tolerance. Ancient Taoist sages spoke of the interrelationship of yin and yang, the dual aspects of existence contrasting such characteristics as dark and light and passivity and activity. When these complementary opposites are out of balance, disharmony brings disease, violence or collapse. When they are in balance, Tao, or harmony, is established and peace returns.

OUT OF BALANCE

Violence
Everybody has a capacity for violence, normally tempered by our gentler side. But popular culture is obsessed with violence, glamorizing it and making force admirable.

Apathy
When society emphasizes power and self-seeking, those left out tend to a sense of helplessness and alienation from reality. Apathy in the face of crisis becomes pervasive.

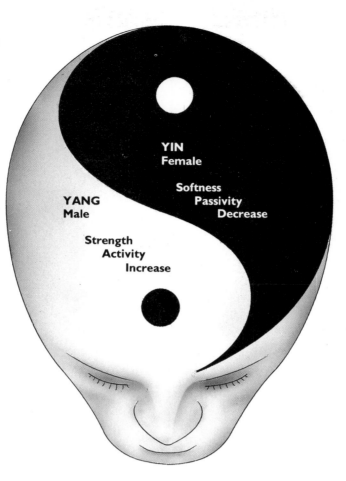

YIN
Female

Softness
Passivity
Decrease

YANG
Male

Strength
Activity
Increase

In search of peace
The imbalance of values polarizes and distorts both yin and yang aspects of society – on the one hand, apathy and anxiety; on the other, violence and hostility. War destroys and divides us even further. But the pursuit of peace helps to reintegrate society, leading people to understand, to tolerate, to respect and to support each other, replacing discord and dis-ease with harmony and health.

Competitiveness
The competitive spirit is now inculcated from childhood in most societies – other people are not partners but adversaries, to be beaten in games, in examinations and in life.

Materialism
Our society defines happiness in terms of material success and satisfaction of the self. But the cult of acquisition and egocentric living isolates people, and ignores deeper needs.

IN BALANCE

Maturity of self
Personal development, to acquire balance and understanding, has little to do with self-indulgence. The mature self is neither over-materialist nor egocentric, but calm, secure and generous.

Co-operation
Through co-operation, people as a whole can achieve more and mistrust and tension are reduced. Common, rather than individual, goals are stressed and each one exploits personal talents for all.

Justice
The law of the jungle is everybody for him/herself. But good laws define limits, so that individual freedoms do not abuse collective well-being. Respect for justice is a mark of wisdom.

Non-violence
There is more to non-violence than just not fighting – rather, it is a philosophy of personal conduct and conflict resolution, rejecting solutions by force in favour of reconciliation and respect.

Human need
Basic human needs are obvious, and until they are met (not the case for one-fifth of humanity) people have little capacity for concern over less tangible desires, and less still for any choice in the matter. But even for those who can choose, defining what people really require, over and above basic needs, poses problems. In our current materialist age, we tend to assume the necessity of video machines and so on. But such an attitude is plainly unsatisfactory – insecurity and alienation are not healed by consumer durables. This has led to a re-evaluation of those social and spiritual needs – such as a sense of community, of self-worth and participation and of personal fulfilment in work and in relationships, and both national and personal security, dignity and rights.

Male/female paradigm
Yin and yang are often loosely referred to as the female and male aspects of being, contrasting such characteristics as gentleness and strength, receptivity and dominance, caring and competing. Modern feminist writers have similarly identified what they see as an unhealthy imbalance towards male principles in modern society, leading to war, aggression, greed and other distortions of "manly" aspects, rather than the more conciliatory and constructive "womanly" virtues. They argue, too, that our patriarchal society, in which this imbalance is enshrined, is a dangerous and an unhealthy one. The logical extension of this argument is that the world would be a safer place if the female element was stressed. But the ideal is a balance between the two, both having a role in the way the world is run and in the nature of every human being.

with about $15,000, which is not seen as enough to provide a living standard – including a house, car, telephone, etc. – that satisfies expectations.

Rapidly growing populations and living standards need more and more energy. To bring developing countries' energy use up to that of the developed countries by the year 2025 (assuming no change in existing policies) would mean increasing global energy use by at least five times. Yet the risk of global warming through effects on the "greenhouse gases" in the atmosphere, and acidification of the environment, rule out even a doubling of energy consumption based on the current mix of energy sources and technologies. Any future economic growth must be based on non-polluting and energy-efficient technologies and policies.

Even assuming that we adopt measures to conserve energy enabling us to "buy time" to develop renewable energy sources (*see pp. 182-3*), present rates of population growth are unsustainable. In many low-income countries, they outstrip any reasonable expectations of modest improvements in housing, health care, food security or education. And while living standards remain so poor, more children are the best form of social security.

Herein lies the dilemma. Rising expectations and need make demands for more industrial growth politically irresistible, however ill-founded our faith in it. And, with conventional top-down approaches, the rate of growth required is mind boggling – a ten-fold increase in world manufacturing output, according to the Brundtland Report, to raise developing-world consumption to developed-world levels by the time population stabilizes next century.

Yet many ecologists are seeking a limit to growth, and ultimately a steady-state use of resources. The argument lies in our definitions: growth for whom? The poor cannot be left in their poverty; and their plight in itself fuels environmental destruction and population increase. But what policies will create true economic growth in the poorest sector? Industrial growth trickle down is a wasteful approach.

Even if we do achieve replacement-only fertility by 2035 (no mean task), population will not stabilize until 2095, and then at 10 billion – double the present world population. Most will live in cities, in conditions that could be indescribably grim. How many of these people will be adequately fed? So far, annual food production has managed to keep ahead of population growth. Between 1950 and 1985, cereal production grew at an annual rate of 2.7 per cent, while the world population increased at an annual rate of 1.9 per cent. In the next few decades, food production will have to increase by 3 to 4 per cent each year, to satisfy the extra demand, if current approaches continue. But food security could equally be met by reducing distortions in the world food market, by altered land distribution and use, and by sustainable management. Equitable distribution is a key factor – today we have abundant food, yet mass starvation. We have some very real choices ahead of us – choices that could make a difference of billions to the

Growth vs steady state

Natural populations experiencing explosive growth can expect to crash: outstripping resources and encountering new diseases and competitors. Human society seems to believe itself immune from this law; when faced with the multiplying symptoms of crisis, we advocate yet more unsustainable growth. We are engaged in exponential growth (as the curves suggest) in numbers, in consumption of resources and in disturbance of the planetary ecosystem. Yet the environment is finite. The doubling time of human population is shortening: there are now about 20 times as many people as there were at the time of Christ. In less than a hundred years there will be 40 times as many – if the crash does not overtake us before then.

There is an alternative: life communities can, and do, flourish over long periods of time, once they achieve a stable relationship with their environment. Such populations are mature – "climax" communities that grow, not in size, like a child, but in richness and strength, like an adult. The path towards maturity is not easy: but it is imperative we choose it. Otherwise nature will choose on our behalf.

Energy
The fossil fuel age ushered in our energy-consuming society. Predictions that present global energy consumption of around 13 terawatts may triple, or even quadruple, in 35 years, imply environmental catastrophe.

Population
It took 33,000 years for the human population to reach 1 billion (in the 1830s), and then only a hundred years for it to double to 2 billion. Less than 50 years later it had reached 4 billion. The prospect by the end of next century is between 8 and 14 billion.

Impact on Gaia
We are living out of balance with Gaia, changing the climate and pouring out pollution faster than natural systems can cope. Extinction threatens at least 25% of all species by the middle of the next century. By this time, we could have wasted a third of cultivable land, half of tropical forests, and face famine and irreversible climate change.

Steady state

The obvious way to avoid a crisis and crash is to halt the global rise in population and resource consumption *before* it is too late, producing a steady-state economy and society that is sustainable in planetary terms. Without corrective action, the population may stabilize at 10 billion; with it, we could reduce this by 2 billion, or possibly even more. Stabilizing consumption is even more problematic in a world with over 1 billion people in "absolute poverty", while the lion's share of resources supports fewer, more affluent people.

A fairer use of resources is a prerequisite to a steady-state economy; so, too, is a more careful, conserving use of resources. Both would enable an improvement in conditions of the poorest, without the damaging effects of competitive economic growth. Ultimately, a steady-state human society, using a sustainable flow of resource "income", but conserving non-renewable resource "capital", could produce a mature, "climax" civilization in which all of us could flourish.

Post-expansion crash

The likely outcome of uncontrolled growth is a crash – preceded by violent instability, as the graph shows. This type of growth in a finite environment will inevitably provoke resource crises and chaos in financial systems. Increasing numbers of people will be unable to meet their basic needs, leading to widespread famine and disease. The disintegration of society and the environment will lead to mounting death rates; the outbreak of endemic violence and repressive wars will speed the process. Many believe we are at the "unstable" point now, with the onset of the new dark age, at best, only 50 years off, and, at worst, approaching with the millennium.

The choice

We are at a crossroads. Following the old values of growth, expansion, competition, conflict and dominance of others and of nature all lead to an inevitable crash. If we now, instead, adopt values of maturity, stability, co-operation and peaceful "symbiosis" with each other and nature, we will be taking a path that can lead to a sustainable future. The choice is ours.

world population in the next century, bring an end to poverty or perpetuate it, and save or destroy our environment.

Future technological choices

We live in what is called a "technological cycle", a period in which technological advances occur at an unusually fast rate. There are, therefore, many choices open to us, many directions to follow, in deciding which technologies to adopt to solve specific global problems. The technologies we choose will depend on our choice of future. And, in turn, our future will depend on which technologies we develop. A future society based on, for example, solar power energy would probably be hugely different from a society based on nuclear breeder or fusion reactors (*see pp. 180-1*).

Complex technologies tend to accompany increasing industrialization. We then have to ask ourselves, can a society have such things as complex medical equipment, the most modern dental equipment, and effective transportation systems, without much industrialization? And can a society industrialize to such an extent without bringing on the environmental, social and other problems associated with today's industrialized societies?

Once again, there are choices to be made. For example, what expectation of life should we aim for? Do we want to invest the huge sums in developing and acquiring the medical technologies needed to keep people alive for the maximum time possible? Should people be kept in intensive-care units at great cost irrespective of the quality of their lives? Or should the money be invested for wider health for all?

The question of life expectancy is important for developed and developing countries. Rich countries are having to face escalating costs of medical services, particularly, to cope with an increasing number of old people. Developing countries have to face the fact that the degree of industrialization they will need to reach may depend on the infant mortality rate and the death rate they aim for. Does a life expectancy at birth of, say, 75 years and infant mortality rates of about 7 deaths under one year of age per 1000 live births require industrialization like that of, for example, Sweden? Or is there another route? Is this standard itself too high? In very poor countries, infant mortality rates may be more than 200 and life expectancy as short as 40 years. A broad spread of local social investment would improve matters far faster than capital-intensive industrial spending.

Another vital choice is the importance placed on the quality of the environment. Developing countries in the process of industrializing are often less sensitive about local environmental issues than countries already industrialized – at least, their governments are. The air and water in cities like Calcutta or Colombo are much more polluted than those in London or New York. But developed countries are often very insensitive about pollution that affects other states. Thus, the countries that inject into the atmosphere the most carbon dioxide, sulphur dioxide and chemicals that destroy the ozone

Quality or quantity of life

How can we provide a decent quality of life for 8 or 10 billion people – when, even with 5 billion, many go hungry and lead shortened lives? Everything depends on how we define and measure quality of life, and how we then perceive what creates it. Life expectancy and infant mortality rates, for instance, are common indicators, and the figures are far better in the North. But the assumption that industry and hi-tech medicine provide this advantage is false; nutrition, sanitation and social caring are far more important. Another measure is "satisfaction of need" – with emphasis on consumer needs and thus the endless, destructive pursuit of "progress". But true human needs are deeper: physical well-being and a sustainable lifestyle; the chance to express one's human potential and contribute to society; to live, love and share in a flourishing natural world. These needs we can meet – if we learn to seek not quantitative consumption and longevity for the minority, but a qualitative well-being for the whole human family and the environment. This choice of future comes down to practical decisions by governments and policymakers at work today. And it is of huge significance: raising the quality of life and potential of the majority is the fundamental first step to safeguarding the environment and bringing population growth to a halt, sooner rather than later.

The unequal world today

Everyone is equal in the eyes of God; but not in the eyes of most governments, nor in the accident of birth. Today, a person born in a developed nation can expect an average life span of 73 years. But for those born into the majority of humanity in developing nations, this life expectancy is at once reduced by over a fifth – 14 lost years. In Africa, overall life expectancy is two-thirds that of Europe, in some areas only half, while infant mortality is 8 times higher. High mortality is a spur to population growth – 90% of which is expected in the poor South of the world.

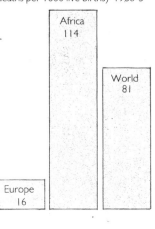

Life expectancy (years) 1980-5

Developed 73
Developing 59
Africa 49

1.2   0.56   3.6
Population (billions) 1985

Infant mortality (deaths per 1000 live births) 1980-5

Africa 114
World 81
Europe 16

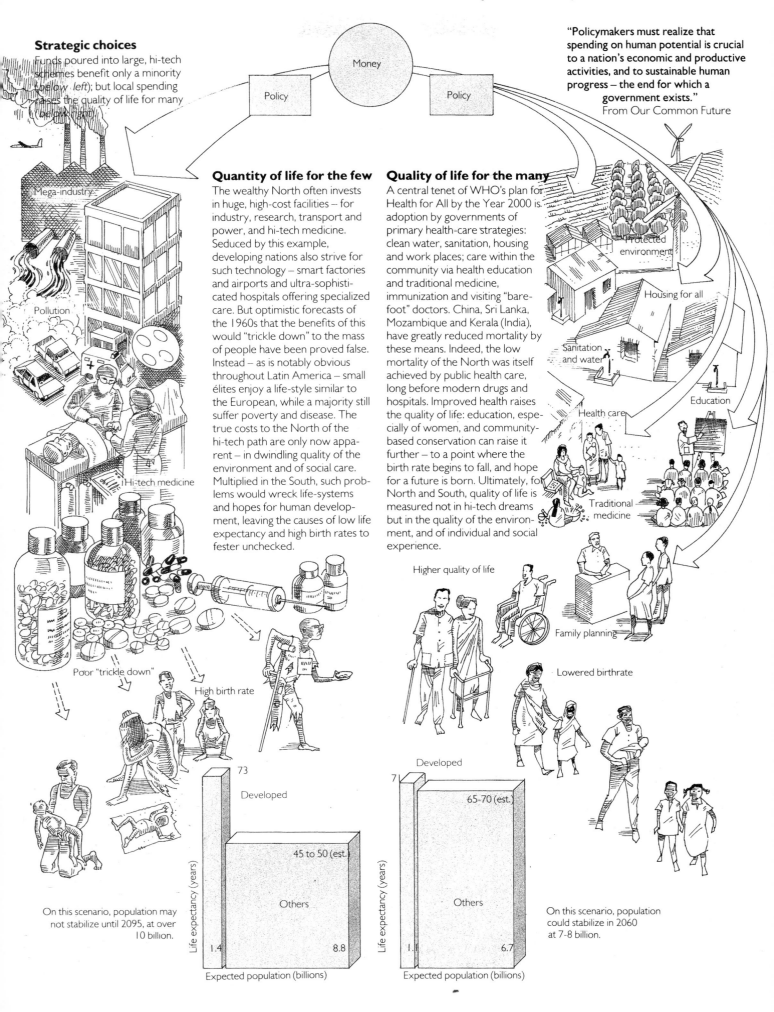

Strategic choices

Funds poured into large, hi-tech schemes benefit only a minority (below left); but local spending raises the quality of life for many (below right).

"Policymakers must realize that spending on human potential is crucial to a nation's economic and productive activities, and to sustainable human progress – the end for which a government exists."
From Our Common Future

Quantity of life for the few

The wealthy North often invests in huge, high-cost facilities – for industry, research, transport and power, and hi-tech medicine. Seduced by this example, developing nations also strive for such technology – smart factories and airports and ultra-sophisticated hospitals offering specialized care. But optimistic forecasts of the 1960s that the benefits of this would "trickle down" to the mass of people have been proved false. Instead – as is notably obvious throughout Latin America – small élites enjoy a life-style similar to the European, while a majority still suffer poverty and disease. The true costs to the North of the hi-tech path are only now apparent – in dwindling quality of the environment and of social care. Multiplied in the South, such problems would wreck life-systems and hopes for human development, leaving the causes of low life expectancy and high birth rates to fester unchecked.

Quality of life for the many

A central tenet of WHO's plan for Health for All by the Year 2000 is adoption by governments of primary health-care strategies: clean water, sanitation, housing and work places; care within the community via health education and traditional medicine, immunization and visiting "barefoot" doctors. China, Sri Lanka, Mozambique and Kerala (India), have greatly reduced mortality by these means. Indeed, the low mortality of the North was itself achieved by public health care, long before modern drugs and hospitals. Improved health raises the quality of life: education, especially of women, and community-based conservation can raise it further – to a point where the birth rate begins to fall, and hope for a future is born. Ultimately, for North and South, quality of life is measured not in hi-tech dreams but in the quality of the environment, and of individual and social experience.

Mega-industry

Pollution

Hi-tech medicine

Poor "trickle down"

High birth rate

Protected environment

Housing for all

Sanitation and water

Education

Health care

Traditional medicine

Higher quality of life

Family planning

Lowered birthrate

Developed

73

45 to 50 (est.)

Others

1.4   8.8

Life expectancy (years)

Expected population (billions)

On this scenario, population may not stabilize until 2095, at over 10 billion.

Developed

7

65-70 (est.)

Others

1.1   6.7

Life expectancy (years)

Expected population (billions)

On this scenario, population could stabilize in 2060 at 7-8 billion.

layer are the rich countries. And the developed countries often export their pollution to the South, either by dumping toxic waste there, or by manufacturing toxic materials (often banned in the North) there.

All countries must make choices about the quality of the environment, and the quality of life for peoples within it. And if these choices are to improve the lot of *all* peoples, not just those who presently have power to make them, we shall need wisdom and a willingness to devolve choices to those they affect.

What balance should be struck between industrial efficiency and controlling pollution? Which is better – a shorter life in a relatively unpolluted and natural environment or a longer life in a polluted and industrialized one? Who should be responsible for controlling pollution? What penalties will deter it?

Entering the biological age

By the 1980s, species extinctions were running at about one per day – 400 times the natural rate; by the 1990s, it may be one per hour; by 2000 one every 10 minutes. The apparent causes, rising human numbers and needs, conceal a deeper one – our inability to control technology.

While our brains may be very inventive at science, we are pretty poor at using heart and mind to direct it for good, or to devise social and political institutions to do this for us. Nor are we able to predict its effects.

An escalating arms race, ill-considered schemes for "development", pollution and climate change are all symptoms of this malaise, which wrecks the promise of each new technology. Many look to emerging technologies for solutions: for ways to replace scarce raw materials, make industry more "competitive", and create wealth. But, on past performance, these new technologies also may bring toxic wastes, unforeseen environmental kickbacks, and catastrophic accidents.

Today, our fastest growing industry is biotechnology, which offers to feed and fuel the coming billions. But it, too, may prove, like the Green Revolution, socially divisive and environmentally malign, fuelling genetic loss and creating the new threat of microbial pollution. And just as Star Wars research continues though space war is banned, prohibitions on germ warfare do not stop research into hostile pathogens.

Technology remains uncontrolled because it has no appropriate value framework. Commercially driven, its course is determined by short-term gain and political interests often remote from the point of impact. And it is rooted in Descartian science, with its mechanistic view of the world and grandiose belief in the "mastery of nature". The holistic view of ecology has, so far, barely shaken the technocracy. But change is coming.

Fifteen years after the Gaia Hypothesis was first put forward, this most lucid way of looking at our planet and ourselves is steadily gaining credence (*see pp. 254-5*). It may well signal the birth of a mature science that seeks not to manipulate, but to co-operate and participate with nature. It could take years to influence commerce and governments, and shape a non-invasive

Biological choices

We are entering the age of biology. So far, humanity has abused its growing power over nature, but the new age may offer us the skills to make good the damage. Do we, though, have the wisdom? Or will our intervention in biological systems be so great, with such unforeseen interactions, that we must expect shocks to come? Two sciences are leading the way, but with very different credos. Ecology is the elder: increasingly drawing on Gaian ideas (*below*), it studies whole biological systems – from planetary climate to soil communities – and seeks to guard the diversity and genetic wealth of the planet, and develop a technology in harmony with nature. Biotechnology, by contrast, is an *enfant terrible*. One of the youngest, fastest-growing industries in the world, it offers new medicines, crops, pest controls and energy sources, with great potential for sustainable use – or for evil. Can we control it? After synthetic chemicals, which persist and accumulate in food chains, might we now face rogue synthetic living organisms, multiplying with potentially devastating effect? Is it folly to meddle with the genetic code – our wealth for the future? How can we ensure that biotechnology serves human need, and ecological wisdom, in harmony with Gaia?

A partnership with Gaia

Scientists seeking to detect life on other planets first discovered the phenomenon of the Earth's self-sustaining biosphere, and named it Gaia. Within Gaia, every organism is linked. All are caught up in the cycling of energy and nutrients via earth, air and water. But human kind grossly interferes, threatening its continuity. In place of the fabric of Gaia, we see only "resources" to exploit. Perceiving and acting in harmony with Gaian systems may be crucial. This does not mean a reactionary "back to nature" approach, but rather a radical reassessment of human needs, and the technologies used to meet them. Governments, commerce, science and individuals all must assess actions by new criteria – to work with Gaian systems, and do the least harm to them.

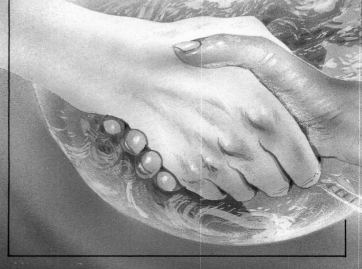

Genetic resources

The 5-10 million species thought to exist represent a vastly greater genetic diversity – races, strains, and local varieties, both wild and domesticated. As this is eroded, concerned groups such as the CGIAR and IBPGR are building up gene banks and reserves in an attempt to preserve it, a common heritage for humanity. But as the economic importance of genetic resources grows, they are becoming, instead, a divisive political issue. The world's gene wealth lies mainly in the South, which is challenging the right of Northern industries to appropriate and profit from it.

Guarding diversity

Humanity tends carelessly to "simplify" nature, replacing its diversity with fewer and fewer species. As the great wild centres – the tropical forests – shrink, species decline is hugely accelerated. We are losing the diversity of traditional crops, too, as modern agriculture spreads vast monocultures of engineered Green Revolution strains – Greece, for example, has lost 90% of its native wheat strains in just 40 years. Our dependence on ever fewer, inbred crop strains risks massive failure through pest or blight. Ecology warns that reducing diversity weakens the resilience of systems. "Guard diversity" should be our first law, in all future choices.

Controlling biotechnology

Now worth about $4 billion a year, the biotechnology industry devotes 60% of this to genetic engineering, 30% to cellular biology and 8% to fermentation techniques for new energy and protein sources. The science promises a "non-invasive" agriculture – crops that flourish without chemicals, natural reclamation and pest control. But its promise is undermined by the loss of its raw material – genetic wealth. And there are cries of alarm – about the ill-considered release of new microorganisms; and about exploitation that cares for neither people nor planet.

The human seed

No issue raises more debate than the sanctity of the human embryo. Halting population growth is an urgent task. But what means are justifiable? Some religions still oppose contraception; democrats resist legal or state controls. Moral objections to abortion are met by feminist claims to "rights" over their bodies. Grave legal and ethical problems are posed by science, too: who is the parent of a surrogate baby? Should medical research with human embryos be banned?

agriculture and industry. But the image of Gaia, the "blue pearl hanging in space", is powerful. It offers a code for technology similar to the ancient Hippocratic Oath of medicine: "do nothing that may harm the planet – or her peoples."

Prospects for the information age

Can democracy survive in the post-industrial society? Large computers that can store and very rapidly analyse vast amounts of information are producing social effects as far-reaching as those of the Industrial Revolution. Few realize how rapidly computer technology is advancing. A computer equivalent to the small pocket calculator so common today would, 30 years ago, have filled a large room. Within the next decade the capacity of computers will be increased a thousand-fold. Very-high-speed integrated circuits will account for a hundredfold of this; improvements in software for another tenfold.

Already, many adults of developed countries feature in computer data files on credit rating, driver status, marketing targets, and a range of less comfortable statistics such as criminal record or political activity. Such systems will be more developed in future; guarding freedoms will need a watchful citizenry.

Coupled with communications satellites, information technology produces almost instant global communications. Information can be transmitted around the world in one-tenth of a second. Transistor radios and, increasingly, television sets, are widely available, even in poor regions. In the information age, all countries know what is going on in all other countries, often while it is going on. Developing countries compare the standard of living enjoyed in developed countries with their own.

This causes discontent. It also becomes obvious to poorer people that the wealth in their own countries is not equitably distributed. Revolutionary movements then gain credibility and support. And what people in the South see in television programmes and hear on radio is often dictated by short-sighted Western commercial interests. It is these that control most satellite communications. The consequence is to promote the worst of Western values and consumerism – the "coca-cola civilization" – and to prevent true communication between North and South, and within the South. Indigenous cultures deteriorate under the bombardment.

The global village and its caretakers

Information storage and flow are characteristics of life; one way of looking at natural systems is as complex information networks and exchanges. The human species has increased information transfer and accumulation within Gaia enormously – both in speed and in volume. This is one argument for proposing humanity as the "brain" of the planet, our communications as its "nervous system" – alongside the slower, "hormonal" communications of nature via life-forms, oceans and air, and genetic transfer.

The age of "Big Brother"

In the 1980s, the hope that the information revolution would lead to greater freedom of knowledge may have started to fade. In many countries, the abuse of new information-gathering and surveillance techniques means that centralized "information power" seems to be winning. Governments across the political spectrum are determined to have not only as much information as possible about other countries, but also about their own citizens.

Many strands of the state machinery enmesh and bind the individual to the system. Large computers that can store and rapidly analyse vast amounts of information are producing social effects as far-reaching as those of the industrial revolution. Information will probably be stored on centralized computers capable of providing instant access to data on every citizen – data about health, criminal record, marital history, employment and academic records, character references and personal finances. The use of credit cards, automatic cash dispensers and soon, perhaps, "plastic money" means that, at key points during any normal day, the authorities will know our precise movements.

The new underclass

The microchip has led to a second industrial revolution, one that has sharply reduced labour requirements, especially in the more technology-dependent North. The danger is that the world will become a society divided between a rich, information-using minority with jobs utilizing complex communication systems or technological skills, and a poor majority, an uninformed underclass of the unemployed or those consigned to low-paid menial tasks. For the many, the future holds the prospect of decreasing involvement in the decision-making processes and increasing dependence on welfare and easily accessible mass-media output.

Media control

In many Communist and developing countries, the government or ruling party has direct control of the press. By extension, it therefore controls most of the news. In Western democracies, in principle, there is freedom of the media. But in practice, the tendency is towards large conglomerates, with ownership more and more in the hands of a few powerful individuals or concerns, some of whom have media empires verging on monopolies. Thus, they too can influence what people know and what is kept out of the public domain.

The international flow of news is controlled largely by a small group of Western news agencies, transmitting news through the wire services carefully tailored to the tastes and preconceptions of their Western readership. In an attempt to counter this, some developing countries tried through UNESCO to have a new international information order accepted, which would have reduced such biased coverage.

The losers

Individuals without access to new information tools will be at a huge disadvantage in the world of the near future, as will those without the skills to use them. The poor are excluded by reasons of their poverty – which is as true for nations as it is for individuals. In many fields even today, lacking a personal computer is as great a disadvantage as lacking access to a telephone. It is how the information provided by worldwide computer link-ups is used, however, that gives cause for concern: commodities buyers in a European stock exchange may know, for example, of a blight threatening a coffee crop before the farmers in a neighbouring region.

Centralized data

It is not only governments that maintain detailed computerized records on individuals. Banks, private companies, employment agencies, credit card companies, magazine and book distributors and many others all maintain computerized lists of clients or of people relevant to their clients' businesses. It is now common practice for these lists to be sold to other interested parties for straight financial gain, with little or no regard for the privacy of the individuals concerned.

At a governmental level, countries are increasingly making use of personalized computer codes assigned to each citizen at birth. This code is entered on all official interactions – school records, hospital records, social security records, dealings with licensing authorities, the courts and so on – and information logged in centralized data bases. Anybody with a high enough security clearance (or ability to "break into" the computer system) can gain personal information on any individual.

Whether this somewhat presumptuous idea actually does Gaia or us any good will depend on how we use our growing communications skill. It could help us to build a global village, where every individual can talk to any other, anywhere in the world, be they peasant or prince. And where each can learn anything they need or want to know, at a moment's enquiry, via databases and satellite links. And it is already helping us to observe and monitor the environment, and our own impacts, from outside.

Various countries are now beginning to exploit remote sensing of the Earth using satellite technology, for a number of purposes including geo-ecology and landscape planning, geology, hydrology, environmental control and monitoring of vegetation. Remote sensing can also give early warning of natural disasters, optimize the use of resources, such as arable land, and identify at an early stage changes in the natural environment. Currently satellites are exploring natural resources, measuring the quality of the Earth's vegetation, the moisture content of soil, biogenic zones in the oceans, water pollution, and the temperature and chemical composition of the atmosphere. These measurements would be very difficult or very expensive without space technologies.

In much of our daily lives, we are already dependent on space communications – for long-distance radio and television programmes, or telephone calls; to hear the weather forecast or travel by plane. In future, this benign technology may help create and monitor peace.

Information technology and robotics go hand in hand. This siamese twin promises to revolutionize almost all aspects of life – economics, the work place, education, leisure, development of poor countries, and political and military activities. In the industrialized world, within a decade or so, the vast bulk of the population will be employed in the service industries or unemployed, at least in the traditional sense.

But this technology has a dark side. Unemployment is already a scourge. Do we want to worsen it, and waste human potential and skill? And do we want mass production of goods to pour off automated lines, further indebting us to the environment and producing yet more cultural uniformity? The same dilemma confronts us: cheap goods are needed and wanted; but would not local work, and craft-based, more individual, production, help us more?

Military nightmares

The dangers of automation and information technology in military activities are clear. Technologically, fully automated warfare is foreseeable within the next 20 years. A war that involves automated attacks and defence in an area cleared of humans, with remote, if any, human control, raises some fundamental questions. How would victory be defined? If no blood flows – a benefit on the face of it – how would war ever end? The danger is that such wars would be seen to fail to determine anything, and rapidly escalate to wider violence on a nuclear scale.

The information revolution

What future will the information age bring? Already, satellites swarm above the Earth like bees. One communications satellite in geostationary orbit can simultaneously relay several thousand telephone calls and many television pictures between, say, Europe and the US. Three together can cover the entire globe. On the ground, the telephone, telex, television and video are becoming the ears and eyes of the world, while "spacebridge" television links together people in such diverse locations as China and New York or Red Square and rural India, to see and hear each

Looking after the land
Radios, and radio telephones, are already valuable to farmers in remote regions of the world. They can bring early warning of livestock diseases or crop blights, of drought, flood, locusts or fires, as shown here. They could in future also bring advice specific to local needs, based on satellite surveys monitoring a huge range of factors.

The liberating computer?
Low-cost, mobile communication or computer equipment, which can be used at home, will free many industrial nations from the grind of long travel to work, or city living. It can also help small-scale local industry and co-opera-tive work schemes in developing regions, and enable women and the self-employed to earn extra money to raise living standards. But dreams of free data access, with its huge educational potential are fading.

other and debate global issues. Computers are becoming ever smaller, more mobile and cheaper: eventually the benefits may reach beyond the affluent – to help human and sustainable development for the poor, and join the local and global in a network of co-operative effort and true democracy. At present, secrecy and "data power" – whether of states or big business – block the way. Such a future depends on the will and vision to share, both information and technology. The greatest gift of the information revolution is this vision. Up in their polar orbits, remote-sensing satellites are allowing us to "see" the planet from outside – and our own impact on it – bringing a new sense of self-awareness and of our common humanity.

The world's largest machine

Pick up a telephone today, and you have access to 600 million others. What will the world be like if, one day, the dream of Alexander Graham Bell comes true: that any person can talk to any other? We are far from this yet. There are still more telephones in metropolitan New York than in the whole of black Africa. But once radiophones and satellites free us from the cable, and with the impetus of communications spread, even in remote, poor regions the telephone may eventually arrive. Unit costs per call are becoming astoundingly low. The telephone user increasingly taps into the whole information age – via telex, fax, television, data services, computer nets, radio phone-ins and recorded advice. The telephone system – "the largest machine in the world" – may give humanity its voice.

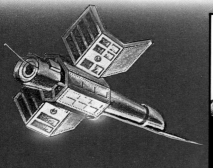

Bridging the literacy gap

In areas where literacy is low, films, slide shows, and television, can span the "literacy gap". In India, satellite television is used for education programmes. People need information – on health, contraception, farming and markets, as well as on world and local events. For women especially, like this group in Nigeria, access to media can be a powerful force for change.

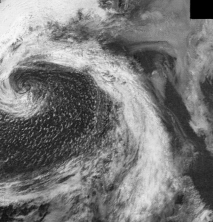

Observing Gaia

Remote-sensing satellites give us "eyes in the sky" which may help us to understand the life-cycles of our planet, and the damage we do. NOAA weather satellites, for instance, map cloud cover, ozone patterns, and atmospheric changes, study marine pollution, and even the biological vigour of land and sea life; LANDSAT spacecraft have been used to measure the eroding effects of deforestation.

Media for peace

The information revolution could help create a peaceful world. But Northern and commercial dominance has led to cries from the South for a more effective voice, and to proposals for a New World Information and Communication Order. A Non-aligned News Agency Pool was set up in 1977. Calls for a code of journalism to ensure fair reporting of South issues, however, raised fears of state media control; the 1981 Talloires Declaration in support of press freedom was signed by journalists from 20 nations. Since then, the NWICO has evolved with much debate. Recent years have seen a marked increase in the flow of news and cultural media from South to North – an exchange vital to understanding in the future.

Moreover, automated wars would use weapons at a very fast rate, and continue until one side or the other ran out of resources. This would necessitate establishing large-scale production facilities for military robots, unmanned vehicles, autonomous missiles, computerized command and control systems, and so on, and doing so well in advance of the battle. Automated war could lead to the total militarization of economies and societies.

The effects of uncontrolled military technology are most obvious in the nuclear arms race, and the policies of strategists who are seduced by ideas of technical "mastery". Its effect on future American policy, for instance, is indicated by the 1988 report of an American Presidential Commission, *Discriminate Deterrence*. The "blue-ribbon" commission contained 13 members, chaired by Mr Fred Ikle, the American Under Secretary of Defence for Policy Affairs. A number of distinguished strategic experts served on the commission – names such as Dr Henry Kissinger, Dr Zbigniew Brzezinski and Mr William Clark, all former National Security Advisers.

The commission was asked for a long-term "integrated strategy" for meeting the US's security needs until the year 2010. According to its analysis, the next 20 years are likely to bring dramatic changes in international relations. China, Japan and other countries will acquire very destructive conventional weapons and some will have weapons of mass destruction. The USA and USSR will no longer stand out as the military giants they now are.

A world with three or four superpowers will confront American military planners with a much more complex environment than today's bipolar world. The US will have to manage relations with several different global powers and form appropriate coalitions with them. Wars may break out between superpowers not aligned with the US. Alliances may shift. The next 20 years will be a period of transition to this new, complex and unfamiliar world.

To meet the new threats, the report recommends the use of high technologies, repeatedly emphasizing that they must be exploited by the military to the utmost – not only to deter wars but also to fight them. Senior Americans have obviously not dropped the myths of limited nuclear wars, of fightable and winnable nuclear wars, or of "surgical" nuclear strikes. The commission, in fact, suggests that NATO's policy of "flexible response" is replaced by so-called "discriminating nuclear responses".

Low-yield nuclear weapons, accurately delivered, are recommended for future warfare because they would be perceived as causing less than massive damage. The commission believes that such weapons would be more publicly acceptable than today's nuclear weapons. New conventional weapons are also needed for the "controlled, discriminate use of force".

The commission thinks that the US military should become more involved in conflicts in the South to counter what it calls "low-intensity conflict". This, the

Automated battlefield

Military and civilian activities are becoming increasingly automated. Within the foreseeable future almost all the food and consumer goods needed in the industrialized countries will be produced by about only 4 or 5% of the workforce. Automated, robot-intensive industries will be run by a small working élite with the potential to accumulate considerable economic and political power.

Eventually warfare could also be automated. Battles could take place on strips of evacuated border territory fought between unmanned vehicles and robots and automated, autonomous missiles. Victory could go to the side able to keep the battle going longest. In an automated battle, weapons would be used at a tremendous rate. This would put a high premium on establishing, before war began, industries able to produce unmanned vehicles, remotely piloted planes, autonomous missiles and other weapons systems. Automated warfare could, therefore, lead to the total militarization of the economy and society.

The end point of military and civilian automation may well be totalitarian societies headed by the élites who control the computers running the automated industries.

Automated scenario

In its simplest form, an automated battle would take place in territory around the border of two countries from which civilians had been evacuated. The "attacker" would invade the area with unmanned vehicles and robots; the other side would respond with autonomous missiles.

Even this automated scenario could progress along fairly tradi-tional lines: first, the enemy would be located and assessed; second, command decisions would be made regarding the best response; third, weapons would be selected and unleashed; and finally, the effectiveness of the attack would be assessed before deciding if the whole process needed to be repeated.

On the automated battlefield, however, the location and assess-ment of the enemy would be by reconnaissance satellites, ground sensors and by RPVs (remotely piloted vehicles). These pilotless planes would not only feed intelli-gence back to central battle com-puters (much as they do already), they would also be equipped with laser guidance systems to direct missiles on to their targets.

Although not strictly essential, if the need for the shedding of blood was felt necessary, small squads of highly mobile troops could be infiltrated into the battle zone. These would be equipped with advanced manual-launch mis-siles powerful enough to take out even the most heavily armoured enemy vehicles missed by the initial barrage.

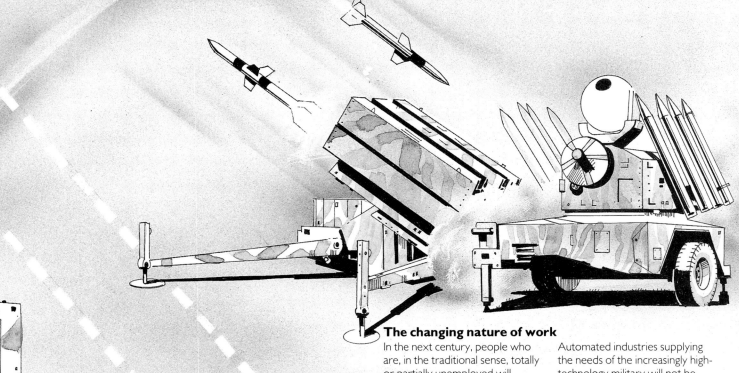

The changing nature of work

In the next century, people who are, in the traditional sense, totally or partially unemployed will include most women, all those over, say, the age of 40, the disabled and the young – hun-dreds of millions of people in the industrialized countries alone.

Automated industries supplying the needs of the increasingly high-technology military will not be able to take up the slack, concen-trating, instead, its labour needs from among the cream of the technologists and research scien-tists.

The dangers

The automation of warfare is occurring for a number of reasons. Manpower shortages and the increasing lethality of the bat-tlefield make attractive the use of relatively cheap and expendable robots. In the automated society of the near future, there are likely to be few people, other than the working élites, able to operate complex and sophisticated weapons. And the élites will not willingly go to war.

A major reason for automation, though, is simply that the tech-nologies are becoming available, and every conceivable technolo-gical advance is used for military purposes. The pressures for this military use of technology has so far proved politically irresistible. There is no reason to believe that the élites controlling automated industries will, in this respect, behave differently to today's vested interests.

If warfare is becoming a battle between robots and missiles, why not, one may ask, simply decide the issue by having the generals play computer-simulated war games? In fact, is not the concept of automated war so absurd as to make it incredible? Herein lies the danger – automated war may make the concept of conventional tactical warfare in Europe incredi-ble. Any conflict in Europe is then likely to escalate rapidly to an all-out strategic nuclear war. Moves towards automated war-fare are, therefore, likely to decrease global security.

report says, will considerably increase over the next 20 years. The term "low-intensity conflict" includes insurgencies, terrorism, paramilitary crime, sabotage, and other forms of violence in the shadowy area between war and peace.

"Low-intensity conflict" has become, according to the report, a permanent form of warfare in which the "enemy" is unlikely ever to surrender. New weapons should be developed to fight it – including special communications systems and "smart" (precision-guided) missiles – and the US's allies in the South should be equipped with them.

The commission also wants much more covert action, not necessarily run by the CIA, with fewer legislative restrictions. And it recommends that the US keeps strike forces available for use in conflicts in the South. These would be "versatile, mobile forces, minimally dependent on overseas bases, that can deliver precisely controlled strikes against distant military targets".

The views expressed in Discriminate Deterrence should be taken seriously, given the distinction of the members of the commission. In this context, the report makes depressing reading. Hopefully, the American public will realize that American security cannot be had at the expense of world security, and persuade their political leaders to fashion their future foreign policy accordingly.

What kind of world?

Certainly, the world of the future will be politically and technologically altered even more than we imagine now. How will money be circulated in an automated, largely unemployed, society, for instance? Someone will have to buy the goods the robots produce. Will a whole new range of activities – from running a local community radio station to looking after one's grandparents – become paid work? Perhaps the government will send cheques through the post to anyone engaged in one of a huge number of "approved activities". Or perhaps everyone will get a cheque through the post anyway.

Everyone whose government can afford it, that is. In large parts of the world where young populations and strained resources coincide, will new models of local development have grown alongside modern communications, to enable people here, too, to share in the global village? And how will the shifts in population power in favour of the East, and of ethnic minorities within the Western nations, alter these patterns?

Whatever solutions are chosen will transform current ideas on economics and the meaning of work. Protestant ethics about the social value of work, the role of money and competition, and the responsible "breadwinner", will no longer be a sound basis for life. On the contrary, there will be more social value in not working.

Will a new ethic evolve without great disruption? Will political parties representing the new majorities arise, or will more authoritarian parties fight for the old guard? If traditional jobs, notably in manufacturing, do not

The future majorities

How will we live in, say, fifty years from now? Our technology, and the social and demographic profiles of the world are going through profound changes. It is difficult to predict how these changes will interact – though it is certain that future lifestyles will be as different from what we know now as today is from the Victorian past. There is a marked contrast, however, between the expectations of different regions of the world. Low birth rates and better geriatric care in the North means the population is increasingly elderly, and the workforce is shrinking – taken with automation, this may create a majority outside the formal work ethic. Declining cities, and growing ethnic minorities, also imply social change. Much of the South, by contrast, with continuing high birth rates, is facing a huge young population clamouring for work; swelling cities, and a declining resource base mean an intensified effort to meet basic needs. Such trends have far-reaching consequences for planning. Whereas high-tech, low-labour economies may be appropriate to the North, with prospects for a leisured society, such strategies may be wildly inappropriate at this stage in the South. If we would build an equitable and sustainable world for the future majority, we must choose with care.

Future lifestyles

US workshops in "future imaging" are described in *Citizen Summitry*, by D. Carlson and C. Comstock (1986): "Participants see a very localist world, imbued with a strong sense of planetary consciousness, an earth-sense, a Gaia sense. What emerges is . . . an active local community . . . The bulk of work involves human services . . . with emphasis on life-long training in conflict-resolution skills . . . "

Southern profile: newly industrial and urban

Industrializing countries, such as Mexico and Brazil, have more potential jobs and markets than less-developed ones. But huge cities will create demands to construct public health utilities, housing, water supply and an energy infrastructure. These countries need technologies that are humanly accessible to their work-hungry people. Automation brings leisure only to the rich, and harms the poor majority; rather, world financial reform, and national recognition of ordinary people's needs and skills, are required for a sustainable future lifestyle.

Northern lifestyles: US and Europe

Formal employment is likely to take a diminishing role in most people's lives. Computers could permit people to work at home. Education in self-employed and leisure skills will be needed. But with a small workforce, generating income to support the workless and the health and social services may be difficult. A growing under-class of poor already exists. In the US, the added influx of minorities could lead to a "poor majority" – with English not even their first language – and major social and political changes.

Asian resurgence: Japan

The peoples of Asia already dominate the world in numbers. Increasingly, their new technolo-gies and philosophies are becom-ing dominant, too. Japan in par-ticular is demonstrating an unmatched economic power. Free of a heavy military budget, and with advanced technology and futurist thinking, Japan's eco-nomy grows out of new princi-ples: shared government and commercial risk, and co-operative competition. It may ultimately be this fresh model of economic participation, rather than its hi-tech image, which is Japan's gift to other nations.

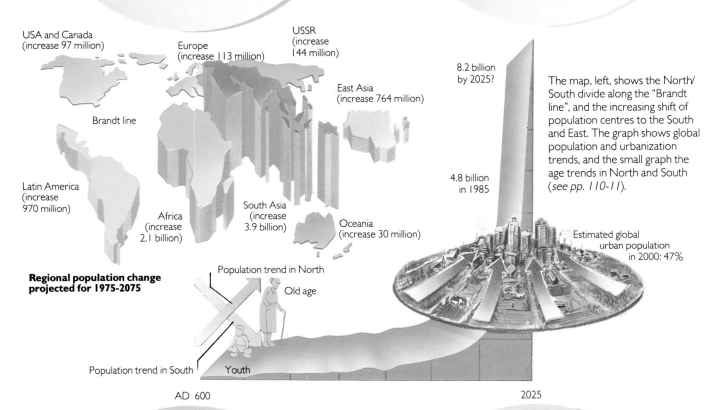

USA and Canada (increase 97 million)

Europe (increase 113 million)

USSR (increase 144 million)

East Asia (increase 764 million)

Brandt line

Latin America (increase 970 million)

Africa (increase 2.1 billion)

South Asia (increase 3.9 billion)

Oceania (increase 30 million)

8.2 billion by 2025?

4.8 billion in 1985

The map, left, shows the North/South divide along the "Brandt line", and the increasing shift of population centres to the South and East. The graph shows global population and urbanization trends, and the small graph the age trends in North and South (see pp. 110-11).

Regional population change projected for 1975-2075

Population trend in North

Old age

Population trend in South

Youth

Estimated global urban population in 2000: 47%

AD 600

2025

Southern profile: least developed and rural

Future lifestyles in the poorer Southern countries may be grim indeed, unless improved terms of trade, debt remission, and help with sustainable technology and funding from outside is given. High birth rates and infant mortality, and an overstretched land and water base, afflict areas, such as Africa. Local health, industry and sustainable agriculture could all benefit from a mix of small-scale new and traditional technology, and from communication and education via satellite, radio and television.

South strategies: China

With nearly a quarter of world population, China has pursued decentralized, labour-intensive strategies that have eradicated real poverty. Appropriate tech-nology for rural self-sufficiency and small-scale industry, and major efforts to reforest and protect watersheds are coupled with traditional and local health care. Automation of industry would be inappropriate in much of China now, but information technology could be of enormous benefit in such a decentralized economy.

exist, how will people pass their time? Sitting at home playing computer games? In sports and leisure activities? In education? Or in efforts to survive via barter and self-sufficiency, and the black economy?

Is nuclear energy acceptable?

Future energy projections, both high and low, assume a certain growth of nuclear power. In a post-fossil-fuel world, nuclear power is seen as a clean form of energy, although, as the public is all too well aware, it comes with a number of serious drawbacks. Not least is the problem of radioactive waste disposal. There is also the military connection: can we guarantee the separation of civilian and military nuclear activity?

Fusion power is seen by some as a great future source of energy. This thinking is stimulated by the fact that there is enough deuterium in the oceans to supply humankind's energy needs for millions of years. Fusion, in which two light nuclei, such as hydrogen nuclei, are fused together to form a heavier one, can only take place at very high temperatures – over a hundred million degrees Centigrade. But no existing material can withstand temperatures higher than a few thousand degrees. The major problem of fusion reactors is to isolate the fuel from the walls of the containment vessel.

It is difficult to predict if and when fusion reactors will be commercially developed. If they are, it will probably be well into the 21st century. A fusion reactor will probably use a plasma (a very hot gas consisting mostly of electrons and positive ions) of deuterium and tritium contained in a toroid (a volume in which magnetic fields isolate the plasma from the container wall). The plasma may be surrounded by a "blanket" through which a coolant will flow to remove the fusion energy from the reactor. The heat produced will then be used to generate electricity as in a conventional power station.

Fusion produces high-energy neutrons that could be used to produce plutonium, in uranium placed, for example, around the reactor core; the plutonium could, in turn, be used to make nuclear weapons. Fusion reactors will, therefore, not reduce the risk of the proliferation of nuclear weapons. Nor will they be environmentally benign. The high-energy neutrons produced during fusion will make radioactive materials in and near the reactor. There will, therefore, still be considerable problems of disposing of large amounts of highly radioactive waste.

Energy for all our futures

Clearly, a, if not the, main requirement for sustainable development is an economically viable and environmentally benign mix of energy sources that will sustain human well-being in the medium and long term. Energy efficiency must become the key-stone of development. Greater energy services must be supplied, but with a fraction of the primary energy inputs currently used per each output.

An acceptable global energy structure in the next century must obviously be based on renewable

Energy: A hi-tech centralized utopia

Science fiction envisages a future where the wheels of power hum effortlessly in a peaceable and nature-loving society. Reality is different: dwindling and pollutant fossil fuels; socially divisive nuclear technology; one-quarter of peoples using three-quarters of energy supplies; half of all peoples dependent on shrinking tree cover for fuel.

Some estimates suggest energy use will triple by 2020. The environmental and social costs of this would be huge. Centralized industries tend towards secrecy, especially where nuclear power is concerned. The risk of nuclear terrorism posed by large-scale reprocessing make draconian security measures likely. It is doubtful whether in an open society such measures would be legally, politically and socially acceptable. Democracy may not survive in a plutonium economy.

The fuelwood crisis

In 1980 half the existing world population depended on biomass fuels – wood, straw, dung, or charcoal – for cooking, heating, and local industry; 70% of these people already experienced scarcity, fuel collection involving 100-300 days of walking time per family year. By 1990, 2.5 billion, and by 2000, nearly 3 billion people will be in the same distress. Large central energy supplies will not solve this problem. There is no infrastructure to supply it, no money to pay for it. Half the world needs a different energy strategy.

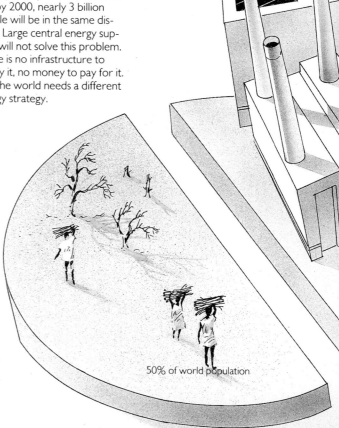

50% of world population

Centralized control of energy

Huge, high-technology industries require large, centralized bureaucracies, which soon become unable to conceive of small industrial units. Instead they agitate for yet more expansion. In the 1960s, a nuclear power station generating 2-3 Mw was considered large; those now being built generate more than 1,000 Mw; breeder reactors will generate several thousand Mw. A similar trend in all power source technologies is apparent, and the problems of environmental impact, and resistance to democratic control increase exponentially with size. And if the technology proves dangerous, costly or shortlived, the expense of the failure makes it hard to admit to or to correct.

Fossil fuels

Fossil fuels supply nine-tenths of world commercial energy. Consumption, though, is grossly unequal – developed nations, with only a quarter of world population, consume nearly four-fifths. Oil is presently fairly cheap, but stocks may last only 30 years and price shocks will come, hitting hardest at developing, oil-importing nations. Coal will last much longer, but it is the dirtiest of all fuels. Acid rain is now affecting the South as well as the North, and climate change due to the "greenhouse effect" is global. The best use of oil energy is on the land – as fertilizer badly needed in developing regions – not as fuel.

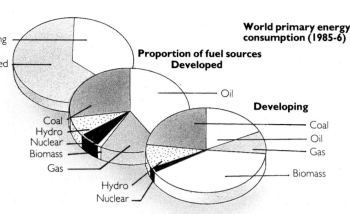

World primary energy consumption (1985-6)

Developing

Developed

Proportion of fuel sources Developed

Oil

Coal
Hydro
Nuclear
Biomass
Gas

Hydro
Nuclear

Developing

Coal

Oil

Gas

Biomass

Nuclear futures

Nuclear energy now has a questionable future. Expensive, dangerous and environmentally suspect, its links with the nuclear arms race provoke government secrecy and public distrust. Yet it is abundant, and could be "clean" if controlled. Current programmes are for breeder reactors, which produce surplus plutonium, and so promote large-scale reprocessing with all the associated risks (*below*). But it is fusion that is the future hope. Fusion processes require huge temperatures, and the technology to build reactors that can withstand them is not yet available. But the fuel – deuterium and tritium – is abundant: in theory the oceans could supply enough to last millions of years.

Large-scale renewables

The energy industry is putting increasing effort into renewable potential: wind, solar, hydro, geothermal and ocean power. Hydropower provides nearly a quarter of all electricity worldwide, and up to 70% in some countries, and ocean power has huge potential. Once again, however, the "corporate bureaucracy" factor tends towards the large-scale. Huge dams, such as the Aswan, have immediate and long-term environmental effects. Ecologists protest that tidal barrages planned for the British Severn Estuary were on such a scale as to threaten disruption of the whole region. The very quality of renewable sources that makes them so attractive – wide-spread distribution, low-price, small-scale, non-invasive technology – is negated by this corporate enthusiasm.

Energy split

Two-thirds of global primary energy use, including domestic, goes to the developed nations (with only 25% of world population), while one-third goes to developing countries. (If domestic use is excluded, the North/South imbalance is clearer: three-quarters of commercial consumption to the North; one-quarter to the South.) The South depends for almost half its energy on biomass fuels, which are, theoretically, renewable.

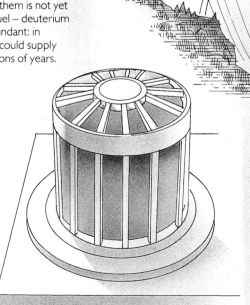

Threats to the nuclear industry

Nuclear reprocessing raises the problem of theft of plutonium, including terrorist hijacking of transports. Also implied are on-going security measures, such as continuous observation of workers, their families and friends, and on- and off-site, searches, including body searches. Protection of reprocessing plants will require guards and commando teams at many locations.

resources, such as solar power. But it must be remembered that the main source of energy for domestic use in the South is wood. And the number of people that rely on wood for fuel is growing. It is important that developing nations reorganize their agriculture to produce a large amount of wood and other plant fuels, and more efficient and less polluting local technologies to use them.

The changes needed in global energy policies will not come from market forces. At least, they will not come in time. Oil is presently cheap, encouraging nations to persist with, or invest in, oil-based energy, with likely severe consequences later – in Greenhouse effects, and in further debts when oil prices rise. Energy prices to consumers must be adjusted by governments (who are, after all, the main producers), to ensure that energy is saved and that environmentally benign energy sources are developed. Unless the political will and co-operation arise to achieve sensible energy pricing and resource policies, the outlook is bleak.

The choice of technologies for energy sources and for economic growth will determine whether or not we avoid global catastrophes, such as severe climatic changes and reduction of the ozone layer, and will determine the quality of life in the 21st century. The extremes of choice are "low", decentralized technologies and hi-tech central supplies. The developed countries will probably retain the technological and industrial base they now have and move steadily to higher technologies, particularly those based on computers. But they will also probably choose more efficiency, and greatly reduce energy consumption.

In the South, low or intermediate technologies could allow large reductions in infant-mortality rates and raise life expectancy. Infant-mortality rates of, say, 20 per 1000 live births, and life expectancy of, say, 65 years could probably be achieved by "soft" energy paths that would not seriously damage the environment. Using a mix of solar, wind, hydro and biomass energy, developing countries could supply domestic and local energy needs with relatively small capital investments. Similar, low or intermediate technologies for fertilization and pest control, more efficient use of food, and more sustainable agriculture could greatly increase food production in developing countries.

But this approach would not give the South the hi-tech industrial base which has allowed the North to develop sophisticated medical techniques to prolong life. The developing countries would risk sacrificing ideal infant mortality and life expectancy for a higher quality of life and environment. The challenge for the South is to achieve a mix of low and high technologies that will eradicate poverty from the bottom up, and yet allow them to participate in benign aspects of the technological revolution – communications, especially.

The militarization of space

Will the military use of space lead to its domination by the superpowers? How can this militarization of space, now declared a peaceful common heritage, be pre-

A sustainable energy supply

Energy is a key "growth indicator" – it brings wealth, food, warmth and power, as well as health, work and leisure. Rapid industrial growth this century has been based on fossil fuels – resources which we must seek to replace as stocks run out. Even more urgent is the fuelwood crisis threatening one half of humanity. We shall need more energy, but "hard" sources (especially coal, oil and nuclear power) will bring more pollution and huge financial and political risks. There are alternatives. Energy-efficient technologies and conservation could alter our lives, radically reducing energy demand – a trend that has already begun in the North. And whereas many developing countries lack stocks of fossil energy, most are rich in renewable energy. Many age-old techniques, discarded in the rush for modernization, are now being reappraised. Much of the technology is new, but it is as appropriate to local areas without any existing supply structure, as it is to the needs of burgeoning cities. Only ten years ago, the proponents of alternative energy and appropriate technology were dismissed as cranks: now they are taken much more seriously. The choices we make today on energy investment will determine our ability to head towards a sustainable future, or our failure to do so.

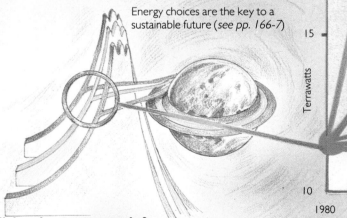

Energy choices are the key to a sustainable future (*see pp. 166-7*)

30
25
20
15
10
1980

Terrawatts

High or low energy paths?

How much "consumable" energy will we need by 2020 to provide for the 8-10 billion population? Experts differ hugely (see graph) – from a 300% increase over present supply (IIASA 1981), or worse, to a modest 10% rise (Goldenberg 1985).

Present energy policies – reliant on centralized supply, declining fossil fuels and growing nuclear capacity (with a neglect of energy efficiency or appropriateness to local need) – are leading us on the "high" path. Poorer nations, and even rich ones, will find the cost insupportable; acid rain, nuclear pollution and climate change will worsen; conflicts will multiply.

This "high" scenario assumes a conventional GNP growth rate of 2.1%. The alternative "low" path allows real growth (in well-being) at rates of 3% globally, 6% in the developing regions. It requires localized supply and investment in renewable energy technology and forestry, increased energy efficiency (domestic and commercial) and pollution control.

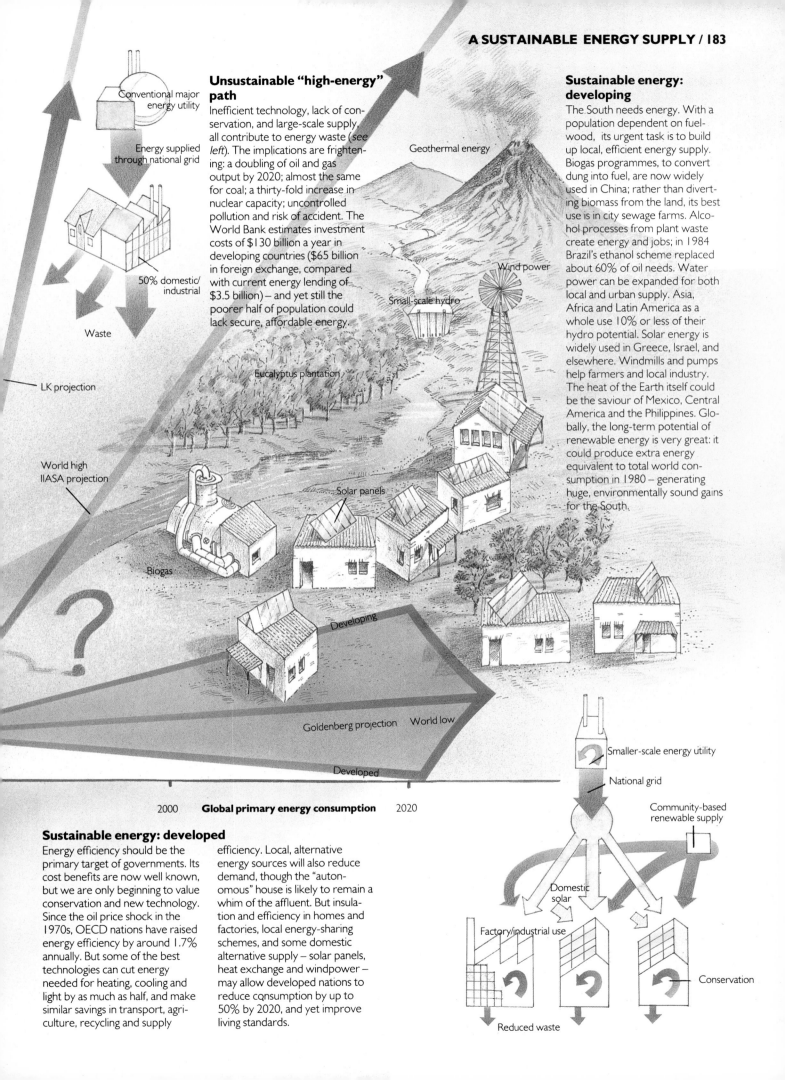

Conventional major energy utility

Energy supplied through national grid

50% domestic/ industrial

Waste

LK projection

World high IIASA projection

Biogas

?

Developing

Goldenberg projection   World low

Developed

2000   **Global primary energy consumption**   2020

Geothermal energy

Wind power

Small-scale hydro

Eucalyptus plantation

Solar panels

Smaller-scale energy utility

National grid

Community-based renewable supply

Domestic solar

Factory/industrial use

Conservation

Reduced waste

Unsustainable "high-energy" path

Inefficient technology, lack of conservation, and large-scale supply, all contribute to energy waste (*see left*). The implications are frightening: a doubling of oil and gas output by 2020; almost the same for coal; a thirty-fold increase in nuclear capacity; uncontrolled pollution and risk of accident. The World Bank estimates investment costs of $130 billion a year in developing countries ($65 billion in foreign exchange, compared with current energy lending of $3.5 billion) – and yet still the poorer half of population could lack secure, affordable energy.

Sustainable energy: developing

The South needs energy. With a population dependent on fuel-wood, its urgent task is to build up local, efficient energy supply. Biogas programmes, to convert dung into fuel, are now widely used in China; rather than diverting biomass from the land, its best use is in city sewage farms. Alcohol processes from plant waste create energy and jobs; in 1984 Brazil's ethanol scheme replaced about 60% of oil needs. Water power can be expanded for both local and urban supply. Asia, Africa and Latin America as a whole use 10% or less of their hydro potential. Solar energy is widely used in Greece, Israel, and elsewhere. Windmills and pumps help farmers and local industry. The heat of the Earth itself could be the saviour of Mexico, Central America and the Philippines. Globally, the long-term potential of renewable energy is very great: it could produce extra energy equivalent to total world consumption in 1980 – generating huge, environmentally sound gains for the South.

Sustainable energy: developed

Energy efficiency should be the primary target of governments. Its cost benefits are now well known, but we are only beginning to value conservation and new technology. Since the oil price shock in the 1970s, OECD nations have raised energy efficiency by around 1.7% annually. But some of the best technologies can cut energy needed for heating, cooling and light by as much as half, and make similar savings in transport, agriculture, recycling and supply efficiency. Local, alternative energy sources will also reduce demand, though the "autonomous" house is likely to remain a whim of the affluent. But insulation and efficiency in homes and factories, local energy-sharing schemes, and some domestic alternative supply – solar panels, heat exchange and windpower – may allow developed nations to reduce consumption by up to 50% by 2020, and yet improve living standards.

vented? Urgent action is needed, or the Star Wars programme may provoke an out-and-out US-USSR arms race in space.

The Strategic Defense Initiative (Star Wars) programme was launched by President Reagan in March, 1983. Ever since, fierce arguments have raged about the feasibility of Star Wars. Its purpose is to shoot down Soviet ballistic missiles and their warheads before they reach their targets. Is Star Wars science fact or science fiction?

First, Soviet ballistic missiles would be attacked with kinetic-energy weapons just after they have been launched. Nuclear warheads released by the Soviet missiles that survived this initial attack would then be attacked as they pass through space. Lastly, any nuclear warheads that survived in space would be attacked when they re-entered the atmosphere.

The Star Wars weapons deployed in the first phase would, according to Pentagon plans, be small projectiles, like bullets. They would be fired from platforms in space or fired from the ground using relatively small rockets. They would be manoeuvrable so that they could seek out and destroy their targets. And they would, by Pentagon standards, be so cheap that large numbers could be deployed.

Once the first phase of Star Wars is deployed, it can be added to as new technologies develop. In particular, the Pentagon has great hopes that high-energy chemical lasers, X-ray lasers and beams of particles – so-called directed-energy weapons – will be developed.

But are such sophisticated weapons really feasible? The American Physical Society is sceptical. Their report is the result of a thorough examination of feasibility of advanced Star Wars weapons. The study took 21 months to complete and was carried out by 17 leading American physicists.

The report concludes that at least another 10 years of research are needed just to decide if directed-energy weapons could be developed into effective Star Wars weapons. The actual deployment of a significant number of these weapons in a ballistic missile defence system, if ever sensible, is, the report says, not feasible in this century. This contrasts sharply with the views of General James Abrahamson, the Director of the Strategic Defense Initiative Program, who says that continued research at current levels will allow a decision about deploying high-energy lasers and other sophisticated Star Wars weapons in space in the 1990s or earlier.

The sceptical American physicists agree that Star Wars research has produced some working laser and particle-beam devices. But these are simply not powerful enough for use in Star Wars. To make them powerful enough would be a very difficult task.

If high-energy lasers and other directed-energy weapons are ever used as Star Wars weapons to attack Soviet ballistic missiles as they rise in the Earth's atmosphere and Soviet nuclear warheads in space, the weapons will themselves have to be deployed in space, on space battle-stations. The American Physical

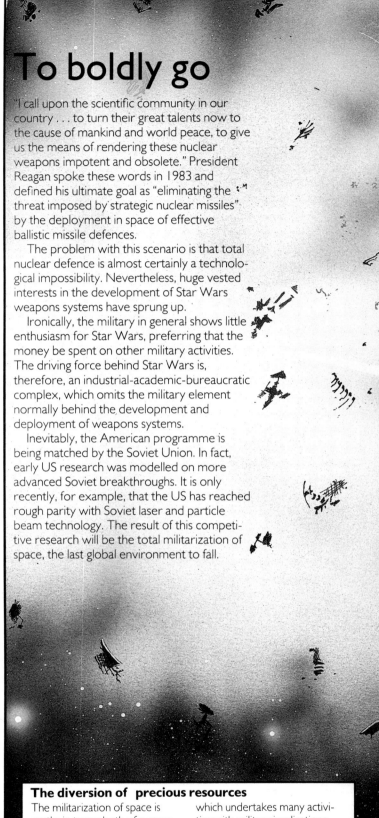

To boldly go

"I call upon the scientific community in our country . . . to turn their great talents now to the cause of mankind and world peace, to give us the means of rendering these nuclear weapons impotent and obsolete." President Reagan spoke these words in 1983 and defined his ultimate goal as "eliminating the threat imposed by strategic nuclear missiles" by the deployment in space of effective ballistic missile defences.

The problem with this scenario is that total nuclear defence is almost certainly a technological impossibility. Nevertheless, huge vested interests in the development of Star Wars weapons systems have sprung up.

Ironically, the military in general shows little enthusiasm for Star Wars, preferring that the money be spent on other military activities. The driving force behind Star Wars is, therefore, an industrial-academic-bureaucratic complex, which omits the military element normally behind the development and deployment of weapons systems.

Inevitably, the American programme is being matched by the Soviet Union. In fact, early US research was modelled on more advanced Soviet breakthroughs. It is only recently, for example, that the US has reached rough parity with Soviet laser and particle beam technology. The result of this competitive research will be the total militarization of space, the last global environment to fall.

The diversion of precious resources

The militarization of space is costly, in terms both of money and skilled scientific and technical personnel. Huge resources are being diverted into space activities that could otherwise be used to bolster aid to the developing world.

The US military space budget, for example, is running at approximately $10 billion a year, and the budget of the National Aeronautical and Space Administration (NASA),

which undertakes many activities with military implications, is presently about $7.5 billion a year. The cost of the Soviet military space activity must be at least roughly that of the USA. The scientists and engineers working on space research, as well as related projects, regarded as one of the most glamorous of scientific careers, are among the world's most highly qualified and resourceful.

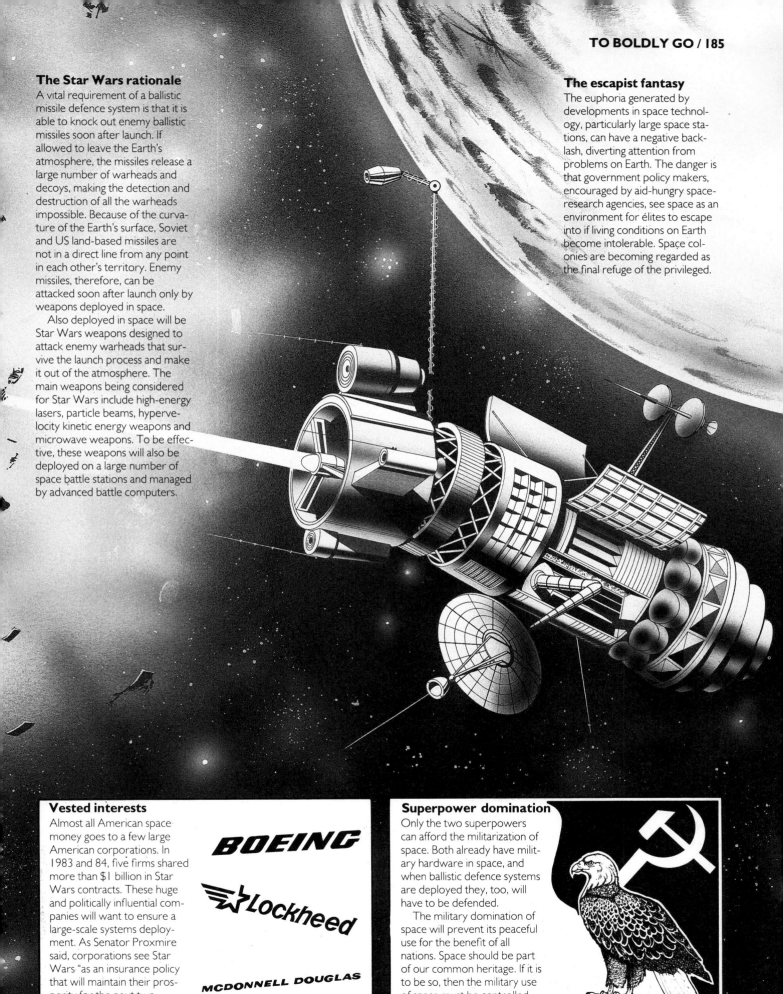

The Star Wars rationale

A vital requirement of a ballistic missile defence system is that it is able to knock out enemy ballistic missiles soon after launch. If allowed to leave the Earth's atmosphere, the missiles release a large number of warheads and decoys, making the detection and destruction of all the warheads impossible. Because of the curvature of the Earth's surface, Soviet and US land-based missiles are not in a direct line from any point in each other's territory. Enemy missiles, therefore, can be attacked soon after launch only by weapons deployed in space.

Also deployed in space will be Star Wars weapons designed to attack enemy warheads that survive the launch process and make it out of the atmosphere. The main weapons being considered for Star Wars include high-energy lasers, particle beams, hypervelocity kinetic energy weapons and microwave weapons. To be effective, these weapons will also be deployed on a large number of space battle stations and managed by advanced battle computers.

The escapist fantasy

The euphoria generated by developments in space technology, particularly large space stations, can have a negative backlash, diverting attention from problems on Earth. The danger is that government policy makers, encouraged by aid-hungry space-research agencies, see space as an environment for élites to escape into if living conditions on Earth become intolerable. Space colonies are becoming regarded as the final refuge of the privileged.

Vested interests

Almost all American space money goes to a few large American corporations. In 1983 and 84, five firms shared more than $1 billion in Star Wars contracts. These huge and politically influential companies will want to ensure a large-scale systems deployment. As Senator Proxmire said, corporations see Star Wars "as an insurance policy that will maintain their prosperity for the next two decades".

BOEING

Lockheed

MCDONNELL DOUGLAS

Superpower domination

Only the two superpowers can afford the militarization of space. Both already have military hardware in space, and when ballistic defence systems are deployed they, too, will have to be defended.

The military domination of space will prevent its peaceful use for the benefit of all nations. Space should be part of our common heritage. If it is to be so, then the military use of space must be controlled.

Society report estimates the power needed for such space-based systems. It shows that the only way of providing this power would be to provide each space battle-station with a nuclear reactor. The idea of having hundreds of nuclear reactors launched into space is a frightening one.

Why is the Pentagon so optimistic about Star Wars when so many eminent scientists say that an effective missile defence is probably not technically feasible? Perhaps the reason is that many Pentagon Star Wars advocates do not see it as a defensive system at all but as an offensive one. Some scientists who have been with the programme have expressed that this is the case. In other words, the true purpose of Star Wars is to restore the US's strategic nuclear superiority over the USSR, a superiority it lost in the 1960s. One way in which the US could regain superiority would be to acquire a nuclear first-strike capability. Star Wars would be an essential element of such a capability.

The pursuit of a nuclear first-strike capability is bound to increase the danger of a nuclear world war, both by design and accident. This is why Star Wars is such a dangerous activity. It would also lead to the superpower military domination of space, thereby preventing its peaceful exploitation.

Space – is it the last frontier?

Space enthusiasts believe that the continued exploitation of space for peaceful purposes will go a long way towards solving some of the fundamental problems facing humanity. They argue that space activity will benefit individuals, help solve economic and social problems in all countries and play a key role in creating the international co-operation needed to solve global problems and reduce the risk of catastrophes. Space technology could, it is said, be used to help prevent war; to resolve conflicts; to increase security; to contribute to development in the South; to meet needs for energy, food and raw materials; and to maintain and monitor a viable environment.

Spending on space activities by modern industrialized countries is increasing rapidly. So far, peaceful space activities have been mainly confined to research but they have stimulated new technologies from titanium use and microelectronics to automated control systems, sensor technology and robotics. This technological "spin-off" is seen to be an extra benefit.

The main current areas of peaceful space research are investigations in materials science, to see which special materials could be economically manufactured on spacecraft; space communication technology, particularly to make available new transmission channels at ultra-high frequencies; meteorology, particularly to improve the reliability of weather forecasting; space biology and medicine and the production of drugs; and remote sensing.

For the space production of such materials as alloys, semi-conductors, and vitreous and biomedical materials the expected economic benefits are attractive. There is also increasing interest in the possibility of extracting

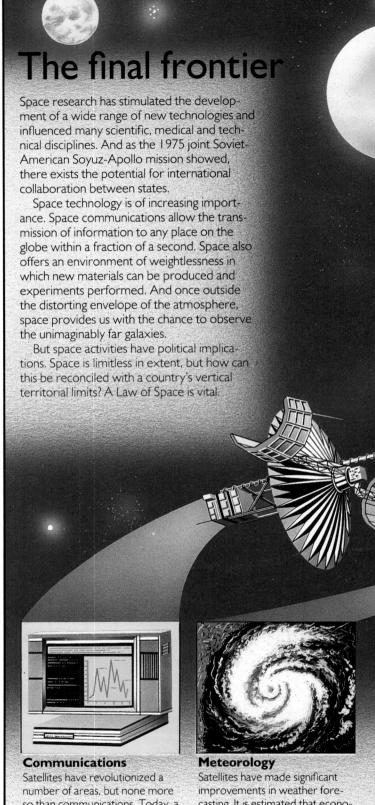

The final frontier

Space research has stimulated the development of a wide range of new technologies and influenced many scientific, medical and technical disciplines. And as the 1975 joint Soviet-American Soyuz-Apollo mission showed, there exists the potential for international collaboration between states.

Space technology is of increasing importance. Space communications allow the transmission of information to any place on the globe within a fraction of a second. Space also offers an environment of weightlessness in which new materials can be produced and experiments performed. And once outside the distorting envelope of the atmosphere, space provides us with the chance to observe the unimaginably far galaxies.

But space activities have political implications. Space is limitless in extent, but how can this be reconciled with a country's vertical territorial limits? A Law of Space is vital.

Communications
Satellites have revolutionized a number of areas, but none more so than communications. Today, a series of communications satellites in geostationary orbit encircles the Earth at a height of 36,610 km above the equator. Via these satellites, a continuous exchange of data, video and audio signals is possible between transmitting and receiving stations anywhere on the world's surface.

In fact, for transmissions over distances greater than a few hundred kilometres, space communications systems are far superior to conventional terrestrial, relay-operated lines.

Meteorology
Satellites have made significant improvements in weather forecasting. It is estimated that economic benefits worldwide of the improved reliability of weather forecasts are in the region of $60 billion a year, with agriculture particularly benefitting.

Meteorological satellites carry equipment for measuring infrared radiation emitted from different heights within the atmosphere, the density of precipitating electrons, the oxygen and nitrogen content of the thermosphere and the temperature and water vapour content at various altitudes.

The space race

Nearly 3000 satellites have been launched into space, mainly by the USA and the USSR, but also by France, China, Japan and India. Other countries, such as Brazil, have advanced, high-altitude rocket programmes and will, no doubt, develop space launchers.

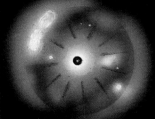

Bio/medical

Space technologies are already making significant contributions to the study of biology and the development of new medicines. The manufacture of certain drugs on Earth is adversely affected by gravity. Experiments conducted on satellites and within the Soviet Salyut space stations have shown that these types of drugs could be economically produced in space.

In fact, the large-scale production of biomedical materials in space is likely to be carried out alongside the production of semi-conductors, vitreous materials and some special alloys in extremely profitable space factories.

Remote-sensing

This type of satellite can bring benefits to both developed and developing countries alike. As well as discovering new reserves of minerals and other resources, they can also accurately assess the extent of existing ones, thus helping to conserve and extend their use. They can also identify at an early stage changes in the natural environment, such as in vegetation.

The collection of data by the remote sensing of land areas, the oceans and atmosphere, coupled with rapid communications and virtually instantaneous access to vast data banks, is providing a service of immense value.

Solar power

Many satellites are powered by solar energy: the next step is to use them as solar energy collectors capable of producing power beyond their own needs. In this way, future satellites may be able to supply the planet's energy requirements. This energy would be focused and beamed to receiving stations below. This type of technology will be feasible, however, only when the cost of transporting heavy loads into space is reduced.

By that time, large areas of the planet's surface may be lit by reflectors in space, so conserving conventional electric power.

Planetary awareness

The photographs of Earth seen as a whole from outer space had a profound effect on many people. For the first time it was possible to see not only the beauty and unity of the planet, but also to gain a real sense of the fragility of the environment common to all.

The development of space could greatly benefit humankind. It could play a key role in preventing war and providing greater security and international co-operation. It may, in the third millennium, meet the demands for energy, food and raw materials and help produce and maintain a clean environment for all.

mineral resources on the moon and other celestial bodies. The idea is to mine raw materials, process them in space and transport them to Earth using energy from cosmic sources, thereby protecting the Earth's environment.

Space meteorology already brings significant economic benefits. An estimated $600 million is now saved each year because of space weather forecasts. When the reliability of weather forecasts increases to 95 per cent for periods of three days, it is calculated that $60 *billion* a year would be saved worldwide. Space communications systems have also proved economically beneficial. In fact, for transmitting information over distances greater than a few hundred kilometres, space communications systems are by far the best. The capacity of satellite technology to bring understanding of natural and human systems – to give us "eyes in space" to see ourselves, promises much (*see p. 175*).

One very ambitious space proposal is the construction of a system to supply the world's energy: the idea is to station some 60 satellites in geosynchronous orbits, to collect solar energy over a surface of 50-100 square kilometres of solar cells, and to focus and beam it by microwave to ground antennae. Another is to establish a huge system of reflectors to illuminate cities and agricultural areas. These projects await reductions in the cost of transporting heavy loads into space.

These costs will be reduced as large-scale space activities proceed. For example, both the USA and the USSR will construct large, permanently manned space stations. Eventually, space enthusiasts hope, these will develop into full-scale, autonomous space colonies that will have little or no contact with Earth.

Motives for developing these colonies are mixed. Some see them as a natural and inevitable evolution of space activity. But others argue that they will become welcome havens from an Earth that has become unacceptably over-populated and polluted – the final denial of Gaia, and of our own humanity.

Visions of the future

Favoured solutions to global problems will depend on one's vision of the future. The most extreme pessimistic vision is that humankind will be destroyed. Unless the nuclear arms race is stopped, a nuclear world war is, in time, inevitable.

Ecological disasters seem, to the pessimist, even more certain; on our present course, either major climatic change or slow famine will bring us to our knees. Local nuclear wars or nuclear terrorism will be more likely as shortages of water, food, land and strategic resources, and demands for a more equitable distribution of wealth cause rising conflict in the South. In the North, our inability to grapple with the post-industrial society may lead to societal disintegration.

A major reason for pessimism is that we have not yet begun to invent the social and political institutions needed to control technology. We have also failed to set up a satisfactory method of international governance.

In contrast, the most optimistic views of the future

The non-sustainable nightmare

"The next twenty-five years, possibly the next decade, will bring starvation to hundreds of millions, and hardship, disorder or war to most of the rest of us."
Ronald Higgins *The Seventh Enemy* 1975

Human and industrial development cannot continue along present lines without catastrophe. We are no longer living in harmony with the planet, and are critically jeopardizing our own future. There can be no food distribution if we destroy the land that grows it; no development, the dream of the world's poor, without sustainable and non-polluting energy. With rising numbers and expectations, and failing resources, conflict is almost inevitable.

In the 1980s, with enough food for at least one and a third times the world population, we have let millions starve and tens of millions go hungry. Countries with fertile land are reducing food output because of gluts, while famine stalks the South. Debt and militarism are pumping away the wealth of poorly endowed agricultural regions in export crops for cash, while the hungry work fragile lands to exhaustion. How are we to feed 10 or even 8 billion people if, with enough to go around, we cannot equitably feed half this number? Even if we could double food production, it would put impossible strains on the environment – and, on present showing, the poor would still starve. Famine is increasing in frequency and severity across a wide "hunger belt", from South Asia through the arid tropics of Africa to Latin America.

Human pressures are causing desertification, erosion, poisoning and "development" of about 18 million hectares of usable land a year. By 2025, we may be trying to feed double the numbers on a third less cropland, and this weakened, or subject to flooding and drought. Acid rain is spreading to the South, to attack forests already under extreme pressure. CO_2 pollution is following suit, accelerating atmospheric warming to threaten fundamental change to global patterns of temperature, wind, rainfall, and ocean currents. Already, southern Europe is experiencing hotter summers, Northern grain belts show greater aridity, monsoons are unpredictable. If the grain belts fail, famine, political instability and war may afflict North and South alike; if sea levels rise, massive disturbances unlike any we have ever known will affect low-lying countries, and the coastal cities with their growing millions.

Driven off their land by hunger, poverty, injustice, or war, the people of the rural South are drawn to the cities as if by a magnet – to swell the overcrowded and polluted shanty towns. In Africa in 1950, only 14% of people lived in cities; that percentage has more than doubled. Predictions of future Southern megacities of 10 million people or more are appalling to contemplate – and challenged by those who say that when there is no water to drink, people will die faster than the newcomers arrive. Already public utilities of swollen conurbations such as Cairo and Mexico City cannot cope. And alongside poverty and physical misery, there is social breakdown. Alternative or "black" economies, from crime and prostitution to arms smuggling, find fertile ground among the embittered and hungry. So, too, do political extremism and support for terrorist activity – with the risk, ultimately, of nuclear terrorism, bred amidst the anarchic "other society" of unmanageable cities, and savage repressive measures threatening the death of democratic freedoms.

assume that technology will solve many of the world's problems with appropriate and ecologically benign energy sources, safe water, cheap housing, immunization, and so on. Optimists also believe we can produce enough food to feed up to 11 billion – if price and distribution problems are solved. Information technology is seen as producing revolutionary changes in perception, and the optimists assume that politicians will acquire the will to put into practice the solutions technology allows. They have also to believe that people in the developed countries will agree to the transfer of resources to the South – from altruism, or long-term self-interest.

Sustainable development

Sustainable development is a dynamic process in which "the exploitation of resources, the direction of investments, the orientation of technological development and institutional change are made consistent with future as well as present needs" (Brundtland). Sustainability becomes the main criterion by which human activities are judged, rather than economic or industrial growth.

Remembering that the world population is likely to reach 8 billion within 40 years, we need to achieve sustainable development very soon.

According to the UK Greens: "In the long run, all nations will *have* to manage the demands of their people in a stable-state economy. The characteristics of such an economy are clear: reduced industrial throughput, greater self-reliance and sustainability through largely decentralized economic activity, maximized use of renewable resources and conservation of non-renewable resources, a far-reaching redistribution of wealth, land and the means of production, with the possibility of more fulfilling, personally satisfying work, all set within a more co-operatively based framework, and enhanced by use of new technologies where they complement the above features."

The global mix of high and low technologies needed to support reasonable living standards and a reasonable quality of life for all, depends on the emergence of political leaders in the developing countries strong enough to control the entrenched interests in them and push through development plans that benefit the masses rather than the privileged few. It also depends on the emergence in the developed countries of the political will to transfer resources and technology.

It is hard to see the political, social and economic developments needed for sustainable development taking place without a spiritual revolution of global dimensions – leading to an equitable share of the world's resources, a support for ecological living, rich and poor, and a belief in peace and the rule of international law, human rights and social justice.

In any optimistic vision of the 21st century, emphasis on quality of life, rather than consumerism at all costs, is fundamental. Sensitivity to nature and the interests of others is the stuff of spirituality. The future rests on educating ourselves and our children to see that the good life depends on quality rather than quantity.

A sustainable future

"This task before us now, if we would not perish, is to shake our ancient prejudices, and to build the earth."
Pierre Teilhard de Chardin, 1936

For too long, we have equated security with weapons, progress with "growth" – and growth with industrialization, seen as the essential route to "development". But in the words of Rudolf Bahro "if the industrialization of the world were to be completed, life on earth would be destroyed". Escape from the nightmare of ecological failure and war is still possible. But to achieve true security, real wealth, and growth in the quality of life, we must do an about-turn. It is not enough to talk of conservation and management of resources, or of "sustainable" development, encouraging though these new approaches are. We must transform our relationship with Gaia and each other, profoundly, and soon.

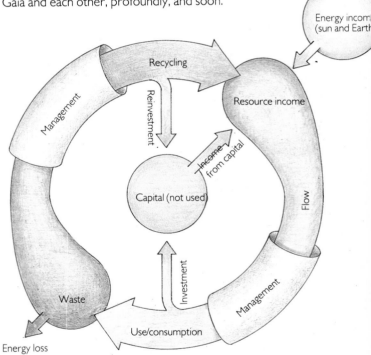

Steady-state resource flow

The fertility of soil, the diversity of species, clean water and air, equable climate – these are the real wealth of the planet, its capital resources. In a steady-state world, we would not deplete this capital by careless exploitation. We would guard and replenish it, living on the income generated by seasonal growth and the energy of the sun and Earth, and by the recycling of used resources. The old economic imperative, defining "growth" as rising consumption and GNP, is discredited in such a system. But *real* growth is possible – the better we care for the capital base, the more efficiently we conserve, recycle and renew the income, the greater the "flow" of resources. Even with abundant, clean energy, however, there are finite limits to a sustainable income. One cannot deny poor countries the right to a better future; rather, living standards in rich countries may have to fall. Both must seek to replace ethics of materialism with desire for shared well-being.

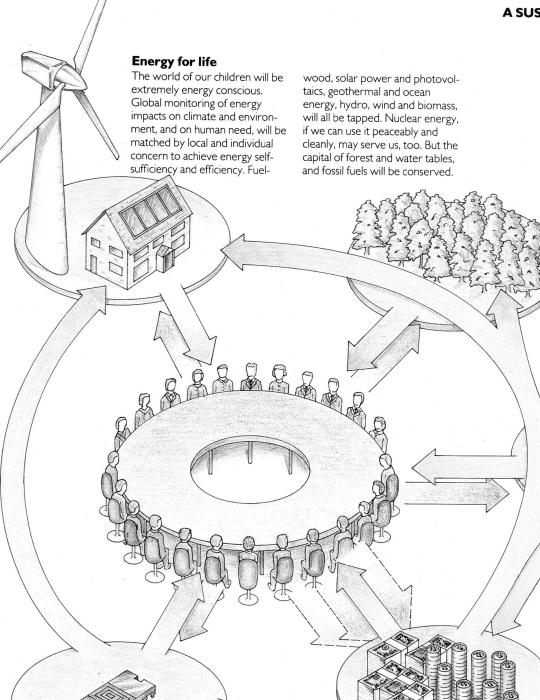

Energy for life

The world of our children will be extremely energy conscious. Global monitoring of energy impacts on climate and environment, and on human need, will be matched by local and individual concern to achieve energy self-sufficiency and efficiency. Fuelwood, solar power and photovoltaics, geothermal and ocean energy, hydro, wind and biomass, will all be tapped. Nuclear energy, if we can use it peaceably and cleanly, may serve us, too. But the capital of forest and water tables, and fossil fuels will be conserved.

A new environmental concern

In a sustainable society, all people will come to regard protection of the environment as a healthy insurance policy for the future. This will require massive international action in many cases. The new sciences of the information and Gaian age, too, will have to do much to help, and new economic and social criteria be used to judge our activities and schemes. But the true guardians of the land will be local communities and individuals – planting trees, clearing away pollution, changing farming practices and daily living habits, monitoring and controlling the use of the local environment and its health and diversity. Educating the next generation to be ecologically aware citizens is vital.

A redistribution of wealth

Poverty bars the way to the future – sustainable development requires a redistribution of wealth between and within nations. Steps to halt negative wealth flow from South to North via debt, arms purchase and trade, and to create a positive wealth transfer to the South are urgent. Within nations, we must close the income gap – by land reform, co-operative ownership, taxation, social services and technology.

Appropriate technology

The first stages of industrialization entailed an accelerating and destructive use of resources. But new technologies – especially in communications and information – can actually reduce the exploitative nature of development. They can cut wastage and energy needs, lessen oppressive work patterns and enable sustainable practices. But the future depends most on how we use technology – out of concern for people and the planet, or out of short-term greed.

Participation and conflict resolution

Moving to a broader base of power, and to more co-operative forms of governance and decision making, will be crucial in bringing about a sustainable future. Conflict resolution and problem solving, rather than conflicts themselves, will become a major priority for those in positions of power. Education in such skills will begin in early childhood. We will learn to replace force with words, and to persist with patience and goodwill against oppression or conflict, recapturing the co-operative and sharing skills of simpler societies than ours. All our institutions of governance will be transformed in this process. But a start on the road to this future could be made now – with the help of regional groups, such as the European Community or Organisation of African Unity, or the United Nations, and of the multiplying peace groups and educational movements.

Decentralized economy

The industrial age centralized economies, placing control and decision with élite business and finance groups, both globally – in economic centres such as New York or Tokyo – and locally, within nations. In the information age, this is unnecessary. Restructured economies with greater involvement of regional, or even local, centres and communities will allow less stressful lives in the North, and a rebirth of rural industry and self-sufficiency in the South.

8 Short-term steps for survival

Introduced by Inga Thorsson

"Our small planet is becoming endangered: by the arsenals of weapons which could blow it up; by the burden of military expenditures which could sink it under; and by the unmet basic needs of two-thirds of its population which subsists on less than one-third of its resources. We belong to a near universal constituency which believes that we are borrowing this Earth from our children as much as we have inherited it from our forefathers. The carrying capacity of Earth is not infinite, nor are its resources. The needs of security are legitimate and must be met. But must we stand by as helpless witnesses of a drift towards greater insecurity at higher costs?" These words are from the 1986 UN Declaration on Disarmament and Development.

Almost 30 years ago, at an international conference in Copenhagen, the brilliant Danish Gruk-poet Piet Hein said: "We are global citizens with tribal souls." Since these words were spoken, we have acquired much technical knowledge and our ways of life have been revolutionized – at least in the industrial world. But thinking has remained the same; there is no new thinking, no redefinition of old and outdated concepts.   What is needed immediately are short-term survival strategies – strategies aimed at giving us a "breathing space". Existing institutions of security and development, at the international level, are still, as we approach the last decade of the 20th century, not entrusted by the big and mighty with the power and the resources necessary to present these short-term solutions and thus provide that all-important breathing space. With global threats to survival having been brought to their present heights, even short-term solutions require such a reversal of old and outdated political thinking that they approach the long-term change needed to ensure survival.

What is needed, urgently and immediately, is a new global thinking, in the enlightened self-interest of all nations, a revival of multilateralism through the United Nations. This would represent a "Copernican leap" for which I am not sure the conditions are present. Sometimes I think that a popular uprising is what is needed in order to bring about the necessary and urgent changes in behaviour and action. We live in a period of grace – for how long, no-one knows.

I spoke, quoting my late friend Barbara Ward, of the need for a new Copernican leap. Let me, in conclusion, make another quote, from an almost contemporary of Copernicus, the poet John Donne (Devotions XVII):

No man is an Island, entire of itself;
Every man is a piece of the Continent,
A part of the main.

Any man's death diminishes me,
Because I am involved in mankind;
And therefore never send to know for whom the bell tolls;
It tolls for thee.

If the present generation of mankind should be made to understand the wisdom of these sentences, they might be brought to their senses and provide possibilities for both short- and long-term solutions to the predicaments of the present human existence.

"Boldness has genius, magic and power in it. Begin it now." Goethe

Humanity is facing the twin threats of nuclear world war and ecological catastrophe. The two drive each other on. Nuclear war would be the ultimate eco-disaster. The militarism that brings it near also fuels environmental collapse. Relations between states then deteriorate and crises intensify, increasing the risk of nuclear war.

The situation is urgent. As the opening of this book states, we may have only 15 years left – five thousand days – if we persist in our ways before catastrophe strikes. That may be all we have in which to reverse the nuclear arms race and halt poverty, famine and world climate change – or it will be too late.

We have to gain time, to buy a breathing space during which the drift to eco-disaster and nuclear catastrophe can be stopped and reversed, and long-term planning can begin for sustainable peace in the Third Millennium (*see Chapter 9*). Buying this time demands bold action.

What we need is an emergency programme to allow human survival into the 21st century. And this has to rely on existing institutions – governments, regions, NGOs, financiers and the United Nations – for its success.

At least, this programme must include measures to: halt the nuclear arms race, control military technology and reduce arsenals severely; prevent the spread of nuclear weapon ownership; increase détente and regional security; restrict, and then end, the arms trade; reduce conventional forces and military budgets in all nations and divert the manpower and finance so released to development; reform terms of trade and resolve the debt crisis; achieve food and livelihood security, population control and an "ecofreeze".

The actions needed to achieve all of these are, in many cases, known, as the case studies following show. But the political will is lacking. Huge public pressure will be needed to carry such a programme through, and a spirit of internationalism that outweighs sovereignty. And we have to break the link between security and militarism and act instead for true, common security.

Reducing the risk

Both superpowers recognize the need to reduce the risk of nuclear war. But their approaches differ. General Secretary Gorbachev proposes to reduce it radically by eliminating nuclear weapons via negotiation between the nuclear powers, beginning with the USA and USSR. He proposes that both aim at total nuclear disarmament by the year 2000. It is unclear if he envisages reducing nuclear weapons held by each side to zero by this date, or means each to be left enough for "minimum deterrence" – a few hundred (compared with 25,000 or so now). The Gorbachev proposal is desirable, and technically feasible. But it conflicts with NATO policy of using nuclear forces to halt a conventional Soviet advance.

President Reagan plans to reduce the risk of nuclear war by replacing deterrence with nuclear defence, via the Strategic Defense Initiative, or "Star Wars" (*see*

General Secretary Gorbachev and President Reagan shake hands after the signing of the historic INF Treaty on 8 December 1987.

One of the great hopes for the solution of global problems through internationalism is the coming to power in the USSR of Mikhail Gorbachev. He and his US presidential counterpart may well together set up the institutions needed for far-reaching disarmament, managing a de-militarized world and re-channelling the financial and skilled manpower resources now used by the military into sustainable development. After a series of aged and reactionary Soviet leaders – Brezhnev, Andropov and Chernenko – Gorbachev is relatively young and likely to be in power for many years, a reformer, if not a revolutionary. And he seems intent on modernizing Soviet foreign policy as well as the country's domestic economy.

Gorbachev's new foreign policy concepts are centred on the need to get rid of nuclear weapons, the need to boost and encourage developing countries and the relationship between these two essential steps. He talks of the "wrath bred by dramatic polarization of poverty and wealth and the contrast between possibilities and realities". He paints a much more complex picture of the South than any of his predecessors have done.

Gorbachev argues that "the international and economic processes of our time" have the force of "an objective law", and will lead to either a global disaster or "a joint quest for a new economic order taking into account the interests of all on an equal basis". And he sees the best route to this new international economic order as the concept of disarmament and development.

To implement his new foreign policy concepts, Gorbachev seems intent on forging fresh Soviet relations with developing countries and encouraging more Soviet participation in international institutions – for example, the World Bank and IMF, as well as regional and international institutions dealing with development for the South. Given his emphasis that, despite the radical differences between political and social systems, the countries of the contemporary world are "interrelated, independent and integral", we can expect the USSR to show a new and positive attitude towards internationalism.

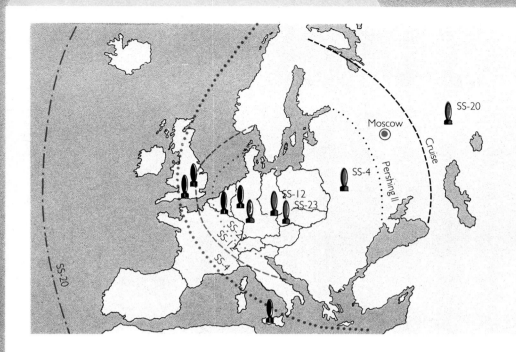

Maximum range of missiles

SS missiles

Pershing missiles

Cruise missiles

The map shows the location and type of intermediate-range missiles eliminated under the terms of the 1987 INF Treaty.

On 8 December 1987 President Reagan and General Secretary Gorbachev signed the Soviet-American Treaty on the Elimination of Intermediate-range Nuclear Forces (INF for short). The INF Treaty obliges the USA and the USSR to eliminate all of their ground-launched ballistic and cruise missile systems with a maximum range of between 500 and 5,500 kilometres over a period of 18 months to three years.

This is the first treaty in history to promise the elimination of nuclear weapons. It is, therefore, also hoped to be the first step in a far-reaching nuclear disarmament process. Already, the two sides have begun negotiations concerning the next phase, seeking to agree considerable reductions in strategic nuclear weapons. The signing of the INF Treaty was welcomed with great enthusiasm by ordinary members of the public and peace campaigners alike. (Right-wing commentators were, of course, euphoric because they saw the new situation as undermining the authority of the peace movement.) But we should beware of being lulled into a false sense of security.

Out of a total of 50,000 nuclear warheads, half of which are deployed in tactical and half in long-range strategic systems, only about 2000 will be destroyed under the terms of the INF Treaty: 23,000 nuclear artillery shells and tactical missiles with a range of less than 500 kilometres are not going to be affected.

The INF Treaty is being presented as a major breakthrough, a cause of relief to the whole world – as indeed it is. Yet the result could be that we could end up with *more* nuclear weapons than existed before. Even before the signing of the Treaty, plans were being laid in NATO to deploy new nuclear weapons, to compensate for those axed, and to "modernize" existing systems. The new weapons being considered are missiles carried by aircraft or ships – since the Treaty affects only ground-launched missiles.

Verification, however, is a truly optimistic and radical achievement of the Treaty. Always a stumbling block in previous negotiations, for the first time it promises to be surprisingly open and frank. Before signing, the US proposal was for detailed exchange of data; notification of movement; baseline inspection until missiles are eliminated; "close-out" inspection to ensure activities have ended; and short-notice inspection of certain facilities if illegal activity was suspected.

The Soviets were in agreement in principle with many aspects of the US proposal.

Washington and Moscow have established a staged verification regime, the first step being to check that the declared baseline of weaponry actually exists. Over 3 years, inspectors will then visit missile sites to see that weapons are being removed, ensuring that the superpowers are left with equal numbers of longer-range INF weapons. After this, a close-out inspection will take place to check that all the agreed missiles have been removed. Provision will be made for short-notice inspection of suspect sites on both sides.

The terms of the Treaty
The following missiles must be eliminated:
US intermediate-range missiles
Pershing-II ballistic missiles
108 deployed missiles plus 12 deployed spares plus 127 non-deployed missiles = 247 Pershing-IIs
Ground-launched cruise missiles
256 deployed missiles plus 35 deployed spares plus 133 non-deployed missiles = 424 ground-launched cruise missiles
Pershing-IB
170 non-deployed missiles
Soviet intermediate-range missiles
SS-4 ballistic missiles
65 deployed missiles plus 105 non-deployed = 170 SS-4s
SS-20 ballistic missiles
405 deployed plus 245 non-deployed = 650 SS-20s
SS-12 ballistic missiles
220 deployed plus 506 non-deployed = 726 SS-12s
SS-23 ballistic missiles
167 deployed plus 33 non-deployed = 200 SS-23s

Therefore the US will eliminate a total of 841 missiles; the USSR a total of 1746 missiles. The total number of missiles (deployed and non-deployed) eliminated under the INF treaty will be 2587. The total number of deployed warheads destroyed will be 2096, or about 4% of the total number of nuclear warheads held by both sides.

p. 184). He envisages erecting a shield over the US and its allies against nuclear attack. Elimination of this threat would pave the way to disarmament. The problem with Reagan's plan is that few scientists believe it is technically feasible. And any shield less than 100 per cent effective will be interpreted by the Soviets as part of a US nuclear first strike capability. The Soviets have a parallel programme, revealed under the new *Glasnost* (openness). Star Wars perpetuates "enemy" images, destabilizes the US-USSR strategic balance and thus increases, rather then decreases, the risk of war.

Arms reduction efforts by the superpowers need all our support. Their success is a measure of détente and also lowers the risk of accident. But INF, and START if it succeeds, will not alone stop the nuclear arms race. Technology advances so fast that the cuts are seen to eradicate "obsolete" weapons, to make way for new ones that bring "first strike" capability nearer. NATO is already in process of this updating, despite opposition.

We can halt the drift to nuclear war, and the nuclear arms race, by the following minimum first steps:
1 The USA and USSR must adhere *strictly* to the Anti-Ballistic Missile Treaty.
2 The US and USSR must achieve, in the START treaty, major cuts in strategic nuclear forces, and until this time adhere strictly to SALT II limits on these.
3 Meanwhile, the powers should agree a verifiable freeze on testing, production and deployment of nuclear weapons. The crucial element in this would be a complete and permanent test ban. Britain, the US and USSR should conclude the comprehensive test ban treaty.
4 A treaty banning the testing and deployment of anti-satellite weapons should be negotiated and implemented, to maintain the invulnerability of early warning and reconnaissance satellites, reducing the likely success of a first strike, and the fear of it.

These measures would halt development and deployment of increasingly destabilizing new nuclear weapons and evolution of a first-strike capability. The military, unable to take nuclear weapons out of the arsenals to test them would, within a few years, lose confidence in their reliability and so be unwilling to launch a first strike, though deterrence would still be possible.

Preventing the spread of nuclear weapons

Emergency measures to pull us back from the slide to nuclear world war also demand immediate strengthening of the nuclear non-proliferation regime – the spread of nuclear weapons to other countries gravely raises the risk of nuclear war in international crises to come.

Our main safeguard against proliferation now is the 1970 Non-Proliferation Treaty (NPT). Unfortunately, a number of important countries have not joined. They include Pakistan, Argentina and Brazil, as well as India, which has exploded a nuclear device; China, France and Israel, which have nuclear arsenals; and South Africa, which is generally believed to have nuclear weapons.

The British Freeze campaign sees educating public opinion in the need for a nuclear freeze as one of its main objectives. The use of banners helps to draw attention to the message.

Non-proliferation is an essential step to nuclear disarmament. Many groups are now working towards this. Their common aim is to halt the arms race, as a prerequisite to staged disarmament and conversion of military industries.

FREEZE began in the US in 1980, where it received considerable support: interest waned, however, due to the Star Wars initiative. A new campaign was launched in Britain in 1985, seeking "a verifiable world-wide halt to the testing, production and deployment of nuclear weapons . . . as a first step to mutual and meaningful reductions in nuclear arms". Its "freeze and reduction" programme moves step-by-step from a comprehensive test ban treaty through a reduction in existing nuclear weapons to a halt in the manufacture of new ones. It also includes a strengthening of SALT II and the ABM Treaty, and a conversion programme.

IGRAT (International Group of Researchers on the ABM Treaty), founded 1986, provides a focus for issues related to the 1972 ABM treaty, the backdrop to any other arms control talks. IGRAT acts as a monitor of all such negotiations.

EPIC (European Proliferation Information Centre), set up in 1984, serves media, politicians, unions and NGOs with information on such issues as: the spread of nuclear, biological and chemical weapons; the Nuclear Non-Proliferation Treaty and its links with a comprehensive test ban treaty; and the feasibility of conversion.

CAAT (Campaign Against the Arms Trade) is a UK-based coalition, set up 1974, committed to ending the arms trade and its adverse effects on developing countries. CAAT's work includes campaigns for "Bread not Bombs" and the CAAT Development Education Project (1986), which is funded by Oxfam, Christian Aid, CAFOD and the EEC.

NRDC (National Resources Defense Council), set up 1970, is a US national NGO of lawyers and scientists working for the environment and seeking a comprehensive test ban treaty.

FILE: NON-PROLIFERATION
New Zealand and the Pacific

In 1984, in an historic decision, New Zealand's Prime Minister David Lange declared New Zealand a nuclear-free zone and banned nuclear weapons from its land, air and sea.

Only a few months later this policy was put to its first major test by the United States. The Reagan administration had asked for permission to send a Navy destroyer, the USS Buchanan, on a port-of-call visit to New Zealand as part of annual ANZUS Security Treaty exercises. For reasons of security, the United States refused to deny or confirm whether the ship would carry nuclear weapons. Supported and encouraged by an active, broad-based, local peace movement, Lange denied the request, stating his reason as being "If we don't know whether or not they are nuclear armed they can't come". He further stated that this was going to be New Zealand's continuing policy. Lange went on to say that New Zealand's policy "is not anti-American, it is not anti-alliance, it is anti-nuclear".

In a furious response, the Reagan administration cancelled the ANZUS exercises altogether. Since then, New Zealand has virtually been expelled from ANZUS but has confirmed its anti-nuclear stance by the New Zealand Nuclear Free Zone, Disarmament and Arms Control Act of June 1987. The territory of New Zealand is declared nuclear free; no citizen can manufacture, acquire or have control over nuclear weapons; no person may station them in New Zealand, and no vessels or aircraft may enter carrying them.

New Zealand also helped in 1971 to initiate the South Pacific Forum. The 13 members of the Forum – Australia, Cook Islands, Fiji, Kiribati, Nauru, New Zealand, Niue, Papua New Guinea, Solomon Islands, Tonga, Tuvalu, Vanuatu and Western Samoa – have from its inception been especially concerned with the problem of nuclear testing in the Pacific. The Treaty of Rarotonga (effective since December 1986 – see pp. 152-3) establishes a South Pacific Nuclear Free Zone (SPNFZ). Its signatories agree that none will possess, build, or control nuclear weapons. In 1986 it was decided to ask the five nuclear powers to associate themselves with the Treaty. The USSR and China signed the two protocols open to them; France refused; the USA and Britain said they would not sign but were willing informally to abide by the Treaty.

The US submarine "Queenfish" runs the gauntlet of more than 100 anti-nuclear protest vessels in Auckland Harbour, New Zealand in 1984. That year Prime Minister Lange (*right*), encouraged by a popular anti-nuclear movement, declared New Zealand a nuclear-free zone.

The Treaty of Rarotonga states in moving words that: **"the bounty and beauty of the land and sea in their region shall remain the heritage of their peoples and their descendants in perpetuity, to be enjoyed by all in peace".**

FILE: NON-PROLIFERATION
Stop the neutron bomb

In November 1981 more than 100,000 Dutch people demonstrated as part of the movement "Stop the Neutron Bomb – Stop the Nuclear Arms Race", which has proved to be one of Europe's more successful anti-war lobbies.

The neutron bomb, or ERW (enhanced radiation weapon), was invented in 1958 by Edward Teller. At first it was justified in terms of anti-ballistic missile defence development, but after the ABM Treaty of 1972 the weapon became known for its anti-tank capabilities.

On 19 August 1977 a small group launched the appeal "Stop the Neutron Bomb", hoping to create a broad-based opposition to deployment of this particular weapon. The organization collected 1.2 million signatures within six months and mounted local meetings, a National Forum, an International Forum and a national demonstration of 50,000 people in Amsterdam. These pressures assisted the political rejection of the neutron bomb on 4 March 1978, following the resignation of the Dutch Minister of Defence, Dr Kruisinga. After this initial impact the campaign broadened. In August 1978 it was decided to campaign against the nuclear arms race in general, with the focus on Europe. A wider slogan was devised: "Stop the Nuclear Arms Race".

Continuing protests led to an Action Week against nuclear weapons and this "Die-in" in Dam Square, Amsterdam in May 1984.

Until these countries, and others with significant civil nuclear energy programmes, commit themselves not to develop or acquire nuclear weapons, the nuclear non-proliferation regime will be in constant danger.

All efforts must be made to persuade them, but these will carry more force if the nuclear weapon parties to the Non-Proliferation Treaty – the USA, the USSR and the UK – are clearly seen to be fulfilling their obligations under it. Article VI commits the Treaty powers "to pursue negotiations in good faith on effective measures relating to *the cessation of the nuclear arms race* at an early date and to nuclear disarmament". So far, the parties have not met this obligation – INF is a hopeful beginning, but seen not to be enough. By continually increasing the quality and "fightability" of nuclear weapons, the nuclear powers show that they believe nuclear weapons have great military and political value.

If the nuclear-weapons states negotiated the measures listed above, they would show that they believed nuclear weapons had little or no utility. They must now do so. They must set an example to persuade other countries not to acquire nuclear weapons, and so prevent their spread. And for a start, they could stop intimidating those countries, such as New Zealand and, recently, Denmark, who seek nuclear-free-zone status.

Non-proliferation is a crucial transitional stage in the disarmament process. But it is only a temporary freeze on one small element of the global nuclear-weapon picture. The main disarmament measures must be taken by the superpowers. The prerequisite for any plan to reduce the danger of a nuclear world war is to re-establish lasting détente between East and West. In order to reduce military competition there must be a reduction in political and ideological tension between the superpowers. How can the wider community help?

European security and détente

The superpowers face each other eyeball to eyeball across the East-West German border. Any war in Europe would almost certainly escalate to an all-out strategic nuclear war. One immediate aim must be to reduce risks of war and increase détente in Europe.

To some extent this is already happening. Increasing economic, social and cultural relations between East and West considerably improve the atmosphere, as do medical, scientific and other academic exchanges. The experience of Östpolitik, too, has much to teach the European community. As Willy Brandt says: "we now have to think of security together with instead of against the adversary. Perhaps it was no accident that this concept was developed in divided Germany. In the case of military conflict the Federal Republic of Germany would be destroyed, and the same would happen to East Germany. 'United we perish' has never been our perspective of German unity. Therefore, as a German I say that without peace there is no chance for my own country."

Reducing East-West tension means getting rid of images of "the enemy". Governments on both sides must stop exaggerating the military threat from the

Armand Hammer

The extraordinary potential of an individual without political office to alter the course of history is demonstrated by the veteran American multi-millionaire businessman Dr Armand Hammer, self-styled citizen of the world. Born in 1898, he went at the age of 21 to fight typhus in the Soviet Union where, confronted with mass hunger, he started shipping in food – and soon came to a trading deal with Lenin. Since that period, he has had an intimate working relationship with every Soviet leader, with the exception of Stalin, and throughout his long life he has used his wealth and personal drive to play an unparalleled role in fostering East-West relations. Involved in ceaseless travel, telephoning and personal approaches to political leaders and people of influence, he was, for instance, responsible in 1986 for sending US specialists to the Soviet Union after the nuclear disaster at Chernobyl, and in 1987 for helping to set up summit meetings between Reagan and Gorbachev. Asked at age 89 what his current priorities were, he replied, "finding a cure for cancer and achieving world peace".

Amnesty International

Human rights issues are as critical to détente as to justice and compassion. In 1961, a British lawyer, Peter Beneson, called on all people to press for the release of prisoners of conscience, and Amnesty International was born. Now the world's largest voluntary human rights organization, its 700,000 members and supporters, in local and national groups in more than 150 countries, work for the release of "men and women detained anywhere for their beliefs, colour, sex, ethnic origin, language or religion who have neither used nor advocated violence". The International Secretariat receives and analyses information from newspapers, humanitarian bodies, lawyers, prisoners and their families. Once news of an arrest arrives, facts are examined and valid cases "adopted" by a group, which floods authorities and newspapers with protest letters, and sends relief and support to prisoners. Amnesty conducts fact-finding missions, observes trials, meets detainees and government officials, and publicizes the brutal treatment of prisoners of conscience. It has adopted more than 30,000 individual cases – of the 4200 in 1986 alone, 1900 have been released. In 1977 Amnesty was awarded the Nobel Peace Prize for "its defence of human worth against degrading treatment, violence and torture" and in 1978 the United Nations Human Rights Prize.

Human Rights League Table 1986
(Percentage of rights secured)

TOP	%	BOTTOM	%
1 Aotearoa (NZ)	98	1 Ethiopia	13
Denmark	98	2 North Korea	17
Finland	98	3 Iraq	19
Holland	98	4 Romania	20
Sweden	98	USSR	20
6 Norway	97	6 South Africa	22
W. Germany	97	7 Bulgaria	23
8 Austria	96	China	23
Belgium	96	Libya	23
Canada	96		

Charles Humana's *World Human Rights Guide* provided the source for "New Internationalist's" chart (*above*). Participating governments were awarded a rating based on their freedom from state violence and tolerance of dissent.

FILE: DÉTENTE
Östpolitik

Few political leaders attain such international stature as the former West German Chancellor Willy Brandt, who was awarded the Nobel Peace Prize in 1971 for his Östpolitik. Though primarily aimed at improving the Federal Republic's relations with the Soviet Union and eastern Europe – Brandt's Östpolitik was a key element globally in reducing Cold War tensions and promoting détente. Brandt had been the figurehead of the Western Alliance's determination to stand up to Communist intimidation, thus giving added weight to his later efforts for reconciliation and understanding. These efforts were not always appreciated by the more hawkish elements in West Germany and in Washington, and Brandt was frequently a controversial figure. Divided Europe is a focus of East/West ideological tension. Détente between the two Germanys is a prime necessity for future disarmament and a new world order. The concept of Östpolitik as promoted by Brandt has been adopted and developed by West Germany's Helmut Kohl and East Germany's Erich Honecker. These two politicians have recently tried to broaden the idea to include wider ecological security concerns. In 1987, Mr Honecker made a largely symbolic journey to the West. He and Chancellor Kohl tabled a joint communiqué in which they committed themselves to intensifying all-round co-operation, to improving travel between the two states and to promoting arms control. They also signed agreements on scientific co-operation, exchange of information on nuclear safety and efforts to fight environmental pollution.

Honecker and Kohl cementing friendlier East/West relations.

FILE: DÉTENTE
China: where East meets West?

Since 1964 China has been committed to a nuclear defence policy of "no first use" (and "no use" against states without nuclear arms). Although its own nuclear capacity is insignificant compared with the vast arsenals of the superpowers, China views a minimum deterrent as indispensable for two reasons: first, Soviet threats of a nuclear strike effectively pressurized China into resolving the border skirmishes in 1969; second, Soviet hostility led Chinese representatives to seek allies in the Nixon administration, and thus form the third point of a triangular relationship between the major nuclear powers.

China has a growing interest in international affairs. On peace and disarmament, its attention is focused on non-aligned movements in NATO and Warsaw Pact states and the Pacific. The Chinese Association for International Understanding (CAFIU, 1981) has contacts with many such groups, while the Chinese People's Association for Peace and Disarmament (1984) is affiliated with Trades Unions, the Women's Federation, the Youth League and other mass organizations. China's active role in peace diplomacy has gone a long way towards breaking the US/USSR monopoly of armaments issues, and shown the country as increasingly confident in its policy of non-alignment.

The Chinese economy still lags far behind Western industrialism, with little scope for defence spending. But the country has opened its doors to foreign investment and intends to be considerably stronger and more affluent by 2050. The Chinese arms trade is growing and there is a real danger that it may overstep the limit of minimum deterrence. Though China declares it will never become a superpower, it would be difficult to view a country with a population of over a billion and an enhanced economic and nuclear capability as anything else. As an emergent superpower, China's attitude to détente and peace will be of great significance.

Representatives of the Chinese People's Association for Peace and Disarmament at the Greenham Common women's camp, Berkshire, England, in June 1986.

other. Political leaders still claim that the other side has superior forces to justify maintaining or increasing military budgets. Yet in reality neither side is militarily strong enough to be sure of victory by attacking the other with conventional forces. In making the public aware of this, the media could do much.

A greater openness and exchange is crucial to détente. Gorbachev's reforms in the Soviet Union give a great chance to achieve this and deserve a strong and positive response. We can reduce fear of surprise attack by bilateral deals on open verification and surveillance and publication of armaments statistics. We can make efforts to increase communication, from military and intelligence personnel exchanges to updating the "hot-line" (a joint crisis-control centre is being discussed). We can create confidence-building and "fair exchange" deals in as many areas as possible: food and energy policies, technology swaps, passport and work permit status, exchange residencies of senior officials, and human rights concessions.

But major reductions in tension and the risk of war can only come by seeking a demilitarized Europe, and here economic constraints will increasingly lend their weight. All citizens of Europe should press for steady cuts in conventional and tactical nuclear weapons.

Increasing the pressure for peace

Nuclear-weapons cuts can be successfully negotiated only by direct talks between the parties. But the United Nations Assembly and special committees can do a great deal. The Geneva sessions can press the superpowers for a timetable of cuts and for movement on the urgent test ban agreements, proposing deadlines for various stages. Though these would lack power of enforcement, they would have considerable moral impact and, if widely publicized and endorsed by Non-aligned states and peace movements, would place the nuclear powers in a position where they have to be seen to be respecting world opinion.

Geneva can also move faster to conclude a complete chemical weapons ban treaty. And they can offer help in practical ways. Disarmament and an end to competition in military technology can only come if the military and industrial establishment perceive them as feasible and, if not desirable, at least posing no threat of economic loss. UN disarmers should be proposing realistic and detailed plans for verification, for redeployment and conversion of equipment, manufacturing and personnel.

Conversion research (*see Chapter 9*) and strategies for the entire world military community are urgently needed, and have hardly begun. How, for instance, are the 50-60,000 nuclear missiles to be eradicated in our "five thousand days"? Disarming them is simple, and the 200 tons or so of plutonium they contain could be added to the civil energy stockpile. But the missiles, the ancillary equipment, and their fuel – what is to be done with these and the industries that support them?

Academic research answers will have little influence alone; industrialists and lawyers must be involved, and politicians, if the results are to have any weight. The

communities of NGOs too could give valuable advice from their own work. Broadly based committees of such elements are needed. The UN could lead and co-ordinate world research into conversion and the potential of military resources for peace.

Controlling the global arms trade

Conversion plans are also a key to ending the arms trade. Since the major nuclear powers are the main arms suppliers, here too they should directly negotiate – seeking staged limits on the trade via a treaty that other nations can then join. Again, the United Nations can help in practical ways with legal and economic studies and proposals for conversion time-tables.

The first stage should be an agreement for no sales to any countries where armed conflict is occurring, or has occurred within a past specified period – whether civil or international. This could be extended to ban sales to military or non-consensus regimes and to those with poor records on human rights and basic needs; and ultimately to a blanket ban on overseas sales.

As with nuclear weapons, controlling the technology itself is critical. We need a treaty banning testing of conventional weapons of high lethality and national laws on weapons lethality too. With co-operation in control of illegal arms, we should aim for a world where all international weapons sales require a UN licence.

Strengthening regional security

All these agreements – on nuclear arsenals reductions, on non-proliferation, on chemical weapons and arms trade controls, are less likely to succeed while regional conflicts continue and the superpowers remain involved in them. Wars outside Europe could easily spread to Europe and thus escalate to nuclear world·war. It is essential and urgent that we resolve regional conflicts, cool down the "hotspots", and build regional security.

Regional councils, as in Latin and Central America, need strengthening and world support for initiatives at planned and staged regional conflict solutions and security-building. Concerned groups and individuals of all types can help – UK specialists in international conflict resolution (*see pp. 218-19*) are studying the Gulf war, for instance. The world oil industry could work for a Gulf resolution, too. Grass roots groups and NGOs should seek analyses and proposals for solutions, and press them at every opportunity, in all quarters.

The shocks that trigger international crises are too seldom foreseen. We need better crisis anticipation and thus more attention to the roots of conflict and the patterns of its emergence. It might also help if permanent groups of regional or supranational (for instance, UN) mediators were trained in conflict recognition and resolution, and briefed as "watchdogs" and mediators to observe, respond to and defuse crises ahead of time.

The resolution of a conflict is much more than its settlement. Resolution requires the creation of a new set of relationships between the parties, which is self-sustaining and independent of coercion. Conflict cannot be resolved by military victory or threat, nor can

Mineral riches are Southern Africa's common heritage. But their strategic value draws superpower rivalry, and the risk of rapid escalation of any conflict. Thus South Africa's internal struggle; its illegal occupation of Namibia and war with SWAPO; its attacks on neighbouring states and use of proxy rebels, such as Angola's Unita or the Mozambique National Resistance, to destabilize them, all pose a grave threat to security. Moreover, South Africa may have a nuclear capability – and any threat to use it would provoke a world crisis. The great powers have a prime need to help resolve this regional conflict and prevent a civil war in South Africa.

Real resolution cannot begin until apartheid ends in South Africa and popular government established. If there is not to be a blood bath, the regime in Pretoria must negotiate with the African National Council and SADCC. The black trade unions and COSATU (the trade union confederation) are increasing pressure internally, but need support from the Front-line African states. Yet the SADCC states face a cruel dilemma: economically tied to Pretoria, they require aid – Zambia, Angola and Mozambique particularly – before they can apply pressure freely to the regime.

Internationally, trade and financial sanctions are the most effective non-violent ways to force change on Pretoria. Though supported by the Non-aligned Movement, the Commonwealth (except the Thatcher government), the OAU, and others, for sanctions to carry great force they must be applied by the Western industrial nations.

The conflict would be less violent if South Africa felt less isolated – and if Southern Africa's problems, rather than its enmities, were the focus. This is an argument for involving, as a first step, Pretoria and the ANC in regional discussions of, say, strategic resources and economic need, or famine prevention. South Africa has, after all, the strongest economy in the region.

Archbishop Desmond Tutu (*above*) is one of the most active figures in the fight for black African liberation.

Members of Southern African Development Co-ordination Conference (SADCC)

FILE: CRISIS RESOLUTION
The Middle East

Resolution of the Middle East conflict ultimately rests on the establishment of mutually satisfactory relations between Arabs and Jews. As Aaron Cohen concludes in his book *Israel and the Arab World*, this requires:

"1 Recognition by the Arabs of the state of Israel and the integration of Israel into the political totality of the area, which is basically Arab.

2 Satisfaction of the personal and the national-political rights of the Palestinian Arabs – permanent population and refugees alike."

The process of creating new relationships must start from scratch. Most Arab states refuse to sit down and negotiate with Israel, and the Israelis refuse to talk to the Palestinian Liberation Organization. An international peace conference would obviously help. Direct Arab-Israeli peace talks could begin under the umbrella of the permanent members of the UN Security Council. The implied international guarantees might then provide enough mutual confidence for subsequent negotiations between Arabs and Israelis only on regional problems – especially water, and nuclear-weapon-free status.

Israel's unwillingness to lose control of the water table on the West Bank is a prime source of tension. Agreement on the waters of the River Jordan would be a major step towards resolving Middle East conflict. World security would also be greatly enhanced if nuclear weapons were banned from the region. This could best be achieved by direct negotiations between Israel and the Arabs – including the PLO, whose presence would help Israeli/Palestinian relations and avert the risk of the PLO acquiring nuclear weapons.

Clearly, lasting security in the Middle East must be self-sustaining, and achieved by the parties themselves. A bi-national state may be the best hope in the long-term.

An Arab refugee with all his belongings crosses the Allenby Bridge, near Jericho, under the supervision of Israeli soldiers.

Occupied territories

Lebanon

Golan Heights

Israel

River Jordan

West Bank

Mediterranean Sea

Jerusalem

Jordan

Gaza Strip

solutions be imposed from outside. Although third-party and international efforts can prepare the ground and seek to bring the parties to the conference table – as in present US efforts in the Middle East – long-term solutions depend on patient problem-solving by all the states and interests involved in the region.

One fertile approach, in particular, is attention to common heritage or development problems rather than to hostilities. Conflicting parties must be encouraged to talk about issues of conservation, wealth, development and human insecurity – the Jordan waters in the Middle East, oil in the Gulf, famine relief in Africa – where co-operation may be possible. The establishment of peace and conservation zones in border disputed regions in Nicaragua is an example that might be adapted elsewhere. The involvement of NGOs and multinationals in regional conferences on true security-building in environmental and human terms would bring hostile parties together in a new context.

Minorities and international law

Human and minority rights issues are more difficult, impinging on questions of sovereignty. Establishment of "minorities" councils at both regional and international levels could reduce conflict while "joint nationality" might well provide solutions in some cases. New laws must be introduced for nomadic cultures who could be protected, too, by transborder agreements.

Here again, the United Nations should consider new approaches. Under present international law, minorities have no legal existence: and thus cannot be parties to any international treaties nor subject to international laws of peace or war. Lawyers of the International Court of Justice should seek a new, acceptable legal status for minorities enabling some definition of their rights and obligations under law. This would be a start on studying the legal definitions of national sovereignty we now employ, and seeking their modification in the light of international realities today.

The International Court could also put to the UN proposals for a new treaty on international law – under which nations would commit themselves to embody within their own national law a recognition of the supremacy of international law. This might begin via national laws honouring the priority of regional court rulings, as in Europe; and regional laws recognizing international law and the authority of the International Court of Justice.

Ending foreign military involvement

Foreign military support for combatants, and even more so direct involvement, always worsens the prospects for its solution. Control of the arms trade is essential to regional conflict resolution. The other prerequisite is negotiation of a non-intervention treaty. Bilateral, less-formal agreements between the Soviets and Americans on particular conflicts are beginning. Ultimately a non-intervention treaty must be implemented.

There are major obstacles to such a superpower

The Gulf

Resolution of the Gulf conflict is bedevilled by foreign interests, and the focus of this interest is oil. Europe, Japan and South East Asia have long depended on Gulf oil. But it is less often realized that the USA and USSR, too, will soon compete for it. By 1990, for example, the US hopes to obtain up to 50% of its oil from the region. The strong US presence in the Gulf reflects Washington's strategic oil interests. The USSR is equally anxious to assure future oil and gas for its East European allies. And neither superpower is keen to see a "winner" emerge from the Iran/Iraq war, or both parties freed to pursue their former power interests in the region. Other oil producers may also have an interest in the continuation of the war, since it restricts oil output and keeps prices up. An embargo on Gulf oil to force a peace would benefit non-Gulf producers, but this would prove economically damaging to developing, oil-importing countries.

Superpower competition in the Gulf has profound consequences for any efforts at regional resolutions. Such efforts are also hampered by local instabilities. Some regimes – as in Saudi Arabia, the Emirates and Kuwait – face social and political revolutions; Islamic revivalism and Iran's hatred for Kuwait and Saudi Arabia are further barriers. And when Soviet forces leave Afghanistan, a new civil war may erupt. Relations between Gulf countries must improve and stable regimes with popular support emerge before conflict resolution can succeed. The situation is so complex that true peace will only be built by a patient, determined approach to

Central America

Members of the Contadora countries (shown on map) have proved to be an effective regional pressure group. Shown *below* are ambassadors and ministers, representatives of the Contadora and Contadora support countries, meeting in London in September 1987.

regional security and understanding by all concerned.

International, especially UN, efforts for peace are highly desirable. An arms embargo makes sense, as does a UN force in the Gulf. But while the US will not retire in favour of the UN nor Moscow endorse any international action, the UN should explore contexts for direct local conflict resolution. The thorny question of who began the Iran/Iraq war needs attention under international law; meanwhile, efforts to resolve other main conflicts, such as the Kurds' fight with Iraq and Turkey, and to shape regional agreement on conservation, and minority and religious security, could be pursued.

Since oil is at the heart of the conflict, it is the oil community that should seek a long-term resolution. The creation of a new world oil order is so much to the advantage of oil producers that pressures for it will surely increase. But it will only be achieved if the regional conflicts are resolved. The need to optimize use of oil reserves may be the greatest spur to peace in the region. And the need of oil-importing states to secure supplies into the 21st century may encourage them, too, to cease hampering local and international efforts to resolve the conflict.

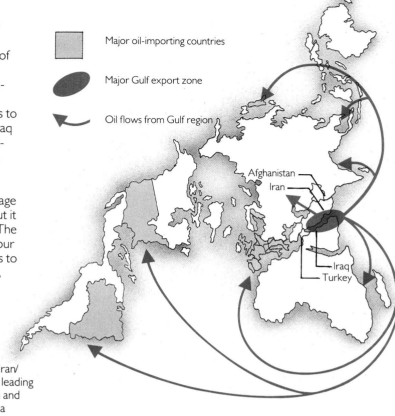

Major oil-importing countries

Major Gulf export zone

Oil flows from Gulf region

Afghanistan
Iran
Iraq
Turkey

Despite an abundance of oil in the market place at present, the Gulf region, with its huge reserves, represents a major source of energy for the world well into the next century. Political instability in the region (the continuing Iran/Iraq conflict, for example), leading to uncertain oil production and wild price fluctuations, has a generally destabilizing effect on world economies.

Of all the world's hotspots, Central America has the most established frameworks for resolving conflict. The peninsula, linking as it does two great continents and two great oceans, has a rich culture and long history of strategic importance, and has been responsible for a good many institutions to discuss common regional problems. The Organization of Central American States, the Central American Common Market, the Commission for Peace, Regional Security and Democracy, and the Central American Common Market are examples. The Andean Pact – Bolivia, Colombia, Ecuador, Peru and Venezuela – seems particularly active at present, and the Contadora group was set up in 1983 specifically to find a regional solution to disputes in Central America.

But there are still serious barriers to be overcome before regional conflict resolution can work. Many of these are environmental problems at root. Population increases and higher expectations in most Central American countries are putting intolerable pressures on scarce resources of land. Land reform is, therefore, a prerequisite for conflict resolution. Deforestation, too, is severe: Central America has some of the rarest and most valuable ecosytems in the New World, all of which need concerted protection. Upland forest loss threatens, for instance, to wreck the Panama Canal lock system by siltation and reduced water flows; it may also be changing local climate, and even threatening more arid conditions in the southern United States.

Human rights are another major issue. And the combined effects of land shortage, poverty, oppression and conflict are sending waves of migrants northward to put pressure on Mexico and the States. But positive signs are the use of bodies such as the Latin American Economic System as forums for improving regional relations and development stategies.

Politically, the unresolved border disputes between Peru and Ecuador and between Venezuela and Colombia still cause problems. But the main barrier to conflict resolution is Washington's continuing military support for the Contra rebels in Nicaragua. This jeopardizes any peace plan, such as that of President Oscar Arias Sanchez of neutral Costa Rica.

The US attitude is well described in a recent report, Discriminate Deterrence: "If the Sandinista regime consolidates its power in Nicaragua and continues to receive Soviet support, hostile communist regimes might gradually become established elsewhere in Central America – for example, in El Salvador, Honduras and Panama. Any such trend could be expected to endanger control of the Panama Canal and threaten the political stability of Mexico. These developments would force the United States to divert far more of its foreign policy resources and defense assets to the Caribbean region."

Clearly, the resolution of conflict in Central America cannot take place if the USA seriously objects to the arrangements. The first requirement, therefore, is a change in America's obsessive perceptions concerning the possible spread of communism in the western hemisphere.

Participation of the US government in a joint effort at conservation planning and climate research for the region might help. The recent initiative by Costa Rica and Nicaragua, for instance, in declaring some of the tropical forest lands in the Contra war zone a "Peace Park", partly funded out of discounted debts purchased in a "conservation swap" scheme, seems almost an invitation to the US to change from a confrontational stance to one of co-operation with its hard-pressed neighbours.

agreement. Human rights and foreign policy are deeply divisive issues; the two powers are locked in a battle for ideological and economic influence in the South, and each has hardliners to satisfy, the US particularly. America is the world's most democratic power. But its foreign policy is relatively hawkish, and may remain so if a 1988 policy proposal by prestigious US strategists, "Discriminate Deterrence" (*see p. 176*), is endorsed.

This recommends, for instance, yet greater reliance on military technology, with smaller, more "acceptable" (and usable) nuclear weapons, forces ready for regional interventions at short notice, and increased military aid to allies to counter continuous "low-intensity conflict" – which it foresees in a future of heightened struggle for democratic freedoms and three- or four-way nuclear-power rivalry. The prospect is alarming, and in opposition to Soviet thinking as Gorbachev propounds it – regional stability not by superpower intervention but by withdrawal. With such divergent views, can the superpowers avoid continuing regional confrontation?

The paradox of democratic America pursuing such a hawkish policy abroad is explained by the US belief in democratic freedoms and economic competition; the corresponding almost obsessive fear of communism; the US faith in its own economic and military power as the best guarantee of liberty for itself and its allies; and the power of the military-industro nexus to spread a blind political faith in military technology.

But more than in any other country, public opinion is the final arbiter of American policy. As with the anti-Vietnam War movement, it can modify government behaviour. Nor is all US policy geared to nuclear expansion. President Reagan's State of The Union address to Congress in 1988 stated that America will "continue to assist developing countries to realize sustained non-inflationary growth, since we understand this is in our mutual economic and security interests".

Preventing ecological disaster

While negotiating measures to reduce the risk of nuclear war, the world's political leaders must at the same time produce an emergency programme to halt the slide to eco-catastrophe. Some of the money may have to be found from the military, from taxation, and by economic reform to free the South's resources.

The need for such action has been voiced time and again by NGOs and commissions of all kinds, and most recently in *Our Common Future*, the report of The World Commission on Environment and Development, chaired by Norwegian Prime Minister Gro Brundtland. Taking evidence from government officials, scientists, industrialists, non-governmental organizations and the general public, from all regions of the world, the Brundtland Commission has provided the best and sharpest analysis available of major global problems, and the interlinked crisis of the environment, human development and true security.

The overriding need the report recognizes is for the elimination of poverty – without which all efforts at environmental protection and development will fail, and

peace itself will be continuously threatened. The report stresses that the world has real choices – on population control measures, for instance, choices by governments now could make a difference of thousands of millions to the ultimate global total in the 21st century. Choices in energy policies and investment, in economic priorities, agriculture and so on are equally critical. And it claims that we have the ability to make development sustainable – "to ensure that humanity meets the needs of the present without compromising the ability of future generations to meet their own needs."

Such a future requires greater and more fundamental changes than the programme outlined in the Brundtland report. Its achievement will take reform of economic systems and values, new social and political institutions, new leadership and a radical shift in human relations with the biosphere (*see Chapter 9*). We shall have no hope of this without a bold emergency effort now.

Emergency economic reforms

The poor must not be left in their poverty. Frequently the least visible sector of need, until disaster comes, they need some permanent global watchdog body, born of the poor themselves, to keep their voice constantly in the ears of politicians, financiers, "experts" and all who run the affairs of the world.

A programme to reduce the North-South economic gap should then be undertaken. It must involve a firm agreement on commodity prices and agreement by all trading nations to end protectionism and the dumping of subsidized foods from richer nations at artificially low prices. Instabilities and overproduction in agriculture in the North are anyway under review; the EEC could take the lead in a new deal with the South on trade.

And it must include far-reaching debt reform to end the absurd situation where wealth and resources flow, not from the rich to the poor nations, but vice versa – from the poor into the rich North.

The new idea of using debts as a lever to achieve environmental protection – whereby conservation agencies buy up discounted debts and debtor countries repay them in conservation measures – could start a world "debt conversion" programme, debt into development, of major scale. But the North should also join with the South in setting up a negotiated limit on interest rates, back dated, and in planning how the returned overpaid amounts are deployed for sustainable development for the poor.

The financial community should also agree a large increase in development aid, conditional on its use in bottom-up development administered by communities themselves with the aid of NGOs and intermediate-technology specialists. Such aid could also be drawn as taxation from multinational corporations operating in the countries concerned, from debt conversion, and by offering extra aid in return for reduced militarism, and for regional security and conflict-resolution schemes.

Most of all, we must change our way of thinking and adapt our economies to serve real long-term interests. The environment must be regarded as productive

Debt and artificially high interest rates are acting to transfer wealth from the South to the North. Low commodity prices force the South to export to creditor countries large amounts of their natural resources, a drain increased by the arms trade. The environment and peoples of debtor nations are increasingly bankrupted by this flow. Many cannot service their debts, and some see the debts themselves as illegitimate – whether because loans were acquired by undemocratic regimes (and then, all too often, salted away in foreign bank accounts, or wasted on non-productive schemes), or because the greater part of the debt is due to interest rises.

There are many solutions proposed: cancelling all or part of the debt (but this might leave debtor countries "blacked"); lending new capital to the most indebted (more of the same); rescheduling debts (organized postponement); and "structural adjustment" in debtor countries (more private enterprise) and more growth in industrialized markets (which has not worked thus far). Newer ideas include: valuing debts on world markets and discounting them; converting discounted debts into securities, or debt-swap schemes; and reducing rates to original levels and repaying the overpaid interest.

> Any lasting solution to debt must encourage:
> **1** Reversal of the flow of wealth, back to the South.
> **2** Diversion of military resources to development.
> **3** Investment in real wealth, environmental and human, and wise use of materials, by developing countries.
> **4** Movement of global economy towards a "steady" state.
> Moreover it must reasonably satisfy the interests of all parties, avoid a market crash, and be seen to be a fair sharing of the financial burden of a resolution.

The Alfonsin plan

One proposal that fits the criteria reasonably well is that of Argentinian President Alfonsin. Devised for Latin American countries, but certainly adaptable for others, his plan is based on the concept of "debt legitimacy". The debt would be reduced to its "legitimate" size by discounting all increments in international interest rates over a basic rate of 6%, back-dated to 1976. Debtor nations would then be compensated for the sharp price drops in raw materials and commodities since 1980, and the monetary value of the remaining debt would be converted into amounts of

materials and/or manufactured products, using fair prices.

Other aspects of the Alfonsin plan call for yearly rates of interest not to rise above 6%. There would also be a 25-year repayment period for the capital, during which time commodity prices would be held stable and no new long-term loans or debt renegotiations would be asked for. All capital illegitimately sent out of Latin American countries since 1976 would be repatriated.

Swap and conservation schemes

The discounting of debts on the world money markets, and lateral thinking by conservation bodies, has led for the first time to positive action towards converting debts into wealth. This innovative idea was first proposed by Dr Thomas E. Lovejoy of the US World Wildlife Fund in 1984.

In Costa Rica, for instance, the World Wildlife Fund has relieved the country of $270,000 of its debt by purchasing it at a discount from the lending sources; and in return Costa Rica will deposit 75% of this sum in local currency in a special account used for conservation purposes – in this case, towards the purchase of 40,000 acres of protected land. In Ecuador, the World Wildlife Fund and Fundacion Natura have agreed a similar debt-for-nature swap, involving the purchase of Ecuadorean debt with a face value of at least $1,000,000.

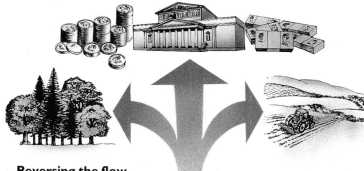

Reversing the flow

The South's debt is pumping resources to the North. Any solution must reverse this, to create environmental and human wealth in the South.

Extending debt conversion

Debt swaps might help other Latin American countries, but in Africa (where debts are owed to governments rather than to banks) their value is uncertain. There are moves to involve the World Bank in debt swaps, and for "debt donations" to conservation bodies, in return for donor tax relief. The author Susan George, in *A Fate Worse than Debt*, proposes a radical "3-D solution" – debt, development and democracy – deals between lenders and borrowers.

Whereas debt swaps alone cannot solve the $1 trillion debt crisis, they do provide a model for the creation of real wealth out of what seemed an intractable economic decline. Such a scheme could be adapted by any development agency already spending funds in a debtor country. One can even envisage a broader scheme for "debt to sustainable development", involving agencies, banks, commerce, and community groups, and the creation of a global debt-swap fund invested in world markets to increase its value.

In November 1987, stock markets went wild (as can be seen in this picture taken in Tokyo's foreign exchange market). The debt crisis was a trigger to this shock to the world financial system.

capital, even if it is not used as such. When we destroy forests, over-work croplands until the soil erodes and engage in industrial activities that pollute the air and waters, our income, as measured by Gross National Product (GNP) actually registers an increase. When we take measures to reduce or repair environmental damage, they are also registered as increases in GNP.

This is patently misleading. It also disguises the fact that the destruction of the natural resource base is, in reality, a serious economic loss. We urgently need a unified system of accounting that reflects the total picture of a nation's economy and of its resource base.

Food security
Between 1950 and 1985 cereal production outstripped population growth, increasing from about 700 million tons to over 1,800 million tons, an annual growth rate of about 2.7 per cent. During this period, the annual growth of the world population was 1.9 per cent. In 1985, the world produced nearly 500 kilogrammes per head of cereals and root crops. In Europe, meat production more than tripled between 1950 and 1984 and milk production nearly doubled. World meat exports have risen from some 2 million tons in 1950-2 to over 11 million tons in 1984. To produce this meat and milk in 1984 required some 1,400 million cattle and buffaloes, 1,600 million sheep and goats, 900 million pigs and a huge number of chicken. These animals weigh in total more than the people of the world.

Nonetheless, nearly 800 million people are without enough food to sustain an ordinary working day. And short-sighted policies are degrading the agricultural resource base almost everywhere – soil erosion in North America, soil acidification in Europe, deforestation and desertification in Asia, Africa and Latin America, and waste and pollution of water virtually everywhere. It is estimated, for instance, that about 10,000 people die each year in developing countries from pesticide poisoning.

The problem of raising nutritional supply while retaining "the essential ecological integrity of production systems" is colossal. But it can be done, most particularly if the criterion of "sustainable livelihood security" is applied. This approach to food production takes as its basis the needs of the poor and the local community. It requires changes in agricultural policies at government and international levels, plus redistribution of land, the ecologically responsible use of traditional or new technology and an overriding principle of long-term perspectives.

Governments usually control national agriculture quite closely, with incentive schemes and pricing. These controls must now, in many instances, be turned on their heads – to favour reduced production in the North; increased food for local consumption, rather than luxuries for export, in the South.

And the local community must be involved in all land reclamation and new agricultural directions and development. Wood-fuel plots and afforestation; water and sanitation supply schemes; fish farming and irriga-

tion; terracing and windbreaks; mixed smallholdings and forestry combined with interplanted crops – "agroforestry"; chemical-free organic pest control and locally adapted crops and livestock; game management and small-scale industries; direct marketing to wholesalers or overseas "friendly" concerns – all these, and more, are "bottom-up" approaches to sustainable livelihood and food security for all the world's peoples.

Community and human security
Dag Hammarskjöld spoke of "another development", which would be: need oriented – that is, designed for the people it served; endogenous, that is, created and managed by the people it served; self-reliant, that is, able to thrive without outside help if need be; ecologically sound, that is, guarding the environment and productivity of the land; and structurally transforming, that is, involving changes in the society away from oppression and violence.

Many NGOs have begun to adopt these criteria; but governments are slow to follow, financiers even slower. If human and community security needs – for livelihood, for independence, for participation and dignity and freedom – are to be met, major rethinking is needed at the top, to match the potential at the bottom.

Development financing, for instance, needs new financial models: local control of the funds; long-term and "in-kind" returns on investment over periods that truly reflect the time-scales of natural systems, from forests to fisheries; back up services of specialists in local community revival and intermediate skills indigenous to the culture; partnership schemes between commerce, government, bank and community.

A broad committee of the main NGOs, community representatives, commerce, insurance companies and co-operative and labour movements, together with world money sources and legal advisers, should address these requirements of "sustainable financing".

Population control
One of the toughest problems facing us is the population explosion. Rather than straining our overloaded planet to the limit to cater for twice as many people within just another 35 years, we must try to call a halt. If we were to achieve a replacement level of fertility (namely a two-child family on average) by the year 2005 – 20 years earlier than assumed by the United Nations in its medium projection – the global population would stabilize at around 8, rather than 10, billion persons. If, however, replacement levels of fertility are not reached until 20 years after the date anticipated by the UN, then 2.8 billion more people would be added to the projected total (unless AIDS or other unknowns change this pattern) – a difference of 4 billion more mouths to feed.

Reducing the birthrate to replacement level by the year 2000 would be a demanding task. But it is not impossible. There have been startling declines on the part of certain communities – China, Taiwan, South Korea, Java, Thailand, Kerala in India, Sri Lanka, Cuba, Mexico, Costa Rica and Colombia – countries with a

Ethiopian farmers working on a co-operative sow food crops after a few days of rain.

In 1970, the world produced about 700 million tons of cereal; today, cereal production exceeds 2 billion tons a year. In Europe, meat production has nearly tripled since 1950 and milk production doubled. Yet in the midst of plenty there is widespread starvation and malnutrition. If we are to feed the 1.1 billion people that will be added to the planet before the year 2000, we must increase global food production by 3 or 4 per cent each year. This was one of the problems studied by the UN World Commission on Environment and Development, headed by Gro Brundtland. One of the reports that grew out of its three-year research period was *Food 2000*.

In the past few decades food production has been increased, due largely to rises in productivity rather than to increases in the amount of cultivated land. This has been achieved by using new, high-yield seed varieties and huge amounts of fertilizers and pesticides. The often indiscriminate use of these substances is, however, taking a heavy human and ecological toll. Water supplies, for example, are poisoned by nitrate run-off, while improper use of pesticides can kill.

To reach the goal of a 3 to 4 per cent yearly increase in global food production in a sustainable way, the Brundtland

Commission makes several recommendations. Developing countries must turn the "terms of trade" in favour of farmers through better pricing policies for food crops and increasing investments in the agricultural sector by providing farm support services and a better market infrastructure.

Rural poverty must be tackled head-on, with comprehensive land reforms, expansion of the technological base, and integrated "bottom-up" development schemes, to create sustainable livelihood security and thus protect the agricultural base. The Commission goes on to suggest that agricultural land should be classified as "enhancement", "prevention" or "restoration" areas.

Enhancement areas are those capable of sustaining intensive cropping and higher population and consumption levels. Prevention areas are not to be developed for intensive agricultures or, where already developed, converted to other uses. Restoration areas are once productive land now stripped of vegetation and in need of resuscitation.

In the South agriculture is in crisis. This is also the case in the industrialized North. Huge farm subsidies – in 1986, these

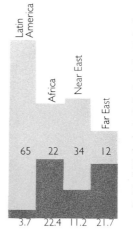

On present evidence, conversion of land from often inefficient large land holdings to more intensely cultivated smallholdings is one of the most politically sensitive of all social reforms. The bar chart, *left*, shows the percentage of land in four major regions presently farmed as smallholdings (red), and the percentage of "excess" land that could be cultivated as smallholdings (pink). In Latin America, "excess" means holdings over 100 ha; Asia, between 10 and 20 ha; and Africa, 10 ha.

amounted to about $26 billion in the USA and $21 billion in the EEC – help depress the prices of Southern commodities and harm agriculture. It is usually cheaper and politically expedient to export food surpluses as food aid rather than store them. Such food aid and low-priced food imports further depress prices for Southern farmers as well as reducing incentives to produce food indigenously.

Less environmental pressure
Less refugeeism and conflict
Lower population growth
Less urbanization

Land redistribution

Technology transfer

Community support

Ecologically sound
agriculture and energy

Sustainable livelihood
(food, water, energy, health, work)

POVERTY

Assistance coming in at the bottom to remove poverty and provide a sustainable livelihood has advantageous effects for the whole society.

Food is not our only problem. The long-term management of global agriculture must be improved. Food production must be increased without environmental degradation. *Food 2000* suggests a seven-point Action Plan.
1 Develop an international code for the sustainable and equitable use of life-support systems.
2 Include sustainable development livelihood for all in the UN Declaration of Human Rights.
3 Initiate a new agricultural system for nutrition security.
4 Ensure equality of opportunity for access to technology.
5 Organize skills for sustainable livelihood security in every country.
6 Reorientate international action and assistance so that it is consistent with integrated national conservation and sustainable livelihood strategies.
7 Promote political commitment and accountability.

broad range of cultural backgrounds. Replacement rate by the year 2000 would bring great benefits to many hard-pressed countries. If Nigeria, for instance, were to achieve this goal, its ultimate population size would not be 532 million but 227 million, greatly expanding its options for ending poverty and achieving sustainable development. In the case of Central America, the ultimate population figure would fall from 81 million to 55 million, with all that would imply for enhanced stability in a region with long-standing antagonisms.

Besides increased security in old age, to reduce their child-bearing most couples need motivation as well as contraception. More education and greater freedom for women are essential. When women can earn, and make reasoned choices about their own lives, they have fewer children. And we could make a dent in the problem now merely by taking care of "unmet needs" of women who want contraception but cannot get it.

These make up, as a rough average, 20 per cent of the 400 million women without family planning in developing countries. Provision for this 20 per cent would add only $1 million to world family planning budgets of about $1 billion (excluding China). But it could cut the ultimate population by almost a billion people over several generations.

We can also take measures to reduce the impacts of high populations; efforts to create livelihood security in the rural areas and to reclaim damaged environments will reduce the flow of migrants to the cities.

But the fundamental problem is poverty itself. The world community has to weigh its choices. Which will cost richer nations, and leaders of poorer ones, less: to neglect the economic reforms and increased aid which are needed to tackle poverty – and so face a world of 11 billion people? Or to act now to provide the poor with the basic social security for old age, education and health services that would remove the need for children as providers, and bring that total down?

Ecofreeze

The most critical element of an emergency programme for survival is the "ecofreeze" – calling a halt to deforestation, desertification, genetic loss and atmospheric pollution with its attendant acid rain, ozone depletion and global warming. Gaia is running a temperature – and threatening us with massive flooding and upset to agriculture as a result, while long-term failure of managed ecosystems may plunge us all, sooner or later, into famine and disease.

Ecological changes are slow to take effect, slower by far than human timescales. We are only now, for example, appreciating the damage of the industrial revolution. Civilizations in the past have taken hundreds of years to observe their own impact. And we do not yet know what our pollution of rivers and oceans with thousands of newly added toxic chemicals is doing – or what "communications pollution" (radio spectrum interference) or "biological pollution" may do. But though the build-up period of trouble is long, the break-down can be swift when it comes – witness the

Stabilizing world population

An exploding population is one of the most urgent problems facing the world today. To achieve sustainability, it is essential that global population is stabilized at around the 8 to 10 billion mark, which means reducing the fertility rate to replacement level by the year 2000, or soon afterwards. Much has already been accomplished in countries such as China and Singapore, but much remains to do for the millions of women in the developing world in terms of adequate, safe, contraception and birth control technology. Population policies and provision alone will not, however, reduce fertility rates; they must be accompanied by improvements in living standards and in the quality of life.

Singapore: girl or boy, two children is enough
Singapore has the second highest population density in the world after Hong Kong. But it also has what has been hailed as one of the most successful birth-control programmes. Family planning in Singapore dates back to 1949 when a voluntary organization was set up to provide health care for mothers and children, and to advise on birth control. In 1966 this organization was replaced by the government backed Singapore Family Planning and Population Board (SFPPB).

The SFPPB's initial aim was to provide family planning services to 60% of all married women aged between 15-44; by 1971, 62% of eligible women were registered at clinics. In 1969 both abortion and sterilization were legalized, and at the same time a number of disincentives were introduced to prevent large families.

Since 1975, the SFPPB has been actively promoting a two-child family. Posters displaying two-child families adorn most public places, and the SFPPB makes use of radio, television, schools and exhibitions to get its message across. Awareness of family planning is widespread and at least 90% of the population is either practising or has practised some method of contraception. To a great extent, this reflects the situation in Singapore itself. Industrial progress has been rapid and GNP is high. The average age of marriage is also high and most couples prefer to establish their careers before having children.

Safe Motherhood Initiative
Every minute a woman dies from a pregnancy related cause; 95% of these occur in developing countries. In February 1987, 140 health experts from 30 countries met in Nairobi to discuss the level of maternal mortality and to launch the Safe Motherhood Initiative. The meeting was organized jointly by the World Bank, the World Health Organization, and the UN Fund for Population Activities. Other participants included the administrator of the UN Development Programme and the Secretary General of the International Planned Parenthood Federation (IPPF).

The Conference called for adequate primary health care, nutrition, and the widespread availability of contraception. Birth rate is higher in developing countries and women will have at least six or seven pregnancies. Increasing the availability and use of contraception would not only reduce the birth rate but make birth a safer process when combined with good basic health care schemes.

India welcomed the Conference's call to action, and hopes within three years to raise the marriage age from 18 to 20, thus effectively reducing births by 10-15%. At the other end of the spectrum, contraception or sterilization for women over 30 years who already have families and are in the high-risk pregnancy category, will reduce the birth rate by 25% in urban and up to 28% in rural areas.

实行计划生育　是我国的一项基本国策
FAMILY PLANNING — A BASIS NATIONAL POLICY OF CHINA

Huge posters in China (*above*) extoll the virtues of one-child families: in Singapore (*far right*) and Africa (*centre* and *near right*) the process of educating young mothers also continues.

China: A unique experiment

With a population of some 1 billion people, China accounts for 23% of the world population but only has 7% of its land. Faced with the possibility of a 3 billion population by the year 2030, in 1978, Chinese policymakers set a target of only 1.2 billion for the year 2000. To achieve this they implemented an ambitious one-child, one-couple policy and launched what has been described as "the most stringent birth control programme in history".

Using extensive education, official propaganda, peer and group pressure, provincial officials and family planning workers throughout China urged couples to restrict their families to one child. Couples who conceived a second child were encouraged to have an abortion, and those who produced one were fined or forced to pay back benefits. Nationally, the number of sterilizations soared, reaching 8.86 million in 1984. Since then, there has been a change of emphasis and Chinese authorities are taking more account of people's wishes. Research into popular attitudes has revealed that a two-child family is acceptable in rural areas. So while the one-child policy is still stressed, a more permissive attitude is being taken towards having a second child.

Zaire: Traditional midwives provide "unmet needs"

The region of Karawa, Zaire, suffers from high fertility as well as high infant and maternal mortality rates. Since contraception is confined to 2% only of the population, there is an enormous unmet need for family planning services.

In 1982, Karawa implemented an experimental community-based health initiative which relies on Traditional Birth Attendants (TBAs). These are local women, chosen by village health development committees for training in modern maternity techniques and family planning. Many of the TBAs are illiterate but are experienced midwives, trusted by the women they are trying to reach. Since 1982, 170 women have been trained in improved delivery practice as well as referral of high-risk women to hospital.

The community itself helps to finance the TBAs. Local families pay a small delivery fee. There are 20 health centres in the region, each serving between 6,000 and 20,000 people. Since the programme was initiated, an increasing number of women have been attending clinics. The use of non-doctors, especially TBAs, who have the full support of the community, is considered to be the best means of providing health care for village women and children.

alarmingly rapid growth of exotic weed species when they take over, the expanding hole in the ozone layer, the marching deserts of Africa.

Ecosystems, and the biosphere as a whole, need a diversity of species and of genetic material to thrive. Species are disappearing at unprecedented rates. On average some 900,000 species of plants and animals have become extinct every 1 million years during the past 200 million years, an average of 1 extinction every one and one-ninth years. Currently, human-caused extinctions are occurring at rates hundreds or perhaps thousands of times higher than this. Accurate figures are not known but estimates range from one per day, to one per hour.

Most of the species vanishing are the least known and in the tropical forests. These, which contain 90 per cent or more of all species, are being destroyed at a great rate. (Out of about the 1.5 thousand million hectares that once stood, only 900 million remain and these are going at the rate of about 11 million hectares a year.)

Not only is an ecofreeze the most critical emergency programme, it is the most difficult, and demands huge effort. Some governments are moving to conserve species and genetic diversity, mainly by establishing protected areas. Worldwide about 4 million square kilometres are protected – 3.9 per cent of the territory of Europe; 2.5 per cent of the USSR; 8.1 per cent of North America; 6.1 per cent of Asia; and 4.3 per cent of Australia.

But the total area protected must be at least tripled if it is to include a representative sample of Earth's ecosystems. And we need massive investment in the existing and new action plans to halt the assault on tropical forests, to plant new forests, combat desertification, introduce widespread soil conservation and programmes to protect watersheds and supplies.

To bring poorer countries up to the energy use of the developed countries by the year 2025 could increase our world energy use by a factor of five. Yet the risks of global warming and acidification of the environment rule out even a doubling of energy use based on the current mix of energy sources. As *Our Common Future* points out, investment now in clean and sustainable alternative energy technologies "is imperative. It is also possible. But it will require new dimensions of political will and institutional co-operation to achieve it."

Meantime, we must seek emergency measures to limit our outpourings: taxation penalties; pollution control incentives; new pollutant extraction technologies. And if every person on Earth with power to do so helped plant trees – trees everywhere – we might have a chance.

Changing attitudes to security

Security is normally defined as the protection of the people in a country as a whole from dangers and threats. Until recently this meant protection against the use or the threat of the use by another country of its military forces to jeopardize the governments (or

FILE: ECOFREEZE
Tackling the Greenhouse effect

Governments and scientists are now well aware of the risks of global atmospheric warming, and the Montreal Treaty on ozone layer protection is evidence that the world community can act in the face of a crisis of transnational impact. But our failure to control the emissions that cause acid rain – even though we have the technology – bodes ill for our capacity to tackle the Greenhouse effect. Technology to reduce CO_2 emissions at source is still undeveloped (though efforts in Sweden show that power station releases can be controlled). We need clearer understanding, too, of the role of forest burning, or of methane from livestock, fertilizers and sewage – CO_2 makes up only 50% of the Greenhouse gases.

While we wait, the problem is worsening. We have to buy time. Reafforestation on a grand scale is one strategy we know will help local climate, and possibly reduce CO_2 levels in the atmosphere. Public support for energy conservation and reduced private transport, with bans on stubble and forest burning, creation of more smokeless zones, and tight controls on industrial, urban and agricultural pollution, would do much.

Most of all, we need to prevent worse pollution in the future: the Brundtland report calls for a world strategy on energy and the environment, matched by national plans that emphasize conservation, efficiency, phasing out of fossil and wood fuels, and steady substitution with clean, sustainable energies. Such an approach also needs input from climatologists and Gaia scientists, and from NGOs and agencies aware of local demands and culturally appropriate solutions. In an increasingly unemployed world, community and craft-based human labour and skill can be far less polluting, and more conducive to well-being than large automated industries. Even with a major effort at a pollution "freeze" now, however, warming is likely to continue while fossil-fuel reliance continues. The community of nations should consider contingency plans for the predicted consequences now.

FILE: ECOFREEZE
Protecting the ozone layer

In order to protect the ozone layer (*see pp. 120-1*), the world's main producers and consumers of chlorofluorocarbons (CFCs) signed an agreement in Montreal in September 1987 to freeze, and then reduce, emissions of these chemicals in aerosols. Campaigns by NGOs, such as Friends of the Earth, had led in 1980 to UNEP requesting governments to reduce CFC manufacture and use. In 1985 the Vienna Convention for Protection of the Ozone Layer was adopted by the EEC and 21 other states. In 1986 Dupont announced it would produce alternative aerosol carriers within 5 years.

The Montreal Treaty freezes CFC use at 1986 levels, with a 20% cut by 1994 and 30% more by 2000. Production will be cut by only a third, and sales may increase in developing countries (many are exempt for 10 years). Low-consumer states can raise use up to 0.3 kg per capita.

These terms do not go far enough, quickly enough. CFCs are now banned in the US, Canada, Norway, Sweden and Denmark with voluntary restrictions in West Germany, Australia, Switzerland and Japan. A total world ban should follow, but powerful counterpressures from the giant chemical manufacturers demand stronger incentives to abandon CFCs. Meanwhile, more recent evidence (1987) suggests the Treaty is already out of date. The hole in the ozone layer is now 15% bigger than in previous years.

Forests are vital to life. When trees go, soil bleeds from the land. Watersheds no longer hold rain in the forest "sponge" to feed rivers throughout the year, and so a cycle of devastating flood and drought sets in. Rain becomes erratic and the climate hotter and drier; crops fail; deserts spread. Globally, forest loss reduces solar gain and evaporation, leading to disruption of convection and major climate shifts. When forests are burned, CO_2 is released: but no matter how they are cleared, the reduced tree cover reabsorbs less CO_2 and new farm lands add to methane flows. Acid rain further weakens forest cover and absorption, and the Greenhouse threat grows.

The chainsaws in the tropical forests are driven by land hunger and an insatiable demand for timber – often to supply products to the North. Land reform, agroforestry and new, more self-reliant, agricultural policies would strike at the root of the problem. Every year, too, several million ha of forest, woodland and scrub are stripped for fuelwood. "Tree farm" schemes (with provision for immediate need so that young trees are not cut) are wanted almost universally.

Much work is already in hand – from local NGO efforts to the World Bank Forest Action Plan, which calls for $8 billion over 5 years. There have been many success stories (*see below*), particularly those projects where local communities have been wholly involved and schemes are economically and ecologically beneficial. But the total is neither fast nor far-reaching enough.

The ecological crisis is grave and urgent. Mass reafforestation, land reform, reserve creation and a freeze on further clearance must move to the top of the world agenda – and to the heart of every community.

Open dry woodland

Tropical moist forest (evergreen and seasonal)

Frontiers of forest loss

The highlands of Nepal have seen some of the world's worst erosion following large-scale deforestation. Here, a woman in the Gurung District, in the Himalayan foothills, plants fast-maturing fodder and fuelwood tree seedlings.

The greening of China

China's target of 30% tree cover involves the whole nation. Land workers are entitled to long-term management of afforestation plots while urban roadside and railway plantations are common. Incentive schemes are matched by heavy fines for illegal felling or failure to meet afforestation targets. Even "honeymoon" plantations encourage newlyweds to plant a tree.

Community forestry in Nepal

Current rates of deforestation could destroy Nepal's hill forests in 15 years. A major community forestry effort to save them, run by the Nepalese government with the World Bank, FAO and UNDP, involves local people at every stage. A quarter of a million trees have been planted; dams, canals and terraces built or renovated; and 15,000 energy-saving domestic stoves introduced.

Jordan: Fruit trees save the soil

Jordan's steep, arid land makes cultivation hard, and erosion is silting up irrigation dams. Under a new government scheme, farmers have turned from wheat and barley planting to fruit trees – peaches, olives, almonds – on terraces, to stabilize the soil. Training, 40% of terracing costs, and food stocks are provided by the World Food Programme, encouraging a return to the land.

Sahel: Restoring soil fertility

Funded by Finland and the World Food Programme, villagers are using community forestry to tackle desertification and fuel scarcity in the Sahel. Groundnut yields have dropped alarmingly. Efforts to raise them have led to exhausted soil and need for costly fertilizer. The new forestry programme offers training and payment, as acacia and eucalyptus are interplanted with groundnuts.

New Zealand: Staggered planting

Woodhill Forest, started in the 1930s to halt an encroaching 150m-high dune, is now densely covered. Staggered plantings of grass, shrubs and pines checked the sand. The wood supplies Auckland, and cattle are pastured, their grazing preventing the smothering of saplings by invasive grass. Foresters, farmers and wildlife are brought together.

Ecuador's forest plan

Although largely jungle, Ecuador has lost 90% of tree cover in the southwest due to land pressure. Its Forest Plan, launched in 1985 from petroleum revenues, is one of the best in South America. Loans enable farmers to plant and maintain forests, with repayment deferred until the trees mature.

parliament's) freedom of decision-making, the human rights of the citizens, the independent development of the society or the viability of the state. In other words, security meant the protection of the territorial integrity and political independence of the country. This security against external military threats was to be achieved by armed forces. This view of security is leading us to destruction, nuclear and ecological.

Fundamentally, we need a change of attitude. We need it in the establishment of a real détente between the USA and the USSR, between North and South, East and West. We need it in ridding ourselves of "images of the enemy" and in putting the military threat in its true perspective. We need it in a renewed and resolute effort to achieve the control of military technology, nuclear disarmament and an end to the arms trade. We need it to banish poverty, use our economies to support long-term survival, and act out of concerted care for Gaian systems and species.

Until this time, people will demand some military defence as the nuclear arsenals and conventional forces are reduced. Conventional weapons today are extremely destructive; the choice for many, Europe especially, is not between nuclear or conventional war, but between war – and destruction – or no war. The sole aim of any interim military defence should be to reduce the risk of war. Limited lethality of weapons, purely defensive technologies, and restriction within national borders would all serve as safeguards.

And until sustainable livelihood and relationships with resources are established, we may face some fairly draconian measures to protect environments, and need to take drastic and expensive holding actions – to provide a minimum income for the poor, to redistribute land and wealth, to prevent further inequities arising.

Redefining security

In the long run, though, we can only survive in a disarmed world, where military technology is forbidden ever again to lead us down this path. In such a world, how "policing" and "sanctions" will be managed will no doubt not be difficult to arrange – nations no longer in fear will not find it so difficult to concede sovereignty.

And in the long run, we can only survive in living partnership with natural resources, through sustainable and co-operative technologies and human behaviour. How sanctions and policing will be applied here, too, will be much easier to decide for generations not plagued by poverty and distorted sets of values, but participating in local and global governance.

We must redefine security. True security rests on a supportive and sustainable ecological base, on spiritual as well as material well-being, on trust and reliance on one's neighbours, on justice and understanding in a disarmed world. Getting there requires all our present institutions – nations, states, the United Nations, the banks and commercial companies, the major alliances, the superpowers – to take concerted action. Real security is common security. It can only be won *with*, not against, all people, and all species, of Gaia.

Redefining security

As we approach the end of the 20th century the concept of security is being redefined. This redefinition is urgent because the daily survival of people in all countries, their human rights, and the viability of their governments are being jeopardized by problems of local, regional and global scale. The new security recognizes the growth of political, social, economic, and even military interdependencies between nations. And it seeks to address the threatening crises of economic collapse, pollution, population pressures, widening poverty gaps, food shortages, climate change, and decline of life systems such as soil, fresh water, genetic material, and forests. Security is also coming to mean security of the foundations of peace – consensus, law, social justice and sustainable development.

Environmental security

True environmental security will depend on an ecologically wise economy, sustainable livelihood for all, and a re-integration of human and natural systems. It will seek to achieve:

- Prevention of climate change
- Population stabilization
- Forest and wilderness protection

- Soil conservation
- Security of gene base
- Security of ecosystems and species
- Security from toxic pollutants
- Waste management and re-use
- Access to efficient, clean energy
- Management of nonrenewables
- Protection of global commons
- Protection of water cycles
- An end to environmental refugeeism

Human and civil security

Human security rests on economic, environmental and spiritual security, and on the eradication of structural violence within society. It seeks to provide:

- Adequate life and health expectancy
- A secure home and shelter
- Secure food and water supplies

- Security of land and tenure
- Security of income and sustainable livelihood
- Social security
- Human rights security
- Participatory governance
- Access to rewarding work
- Access to law and justice
- Access to education
- Equality of opportunity for sexes, races, religions, ages

Security is thus redefined as the provision of basic human needs – food, water, shelter, health, education, and so on – on a sustainable and permanent basis, and also of social justice, human opportunity and freedom from oppression. (The diagram below is adapted from one originated by the London Centre for International Peacebuilding, discussed by the Generals for Peace and Disarmament.) Security covering this wide range of elements can no longer be achieved through military force – if it ever was – nor can it be achieved unilaterally. Security for one's own country must take into account that of one's neighbours. Security in the broad sense can, in today's world and tomorrow's, only be achieved with other countries; it can no longer be achieved against them.

Peace-keeping security

The best defensive strategy is to remove any aggressor's desire to use force by – lessening fear and tension; reducing the likely gain; and increasing the likely cost. Lessening fear depends on co-operation and disarmament. Reducing gains depends much on civil non-co-operation; increasing likely costs depends on sanctions by the global community.

Ultimately, fear can only be removed by gaining environmental, economic, human and spiritual security and by general disarmament. With verification that no military build-ups occur, peace-keeping will be needed:

1 Locally – via policing, conflict resolution and law.
2 Nationally – via law, police and diplomacy. No military.
3 Regionally – via policing for control of terrorism, crime, etc., and via negotiated conflict resolution. No military.
4 Globally – via UN forces, conflict resolution teams and international courts.

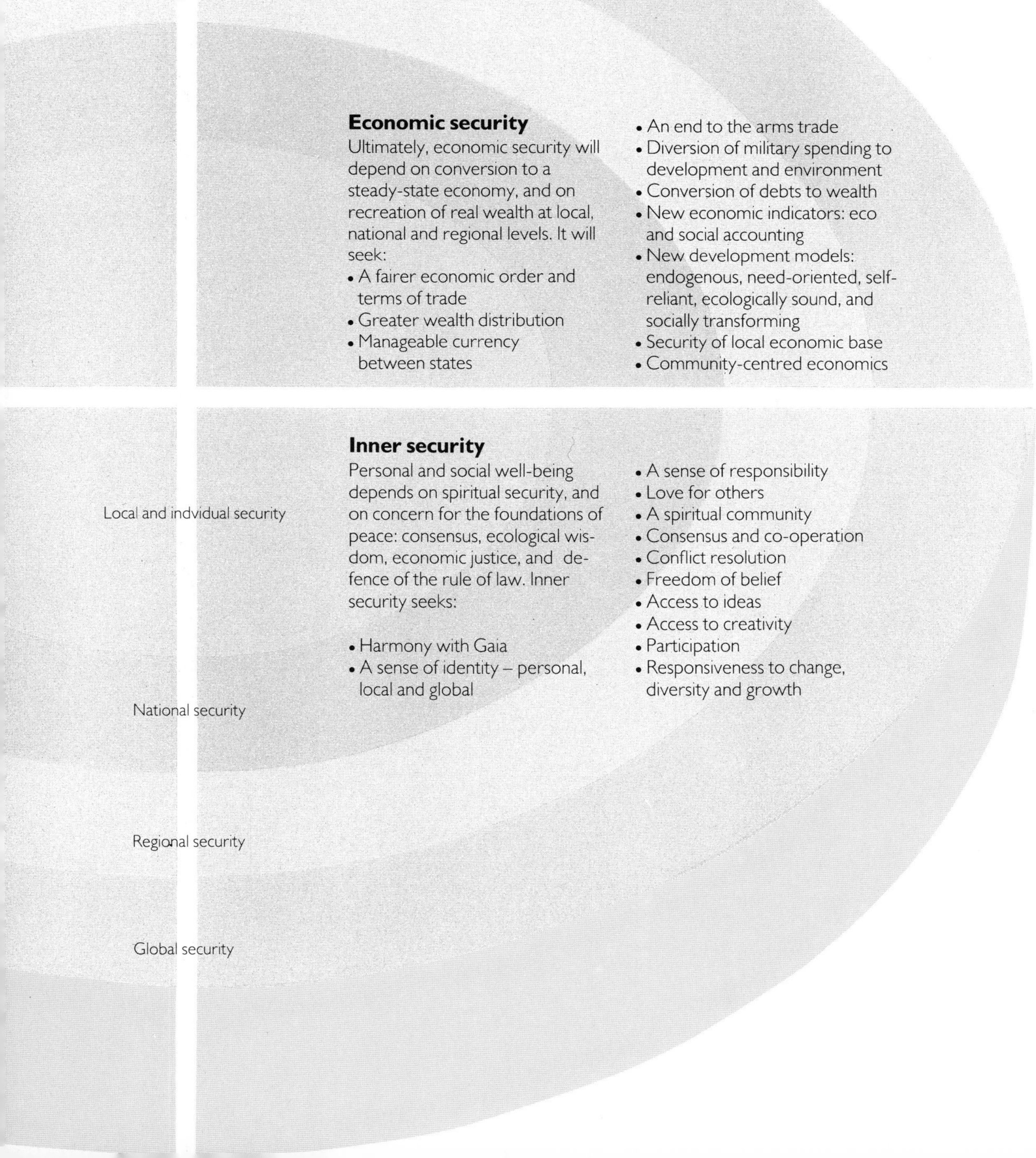

Economic security

Ultimately, economic security will depend on conversion to a steady-state economy, and on recreation of real wealth at local, national and regional levels. It will seek:

- A fairer economic order and terms of trade
- Greater wealth distribution
- Manageable currency between states
- An end to the arms trade
- Diversion of military spending to development and environment
- Conversion of debts to wealth
- New economic indicators: eco and social accounting
- New development models: endogenous, need-oriented, self-reliant, ecologically sound, and socially transforming
- Security of local economic base
- Community-centred economics

Local and individual security

Inner security

Personal and social well-being depends on spiritual security, and on concern for the foundations of peace: consensus, ecological wisdom, economic justice, and defence of the rule of law. Inner security seeks:

- Harmony with Gaia
- A sense of identity – personal, local and global
- A sense of responsibility
- Love for others
- A spiritual community
- Consensus and co-operation
- Conflict resolution
- Freedom of belief
- Access to ideas
- Access to creativity
- Participation
- Responsiveness to change, diversity and growth

National security

Regional security

Global security

9 Redirection: A sustainable future

Introduced by Maurice F. Strong

The arrangements that people have made for governing their relationships with each other have, since the dawn of human history, progressed through a number of levels: from the family to the tribe to the village to the town to the city to the city-state, and in our own times, to the nation state. The process was an integral aspect of civilization itself – increasing complexity, specialization, interdependence, and economic and social development and common security needs.

While nation states vigorously defend and assert their own sovereignty and resist threats to it from whatever source, the world which gave rise to them has continued to change at an accelerating pace. The increasing intensity and complexity of human activity, which science and technology have made possible, and the emergence of a global economy, and the equally global capacity for nuclear destruction, have created a situation in which no national government, however powerful, can effectively care for the interests or secure the future of its people on a unilateral basis. The same imperatives which led to the creation of the present nation state system inevitably and inexorably are moving us towards the creation of a world system of governance.

Yet everywhere today we see disturbing signs of a retreat from the concept of co-operative internationalism on which creation of such a system depends. This has reached crisis proportions. Today we have the paradox that, in a world where the objective need for an effective international system of governance has grown immensely, the United Nations, the essential element in that system, is weaker, less effective, and enjoys vastly less confidence and support from both public and governments than it did at the time of its creation.

The majority of the UN membership, eg. the non-great powers, must take the lead in remaking the United Nations. Even without revision of the Charter, there is much they can do. They can take the UN much more seriously themselves, and commit to being bound by its decisions. Majority votes must begin to have real meaning. And there must be a greater identification of the United Nations with the constituencies on which it depends, the ministers of governments and officials of world institutions, key actors in international affairs. The United Nations must also reach out to the great variety of constituencies, and potential constituencies, represented by non-governmental organizations.

Revision of the UN Charter will ultimately come. The present anomalous situation, in which the United Nations differs from all other levels of governance, gives it neither a direct access to its constituency nor taxing power. It is unlikely that any nation could function on this basis. When Charter revision comes, I hope we will have advanced to a point at which these deficiencies in the United Nations as the prime organ of the global level, the ultimate level, of governance can be redressed.

These changes will come about not because people embrace the concept of world government. World *government* as such is not, in my view, either practicable or desirable. But the evolution of a world *system* is an absolute imperative if civilized life is to continue. The United Nations is the essential centrepiece of that system. If it did not exist we would have to create it. Even more today than when it was created, the United Nations continues to reflect and enshrine the hopes and aspirations of the entire human family and the imperatives for its future survival and well-being.

"With a terrible ferocity I want you to be born whole. I want clean air for you to breathe and safe water to drink and living woodlands and fields for you to run in. The chances for that seem slim, given the destructive forces our society has unleashed. Yet more and more of us are waking up, more and more of us are working together to try to heal the world. Because it is your world too."
Joanna Macy: *To Our Children's Children*

Future society cannot be much like the present. Unless we solve the problems facing us, we shall not survive: and they will not be solved by the means we use today. The most present institutions can achieve is emergency measures to get us as far as the 21st century. Unless we evolve longer-term solutions, poverty, pollution, pestilence, urban violence, and war will increase until we destroy our civilization, and perhaps even humankind. Some believe that increasingly authoritarian control, perhaps even an authoritarian world government, will emerge – able to conserve resources and ensure law and order, but severely restricting basic freedoms. Others pin their hopes on science and high technology, and a greatly accelerated industrial development and economic growth.

This book argues that neither authoritarianism nor technology is the answer. We need a radical change of direction – to global *self-governance*, decentralized societies and a partnership between human and Gaian ecosystems, leading to a peaceful world that encourages social justice through sustainable development.

The last chapter spelled out the measures that must be taken, and in some cases are being started, to improve immediate security and development. They fall far short of what we need for a peaceful and sustainable civilization. But they can gain us time and lay the framework for such a world. While these measures are taking effect, we must start work now, to end the threats of nuclear and ecological catastrophe for good.

The framework for a future

The Earth's carrying capacity is finite. Technology can increase this capacity, but only to a limited extent. Our population may reach 8 billion, but no technological fixes are likely to allow a much higher number to be supported. If population goes higher, disasters – world war, pestilence, famines – are inevitable. A levelling off of population is likely to be achieved partly by birth control, partly by rising standards of living created by a better use of fuels, technology and land, which will reduce the necessity for large families.

More energy efficiency and conservation in industrial countries could reduce the demand for energy by 20 per cent or so over the next two or three decades. This, and production efficiency generally, will reduce the demand by the North for scarce resources. Efficiency will also mitigate the demand for energy and resources in the developing world, bringing larger increases in living standards for each increment of extra energy.

Economic constraints will increasingly limit military budgets. Higher expectations and life expectancies of

Eradicating the roots of war

War is deeply rooted in society. For society to develop to its full potential, we must learn to eradicate the roots of war. This involves far more than just curtailing physical violence: *structural* violence must be minimized, and the problem of élites and vested interests tackled. The deprivation of the one billion undernourished is the most pressing issue, but all the roots of peace need to be restored if we are to effect genuine, lasting change. And all these changes are entirely dependent on raising the consciousness of the world population. On what do we base a choice about the world's future if not on an understanding of its problems? This may seem like the most impossible part of the task, but the seeds are already there: religious leaders are more aware of their role and the NGOs are also sharing the burden with the traditional education system. A difficult challenge is facing humanity. But we have nothing to lose, everything to gain and, in the words of Abdu'l-Baha, a leader of the Baha'i faith: "Why not try peace for a while? If we find war is better, it will not be difficult to fight again."

Consensus achieved
Attempts to maintain the unity and stability of society by force are a root cause of upheaval and war. Conversely, the dramatic social changes now needed can only be achieved with strong public support. Humanity must have a sense of belonging to a larger whole. The major religions already promote global consciousness and we may gain this unity through spirituality.

Ecology sustained
Our relationship with the environment needs to be sustainable at all levels. To help ensure this, the responsibility for monitoring and controlling ecological sustainability can be vested in existing councils at village, town and regional levels. The individual household has to understand its impact on the ecology as much as any large corporation, and the work of NGOs is vital to this.

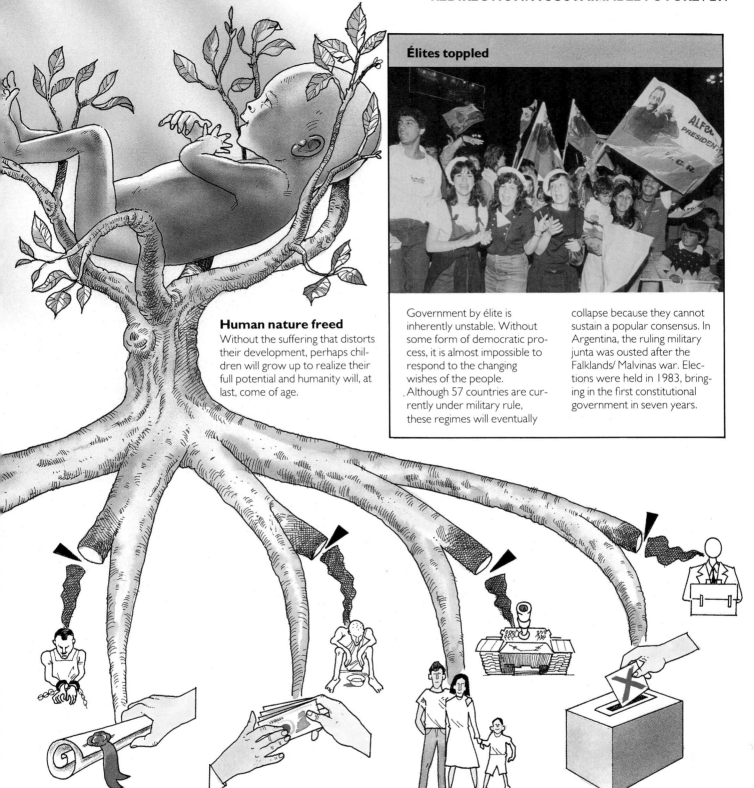

Élites toppled

Government by élite is inherently unstable. Without some form of democratic process, it is almost impossible to respond to the changing wishes of the people. Although 57 countries are currently under military rule, these regimes will eventually collapse because they cannot sustain a popular consensus. In Argentina, the ruling military junta was ousted after the Falklands/ Malvinas war. Elections were held in 1983, bringing in the first constitutional government in seven years.

Human nature freed

Without the suffering that distorts their development, perhaps children will grow up to realize their full potential and humanity will, at last, come of age.

Law empowered

International law must override national law on issues concerning human rights, the environment and global security. This requires the explicit support of individual nations. Individuals and minority groups should be allowed access to international courts, and there must be an international code of practice governing the many different activities of transnational groups and corporations.

Wealth redistributed

Before any other changes can be wrought, deprivation must be tackled. This will require decentralized control of the means of wealth creation. With all investment managed locally we can ensure that the returns on that investment accrue to the local populace. Globally, reform of the international financial system is needed, plus transfer and conversion of the South's debt.

Real security

Security must be redefined to take account of non-military threats, and greater emphasis on conflict-resolution techniques at all levels of society is essential. It will be necessary to retain local civil policing and, in order to maintain enough global stability for other changes to take place, the UN must have the power to enforce sanctions – there must be a supranational police force.

Just governance

If we are to achieve popular world governance in the foreseeable future we will do best to modify existing institutions rather than trying to start fresh ones. A world government is no solution – it would be susceptible to the same distortions as any élite organization. The UN, with the addition of a second (peoples') assembly, has the potential to be a just system of world governance.

people in the industrialized countries will require more and more resources for social welfare systems. And the demand for more equitable distribution of wealth between countries will require a flow of capital from the North to the South. The money can only come from military budgets. The need to balance trade and national budgets will also constrain military spending in many developed countries. In developing countries, pressures for more social justice will equally limit the financial and personnel resources devoted to military activities. Economic necessity will steadily produce a worldwide diversion of funds from military to civilian use.

We can expect some success in the next few decades in reafforestation; in control of soil erosion and desertification; in reduction of atmospheric pollution – and, therefore, the slowing of climate change; in provision, where needed, of food, safe water, medical services, sanitation; and so on. The international economic order is likely to become less chaotic. The world debt crisis will be at least partly resolved and a fairer system devised to set commodity prices and the terms of trade.

While such changes are occurring, the education system will be preparing citizens' minds for the 21st century. The world a hundred years from now will be as different from that today, as today's world is from the 19th century. People's thinking will be equally changed.

Education will teach people what real security is; that there are many non-military threats to security; that an eco-disaster is as great a threat as a nuclear world war; and that the link between military force and security is no longer valid. More contact between people, more travel, more cultural exchange, and, above all, the universal spread of mass media will change our images of each other, including images of the enemy.

People will no longer judge affairs in terms of what is good for national security, but what is best for the human family, for regional and world security. Global loyalty will replace national loyalty; Gaian planetary concerns outweigh short-term difficulties and concerns. Internationalism will replace nationalism, as the strongest driving force at all levels of society.

This educational task will not be as difficult as it may seem. Organized violence and warfare are relatively recent phenomena; co-operative drives are stronger than aggressive ones; people desperately want to live their lives in peace. Few will deny the need to renounce war, eliminate structural violence, and achieve a peaceful, co-operative, sustainable and creative world. We may enter the next millennium prepared for peace.

Converting military industry for peace

The global arms race is not only a permanent threat to peace but also an enormous, pointless waste of human, scientific, technical, natural and economic resources. Examples abound. Just half a day's military spending would pay for the whole programme of the World Health Organization to wipe out malaria. For the cost of one modern main battle tank 1000 classrooms could be built for 30,000 children; another two would pay for the equipment in the classrooms. A jet fighter would pay for

40,000 village pharmacies; a destroyer provide 9 million people with electricity. And a ten-year programme to provide the main food requirements for all the developing countries and wipe hunger off the face of the earth would cost *less than six months' expenditure on arms.*

There are growing demands that military spending be cut back in all countries and at least some of the resources freed devoted to development – "swords into ploughshares, tanks into tractors". That military industries can be converted to civilian purposes is shown by the outcome of the 1972 Biological Weapon Convention. This banned the production and development of biological weapons. American biological weapon establishments and personnel were then converted to civilian medical establishments.

The major barriers to conversion are the fears of unemployment among workers, and of loss of profit-making among management, in armaments industries – fears that are played on by establishment and military hawks. The European Trade Union Institute believes these barriers would be reduced by: National Conversion Agencies, working to attract alternative employment and industries to areas affected by reductions in military production; guaranteed continued employment for workers affected by reduced military budgets; and staged "diversification" agreements concluded between governments and major defence contractors.

Conversion is a key to disarmament. Conditions for its success must be established, because until it is proven that conversion can succeed without social and economic disruption, achieving far-reaching arms cuts will be politically difficult. Conversion can hinder progress – or oil the wheels of a global society that disarms and develops until militarism yields to peace.

Conversion and development

Conversion is essential, too, for sustainable development: and not only for financial reasons, but also to divert skilled scientific and technical manpower. The South's development problems – particularly those of dealing with the increase in populations, the food crisis, natural disasters and the effects of war; of pollution control, of providing new sources of energy and transport and resources while preserving the environment; of urbanization; of reducing poverty and improving standards of health, diet, education and housing – all make claims on investment, research and other resources in direct competition with military sectors.

So many of the world's scientists and engineers are working in military science only that there are too few left to deal with problems of development. The skills tied up in military research and development and the managerial, administrative and logistical ability of the armed services are vital for, and could rather quickly be diverted to, the work of sustainable development.

Military training produces operationally oriented people, who like to get things done efficiently. They could be a crucial resource. The fight against infectious diseases, particularly those of childhood, for example, offers a challenge suitable for military logistic planning.

The TGWU Arms Conversion Strategy

The 1.35 million strong Transport and General Workers' Union (TGWU) has been a consistent opponent of nuclear weapons since the 1950s, when it led the campaign against Britain's H-Bomb. In 1981 the Biennial Conference reaffirmed Union policy in favour of unilateral disarmament and asked its members to support the World Disarmament Campaign.

The TGWU believes that conversion from arms to socially useful production would facilitate the disarmament process; produce greater stability and enhance employment prospects for armaments workers; provide a stimulus to economic growth by diverting resources to civil production; and allow urgent social needs to be met. The Union is aware that, since 1963, 600,000 jobs have been lost in the defence industry, despite massive increases in spending.

During March 1987, the TGWU organized a Conversion Conference. Twenty-two unions from ten European countries took part. An analysis presented at the conference showed that defence workers were losing jobs because of the Western switch to nuclear weapon dependency, the increasing technological sophistication of weapons, and the intense world competition in the arms trade. The conference explored the broader economic and social arguments for employing capital in socially useful production as opposed to weapons manufacture. These had to be seen in the context of massive Third World problems and Western unemployment.

From the conference it was evident to the TGWU that there existed a real foundation in private and public defence sectors for developing the basic ideas of arms conversion. Such ideas will now be developed in full through international trades union conferences. Conversion provides a positive alternative to the imminent self-generated crisis faced by Western arms industries. But any progress also requires unions to campaign actively for peace and disarmament.

Trade unionists pledging their support for CND. From left to right are Brian Nicholson and Walter Greendale of the TGWU, and Rodney Bickerstaffe of the National Union of Public Employees (NUPE), 24 October 1984.

Socially useful products

As the defence industries become increasingly capital intensive, many defence-dependent jobs are being lost. Aware of the need to redeploy armaments workers in civil industry, both local and central governments are responding to union initiatives on arms conversion. Proposals first put forward by union leaders at Lucas Aerospace in the UK have now been taken up by local authorities around the country. The Sheffield City Council has spent five years developing a conversion initiative which has culminated in a complex for socially useful products. This facility, known as SCEPTRE, is sited in the Sheffield Science Park. The City Council is currently bidding to locate a National Product Development Network in Sheffield and encouraging other local authorities to follow suit. Indeed, central government in the UK has set up Defence Technology Enterprises to explore how technology could be transferred from military to civilian applications.

In Minnesota, USA, an Economic Conversion Task Force was set up in 1985 with the financial backing of two state departments. Delegates from the Task Force attended the UK Local Authority Conference on Economic and Arms Conversion, held in 1987 in Sheffield. They were so encouraged by the conversion initiatives taken in Sheffield that representatives were invited back to Minnesota in March 1988. The Task Force hopes to expand similar schemes in the US. A product development centre has been established and research undertaken into the durability of military contracts in Minnesota. Vulnerable contracts are identified for potential state assistance with future conversion plans, and the Task Force is investigating the feasibility of using defence electronics workshops to make medical equipment.

Interior and exterior views of the Sheffield Science Park in the UK – a business and innovation centre developed with financial backing from central government and the EEC, which opened in March 1988.

The military has always paid attention to epidemic disease, to food hygiene, and to the management of water and waste under field conditions. In 1963-4, when cholera hit Iran, the army implemented nation-wide measures, establishing a *cordon sanitaire* and organizing chemoprophylaxis and vaccination. In Brazil, too, vaccination has drawn on military assistance.

Some 90 million children are born annually in the developing countries. Less than 10 per cent receive immunization. Consequently, 5 million children die each year and the same number are crippled, blinded, mentally retarded or otherwise disabled for life because they contract diphtheria, pertussis, tetanus, measles, polio or tuberculosis. The fact that the risk of dying before adolescence is twenty times higher in some African states than in the industrialized countries is an unacceptable example of structural violence. The cost of immunizing each child is less than $5.

The scale of the problem cries out for military assistance. If the military in each developing country took on the job of vaccinating children we might have a chance of reaching the World Health Organization's stated goal: that infant mortality be reduced to less than 50 per 1000 live births (compared with 110 at present), and life expectancy increased to considerably more than 60 years (compared with 56 years at present) as measures of "health for all by the year 2000".

A military effort focused on childhood diseases could lead to expansion into other fields. Instead of fighting wars, the military could become preventers of war, the defenders of common security, with prestige to match – showing both the development, and the career, potential of conversion. Without conversion we cannot make the economic move to a peaceful and sustainable world.

Peace education

Adults are so imbued with old views of security – the belief that the main threat to society is the military ambition of another country to invade and occupy one's own – that it is extremely difficult to get them to accept new ideas. The radical change of re-defining security to take into account and address non-military threats to survival will demand education.

We are leaving a malign legacy to our children: yet we look to them with hope – hope that education will create a new generation who can grapple with the global problems facing us and evolve the institutions needed to solve them. Children, however, learn from all the adults they meet, not just teachers. And it is the present generation who must gain the world its breathing space. Parents and decision-makers have to be re-educated, too – so that they unlearn old attitudes, understand the need for radical change on a global scale, and apply this in their lives, work, and upbringing of citizens-to-be.

Peace education is gradually being introduced into schools, colleges, workers' associations and forward-looking businesses in various parts of the developed world. Peace educator David Hicks defines it as working in three ways. It sharpens young and adult awareness – about the existence of conflict between

Swords into ploughshares

"They shall beat their swords into ploughshares, and their spears into pruninghooks: nation shall not lift up sword against nation, neither shall they learn war any more." Isaiah 2:4

In a militarized world, we cannot assume that the fabric of the military order will come apart smoothly in response to political pressures for disarmament. If disarmament is to be achieved, the vested interests must be tackled and a comprehensive programme of econo-mic converson established. Policies will have to be developed to maintain the level of aggregate demand and provide employment for those whose jobs formerly depended on military spending. This would improve pro-ductivity in target industries and encourage further investment. Conversion involves far more than switching armaments factories to the production of socially useful products. It also involves redirecting people's skills into the development of alternative technologies and the conversion of the highly trained military to peaceful ends. In addition to their potential as a war-prevention force and conflict-resolution specialists, military personnel constitute a large labour force for economic reconstruction.

The role of the people
The necessity of military security is firmly established in the public consciousness. Yet the release of military resources for economic and social development can only happen with public support. For only then will the politicians have an incentive to change the current system. If we are to break the circle of poverty and deprivation that stifles the South, and leads to instability and conflict, the princi-ple of global sharing must be grasped by all. Humanity must understand that our "choice" is between reshaping global society or perishing.

The vested interests

Militarism is entrenched in financial and social institutions, and a large part of the world economy is devoted to supporting military security. Those who manage and benefit from the military machine project images of unemployment, economic suffering and invasion as the consequences of demilitarization. Although their support, and their power, will fade with public awareness, it will be a slow process.

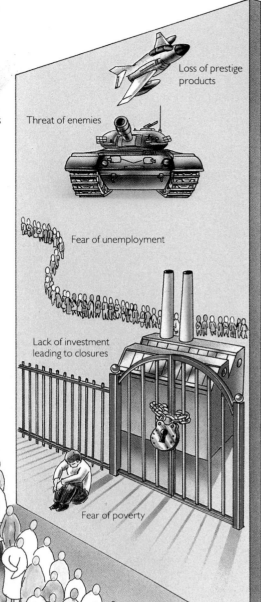

Loss of prestige products

Threat of enemies

Fear of unemployment

Lack of investment leading to closures

Fear of poverty

Ploughshares and pruning hooks

The potential rewards from arms conversion are enormous, even in those countries that earn a substantial income from the sale of armaments. Shifting to the manufacture of socially useful products strengthens the economy and generates greater employment opportunities as well as improving living standards. But each region requires an individual approach. It would be inappropriate to apply the same hi-tech solutions to the South that are beginning to have so much success in the North.

Afforestation

Hospitals

Housing

Water supplies

Education

If the control of this technology remained with the supplier countries it could only aggravate the problems of the South. More important, and more urgent, is the fulfilment of basic needs. The creation of an efficient and reliable infrastructure for the provision of essential services is imperative. Local peoples should also be encouraged to be self-sufficient, and to develop for themselves the necessary technology that will ease their transition out of the poverty trap.

The military workforce

The armed forces are an important resource and could help greatly with the process of conversion. They are an élite, highly trained and motivated potential labour force. In most countries, the military are called in to help in civil emergencies, and could, on a more or less permanent basis, help with development schemes – draining marshland, building homes and even reafforestation. There is also a considerable body of technical expertize in the military ranks – a help rather than a hindrance to conversion.

people and within and between states. It teaches us to investigate the causes of conflict and violence that are embedded within our individual perceptions, values and attitudes, and also in the social, political and economic structures of society. And it encourages a search for alternatives, including non-violence, and development of the skills, attitudes and knowledge we need to resolve conflict peacefully, and so work for a more just, sustainable and less-violent world.

Peace is more than the absence of violence; it is the positive presence of co-operation in society. Peace education thus tries to raise our understanding of the interdependence of individuals, groups and nations, and an appreciation of the biological and social factors that influence human behaviour. It encourages respect and a sense of responsibility for individual freedoms, for human rights, cultural diversity, and the environment, and thinking within global frameworks. And it develops the interpersonal skills needed to build more just and peaceable relationships – particularly our understanding of the nature of power, and the power relationships between individuals, groups and nations.

Various closely related subjects to peace education are now entering the fray. World studies, for example, promotes the knowledge, attitude and skills relevant to living responsibly in a multicultural and interdependent world. Studies include cultures and countries other than one's own, and the ways in which they are different and similar; major issues that face different countries and cultures; and how everyday life and experience affect, and are affected by, the issues of the wider world.

A pioneer in this field is World Studies 8-13. Jointly run by the One World Trust charity, and the Centre for Peace Studies in Lancaster, UK, the project is operating in some 45 local education areas in England and Wales. It offers a published framework for planning curricula on world studies, including a set of objectives and key concepts, and suggests strategies for running workshops and in-service courses with a world dimension. World Studies 8-13 is the only national curriculum project of its kind looking at global education in schools.

Education in peace and sustainable living is vital to our future – in schools, work places and adult classes; in the staff training of enterprises large and small; in commerce or professions or governments. Citizens of today and tomorrow have to begin, somehow, anywhere they can, to handle and resolve conflict well and to apply the environmental restraint and respect we must use. If national leaders were trained in these skills, and the bureaucrats and élites who presently obstruct change, we might see a very different world.

The new skills of conflict resolution

Conflict may be endemic in complex, changing systems, and even necessary and creative in many human relationships. But if unresolved, it will also be destructive. Human societies already have many institutions for conflict resolution, but these are failing us in our troubled world – and so too, it seems, are our personal conflict-handling skills. The escalation to coercion,

Neve Shalom – school for peace

The peace of the world will depend on future generations being trained from youth in conflict resolution and co-operation. This is particularly important in communities divided by ethnic hatred and suspicion, such as Sri Lanka, South Africa, Northern Ireland and the Middle East.

The community of Neve Shalom, which means Oasis of Peace, was founded in Israel by a Dominican monk in 1972. Independent of any outside control or political affiliation, Neve Shalom aims to foster universal acceptance of the principle of harmonious co-existence in Israel. Within its walls, Jewish and Arab (Christian and Muslim) families and individuals live together peacefully, free from prejudice and in a spirit of mutual tolerance and respect. The Friends of Neve Shalom, which promotes and raises funds for the community, has branches in 12 countries throughout the world.

The School for Peace at Neve Shalom was set up by members in 1978 as a separate project strictly for those not living within the community. Aimed primarily at teenagers, some of whom are shown in the photograph below, the school offers workshops, seminars and summer camps with places split equally between Jewish and Arab participants. Qualified staff teach students the importance of an awareness of their own cultural and religious heritage, and respect for the differing views of their neighbours. Students learn to agree to differ, and the living proof of this positive outlook can be observed in the daily life of the Neve Shalom community. In Israel, the Ministry of Education has given official recognition to the School for Peace, recommending that pupils from all schools should participate in the workshops. Teachers and counsellors attend groups and courses in towns and villages, both Jewish and Arab, throughout Israel. Only two problems have arisen: the shortage of staff to cope with the great demand for teaching, and the need for additional accommodation to cater for increasing numbers of visitors.

Links with Northern Ireland

In 1984, a Northern Irish group called Holiday Projects West invited two Jewish and two Arab counsellors from Neve Shalom to visit them and demonstrate the community's techniques and ideas. Holiday Projects, a registered charity, provides holidays and work-camps for needy children and teenagers from both Protestant and Catholic backgrounds. Its aim is to improve relations between the two conflicting sections of the community. Holiday Projects felt that it could learn much from the techniques of co-operation, affirmation and conflict resolution taught in the School for Peace. The visit was wholly successful, and in 1987 a group of Protestant and Catholic Irish teachers visited the School in Israel.

In response to growing concern for the future, peace schools and universities are multiplying around the world. One of these, the Atlantic College, was set up in Wales in 1962 as part of the United World Colleges Movement. There are at present six member colleges – in Wales, Canada, Singapore, Italy, and the US. The Movement brings together 16-19 year old students from all parts of the world, teaching them to live, study and work together in a socially aware and responsible way. At the Atlantic College, students serve the local community by running the inshore lifeboat and other rescue and social services. Developing an international perspective and awareness of cultures other than the students' own are prime objectives of the College. Course requirements include learning a foreign language, world history and a subject called the Study of Man, designed specifically to foster greater intercultural understanding.

Peace Studies is taught as part of the well-respected International Baccalaureate, a six-subject diploma accepted as a university entrance qualification. The Peace Studies syllabus examines issues at three levels – individual, social and international. The roots of human aggression are examined on the individual level; issues such as apartheid in South Africa and the Irish problem are part of the course, which analyses structural violence in society; subjects such as the Arms Race, Superpower Conflict, and the Theory and Practice of Non-violence are part of the international dimension of the syllabus. The rationale of the Peace Studies course at the Atlantic College is education for citizenship in a democratic society so that decisions on international and controversial issues can be made on an informed, critical basis.

Principal Andrew Stuart with students from some of the 60 countries represented at the Atlantic College in Wales.

Continued industrial development and the protection of the environment need not be incompatible. Large multinational companies could play a vital role in pioneering technologies better suited to human and planetary well-being. A number of companies, such as British Petroleum, Glaxo and IBM, now have strong environmental programmes. BP's specialist group, Environmental Services Department, issues guidelines and standards to all its operating companies; caring for the environment is an integral part of each manager's responsibilities, and environmental sessions are incorporated into all the company's management and training courses. BP also uses its expertise to train the staff of environmental charities and other NGOs in business management techniques.

Recognition of BP's concern for the environment came from the World Environment Center in New York, when BP was awarded the Center's 1988 Gold Medal for International Corporate Environmental Achievement. BP was chosen because of its Environmental Protection Management programme, which stringently researches and assesses the environmental impact of any new projects, monitors existing projects and measures the efficacy of protective steps taken to safeguard the environment. Two outstanding examples of BP's policy in action are the Wytch Farm Oilfield development in the UK, and the Prudhoe Bay enterprise in Alaska, where ramps were built over some sections of an oil pipeline to enable migrating caribou to cross.

BP's environmental policy is implemented for all projects from inception to termination, in over 70 countries. Its commitment to educating management on environmental issues can be seen as a model for industry worldwide. But controlling local environmental impact is not enough. The oil industry could do much to find solutions to broader environmental issues, such as the impact of CO_2 on climate.

The large picture shows a trenching machine laying BP's North Sea oil pipeline through a field in Perthshire, Scotland. Inset is a photograph taken from the same spot two years later.

litigation and punishment, or to frustrated violence, is too rapid. If we are to build a peaceful, disarmed world, we shall have to learn how to resolve conflicts by co-operation and consensus, not coercion.

The trick is to see not the conflict, but the problem. Conflicts demand a winner and loser; if we avoid them, or compromise for short-term ends, they resurface. Problems suggest that we seek a solution, to please both parties. As John Groom explains, applying this wisdom to international relations requires choosing situations in which consideration of the parties' joint problem is possible, and avoiding ones where "the prosecution of the conflict by negotiation and bargaining is the main aim". He sees non-violent and non-coercive conflict resolution as "designed to create a situation in which all parties feel that they have, according to their own criteria, 'won' and not merely have done well in a situation where there are winners and losers".

In most conflicts, those involved have incomplete information about the problem, not knowing in any detail the objectives and motives of the other side. A person skilled in resolving conflict non-violently will show the disputants that their definition of the problem needs revision and they may have misunderstood "the perception of other parties about the nature of the dispute". The point is to establish a new set of relationships, self-sustaining and independent of any outside coercion or intervention. It is, in Groom's words, "not a settlement imposed by a victor or a powerful third party, but rather (one) freely and knowledgeably arrived at by the parties themselves".

All too often, those locked in international conflicts cannot win, even though they cannot be defeated; and they feel unable to stop the conflict even though it costs a lot to continue. The goal of problem-solving "is to get what the parties want at least cost, all things and people considered, in the long run. It emphasizes a long-run perspective." Solving this type of deadlock may require a third party facilitator to get the combatants to define the problem and "think about an acceptable future relationship, putting aside, however hard it may be, the past relationship". He or she will help them break the conflict down into "manageable components so that, at the end of the day, there will be something, no matter how trivial, on which there can be agreement".

Whatever technique is used, non-violent conflict resolution depends on the establishment of trust and good communication. In the words of biologist Graham Kemp: "Human contact and communication is essential to the promotion of non-violence, and human perception can alter the reality of our behaviour."

Interconnecting approaches

We have seen that global problems are all interlocked. An increasing world population worsens the North-South poverty gap. Poverty and over-consumption, in turn, increase pollution and the risk of eco-disaster. As we approach such a disaster, the risk of a nuclear world war increases. And so on. Just as the problems are interlocked, so must the solutions be. To eradicate

Conflict resolution techniques

Conflict will not disappear from the world when we have done away with armaments. The conflicts that do exist must be recognized, managed and resolved. With a genuinely co-operative attitude, techniques of conflict resolution can be applied to solve the underlying problem. Such techniques are equally applicable to international diplomacy, industrial relations or personal relationships. They rely on a clear definition and analysis of the problem, open communication, trust, good faith, a desire for security, an understanding of the needs and goals of both parties involved, and on their willingness to co-operate. Each side *must* be able to drop its preconceptions about the other, and to focus on the problem rather than the personalities involved. There must also be an absence of coercion or threats. Training in conflict-resolution techniques often involves role-playing games such as those described here. The Prisoner's Dilemma is familiar from superpower negotiations. The ultimate aim of effective conflict resolution is to move away from a framework in which one side wins and the other loses, to a "win-win" situation which satisfies both parties.

Responses to conflict
People faced with a conflict may behave in one of five ways, but only the approach that attempts to solve the problem will resolve the conflict in the long term:

1 Coercion One side forces the other to acquiesce, getting what it wants at the other's expense – leading to further conflict.
2 Avoidance One or both parties withdraw from or avoid conflict. But the conflict does not go away.
3 Smoothing The emphasis is on areas of agreement. Disagreements are completely ignored. Again conflict is likely to recur.
4 Compromise Parties bargain so that each side gains part of what it wants but relinquishes the rest. This may provide a short-term solution, but does not get to the root of the problem.
5 Problem solving Parties face up to the conflict and agree to co-operate in finding a solution that meets the needs of both sides, without either side feeling that it has lost.

START HERE

Playing the game
Ugli orange game
Role-playing games provide an experimental approach to understanding conflict. One, devised by the Centre for Conflict Resolution in Wisconsin, involves two fictional competitors, one of whom has developed a synthetic vapour made from the rind of the rare Ugli orange. The other has developed a synthetic serum made from the juice. There is only a limited number of Ugli oranges available, creating a competitive situation. The purpose of the game is to see how both competitors can arrive at a satisfactory solution that meets both their needs. At the start neither is aware that they can share the oranges.

Prisoner's dilemma
This game was developed with the aim of discovering the most effective strategy for encouraging co-operation: two suspects are questioned separately by the police. If both stick to their story they will be charged with a lesser crime. If both turn State's witness they will be punished. If one defects, while the other sticks to the original story, one will be punished, the other will be rewarded. It was found that long-term co-operation can be encouraged if certain ground rules are followed: avoid envy and cleverness and co-operate for as long as the other person does – that is, do not be the first to defect.

Lost in space
This game demonstrates that group decision making can work very smoothly if consensus is used to arrive at decisions. Played by a group of about six people, the game revolves around a space crew stranded in a damaged spacecraft. The crew has been left with 15 intact items: a box of matches; food concentrate; 50 feet of nylon rope; parachute silk; portable heating unit; two pistols; dehydrated milk; two oxygen tanks; stellar map; life raft; magnetic compass; five gallons of water; flares; first-aid kit; solar-powered receiver/transmitter. The group must prioritize the items using consensus.

Co-operation is better than conflict
Neither donkey will eat while it perceives only its own hunger and the food under its nose. But with an awareness of each other's needs they can co-operate and share the food. Conflict and competition are frequently presented as endemic to humankind, natural instincts without which there can be no success. By contrast, thinkers have argued that the urge to co-operate is a fundamental impulse without which species cannot survive.

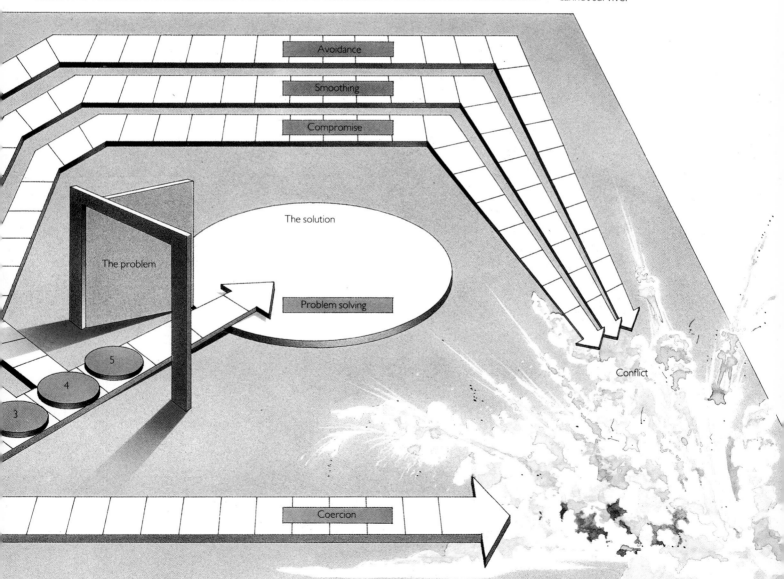

present structural violence we will have to achieve sustainable development; this will take a harmonious integration of human systems with the planetary ecosystem. Building positive peace and social justice is a long-term process, involving the efforts of governments, non-governmental organizations and of all of us.

If we are going to evolve the political and social institutions needed to achieve sustainable development, we shall have to give up some national sovereignty. Since governments are unlikely to relinquish sovereignty unless prompted by considerable pressure from public opinion, NGOs and citizens must become involved in the process of change.

We have to evolve new systems of governance. Our major institutions, set up in the 1940s or earlier, are out of date. The functions of state governments, whether capitalist, socialist or communist, and our models of economic systems and of international and regional bodies, do not reflect the complexity and dangers of today's world. National governments and international organizations are increasingly unable to cope.

Governance is no longer achieved by governments alone. The functions of governance, involving all the co-operative interactions between people, are increasingly administered by transnational organizations – NGOs, multinational corporations, professional bodies (medical, scientific, legal, etc.), financial institutions, and so on – that operate independently of nations.

The future demands a wider understanding of the complexity of the global community – in particular, of the interlocking and overlapping nature of all our systems of governance, whether dealing with law, economics, environmental matters, politics, commerce, or whatever. We need to understand that action in one field has reactions elsewhere and that action on one level – local, national, regional or international – has repercussions on others. The old type of narrow thinking – based mainly on jealously guarded national and commercial interests – is no longer adequate.

Shaping a new society

Instead, we need to adopt a holistic approach, based on complex networks of responsibility and interaction. And one that recognizes that all systems of governance are comprised of people, and each of us is a producer, a consumer and a participant in governance. Our own actions create the systems that are often oppressive.

Today's systems of governance exploit the environment and damage people. They produce direct and structural violence, are divisive, increase social injustice, and often disregard human rights. But change is coming, from within the human community. Richard Falk describes this change as a series of local and specific responses by people to destructive forces that impinge on their own lives. This new wave of response is characterized by: "an emphasis on local, grass roots; the realization that information is power; the realization that how we act in 'private' spheres of family, workplace and personal relationships is 'politics'; and an understanding that religious traditions and institutions

Interlocking systems

Humanity's problems are inextricably intertwined. Multiplying population adds to the South's economic problems; poverty fuels environmental decline. These spark off local conflicts, drawing in Northern arms suppliers; and nuclear war in response to these conflicts is an ever-present threat. The cure for these ills will depend, too, on interlocking approaches.

Every person is both a producer and a consumer of goods, with an economic impact. Each of us also participates in systems of governance and law. And everybody has a spiritual and creative potential. Collectively, our influence at the local level is capable of defining national policies and regional agreements. Denying this influence, and our personal responsibility as organizers of society, we effectively disempower ourselves – and, indirectly, help to maintain global inequalities.

We have to recognize that we can act in a small way in our own lives – in the family or workplace – and can eventually influence even the most authoritarian government, if we express a firm commitment to honest action. Throughout the world, grass roots groups are emerging that attempt to address global problems locally. The Right Livelihood Award (*see below*) honours and supports such work.

Right livelihood

"Right livelihood" means living in equilibrium with the Earth, not extracting an unsustainable amount of resources, and taking responsibility for the consequences of our actions. A Right Livelihood Award was introduced in 1980 to honour and support work that faces the problems of humanity holistically and which pioneers practicable, replicable solutions. Since then, 27 people and projects have received the annual Award, popularly known as the "Alternative Nobel Prize". The main purpose of the Award is to project a message of hope and encourage small groups to work for the common good of humanity. It supports those who are working for peace and disarmament, human rights, sustainable economic development, environmental conservation, or human development, whether through the improvement of health and education, cultural and spiritual renewal, or by developing benign technologies. The photograph shows Wangari Maathai (*see page 91*) receiving the Award in 1984.

Governance

New systems of governance – no longer the responsibility of governments alone – must replace outdated ones. There must be greater understanding in the global community, of the way systems interlock. Action in one area has reactions elsewhere. Action on one level has repercussions elsewhere. Governance requires a holistic approach recognizing such interdependence.

Religion

The spiritual dimension of life is a positive, constructive force. Much religious activism supports peace and justice and "liberation theology" exists in several religions, particularly noticeable in churches in South Africa. The feminine emphasis, love of nature, and the creative imagination will be acknowledged more and more, challenging accepted conceptions of power and authority.

Law

Positive peace embodies sustainable development and human rights. Since these are predominantly supranational issues, peace will be achieved only if international law supersedes much of national law. International law has a role to play in protecting movements for radical change from the often limited vision of governments. For example, upholding the right to anti-nuclear protest.

Producer

Organizer

Consumer

Commerce

Private enterprise can play a constructive role, especially in agriculture. It no longer makes business sense to overwork tropical soils, or over-cut forests. Exhausted resources cannot provide a future income. The poor in the South and commercial investors can be brought together in a partnership that has benefits for both.

The arts and sciences

Art has a greater role to play in tomorrow's world. It will be made more accessible to all, instead of being the pursuit of a tiny élite. Scientific and technical skills, including those of the military, will become public property and be directed towards problem solving rather than creating weaponry.

Ten key values of the Green movement

The following list was devised in America by a "diverse group of people . . . working to build a new politics, which has kinship with Green movements around the World". It represents the basic values humanity must have.

1 Ecological wisdom

Humanity must operate with the understanding that we are a part of nature, not its owners.

2 Grass roots democracy

Developing systems that enable and encourage us to control decisions that affect our lives.

3 Responsibility for society

We each have a role to play in responding to human suffering in ways that promote dignity.

4 Non-violence

Developing effective alternatives to our current patterns of violence, at all levels.

5 Decentralization

Restoring power and responsibility to individuals, communities, institutions and regions.

6 Community-based economics

Redesigning work structures to encourage employee ownership and workplace democracy.

7 Post-patriarchal values

Replacing the ethics of dominance and control with more co-operative ways of interacting.

8 Respect for diversity

Honouring cultural, sexual and spiritual diversity within the context of social awareness.

9 Global responsibility

Trying to be of genuine assistance to grass roots groups in the developing countries.

10 Future focus

Thinking of the long-term future and not just in terms of our short-term self-interest.

can be and are being mobilized for constructive roles." People are learning, too, that the law and government can be involved positively in radical change; and that feminine energies are "contriving alternative images and conceptions of power, authority and order". "New tendencies," Falk says, "seek a non-violent, democratized, ecologically prudent, spiritually fulfilling, and joyous destiny for the species and planet earth."

Economics for a sustainable world

Yesterday's vision of continual economic growth and indefinite expansion is impossible in a planet of finite natural resources. And as ecological refugees in Africa flee from the breakdown in their environment, the old idea that development could come from the "trickle down" effect of economic growth in the rich industrialized countries has proved a deadly trap.

Tomorrow's world will depend on a radical transformation of our economic and monetary systems and values. The new economics will reflect the finite limits of the planet's resources and the overriding requirements of sustainable development and social justice. "Growth" must be in quality, instead of quantity.

For a start, we need to revise our indicators of growth. The GNP figures we now use measure personal and government expenditures on goods and services, plus investments – including spending on weapons, on health repair, prisons and pollution control. Thus, the more wars, ill health, alienation and mess we create, the more "productive" we seem to be. GNP measures neither the real costs of the damage to the environment by human activities, nor true wealth and income. True wealth includes, forests, water, soil, energy, human skills, social well-being, and the capital infrastructure of civilization. True income is the work of humans, the productivity of land, the flow of solar energy, the reproduction and diversity of species.

Current economic wisdom fails to distinguish between renewable and non-renewable resources. We cannot rely on market forces and the price mechanism to do this, and achieve a sustainable use of resources. The market will not provide clean air – because atmospheric polluters are not penalized until a disaster occurs; it will not guard the forests, because "managed" land is classifed as more "valuable" than the wild. We rely too much on measures of "throughput" in our economies, which ignore the health of the environment from which that income comes.

And when we measure economic performance, we ignore the true productivity of human beings. The "invisible" work of caring for families and voluntary work, and of arts, media, gardening, athletes, and so on, is excluded, even though it contributes greatly to social well-being and the quality of life. Even in the paid work sector, our economics seem upside down – those who care for the land or health, are paid least of all.

Eco-economics proposes a new economic framework. Social costs, military costs, the costs of cleaning up pollution, the loss of natural resources, and all the costs of structural violence are *subtracted* from,

TOES: The Other Economic Summit

The growth of new economics led, in 1983, to the formation of TOES – an independent, international forum bringing together pioneering economists from around the world. TOES meetings are held to coincide with the annual Economic Summits of the seven richest Western nations. The forum is committed to promoting and developing a new economics, which provides for the range of human needs, social justice, personal development, and sustainable use of resources and the environment. It presents these matters to the ministers and press prior to the Summit meetings.

TOES has held international conferences focused on the London, Bonn, Tokyo and Venice Economic Summits (in 1984, 1985, 1986 and 1987). In 1987, it studied the economics of urban regeneration for the International Year of Shelter for the Homeless, and issues of environment and development to coincide with the Brundtland Commission's report. TOES aims to raise the profile of neglected fundamental economic issues and to promote practicable solutions, from local self-reliance to global economic reforms.

TOES has won considerable recognition, and its work has been widely published, notably in Paul Ekins's *The Living Economy*, which collects the thinking of more than 40 new economists. "Money as if people and environment mattered" is a new economic principle which is gaining ground. Industry is becoming more responsive to Green economics (less so to peace economics), as are consumers. In the words of Paul Ekins: "People's ordinary spending is the most powerful agent of social change they possess."

Wangari Maathai (standing), Kenyan Green Belt movement, and Jonathan Porritt (to her right), Director of Friends of the Earth, at TOES 1985.

The Homegrown Economy Project

In the future, economists will apply a multi-level approach, with emphasis on local development. Most wealth will be generated in increasingly self-reliant communities in which investment and employment are under local control.

Cut-backs and unemployment caused by conventional top-down policies have already led to several attempts to revive economies by local effort. The city of St Paul's, Minnesota, has set up the Homegrown Economy Project, to "extract the maximum value from the community's human, natural and technological resource". Support is given to new enterprises that place an emphasis on local ownership, diversifying the city economy, direct benefit to the commun-

Economics is affected by the values of a society, relationships within it and its relationship with the natural world. In the past, we have viewed the world as a limitless expanse, where new resources could always be exploited, and where waste could be dispersed and lost. We have seen economic growth in terms of an increased "throughput" of production and consumption, and competition as the main motive for "progress". The distinguished economist Kenneth Boulding has described this as a "cowboy" or "frontier" economy. He proposes that we now replace it with one recognizing that we live not on a limitless plain but in a closed sphere, a planet of finite limits: a "spaceship Earth" economy.

A spaceship inhabitant would not "extract resources" by mining the vessel on which life depends, nor "throw away" waste to accumulate and damage the ship. A spaceship economy depends on the recycling of materials, and the protection of reserves. Success is measured in terms not of throughput, but of "the nature, extent, quality and complexity of the total capital stock" including human well-being. In fact, the less throughput needed to achieve this conservation of capital, and of well-being, the better – an idea that runs counter to the present-day emphasis on unlimited growth of production.

The analogy, however, goes only so far. Gaia is not a spaceship, a machine, but alive – thriving on an income of solar energy, capable of growth and renewal, and with a generous capacity to disperse and recycle waste. But these capacities are, as with the spaceship, finite – and we are over-stretching them to our peril.

The new economics does not seek an end to growth, but a redefinition in real and sustainable terms. Growth in GNP is the conventional indicator of progress. But it clearly does not indicate this adequately for the poor, nor at all for the environment. GNP figures do not distinguish between non-renewable and renewable resources, for example, nor do they measure the pollution costs of their use in production; and they mask inequities in consumption.

The design of a spaceship or Gaian economy is a great challenge to economists. We need economic indicators that will measure sustainable growth, and that can more accurately measure social and environmental costs and benefits, including future ones. We need to address the question of damages – pollution, degradation of land and loss of human security – and how these are accounted for under law and taxation. Economists are also attempting to put values on environmental repair, social recovery and security as "economic goods", in hard figures that businesses and governments can understand. A reframing of conventional economics is urgently required – without it, poverty, deep social divisions, environmental decline and conflict will continue until civilization fails.

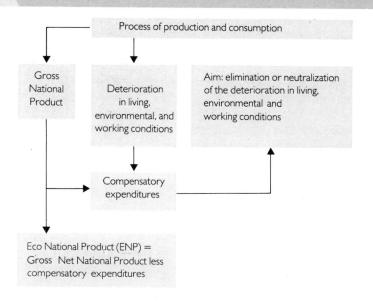

| Process of production and consumption | | |

Gross National Product

Deterioration in living, environmental, and working conditions

Aim: elimination or neutralization of the deterioration in living, environmental and working conditions

Compensatory expenditures

Eco National Product (ENP) = Gross Net National Product less compensatory expenditures

New economic indicators

Christian Leipert, in *Social Costs of Economic Growth* has proposed a new economic indicator – the Eco National Product, or ENP. It is calculated by subtracting social and environmental compensatory costs incurred in production from the GNP figure (*see above*). These costs are of four kinds: expenditures to prevent or repair damage; the cost of pensions and health insurance; environmental and human damage and lost well-being; and the real damage from failing to respond in time.

ity in terms of products and services, and economic self-sufficiency. The city manages, for example, a fund from investment portfolios of local insurance companies to provide venture capital at lower than market rates, and a revolving loan scheme to finance businesses that meet the Homegrown criteria. The main results so far are increased local wealth, higher employment, a more varied economy, greater citizen participation in local government, and self-reliance.

Many older Northern cities may have to adopt similar systematic approaches to local revival and development; even more so the poverty-stricken local communities in the burgeoning cities of the developing world.

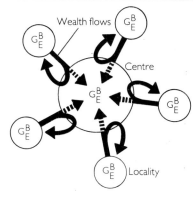

Wealth flows

Centre

Locality

In the future, localization of economies will be as important as internationalization. Finance sources (B), employment (E) and governance of the economy (G) will increasingly be based at local level, so that wealth flows within communities rather than draining from them. The main criteria are: local needs met by local work and resources; more money circulating locally; and local savings invested and loaned locally.

rather than added to, the GNP. All services and the capital gains to the environment by, for example, reforestation, and so on, would be added to the GNP. This would give a real impression of the benefits of human activities and the true cost of growth. It would also indicate whether development was sustainable.

Future economic models will lead to a redefinition of human needs, recognizing spiritual, social and emotional satisfaction as well as material needs. This will be assisted by a just currency between nations, a guaranteed basic income for all individuals, and socially responsible investment and financial dealings. Much greater value will be put on long-term returns on investment – giving a weight to the future in all accounting. Above all, there will be a dispersion of government and economic power, which will allow more interplay between different levels of society – from local to global.

Eco-economics seeks a revitalized, self-reliant future – for communities, nations and regions – but also greater integration of the global community. Sustainable development will require economic units of appropriate size at each level – and a localization of control and management to ensure human and ecological guardianship. Production and goods that damage the environment or use energy inefficiently will be very heavily taxed. Activities that encourage sustainability and diversity, are environmentally benign and improve human well-being will carry incentives.

The vision of today's eco-economists is bold, and full of challenge. It offers a way out of the impasse in which present systems are locked, and one which is achievable – a redirection of effort toward a new civilization.

A sustainable society: new models

Underlying the transformation of economic realities is a more profound transformation – in our relationship with the living planet and with each other. Governments and international organizations do not yet have the political will to evolve solutions to global problems. But peoples around the world crave for a positive evolution of human destiny. They are, therefore, beginning to take matters into their own hands and apply new models and values, at grass roots level, to their activities. The new models in developing countries range from co-operative village and urban self-development to a revival of traditional skills with new appropriate technologies.

Changes of lifestyle and a new spirituality are emerging in the affluent West, too. These often reflect a recognition that both Eastern philosophies, and the older values of "primitive" or rural peoples, with their closeness to the soil and reverence for nature, and their traditional skills and beliefs, have much to offer.

We are seeing, in effect, the seeds of non-violent revolution from below, leading to a new world. What could this world be like?

When the birth rate is limited to the replacement rate or less, there may be a resurgence of more neighbour groupings. This may help reduce the consumption of goods by individuals and increase local self-reliance.

New models

We now have both the understanding and the appropriate technology to create a sustainable civilization. The new models for agriculture, forestry, common heritage resources, and industry, energy, and human settlements are at the same time cost-effective, productive, and, above all, possible. New ideas on accounting, and accountability, already exist. We are capable of drawing up a balance sheet of sustainable living, both in terms of capital and through-put, and applying it.

Managed lands
In the recent Ottawa Declaration on agricultural practice, scientists urged all relevant groups to adopt the aim of eco-sustainability. We already have the knowledge to build a new agriculture and the same is true of forest lands. Community involvement in planning sustainable land use is vital. Future managers will draw up a balance sheet of the land – keeping track of resources used, energy inputs, toxin levels, and diversity.

Common heritage
The new Law of the Sea has established the principle of "common heritage", or shared guardianship of resources, replacing the concept of the planet "up for grabs". So far, we have applied this only to remote oceans, the poles and outer space. But the dependence of all peoples on water, air, climate, soil, forests, and genetic diversity adds urgency to the call for a new Charter for the Environment, and laws for its protection.

Industries and services
Technology for energy efficiency, materials recycling and pollution control is rapidly advancing. An eco-accountable society will invest in renewable and clean energy sources, and prefer small-scale, community-run outfits where re-use of materials is central. Future industries may be taxed on "real" capital depletion – and throw-away consumer goods may carry steep price disincentives.

Human settlements
No sustainable models can be applied to the hard-pressed inner cities or shanty towns without community-renewal policies. According to TOES (*see p. 228*), some key approaches are: encouraging local investment, community education and start-up schemes for local enterprise; creating partnerships between government, business, labour and the community to bring in "packages" of work; putting a limit on unemployment time; and voluntary care.

Managed lands balance sheet

Capital Soil fertility, water flows, tree cover and diversity all conserved, and replenished by: reafforestation, hedgerows, wind breaks, adapted plants, terracing, fallow lands, agroforestry and reclamation. **Throughput** Lower oil energy inputs through more human labour, and organic farming; pesticides cut; reforms reducing pressure on resources.

Common heritage balance sheet

Capital Global protection agreements for all common heritage areas, and gradual extension to the gene base, climate, atmosphere, water, species diversity and ecosystems, with clean-up/repair programmes. **Throughput** Before drawing any "income" from capital, full cost accounting of effects on environment; bans on pollution and depletion.

Industrial balance sheet

Capital Human knowledge and craft skills protected; material resources conserved and recycled; energy efficiency improved; diversity and lifespan of products increased. **Throughput** Full costs of resource depletion, nonrenewable energy use, waste, pollution and ill health entered on balance sheet and taxed or passed to consumer after benefits of capital improvements offset.

Human settlements balance sheet

Capital Sanitation, water supply and housing improved; green areas extended; human capital enhanced; support base from water-sheds, soil, forests and rural communities protected. **Throughput** Resources consumed and costs of health and pollution repair and environmental impacts (near and far), balanced against benefits.

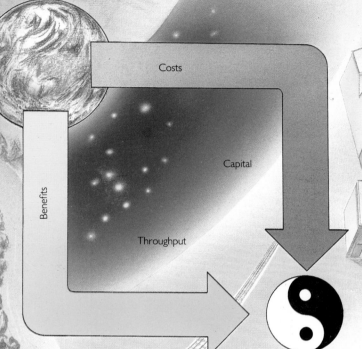

The balance sheet of use and resource

Attempts to monitor and control our impact on nature are not new. Major contractors are accustomed to preparing an Environmental Impact Assessment on a scheme, and expect public hearings before proceeding. Some large corporations (BP and ICI, for instance) attach weight to having a "good" conservation image and policy. And some states are developing National Conservation Strategies. But no balance sheet – corporate, governmental, or ordinary domestic – yet shows the true balance of our "account" with nature.

Such a balance sheet would state how the real "capital stocks" – species diversity, soil fertility, forests, water, air, mineral and energy reserves, and human potential – had fared in the past year. It would also analyse the "throughput" of production and consumption in terms of costs and benefits. Costs include protecting or repairing the stock, unrepaired damage or depletion, and all nonproductive costs such as military budgets. Benefits are the goods and services supplied. Only if the capital is conserved, throughput reduced or steady, and benefits balance costs, is any enterprise sustainable long term. Broad parameters for such balance sheets are proposed above.

From local to global

In time, we will come to apply the principles of sustainable living at every level of society, whether as individuals, local communities and enterprises, large corporations, governments or regional and global bodies. Cities and farms, industry and the arts, will all balance the account with nature as best they can. Increasing localization of all decisions will allow a community both to create and protect its own sustainable base. Law and taxes will control and price-out damaging goods. As global citizens, we will seek to:

* conserve energy
* recycle materials and wastes
* ban all toxins and pollutants
* conserve and improve capital
* reduce or stabilize throughput
* achieve growth in well-being for all peoples.

With the widespread use of information technology, the distinction between work and leisure will become blurred. All sorts of activities – looking after aged relations, running a local radio station, and so on – will be seen as "productive", worthy of reward. There will be more involvement in community life, more urgency about, and willingness to clear up, pollution, more responsibilities on citizens, and greater awareness of rights under international law. There will be more emphasis on organic agriculture, forestry, environmental work, greater concern for the arts and greater interest in cultural heritage.

It should be a more democratized world with more accountability. Mass communications will ensure more transnational links and the global spread of ideas about how to obtain peace and justice. Recent sudden transitions from autocratic to democratic forms of governance in Argentina, Brazil, the Philippines, Uruguay and other countries are signs of things to come.

Appropriate science and technology

The Manhattan project to develop nuclear weapons in World War II gave a new boost to the myth that science and technology would solve the problems of development. President Eisenhower's Atoms for Peace programme was an example of a vision in which technology would transform scarcity into abundance, bringing unheard of riches to all countries. The grandiose visions of technological paradise began to fade in the 1960s. Bhopal, Windscale, Three Mile Island and Chernobyl were all nails in the coffin that finally laid them to rest.

We now know that "technological fixes" alone cannot be relied on to save us. Nevertheless, many positive visions of the future rely on continual breakthroughs in science and technology. Nobody can deny that they have had some remarkable successes. Infant mortality rates have been greatly reduced; life expectancy has been considerably increased; machines have taken much of the drudgery out of life; the computer has revolutionized many fields of human activity. By increasing productivity dramatically, technology has made possible in some countries generous social welfare schemes. Many scientific innovations have improved the quality of life, sometimes beyond all recognition, and enriched our experience.

Future technologies could also bring great benefits: conservation technologies, sustainable agricultural techniques, and improved fishery and forestry practices, for instance; and information technologies leading to greater access to knowledge and reduced mass commuting. Or technologies that bring efficiency and durability; alternative and renewable energy sources; and non-polluting, space-based co-operative efforts.

We can also predict some breakthroughs: biological energy supplies through photosynthesis; cheap photovoltaic cells leading to cheaper solar energy; pollution extraction at source, such as the removal of carbon dioxide from power station outflows. Such technological advances could transform the future – if they are applied with sustainable development in mind. Unfortu-

Global Challenges Network

Conceived by the German professor Hans-Peter Dürr, Global Challenges Network aims to link up groups worldwide that are committed to solving urgent problems threatening human survival. The first meeting, in Munich in July 1987, set up an International Science and Technology Study Group, and planned a data-based computer network between its members, linking many different countries and professions. Members must have a global, holistic view, broad experience and specialist knowledge. The data base will inform the Group on projects, methods and people involved, and attract others to join The Network. The Network's goals are to: reduce pollution and radiation; retard depletion of resources; prevent poverty, hunger and disease; reorganize the economy for redistribution of wealth; and establish human rights for all.

Global problems are not soluble by science and technology alone. Indeed, Professor Dürr believes that their solution demands a radical shift in the way we perceive, think and communicate. Many scientists are concerned about their involvement in research and development that is ultimately life-threatening. Those who feel impelled to disassociate themselves have the skills, contacts, and experience in transnational collaboration to take up global challenges. An International Foundation for Survival and Humanity was formed in 1987 at a world forum in Moscow. Similar foundations are being established. Scientists who are freed from military and commercial constraints can serve as catalysts in a process of global co-operation.

Hans-Peter Dürr (centre) and supporters.

The coming of age of Gaia

In March 1988 the prestigious Chapman Conference took as its theme the Gaia Hypothesis, 15 years after British scientist James Lovelock first proposed the revolutionary principle that the Earth is alive. He named this newly recognized organism Gaia, from the Greek Earth goddess. Convened by the American Geophysical Union in San Diego, California, the conference drew together leading physicists, biologists and climatologists to consider the evidence for Gaia, and the implications for the future of science. The event marked the coming of age of the Gaia principle as a respectable subject within the scientific establishment.

According to the Gaia Hypothesis, life shapes and controls the environment, rather than the other way around. The two have evolved together, and every individual life form, from microbe to man, is involved – simply by its own life processes – in homeostatic systems that have evolved to operate on a global scale. Just as a living creature keeps its temperature and chemistry in balance, so Gaia – all of life – maintains

Intermediate Technology (IT) was set up in 1965 to put into practice the alternative approach to economic development advocated by Schumacher in *Small is Beautiful*, a study of "economics as if people mattered". For over 20 years, IT has provided choices of technology intermediate between the traditional methods of agriculture and manufacture in many developing countries, and Western technology – aiming for "a happy medium between a sickle and a combine harvester".

IT engineers, economists and advisors concentrate on helping local people to become more independent, self-sufficient, and able to overcome their problems themselves. They match technology to the needs and skills of the people by the sensitive introduction of more efficient means of livelihood. Working in more than 60 countries, IT has designed, developed and tested many new types of tools and equipment, and published hundreds of manuals, case studies and buyer's guides. It also advises leading aid agencies, government ministries and The World Bank.

Typical current projects are the development of rainwater catchments in Kenya, and of fishing boats in Quilon, South India. In Kenya, IT is helping semi-nomadic pastoralists to extend the areas where food and fodder crops are grown by building earth bunds – small sunken fields. These trap the region's scarce, irregular rainfall so that sorghum can be grown. Three groups, involving more than 120 families, are now planning, building and maintaining these sites in traditional wet season grazing grounds.

In Quilon, 5000 fishermen and their families were faced with destitution when it became illegal to cut down the mango tree from which they fashioned their boats. IT came up with a solution in the form of a low-cost plywood boat that could be made locally from plentiful supplies. Villagers have now started their own boatyard and are pleased with the new boat, which, thanks to Intermediate Technology's expertize, is not only more spacious, stable and safe, but costs the same as the traditional design.

Intermediate Technology at work in Turkana, Kenya: oxen being trained as part of the Water Harvesting Project.

harmonious conditions on Earth. Gaia is a challenging, and to some, a disturbing idea.

There have been plenty of scientists to argue against it, and few with the curiosity and freedom of mind to go out and investigate. Yet the science is growing fast. Most now accept, for instance, that the exchange of chemistry between life and the environment does influence the mix of gases in our atmosphere; tiny organisms in the sea mediate cloud cover over oceans, their dimethyl sulphide emissions "seeding" cloud formation.

Clouds reflect heat back to space; atmospheric gases retain heat by the Greenhouse effect; life is known to be involved in both processes. But critics argue that for Gaia to use these means to keep temperatures comfortable for life, presupposes a conscious planetary intelligence. As Lovelock explains, this need not be so: simple feedback mechanisms between the environment and organisms could achieve exactly the same result.

If Gaian life-systems are homeostatic mechanisms, what is their tolerance to human attack? Lovelock speaks of the "vital organs" of Gaia: the algae of the sea, and of the soil – "the skin of Gaia" so named by Gaian biologist Lynn Margulis – and the microflora of mud beds on the sea floor, in wetlands and rainforests. Damage here could critically alter the carbon cycle, and so temperatures, even rendering life on Earth impossible. If we are to find a sustainable relationship with Gaia, we have to seek fuller knowledge of how her systems work and learn to respect them.

The qualities we shall demand of future scientists are very different from the mechanistic, "power over nature" ethics of the past. The emergence of Gaia marks just such a change; its acceptance into the official science agenda is a sign of great hope. Asked if Gaia could be proved, Lovelock replied: "I don't think it matters. We should just be curious. Go out and wonder about it."

nately, investments in the most important of these technologies – notably conservation technology – are low. So, too, is investment in cross-disciplinary approaches to predicting unexpected malign effects of technologies. And in technologies for peace – for the verification of arms control and disarmament treaties, and for new global security systems – the investment is virtually nil.

What we need most is a new and mature morality and philosophy of science and technology. We can already see the seeds of this revolution – moves among NGOs and some governments to ban nuclear technology, some forms of bio-technology, and some agricultural technologies, notably pesticides. And there is some movement to a more socially responsive science and technology, for treaties protecting sources of knowledge, genetic resources and so on.

But we need to go much further. We need a holistic science and technology to develop more understanding of the biospheric regulatory mechanisms of Gaia, and of how human activities interact with natural changes. And we need to find out how human governance and social values interact at all levels – a "systems theory" of social well-being. And we need a more humble science – one that acknowledges its limitations, and respects spiritual and creative values, leaving behind mechanistic ideas and the "mastery of nature". This will mean freeing science from corporate and, particularly, military control.

Future science and technology will be both internationalized, with many countries participating in the more ambitious projects, and localized, with technology transferred to developing countries, to shanty town and village, to the individual. And it will interact with other sectors of society – communities, the arts, planners, children. More and more, the science of prevention will outweigh that of cure, and both will marry modern medicine with traditional healing. Human health will be seen to be linked with planetary well-being.

Can technology be controlled? Can we create a people-centred, Gaia-respecting science? Will Schumacher's vision of "small is beautiful" come? There has been much progress in appropriate or intermediate technologies, which mix traditional and new skills – from waterwheel to dynamo. These technologies are appropriate to the needs of people and the land, in scale, cost, use and repair, in culture and traditions. Their success gives hope that we will evolve a science and technology in harmony with the planetary ecosystem and human well-being.

Broadening the base of power

If we are to meet the challenge of the future, to take the radical steps we must to grapple with the intractable present, broadening the base of our decision-making and governance is essential. All those actors on the human stage who are seeking new approaches – from pressure group to village, from scientist to teacher – must have a voice in governance. Political leaders have shown that, left to themselves, they will not take the

Grass roots

"The way to deal with this dual challenge facing us (of war and poverty) lies not in some blind faith in technology and its continuous expansion but rather in bringing the human community back at the centre of the development process . . . The saviours of peace (if they succeed) will be . . . ordinary men and women, in their consciousness, in their comprehension of the multidimensional and interrelated nature of the problem, in their courage, their capacity to overcome fear and insecurity, their willingness . . . to collectively create the conditions and the compulsions for peace."

Jimom Omom-Fadaka, Environment Liaison Centre, Nairobi

This grass roots decentralization and democratization is spreading through law, politics, and commerce, challenging existing power structures. Many of the new initiatives are being taken by women.

The Greens in Italy

The growth of grass roots movements has helped the Greens to gather strength throughout northern Europe, and they have had considerable electoral success in West Germany. Their influence is now extending to Italy, where polls reveal that voters are becoming increasingly sympathetic to ecological and pacifist ideas. Pollution, environmental degradation and metropolitan chaos are all issues of public concern, and are causing the electorate to look for change beyond the established political system.

Zimbabwe's co-operatives

Since independence in 1980, the co-operative movement in Zimbabwe has grown rapidly. It now consists of over 800 collectively owned and managed co-operatives. Many communities are now not just self-reliant, but actually have surplus output in activities ranging from farming and fishing, shoe-making and tailoring, to printing and design, fencing and security services. Many of the workers were former combatants in the war of liberation, or were previously unemployed.

The Seikatsu Club

A wholefood co-operative with a difference is the Seikatsu Club Consumers' Co-operative in Japan, which represents half a million people, the majority of whom are women. It is concerned not merely with supplying material goods and services, but seeks to integrate the roles of producer, consumer and investor, so that all aspects of the production process, including the ecological impact, are understood by its members. Recently the Club has become involved in local government, focusing on issues such as health, safety, environmental protection, peace, women's rights, social welfare, and the promotion of greater participation in the wider political process.

The fifteen-strong team which makes up the Green representation in the Italian parliament.

SEWA

The Self-employed Women's Association (SEWA) is an Indian trade union movement whose membership consists of scattered, self-employed and home-based women workers. Founded in 1972, SEWA has some 25,000 members in a variety of professions. Although the poorest and most exploited section of the community, the lives and working conditions of these women have been transformed by SEWA. The co-operative arranges training programmes to upgrade skills, provides welfare, it negotiates minimum wages and gives access to special credit terms.

Latin American and Caribbean Women's Gathering in Mexico City in 1987, the theme of which was "What are the politics of feminism?".

The feminist movement in Latin America

Despite ingrained prejudice against feminism, the women's movements that have emerged in Latin America in the 1980s have acquired considerable political influence. After the 1983 elections in Argentina, women's groups formed La Multisectorial, a coalition to lobby on behalf of women's issues, which has already succeeded in changing legislation. In Costa Rica, one Presidential candidate proposed a woman for the Vice Presidency. In Uruguay, a feminist study centre is a leading consultant for a radical programme of social change, and in Brazil, a regional women's health programme is finally incorporating recommendations made by the feminist movement.

GABRIELA

The General Assembly Binding (Women) for Reforms, Integrity, Equality, Leadership and Action is a movement of women workers in the Philippines that pledges to fight for economic self-reliance and for a just and free society. An umbrella organization of more than 70 women's networks, GABRIELA aims to free the Philippines from the economic and military domination by foreign powers, and to educate, organize and mobilize women towards their ultimate goal – eliminating all forms of oppression against women.

necessary measures. Their "business as usual" approach will lead to nuclear and ecological disaster.

This democratization is already happening, but it is too slow. Only a new, inspiring vision of the common good, of our membership of one family, one planet, and the potential of the human heritage will hasten it.

We need to broaden the base of power to reduce the dominant influence of élites and vested interests – and to move governance away from national sovereignty and cumbersome international bureaucracies. Broadening the international dialogue will also reduce the tensions between East and West, and North and South.

We need to see "the peoples of the United Nations" break the stranglehold of narrow national and commercial interests and insist on sustainable development in the global, rather than national, interest. This can only happen if human potential, particularly traditional and local knowledge, is maximized. Democratization is the only way of achieving this, and allowing communities to develop self-reliance and self-administered economies.

"Think globally, act locally" is the great rallying cry of the new world. Broadening the base requires both local and international action, and communication between them. Individuals in communities need to think of the global effects of their activities; international civil servants need to think locally, to listen to the voice of the village. Local self-reliance is a buffer against world economic and employment crises as well as a route to sustainable living. Effective sustainable development must be carried out from the grass roots ("bottom up"); it cannot be commanded and controlled ("top down") by the large bureaucracies of central government.

In a society that is flourishing from the grass roots up, decisions for sustainable development are best made at the lowest effective level, by people who will apply them. The smaller the group, the better – a village of a hundred souls can often act more decisively than a town of a hundred thousand. Higher levels of decision occur only if there are insufficient resources or information to take them locally. Information is, in fact, a resource that should often be gathered, analysed and transmitted at a global level, but relayed back locally. Data from remote-sensing satellites, for example, can be used to improve local agricultural practices.

Most of all, broadening the base means mobilizing the potential of marginalized groups, particularly women, with all their skills and diversity. Traditionally, women had a large role in decision-making – a role that still persists in parts of Africa and in other indigenous societies. Their recent new activities in peace, development and environmental movements is a resurgence of this involvement. Women are carers, for others and for the land, and patient negotiators. Though largely unrecognized in current economic indicators, women already play a key role in the global economy.

The actuality of self-governance need not depend on the agreement of governing élites, nor need it wait until there is a change of government. As Richard Falk points out: "By establishing popular governance at home, at work, in church and social gatherings, among friends, there is a widening zone of autonomy created . . . Transnational bonding by non-violent resistance groups is mutually encouraging" to this rise in self-governance.

Throughout history, human societies have struggled to balance effective governance with control of the abuse of power. We are involved, now, in a greater struggle yet – to achieve this at a global level. The hope of civilization rests on this upspringing life of popular governance, on the vitality and imaginative courage of ordinary people, to seize the future.

A new internationalism

The international community has been growing ever more interdependent – but we are reluctant internationalists. Commitment to the spirit of internationalism is an essential element of broadening the base of power; when it comes, it will bring sweeping reforms in international governance. And it will come. It will grow from the wide transnational links of non-governmental organizations, of trade unions, professional bodies, and so on. It will grow in increased links between North and South, leading to a real dialogue between them.

Governments of smaller powers can apply international governance even when their countries are in military alliances. For example, the Netherlands and Rumania, members of NATO and the Warsaw Pact respectively, often take stands on security issues different from those of the superpower leaders of the alliances. By refusing to be dominated by superpower geopolitics, they contribute to the growth of international governance. In fact, there is and will be a growing role for third-party initiatives by smaller countries. The larger powers are sensitive to global opinion and do not like to be exposed to criticism. They are increasingly loathe to defy the global norms of reasonable international behaviour. This sensitivity presents other countries with opportunities to influence events and thereby broaden the base of power.

The future of governance

Diversity is the stuff of good governance. Involving the integration of all human co-operative activities, good governance is rooted in consensus, co-operation and the non-violent settlement of conflicts; in respect for law, human rights, and justice, and, above all, in the maximum participation of individuals. In the words of Javier Pérez de Cuéllar, in April, 1984: "If you accuse me of appealing to people over the heads of the governments you are right. The work of peace is too important to leave to governments alone."

Recent history shows only too clearly how impotent governments are to deal effectively with global problems. Future governance must go far beyond government based on national sovereignty. Numerous groups and individuals – local communities, multinational corporations, non-governmental organizations, regional organizations, the media, professional bodies, and a host of others – are potential elements. Future governance must be as diverse as the community it

If the global community is to master the immense task of building a sustainable civilization, all its members must be heard. The present Northern dominance and North-South misunderstanding must make way for a broader-based dialogue. One new initiative in this direction is the South Commission, a joint idea of Julius Nyerere of Tanzania and Carlos Andres Perez of Venezuela. Together, in 1987, they made an historic trip to Venezuela, Cuba, Peru, Brazil, Uruguay, and Argentina. This was the first time that an African leader had visited Latin America. The journey was in preparation for the setting up of the South Commission, which aims to strengthen communication between developing countries, and foster collaboration in tackling global and North-South problems. Its strength lies in its independence from governments and institutions, and its ability to draw on the wide network of research centres active in the South.

Initiatives to broaden the global dialogue are also coming from the North. The Council of Europe's new 1988 North-South Interdependence campaign seeks to make people in the North aware of how North-South relationships affect our daily lives. Each European government is responsible for running the campaign in its own country. The emphasis is on education, by means of local exhibitions and seminars, on a wide range of issues – including trade, jobs, environment, education, culture, agriculture, and aid. Established groups, such as schools and churches, are encouraged to explore

Julius Nyerere in conference with members of the Latin American Economic System (SELA).

aspects of their own interdependence with developing countries. The strong educational bias and the creation of wider contacts make this campaign a positive step towards reducing tension between North and South. Policy makers in Europe and the developing countries must establish a more equitable distribution of resources between rich and poor.

FILE: BROADENING THE BASE
Youth Building the Future

Young people hold the future in their hands. Humanity urgently needs a spirit of true internationalism, of common purpose and a sense of global citizenship. This must come through the education of the rising new generation.

The Youth Building the Future Conference was held in Melbourne in August 1987. It brought together young people from all over the world "to inspire international co-operation and search for a way to build a new future". The need for everyone to begin thinking in global terms was made clear from the start. The week consisted of lectures, discussions and workshops involving students who were studying a wide range of subjects in 18 different nations. The Conference addressed itself to such crucial questions as the future of the arms race, the threat of nuclear war, conservation of the environment and natural resources, the North/South poverty gap, and international relations.

The Conference spelt out the need for a change in the

attitudes of governments worldwide. It called for a total ban on the further development of nuclear weapons, the eradication of social injustices, and the removal of the crippling burden of debt borne by the developing nations. Delegates took responsibility for setting up a network to communicate the Conference's recommendations to colleges, schools, the media, and the general public. The week proved to be a great success and all participants felt energized by close contact with students from other nationalities and cultures. Everyone emerged feeling positive and hopeful for the future. As one student remarked: "We are the youth that will act, not just speak. It's up to us."

FILE: BROADENING THE BASE
Transnational codes of conduct

The pervasive role of transnational companies in the world economy requires the formulation of guidelines for their conduct. The UN has drafted a Code of Conduct on Transnational Corporations, which is in the final stages of discussion. Its main recommendations are summarized below.
● Respect national sovereignty and observe domestic laws, regulations and administrative practices.
● Contribute to economic and social development of the host country, eg. by placing sub-contracts locally.
● Long-term contracts between governments and transnationals must be open to review.
● Avoid practices, products or services that run counter to domestic socio-cultural values.
● Respect human rights and fundamental freedoms.
● Do not collaborate with racist minority regimes in southern Africa.

● Do not interfere in internal political affairs.
● Do not interfere in intergovernmental relations.
● Abstain from corrupt practices.
● Make a positive contribution to the host country's balance of payments; avoid potentially destabilizing activities.
● Give priority to employment, promotion and training of nationals from the host country.
● Pricing policies must be based on fair market prices.
● Observe international standards and national laws on consumer protection and environmental protection.
● Disclose all relevant information on potentially hazardous effects of products, processes and services.
● Disclose clear and comprehensive information on the structure, policies and activities of the corporation as a whole, including financial information, annually.

governs, operating effectively at all levels of the community starting, in the words of Richard Falk: "within the inner life of individuals and in family relations between parent and child and men and women."

What will future governance be like? What will be the role of the United Nations? Currently, the United Nations is in crisis; its members can agree neither what the UN should be doing nor how it should achieve it. Most do agree that immediate reform within the Charter, and then radical structural change and a new Charter, are needed. The UN is the only global institution we have. But unless it becomes democratized, the UN will be increasingly marginalized. This would be a tragedy for future international governance.

The organization has an impressive record in dealing with humanitarian issues, from world health and refugees to disaster relief, and in some matters concerning the atmosphere, oceans and outer space. The task is to build on this. The global community must frame a new United Nations able to deal effectively in an interdependent world with economic and political issues, with conflict resolution and security.

Democratizing the United Nations

One bold proposal to democratize and revitalize the UN is to give it an "upper house" with voting power. This would be more radical than the General Assembly and not politically aligned. The UN Charter begins with the phrase "we the peoples of the United Nations . . ." and it is time to honour this intent. The upper house could be made up of representatives of the people. Its members could represent many interest groups, too: non-governmental organizations, multinational corporations, women, science and technology, law, medicine, education, health, cities, villages, shanty towns, human rights groups, financial institutions, farmers, trades unions . . .

Such a body would get around one basic problem with the UN – political and ideological differences between the members of the Security Council and the use of the veto. And it would allow, for example, a further enhancement of the role of the Secretary-General in mediating conflicts. Major UN conferences have stimulated counter-conferences by citizen groups – such as The Other Economic Summit (TOES) – that have shown a better understanding of the issues involved and have emphasized that solutions to many global problems need radical structural changes. The success of these counter-conferences demonstrate the enormous potential of transnational networks of concerned non-governmental groups and individuals.

The Security Council, with an expanded membership and with no veto, could be retained to deal with emergency action. Although the executive body of the UN deciding much of its policy will continue to be national governments, there should be a mechanism through which the smallest village or any individual can appeal to the "supreme court" of human affairs.

Today, the UN itself, and its international efforts – to deal with, for example, pollution – are miserably

Future governance

How will the world be governed in the peaceable society of the 21st century? What we need is not more government, but better governance – a new international system that gives a voice to the "peoples of the United Nations". Governance is more than government: it is the sum of all co-operative human enterprises, at all levels and between all sectors. In future, hierarchical, centralized "authority" will give way to a network of interlocking levels of governance.

Reform of the UN is urgent. We must have a system where national interests no longer mask global issues; where the veto and budgetary dominance of the Great Powers no longer block true democracy; where true peacekeeping and the rule of law are enforceable. We need a democratized UN, with a constituency in the global citizenry and a concern for true security.

Ultimately, governments are the servants of peoples. And it is the people who are the best guardians of justice, peace and morality. Many have proposed a second UN Chamber, a Peoples' Assembly.

Functional sovereignty

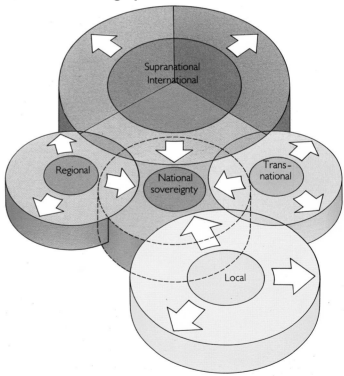

Even today, nations cannot govern alone; they are dependent on a web of interactions in the multi-level world community. In future we will see, if not the "withering away of the state", its redefinition in functional terms. Sovereignty will be eroded from all sides – by supranational laws on peace, human rights and the environ- ment; by international ones on a host of daily affairs; by regional accords and transnational links; and by devolution to local levels. The state will still be a major actor in the world, but autonomous only in specific areas. Its larger role will be as interpreter, enacter and mediator of codes of global, regional and local management.

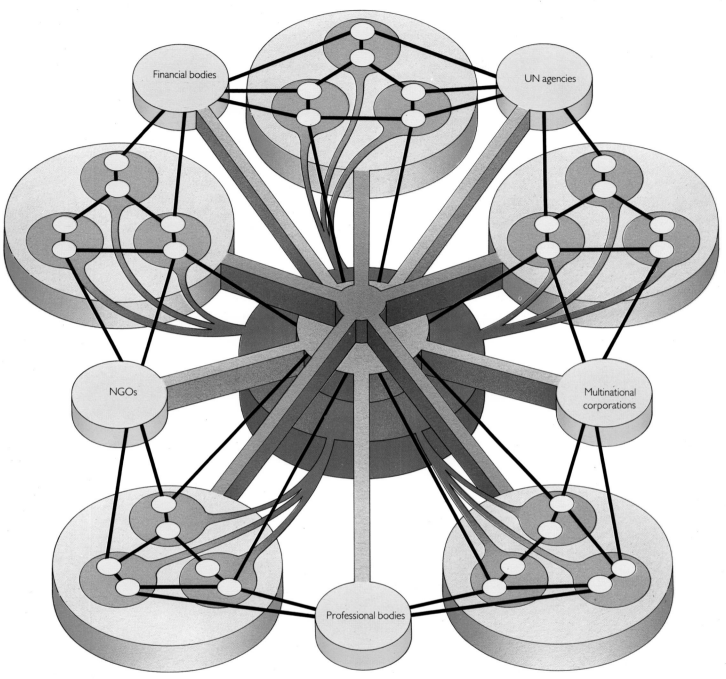

New models of governance

Unlike other systems of governance, which operate at the level of the nation or below, the UN has no direct access to its constituents nor any power to levy taxes. Veteran internationalist Maurice Strong suggests that we need "a bi-cameral system in which directly elected representatives of peoples sit in one chamber and representatives of governments in the other". The UN could be financed through taxation of international economic activity. The International Network for a UN Second Assembly has called for a second chamber of NGOs.

Any successful system of future governance must satisfy the following criteria. It must give the peoples of the world a democratic voice; have global, more than national, concerns; have as many levels as the world it governs; have authority on issues of global security, and consensus support; involve all actors in the world community; use the least centralization compatible with effective action. And it must be open to change.

A system that might meet these criteria is shown above: *Security Council* remodelled to comprise all main regions and powers, with no veto, and a core "guardianship" group of planetary citizens; its brief, the security of Gaia and all peoples: peace, human rights, and the environment. *Upper Chamber or Peoples' Assembly* comprising elected representatives of the "peoples of the United Nations", of Gaia, from local communities – village, city, or farms, and from transnational bodies. Representing, not any geographic grouping, but commonalities of interest worldwide; its brief, to broaden the base of governance and plan for sustainable civilization. *Lower Chamber or General Assembly* of nations, with democratized financing, constituency elections, and taxing powers, its brief to legislate, and integrate national actions with global policy.

Security Council (regions and guardianship group)

2nd Upper Assembly (NGOs, peoples)

1st Lower Assembly (States)

Transnational bodies

Regions

States

Communities

underfunded. And the relationships between population, environment, shortages of resources and conflict are not being addressed. Funding for UN programmes to deal with these problems could and should be provided by taxation – notably of international activities that rely on secure international governance and on non-renewable resources.

But the UN would be better able to cope, too, if its agencies were streamlined and more activities devolved to regional organizations. Shared cultures make them better able to deal with such issues as human rights, agricultural policies, financing, environmental issues, and security. Regional bodies should be strengthened for a role in future governance; but they should work to an international agenda.

To be effective, the UN must have power to apply and enforce sanctions. This may involve UN policing forces, to back up legal decisions and keep the peace. In fact, in a disarmed world all military forces would be under the command of the UN. National forces would be limited to those necessary to maintain internal order.

Humanity has come a long road. From the wandering hunter-gatherers sharing survival, to village, town and city and warring states. The task of shaping global governance for a peaceable, sustainable future is a great creative enterprise – a huge adventure.

Honouring the rule of law

The only basis for a future civilization – indeed for any future at all – is the rule of law. Governments must come to recognize that the requirements of international law always transcend those of national law. National sovereignty is already breached by international law in some areas, but is still jealously, often obsessively, guarded in many others.

Although there should be sanctions for violating international law and a way of enforcing the judgments of the International Court of Justice, the best guarantee that international law will be observed is the opprobrium which a violator attracts. The best international law is consensus law, its strength depending on commitment to peaceful change, respect for legality, and the desire of nations and sub-national groups to seek non-violent solutions to conflicts.

The ultimate sanction is an alert global citizenry – monitoring the behaviour of states and groups, insisting that international laws are obeyed. Governments, commercial and financial institutions are, after all, servants of the public, and should, therefore be made to comply with the wishes of the public. Julius Caesar remarked: "the fault, dear Brutus, lies not in our stars, but in ourselves, that we are underlings." But more and more people are realizing that they are not "underlings", and refuse any longer to be manipulated by the propaganda of governments, advertising agencies, or media.

The Nuremberg Principles and Obligation commit all individuals and groups to honour international law in war and peace, as a legal and moral duty. The planning and preparation, as well as the waging, of an aggressive war

Shaping supranational law

No subject today bears more closely on the survival of humanity than our willingness to accept and honour the rule of law. There are, according to the World Federalists, four types of governance: "the rule of force; the rule of custom; the rule of law; and the rule of love." The rule of force we must, for our own safety, abandon; the rule of custom serves only where there is a common culture and consensus; governance by love and co-operation is still a long way off. No one is "in charge" of our world – a great diversity of nations, institutions and cultures is involved in collective self-governance – and the interlocking issues of human and environmental security are too complex for any one to be addressed in isolation. If we are to achieve peace in such a world, it must be by expanding and strengthening codes of supranational law. This law will have new definitions of acceptable behaviour – in terms of the environment, human rights and needs and the concerns of peace. In these areas it will embody new principles of responsibility and accountability, covering all actors in the global arena – national, subnational and transnational.

The laws of sustainability

We must frame laws to "keep human activities in harmony with the unchanging laws of nature" and "recognize the reciprocal rights and responsibilities of individuals and states for sustainable development" (Brundtland Commission).

In 1984, methyl isocyanate gas leaked from the Union Carbide plant in Bhopal, India, killing at least 2,500 people and leaving tens of thousands permanently handicapped. Four years on, Union Carbide and the Indian government are still wrangling over compensation, while thousands wait for some of the meagre $114 per person promised two years ago. Under future international law such a situation would not be tolerated. Union Carbide would be accountable from day one, under codes regulating the actions and responsibilities of transnational bodies.

As things stand, there has been little support for the survivors and the effects of the leak have not been

Lawyers for Peace

In January 1985, the British group Lawyers for Nuclear Disarmament organized the four-day London Nuclear Warfare Tribunal. Its aim was to put nuclear weapons on trial, assessing their manufacture and use against standards of international law. The tribunal judges included three Nobel Prize winners – Sean MacBride, international jurist and former Assistant Secretary-General to the United Nations, Professors Dorothy Hodgkin and Maurice Wilkins – and an American professor of international law. The Tribunal heard evidence from 40 witnesses from nine different countries, all of whom were cross-examined by barristers. The British Government refused to take part in the proceedings.

The Tribunal concluded that the procurement or use of nuclear weapons was illegal because they infringed the Charter of the UN, the Hague Conventions of 1899 and 1907, the Geneva Convention of 1949, and the Geneva Protocol of 1977. The Tribunal recommended that immediate steps be taken to renounce unconditionally any reliance on nuclear weapons for first-strike use, and government

There is some groundwork on which to build. The 1972 Stockholm Declaration recognized the "fundamental right to freedom, equality and adequate conditions of life in an environment of quality". Five years later, the Enmod Convention prohibited the hostile use of environmental modification techniques – a principle that could be extended. And in 1982 the "common heritage" principle was encoded in the Law of the Sea Treaty. But despite these and other environmental conventions, the law is very weak, lacking supranational force.

The 1987 Brundtland report puts forward 22 new legal principles for sustainable development, from the right to "an environment adequate for health and wellbeing" to the responsibility and accountability of states for maintaining ecosystems, the biosphere and biological diversity, and providing compensation for damage. The Commission proposes that the new principles be incorporated into national laws or charters setting out the rights and duties of citizens and state, and into a world convention on the sovereign rights and reciprocal responsibilities of all nations.

The Commission further recommends that such existing institutions as the General Assembly, the International Court of Justice and the Permanent Court of Arbitration be strengthened to deal with environmental and resource problems, and that public bodies and NGOs help provide expertise, especially to settle disputes.

The laws of peace

The world already has laws of peace. Under the UN Charter, wars of aggression are illegal, as are various classes of weapons (including nuclear weapons) and acts in war. But the law is constantly flouted, and the proviso that force may be used in self-defence or to aid an ally is used to disguise many crimes. Present laws, moreover, refer only to nations; subnational or transnational combatants are not covered.

International criminal law must also be strengthened, and appropriate international criminal proceedings created where parties other than nations can bring suit. Our definitions of criminality may have to widen, too – arms manufacture and trading, for instance, and certain types of economic exploitation may be classed with drugs trading and blackmail as crimes. The accountability of leaders, groups and individuals should be extended – a precedent already exists in the Nuremberg Trials (*see p. 68*). And the Nuremberg Obligation, which imposes a duty on all individuals to oppose criminal or aggressive policies by governments, could become a civil right incorporated into national and international charters.

FILE: FUTURE LAW
Bhopal

monitored. A report in 1986 discovered a large number of serious medical problems in the population and possibly as many as 2.5 million people have claimed compensation. Medical conditions include eye and respiratory problems, frequent miscarriages, and psychological difficulties. There is no sense of urgency for a legal settlement. Union Carbide admits a "moral responsibility" for the accident, but at the same time claims that the leak was caused by sabotage. It is in Union Carbide's interests to delay the case as long as possible while reorganizing assets and fighting a publicity battle. As Bob Berzok, Director of Corporate Communications said "I can put my hand on my heart and say Union Carbide didn't lose a single major customer as a result of Bhopal".

Bhopal victims being treated at a hospital; many suffering serious eye injuries.

Left to right: Dr Richard Falk, Sean MacBride QC, Professor Dorothy Hodgkin and Professor Maurice Wilkins – four judges at the Nuclear Warfare Tribunal.

studies to consider long-term alternative security policies. All those who participate directly or indirectly in preparations for nuclear war were called on to consider their own moral and legal responsibility, while peace groups and individual taxpayers were encouraged to adopt non-violent direct action to increase public opposition to nuclear strategies. The judgment was circulated to world leaders, the United Nations, lawyers worldwide, and non-nuclear states for their endorsement.

The Tribunal warned that the outbreak of nuclear war was virtually inevitable if the development of nuclear weapons and nuclear war strategies continued. Lawyers are awakening to their responsibilities to human life and development. As individuals, we now have the right to object to active or passive participation in the preparation for nuclear war on the grounds that it has been declared illegal.

is a punishable crime under international law. It should be recognized that this commitment applies to the nuclear arms race, associated as it is with deployment of nuclear first-strike weaponry, nuclear war-winning strategies, and threats to use nuclear weapons. The Nuremberg Obligation commits each and every citizen of the world – all of us – to resist governmental policies that involve aggressive militarism and repression. Individuals and transnational NGOs should work for the implementation of the Nuremberg Obligation.

New laws often evolve from voluntary codes of conduct. Such new codes – for instance, on the accountability and conduct of multinational corporations – are now being formulated by non-governmental organizations. Some will become incorporated into international law. Particularly important will be codes of environmental practice. We need a code for the environment similar to the UN Convention on Human Rights, a code that could form the basis of a future international environmental law. This may best develop from existing regional codes – but it cannot wait.

Just as the Nuremberg Obligation makes leaders accountable for their behaviour, and criminally and individually liable for violations of international law, they should be similarly accountable for crimes against nature. This should be a fundamental premise of future international law. Moreover, citizens or interest groups should have an ultimate access to a supranational judgment, binding on governments, on issues of international law, including human and environmental rights. As a first step, the statutes of the International Court of Justice should be modified to allow individuals to plead cases involving violations of international law by states or groups.

Spirit of Peace

"Goodwill is the mightiest practical force in the universe." The Talmud "Not women as such, but the feminine, seems capable of activating the political imagination in important ways – especially helping organized society to disentangle its understanding of effective authority from violence; to rescue law and order, and government, from hierarchical arrangements of top-down bureaucratic structure; to separate power generally from destructive capability and military/police techniques; and to distinguish political leadership from concentrations of wealth, egoistic prestige and royalist pretensions. Women are the leading, but the exclusive, bearers of feminine creativity". Richard Falk

Virtually all positive visions of the future include a spiritual revolution, conscious of the sense of divine in life and of the beauty and diversity of nature, as a fundamental, rising force for radical change.

Such a spiritual revolution should not be confused with current revivals of fundamentalist religions – such as the Moral Majority in the USA, the Islamic revolution and so on. These sorts of fundamentalism are backward looking and energized by violent images, rather than seeking non-violent solutions.

The spirit of peace

Visualizing a peaceful and positive future for humanity requires a spiritual revolution. We need to change the way we think, feel and act towards each other and our planet if we are to survive.

We enter into the spirit of peace when we move away from analytical, separatist thinking and towards a more co-operative, holistic world view. A belief in the interconnectedness of all living things is an expression of spirituality. This philosophy has long been held by Native Americans, Buddhists, and Taoists. Qualities traditionally considered as feminine – such as caring, co-operation, and intuition – must be expressed by men and women alike. Present concepts of peace and security are founded on more masculine notions of defence by force and increasing militarization. The way of non-violence and co-operation is open to everyone. A more spiritual society with greater freedom of expression is fundamental to our future.

"We utterly deny all outward wars and strife, and fightings with outward weapons, for any end, or under any pretence whatever; this is our testimony to the whole world. The Spirit of Christ by which we are guided is not changeable, so as once to command us from a thing as evil, and again to move unto it; and we certainly know, and testify to the world, that the Spirit of Christ, which leads us into all truth, will never move us to fight and war against any man with outward weapons, neither for the kingdom of Christ, nor for the kingdoms of the world."
Quakers' declaration to Charles II, 1660

"How can you buy or sell the sky, the warmth of the land? The idea is strange to us. If we do not own the freshness of the air and the sparkle of the water, how can you buy them? . . . We know that the white man does not understand our ways. One portion of land is the same to him as the next, for he is a stranger who comes in the night and takes from the land whatever he needs. The earth is not his brother, but his enemy, and when he has conquered it, he moves on . . . He treats his mother, the earth, and his brother, the sky, as things to be bought, plundered, sold like sheep or bright beads. His appetite will devour the earth and leave behind only a desert . . .

Teach your children what we have taught our children, that the earth is our mother. Whatever befalls the earth befalls the sons of the earth. If men spit upon the ground, they spit upon themselves. This we know –

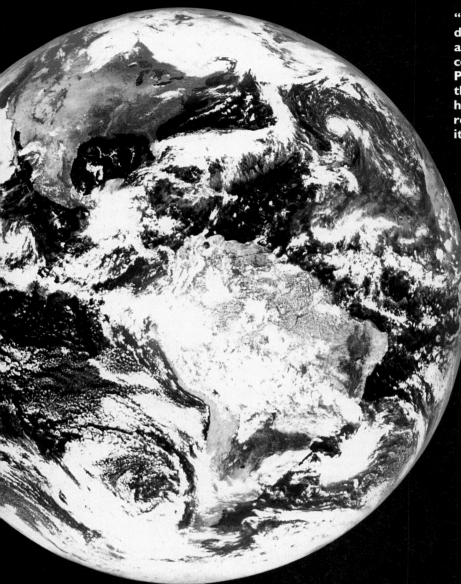

"If the earth were only a few feet in diameter, a ball floating a few feet above a field somewhere, people would come from everywhere to marvel at it. People would love it and defend it with their lives, because they would somehow know that their lives, their own roundness, could be nothing without it." Friends of the Earth

"The cause of war is preparation for war." A. J. P. Taylor

"No leader is going to give us peace, no government, no army, no country. What will bring peace is inward transformation which will lead to outward action. Inward transformation is not isolation, not a withdrawal from outward action. On the contrary, there can be right action only when there is right thinking, and there is no right thinking when there is no self-knowledge. Without knowing yourself, there is no peace." Krishnamurti (1895-1985)

the earth does not belong to man, man belongs to the earth. All things are connected like the blood which unites one family. Whatever befalls the earth befalls the sons of the earth. Man did not weave the web of life: he is merely a strand in it. Whatever he does to the web, he does to himself . . . This earth is precious to him, and to harm the earth is to heap contempt on its Creator. The whites too shall pass: perhaps sooner than all other tribes. Contaminate your bed, and you will one night suffocate in your own waste. But in your perishing you will shine brightly, fired by the strength of the God who brought you to this land and for some special purpose gave you dominion over this land and over the red man. That destiny is a mystery to us, for we do not understand when the buffalo are all slaughtered, the wild horses are tamed, the secret corners of the forest heavy with scent of many men, and the view of the ripe hills blotted by talking wires.

Where is the thicket? Gone.

Where is the eagle? Gone.

The end of living and the beginning of survival."

In 1854, the "Great White Chief" in Washington made an offer for a large area of Indian land and promised a reservation for the Indian people. Chief Seattle's reply, excerpted here, has been described as the most beautiful and profound statement on the environment ever made.

Peace, the absence of structural violence, requires new human relationships, new moral codes – a positive spirituality emphasizing neighbourliness as a criterion for all policies. If change is regarded as "good" only if it increases one's income or wealth in the short term, we will never achieve a non-violent, sustainable democratized world. A spiritual revolution would also run counter to today's psychology that "national security" can come only from tanks, bombers, warships and missiles, and that rich and powerful élites can best run society and organize the future. Peace demands a resurgence of our human spirit of co-operation.

The personal and the political

Many citizens believe that the individual is powerless to influence the drift towards nuclear world war and eco-catastrophe, or to do much about the arms race or the destruction of the environment. But it is a mistake to underestimate what the individual can do.

Information is power. The first task for responsible citizens is, therefore, to inform yourselves of the facts. You can then make educated judgments of the issues. Well-informed citizens are a challenge to the abuse of state power. Objective information, frequently at odds with that released by governments, is regularly published on nearly all issues by respected institutions. Amnesty International, for example, publishes reliable information on human rights issues; the Stockholm Peace Research Institute objective data on the arms race; and Friends of the Earth and Greenpeace on the environment.

Once citizens have learnt the facts, most want to do something. Each individual can contribute: all of us can achieve change by our own lifestyles, by insisting on measures of energy conservation and reducing pollution, by educating our children, and by exposing exploitation, corruption and illegality. If enough people decide that a certain course of action – such as nuclear disarmament, or reducing atmospheric pollution – is called for, political leaders, even very reluctant ones, are likely to respond. Public opinion is crucial.

Some people will participate in non-violent demonstrations; some will join non-governmental organizations dealing with issues that concern them; others may discuss the issues with colleagues, family members, and friends; writers can write about global issues, teachers discuss issues with students; individuals will write letters to their MPs, the local and national press.

Some people have special responsibility. Scientists, for example, have a duty to consider the possibilities of converting military industries to peaceful use. Military personnel should make clear the horrors of war and evil nature of nuclear weapons, the obscenity of the North/South poverty gap, waste of resources on militarism, and need for more social justice. Journalists and other media professionals have a responsibility to disseminate correct information and counter propaganda.

You can play your part by thinking globally, acting locally, being persistent, and participating. The alternative is to sit back and wait for armageddon.

Mothers of the disappeared

The individual has the right to challenge the actions of the state. When their desperation and courage lead ordinary people to confront state power, personal feelings can become a political force.

From 1976 to 1983, Argentina was under military rule. The repressive juntas were responsible for the disappearance of 30,000 people – mostly young trade unionists, students, professionals – anyone who dared to question the regime. They were kidnapped from their homes, held in detention centres, and refused all contact with the outside world. These young Argentinians, the "disappeared", officially did not exist.

Los Madres de La Plaza de Mayo is the organization formed by the mothers of those victims. They took their name from the square in which they used to gather outside Government House in Buenos Aires – the Plaza de Mayo. They wore white headscarves to identify themselves and began to wage a campaign against the military authorities for the return of their children The Mothers are women with no previous political experience and very limited formal education. They found little support for their campaign: the Catholic Church was hostile, and even their own families criticized them for venturing outside the traditional female confines of the home. The Mothers were harassed by the police, arrested, imprisoned, and constant threats were made against their lives. In 1977 their own president was kidnapped and herself became one of the disappeared.

As the Mothers campaigned nationally and internationally, support for their cause grew. They presented a novel form of political threat for which the juntas had no effective answer. The juntas were ousted in 1983 but there seems little hope that any of the disappeared are still alive. Yet the Mothers refuse to give up their search. Popular support increases: thousands joined in their seventh annual "March of Resistance" and 24 hour vigil in the Plaza de Mayo in December 1987. The Mothers' courageous and uncompromising stance strengthens the growing human rights movement in Argentina.

The Great Peace Journey

Governments should represent the interests of the people. Ordinary people have a right to insist that the governments of the UN member states accept their duties under the Charter that they have all signed. The Charter opens with a clear obligation on the part of nations "to save succeeding generations from the scourge of war". The Great Peace Journey seeks to make nations, collectively and publicly, commit themselves to abide by the UN Charter. Since May 1985, delegates have travelled to the capitals of 105 UN member states to pose the following five questions (requiring "Yes" or "No" responses) to government representatives:

1 Are you willing to initiate national legislation which guarantees that your country's defence forces, including "military advisers", do not leave your territory for military purposes (other than in UN peacekeeping forces) – if all other Members of the UN undertake to do the same?
2 Are you willing to take steps to ensure that the development, possession, storage and employment of mass-destruction weapons, including nuclear weapons, which threaten to destroy the very conditions necessary for life on this earth, are forbidden in your country – if all other Members of the United Nations undertake to do the same?

Greenham Common

At dawn on New Year's Day 1983, 44 women from the Greenham Common peace camp climbed the perimeter fence and danced in a circle on the nuclear silos.

The peace camp at the US Air Force base on Greenham Common began in 1981 as a women-only protest against the introduction of cruise missiles to Britain. After six years, cruise missiles are finally to be dismantled under the INF treaty. This gives enormous satisfaction to the Greenham women. Their passive but determined resistance has done much to raise public awareness of the nuclear threat.

The Greenham peace camp has also had a wider social impact. It has become a symbol of non-patriarchal values, of endurance and non-violent resistance, and of the ability of ordinary women to oppose government intransigence and power. The occupation has also been a political education for many of the women who went there, marking their transition from personal belief to political action.

The Greenham women have gained worldwide recognition with their long, arduous and creative protest. In December 1982, 300,000 women linked arms around the nine-mile perimeter fence. In October 1983, 2000 women cut down four and a half miles of fence. The missiles arrived in November 1983, and 50,000 women encircled the base and used mirrors to reflect the base back on itself. The women established Cruisewatch in 1984 to monitor, publicize, and disrupt convoys of cruise missiles on their journeys to and from Greenham Common.

In April 1985, trespass on common land became a criminal offence. Hundreds of women entered the base as a protest and were then sent to prison. They contested the validity of the law, and in 1988 a High Court judgment was passed in their favour. The contention of the women, that they had right of way through the base, was upheld.

3 Are you willing to take steps to prevent your country from allowing the supply of military equipment and weapons technology to other countries – if all other Members of the United Nations undertake to do the same?
4 Are you willing to work for a distribution of the earth's resources so that the fundamental necessities of human life, such as clean water, food, elementary health care and education are available to all people worldwide?
5 Are you willing to ensure that any conflicts, in which your country may be involved in the future, will be settled by peaceful means as specified in Article 33 of the UN Charter, and not by the use or threat of force?

Of the nations interviewed, 84% answered "Yes" to all five questions and a preliminary report was presented to the UN Secretary-General in December 1986. The present goal of the Great Peace Journey is to organize a Global Popular Summit in New York in September 1988. Here, at the opening of the UN General Assembly, the results of the questionnaires will be published. The aim of this Summit is to outline concrete proposals for world peace to be presented to the UN. It will reinforce the right of people from all nations to participate in, and influence, world peace policies.

A personal code of action

We have to choose our own personal code: the points below are merely a guide. But we should never forget that governments are ultimately the servants of peoples, and it is their duty to represent our wishes. When governments fail us, our own actions *can* change the world. If we want an alternative future, the choice is ours.

As a producer Choose work free of violence, oppression, or unsustainable practices. Keep to two children per couple.
As a consumer Be aware of your impact on resources and people, and use your consumer power wisely.
As a thinker and communicator Honour Gaia, justice, and the rule of law and reject the values of dominance. Learn, educate the young, spread the word, write, speak, campaign.
As a participator Protect your local ecosystem and community. Join a local, and an international voluntary organization. Use your vote. Seize opportunities. Expose dangers, lies and corruption. Speak out against oppression and honour the Nuremberg Obligation. Use the law and constitution to challenge the legitimacy of state actions.

If every person in the world declined to manufacture, bear or use arms, or tolerate injustice, peace would break out.

Voices Our children's children

> "War in primitive societies was fought with simple weapons, was highly ritualized, and led to few casualties. Its goal was largely to provide an avenue for social prestige, successful warriors in warlike societies being held in high esteem. It was not fought, as in the modern world, to acquire land, to secure a source of cheap labour and raw materials, or to establish or protect a market for manufactured goods.

This is clear since a tribal society had ample land for its purposes, its population was stable, it used agricultural methods which did not lead to soil erosion and desertification, and required limited mineral resources, while its farmers and artisans produced largely for local consumption.

With economic development, populations exploded and more land was required on which to settle the extra people or to provide food for them. Both agricultural and industrial production became increasingly dependent on energy and natural resources, and expanded to satisfy the escalating consumption of consumer goods. As local supplies were exhausted, dependence on foreign supplies increased as did competition among producers for external markets.

In other words economic self-sufficiency gave rise to economic interdependence. This means that changes in the socio-economic policies pursued by one country can now spell economic ruin for others.

With economic development also goes that of science and technology, which dramatically increases the destructiveness of the available weaponry. It also gives rise to the most disastrous environmental destruction, which is one of the main causes of impoverishment and famine.

Clearly such conditions could not be more favourable to the increasing incidence and destructiveness of warfare. For this reason it seems totally unrealistic to draw up a plan to reduce warfare and promote peace outside of a wider programme of systematic economic development."

Teddy Goldsmith
Founder, *The Ecologist*

> "Where spirituality and politics can be seen and experienced at all as opposites, there is something fundamentally wrong with the world, both internally and externally. Of course what we generally understand by politics does not deserve the name, but is miserable politicking which flickers across the TV screen and drips out of newspaper columns. And what we usually understand by spirituality is the individualistic private enjoyment of more or less "alternative" members of the affluent society who have not even assumed responsibility for themselves. It is ridiculous to want to achieve reunification with the very great Whole, the Cosmos, and at the same time to believe it is possible to leave out the most obvious social Whole, the many fields of social practice right down to human destiny. Anyone who celebrates in the Buddhist meditation of love, the unity of all feeling beings, and, for example, spiritually and practically discards this monstrous practice of slaughter-houses or of the animal experiments which lies behind our cosmetics, our use of medicines, etc., is with difficulty heading for the kind of awakening we need in view of our collision with all realms of life. And anyone simply wanting to do away with animal experiments would soon learn that in order to do so we must change our whole basic attitude and way of life, not only our "energy" for reflective hours, we must empty ourselves, above all, of the countless ways we unconsciously identify as white people of the West and for the unbiased blueprint of a new culture compatible with nature, which rests more on love than on power. And this blueprint we must transform with European activity energetically into deeds. We must pull the cart out of the mud we have driven it into.

Spirituality, therapy, etc., as commercially motivated weekend culture, even combined with political reflection, does not lead far enough. The blueprint I have drawn awaits male and female collaborators who already have of themselves the same goal, a similar path and perhaps the longing for life in a completely loving and viable community. I want to prepare, promote and help to realize on a spiritual basis a political reformation to stop our suicidal machinery, a social transformation in the grand manner, a new building for our culture. Who else wants the same?"

Rudy Bahro
Co-founder, Die Grünen

" 'Our children's children' is a common concept among many indigenous people when making any sort of community or tribal decision. For them the notion of a sustainable future is built into each present moment and activity. There are still tribes in Columbia who try to take decisions with regard as to how they will affect even the seventh generation!

Unfortunately industrial man threw out such concepts when he accepted the principles of economic Darwinism. The Earth was plundered and mined in the interests of immediate profits. Consumerism replaced conservationism and within the compass of three generations so much effluence was created for the sake of affluence, that even the seas, rivers, lakes and atmosphere had to be requisitioned as repositories for the man-made debris. The Earth by itself can no longer cope!

Technocratic man became blinded to the fact that we are all chronologically and geographically connected, with all parts related to the whole: scientific specialization harnessed to material greed had made him arrogant beyond belief! In a few decades he had squandered resources silently guarded by nature for millions of years.

So what are we leaving for our children's children? We have already mortgaged their earthly home and rendered practically all their life support systems environmentally hazardous and potentially dangerous. For the sake of future generations, peace with the Earth itself must be restored. This we should do immediately through right livelihood before it is too late and we can no longer negotiate a truce.

We cannot, on any account, leave this planet to our children irreversibly damaged. Although the damage already caused is derived from pursuing false values and being mesmerized by crazy illusions, a change of heart, and a deepening spiritual awareness of our responsibility for the universe is always possible.

The material structures of our earthly home, however, may take hundreds of years to repair even if we begin today. We must at all costs prevent those policies which cause irreversible damage. These are sum-

med up as the 5 damnable D's: Destruction – of the human species and the environment caused by war and pollution. Depletion – of non-renewable resources and the creation of waste. Dismantling – of traditional values without replacing them with more sustainable and holistic alternatives. Denial – of human rights, including the right to clean air, water, seas and uncontaminated soil; the right to food and resources; denial of the rights of the Earth itself. Desecration – of the biogenetic and spiritual links which bind the Creator with the creation of mankind and nature. The 5 D's are negative forces to be overcome – only then can humanity live in true security.

Let us not lose one moment on regret. In this one-world context, each of us must become a vehicle for positive change. We shall find that a small amount of wisdom is more valuable than vast quantities of knowledge and that even the poorest among us can be bountiful in wisdom. But we must 'walk our talk'. To ensure peace with man we must be prepared to be the first to love and to love universally. To secure future peace with nature we must be the first to act, each of us in our own way.

The astronauts' first Moonlanding was claimed as a small step for man but a great step for mankind. Another such significant step in which all could participate is the planting of trees. Trees are for me prominently symbolic. They feature in all the world religions since they unite the forces of the Earth with those of the heavens. Trees are symbols of non-violence and future life as well as being essential to the biosphere. They have traditionally been planted in commemoration of loved ones. Today if just one sapling could be planted by a parent or relative in the name of every child who enters this world – the child's special tree for life – our children's children would find themselves with more reverence for nature than their forefathers of today had ever had. **"**

Diana Schumacher
Ecologist

Voices 2

❝ The unexpressed assumption that human problems ought to have technological solutions is an example of a failure of humility. It is very tempting for those who have learnt to use powerful problem-solving techniques, to assume that they can know enough about the complexities of human life to apply these techniques without substantial risk of error. But technological solutions to the problem of war, or even of riot control, for instance, have not been a conspicuous success.

A Christian approach to purpose in the technological society must endeavour somehow to do justice to the ambiguity of technology. It is a tool in the hand of man, which can be used for good or ill. There is no absolute value in technological advance . . .

Yet on the other hand, there are no good grounds within the Christian faith for despising or failing to appreciate the enormous achievements of technology. A sacramental view of life should lead to a reverence for material things which, like the sacraments themselves, can become a means to spiritual ends.

Humility is necessary, because the Christian sees himself as holding the world in trust from God. It is not his to exploit unmercifully, but to use with respect. Hopefulness is possible, and can motivate human effort, because in Christian belief the universe is not ultimately hostile or meaningless.❞

John Eton
Archbishop of York

❝ The world is now faced by an acute crisis of more universal dimensions than any since the Flood. I cannot believe that such a crisis, threatening the very collapse of our civilization, can occur. I cannot believe that nations have become ungovernable, that technological advances as well as vice and violence have outstripped our capacity to control them; that we witness the end of the era of affluence, and of the hegemony of the industrial nations. I cannot accept that powerful governments must capitulate to the economic and political dictates of a handful of persons ruling over medieval serfdoms which still practise slavery and polygamy. I cannot accept that the majority of the world's nations must agree to confer legitimacy to a murderous organization dedicated to diabolical terror against innocent air-passengers, sportsmen and schoolchildren. In short, I cannot believe that the civilized world as we knew it is inevitably coming to grief and ruin in a convulsion of unprecedented proportions, simply because some effective political and economic formulae have eluded us.

The wave of indiscriminate violence is only one aspect of the current assault on the supreme value of life. There is the threat to life from the atomic bomb tests prompted by a false national vanity. There is the ecological peril to our environment, which, through our reckless abuse of the bounty of nature in the name of economic progress, threatens to poison our food, pollute our rivers and choke us in the very air we breathe.

By consecrating public life no less than individual conduct, religious perceptions and commitments can offer our stricken generation the solace, the strength, and the faith to see ourselves horizontally bound together as human brothers in a fellowship of peace, and vertically linked with the generations before and after us to consummate our human evolution, from the time we were created in the image of our Maker to the time we shall live in his image.❞

Immanuel Jacobovitz
Chief Rabbi, UK

❝ All living things are subject to the compassion of the Great Sage, the World-Honored One. That is the reason for the Buddha's appearance on this Earth. Big or small, good or bad, without discrimination, all living beings are recipients of the Tathagata's compassion. The life given to me in this saha world also made me subject to the compassion of the World-Honored One. The compassion of the Tathagata is like that of parents towards their children: each child is held equally dear whether they are boy or girl, good or bad.

We are in pursuit of an extensive and perfect freedom at its highest level. Perfect freedom is what we seek now – not in the future. What must be done to obtain perfect freedom? Yokawa believes it can be materialized through persistent denial of all forms of violence. All forms of violence would include killing and destructive powers of atomic and hydrogen bombs as well as the might of various weaponry such as aircraft-carriers, submarines, heavy guns, machine guns, tanks and rocket bombs. The United States, the United Nations and communist countries are all competing to proliferate these weapons.

Civilization is neither to have electric lights nor airplanes, nor to produce nuclear bombs. Civilization is to hold mutual affection and to respect each other.❞

Nichidatsu Fujii
Founder, Nipponzan Myohoji
Buddhist Order

"I am deeply convinced that to reflect together on the priceless treasure of peace is in a way to begin to build it. Peace, which is built up and consolidated at all levels of human association, puts down its roots in the freedom and openness of consciences to truth, and every violation of religious freedom does fundamental damage to the cause of peace. Millions of people are still suffering for their religious convictions: they are victims of repressive and oppressive legislation, victims sometimes of open persecution, but more often of subtle forms of discrimination aimed at believers and communities. This state of affairs, in itself intolerable, is also a bad omen for peace.

Everybody is aware that the religious dimension, rooted in the human conscience, has a specific impact on the subject of peace, and that every attempt to impede or to coerce its free expression inevitably has grave negative effects upon the possibility of a peaceful society.

At the same time there is reason to rejoice that both the leaders of the religious bodies and the ordinary faithful are showing an ever keener interest and a livelier desire to work for peace. These intentions deserve to be encouraged and appropriately co-ordinated in order to increase their effectiveness. For this purpose, it is necessary to go to the roots.

Last year in Assisi, in response to my fraternal invitation, the leaders of the world's main religions gathered in order to affirm together – while remaining faithful to each one's religious conviction – their common commitment to building peace.

In the spirit of Assisi, there is here a question of a binding and demanding gift, a gift to be cultivated and brought to maturity: in mutual acceptance and respect, renouncing ideological intimidation and violence, promoting institutions and methods of joint action and co-operation between peoples and nations, but especially in education for peace, considered at a level well above the necessary and hoped for reform of structures – peace that presupposes the conversion of hearts.

Brothers and sisters in the faith: the commitment to peace is one of the testimonies which today makes us credible in the eyes of the world, and especially in the eyes of the younger generation. The great challenge facing modern man, the challenge to his true freedom, is found in the Gospel Beatitude: 'Blessed are the peacemakers' (Matthew 5:9).

The world needs peace, the world ardently desires peace. Let us pray that all men and women, enjoying religious freedom, may be able to live in peace."

Pope John Paul II

"We ought to have learnt the lesson a very long time ago. It is all set out in Psalm 33 'A King is not saved by his great army, a warrior is not delivered by his strength, the War Horse is a vain hope for victory by its great strength it cannot save.'

We have had to travel many centuries over long roads to the edge of the nuclear abyss before the futility of the War Horse started to be grasped. For all our nuclear weapon mountains and our contorted arguments about deterrence, we have only managed to make the world an ever more dangerous place.

Now we have only one choice. The threats that face us, from Aids and famine to war and pollution face us as one people. They recognize no frontiers. Yet we have behaved as if we had the world's freehold in our hands, each of us under different and demanding national flags and each exploiting that freehold in the most selfish ways. But we are not freeholders, but tenants only for a short time, of different rooms in one and in the same house. Our dangerous and barbaric security policies have only succeeded in putting the whole house in greater and greater danger.

We still have time to change our ways. Today's security can only be common security. We are citizens of one small planet and we have now to turn the rhetoric of 'one family' into practical political reality. We have to build and fund the international structures of justice and peace. International law must take priority over national law. Education for peace and non-violent conflict resolution should have pride of place in every syllabus. Teilhard de Chardin warned us long ago: 'The age of Nations is past. The task before us now if we would not perish is to build the earth.' It is time we started."

Bruce Kent
Campaign for Nuclear Disarmament

Voices 3

“During my space flight, I came to appreciate my profound connection to the home planet and the process of life evolving in our special corner of the universe, and I grasped that I was part of a vast and mysterious dance whose outcome will be determined largely by human values and actions.

As I floated outside Apollo 9 with sunlight streaming past me, streaking over the Pacific at 17,000 miles an hour, I realized I was there on behalf of all humanity, that it was my responsibility to communicate this experience to my fellow beings.

By any measure, we are a marvellous experiment. But we are now capable of terminating this cosmic experiment. Anyone could trigger events that would lead to hundreds of millions of deaths, if not planetary extinction.

Our future – indeed our survival – is closely tied to the idea of our common destiny, and we must act, individually and together, out of an appreciation of that grand vision.

Many years ago I was a fighter pilot stationed in the Philippines. I was assigned to an F-100 squadron, and every fourth week or so it would be my turn to stand nuclear alert at an airbase on Taiwan. We would lounge inside the alert shack, waiting for the red phone to ring – and hoping it never would.

About once a week each of the planes would have to be exchanged for a fresh one. The pilot who was assigned to that plane would be notified and he would go out to the ramp to monitor the operation. The ground crews would roll a cradle under the nuclear weapon; it would be lowered from the plane, wheeled off to the side, and the flight crew would tow away the old leaker, move in a fresh plane, and reload the weapon.

Whenever it was my turn to go through this drill, I would climb on top of it and lie there, looking up at the stars. My back pressed to the bomb, I would search my soul for the moral basis on which I might decide whether or not to release the bomb if called upon to do so. I knew I would have very little knowledge of what was going on in the rest of the world. Was half of it already gone? What about my family?

My home town? I would not know their fate.

Will our vision of the human future be large and clear enough to lift us beyond the uncertainties and fears of our cosmic birth? Or will we defer to experts and impersonal systems of authority in the false belief that in them reside greater wisdom and morality? In how we answer these questions may lie the outcome of the great experiment of life.”

Rusty Schweickart
Astronaut, Apollo 9
(*Discover*, 1987)

“Since 1900, conventional wars have killed nearly seventy-eight million human beings. No citizen of this century needs to be told that conventional war is tragic.

Nuclear war, though, would be different in kind, a new phenomenon in human history. Nuclear war would change the issue from victory or defeat to survival. After conventional war, nations or their peoples survive. They recover. They rebuild. They go on. It would not be so after nuclear war. The participating nations would see their national fabrics and their cultures destroyed. Most of their populations would be killed; the survivors would be reduced to a primitive existence in a poisoned land. Other nations would feel many of the same effects. Damage, disruption, fall-out, famine, nuclear winter would be widespread, perhaps global. It would be an unimaginable catastrophe.

Preventing conventional war is a goal to be pursued by all of us, a splendid goal. But preventing nuclear war is a necessity, an immediate, grim necessity, for the whole human race.

What is required to prevent another nuclear war, to allow us to survive, over the long run, in the nuclear age? In essence, we must act on the warning Albert Einstein gave us forty years ago. He told us then that the nuclear weapon had changed everything except the way we think, that if we failed to change our thinking to accord with nuclear reality, we moved towards disaster.

We still have not changed that pre-nuclear thinking. We still think, and act

on the thought, that these appalling devices are weapons – tools that we can use or threaten to use to accomplish human purposes. For decades, we have gone trying to find rational ways to use them as weapons. We have not succeeded. It should be clear by now that we are not going to succeed. We are not going to devise some further technological miracle, whether for attack or for Star Wars defense, that will enable us to enforce our will or to survive major nuclear attack by others.

We must get nuclear truth into our heads, that the nuclear weapon is too powerful, the fabric of human civilization too fragile, the global ecosystem perhaps too vulnerable – too unreliable – to permit using nuclear weapons in action or in threat. Unless we do absorb these truths, there is a prohibitively high probability that, sooner or later, Einstein's prediction will come to pass, and an apocalyptic nuclear disaster will take place.”

John Marshall Lee,
Vice Admiral, US Navy (Ret.)

" UNICEF's experience suggests that the preparation for war is as wasteful and tragic as war itself. The diversion of the Earth's treasure on armaments in some of the poorest countries takes national attention and scarce resources away from social programmes of health education, and development, causing needless suffering and deaths among millions of children, the most vulnerable members of the national population. UNICEF's protégés are children below 15. It is a serendipitous and suggestive coincidence that we have approximately 15 years remaining in this millennium to do what is needed to correct the distortions in human relationships which now exist. If we are successful, the children now being born will have a chance of survival and of inheriting a new millennium free of the gross poverty and underdevelopment which now disfigures the Earth."

James P. Grant
Director, UNICEF

" More people are becoming aware of some disquieting features of our society. These include the distrust both of the State and of politicians, and transnational corporations, together with periodic evidences of corruption; from the inability or unwillingness of governments to heed ecological warning signals; from the dissatisfaction with consumerist lifestyles; from the growing militancy of disadvantaged minorities and the proliferation of single-issue campaigns. Some, though by no means all, of these movements and campaigns are loosely related, even loosely linked. But they are all strands in an inchoate effort to reach out to an alternative development, a different lifestyle. They are signs that people are no longer content to be mere election fodder. They represent an attempt by ordinary men and women to reassume some measure of control over their own destiny. As such, they should be welcomed, cherished, rejoiced over.

Yes, rejoiced over! Many people forget that George Orwell's gloomy forecast for 1984 applied to both sides of the Iron Curtain, not just to one. So wherever we see ordinary men and women banding together, making a stand, saying 'Enough is enough! We want a hand in deciding our future and our children's future', we know that people have stopped being zombies and have decided to resume membership in the human race. These are the action stations for democratic process. This is where we should all be, in spirit if we cannot be there in flesh, whether the station is called Greenham Common, Kelly's Bush, or the Danzig Shipyards."

Jack C. Westoby
Former Director UN Forestry
Division

" Two truths are now beginning to penetrate our minds concerning the crucial problems threatening our survival: the globality of issues and the commonality of issues. Following the publication of the Brundtland Report, *Our Common Future*, I chaired a subcommittee on the interrelationships between population, environment, resources and development, which called for radical reversals of traditional thinking about development priorities, policies and strategies.

Despite the fact that we live in a global community, political leaders, particularly those of the superpowers, have displayed an attitude of arrogance in their international relations, based on shortsighted, narrow and egoistic thinking. Hopefully, however, there are now some signs of new possibilities to create more of an equilibrium in world affairs, perhaps even a restoration of real influence of the United Nations.

If that trend continues, it is my firm conviction that the peoples of the world must be mobilized in defence of their right to survive in human decency and dignity. After all, governments of UN member states are – or should be – accountable for the way in which they face and solve the problems threatening the survival of humankind."

Inga Thorsson
Ministry of Foreign Affairs,
Sweden

Voices 4

" The destinies of the world and the future of humanity have concerned the best minds in various lands ever since man first thought of the morrow.

Until relatively recently these and related reflections have been seen as an imaginative exercise, as the other-worldly pursuits of philosophers, scholars and theologians. In the past decades, however, these problems have moved on to a highly practical plane. The reasons are obvious.

The development and subsequent stockpiling of nuclear weapons and of their delivery vehicles beyond all reasonable bounds have made man technically capable of terminating his own existence. The simultaneous accumulation of explosive social material in the world, and attempts to continue tackling forcefully with stone-age methods the problems of a cardinally altered world make catastrophe highly likely in political terms as well. The militarization of mentality and of the way of life weakens and even removes altogether any moral inhibitions with regard to nuclear suicide . . .

There would be no second Noah's Ark for a nuclear deluge. Everyone seems to understand this. So it is time to realize that we can no longer expect things to take care of themselves. There are still quite a few people in the world who think precisely in this way. International contacts and the policy of governments and states have to be brought without delay into line with the realities of the nuclear age.

In all human affairs, and especially in international politics, we should not for a moment forget the currently dominant contradiction between war and peace, between the existence and non-existence for humanity, and we must work to resolve it in good time in favour of peace.

This requires us to seek out, foster and share with each other all the best that history has produced, to look for new creative approaches to chronic problems.

The very survival, and not just progress, of the human race, depend on whether or not we find the strength and courage to overcome the threats hidden in the modern world.

We believe that there are grounds

for expecting so. A notable feature of recent decades has been that for the first time in its history mankind as a whole, and not only individual representatives, has begun to feel that it is one entity, to see global relationships between man, society and nature, and to assess the consequences of material activities.

This feeling did not come alone, it has brought with it a struggle to remove the nuclear threat. And it cannot be denied that it has already become a great moral and political school in which the masses of the people and whole nations are learning the difficult but necessary art of living in peace with each other, of striking a balance between general and particular interests, of looking at the present and future boldly, square on, of comprehending them and, in doing so, drawing conclusions for action.

Now allow me to deal with another major reality of our time. It also requires a new way of thinking. I mean the unprecedented diversity and increasing interconnection and integrity of the world. Our world is united not only by internationalization of economic life and powerful information and communication media, but also faces the common danger of nuclear death, ecological catastrophe and global explosion of the poverty-wealth contradictions of its different regions.

The world today is a multitude of states, each having its unique history, traditions, customs and ways of life.

Each people and country has its own truth, its own national interests and its own aspirations. This is the most important reality in today's world. It did not exist 30-40 years ago. This is a reality that manifested itself as a result of the choice made by the peoples themselves. They have chosen their path of social development . . .

We know that some leaders still view the world as their domain and declare their 'vital interests' wherever they like. This stimulates the arms race because such views result from a policy of strength designed for political and economic domination. This is an in-grained, antiquated mentality of the time when it was considered 'right' to exploit other peoples, manage their resources and decide their destinies.

These views lead to new regional conflicts and incite hatred. Such conflicts assume dangerous proportions, involving more and more countries as their interests are affected directly or indirectly. Regional conflicts have a very negative impact on international relations as a whole. People are being killed in wars declared and undeclared, at the front and in the rear. Countries suffering from abject poverty and mass hunger are being drawn into a wasteful arms race.

Settlement of regional conflicts is a dictate of our time. And our initiatives on the Middle East may serve as an example of our approach to the problem. It is a major nerve centre on our planet. The interests of many nations, and not only the Arabs and Israel, intersect there. It is a crossroads of histories, religions and cultures. Therefore we believe in the need for a very responsible, cautious and even delicate approach. Power politics, piracy and constant threats of force are unacceptable.

We say: let us search and act together. This applies to the Iran-Iraq war, the Central American crisis, the Afghan problem and the situation in the south of Africa and in Indochina. The main thing is to honour the rights of the peoples to decide their own destiny themselves, and not to interfere in the internal affairs of other states.

Mikhail Gorbachev
USSR General Secretary

66 The possibility of nuclear war is a direct threat to most of the world . . . If a nuclear war occurs, there is a chance, remote no doubt but undeniable, that the human species and many other species as well will be destroyed. At best, the world might return to some very early stage of evolution . . .

Our major problem perhaps is that we find it difficult to make the transition into not only a technically new world but also into a new way of thinking which alone will allow us to live under these fundamentally new conditions. We cannot risk another major war. But our states were founded on wars, our national heroes were almost without exception soldiers or admirals. Wars have in the past also been stimulants of technological and social change; they have even brought to countries some kind of spiritual peace otherwise rarely obtainable.

This will not be the case in a nuclear war. Therefore, avoiding such a war must be our first priority. It is in the interest of all states and all people. However, to accept this verdict and to draw the proper conclusions for political decisions seems to be rather difficult. This may have to do with the fact that most of the politicians who direct modern states are at a loss in the scientific and technical labyrinth which gives the states their power and opportunities . . .

What then is our conclusion? What is our message to the 21st century?   In view of the renewed Cold War between the two superpowers, the assurances of goodwill and friendly intentions are a welcome sign but not good enough as a response to the challenges of our times. What we need in all states and systems is a well-devised policy, a mobilization of strength and willpower, both in theory and practice, in design and implementation, to strengthen world peace and make it unbreakable . . .

The new concept of security can only be based on a radically different world view which no longer tries to secure peace against but rather together with the adversary. A common effort is required to achieve 'common security' . . . [which] requires a process of rethinking and of abandoning old concepts . . .

Mutually Assured Destruction has removed any hope for final victory as far as the superpowers are concerned. Any attempt to change this situation through unilateral development of new arms destabilizes security between nations. It is for this reason that my friends in this part of the world are against all aspirations for military superiority or military hegemony, and why we consider them as dangerous.

We know very well . . . how difficult it is for the United States to accept the idea of common security as a basic principle. We also know how difficult it is for the Soviet Union to abandon the idea of the 'just war'. But nothing less is required. If mankind cannot control the forces which it was able to invent and which may destroy it – then indeed it will perish.

Therefore: 'Since wars begin in the minds of men it is in the minds of men that the defenses of peace must be constructed' – this I think is our basic message on war and peace to the 21st century. We must give up the long-held view which came down at least from the days of the Romans: *Si vis pacem, para bellum.* It is no longer true in that narrow sense that 'if you want peace, prepare for war'. This is a radical and fundamental change indeed. We must understand it or mankind will not survive."

Willy Brandt
President, Social Democratic
Party, W. Germany

66 One of the greatest contributions the United States can make to the world is to promote freedom as the key to economic growth . . . This movement we see in so many places toward economic freedom is indivisible from the world-wide movement toward political freedom – and against totalitarian rule. This global democratic revolution has removed the specter – so frightening a decade ago – of democracy doomed to a permanent minority status in the world.

Yet, even as we work to expand world freedom, we must build a safer peace and reduce the danger of nuclear war . . . the resolve of America and its NATO allies has opened the way for unprecedented achievement in arms reduction. Our recently signed INF treaty is historic because it reduces nuclear arms and establishes the most stringent verification regime in arms control history, including several forms of short-notice, on-site inspection . . .

As I mentioned earlier, our efforts are to give future generations what we never had: a future free of nuclear terror. Reduction of strategic offensive arms is one step. SDI another . . . SDI has the same purpose and supports the same goals of arms reduction. It reduces the risk of war and the threat of nuclear weapons to all mankind. Strategic defenses that threaten no one could offer the world a safer, more stable basis for deterrence.

Ronald Reagan
US President

Gaia and the unknown

"For now we see through a glass darkly…" Corinthians
In our rational, materialist world, we tend to believe that science can explain everything – that we have "mastered nature" and can predict what outcomes to expect. Nothing could be further from the truth.

Scientists, for instance, have been developing more and more sophisticated computer models of the atmosphere. Yet none of these predicted the Antarctic hole in the ozone layer. Medical experts believed they were bringing viral disease under control; not one of them predicted AIDS. Our corrective efforts, too, are also shots in the dark. Clean air acts produced the complacent view that we had "dealt with" urban pollution; no one predicted the death of distant forests. Gaia has a knack of taking us by surprise.

We are equally caught unawares by ourselves – from the savagery of war to the failure of civilizations, events overwhelm us. No one anticipated the oil shocks of the 1970s, or the divisive economic problems that now threaten us. Nor can we guess what crises the growing underclass may bring about, what new resource shocks may emerge, or which may trigger nuclear madness.

We also tend to think that change is always gradual – that the Greenhouse effect, for example, will take decades to produce any major consequences. Yet science is beginning to fear not only surprises but suddenness. Systems theory teaches us that homeostatic mechanisms under strain can undergo abrupt collapse. What if today's warming atmosphere triggered a shift in ocean circulation, suddenly "switching off" the Gulf Stream that creates the mild climate of Europe? Suddenness is equally a characteristic of human affairs – nuclear war could seal our fate in an afternoon.

Surprises are becoming a serious research area – we need urgently to ask questions about Gaia and about ourselves. Yet it will always be the unexpected that brings disaster. Belief that we are in control is the ancient sin of *hubris*, or pride. All religions, all the greatest scientists, recognize the limitations of human understanding. So, too, do many older cultures, who also know that we are not masters, but a part, of nature.

We have no inalienable right of tenure on this Earth. If we wish to survive we have to recognize that neither our technology nor our knowledge are infallible. We have to face moral choices. It is time for humanity to grow up. Only by abjuring war and oppression, by respecting Gaia and ourselves, can we find a sustainable future. We must guard diversity, our best hope of resilience to change. Most of all, we should seek the philosophy of "no harm" – no harm to Gaia, to the human spirit, to that which we do not understand, yet which supports our lives. If we fail, Gaia will still continue – but we will not.

The unknown

Anticipating surprises is a new concern of science. Researchers are seeking models that can predict seemingly unlikely events and the interactions and knock-on effects of multiple human impacts on planetary mechanisms. The International Geosphere-Biosphere Program, for instance, attempts to answer such questions as: If all the Amazon forests go what will happen to rainfall and the Greenhouse effect? If we are to survive and build a sustainable future we have to understand how the planet works and how we disturb systems. Applying similar models to predict surprise and disaster in human affairs is as important. Yet in studying "mechanisms" we still make a fundamental error. Neither we nor Gaia are machines. We are alive, and bound together in a partnership of unpredictable adventure. Unco-operative partners seldom last the course.

Gaia and humanity

For around 3 billion years, life has persisted on this planet, evolving and co-operating to shape and sustain its own environment. Humanity is no more than 2 million years old; civilization only a few thousand years. In the last 200 years, and particularly the last half century – a blink of an eye in Gaian time – we have come to threaten much of life on Earth. A nuclear exchange would probably exterminate the human species. Our disturbance of environments may provoke major system shifts, equally rendering much present life extinct. We do not even know what we would be destroying – we are more ignorant of much of Gaia than of the moon. There are those who view humanity as a cancerous organism, while others promote us as the emerging consciousness of Gaia. Why can we not see ourselves just as we are – members of a democratic, living community?

The peace of Gaia

A world at peace will not be some sleepy utopian dream. Change and experiment, creativity, risk and surprise are drives we share with life itself – as we do its search for order, stability, organization and homeostatic regulation. It is time we made peace with Gaia – an enterprise that will challenge all our ingenuity, courage and skill. And it is time we recognized that war is neither a necessary evil, nor part of "human nature", but a failure of our nature. The peace of Gaia is a great venture into the unknown.

"Every part of this earth is sacred to my people . . . The sap which courses through the trees carries the memories of the red man . . . Our dead never forget this beautiful earth, for it is the mother of the red man. We are part of the earth and it is part of us . . . The water's murmur is the voice of my father's father. The rivers are our brothers, they quench our thirst . . . The air is precious to the red man, for all things share the same breath . . . We know that the white man does not understand our ways . . . The earth is not his brother, but his enemy, and when he has conquered it, he moves on . . . His appetite will devour the earth and leave behind only a desert . . . Perhaps it is because I am a savage I do not understand. What is man without the beasts? If all the beasts were gone, man would die from a great loneliness of spirit. For whatever happens to the beasts soon happens to man."

From Chief Seattle's reply to the US President, 1854

Epilogue

"No great improvements in the lot of mankind are possible until a great change takes place in the fundamental constitution of their modes of thought." John Stuart Mill, philosopher

"Breakthroughs in physics are sometimes easier than breakthroughs in psyches." President Ronald Reagan

Preparing this book has been both depressing and exhilarating. It has brought home to me yet again the inability of today's political leaders to grapple with grave global problems. But I believe that public opinion will exert itself before these problems pass the point of no return, and insist that reluctant politicians act in time.

The human drive for survival is strong. Recent history shows that ordinary people recognize, instinctively, when their survival as a society is threatened. And then they act. They do not need a deep knowledge of the subject. The mass European reaction against deployment of neutron bombs is a good example. People didn't know much about neutron bombs, in particular, or nuclear weapons, in general. They just had a gut feeling that the nuclear arms race was out of control. And they took to the streets in such numbers that politicians felt compelled to ban neutron bombs from Europe.

The main barriers to solving the global problems outlined in this book are the powers, who, through their vested interests, will lose short-term profits or influence, and are convinced that they are defending our "security". It often seems that little short of a revolution will shake this view. But economic constraints will work in favour of solutions. The Pentagon, for example, is asking the US Congress to give it just under $300 billion to spend in the fiscal year 1989. This is a huge sum of money. Nevertheless, the American military had originally intended to ask for much more. But given Congress's aim to reduce the US's large budget deficit, the military have realized that they are unlikely to get more money next year than they have this year. Similarly the need to pay for economic reforms will constrain future Soviet military spending.

It is very difficult to imagine what a huge sum like $300 billion really means. For comparison, this spending in one year equals the total gross domestic products of the countries that contain the poorest 25 per cent of the world's population – about 1.5 billion people. The USSR spends about the same amount of money on its military. Together, the superpowers spend on the military as much as the 3 billion people in the 44 poorest nations earn. Bearing in mind the abject poverty in which so many people live, to give such resources to the military is intolerable.

The world's governments spend more on the military than on health or education. Yet 770 million people do not get enough food to sustain an active working life; 1300 million have no safe water to drink; 1 billion live in poverty, unable to meet minimal needs; 880 million adults cannot read or write; 14 million children under the age of five die of hunger-related diseases every year, and so on; one depressing statistic after another.

A five-year programme to immunize the world's children against the six deadly diseases of childhood, which each year kill one million children before their fifth year, would cost about $1.5 billion. The world's military spends twice this sum *every day*. The poorest fifth of the world population has less than 2 per cent of the world's economic product; the richest fifth has 75 per cent. This gross inequality, and the increasing North-South tension it produces, is a serious threat to the security of all. We would greatly improve our own security if we spent less on the military and used the money to reduce global injustice.

If the world's military spent less, fewer people would die when conflicts occurred. The smart new weapons that governments buy kill ever-larger numbers of people. In the 20th century, so far, 99 million people have been killed in wars – ten times the deaths in the two preceding centuries put together. Moreover, modern wars kill far more civilians than soldiers. In the 1980s, civilians have accounted for as much as 90 per cent of the deaths in wars. Our century is certainly a barbarous one.

Technology continually develops more efficient ways of killing people. It is also responsible for many of the environmental problems we face. On the other hand, technology has considerably improved our expectation of life, and if used appropriately could do much to ease our future. Choosing between destructive and life-enhancing technologies is one of the major dilemmas of our age. Our species has evidently evolved with excellent scientific and technical capacities. But we are, it seems, less well endowed with the moral understanding, or the inventiveness, needed to create the social institutions that could control this technology.

Necessity, however, is the mother of invention. Surely we must discover how to control technology and use it for benign purposes, before it destroys us.

Frank Barnaby

Appendices

Data

Although there is a wealth of literature analysing war and its origins, there is little dealing with co-operation and how to achieve a peaceful society. Yet war and peace are, in truth, two sides of the same coin. We cannot hope to achieve a peaceful and sustainable global society unless we understand our capacity for both good and bad. The dearth of balanced information has made the preparation of this book, at times, very difficult.

Delving into the past has proved frustrating. Archaeology is essentially the study of physical remains and as such reveals very little about social structures. Trying to learn from existing peaceful and egalitarian societies we have come up against the resistance of anthropologists who, like other social scientists, are often reluctant to tackle contentious issues. There are very few anthropological studies devoted to either the analysis of warfare or to the factors that make a society peaceful.

In contrast, a growing number of organizations are concerned with documenting the full extent of current global militarization and its impact on humanity. The list of lost opportunities for development, meeting basic needs and halting the destruction of the biosphere is growing every day. Due to a lack of public awareness, the research organizations understandably put most of their energy into identifying the problem, and consequently devote little time to coming up with solutions. Research is urgently needed into policies and strategies for preventing and resolving conflict and structural violence.

Throughout this atlas we have used the most reliable information available but national statistics do rely on a country's ability to collect, and willingess to reveal, reliable data about themselves. In some countries, systems of data collection are very basic. Others limit disclosure of statistics or even distort them for political ends. To offset uncertainties we have used case studies, informed analysis, and our own research and contacts as a countercheck wherever possible. Where we have had to rely on estimates – for example, the number of refugees or the extent of human rights violations – it is worth bearing in mind that most data on the extent of militarization and human suffering tend to be under- rather than overestimated.

Essential reading

The Gaia Peace Atlas is a companion volume to *The Gaia Atlas of Planet Management* and Gaia's *State of the Ark Atlas*, and readers will find both helpful for their further statistics and analysis. There are, in addition, a handful of outstanding books dealing with peace and sustainable ecology which should accompany *The Gaia Peace Atlas* on your bookshelf. Most are readily available in both the USA and the UK; all can be ordered from a bookshop with the information provided below. We recommend the following for the insight and information they provide:

B. Brock-Utne *Educating for Peace*, Pergamon Press (1985)
L. R. Brown et al *State of the World 1987*, Norton (1987)
F. Capra *Turning Point*, Collins (1983)
G. Chaliand and J. P. Rageau *Strategic Atlas*, Penguin Books (1985)
L. Durrell *State of the Ark*, Doubleday (1986)
P. Ekins (ed) *The Living Economy*, Routledge and Kegan Paul (1986)
E. Fromm *The Anatomy of Human Destructiveness*, Pelican Books (1982)
The Hunger Project *Ending Hunger*, Praeger Publishers (1985)
P. Kome and P. Crean (eds) *Peace: A Dream Unfolding*, Sierra Club Books (1986)
J. E. Lovelock *Gaia: A New Look at Life on Earth*, Oxford University Press (1987)
N. Myers *The Gaia Atlas of Planet Management*, Pan Books (1985)
P. Russell *The Awakening Earth*, Routledge and Kegan Paul (1976)
W. and D. Schwarz *Breaking Through*, Green Books (1987)
Third World Guide 86-87, Third World (1986)
A. Toffler *The Third Wave*, Collins (1980)
The Universal House of Justice *The Promise of World Peace*, One World Publications (1986)
WCED *Our Common Future*, Oxford University Press (1987).

The following comprise an important additional bibliography:
P. Calvocoressi *A Time for Peace*, Hutchinson (1987)
E. Fromm *To Have or To Be?*, Abacus, Sphere Books (1979)
A. Huxley *Green Inheritance*, Collins (1984)
T. J. Kaptchuk *Chinese Medicine: The Web That Has No Weaver*, Hutchinson (1983)
M. Kidron and R. Segal *The New State of the World Atlas*, Simon and Schuster (1984)
M. Kidron and D. Smith *The War Atlas*, Pan Books (1983)
R. Leger Sivard *World Military and Social Expenditures 1986*, World Priorities (1986)
SIPRI Yearbook 1987, Oxford University Press (1987)
A. H. Westing (ed) *Global Resources and International Conflict*, Oxford University Press (1986)
WCED *Energy 2000*, Zed Books (1987)
WCED *Food 2000*, Zed Books (1987)
R. Whitehouse and J. Wilkins *The Making of Civilization*, Collins (1986)
The World Bank *World Development Report 1986*, Oxford University Press (1986)
The World Defence Almanac: The Balance of Military Power, Military Technology, No.13/86 (1986)
World Encyclopedia of Peace, Pergamon Press (1986)
World Resources Institute and IIED *World Resources 1986*, Basic Books (1986)

Abbreviations

ABM Anti-Ballistic Missile
ANC African National Congress
ANZUS Australia-New Zealand-US Security Treaty
ASEAN Association of South East Asian Nations
AWACS Airborne Warning and Control System
CAAT Campaign Against the Arms Trade
CEP Circular Error Probability
CGIAR Consultative Group on International Agricultural Research
CIA Central Intelligence Agency (US)
CITES Convention on International Trade in Endangered Species of Wild Flora and Fauna
CND Campaign for Nuclear Disarmament
COMECON Council for Mutual Economic Assistance (Communist nations)
EEC European Economic Community
EEZ Exclusive Economic Zone
EPIC European Proliferation Information Centre
ERW Enhanced Radiation Weapon (neutron bomb)
FAO Food and Agriculture Organization
GATT General Agreement on Tariffs and Trade
GCD General and Complete Disarmament
GNP Gross National Product
IAEA International Atomic Energy Agency
IBPGR International Board for Plant Genetic Resources
IBRD International Bank for Reconstruction and Development
ICAO International Civil Aviation Organization
ICBM Intercontinental Ballistic Missile
IDA International Development Association
IFAD International Fund for Agricultural Development
IFDA International Foundation for Development Alternatives
IFC International Finance Corporation
IGRAT International Group of Researchers on the ABM Treaty
IIASA International Institute for Applied Systems Analysis
IIED International Institute for Environment and Development
IISS International Institute for Strategic Studies
ILO International Labour Organization
IMF International Monetary Fund
IMO International Maritime Organization
INSTRAW International Research and Training Institute for the Advancement of Women
IPPF International Planned Parenthood Federation
ITU International Telecommunications Union
IUCN International Union for the Conservation of Nature and Natural Resources
KGB Committee of State Security (USSR)
MAD Mutual Assured Destruction
MIRV Multiple Independently-targetable Re-entry Vehicle
NATO North Atlantic Treaty Organization

NGO Non Governmental Organization
NIEO New International Economic Order
NRDC Natural Resources Defense Council
NUTS Nuclear Utilization Targetting Strategy
NWICO New World Information and Communication Order
OECD Organization for Economic Co-operation and Development
OPEC Organization of Petroleum Exporting Countries
OXFAM Oxford Committee for Famine Relief
PLO Palestine Liberation Organization
R and D Research and Development
RPV Remotely Piloted Vehicle
SADCC Southern African Development Co-ordination Conference
SALT Strategic Arms Limitation Talks
SDI Strategic Defense Initiative
SIPRI Stockholm International Peace Research Institute
SLBM Submarine-launched Ballistic Missile
START Strategic Arms Reduction Talks
SWAPO South West Africa People's Organization
TNT Trinitrotoluene (an explosive)
TOES The Other Economic Summit
TOW Tube-launched, Optically-tracked, Wire-guided missile
UNCTAD United Nations Conference on Trade and Development
UNDOF United Nations Disengagement Observer Force
UNDP United Nations Development Programme
UNEP United Nations Environment Programme
UNESCO United Nations Educational, Scientific and Cultural Organization
UNFICYP United Nations Peace-keeping Force in Cyprus
UNHCR Office of the United Nations High Commissioner for Refugees
UNICEF United Nations Children's Fund
UNIDO United Nations Industrial Development Organization
UNIFIL United Nations Interim Force in Lebanon
UNITAR United Nations Institute for Training and Research
UNMOGIP United Nations Military Observer Group in India and Pakistan
UNRWA United Nations Relief and Works Agency for Palestine Refugees
UNTSO United Nations Truce Supervision Organization
UNU United Nations University
UPU Universal Postal Union
WCED World Commission on Environment and Development
WCS World Conservation Strategy
WFC World Food Council
WFP Joint UN/FAO World Food Programme
WHO World Health Organization
WIPO World Intellectual Property Organization
WMO World Meteorological Organization
WRI World Resources Institute
WWF World Wildlife Fund

Glossary

Appropriate technology Low-cost technology that utilizes locally abundant resources in preference to locally scarce resources. The term usually refers to small-scale, decentralized, development approaches.

Austerity measures Tight controls on government spending, often a condition of international financial assistance and loans.

Basic human needs Adequate food, clothing and shelter; access to basic services including primary health care, education and safe water. Sometimes includes the right to work.

Biosphere The thin planetary covering of atmosphere, soil and water that includes and sustains life.

Biotechnology The application of biological organisms, systems or processes to manufacturing industry.

Carrying capacity (of land) The maximum resident population that can be sustained by food derived from a given ecosystem.

Cash cropping Growing crops for sale in a market rather than for family consumption, as in subsistence farming.

CFC Chlorofluorocarbons, a synthetic gas which is a byproduct of industrial processes and which depletes atmospheric ozone.

Co-evolution The joint interactive evolution of species and their environment, to form co-operative, self-sustaining ecosystems.

Double cropping The practice of harvesting two crops from the same land in one year.

Ecosystem A community of organisms and their environment. It can apply to a small area of land or ocean or to the entire planet.

Gaia The name given to the Earth, and the mother goddess, in ancient Greek mythology.

Gaia principle Idea that the biosphere is a "super-organism", and that the biota collectively maintain an environment fit for life.

GNP The total monetary value of final products and services produced by a nation in a given year, e.g. a loaf of bread purchased by the consumer is a final product, but not the wheat, flour or labour used to produce it.

GNP per capita The gross national product of a nation, divided by its population.

Governance The management and organization of society, by all its institutions and systems.

Government The institution of ultimate authority in a society, intended to direct the functions of governance.

Green revolution The development and widespread adoption of high-yield strains of wheat, corn, and rice in the South in the 1960s and early 1970s. It now refers to almost any package of modern agricultural technologies introduced into the South.

International Dealings between nations.

Lingua franca Any language serving as a medium between different peoples.

Meso-America An area centred on the modern states of Mexico, Guatemala, Belize and El Salvador. Meso-American civilizations include the Olmecs, Aztecs, Toltecs, Maya and those based around Monte Alban and Teotihuacan, but not the Incas, Nazca or Chimu.

Monoculture When a genetic make-up is replicated to provide a uniform crop.

Multinational Usually refers to a corporation that has subsidiaries, investments or operations in more than one country. Is gradually being replaced by the term *transnational* which puts greater emphasis on the difficulties of controlling their operations.

North Countries above the Brandt line (see South).

NOx Nitric oxide, a gas formed by the combustion of fossil fuels.

Ozone A condensed form of oxygen. As one of the main constituents of ground level smog it is harmful but in the stratosphere it provides a barrier against ultraviolet and other harmful high-energy radiation penetrating through to the Earth's surface.

Peace Three definitions are used: an absence of war; an absence of direct and structural violence; "positive" peace, in which society actively seeks to build a peaceful structure.

Poverty Usually a relative term, describing those people who are "socially deprived" in relation to others. Absolute poverty traps those people who are unable to supply their own basic needs for food, clothing and shelter in a cycle from which they cannot escape.

South The area below a line drawn on the world map by the Brandt Commission in 1980, identifying those countries with low per capita incomes and previously termed "less developed" or the "Third World".

Sovereignty The notion that a national government should have supreme power over affairs conducted within its own borders.

Star Wars A synonym for the Strategic Defense Initiative launched by President Reagan. This term refers to the direct energy weapons situated in space which could destroy satellites or missiles soon after launch. Deployment, but not development, of such weapons is forbidden under the terms of the ABM Treaty.

Steady state economy An economic system in which resource consumption is held level with replenishment through natural cycles or human effort, and the living environment is therefore conserved.

Structural violence Any act which is not directly physically violent but which nonetheless adversely affects average life expectancy. This includes socially damaging actions such as dumping pollutants, public spending cuts, suppression of rights, etc.

Supranational Literally, "above" the national level. Refers to organizations, treaties or values which are not limited by a nationalistic perspective or sovereignty.

Sustainable Meeting present needs without prejudicing those of future generations.

Third World (see South).

Transnational Organization, treaty, or company which operates across national boundaries. Transnational issues, such as desertification and deforestation, are those which require a regional or global forum since they affect more than the countries in which they are happening.

World Bank Actually the World Bank group – three separately funded but closely related agencies: the IBRD, IDA and IFC.

Sources

CHAPTER 1
THE ROOTS OF PEACE
pp. 24-5 Co-operation and consensus
Sources: R. Whitehouse and J. Wilkins *The Making of Civilization*, Collins (1986); M. Harris *Culture, People, Nature*, 3rd edition, Harper and Row (1980).

pp. 26-7 A sustainable base
Sources: R. Whitehouse and J. Wilkins *The Making of Civilization*, Collins (1986); K. N. Cameron *Humanity and Society*, Monthly Review Press (1973); H. Kinder and W. Hilgemann *The Anchor Atlas of World History*, Vol. 1, Anchor Books, Doubleday (1974).

pp. 28-9 The distribution of wealth
Sources: *The Sunday Times*, 8 November 1987; International Labor Office, Geneva; *WMSE86**; M. B. Brown *Models in Political Economy*, Penguin Books (1984).

pp. 30-1 Rule of law
Sources: *The World Defence Almanac: The Balance of Military Power 1986-1987*, Military Technology, No. 13/86 (1986); K. N. Cameron *Humanity and Society*, Monthly Review Press (1973); W. A. Haviland *Cultural Anthropology*, 4th edition, Holt Reinehart and Winston (1983); J. M. Roberts *The Pelican History of the World*, Penguin Books (1980).

pp. 32-3 Governance
Sources: *Third World Guide 86-87*, Third World (1986); *WMSE86**; Swedish Embassy, London; The World Bank *World Development Report 1986*, Oxford University Press (1986); L. R. Brown et al *State of the World 1987*, Norton (1987).

CHAPTER 2
THE ROOTS OF CONFLICT
pp. 36-7 Introduction with quotations from
speeches by Petra Kelly at the International Green Congress, Stockholm (1987), and the Women in Power conference, Dublin (1984).

pp. 38-9 Roots of war
Sources: B. Brock-Utne *Educating for Peace*, Pergamon Press (1985); K. N. Cameron *Humanity and Society*, Monthly Review Press (1973); E. Fromm *The Anatomy of Human Destructiveness*, Pelican Books (1982); S. B. Clough *The Rise and Fall of Civilization*, Greenwood Press (1978); K. F. Otterbein "The Anthropology of War" in J. J. Honigmann (ed) *Handbook of Social and Cultural Anthropology*, Rand McNally (1973).

pp. 42-3 Territory and resources
Sources: G. Chaliand and J. P. Rageau *Strategic Atlas*, Penguin Books (1985); M. Kidron and R. Segal *The New State of the World Atlas*, Simon and Schuster (1984); A. Boyd *An Atlas of World Affairs*, 7th edition, Methuen (1983); M. Kidron and D. Smith *The War Atlas*, Pan Books (1983); *Third World Guide 86-87*, Third World (1986); Ecoropa Information Sheet 11 *Falklands War – The*

Disturbing Truth; Survival International; Frank Barnaby, *The Australian*, 11 June 1986; Western Desert Land Council, Australia.

pp. 48-9 New identities, old ties
Sources: M. E. Chamberlain *The Scramble for Africa*, Longman (1984); P. Curtin et al *African History*, Longman (1978); G. Chaliand and J. P. Rageau *Strategic Atlas*, Penguin Books (1985); M. Kidron and R. Segal *The New State of the World Atlas*, Simon and Schuster (1986); P. Harrison *Inside The Third World*, Penguin Books (1979); *Third World Atlas*, Open University Press (1983); *The Atlas of Mankind*, Mitchell Beazley (1982).

pp. 50-1 Shackled politicians
Sources: R. Hofstadter and B. K. Hofstadter *Great Issues in American History*, Vol. 3, Vintage Books (1982); *SIPRI Yearbook 1986*, Oxford University Press (1986); *WMSE86**.

pp. 52-3 The arms trade
Sources: *SIPRI Yearbook 1981*, Taylor and Francis (1981); *SIPRI Yearbook 1986*, Oxford University Press (1986); *The Independent*, 1 June 1987; F. Barnaby and R. Huisken *Arms Uncontrolled*, SIPRI (1975); *Bulletin of Peace Proposals*, Vol. 17, No. 3-4, Norwegian University Press (1986); *South*, November 1985; H. M. Sachar *A History of Israel*, Basil Blackwell (1977).

pp. 54-5 Multiplying conflict points
Sources: *WMSE86**; M. Kidron and D. Smith *The War Atlas*, Pan Books (1983).

pp. 56-7 3rd World War?
Sources: *International Herald Tribune*, 6 May 1986; *South*, August 1986; R. Leger Sivard *World Military and Social Expenditures 1983*, World Priorities (1983); *WMSE86**; Frank Barnaby.

CHAPTER 3 KEEPING THE PEACE
pp. 64-5 Civil peacekeeping
Sources: *WMSE86**; M. Kidron and D. Smith *The War Atlas*, Pan Books (1983).

pp. 66-7 DisUnited Nations
Sources: United Nations Information Centre, London; H. Kinder and W. Hilgemann *The Penguin Atlas of World History*, Vol. 2, Penguin Books (1978).

pp. 68-9 The law of war and peace
Sources: B. V. A. Röling *The Law of War and Dubious Weapons*, SIPRI, Almquist and Viksell International (1976); *Charter of the United Nations and Statute of the International Court of Justice*, United Nations Office of Public Information, New York.

pp. 70-1 UN peacekeeping
Sources: *Third World Guide 86-87*, Third World (1986); L. Freedman *Atlas of Global Strategy*, Macmillan (1985); M. Allsebrook *Prototypes of Peacemaking*, Longman (1986).

pp. 72-3 The nuclear umbrella
Sources: Frank Barnaby.

pp. 74-5 UN peace building
Sources: United Nations Information Centre, London.

CHAPTER 4 THE EMERGING GLOBAL COMMUNITY
pp. 78-9 Introduction with quotations from a speech by M. J. K. Nyerere on receiving the Lenin Prize, Dodoma (1987).

pp. 80-1 One world?
Sources: The World Bank World Development Report 1986, Oxford University Press (1986); WMSE86*; F. Capra Turning Point, Flamingo, Collins (1983); W.I. Thompson The Pacific Shift, Sierra Club Books (1986).

pp. 82-3 Networks of agreement
Sources: A. J. Day (ed), Keesings Contemporary Archives Treaties and Alliances of the World, 4th edition, Longman (1986); END.

pp. 84-5 International or supranational?
Sources: World Encyclopedia of Peace, Pergamon Press (1986); UN Information Centre, London; A. J. Day (ed), Keesings Contemporary Archives Treaties and Alliances of the World, 4th edition, Longman (1986).

pp. 86-7 The struggle for human rights
Sources: P. Sieghart The Lawful Rights of Mankind; Amnesty International; W. Lacquer and B. Rubin The Human Rights reader, Meridian (1979); World Encyclopedia of Peace, Pergamon Press (1986); World Resources Institute and IIED World Resources 1986, Basic Books (1986).

pp. 88-9 Perceiving the dangers
Sources: Embassy of the Federal Republic of Germany, London; L. Durrell State of the Ark, Doubleday (1986); M. Kidron and R. Segal The New State of the World Atlas, Simon and Schuster (1984); Greenpeace UK; Sarah Parkin, Green Party UK; Mark Halle, World Conservation Centre, Geneva; Mark Carwardine.

pp. 90-1 Redressing the balance
Sources: L. Durrell State of the Ark, Doubleday (1986); World Encyclopedia of Peace, Pergamon Press (1986).

pp. 92-3 A global culture?
Sources: The World Defence Almanac: The Balance of Military Power 1986-1987, Military Technology, No. 13/86 (1986); M. Kidron and R. Segal The New State of the World Atlas, Simon and Schuster (1984); Third World Guide 86-87, Third World (1986); The Economist, 20 Dec 1986; World Encyclopedia of Peace, Pergamon Press (1986).

CHAPTER 5 CIVILIZATION IN CRISIS
Part 1: The price of military solutions
pp. 94-5 Introduction excerpted from statements by G. H. Brundtland to the UN (1987) and to UNCTAD (1987).

pp. 96-7 The dollar cost
Sources: WMSE86*; The Hunger Project Ending Hunger, Praeger (1985); SIPRI Yearbook 1981, Taylor and Francis (1981); SIPRI Yearbook 1986, Oxford University Press (1986).

pp. 98-9 The human cost?
Sources: Children in Situations of Armed Conflict, UNICEF report, March 1986; WMSE86*; B. Brock-Utne Educating for Peace, Pergamon Press (1985); Common Security, Pan Books (1982); press reports; Children on the Front Line, UNICEF report, January 1987.

pp. 100-1 Children and war
Sources: Children in Situations of Armed Conflict, UNICEF report, March 1986; B. Brock-Utne Educating for Peace, Pergamon Press (1985); Children on the Front Line, UNICEF report, January 1987; To us a Child, Thames Television, 10 December 1986; Uganda, Children of the Terror, Panorama, BBC1 24 March 1986; P. Kome and P. Crean Peace: A Dream Unfolding, Sierra Club Books (1986); Peace Pledge Union; Quaker Peace and Service confidential reports.

pp. 102-3 The environmental cost
Sources: Third World Guide 86-87, Third World (1986); L. Durrell State of the Ark, Doubleday (1986); Environment and Conflict, Earthscan briefing document 40; several press reports; M. Kidron and D. Smith The War Atlas, Pan Books (1983); South, April 1987; UNEP; She, February 1987; The Last Nuclear Explosion, Novosti Press Agency (1986); WWF News, No.24; New Scientist, 21 July 1983; World Health, July 1986; N. Myers "The Environmental Dimension to Security Issues", The Environmentalist, Vol. 6, No. 4 (1986).

pp. 104-9 Lost opportunities
Sources: The Hunger Project Ending Hunger, Praeger (1985); WCED Our Common Future, Oxford University Press (1987); N. Myers The Gaia Atlas of Planet Management, Pan Books (1985); The State of the World's Children 1984, Oxford University Press (1983); WMSE86*; US Bureau of Labor Statistics; The Brandt Commission Common Crisis, Pan Books (1983); UNEP; CITES office, Switzerland; Environmental Data Services, London; Frank Barnaby; United Nations and Disarmament 1945-1985: A Fortieth Anniversary review, Disarmament Fact Sheet No. 42, Department for Disarmament Affairs, UN; The International Conference on the Relationship between Disarmament and Development, Disarmament Fact Sheet No. 45, Department for Disarmament Affairs, UN; N. Myers "Population, Environment, and Conflict", Environmental Conservation, Vol. 14, No. 1, Spring 1987; SIPRI Yearbook 1981, Taylor and Francis (1981); SIPRI Yearbook 1986, Oxford University Press (1986); Dr V. W. Sidel "Socioeconomic Effects of the Arms Race", Preventive Medicine, Vol. 16, No. 3, May 1987.

CHAPTER 5 CIVILIZATION IN CRISIS
Part 2: Transnational threats to security
pp. 110-11 Population insecurity
Sources: L. Durrell State of the Ark, Doubleday (1986); C. M. Cipolla The Economic History of World Population, Penguin Books (1962); WCED Our Common Future, Oxford University Press (1987); The Universal House of Justice The Promise of World Peace, One World Publications (1986); M. Kidron and R. Segal The New State of the World Atlas, Simon and Schuster (1984); L. R. Brown et al State of the World 1987, Norton (1987); R. S. McNamara "Time Bomb or Myth – The Population Problem", Foreign Affairs journal; World Resources Institute and IIED World Resources 1986, Basic Books (1986); The Global 2000 Report to the President, Penguin Books (1982); F. Pearce "Welcome to the global old folks' home" New Scientist, 9 July 1987; David Satterthwaite.

pp. 112-13 Economic insecurity
Sources: The World Bank World Development Report 1986, Oxford University Press (1986); WMSE86*; The Guardian, 6 June 1987; The Independent, 23 June 1987.

pp. 114-15 Human insecurity
Sources: The Global 2000 Report to the President, Penguin Books (1982); J. E. Hardoy and D. Satterthwaite Shelter, Infrastructure and Services in Third World Cities, IIED (1987); Norman Myers; Children in Situations of Armed Conflict, UNICEF report, March 1986; N. Myers The Gaia Atlas of Planet Management, Pan Books (1985); World Resources Institute and IIED World Resources 1986, Basic Books (1986).

pp. 116-17 Resource insecurity
Sources: G. Chaliand and J. P. Rageau Strategic Atlas, Penguin Books (1985); M. Kidron and R. Segal The New State of the World Atlas, Simon and Schuster (1984); N. Myers The Gaia Atlas of Planet Management, Pan Books (1985); World Resources Institute and IIED World Resources 1986, Basic Books (1986); A. H. Westing (ed) Global Resources and International Conflict, Oxford University Press (1986); A. Buchanan Food Poverty and Power, Spokesman (1982); WCED Our Common Future, Oxford University Press (1987).

pp. 118-19 Pollution
Sources: IPPNW; L. R. Brown et al State of the World 1987, Norton (1987); Greenpeace International; press reports; New Scientist 19 March 1987; Greenpeace USA; N. Myers The Gaia Atlas of Planet Management, Pan Books (1985); John May; M. Kidron and R. Segal The New State of the World Atlas, Simon and Schuster (1984); State of the Environment, UNEP (1987).

pp. 120-1 Food power and climate change
Sources: Scripps Institution of Oceanography; L. R. Brown et al State of the World 1987, Norton (1987); Warren Springs

Laboratory *Acid Deposition in the United Kingdom*, Department of the Environment (1983); WCED *Our Common Future*, Oxford University Press (1987); World Resources Institute and IIED *World Resources 1986*, Basic Books (1986); C. M. Cipolla *The Economic History of World Population*, Penguin Books (1962); *A matter of degrees*, World Resources Institute Research Paper No. 5, April 1987; H. Smith *Oceans and Seas*, Bell and Hyman (1985); P. R. and A. H. Erlich, and J. P. Holdren *Ecoscience: Population, Resources, Environment*, W. H. Freeman (1977); G. Chaliand and J. P. Rageau *Strategic Atlas*, Penguin Books (1985); *The Observer*, 15 March 1987.

pp. 122-3 Crime
Sources: Barbara Keiser; Interpol, France; N. Lewis *The Honoured Society: The Sicilian Mafia Observed*, Eland Books (1984); G. Servadio *Mafioso*, Secker and Warburg (1976); C. Wilson *A Criminal History of Mankind*, Granada (1984); *Facts on File*, 18 April 1986, 20 March 1987, 17 July 1987; Senator John Kerry and staff *Private Assistance and the Contras: A Staff Report*, 14 October 1986; A. Henman, R. Lewis and T. Malyon *Big Deal: The Politics of the Illicit Drug Business*, Pluto Press (1985); press reports; D. E. Kaplan and A. Dubro *Yakuzo: The Explosive Account of Japan's Criminal Underworld*, Addison-Wesley (1986).

pp. 124-5 Terrorist or freedom fighter?
Sources: *Patterns of International Terrorism 1980*, CIA report, June 1981; *Patterns of Global Terrorism 1984*, US Department of State; C. Dobson and R. Payne *War Without End*, Harrap (1986); *Public Report of the Vice President's Task Force on Combatting Terrorism*, USA, February 1986; D. Hayes *Terrorists and Freedom Fighters*, Wayland (1980).

pp. 126-7 Media and the secret state
Sources: Jonathan Fryer; BBC; Frank Barnaby; *Financial Times*, 8 August 1985; *The Guardian*, 13 March 1987; *IFDA dossier* 61, September/October 1987.

CHAPTER 5
CIVILIZATION IN CRISIS
Part 3: FEAR OF ARMAGEDDON
pp. 128-9 Nuclear war: Likely causes
Sources: Dr H. L. Abrams "The Problem of Accidental or Inadvertent Nuclear War", *Preventive Medicine*, Vol. 16, No. 3, May 1987; R. Davies *Children and the Threat of Nuclear War*, Occasional Paper No. 8, Centre for Peace Studies, St. Martin's College Lancaster; F. Barnaby (ed) *Future War*, Michael Joseph (1984).

pp. 130-1 Nuclear proliferation
Sources: L. Freedman *Atlas of Global Strategy*, Macmillan (1985); *IAEA Bulletin*, Vol. 29, No. 1 (1987); W. C. Paterson *The Plutonium Business*, Paladin Books (1984); *Science*, Vol. 235, 27 March 1987; L. R. Brown et al *State of the World 1987*, Norton (1987).

pp. 132-3 The infernal machine
Sources: Frank Barnaby; *WMSE86**; L. Freedman *Atlas of Global Strategy*, Macmillan (1985); *SIPRI Yearbook 1986*, Oxford University Press (1986).

pp. 134-5 Conventional war:
Horrors of today
Sources: *The Military Balance 1986 -1987*, IISS (1986); Frank Barnaby; *SIPRI Yearbook 1987*, Oxford University Press (1987); *The Independent*, 7 May 1987; other press reports.

pp. 136-7 The bang
Sources: Royal Swedish Academy of Sciences *AMBIO* special issue, "Nuclear War: The Aftermath", Vol. 9, No. 2-3, Pergamon Press (1982); *Effects of Nuclear War on Health and Health Services*, WHO report, 18 March 1987.

pp. 138-9 Nuclear winter:
Nowhere to hide
Sources: Dr H. J. Geiger and Dr J. Leaning "Nuclear Winter and the Longer-Term Consequences of Nuclear War", *Preventive Medicine*, Vol. 16, No. 3, May 1987; *No Place To Hide: Nuclear Winter and the Third World*, Earthscan Press Briefing Document 43, May 1986; *The Long-Term Environmental and Medical Effects of Nuclear War*, British Medical Association, March 1986; *World Encyclopedia of Peace*, Pergamon Press (1986); P. R. Ehrlich "North America After the War", *Natural History*, No. 3, 1984; L. Dotto *Planet Earth in Jeopardy*, Wiley (1986); *Science*, 12 June and 19 June 1987.

pp.140-1 Despair and hope
Sources: D. Rowe *Living with the Bomb*, Routledge and Kegan Paul (1985); John-Francis Phipps; *The Lancet*, 7 April 1984; J. Thompson "The Psychological Aspects of Nuclear Threat and Nuclear War: Analogies from Disaster Research", *Effects of Nuclear War on Health and Health Services*, WHO report, 18 March 1987; R. Davies *Hopes and Fears: Children's Attitudes to Nuclear War*, Occasional Paper No. 11, Centre for Peace Studies, St. Martin's College Lancaster; J. Macy *Despair and Personal Power in the Nuclear Age*, New Society Publications (1983); R. Davies *Children and the Threat of Nuclear War*, Occasional Paper No. 8, Centre for Peace Studies, St. Martin's College Lancaster; J. S. Barbara "Psychological Impact of the Arms Race on Children", *Preventive Medicine*, Vol. 16, 354-360, 1987.

CHAPTER 6
THE STRUGGLE FOR PEACE
pp. 142-3 Introduction with quotations from the speech "The Quest for Peace" delivered by Archbishop Desmond Tutu in Hiroshima (1986).

pp. 144-5 Disarmament talks
Sources: R. Leger Sivard *World Military and Social Expenditures 1983*, World Priorities (1983); press reports.

pp. 146-7 Transnational efforts
Sources: *Ideas Forum No. 22*, UNICEF (1985); The Hunger Project *Ending Hunger*, Praeger (1985); The World Bank *World Development Report 1986*, Oxford University Press (1986).

pp. 148-9 Responses to terrorism
Sources: A. J. Day (ed), Keesings Contemporary Archives *Treaties and Alliances of the World*, 4th edition, Longman (1986); P. Calvocoressi *A Time for Peace*, Hutchinson (1987); N. Chomsky "Libya in US Demonology", *ENDpapers Fourteen: International Terrorism and International Law*, Bertrand Russell Peace Foundation (1987); *Public Report of the Vice President's Task Force on Combatting Terrorism*, February 1986; US Department of State GIST Report *International Terrorism*, August 1985; P. Wilkinson (ed) *British Perspectives on Terrorism*, George Allen and Unwin (1981).

pp. 150-1 Individual pressures for peace
Sources: The Guardian, 4 September 1987; Third World Guide 86-87, Third World (1986); World Encyclopedia of Peace, Pergamon Press (1986).

pp. 152-3 New peace initiatives
Sources: Commonwealth Secretariat, London; Beyond War; *SIPRI Yearbook 1981*, Taylor and Francis (1981); *SIPRI Yearbook 1986*, Oxford University Press (1986); *The Guardian*, 10 April 1987; *South*, August 1986.

pp. 154-5 The peace movement
Sources: P. Calvocoressi *A Time for Peace*, Hutchinson (1987); *World Encyclopedia of Peace*, Pergamon Press (1986); J. Ruddock *CND Scrapbook*, Optima, Macdonald (1987).

pp. 156-7 Voices of peace
Sources: CND; M. Kidron and R. Segal *The New State of the World Atlas*, Simon and Schuster (1984); *World Encyclopedia of Peace*, Pergamon Press (1986).

pp. 158-9 Non-violence
Sources: P. Calvocoressi *A Time for Peace*, Hutchinson (1987); *World Encyclopedia of Peace*, Pergamon Press (1986); J. Ferguson *A Call To Nonviolence*, Fellowship of Reconciliation (1984); T. Augarde *Gandhi*, Peace Pledge Union (1982); The Universal House of Justice *The Promise of World Peace*, One World Publications (1986); Deeper Dimension.

CHAPTER 7
THE CHOICES FOR HUMANITY
pp. 164-5 Moral choices
Sources: T. J. Kaptchuk *Chinese Medicine: The Web That Has No Weaver*, Rider and Co., Hutchinson (1983); P. Ekins (ed) *The Living Economy*, Routledge and Kegan Paul (1986).

pp. 166-7 Growth vs steady state
Sources: T. J. Kaptchuk *Chinese Medicine: The Web That Has No Weaver*, Rider and Co., Hutchinson (1983); WCED *Our Common Future*, Oxford University Press (1987); C. M. Cipolla *The Economic History of World Population*, Penguin Books (1962); N. Myers *The Gaia Atlas of Planet Management*, Pan Books (1985); WCED *Energy 2000*, Zed Books (1987); Norman Myers; *The Green Party General Election Manifesto*, Green Party UK (1987).

pp. 168-9 Quality or quantity of life
Sources: WCED *Our Common Future*, Oxford University Press (1987); *WMSE86**; WHO; World Resources Institute and IIED *World Resources 1986*, Basic Books (1986).

pp. 170-1 Biological choices
Sources: *New Scientist*, 10 July 1986, 22 October 1987, 3 December 1987; N. Myers *The Gaia Atlas of Planet Management*, Pan Books (1985); C. Raghavan "Towards a people-oriented biotechnology", *IFDA dossier 60*, July/August 1987; D. Baltimore "Setting the Record Straight on Biotechnology", *Technology Review*, October 1986; J. E. Lovelock *Gaia: A New Look At Life On Earth*, Oxford University Press (1987); FAO.

pp. 172-3 The age of "Big Brother"
Sources: *South*, November 1985; *New Internationalist*, December 1986; N. Myers *The Gaia Atlas of Planet Management*, Pan Books (1985); UNESCO; press reports.

pp. 174-5 The information revolution
Sources: *The Economist*, 17 October 1987; *Financial Times*, 14 September 1987; *New Scientist*, 3 December 1987; N. Myers *The Gaia Atlas of Planet Management*, Pan Books (1985); *New World Information and Communication Order: The Latest Phase*, UNESCO/NWICO briefing document, March 1983; National Remote Sensing Centre, Space Department, UK.

pp. 176-7 Automated battlefield
Sources: *New Scientist*, 3 December 1987; F. Barnaby (ed) *Future War*, Michael Joseph (1984).

pp. 178-9 The future majorities
Sources: D. Carlson and C. Comstock (eds) *Citizen Summitry*, J. P. Tarcher (1986); N. Myers *The Gaia Atlas of Planet Management*, Pan Books (1985); L. Durrell *State of the Ark*, Doubleday (1986); The Universal House of Justice *The Promise of World Peace*, One World Publications (1986); C. M. Cipolla *The Economic History of World Population*, Penguin Books (1962); WCED *Our Common Future*, Oxford University Press (1987); World Resources Institute and IIED *World Resources 1986*, Basic Books (1986).

pp. 180-1 Energy: A hi-tech centralized utopia
Sources: *New Scientist*, 26 November 1987; British Nuclear Fuels; *International Herald Tribune*, 15 December 1987; Frank Barnaby;

1985 BP Statistical Review of World Energy, British Petroleum UK, June 1985; N. Myers *The Gaia Atlas of Planet Management*, Pan Books (1985); WCED *Our Common Future*, Oxford University Press (1987); Jonathan Fryer; Friends of the Earth; WCED *Energy 2000*, Zed Books (1987).

pp. 182-3 A sustainable energy supply
Sources: WCED *Energy 2000*, Zed Books (1987); WCED *Our Common Future*, Oxford University Press (1987); J. Osmond and A. Graham *Alternatives*, Thorsons (1984); Earthscan/Development Forum *New and Renewable Energies*, IIED (1981); T. Bartlem *Renewable Energy Investment in the Developing Countries*, IIED (1984).

pp. 184-5 To boldly go
Sources: *New Scientist*, 9 July 1987; F. Barnaby *What on Earth is Star Wars?*, Fourth Estate (1987); *The Sunday Times*, 6 December 1987; The World Bank *World Development Report 1986*, Oxford University Press (1986); *WMSE86**.

pp. 186-7 The final frontier
Sources: *South*, November 1985; Frank Barnaby; *SIPRI Yearbook 1987*, Oxford University Press (1987).

pp. 188-9 The non-sustainable nightmare
Sources: A. Singer *Battle for the Planet*, Pan Books (1987); E. Eckholm *Down to Earth*, Pluto Press (1982); *New Scientist*, 10 July 1986; N. Myers *The Gaia Atlas of Planet Management*, Pan Books (1985); David Satterthwaite.

pp. 190-1 A sustainable future
Sources: P. Ekins (ed) *The Living Economy*, Routledge and Kegan Paul (1986); *The Green Party General Election Manifesto*, Green Party UK (1987); The Other Economic Summit conference papers, 1986 and 1987; K. E. Boulding "The Economics of the Coming Spaceship Earth", *Environmental Quality in a Growing Economy*, The John Hopkins Press (1966); J. Robertson "A New Economics by the Year 2000", *New Economics*, September 1987.

CHAPTER 8 SHORT-TERM STEPS FOR SURVIVAL
pp. 194-5 Disarmament
Sources: (Mikhail Gorbachev) *The Guardian*, 18 February 1987; speeches by Mikhail Gorbachev printed in *Soviet News*, 18 February 1987, 4 March 1987; Frank Barnaby; (*The INF Treaty*) *The Guardian*, 5 December 1987; *The Sunday Times*, 15 November 1987, 6 December 1987; *Nuclear and Space Talks: US and Soviet Proposals*, United States Information Agency, 1 October 1987; Frank Barnaby.

pp. 196-7 Non-proliferation
Sources: (Freezing the arms race) FREEZE; CAAT; IGRAT; EPIC; NRDC; *The American*, 5 September 1986; (**New Zealand and the Pacific**) New Zealand High Commission, London;

Sanity, April 1986, January 1988; other press reports; (**Stop the neutron bomb**) Guy Arnold.

pp. 198-9 Détente
Sources: (**Armand Hammer**) Jonathan Fryer; (**Amnesty International**) Amnesty International; *The New Internationalist*, January 1988; Frank Barnaby; (Östpolitik) press reports; (**China: where East meets West?**) L. Mackay *China: A Power for Peace?*, END/Merlin Press (1986).

pp. 200-3 Crisis resolution
Sources: (**Southern Africa**) Frank Barnaby; (**The Middle East**) A. Cohen *Israel and the Arab World*, W. H. Allen (1970) *The Guardian*, 14 September 1987; (**The Gulf**) George Joffe, *Economist* Intelligence Unit; (**Central America**) *Discriminate Deterrence*, US Department of Defense, January 1988; Economic Commission for Latin America and the Caribbean *The Economic Crisis: Policies for Adjustment, Stabilization and Growth*, United Nations (1986).

pp. 204-5 Economic reform
Sources: H. Lever and C. Huhne *Debt and Danger*, Pelican Books (1987); J. Schatan *World Debt – Who is to Pay?* Zed Books (1987); *The Economist*, 19 December 1987, 9 January 1988; *The Guardian*, 22 June 1987; *South*, January 1988; *Costa Rica Reduces Debt in Swap for Tropical Forest*, WWF News Release, 27 July 1987.

pp. 206-7 Emergency development
Sources: WCED *Food 2000*, Zed Books (1987); WCED *Our Common Future*, Oxford University Press (1987); Frank Barnaby.

pp. 208-9 Population control
Sources: All case study material from IPPF.

pp. 210-11 Ecofreeze
Sources:
(**Bring back the forests**) *The Disappearing Forests*, UNEP Environment Brief No. 3; *The Tropical Forestry Action Plan*, FAO/IBRD/WRI/UNDP (1987); The Panos Institute *Panoscope* No. 3, October 1987; Friends of the Earth; (**Tackling the greenhouse effect**) M. Glantz, R. Katz and M. Krenz (eds) *The Societal Impacts Associated with the 1982-83 Worldwide Climate Anomalies*, Environmental and Societal Impacts Group, National Center for Atmospheric Research/UNEP (1987); (**Protecting the ozone layer**) Andy Crump; UNEP; press reports.

pp. 212-13 Redefining Security
Sources: Frank Barnaby; Paul Ekins; Michael and Eirwen Harbottle, the London Centre for International Peacebuilding.

CHAPTER 9 REDIRECTION: A SUSTAINABLE FUTURE

pp. 214-5 Introduction with quotations from "The Future of the International System and the United Nations", a speech delivered by Maurice Strong at the Global Development Week conference, University of Toronto (1986).

pp. 218-9 Conversion
Sources: (Socially useful products) Phil Asquith, Department of Employment, Sheffield City Council; report on the Local Authority Conference on Economic and Arms Conversion, Sheffield 1987; Karen Clark, Minnesota House of Representatives State Economic Conversion Task Force. (**The TGWU arms conversion strategy**) A Better Future, TGWU Conversion Strategy 1983; TGWU report on the 1987 European Nuclear Disarmament Convention.

pp. 220-1 Swords into ploughshares
Sources: D. Smith and R. Smith The Economics of Militarism, Pluto (1983); J. Middleton, J. Routley and B. Lowe "Swords to Ploughshares – Improving the World's Health", Medicine and War Vol.3, 1987; Labour Action for Peace "Vicious Circle – Virtuous Solution", paper presented at the International Conference on the Relationship Between Disarmament and Development, 1987.

pp. 222-3 Learning peace
Sources: (nited World College of the Atlantic) United World College of the Atlantic, Wales; (**Neve shalom – school for peace**) British Friends of Neve Shalom; (**BP – the greening of industry**) J. Elkington The Green Capitalists, Gollancz (1987); British Petroleum press office.

pp. 224-5 Conflict resolution techniques
Sources: A Manual for Group Facilitators, The Center for Conflict Resolution, Wisconsin USA; John Groom.

pp. 226-7 Interlocking systems
Sources: "Ten key values of the American Green Movement", Green Teacher, December 1987; N. Myers "Environmental Challenges: More Government or Better Governance?"; IFDA dossier 62, November/December 1987; Right Livelihood Award press release, 1987.

pp. 228-9 Eco-economics
Sources: (The Homegrown Economy Project) J. Robertson "The Economics of Local Recovery", TOES conference paper, April 1986; (**TOES: The Other Economic Summit**) New Economics, September 1987; TOES information leaflets; (**Spaceship Earth**) K. E. Boulding "The Economics of the Coming Spaceship Earth", Environmental Quality in a Growing Economy, John Hopkins Press (1966); C. Leipert "From Growth to Adjusted National Product" in P. Ekins (ed) The Living Economy, Routledge Kegan Paul (1986).

pp. 232-3 Appropriate science
Sources: (Global Challenges Network) H. P. Dürr "Global Challenges Network", Stockholm 1987 (unpublished paper); (**The coming age of Gaia**) Chapman conference papers, 1988; New Scientist, 17 March 1988; Gaia conference papers, 1988; (**Intermediate Technology**) Intermediate Technology Development Group project reports.

pp. 234-5 Grass roots
Sources: A. Santa Cruz "The Women's Movement: A Latin American Perspective", IFDA dossier 50, November/December 1985; A. Langer "The Greens in Italy", IFDA dossier 47, May/June 1985; P. Ekins "Growing Concern", The Guardian, 13 January 1988; S. Mitter Common Fate, Common Bond: Women in the Global Economy, Pluto Press (1986).

pp. 236-7 Broadening the base
Sources: (Youth building the future) International Student Conference Youth Building the Future, press release August 1987; (**Transnational codes of conduct**) J. Elkington The Green Capitalists, Gollancz (1987); (**North-South understanding**) IFDA dossier 60, July/August 1987; Proposed Programme of the UK National Organizing Committee of the Council of Europe's 1988 Campaign on North-South Interdependence.

pp. 238-9 Future governance
Sources: Maurice Strong; International Network for a UN Second Assembly; IFDA dossier 47, May/June 1985; J. E. Fobes The Future of the United Nations Systems, IFDA dossier 51, January/February 1986; R. Falk Openings for Peace and Justice in World of Danger and Struggle, IFDA dossier 62, November/December 1987; IFDA dossier 64, March/April 1988; Norman Myers; The Stanley Foundation; World Federalists Association.

pp. 240-1 Future law
Sources: (Shaping supranational law) WCED Our Common Future, Oxford University Press (1987); Association of World Federalists; (**Bhopal**) Bhopal – we must not forget, Special Report of the Transnationals Information Centre, London, October 1987; (**Lawyers for Peace**) Lawyers for Nuclear Disarmament; CND; press reports.

pp. 244-5 Personal and political
Sources: (Mothers of the disappeared) Spare Rib, March 1986; Committee for Human Rights in Argentina; (**The Great Peace Journey**) information supplied by The Great Peace Journey, Sweden.

*R. Leger Sivard World Military and Social Expenditures 1986, World Priorities (1986)

Military spending diverted

One billion dollars is a mere one-tenth of 1% of current world military spending. We asked OXFAM what it would do with such a sum:

"OXFAM is about helping the poorest, and what the poorest need, above all, is money. How can one get money or other resources into the hands of those who really need it without it being "creamed off" by clever intermediaries – landlords, traders, some government officials? OXFAM would want to see some kind of social security system set up in the South providing food, clothes, health care and education for everyone. In addition, there should be an old age pension to prevent the old becoming a financial burden . . .

The danger of "welfarism", of whole populations sitting down and receiving basic pensions from re-allocated arms budgets, can only be averted if agencies like OXFAM use their extra resources to encourage the natural dynamism of ordinary people: small businesses would be encouraged by the growth in spending power; and there would be great opportunities for employment on housing and environmental projects in cities. In rural areas OXFAM would encourage employment in service industries, in small shops, workshops, and transport. Water for all, and health for all, would become real possibilities and not just slogans. Where no other employment possibilities existed, OXFAM would encourage its partners, mainly local NGOs, or local government offices, to arrange "cash for work" – paying people to guard trees or maintain village water supplies.

At present, major donor agencies like the World Bank make their aid conditional on recipient countries following certain fiscal and monetary policies. If OXFAM had far more resources at its disposal than it has currently, it would consider making its aid dependent on countries following policies that genuinely assisted the poorest in their societies. Relief and humanitarian programmes would of course be continued regardless of particular government policies, but before OXFAM expanded its aid to any country it would want to be sure that the governments of these countries were following policies that were supportive of the interests of the poorest.

But it would be wrong to suggest that a sudden inflow of cash into agencies like OXFAM would, in the short term, radically improve the life of the poorest. Third World governments, many of them major customers in the arms trade, do not themselves systematically put the abolition of poverty on the top of their agenda; and many poor people suffer not just from poverty but also from oppressive power structures, which might well be strengthened by a sudden increase in foreign aid flows. The challenge is not only to shift resources from arms to aid, but to ensure that the resources released from armaments are really put at the service of poor people and not just given to the governments of poor countries."

Hugh T. Goyder, OXFAM, April 1987

The United Nations

It is the avowed determination of the members of the United Nations "to save succeeding generations from the scourge of war . . . and to establish conditions under which justice and respect for the obligations arising from treaties and other sources of international law can be maintained."

The Charter of the United Nations clearly outlaws the use of force as a method of settling any international dispute. In article 2, paragraph 3 of the Charter, UN members agree to act in accordance with the principle:

"All members shall settle their international disputes by peaceful means in such a manner that international peace and security, and justice, are not endangered." Article 33 states: "The parties to any dispute, the continuance of which is likely to endanger the maintenance of international peace and security, shall, first of all, seek a solution by negotiation, enquiry, mediation, conciliation, arbitration, judicial settlement, resort to regional agencies or arrangements, or other peaceful means of their own choice."

The concept of *real* security is also contained in article 26 of the Charter, in which the members of the Security Council are called upon "to promote the establishment and maintenance of international peace and security with the least diversion for armaments of the world's human and economic resources".

To date, 157 countries have agreed to abide by the terms of Charter. How many are as good as their word? The following is a list of UN member states and their year of membership:

Afghanistan, 1946;
Albania, 1955;
Algeria, 1962;
Angola, 1976;
Antigua and Barbuda, 1981;
Argentina, 1945;
Australia, 1945;
Austria, 1955;
Bahamas, 1973;
Bahrain, 1971;
Bangladesh, 1974;
Barbados, 1966;
Belgium, 1945;
Belize, 1981;
Benin, 1960;
Bhutan, 1971;
Bolivia, 1945;
Botswana, 1966;
Brazil, 1945;
Brunei Darussalam, 1984;
Bulgaria, 1955;
Burkina Faso, 1960;
Burma, 1948;
Burundi, 1962;
*Byelorussia, 1945;
Cameroon, 1960;
Canada, 1945;
Cape Verde, 1975;
Central Africa Republic, 1960;
Chad, 1960;
Chile, 1945;
China, 1945;
Colombia, 1945;
Comoros, 1975;
Congo, 1960;
Costa Rica, 1945;
Cote d'Ivoire, 1960;
Cuba, 1945;
Cyprus, 1960;
Czechoslovakia, 1945;
Denmark, 1945;
Djibouti, 1977;
Dominica, 1978;
Dominican Republic, 1945;
Ecuador, 1945;
Egypt, 1945;
El Salvador, 1945;
Equatorial Guinea, 1968;
Ethiopia, 1945;
Fiji, 1970;
Finland, 1955;
France, 1945;
Gabon, 1960;
Gambia, 1965;
German Democratic Republic,

1973;
FR Germany, 1973;
Ghana, 1957;
Greece, 1945;
Grenada, 1974;
Guatemala, 1945;
Guinea, 1958;
Guinea-Bissau, 1974;
Guyana, 1966;
Haiti, 1945;
Honduras, 1945;
Hungary, 1955;
Iceland, 1946;
India, 1945;
Indonesia, 1950;
Iran, 1945;
Iraq, 1945;
Ireland, 1955;
Israel, 1949;
Italy, 1955;
Jamaica, 1962;
Japan, 1956;
Jordan, 1955;
Kampuchea, 1955;
Kenya, 1963;
Kuwait, 1963;
Lao People's Democratic Republic, 1955;
Lebanon, 1945;
Lesotho, 1966;
Liberia, 1945;
Libya, 1955;
Luxembourg, 1945;
Madagascar, 1960;
Malawi, 1964;
Malaysia, 1957;
Maldives, 1965;
Mali, 1960;
Malta, 1964;
Mauritania, 1961;
Mauritius, 1968;
Mexico, 1945;
Mongolia, 1961;
Morocco, 1956;
Mozambique, 1975;
Nepal, 1955;
Netherlands, 1945;
New Zealand, 1945;
Nicaragua, 1945;
Niger, 1960;
Nigeria, 1960;
Norway, 1945;
Oman, 1971;
Pakistan, 1947;
Panama, 1945;

Papua New Guinea, 1975;
Paraguay, 1945;
Peru, 1945;
Philippines, 1945;
Poland, 1945;
Portugal, 1955;
Qatar, 1971;
Romania, 1955;
Rwanda, 1962;
Saint Christopher and Nevis, 1983;
Saint Lucia, 1979;
Saint Vincent and the Grenadines, 1980;
Samoa, Western, 1976;
Sao Tome and Principe, 1975;
Saudi Arabia, 1945;
Senegal, 1960;
Seychelles, 1976;
Sierra Leone, 1961;
Singapore, 1965;
Solomon Islands, 1978;
Somalia, 1960;
South Africa, 1945;
Spain, 1955;
Sri Lanka, 1955;
Sudan, 1956;
Suriname, 1975;
Swaziland, 1968;
Sweden, 1946;
Syria, 1945;
Tanzania, 1961;
Thailand, 1946;
Togo, 1960;
Trinidad and Tobago, 1962;
Tunisia, 1956;
Turkey, 1945;
Uganda, 1962;
UK, 1945;
*Ukraine, 1945;
United Arab Emirates, 1971;
Uruguay, 1945;
USA, 1945;
*USSR, 1945;
Vanuatu, 1981;
Venezuela, 1945;
Viet Nam, 1977;
Yemen Arab Republic, 1947;
Yemen, People's Democratic Republic of, 1967;
Yugoslavia, 1945;
Zaire, 1960;
Zambia, 1964;
Zimbabwe, 1980;

In addition, there are at least 50 states and territories which are not members of the UN. Some, such as Namibia, Western Sahara and East Timor, are under foreign military occupation. Others, including Hong Kong, Macao, French Guiana and Greenland are content with being overseas colonies of European states. Most are considered too small to qualify for UN membership but only five recognized, independent states with their own diplomatic missions – Cayman Islands, Switzerland, Taiwan, North Korea and South Korea – have chosen not to join the UN.

* Since Byelorussia and Ukraine are its constituent republics, the USSR effectively has three seats in the UN.

Index

Bold entries refer to main entries.

Photographic credits

Abbreviations: t = top, l = left, r = right, c = centre, b = bottom, tl = top left, etc.
Aspect Picture Library: (Larry Burrows) pp. 2-3
Associated Press: pp. 50-1, 68-9, 86-7, 126, 150, 151 (tl, tc, tr), 154 (bl), 155 (l), 158-9, 201; (Bob Daugherty) pp. 194-5, 253 (r), 197 (main picture inset), 199 (tr); (Sadayuki Mikami) pp. 204-5, 241 (t); (Boris Yurchenko) p. 252
Ed Barber: pp. 6-7, 154-5 (background)
British Petroleum Company Ltd: p. 223 (bl)
Pauline Cohen: p. 91 (l)
Daily Telegraph Colour Library: p. 175 (bl)
Francis Deutsch: p. 241 (b)
Patricia Diaz: p. 235 (b)
El Salvador and Guatemala Committee for Human Rights: (Diana Pritchard) pp. 202-3
Susan Farkas: p. 5 photograph of M. Strong
Format: (Melanie Friend) pp. 155 (r), 197 (bl); (Sheila Gray) p. 219 (t); (Jenny Matthews) p. 174 (b); (Raissa Page) pp. 244-5
Frank Spooner Pictures: (Catherine Leroy) pp. 40-1, 134-5
Freeze: p. 196
Gruppo Parlamentare Verde: (Franz Gustinicich) p. 235 (t)
The Guardian: p. 199 (bl)
R. Humphreys: pp. 148-9
Impact Photos: p. 209 (inset r)
Intermediate Technology Development Group: (J. Young) p. 233
IPPF Information Department: (Peter Charlesworth) p. 209 (main)
Museum of London (Henry Grant Collection): p. 154 (br)
Network Photos: (Katalin Arkell) p. 91 (r); (Geoff Franklin) p. 5 photograph of D. Tutu, p. 151 (bl); (Mike Goldwater) pp. 114-15; (Kaveh Golestan) pp. 56-7
Neve Shalom: (Michael Lyons) p. 222
Panos Pictures: (F Botts) pp. 210-11; (Mark Edwards) pp. 175 (tr), 206-7, 209 (inset l c)
Planet Earth Pictures: (Geoff Du Feu) pp. 246-7 (main); (Peter Stevenson) p. 174 (t)
Popperfoto: pp. 216-17, 236-7
Jakob Radloff: p. 232
Right Livelihood, University of Bradford: pp. 226-7
Werner Schuring: p. 5 photograph of P. Kelly
Science Photo Library: (Earth Satelite Corporation) pp. 242-3; (Fermi National Accelerator Library) endpapers (hardback only); (NASA) p. 229, pp. 250-1 (main)
The Scotsman/Scottish CND: pp. 156-7
Sheffield City Council Department of Employment: p. 219 (bl)
Star Bulletin: (Terry Luke) p. 5 photograph of J. Galtung
Arthur Tess: p. 100 Times Newspapers Ltd: p. 127
TOES: p. 228
UNICEF: (Yann Gamblin) p. 101; (Denis Budd Gray) pp. 146-7
UN Information Centre: (Bachrach) pp. 151 (br)
United World College of the Atlantic: p. 223 (tr)
West German Embassy: p. 253 (l)

Artists

Bill Donohoe pp. 32-5, 40-1, 46-7, 50-1, 54-5, 60-1, 64-7, 70-3, 80-1, 84-7, 90-3, 110-11, 122-5, 128-9, 148-9, 224-7
Eugene Fleury pp. 28-9, 102-5, 138-9, 152-3, 158-9, 164-5, 190-1
Chris Forsey pp. 26-7, 38-9, 74-5, 98-9, 114-5, 130-1, 140-1, 146-7, 154-7, 166-71, 176-7, 180-3, 216-17
Hayward Group pp. 42-3, 48-9, 52-3, 56-7, 62-3, 82-3, 88-9, 96-7, 112-13, 116-121, 136-7, 150-1, 194-213, 218-23, 228-37, 240-1, 244-5;
David Housden pp. 88-9
Aziz Khan pp. 16-17, 30-1, 44-5, 68-9, 106-9, 126-7, 132-5, 144-5, 172-5, 178-9
Linden Artists: (Jim Channel) p. 1, (Sebastian Quigley) pp. 10-11, 18-19, 253-4
Mike Nicholson pp. 100-1
Alan Suttie pp. 12-15, 24-5, 184-7, 238-9

Publisher's acknowledgements

Gaia Books would like to extend our warmest thanks and appreciation to Frank Barnaby for his patience with a production schedule that ran considerably over, to Norman Myers for his meticulous reading from half-way around the world, the members of the Think Tank, all our contributors and the many individuals around the globe who answered our telephone enquiries and who took time out from their busy schedules to send us information and articles. Without their unstinting help the preparation of this book would not have been possible. We give special thanks to the patient staff of many picture agencies, CND, END, Greenpeace International, Greenpeace UK, Books for a Change, Quaker Peace and Service, UNICEF, the UN Information Centre in London, and the Imperial War Museum. We would also like to thank our hard-working artists for creating the body of the book, Ken and Barry at Marlin Graphics Ltd for their speedy typesetting, Ian, Jane and Martin at Technographic Design and Print Ltd, Linda Smith at Mondadori Co. Ltd for helpful print scheduling, John-Francis Phipps of Philosophers for Peace for his contributions to pp. 40-1, 48-9 and 140-1, David Lan, anthropologist and playwright, for his ideas on the marginalization of minorities, Shana Magraw, Peggy Sadler, Claire Duffet, Eirwen Harbottle, Ludmila Pakhomova at the Tass News Agency, H. Hellberg, M. D. at the World Health Organization, Joanna Macy, Nick Gallie, Mark Carwardine, Zed Books, On Yer Bike, Mr. and Mrs. Lee, Shirley du Boulay, and especially Jim Lovelock for his continuing inspiration.

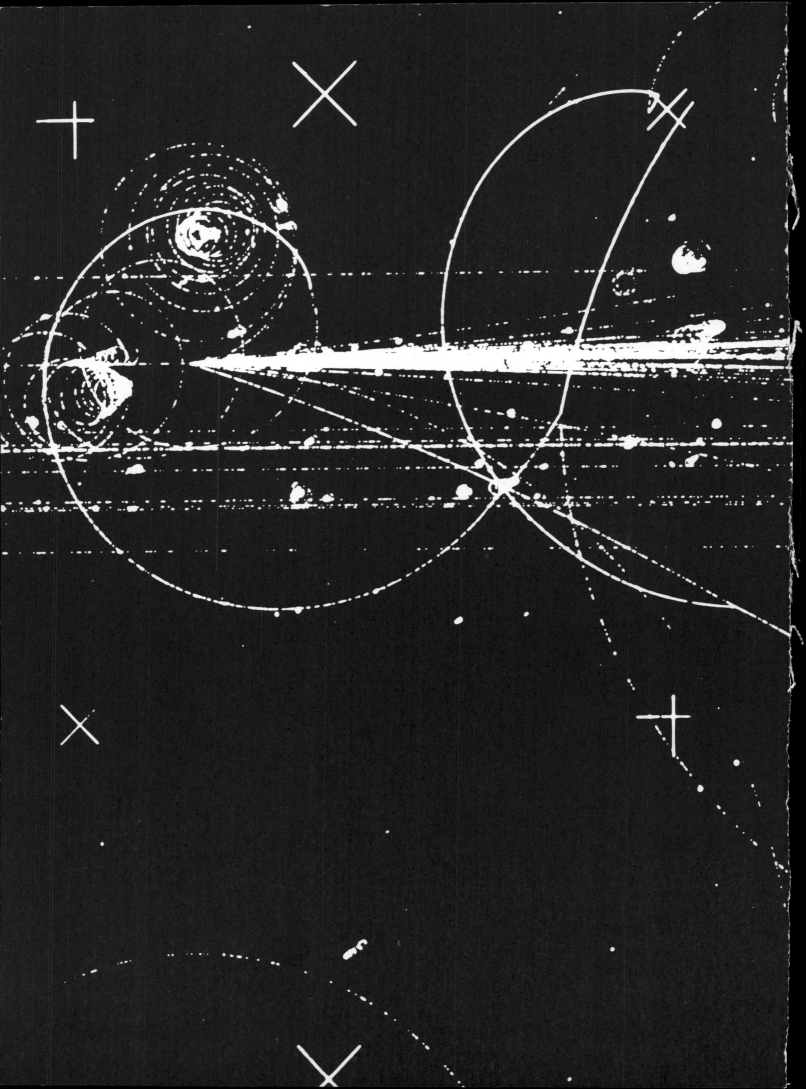